Giftedness is arguably the most precious natural resource a society can have. If one looks back through history and asks just
what it is that made particular civilizations great, so that they
are esteemed and remembered, it is inevitably the gifts of those
who lived in them. The purpose of this book is to present alternative conceptions of giftedness, how it can be measured, and how
it can be developed in both children and adults.

Conceptions of Giftedness consists of eighteen chapters by distinguished contributors to theory and research. It is divided into
six parts. The first, an editorial introduction, constitutes a "map
of the terrain"; it offers a unified perspective on the chapters that
follow. The second part addresses educationally based conceptions
of giftedness; the third, cognitive-psychological approaches; the
fourth, developmental theories; the fifth, domain-specific aspects
in mathematics and music. The final part, an integrative concluding chapter, discusses points of overlap and differences among
the various positions.

Conceptions of Giftedness brings together in one place, for the
first time, comprehensive and readable statements of the main
contemporary points of view by their leading exponents. A wide
audience of psychologists, educators, students, and interested lay-
people will welcome its publication.

Robert J. Sternberg is Professor of Psychology at Yale University,
where Janet E. Davidson is Graduate Fellow in Psychology.

D0081977

Conceptions of giftedness

Conceptions of giftedness

Edited by

ROBERT J. STERNBERG
Yale University

JANET E. DAVIDSON
Yale University

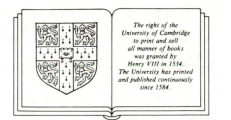

The right of the
University of Cambridge
to print and sell
all manner of books
was granted by
Henry VIII in 1534.
The University has printed
and published continuously
since 1584.

CAMBRIDGE UNIVERSITY PRESS

Cambridge
London   New York   New Rochelle
Melbourne   Sydney

Published by the Press Syndicate of the University of Cambridge
The Pitt Building, Trumpington Street, Cambridge CB2 1RP
32 East 57th Street, New York, NY 10022, USA
10 Stamford Road, Oakleigh, Melbourne 3166, Australia

First published 1986

Printed in the United States of America

Library of Congress Cataloging in Publication Data
Main entry under title:
Conceptions of giftedness
Includes indexes.
1. Genius.   2. Gifted children – Psychology.
I. Sternberg, Robert J.   II. Davidson, Janet E.
BF412.C66   1986   153.9'8   85–15144

British Library Cataloguing in Publication Data
Conceptions of giftedness.
1. Gifted children
I. Sternberg, Robert J.   II. Davidson, Janet E.
155.4'55   BF723.G5

ISBN 0 521 26814 1 hard covers
ISBN 0 521 31879 3 paperback

Contents

List of contributors   *page* vii
Preface   ix

Part I   Introduction

1   Conceptions of giftedness: a map of the terrain   3
    Robert J. Sternberg and Janet E. Davidson

Part II   Implicit-theoretical approaches

2   Giftedness: a psychosocial approach   21
    Abraham J. Tannenbaum
3   The three-ring conception of giftedness: a developmental
    model for creative productivity   53
    Joseph S. Renzulli
4   The educational definition of giftedness and its policy
    implications   93
    James J. Gallagher and Richard D. Courtright
5   A conception of giftedness   112
    John F. Feldhusen
6   Giftedness: coalescence, context, conflict, and commitment   128
    Patricia Haensly, Cecil R. Reynolds, and William R. Nash

Part III   Explicit-theoretical approaches: cognitive theory

7   A conception of giftedness designed to promote research   151
    Nancy Ewald Jackson and Earl C. Butterfield
8   Causes and consequences of metamemory in gifted children   182
    John G. Borkowski and Virginia A. Peck
9   The role of insight in giftedness   201
    Janet E. Davidson
10   A triarchic theory of intellectual giftedness   223
    Robert J. Sternberg

v

Part IV   Explicit-theoretical approaches: developmental theory

11   The self-construction of the extraordinary   247
     Howard E. Gruber
12   Culture, time, and the development of talent   264
     Mihaly Csikszentmihalyi and Rick E. Robinson
13   Giftedness as a developmentalist sees it   285
     David Henry Feldman with the assistance of Ann C. Benjamin
14   The crystallizing experience: discovering an intellectual gift   306
     Joseph Walters and Howard Gardner
15   The achievement of eminence: a model based on a
     longitudinal study of exceptionally gifted boys and their
     families   332
     Robert S. Albert and Mark A. Runco

Part V   Explicit-theoretical approaches: domain-specific theory

16   Youths who reason exceptionally well mathematically   361
     Julian C. Stanley and Camilla Persson Benbow
17   Cognitive issues in the development of musically gifted
     children   388
     Jeanne Bamberger

Part VI   Conclusions and integration

18   Two levels of giftedness: shall ever the twain meet?   417
     Robert S. Siegler and Kenneth Kotovsky

Author index   437
Subject index   443

Contributors

Robert S. Albert
Department of Psychology
Pitzer College

Jeanne Bamberger
Music Section
School of Humanities and Social
    Science
Massachusetts Institute of
    Technology

Camilla Persson Benbow
Department of Psychology
Iowa State University

Ann C. Benjamin
Eliot-Pearson Department of Child
    Study
Tufts University

John G. Borkowski
Department of Psychology
Notre Dame University

Earl C. Butterfield
Department of Education
University of Washington

Richard D. Courtright
Frank Porter Graham Child
    Development Center
University of North Carolina
    at Chapel Hill

Mihaly Csikszentmihalyi
Department of Behavioral Sciences
University of Chicago

Janet E. Davidson
Department of Psychology
Yale University

John F. Feldhusen
Department of Education and
    Psychological Sciences
Purdue University

David Henry Feldman
Eliot-Pearson Department of Child
    Study
Tufts University

James J. Gallagher
Frank Porter Graham Child
    Development Center
University of North Carolina
    at Chapel Hill

Howard Gardner
School of Education
Harvard University
and Boston Veterans
    Administration Medical Center

Howard E. Gruber
Faculté de Psychologie et des Sciences
    de l'Education
Université de Genève
and Rutgers University, Newark

Patricia Haensly
Department of Educational Psychology
Texas A & M University

Nancy Ewald Jackson
Department of Parent
   and Child Nursing
University of Washington

Kenneth Kotovsky
Department of Psychology
Community College of Allegheny
   County

William R. Nash
Department of Educational Psychology
Texas A & M University

Virginia A. Peck
Department of Psychology
Notre Dame University

Joseph S. Renzulli
Department of Educational Psychology
School of Education
University of Connecticut

Cecil R. Reynolds
Department of Educational Psychology
Texas A & M University

Rick E. Robinson
Department of Behavioral Sciences
University of Chicago

Mark A. Runco
Department of Psychology
University of Hawaii, Hilo

Robert S. Siegler
Department of Psychology
Carnegie-Mellon University

Julian C. Stanley
Department of Psychology
The Johns Hopkins University

Robert J. Sternberg
Department of Psychology
Yale University

Abraham J. Tannenbaum
Teachers College
Columbia University

Joseph Walters
School of Education
Harvard University

Preface

Giftedness is arguably the most precious natural resource a civilization can have. There are any number of resources, natural and man-made, that contribute to the development of a civilization. But if one looks back through history and asks just what it is that made certain civilizations great, or remembered, or esteemed, it is inevitably the gifts, whether individual or collective, of those who lived in them. These gifts are what give civilizations such as ancient Greece or the European Renaissance a special place in the history of humankind.

If it is necessary to justify a book – and in these days of seemingly innumerable edited books, it may well be – then we would justify this one in terms of the key importance of giftedness to civilization and to all of its parts, both collective and individual. The key importance of giftedness has not been matched by either theoretical or empirical efforts, and, indeed, the current book is the first to our knowledge that is intended exclusively to bring together conceptions of giftedness from a wide diversity of points of view. We hope the book will serve as a starting focal point for research efforts designed to distinguish among or to integrate these points of view.

Whereas there are many topics in psychology and education that seem to be of considerably greater interest to academicians than to the population at large, giftedness seems to show the reverse pattern: It seems to be of greater interest to the general population than to the professionals in psychology and education. This statement is not made without support. For example, there is today no division of the American Psychological Association devoted to the study and understanding of the gifted (whereas there is one devoted to mental retardation); similarly, there is no special interest group in the American Educational Research Association devoted to the study and understanding of the gifted.* Major journals in these two fields contain only a smattering of articles on the topic, more so in education than in psychology. In neither field is the study of giftedness considered to be mainline. To the extent that

*At press time, such a group was just forming.

there are pockets of psychologists and educators studying giftedness, they tend to be isolated from each other. For example, members of the Social Science Research Council committee studying giftedness have practically no visibility in the National Association for Gifted Children, and "salient" members of the association have no visibility in the council committee. If ever there was a field that needed "bringing together," this one is it, and this book represents what we hope will be a constructive step in this direction. (In fact, it includes among its contributors prominent individuals of both organizations!)

Our goal as editors, then, is to bring together a diversity of viewpoints regarding the conceptualization of giftedness in the hope of promoting the unity and forward movement of the field. We are encouraged by current stirrings in the field, and desire that this book stir things up all the more.

We are grateful to all those who have helped us in "stirring the pot": the Social Science Research Council, which funded a conference of contributors to this volume, and Joseph Renzulli, who did most of the work in organizing the conference; the Spencer Foundation, which has funded our own initial research on giftedness; the scholars who generously gave of their time to write chapters for this book and, in most instances, to attend the conference for it; and, finally, parents and teachers everywhere who have recognized and developed the gifts of the world's children.

It is sometimes said that "every parent has a gifted child." Perhaps not. But parents (and teachers) can help children make the most of whatever gifts they have. In order for them to do so, we all must understand giftedness better, and it is that understanding which this book seeks to develop. We dedicate this book to the parents and teachers of the world who have done their best to nurture the gifts of their children, without making these children give up their childhoods.

RJS
JED

October 1985

Part I

Introduction

1   Conceptions of giftedness: a map of the terrain

Robert J. Sternberg and Janet E. Davidson

Societies tend to dwell on the distinctions among people that they are most easily able to make. Perhaps it is for this reason that differences in race, economic level, and ethnic background have played such an important part in the history of our country, educational and otherwise. Perhaps it is also for this reason that the results of apparently "objective" tests, whether of intelligence or of achievement, tend to dominate selection and placement procedures in educational milieus. But the most psychologically and educationally important distinctions are not always among the most easily made, and because of this it is sometimes important to step back and ask how, ideally, distinctions should be made. This book, based on the premise that the time has come to reassess just what we mean by *giftedness*, provides 17 different conceptions of the construct that, although distinct, are interrelated in certain ways. The goal of this chapter is to foreshadow these conceptions and the nature of some of their interrelations.

There are any number of ways of arranging the chapters in a book like this. We have chosen to use the distinction between "implicit" and "explicit" theories as our primary way of dividing up the chapters.

Implicit theories are essentially definitions that lie within the heads of the theorists, who may be experts or laypersons. Thus, the implicit theorist defines what he or she means by giftedness, and goes on to illustrate the implications of this definition. Because implicit theories are definitional, they cannot be empirically tested, other than in the sense of showing that the proposed implicit theory is in accord with other people's implicit theories.

Explicit theories presuppose definitions, and seek to interrelate such definitions to a network of psychological or educational theory and data. Such theories are testable by the usual empirical means, and thus may be falsified. But the definitions upon which they are based cannot be falsified, so it is important in evaluating the explicit theories to be sensitive to the underlying conception of giftedness that has generated the theory and data, and to evaluate whether this conception is a useful one.

Ultimately, usefulness may be the only test we have of what makes for a better or worse conception of giftedness. Giftedness is something we invent, not something we discover: It is what one society or another wants it to be, and hence its conceptualization can change over time and place. If the definition of giftedness is a useful one, then it can lead to favorable consequences of many kinds, both for the society and for its individuals. If the definition of giftedness is not useful, valuable talents may be wasted, and less valuable ones fostered and encouraged. It is thus important to us all to understand just what it is we, and others, mean by the concept of *giftedness*.

The book is divided into six parts, of which the first, consisting merely of the present chapter, seeks to map out the remainder of the book.

Implicit-theoretical approaches

Part II consists of five chapters, each of which presents a somewhat different implicit theory of giftedness that seeks to define this elusive concept.

In Chapter 2, Abraham J. Tannenbaum proposes a "psychosocial" approach to defining giftedness. He suggests that giftedness is not one thing, but four, in the sense that whether they realize it or not, people classify talents as being of four different kinds: scarcity, surplus, quota, and anomalous.

Scarcity talents are those forever in short supply that make life easier, safer, healthier, and more intelligible. The contributions of Jonas Salk in discovering a polio vaccine or of Freud in proposing a revolutionary theory of mental health and illness represent outcomes of scarcity talents. Surplus talents are those that elevate people's sensitivities and sensibilities. They are embodied in individuals such as Bach or Michelangelo. Such talents enrich the world but do not fundamentally change it in the way a vaccine or a method of psychotherapy might. Quota talents are represented by specialized, high-level skills needed to provide the goods and services for which there is a limited market. Physicians, lawyers, and teachers represent these kinds of talents. Whereas a society could do with an unlimited supply of scarcity and surplus talents, its needs for quota talents are limited by the demands placed upon these skills. Anomalous talents are those that society does not particularly value, or that it may even disvalue, but that are nevertheless recognized as demonstrating a kind of excellence. Many of the listings in *The Guinness Book of World Records* would be of this kind. For example, the abilities to chug beer very quickly or to seduce large numbers of women or men may not arouse great favor, but are nevertheless recognized as abilities that are out of the ordinary.

In Chapter 3 on the "three-ring" conception of giftedness, Joseph S. Renzulli takes a tack quite different from Tannenbaum's in defining giftedness. His focus is on the individual rather than on the society. Rather than defining giftedness from the standpoint of society, Renzulli defines it from the standpoint of the individual. His definition includes three elements: above-average, but not necessarily exceptional, ability; creativity; and task commitment.

Renzulli's definition focuses on the individual but also recognizes the effects of tasks and situations. Renzulli makes no claim that ability, creativity, or task commitment are wholly task- or situation-general. Thus, Renzulli's conception is able to take into account the domain-specificity of many kinds of talents. His conception is largely consistent with but complementary to Tannenbaum's, in that it concentrates on the individual rather than the society. But the two conceptions seem not to be wholly compatible. An anomalous talent like beer-chugging would seem to require little or no creativity, and hence to fit into Tannenbaum's anomalous category of giftedness but not into Renzulli's at all.

The distinction between Tannenbaum's and Renzulli's conceptions of giftedness points out the importance of assessing the domain of inquiry – in terms of what unit or units giftedness is defined. In Chapter 4, James J. Gallagher and Richard D. Courtright explicitly address this issue, making a distinction between psychological conceptions of giftedness, on the one hand, and educational conceptions of giftedness, on the other. Psychological conceptions, which are based primarily on individual differences, (a) consider a full range of mental abilities, (b) use batteries of measuring instruments touching on much or all of this range, (c) more or less ignore ecological factors, (d) have as a primary goal the discovery of the nature of cognitive processes, and (e) have as an outcome the label of "gifted." Educational conceptions, which are based primarily on school performance and assessment, (a) limit the range of predictors considered to those relevant to academic success, (b) use instruments that measure these school-related abilities, (c) are dependent on school and cultural environment for their conceptualization, (d) seek to place children and occasionally adults in their proper educational environment, and (e) yield as a label something like "academically advanced." Gallagher and Courtright seek not to propose any one psychological or educational definition but rather to compare existing psychological and educational definitions, both within and across these two domains. In terms of the distinction between the Tannenbaum and Renzulli chapters, Renzulli's approach is closer to a psychological one, and Tannenbaum's, to an educational one. But Tannenbaum's demarcation of his domain is broader than that of education. In Tannenbaum's conceptualization, the educational sphere would be only one of many that contribute to a societal conceptualization of giftedness. Other spheres might include the arts, politics, science, and so on.

In Chapter 5, John F. Feldhusen proposes a conception of giftedness that would fall squarely into Gallagher and Courtright's psychological domain. Feldhusen's conception has four components: (a) general intellectual ability, (b) positive self-concept, (c) achievement motivation, and (d) special talent(s). Feldhusen reviews literature on each of these components and finds them all to be essential ingredients in gifted individuals. Feldhusen's mission would seem to be similar to Renzulli's, but it is more restrictive. Like Renzulli, he believes in the importance of general ability, but he separates out special abilities or talents from general ability, including creativity in this category. For Feldhusen, then, creativity is not a single thing but rather a more or less domain-specific talent or set of talents. Like Renzulli, Feldhusen places motivation into his definition, but a specific kind of motivation, namely, achievement motivation. Finally, Feldhusen places positive self-concept into his conception, something that does not appear at all in Renzulli's conception (although it may be a by-product of the three components of the Renzulli model).

In the last chapter of Part II, Chapter 6, Patricia Haensly, Cecil R. Reynolds, and William R. Nash also propose a four-component conception of giftedness, but their conception is much more ecologically based and less individually based than is Feldhusen's. Their four components are (a) coalescence, (b) context, (c) conflict, and (d) commitment. (No doubt by coincidence, the letter *c* plays a highly significant role in this conception!)

Coalescence refers to the way abilities come together and work together to produce significant products. For these investigators, the question in defining giftedness is not just what level of abilities an individual has, but how the abilities coalesce synergistically in the production of creative work. Context refers to the situational factors that determine the worth of a product. It is the basis of Tannenbaum's psychosocial conception of giftedness. Thus, a given product might be viewed as worthwhile in one society, and as worth little in another. Or it may not be recognized as valuable in its time but only be "discovered" as a significant product later. For these investigators, then, as for Tannenbaum, giftedness cannot be defined outside a societal context. Conflict shapes and hones the development of the gifted individual. Gifted individuals do not develop in a vacuum but rather respond in certain special ways to the press of the environment. The ways in which they respond determine in large part whether they will produce significant work or not. Finally, commitment (or what Renzulli refers to as "task commitment") refers to an individual's willingness to preserve and stick to the development of excellence. Commitment is persistence in the face of conflict and in the face of obstacles to arrive at the high level of performance of which one is capable, but only in the long run, after much work and travail.

Integrative and recurrent themes

To summarize, then, the contributors in this section propose implicit-theoretical conceptions of giftedness. Several important themes run through these conceptions and will appear throughout the book. First, one must identify the domain that serves as the basis of one's definition, whether individual, societal, or some subset of either of these, such as the educational subset of the societal domain. Second, all of the contributors in this section agree that cognitive abilities are an essential part of giftedness, although there is less than total accord regarding how these abilities are partitioned, particularly with regard to which abilities are domain-general and which are domain-specific. Third, motivation in the form of task commitment is viewed as an essential prerequisite for giftedness, in that without it, latent abilities will never manifest themselves. Fourth, the contributors all believe in the importance of the developmental course of one's various talents for whether or how they are expressed, although these beliefs are expressed in very different ways. The basic theme running through the chapters is that society at its various levels rewards some expressions of one's talents and not others. Throughout the life-span, every gifted individual will be rewarded at some times and nonrewarded or even punished at others. The way the individual reacts to his or her individual course of rewards, nonrewards, and punishments will determine in some part whether an individual is identified as gifted, and in what way he or she is so identified. Fifth and finally, a theme that runs through all the chapters, but is most explicit in the chapter of Haensly et al., is the theme of "coalescence," or of how all of this comes together – not just the patterning of one's abilities, but the combination of one's abilities working together in a motivated way as affected by societal forces that canalize the expression of these abilities. Although some civilizations seem to have had many more gifted individuals than others in terms of contribution to posterity, it seems unlikely it is because those civilizations had better genes. Rather, they presumably structured the environments of their citizens in ways that facilitated rather than inhibited the expression of gifts.

Explicit-theoretical approaches: cognitive theory

Part III of the book presents the chapters of those contributors who most clearly emphasize the explicit theories of cognitive psychology in their writings. This is not to say that all the conceptions of giftedness presented in this section are strictly cognitive, but rather that cognition seems to be the focal point for all of the conceptions, whether or not they are strictly cognitive.

In Chapter 7, Nancy Ewald Jackson and Earl C. Butterfield emphasize the role of metacognition in giftedness. In their own terms, "superordinate processes regulating task analysis and self-management of problem-solving behavior may be important components differentiating gifted from average performance." Jackson and Butterfield's strategy in their chapter is to review various studies of giftedness, and to show how the locus of giftedness displayed in these studies can be understood in terms of metacognitive functioning. The authors do not argue that superior metacognitive functioning is all there is to giftedness or that the evidence linking metacognition to giftedness is conclusive. Rather they argue that the evidence is highly suggestive in pointing to superior metacognitive ability as a key component of giftedness, and moreover, that this component is one that is eminently researchable. They thus present their metacognitive view as one "designed to promote research."

In Chapter 8, John G. Borkowski and Virginia A. Peck elaborate upon the theme established by Jackson and Butterfield. Borkowski and Peck also emphasize the importance of metacognition in giftedness, but they concentrate on a specific aspect of metacognition, namely, metamemory, or one's knowledge and control of one's memory. The bulk of this chapter is devoted to the presentation of a longitudinal study that not only shows the importance of metamemory to gifted performance but also contrasts metamemory to other factors. This strategy of contrasting factors is noteworthy because it is so little used. In the majority of studies the variables under test are confounded with other variables, but no attempt is made to rule out plausible alternative interpretations of the data. The results of the contrast were not entirely clear-cut, however. For example, although Borkowski and Peck built into portions of their study controls for general world knowledge and efficiency of information processing, they end up concluding that these factors also contribute, in greater or lesser degree, to giftedness. Thus, they, like Jackson and Butterfield, recognize that giftedness is plural in its etiology. But they also emphasize, as do Jackson and Butterfield, the importance of isolating a small number of manageable variables if one wishes to conduct experimental research on giftedness.

In Chapter 9, Janet E. Davidson continues in the style of Jackson and Butterfield, and of Borkowski and Peck, by identifying a single variable believed to be particularly critical to giftedness. In Davidson's chapter, this variable is insight. She first establishes the importance of insight in giftedness by showing that most of the major contributions to civilization, as well as many of the more minor ones, have involved insights of greater or lesser degree. She then goes on to establish what insight is, and why it has proven so resistant to experimental analysis.

Davidson suggests that insights are of three kinds: (a) selective encoding, (b) selective combination, and (c) selective comparison. Insights of selective encoding involve distinguishing information that is relevant for one's purposes from information that is irrelevant. Insights of selective combination involve putting together the relevant pieces in just the right way. Insights of selective comparison involve relating these pieces to information already stored in memory. In all three cases, these mental processes become "insights" when they are applied in ways that are nonobvious and inventive. The great insights of history are societally significant as well, and Davidson analyzes several such insights in terms of the theory she proposes. She also presents the results of a set of experiments that isolates the three insight processes and that shows their importance in giftedness.

As do the other authors discussed in Part III, Davidson goes to some lengths to emphasize that no one variable can account for all of intellectual giftedness. But experimental psychologists believe in the importance of first isolating variables and studying them intensively, and only then relating these variables to the other variables underlying a complex phenomenon. Jackson and Butterfield, Borkowski and Peck, and Davidson all follow this strategy of experimental isolation of variables.

In Chapter 10, Robert J. Sternberg places himself squarely in the cognitive tradition by emphasizing the centrality of cognition in giftedness. In his case, the emphasis is on cognitive components, or processes, of intellectual functioning. But Sternberg departs from the style of the other chapters by attempting to place the cognitive aspects of functioning in the context of a theory of intelligence that is not wholly cognitive, namely, his triarchic theory of intelligence. This theory is used as the basis for understanding giftedness.

According to Sternberg, intellectual giftedness has three aspects. The first is cognitive and internal to the individual: The gifted individual can be superior in the functioning of his or her mental processes, including the "metacomponents" that represent the metacognitive functioning dealt with by Jackson and Butterfield and by Borkowski and Peck, and the "knowledge-acquisition components" that represent the cognitive bases for acquiring the knowledge studied by Borkowski and Peck, and, under special circumstances, the insightful functioning dealt with by Davidson. The second aspect is experiential, relating cognition to one's level of experience in applying cognitive processes in particular tasks or situations. The gifted individual can be superior in dealing with relative novelty and in automatizing information processing (that is, in rendering it rapid and outside deliberate conscious control). Sternberg would view the efficiency of information processing studied by Borkowski and Peck in terms of the efficiency with which information processing is automatized. Finally, the gifted individual may be superior in applying the processes of intellectual functioning, as mediated by experience, to functioning in real-world contexts. According to Sternberg, the outward manifestation of giftedness is in superior adaptation to, shaping of, and selection of environments.

Sternberg, like the other contributors to this volume, does not believe that giftedness is any single thing, say, resulting from the conjunction of the skills noted above. Rather, giftedness can come in several varieties. Some gifted individuals may be particularly adept at applying the components of intelligence, but only to academic kinds of situations. They may thus be "test-smart," but little more. Other gifted individuals may be particularly adept at dealing with novelty, but in a synthetic rather than an analytic sense: Their creativity is not matched by analytic power. Still other gifted individuals may be "street-smart" in external contexts, but at a loss in academic contexts. Thus, giftedness is plural rather than singular in nature.

Integrative and recurrent themes

The strategy of the explicit theorists for understanding giftedness is quite different from that of the implicit theorists. The implicit theorists propose a definition or kind of definition of giftedness, and then seek to show that this definition is consistent with the way they and others use the term *giftedness*. Giftedness is an invention, and a major goal of an implicit theorist is to define just what has been invented: What does the invention look like, and how does it function?

The cognitive theorists agree among themselves in several respects, most of which, incidentally, serve to distinguish them from the implicit theorists.

First, the explicit theorists drawing on cognitive theory concentrate not on use of the term *giftedness* but rather on the internal, cognitive antecedents of it. What is it that a person can do well to be identified by this term? In effect, what are the cognitive bases of giftedness? The emphasis in these chapters, then, is on mechanism, not on lexical use.

Second, the cognitive theorists also agree among themselves on the importance of an isolation-of-variables strategy for understanding the cognitive mechanisms underlying giftedness. The implicit theorists, in contrast, placed less emphasis on single variables and more emphasis on lists of variables. The strategy of experimental isolation probably gains depth in the understanding of any one variable, with some loss of breadth in considering other variables and how the variables interact. For example, it is unlikely any of the cognitive theorists would deny that motivation plays an important part in giftedness, and yet none of them directly deal with it, in contrast to the implicit theorists, all of whom do so. Furthermore, their cognitive emphases suggest that they are dealing more with the intellectual forms of giftedness than with any of the other forms, for example, of leadership or of artistic talent. Even Sternberg, who attempts to consider a broader range of variables and their interactions, draws heavily on experiments, including his own, that employ an isolation-of-variables strategy that emphasizes the cognitive in intellectual functioning.

Third, the cognitive theorists agree in their greater emphasis on higher- rather than lower-level processes in understanding giftedness. This emphasis is consistent with that of the implicit theorists and also with that of psychometricians in the tradition of Binet. It is not as consistent with that of psychometricians in the tradition of Galton (who studied psychophysical bases of intelligence), of whom there are few today. But there are a number of cognitive theorists who are more in the tradition of Galton than of Binet. The current contributors, in their emphases on processes of metacognition and insight, side more with the Binetians than with the Galtonians, although they owe exclusive allegiance to neither side: Clearly, lower-level, "bottom–

up" processes are needed in order for high-level, "top–down" processes to function.

Fourth and finally, the cognitivists are committed to theory-driven empirical research as the primary means for advancing our understanding of giftedness. The implicit theorists draw on empirical research in making their points, but this research is not as central to their points as is the research of the cognitivists to their points. Moreover, the research cited by the implicit theorists is more often than not atheoretical. Giftedness is an area in which there has been very little theory-driven research. The cognitivists show a determination to change this situation, and have already started doing so. We believe this is an important development, so long as it is remembered that ultimately, breadth will be as important as depth in obtaining a full understanding of the nature of giftedness.

Explicit-theoretical approaches: developmental theory

The contributors to this part of the book, like those to the preceding one, draw primarily on explicit psychological theories in their work. But whereas the contributors considered above draw primarily on cognitive theories, the contributors in this section draw primarily on developmental theories.

In Chapter 11, Howard E. Gruber makes four main points. First, understanding giftedness requires understanding of the processes of child and especially adult development. Gruber believes the best approach to understanding such development is to study intensively the lives of a small number of extraordinary individuals, a research strategy in marked contrast to that used by the cognitive theorists of Part III, all of whom tend to use the large samples typical of conventional psychological research. Second, the main force in development of an extraordinary person is that person's own activities and interests. Thus, giftedness in extraordinary adults is largely a creation on the part of the gifted person, not just something that "happens to" the person. For Gruber, adult giftedness can unfold only in the wake of self-mobilization of resources and the feeling of specialness that gives rise to it. Third, the meaning as well as the value of any particular kind of gift depends on historical and social circumstances. This position is in accord with that of Tannenbaum in his chapter on the psychosocial factors contributing to giftedness. Fourth, the best way to study extraordinary giftedness in adults is to study closely the lives of creative people. Gruber, for example, has devoted a substantial portion of his career to studying the lives of Darwin and Piaget. Indeed, his thinking has been heavily influenced by both of these scientists.

In Chapter 12, Mihaly Csikszentmihalyi and Rick E. Robinson argue, as has Gruber, that (a) talent cannot be understood or observed except against a background of cultural expectations, and that (b) talent is not a stable trait, because both individual capacity for action and cultural demands for performance change over the lifetime. Note that, like Gruber, these authors emphasize the "unfolding" of giftedness throughout the life-span, a developmental emphasis that simply did not attain any prominence in the cognitively oriented conceptions. Csikszentmihalyi and Robinson suggest that four kinds of development, or "time lines," influence the development of giftedness. Giftedness at one point in development can be a very different thing from giftedness at another point in development.

The first time line is that of life-span transitions of the kind proposed, say, by Erikson. As the developmental tasks of the individual in his or her life change, so do the kinds of contributions that the individual is able to make. The second time line is that of cognitive development. Here, the authors draw on the kinds of stage transitions proposed by Piaget and his successors. Again, the kinds of performances an individual can generate, and that can be described as gifted, will depend on that individual's level of cognitive development. The third time line is that of progression in a given domain of endeavor, such as art, physics, music, or whatever. In art, for example, development in the domain proceeds from spontaneous drawing, to copying, to realistic rendering, to learning the cultural canons and creative experimenting, to the development of a personal style. The fourth time line is that of progression in the field as a social structure. In art, for example, one's unstructured drawing may lead to art courses in school, which then lead to one becoming a full-fledged student of art or an apprentice, which may then lead to one's employment as an artist or art teacher. These four time lines proceed in parallel, and interact with each other to produce what comes to be labeled as gifted performance in some individuals.

Note that these contributors, like Gruber, view development from a life-span perspective. One could not possibly understand giftedness in adults by viewing development as stopping, say, in late adolescence. These contributors are also in accord with Gruber in their stress on interactionism. One cannot understand giftedness merely by looking at the development of the individual in isolation from his or her context, nor can one understand it solely in terms of the context. Rather, one must consider how the individual interacts with his or her context. Whether or not the person will eventually be recognized as gifted will depend upon whether this interaction is a favorable one. For example, no matter how well or rapidly cognitive and socio-emotional development proceed, they will not lead to giftedness if the opportunities are not available both for learning and for expression of the giftedness in some recognized, or at least recognizable, field of endeavor.

In Chapter 13, David Henry Feldman proposes to describe "giftedness as a developmentalist sees it." Feldman emphasizes three features in his developmental view of giftedness. First, he emphasizes the *processes* of intellectual functioning rather than underlying structural *traits*. In this respect, he is in accord with the cognitive theorists of the preceding part, as well as with the developmental theorists considered so far. Second, he views development in terms of a sequence of stages. This view is consistent with that of Csikszent-mihalyi and Robinson, who also posit stages of various kinds, and to a lesser extent with that of Gruber, for whom stages seem to be less clearly demar-cated. Third, and perhaps most critically to Feldman's point of view, devel-opment of giftedness is domain-specific. Supplementing Piaget's universal stages is a sequence of stages that is specific to a given domain. It is the progression through this latter sequence of stages that will determine who is eventually labeled as gifted and who is not. Development through non-universal stages proceeds in parallel with development through universal stages, although not necessarily at the same rate. Child prodigies, for example, show extremely rapid development through the nonuniversal stages, whether or not they show extremely rapid development through the universal ones.

In Chapter 14, Joseph Walters and Howard Gardner continue the emphasis on domain-specific development that was seen in the preceding chapters, in particular that of Feldman. In their chapter, Walters and Gardner emphasize a particularly interesting feature of domain-specific development, namely, the "crystallizing experience," which they define as an experience involving re-markable and memorable contact between a person with unusual talent or potential and the materials of the field in which that talent will be manifested. Such experiences are neither necessary nor sufficient for the development of giftedness, but they appear to play an important role in the lives of many gifted individuals. For these individuals, the crystallizing experience literally changes their lives, steering them in the direction that will later become the domain of a lifetime endeavor.

Walters and Gardner view the crystallizing experience in the context of Gardner's theory of multiple intelligences, according to which intelligence is not a unitary construct but rather a plural one. According to this theory, there are at least seven independent forms of intelligence: linguistic, musical, logical–mathematical, spatial, bodily–kinesthetic, interpersonal, and intra-personal. The crystallizing experience is essentially an encounter of one of these intelligences with the external world, in which one comes to realize the signal importance of that particular intelligence for the unfolding of one's creative potential. It is such experiences that can enable someone brought up, say, in a primarily linguistic environment to realize that his or her main potentials lie elsewhere, and thereby to enable the alteration of a life plan. Without such experience, an individual might never come into contact with his or her own profile of abilities, and the potential bases for creative inspiration.

In Chapter 15, Robert S. Albert and Mark A. Runco derive their conception of giftedness from seven basic assumptions: (a) At high levels of mental ability and talent, intelligence and creativity are not strictly separable; (b) for a gifted person to achieve eminence, his or her early giftedness must be transformed

oh yes they are !

into an appropriate set of values, drives, and skills; (c) the transformation of gifted creativity into eminence begins within one's family structure but is steadily refined through one's formal and informal education, as well as through one's early career efforts; (d) whether a potentially gifted person will actually become gifted will depend in large part on the "informing opportunities" in one's life that enable one either to be steered, or to steer oneself, toward a certain kind of career; (e) the experience-producing and experience-selecting attributes of a family reside primarily in the socioeconomic status, personalities, and values of the family members; (f) family history, as it unfolds in the full interaction of all members of the family, influences the development of each family member, including the potentially gifted one; and (g) the family is a biological and interpersonal organizer of the individual's gifts, focusing and mobilizing both the individual and the surrounding environment in ways that may be more or less favorable for the eventual display of giftedness.

Integrative and recurrent themes

Several themes run throughout the chapters in Part IV. The first recurrent theme is the importance of development, and especially of life-span development, to the emergence of giftedness. Giftedness is not merely something with which one is born, nor does its development stop in late adolescence. Indeed, its development continues throughout the life-span. In developmental psychology today, there is a tension between those who believe that the "interesting" aspects of development stop in adolescence (as did Piaget, for example) and those who believe that interesting development never stops. All of the theorists in these chapters side with the latter camp, at least with regard to understanding giftedness. Some of the theorists, such as Gruber, would even argue that the most interesting aspects of the development of the gifted individual occur later, not earlier, during life.

Second, there is an emphasis among these contributors on the importance of domain-specific, or nonuniversal, aspects of development. None of the theorists deny that there are universal aspects as well. But they do not view gifted individuals as proceeding rapidly through the Piagetian stages or mastering the operations of various universal stages at a higher level than do others. Rather, they see gifted individuals as excelling in one or possibly more domains of talent. Their stagelike development in this domain may be quite idiosyncratic, despite certain regularities associated with progression through stages.

Third, the theorists are all interactionists with respect to the respective roles of the individual and the environment. Although the contributors emphasize varying levels of environmental analysis (family, society, field of endeavor, etc.), all agree that giftedness is defined, shaped, and adjudged in a societal milieu and is not something merely inside a person's head. Tests used to identify the gifted tend to be oversimplifications because of their seeking to find inside a person something that is without as well as within.

Fourth, the investigators all emphasize the importance of the case-study analysis of gifted individuals. This emphasis is not a necessary concomitant of a developmental focus: Many developmental psychologists use large-sample methods. Most of the contributors in this part of the book have themselves used large-sample methods at one time or another, but at the same time they believe that our really trenchant insights about giftedness have evolved from the intensive study of small numbers of cases.

Fifth, the developmentalists all emphasize the role of naturalistic or biographical observation in studying the gifted, as opposed to laboratory methods. Indeed, they often have no choice, as many of the gifted whom they have studied are deceased. But these investigators clearly believe that giftedness will best be understood in the context where it occurs, rather than in laboratory settings.

Sixth and finally, the contributors to these chapters all stress socio-emotional as well as cognitive aspects of development. For them, giftedness is not a solely cognitive phenomenon, as one might measure on an intelligence test or even a creativity test. It is an interaction of systems that involves motivation and affect as well as cognition. Again, strictly cognitive tests provide a rather dim view, if they provide any view at all, of the motivational and affective aspects of giftedness, and of how they interact with each other and with the cognitive aspect.

Although the contributors in this part of the book, like those in the preceding one, all draw on psychological theories, it is interesting to note how different the outcomes are. Indeed, these outcomes differ with respect to all five points above. First, although all of the cognitive theorists in Part III are professionally identified as developmental psychologists (with at least one of their professional hats), none of them in their chapters say much about the role of life-span development of giftedness. Second, all of the cognitive theorists concentrate on universal rather than nonuniversal aspects of the gifted individual. Metacognition, for example, is a universal skill, but the claim is that the gifted possess it in an unusual degree relative to the typical individual. Third, relatively little is said in the cognitive chapters about the role of interaction between the individual and the environment in the development of giftedness, except, perhaps, in Sternberg's chapter. And the part of Sternberg's chapter that deals with this interaction (the contextual subtheory of his theory of intelligence) is the part that he and others would identify as least cognitive. Fourth, large-sample methods are used in all of the studies that are drawn on to bolster the proposed cognitive theories. Case-study methods receive virtually no attention. Fifth, the cognitivists all emphasize laboratory rather than naturalistic studies of gifted performance, and make heavy use of psychometric and cognitive tasks in their analyses. Finally, almost no attention is paid in the cognitive chapters to socio-emotional and motivational factors underlying giftedness.

Lest the cognitivists be faulted relative to the developmentalists, it is important to point out that just as the cognitivists do not follow the themes of the developmentalists, so do the developmentalists not follow the themes of the cognitivists. First, although the developmentalists all talk about mental processes, they do so in vague terms without saying specifically what the cognitive processes are or how they could be identified. Second, none of the developmentalists has employed an isolation-of-variables strategy in his or her research, a strategy that is, of course, difficult to employ in the naturalistic settings favored by the developmentalists. But without such a strategy, it is usually difficult to identify exactly what variable is causing a certain phenomenon. Especially in the real world, variables tend to co-occur so often that without an isolation-of-variables strategy, judgments will inevitably be made on the basis of confounded data. Third, although the developmentalists clearly are interested in high-level cognitive processes as partial bases for giftedness, they do not specify how these processes, even if vaguely defined, might fit into an entire cognitive system of functioning. They may refer to one or more cognitive systems, but there is little detail as to what these cognitive systems look like. Finally, the empirical research of the developmentalists tends to be more exploratory and less theory-driven than that of the cognitivists. All of the developmentalists are theoreticians and use theory in their research. But the designs of their studies do not bear the tight fit to the guiding theory that is the case in the cognitive research. The studies are carried out within a theoretical framework, but their designs are clearly less closely tied to theory than is the case for the cognitive researchers.

To summarize, cognitive and developmental theorists tend to look at somewhat different aspects of giftedness, and to look at these aspects in somewhat different ways. If the discussion in the preceding paragraphs has made anything clear, it is that these ways are largely complementary, and that there is a need to combine the two perspectives and methodologies more fully than is presently being done. There seems to be no reason, in principle, why an approach could not be devised that combines the best aspects of both the cognitive and the developmental approaches to giftedness.

Explicit-theoretical approaches: domain-specific theory

The fifth part of the book consists of two chapters presenting views of giftedness in specific domains. In a certain sense, these two sets of contributors follow the domain-specific emphasis of the developmental theorists in attempting to understand giftedness as it exists in a single domain. The two domains studied are those of mathematics and of music.

In Chapter 16, Julian C. Stanley and Camilla Persson Benbow report on their studies of and interventions in mathematical precocity. They define mathematical precocity in terms of high scores on the mathematics section of the College Board Scholastic Aptitude Test. The authors of the chapter note that their Study of Mathematically Precocious Youth (SMPY) is not much concerned with conceptualizing giftedness. At the same time, there is a clear conception of giftedness underlying the SMPY program, one that emerges throughout the chapter.

A first aspect of this conception is the view of giftedness as early precocity. The investigators administer to young children a test that has been constructed for much older children and that would normally be considered inappropriate for the younger children. They are able to justify this administration by taking the position that they are interested more in measuring attained skill rather than some latent skill that may not be readily accessible through measurement. The Stanley–Benbow view of giftedness is thus a developmental one, but one that emphasizes rapidity of intellectual development in a specific domain.

A second aspect of the Stanley–Benbow conception is the emphasis on the childhood phase of life development. In this respect, these investigators separate themselves from the life-span perspective of the developmentalists in Part IV. Indeed, they question whether so-called late bloomers even exist, in direct contrast to the view of Gruber.

A third aspect of the Stanley–Benbow conception is that of domain-specificity, which puts them in the same camp as the developmentalists. Indeed, Stanley and Benbow argue that they eschew the use of general intelligence tests for their purposes because the tests are not specific enough in the skills they measure. They may be useful as measures of general abilities, but they are nonoptimal for measuring the mathematical reasoning abilities with which Stanley and Benbow concern themselves.

A fourth aspect of the Stanley–Benbow view is that intervention is a proximal goal, not merely a distal goal, following from understanding of giftedness. Probably all of the contributors to this book are concerned, at some level, with interventions that foster the expression of gifts. But none are concerned with the immediacy of Stanley and Benbow. The others view conceptualization and intervention as occurring at two distinct and separable levels. Stanley and Benbow seem not to: In using an operational definition of giftedness, their conception becomes identical to their means of selection for a program of intervention. It is important to note that the focus of their operationalization is not simply on identification, as it might be, say, among some of those who have defined intelligence as what intelligence tests measure. For Stanley and Benbow, identification is simply a necessary first step in the intervention process, namely, the step of selecting those whom the intervention will most benefit.

In Chapter 17, Jeanne Bamberger reports on her studies of musically gifted children. Her main findings have been that (a) gifted young performers have an unusual capacity for representing musical relations to themselves in multiple ways; (b) these multiple representations are conceived of not as distinct but rather as intertwined and as intersecting; (c) earlier representations seem to undergo a transition in adolescence to new forms of representation; these later representations are more formal, more analytical, and more separable from each other; (d) as a result, the functional reciprocity of the network of representations that exists for younger performers no longer exists for older performers; and (e) gifted adolescents must therefore find a way of coordinating these newly separated musical representations so as to make them function in a unified and integrated way.

Bamberger's analysis of unusual musical performers is fascinating, and unusual in its combination of developmental analysis and detailed specification of cognitive representations. Although its author views this as a domain-specific analysis, we wonder whether some or all of Bamberger's findings might be generalizable to other domains. Without intensive analysis of the kind Bamberger has conducted for musicians, we are not yet in a position to know.

Conclusions and integration

In the final chapter, Chapter 18, Robert S. Siegler and Kenneth Kotovsky integrate the various contributions to the book. They distinguish especially between contributors who focus on childhood giftedness in school and contributors who focus on adult giftedness in organized fields of endeavor. They also distinguish among the various levels of analysis of giftedness that the chapter contributors have provided: (a) elementary information processes, (b) processes that operate on products of elementary information processes, (c) rules and strategies, and (d) trait-level descriptions. These levels are further subdivided, and Siegler and Kotovsky show how each of the various contributors addresses one or more of these levels of analysis. This final chapter thus ends the task we have begun: that of placing conceptions of giftedness in perspective. But the time has ended for our perspective setting. It is now time for the perspectives themselves to begin, and for the contributors to speak with their own voices. Although they speak in many different voices and have many different messages to present, we believe the recurrent themes that permeate the chapters demonstrate that different approaches to giftedness are in the process of coming together. We hope that eventually they will merge into a truly unified field of endeavor.

Part II

Implicit-theoretical approaches

2   Giftedness: a psychosocial approach

Abraham J. Tannenbaum

The power center for giftedness is the human brain, which controls both the magnitude and the diversity of individual potential. It can transport an Einstein into heights of abstraction and a da Vinci into flights of creativity that are so far beyond ordinary accomplishments as to seem almost miraculous. It can also generate nearly endless traces of genius ranging from the esoterica of plasma physics, through the visual spectacle of the Taj Mahal, to the magical cadences of a Miltonic sonnet, the sublime sounds of an *Eroica* symphony, the gustatory delights of gourmet cooking, the intricate beauties of Oriental knot designs, and on and on into every possible domain of individual activity.

But whereas the psyche determines the *existence* of high potential, society decides on the *direction* toward its fulfillment by rewarding some kinds of achievement while ignoring or even discouraging others. Rare brainpower has to fit into its own Zeitgeist in order to be recognized and appreciated. For example, it is virtually unthinkable for a twentieth-century gifted dramatist to write a morality play in medieval style or for a composer to create an *Eine Kleine Nachtmusik* to entertain in the salons of aristocracy, since church-centered medievalism no longer predominates, and the royal court of eighteenth-century Europe is an anachronism in today's Western life.

There has to be a perfect match between a person's particular talent and the readiness of society to appreciate it. Otherwise, genius will remain stillborn or mature to serve an unappreciating audience that may regard it either as passé, if it is a throwback to earlier times, or as too avant-garde if the times are not ready for it. There is always room to speculate whether Einstein would have been able to make a contribution to theoretical physics, or whether the scientific world would have been ready for his kind of contribution, if he had been born only half a century before his actual birth. Perhaps he would not have been capable of creating any spectacular theories at all if he had been born in 1950 and others had formulated the theory of relativity ahead of him. This is pure conjecture, but what is clearly evident is that gifted individuals

An elaboration of ideas presented in this chapter may be found in the author's book *Gifted Children: Psychological and Educational Perspectives* (Macmillan, 1983).

who achieve great breakthroughs in the world of ideas do not operate simply as free spirits detached from the temper of their times.

The hierarchical nature of talent

Attempts have been made to define giftedness from a sociocultural perspective that relies heavily on public tastes. Thus, in Western civilization, the most popular talents may be categorized as moral, social, economic, and educational (Holmes, Lauwerys, & Russell, 1961; Phenix, 1964). Society arranges these domains in a prestige hierarchy in which the distances between them are not necessarily uniform. For example, if the social realm were ranked highest, followed by the economic, educational, and moral, in that order, it is possible that the educational would compare more prestigiously with the moral than would the social with the economic or the economic with the educational. To complicate the picture, distances between them are constantly changing. In fact, realms can change places in the hierarchy from one historical period to the next. There are also subcategories of specialized activity within each realm that have their own prestige hierarchy and are always on the move in the same way that the greater realms relate dynamically to each other. Finally, it is important to note that a specific area of specialization within a realm can be more highly acclaimed publicly than one at the corresponding level of a higher realm. It is therefore possible for the most renowned moralists to be more lionized than their counterparts in the economic sphere, even though economics rates higher than morals in the overall prestige rankings.

The categorical nature of talent

There is no way of knowing what accounts for society's seeming fickleness in preferring one sphere of activity over another. Why is ballet classified among the more celebrated art forms, whereas gymnastics, acrobatics, and figure skating never rise above the level of popular entertainment? What distinguishes between highbrow and lowbrow creativity? Surely not the number of neural connections or size of audiences involved. Playing championship chess is surely no less demanding an intellectual chore than is working with complex chemical formulas; yet, research chemists are often more widely acclaimed as gifted than are international grand masters, despite the fact that chess tournaments attract more appreciative spectators than do chemical laboratories.

Equating excellence with the ability to create beauty or to enhance the human condition is also problematic since it can lead to the logical absurdity that pure mathematics should be excluded for failing to measure up on either count. It is a rare person who is sensitive enough to recognize artistry in mathematical abstractions or trusting enough to believe that what is theoretical and obscure in mathematics today could someday lead to practical outcomes. Still, the failure of renowned mathematicians to make sense aesthetically or practicably to all but a tiny handful of gifted colleagues has not prevented them from being revered by the masses for their intellect.

It is hard to know precisely why some extraordinary behaviors are considered gifted and others are not. Much depends on popular beliefs that are too subjective and ephemeral to be captured by rules of logic. But even though we rely so often on "gut feelings" rather than on clear rationales in deciding what belongs in the galaxy of high-level talent, there is remarkable consensus in most instances, and inexplicable disagreements in some. The fact is that dramatic theater is universally accepted as a major art form, whereas sports is far more controversial, despite the fact that both work hard at arousing pity and fear in their respective audiences. Pros and cons about the qualifications of athletics are hardly persuasive because they rely more on emotion than on reason. The same can be said about some types of human performance that attract *unanimous* pros *or* cons.

Perhaps the reasons why only some talents are valued as evidence of excellence will never be fully understood, but this lack of understanding does not necessarily mean that such judgments are whimsical. If preferences are governed by any kind of logic, it may be reflected to some extent in the way people classify individual talents as either of a (a) scarcity, (b) surplus, (c) quota, or (d) anomalous type of giftedness.

Scarcity talents

Of the four categories of talent, those referred to here as scarcity talents are forever in short supply. The world is always in need of people inventive enough to make life easier, safer, healthier, and more intelligible. Although it takes only a single Jonas Salk to achieve the breakthrough in conquering polio, there can never be enough talent like his for the great leaps forward that still need to be made in medical science. The same can be said for an Abraham Lincoln in political leadership, a Martin Luther King, Jr., in race relations, and a Sigmund Freud in mental health. Society will always venerate such talents as they appear, while thirsting for more and more because the shortage can never be filled, principally because the public's motives are more self-preserving than self-serving. It makes sense, therefore, to consider these special abilities as symbols of excellence.

Surplus talents

Those who possess surplus talents have the rare ability to elevate people's sensibilities and sensitivities to new heights through the production of great art, literature, music, and philosophy. Few individuals can excel in this category, and some who do achieve celebrity status, which means that they are the most widely recognizable people in the eyes of the general public. But despite the fame and fortune of a Picasso and a Beethoven, they are treated as "divine luxuries" capable of beautifying the world without guaranteeing its continued existence. Of course, a Michelangelo and a Bach are always welcome as cultural assets; still, the need for such talents represents a *craving* for ways in which to enhance the quality of life rather than a *demand* for finding means of preserving life itself. People are more likely to suppress their cravings than their demands, as evidenced by the vast treasures of art, literature, and music that are widely unappreciated. It is said that multitudes acknowledge the greatness of Dante's *Inferno*, but hardly anyone ever reads it even once in a lifetime. For the nonreaders, such a masterpiece may be considered "surplus" in the sense that it is underutilized as literary fare, although it could never be considered "superfluous," inasmuch as some people, albeit a handful, do read and adore it.

The terms *scarcity talents* and *surplus talents* are not intended to express value judgments, as if one were superior to the other. They are simply different in the *kinds* (rather than the *amounts*) of admiration they elicit from society. Scarcity talents are treated as if they were vital commodities or natural resources that will always be in short supply as long as utopia is yet to be found. Their primary preoccupation is with fathoming the unknown and even the unknowable, and modern Western society has committed itself to investing all it can to further such an enterprise. The physical survival of individuals depends on the existence of scarcity talents, whereas the cultural survival of a civilization depends on surplus-type talents. Alexander Fleming saved countless lives in his and in all subsequent generations through his discovery of penicillin. In ancient Greece, epic poets, dramatists, and philosophers defined the essence of classical civilization through their works; once their voices and voices like theirs were stilled, the distinctive character of Greek civilization died without jeopardizing the physical lives of its people.

There is no doubt that many schools and their supporting communities are more eager to cultivate scarcity talents in order to keep body and soul together rather than to nurture surplus talents for the sake of keeping the human spirit alive.

Quota talents

In this category are included specialized, high-level skills needed to provide goods and services for which the market is limited. The job to be done is fairly clear; there are no creative breakthroughs expected and no way of knowing precisely how long the opportunities for such work will last. Job openings for the relatively few who qualify depend on supply and demand, which can be irregular and geographically bound. Thus, a person with aptitudes for local political leadership has a chance of becoming elected only on the first Tuesday in November, provided that an appropriate vacancy in public office exists on that day. Physicians, teachers, engineers, lawyers, commercial artists, and business executives are but a few of the kinds of highly skilled people whose work is valuable but sought after only for limited numbers of individuals. Sometimes there are scarcities of such talents, as in the case of physicians needed in poverty-stricken communities, and sometimes there are surpluses, such as liberal arts PhDs who are working at unskilled jobs because they cannot find faculty positions that may have been filled by less capable people hired ahead of them and protected by tenure policies.

Like scarcity and surplus talents, quota talents emerge in response to popular demand, but only up to the point where the public feels that its needs for such productivity are being met. For example, major symphony orchestras are kept alive by appreciative audiences that crave and reward first-rate performances played by first-rate musicians. Sometimes there are vacancies to be filled in orchestral sections, and the search is on for candidates who qualify. But the number of such positions is necessarily limited by the number of orchestras the public is willing to support. Hence, there is a quota system against which to measure shortage and surplus.

Schools are probably most responsive to the public's needs for quota talents. These types of advanced skills are easily understood in terms of shortages and superabundance, and therefore schools can be alerted to areas of specialization where there are many openings and the pay is good for those who are bright enough and trained to qualify. In many schools, the advanced training programs designed to fill quotas in various professions constitute the total effort at differentiating education for the gifted.

Anomalous talents

Finally, there are anomalous talents, which reflect how far the powers of the human mind and body can be stretched and yet not be recognized for excellence. They include many prodigious feats, some having practical value, others being appreciated for the amusement they provide, as in the listings of *The Guinness Book of World Records*. Speed reading, mastery of mountains of trivia, gourmet cooking, trapeze artistry, performance of complex mathematical calculations faster than a computer, and even the numbers of sexual seductions boasted by a Don Juan are examples of such talents. This is the only category that contains socially disapproved skills such as wily interpersonal behavior and demagoguery, which may require as much ingenuity as do leadership skills, except that they are detriments rather than benefits to humanity. In this category there are also "extinct" abilities such as oratory and various types of manual craftsmanship that belong among the scarcity, surplus, or quota talents in another era, but can now be considered anomalous talents because they have become anachronisms.

Schools often emphasize the development of some anomalous talents, especially those that attract crowds and build morale, such as sports, glee clubs, and marching bands. The popularity of such activities among students and alumni is communicated to faculties, who respond by mounting elaborate talent hunts and devoting considerable effort to sharpening these talents.

Thus we see that scarcity, surplus, quota, and anomalous types of giftedness are perceived, and sometimes valued, differently by people involved in the education of able children. In the abstract they may accept all four categories as defining the parameters of giftedness, but in practice they allow their predilections to determine which deserves to receive priority attention.

Psychological perspectives

As indicated earlier, giftedness is a psychological phenomenon that can manifest itself as scarcity, surplus, quota, or anomalous talent. It refers to the powers of the mind as they become actualized in rare and precious human performances or products. To date, a great deal more is known about the extent of its strength than about the essence of its functioning. For example, much of the literature has referred to gifted children in terms of their "intelligence" (Miles, 1954). But the meaning of this term as it applies to such children is not much clearer today than it was more than a half-century ago when Boring (1923) defined intelligence as something that is measured by tests of intelligence. What adds to the confusion is a large body of literature that equates giftedness with high IQ. Most modern writers on the subject deny the association as too simplistic, but many ignore their own denials by generalizing about giftedness on the basis of studies of high-IQ children. Of course, it is not easy to avoid such a trap because much of the published research has been conducted on this kind of population; however, those who attempt to define (rather than measure) giftedness from a psychological perspective are well aware that scores on tests of intelligence are intended to provide clues rather than understandings about superior potential.

Emphasis on genius

When genius became the subject of scientific investigation in the nineteenth century (Galton, 1869), the term denoted a degree of eminence rarely achieved in any individual's lifetime. Galton devised a normal curve of ability ranging from idiocy at the lowest level to genius at the highest, with fewer persons categorized at either extreme than at any other of fourteen intermediate points in the distribution. People were then rated according to the probability that contemporaries could do their jobs as well as they. For example, Galton placed prominent English judges and bishops at a level of eminence reached by no more than one individual in four thousand. The illustrious people, or geniuses, were those who could be singled out among millions as candidates for immortality.

Galton recognized genius as a matter of reputation for greatness, judged by contemporaries or by posterity, not as something revealed through psychometrics. Even though he was one of the earliest pioneers in formal mental testing, he never used his instruments to understand the nature of genius or to predict its emergence in young people. Still, his insights into persons who had earned renown in science (1874) led him to the conclusion that these people were endowed with superior intellectual ability, tremendous energy, good physical health, a sense of independence and purposefulness, and exceptional dedication to their fields of productivity. He also felt that they had vivid imaginations, strong, quick, and fluent mental associations, and a drive powerful enough to overcome many internal and external constraints. In short, Galton seemed to regard the genius as some kind of inspired mutant possessing exceptional characteristics, albeit in different combinations, according to the respective fields in which greatness is achieved.

It is noteworthy that Galton's description of the personality traits of geniuses has been essentially confirmed by more than a century of subsequent research on biographies of famous historical and contemporary figures (Cox et al., 1926; Roe, 1953; McCurdy, 1960; Goertzel & Goertzel, 1962; Goertzel, Goertzel, & Goertzel, 1978). What his successors have added, however, is a much better understanding of the environmental factors that contribute to career success. They have also devoted considerable attention to the childhood histories of the subjects under study.

Childhood potential and the IQ

As risky as it is to define and describe talent fulfilled, it is far more precarious to speak with assurance about it in its period of promise when predictions have to be made about the child's future development. Studying high-level potential among school-age children is of obvious interest to educators if there is some reason to hope that proper nurturance at school increases the chances of outstanding adult accomplishment. By far the largest-scale test of the hypothesis that such developmental linkages do exist can be found in the multivolume *Genetic Studies of Genius* conducted by Lewis M. Terman and his associates (Terman et al., 1925; Cox et al., 1926; Burks, Jensen, & Terman, 1930; Terman & Oden, 1947; Terman & Oden, 1959). (Although Terman helped to prepare the 1959 volume, he died in 1957. Several additional follow-up studies have been reported by Melita Oden [1968], Pauline S. Sears & Ann Barbee [1977], and Pauline S. Sears [1979].)

Terman felt justified in measuring general intelligence without formulating a theory about mental structure or process, just as physicists of his day thought it useful to measure electricity without knowing its exact nature. His central argument was that greatness does not reflect a mysterious, freakish mutation; instead, it stems from an extraordinary ability to exercise sensitive judgment in solving problems, to adapt to new situations, and to learn from performing various tasks and experiencing various situations. He felt that all people have these abilities in various degrees, except that the gifted excel in them and are therefore most successful in measuring up to the demands of school and society. He further suggested that these mental traits can be captured in an IQ score and that the gifted are those who rate in the highest percentile on such a measure. So confident was he in equating giftedness with high IQ that he bravely, perhaps brazenly, expressed the view that from the ranks of high-IQ children "and from nowhere else, our geniuses in *every* line are recruited" (Terman, 1924).

The research objectives of Terman and his associates were two-pronged: The first was to identify and conduct a longitudinal study of precocious elementary school age children for the remainder of their life-spans; the second was to conduct a retrospective biographical study of three hundred historical figures judged eminent on the basis of the amount of space they occupied in biographical dictionaries. From the vast amount of data collected over the years, it would appear that some of the original expectations of the study have been verified, whereas others remain doubtful or discredited. One enduring legacy is Terman's insistence that giftedness can be recognized in a continuum of abilities possessed by all people. He saw the gifted and nongifted as having the same organization of abilities but differing in the extent to which they are capable of cultivating some of them. Acceptance of Terman's assumptions about differences in degree rather than in kind means that studies of the nature and measurement of gifted performance can be subsumed under a general investigation of human mentality.

Another outcome of Terman's work that still endures is his conclusion that potential giftedness reveals itself even in childhood. "Early ripe, early rot" is a once popular platitude that has been turned into a canard by his studies of gifted children growing up. There are, to be sure, many case histories written about aborted genius, but they are exceptions to the rule that children with ample mental abilities, reasonably stable personalities, and proper nurturance tend eventually to excel in their careers. And since greatness does not materialize suddenly and unaccountably in adulthood, but instead has roots in its early years of growth, schools are in a key position to help gifted children realize their potential. It suggests the need for special educational programs for the gifted, an idea that would be irrelevant if there were no developmental connection between early promise and later fulfillment.

Other outcomes of Terman's research have not fared so well. Besides creating what promises to become an endless debate over the value of IQ measures in distinguishing between gifted and nongifted children, he contributed to the field two major ideas that have since fallen into disfavor. One of them has to do with the consistency of IQ scores and the inference that giftedness is basically a hereditary phenomenon. There is ample evidence from major longitudinal investigations, including the Harvard Growth Study (Dearborn & Rothney, 1941), the Berkeley Studies (Honzik, MacFarlane, & Allen, 1948), and the Fels Institute research (Sontag, Baker, & Nelson, 1958), that show dramatic shifts in IQ among individual children. Another of Terman's legacies that has fallen into disfavor is his apparent belief in the indivisibility of the organization of mental powers. He never pretended to advocate a theory of intelligence, but his need for a single score and the way in which he obtained it implies an assumption that intelligence consists of one general factor. In more recent years, factor analytic studies of intellectual functioning (Thurstone, 1947; Guilford, 1967) have demonstrated that mental powers may be multifaceted, consisting of special aptitudes that seem to be distinguishable from each other, not part of a single, overall intellectual power.

Differentiated talents

There are many who follow the Terman tradition of defining giftedness as general intellectual superiority that the individual channels into one of many possible areas of specialization on the basis of personal interests, encounters with inspiring teachers, or encouraging job opportunities. For purposes of locating such a gifted pool among children who are too young to choose specific life careers, there is no single, more valid measure than the IQ. But there are others who disagree strongly with the tendency to equate giftedness with high IQ. For example, Robinson (1977) charges that "in the post-Terman era, it has indeed become possible to become a 'gifted' individual without having any noticeable gift at all. We routinely categorize children as 'gifted' if their IQ scores are above 125, 130, 140, or whatever cutoff score we happen to choose, in spite of the fact that they do not do better than average work in school or demonstrate in any other fashion an exceptional degree of talent" (p. 2).

Generally speaking, the movement away from exclusive reliance on IQ and its correlates to define giftedness is not intended simply to devalue the IQ. Instead, the argument is that IQ limits giftedness to traditional academics and is not helpful in distinguishing among different kinds of intellectual functioning. According to Taylor and Ellison (1971), intelligence tests encompass only about 8 intellectual talents, which represent a small fraction of the well over 100 that are known to exist. Taylor and Ellison suggest a "multiple talent" approach to seek out children who are not only learners and reproducers but also thinkers, producers, decision makers, communicators, forecasters, and creators.

So influential has been the multiple talent approach to defining giftedness that the U.S. Commissioner of Education (Marland, 1971) incorporated it into his federal policy statement, as follows:

Children capable of high performance include those with demonstrated achievement and/or potential ability in any of the following areas, singly or in combination: (1) general intellectual ability, (2) specific academic aptitude, (3) creative or productive thinking, (4) leadership ability, (5) visual or performing arts, (6) psychomotor ability. (p. IX)

Although the federal definition has been popular in schools throughout the country, it has been subjected to some vigorous criticism. Renzulli (1978) argues that it omits the nonintellective factors that are vital in characterizing giftedness. He also points to the nonparallel nature of the six categories of giftedness in which two (i.e., specific academic aptitude and visual and performing arts) denote fields of accomplished performance, whereas the other four refer to cognitive processes that may be necessary to bring about superior achievement in many fields. Finally, there is a tendency for practitioners to treat the six categories as if they were independent of each other, and this tendency results in the development of separate identification systems for each category. Gallagher (1979) also sees a possible overlap among the six types of giftedness. In addition, he argues that the listing of leadership and psychomotor abilities is not yet justified because we do not know precisely what they mean and we are not able to identify high potential in either one. Despite these reservations, the federal definition emphasizing various kinds of talent is accepted in many programs for the gifted. Psychomotor ability, however, has been dropped from the list.

Theory without psychometrics

Despite the influence of Terman and the mental testing movement, attempts have been made to capture the essence of genius without relying on measurement instruments. For example, Ashby and Walker (1968) characterize the creative mind as a superintricate information processor. To them, a work of genius seems to have some kind of preexistence that awaits conceptualization and discovery. The great product or performance is actualized by a process of *selection*, or the appropriate means to attain a goal that can be treasured for all time. Successful selection is accomplished through information processing, whereby every alternative that is less than "the perfect" solution to the problem is eliminated. Thus, for example, Bach's *Well-Tempered Clavier* consists of notes, phrases, and rhythms selected by the composer from a universe of possibilities to make up the finished masterpiece. Bach could be regarded as a genius because only he had the ability to select the "bits" of information needed to solve his "problem."

The theory of genius expressed by Ashby and Walker is purely speculative, and these investigations make no use of formal tests to verify it. A somewhat similar departure from the use of psychometrics is also apparent in Sternberg's (1981) "componential" theory of intellectual giftedness. Instead of dealing with stable factors of promise or performance, he emphasizes an understanding of how the organism responds conceptually to external stimuli. Intellectual giftedness may be understood in terms of superior functioning of what he calls "metacomponents," "performance components," and "acquisition," "retention," and "transfer components."

Intellective and nonintellective attributes

Most theories of giftedness from a psychological perspective, including those presented thus far, refer strictly to human abilities of one kind or another. Yet it obviously takes more than brainpower to be an exceptional producer or performer. Without the support of nonintellective traits, such as the capacity and willingness to work hard in achieving excellence, it is impossible to rise above mediocrity. Renzulli (1978) recognized the need for *both* inspiration and perspiration, and he defined giftedness as consisting of three factors representing "above-average abilities," "task commitment," and "creativity," all of which are brought to bear on a large number of general and specific performance areas (see Chapter 3 of this volume for an elaboration of his theory).

Although Renzulli does not specify that giftedness requires the interplay of all three attributes in his model, Lamkins (undated) insists that the three attributes are necessary. However, she also labels children as "talented" if they possess the necessary above-average skills and knowledge and motivational characteristics even while lacking creativity. According to her, the academically talented are hard-working, well-organized high achievers whose performance lacks evidence of innovative ideas. The talented in visual and performing arts are able to perfect their technical skills but with little imagination or daring. Those possessing the necessary skills and creativity while lacking appropriate nonintellective traits for developing high potential are likely to become underachievers, and those combining creativity with the necessary personal drive are unlikely to succeed for want of higher-level thinking skills.

In another approach to the understanding of giftedness through its intellective and nonintellective dimensions, Piechowski (1979) advances the concept of developmental potential (DP), defined as "the original endowment which determines what level of development a person may reach under optimal conditions" (p. 28). DP is made up of special talents and abilities plus what Piechowski calls "overexcitability," an intense visceral reaction to experience that expresses itself in five forms: (a) the *psychomotor* mode, characterized by excessive physical energy, movement, restlessness, and action; (b) the *sensual* mode, of comfort and sensory delectation; (c) the *intellectual* mode, of logic, questioning, and the search for truth; (d) the *imaginational* mode, of dreams, fantasies, and images; and (e) the *emotional* mode, of attachments to other people, empathy, and love. These forms of personal experience are the main channels of human perception and conception. Piechowski likens them to "color filters through which the various external impingements and internal stirrings reach the individual. They determine to what occurrences and in what way one is capable of responding" (p. 29).

A proposed psychosocial definition

The various theories of giftedness discussed thus far seem more additive than alternative in the sense that each regards previous approaches as insufficient, not inappropriate. Those who emphasize the importance of special aptitudes often concede that there is a place for exceptional general ability in the makeup of giftedness, except that it tells only part of the story. Likewise, advocates of nonintellective traits want them as companion factors alongside general and special abilities in their definitions, without compromising the importance of extraordinary intellectual powers.

Furthermore, most theorists tend to agree on some basic issues regarding the nature of giftedness. First and foremost, there is no hesitation to focus on children, since precocity among the young is seen as a fairly valid forerunner of their future distinction. These children are not considered a "breed apart," with unfathomable mental powers or mind-sets for finding and solving problems in ways that seem miraculous for others of their age group. Rather than being characterized as qualitatively different, they are singled out for having quantifiable gifts such as accomplishing unusual and important things *faster*, at a *younger* age than expected, with *greater* efficiency, and *more* imaginatively in comparison to their peers. Finally, the fact that precocious children are heterogeneous in the talents they possess is generally accepted without controversy, although schools still nurture academic skills more ardently than any others.

There is a growing appreciation of diversity even within a particular talent domain. As Nobel Prize–winning zoologist Sir Peter Medawar (1979) suggests, scientists come in a variety of temperaments. There are what he calls collectors, classifiers, and compulsive tidiers-up; detectives and explorers; artists and artisans; poet-scientists and philosopher-scientists; and even mystic-scientists. On the basis of a study of young high achievers in mathematics, Blum-Zorman (1983) hypothesizes the existence of budding mathematicians capable of deep, systematic penetration into complex problems, in contrast to others capable of brilliant leaps of imagination in mathematics. It is therefore reasonable to suspect that, whatever traits are associated with the way in which people create great science or mathematics in their peak years, these syndromes insinuate themselves into the personality structures of such people long before they become renowned, even as early as childhood.

Because childhood precocity frequently leads to adult giftedness, a clear distinction has to be made between them. Work accomplished during a person's maturity can be evaluated by objective standards if its aim is, for example, to prevent rejection of transplanted human organs. Or it can be subjected to critical review, as in the case of poetic composition, to determine whether it deserves to be disseminated and treasured. Not so with children's achievements. Children who are identified as potentially gifted would mostly fail to quality for renown if they were judged on the basis of universal criteria. Instead, they have to be compared with others of their age for early signs of talent that is amenable to nurturance and that promises to live up to high expectations in the future.

Because there can never be any assurance that precocious children will fulfill their potential, defining giftedness among them is necessarily risky. One set of criteria may be *ineffective* because it excludes too many children who may grow up to be gifted; other qualifying characteristics may prove *inefficient* by including too many who turn out to be nongifted. There is inevitably a trade-off between effectiveness and efficiency, and educators invariably opt for a definition that enables them to cast the widest possible net at the outset to be sure not to neglect children whose high potential may be all but hidden from view.

Keeping in mind that developed talent exists only in adults, a proposed definition of giftedness in children is that it denotes their potential for becoming critically acclaimed performers or exemplary producers of ideas in spheres of activity that enhance the moral, physical, emotional, social, intellectual, or aesthetic life of humanity.

Outstanding contributors to the arts, sciences, letters, and general well-being of fellow humans tend often to show signs of promise in childhood. It is therefore reasonable to identify precocious children as the pool from which the most highly gifted are likely to emerge. But precocity only signifies rapid learning of ideas or about people, the ability to grasp abstractions quickly and efficiently, and generally to display skills far beyond those expected at the child's age level. Early schooling is reserved mainly for encountering, distilling, synthesizing, and *consuming* knowledge. *Producing* knowledge with great inventiveness and impact, which is a sign of giftedness, comes later in a person's growth cycle.

Frequently, even voracious young consumers remain that way without ever becoming producers; instead, they grow up as superannuated precocious children. At cocktail parties they are easily recognizable as glib, superficial bores who have ready-made and forceful opinions about any issue under discussion and are always ready to unload their vast storehouses of trivia on audiences of almost any size. Truly gifted children, on the other hand, are sometimes far more limited in what they are capable of absorbing, and their marks on standardized and teacher-made tests show it. Yet, they could someday prove capable of making important contributions to the world of ideas. Generally speaking, renowned producers tend to have a history of extraordinary consumption, and they use their storehouse of understandings to great advantage in making original contributions.

Factors linking promise and fulfillment

Those who have the potential for succeeding as gifted adults require not only the personal attributes often mentioned in definitions of giftedness, but also some special encounters with the environment to facilitate the emergence of talent. The internal qualities of the individual need to interact in a special way with appropriate external conditions in order to produce the magical mix of giftedness. Altogether, there are five psychological and social linkages between promise and fulfillment, each of which deserves clarification independently and in relation to the others. They include: (a) superior general intelligence, (b) exceptional special aptitudes, (c) nonintellective facilitators, (d) environmental influences, and (e) chance, or luck.

The five factors combine in a rare blend to produce great performance or productivity. Each of them has a fixed threshold that represents the minimum essential for giftedness in *any* publicly valued activity. Whoever achieves some measure of eminence has to qualify by *all* of these standards, and the person who is unable to measure up to just *one* of them cannot become truly outstanding. In other words, success depends upon a *combination of facilitators*, whereas failure results from even a *single deficit*. Furthermore, for each of the five intellective, personological, and social-situational factors connecting potential with high-level accomplishment, there is also a threshold level that varies according to *specific* areas of excellence. Thus, for example, the talented artists of Getzels' (1979) sample were able to demonstrate their exceptional talent in various art forms even though their general academic abilities were no better than most other college students'. On the other hand, without high academic promise, no college students could become as distinguished as Roe's (1953) creative scientists. It is therefore reasonable to speculate that the IQ, along with spatial and scientific aptitude thresholds, have to be different for artists and for scientists. Those who fail to measure up to any of these minimum essentials for their respective fields of endeavor could never compare with the Getzels and Roe populations. By virtue of its "veto" power, then, every one of the qualifiers is a *necessary* requisite of high achievement, but none of them has *sufficient* strength to overcome inadequacies in the others.

In essence, it seems as if the causes of extraordinary accomplishment can be described best as resembling some kind of not so clear, complex moving target. The number and variety of antecedent variables preclude any easy designation of a child as gifted on the basis of a few performance measures. Besides, the causes are not the same for all kinds of giftedness. Every area of excellence has its own mix of requisite characteristics, even though general ability, special aptitudes, nonintellective, environmental, and chance factors under which they are subsumed apply to all kinds of talent. These categories could be viewed as "common denominators" that are always associated with giftedness, no matter how it manifests itself. Yet, within each of the categories, the threshold levels, below which outstanding achievement is impossible, have to be adjusted to fit every talent domain, and the need to consider this "goodness of fit" adds to the difficulty of making predictions about the fulfillment of promise.

General ability

General ability can be defined roughly as the *g* factor, which is itself defined roughly as some kind of mysterious intellectual power common to a variety of specific competencies. The *g* factor, reflected in tested general intelligence, figures on a sliding scale in all high-level talent areas. This means that different threshold IQs are required for various kinds of accomplishment, higher in academic subjects than, for example, in the performing arts. There is no basis for making extreme assertions about the IQ such as discounting its relevance to giftedness entirely or claiming that all those destined to become great producers or performers in any area of human activity need to score at the 99th percentile or better. Instead, positions along this continuum should be adjusted according to the talent area, which means taking a stance closer to one extreme for some kinds of giftedness and nearer the opposite extreme for others.

Terman's longitudinal studies of high-IQ children show that those scoring in the highest percentile on a Stanford–Binet-type measure are more likely to become high achievers in school and in the world of work than are agemates with scores closer to average. There is even evidence to show that the higher the IQ within the upper decile, the higher is the likelihood for outstanding scholastic achievement. For example, in a follow-up study of children with superior tested intelligence, Lorge and Hollingworth (1936) found that those who scored at about Terman's cutoff point of IQ 140 had college records roughly comparable to the highest 25% of the collegiate population of the country. Those with IQs of 160 and above tended to win honors at first-rate colleges, and children who tested at and above 180 IQ were often at the top of their graduating classes in college. It is therefore safe to assume that the mental processes assessed in the measure of general intelligence figure significantly, at least in some areas of accomplishment.

On the other hand, it would be naïve to suggest that only IQ makes the difference between giftedness and mediocrity. Obviously, children with high

IQs possess other attributes that can make or break their chances for success. Reinforcing traits were undoubtedly present even in Terman's sample, for as Hughes and Converse (1962) point out, if Terman had selected the children strictly on the basis of IQ, many more would have qualified. Instead, he chose children from a list nominated by teachers as particularly accelerated in their schooling, and undoubtedly many high-IQ children were left off the list of nominees because they lacked the scholastic and personality attributes that attracted teachers' votes.

More frequently heard is the charge that Terman's children never represented the full spectrum of giftedness, nor are any of them likely to achieve immortality. Typical of such objections are those expressed by Laycock (1979), who argues that the sample succeeded primarily in fields that are tied to schooling but is notoriously underrepresented in equally important careers for which success hardly depends on high scholastic aptitude. But despite the limitations in Terman's methodology, his data are so abundant and the message they carry about the high-IQ individual over much of the life-span is so powerfully consistent that it would be naïve to gainsay the importance of high intellectual abilities as measured by the IQ test in the development of at least some kinds of giftedness.

However, more equivocal conclusions about the predictive validity of extremely high IQ were drawn by Feldman (1984) after his follow-up study of all individuals (19 men and 7 women) in Terman's sample whose IQ scores were 180 or above when they were tested as children some 60 years earlier. Comparing them with a random sample of 26 persons (15 men and 11 women) taken from the remaining Terman population and representing the IQ 150 range, Feldman reports the following information: For the women above IQ 180, 5 out of 7 pursued some kind of professional career, as compared to only 3 out of 11 in the IQ 150 group, most of whom reported having served as housewives. In contrast to the women, however, most men in both groups pursued careers as professionals or as business executives. Yet, despite the fact that 4 out of the IQ 180 men (versus none of the IQ 150 men) are described by Feldman as "distinguished," he suggests that "the overall impression is one of lower achievement than the traditional view of IQ would have predicted for both groups" (p. 520). Feldman discloses little about the men he labels as "distinguished," referring to them only as "an internationally known academic psychologist, a highly honored landscape architect, a judge, a promising pollster..." [p. 520]. Hitting the mark in only 4 out of 19 cases may not seem impressive, but considering the facts that (a) distinguished men are rarities by any definition, and (b) the 70-year-olds who were subjects of this study were classified on the basis of IQ scores obtained when they were about age 10, Terman probably deserves more credit than he is given as a talent scout. In other words, Feldman's data can be interpreted to *reinforce* rather than disparage the predictive power of the IQ on grounds that it enabled Terman to locate a small pool of only 19 boys, age 10, as many as 4 of whom were destined to earn reputations as "distinguished" and to retain such a level of esteem 60 years later!

As for the failure of the IQ to lead Terman to a budding Shakespeare or Newton, perhaps he could not find any because there was none to be found in the state of California when he collected his sample of precocious children in 1921 and 1922. A full listing of the longitudinal study population has never been published, but a few names have been leaked through word of mouth and into publications. They include Henry Cowell, one of the greatest American composers of the twentieth century, and Lee Cronbach and Robert Sears, two famous psychologists who have published widely. Even if their renown fades in years to come, it would be difficult to find a Californian of their generation who achieved comparable stature in the arts or sciences and yet was overlooked in Terman's search for high potential. Nevertheless, the popular feeling is that general intelligence, as depicted by the IQ, is too narrowly conceived to capture the full range of talents at school.

There is no end in sight to the debate over the meaning of IQ, its measurement, and the nature–nurture issues that revolve about it, all of which arouse powerful emotions as well as scientific interest. Some behavioral scientists (Estes, 1976; Voss, 1976) have foreseen a decline in the concept of intelligence as a useful description of higher-level cognitive powers and expect it to be replaced by more diagnostic analyses of the patterns and processes of human functioning. This kind of orientation to describing intellectual functioning conforms to the pioneering approach taken by Piaget (1952) in monitoring clinically the development of children's problem-solving behavior.

Thus far, there is little evidence about precocious children's movement through the Piagetian periods of cognitive development. One major effort in this direction is reported by Keating (1975) in a study of preadolescents (fifth- and seventh-graders), with each age group divided into subsamples of bright and average pupils, based on scores obtained on the Raven Standard Progressive Matrices. When Piagetian tasks were administered to the four groups, results showed that the brighter children outperformed their average peers on the formal operational exercises. No significant difference on total score was obtained between the bright seventh- and fifth-graders, but the important fact is that the bright fifth-graders outperformed the average seventh-graders. Keating suggests that, where growth is tied more closely to physiological maturation, as in the child's moving from one developmental period to another, there is less evidence of precocity than where growth depends more on interaction with the environment.

In a more recent study comparing 125 high-IQ (130+) children with 98 age-mates within the normal IQ range of 90 to 115, Carter and Ormrod (1982) produced unexpected results on the relationship of IQ and Piagetian tasks. Unlike previous researchers, they discovered that high-IQ children acquired formal-operational thought at an earlier age than did those with normal IQs, thus indicating a quicker transition from one Piagetian stage to the next. They explained their unusual discovery as resulting from the use of more sensitive instrumentation in assessing thought processes. These beginning efforts to examine ways of thinking, not just powers of intellect, may help considerably in the understanding of giftedness.

Also worth mentioning as important beginnings in the study of cognitive processes are works of Getzels and Csikszentmihalyi (1976) on tactics for problem finding, Feldman (1980) on reaching beyond universals in mental development, and Borland (1981) and Blum-Zorman (1983) in their investigations of differential leveling/sharpening problem-solving styles among potentially gifted children. These are only promising probes of what may someday develop into major contributions to defining the essence of individual differences in cognition.

Special abilities

The idea of a general factor in intelligence has stirred up considerable controversy, some of it concerning its very existence. Spearman (1927) recognized the g factor as an intellectual force necessary for every kind of problem solving. He also discovered specific abilities that share common variance with the g factor and are partly independent of it. These aptitudes presumably relate to narrow areas of specialization. Later, his data convinced him that special abilities combine into clusters, each of which shares a common variance, and he called them *group factors*. This three-tier pyramid consisting of general, group, and specific factors was eventually confirmed by Vernon's (1950) investigations, and he likewise emphasized the importance of the g factor in various kinds of human performance. However, Guilford (1973) is less "evenhanded" when he asserts "that the 'group' factors that Spearman relegated to minor roles, are the most significant components of intelligence and the existence of a g component is extremely doubtful" (p. 632). To support his contention, he cites more than 7,000 correlations among numerous measures of intellect with as many as 17% of the coefficients hovering around zero. These outcomes seem to be in line with Anastasi's (1970) report of low correlations between tests of general intelligence and various special abilities.

Guilford's (1959, 1967) multifactor theory of intelligence defines *intellect* as information processing and *information* as anything the organism can discriminate in its field of perception. *Intelligence* is a qualitative tag referring to the proficiency with which the intellect functions. His structure-of-intellect model is usually presented in the form of a cube to show three dimensions:

operations, contents, and products. Operations is the engineering dimension denoting the alternative ways in which the organism can process any kind of informational content and develop out of it products that take any form. There are five categories under operations, five under contents, and six under products. Altogether, 150 factors are identified, and they consist of every possible combination of categories representing the three rubrics.

The Guilford model is not without its critics. Carroll (1968) and Horn and Knapp (1973) concede that it has considerable heuristic value but are doubtful about the empirical supports. They express skepticism over what they call a "Procrustean" approach to factor analysis, which confirms hypotheses in as many as 93% of the tests. McNemar (1964) is even sharper in his attack on what he calls the practice of fragmentizing ability into "more and more factors of less and less importance" (p. 875). Nevertheless, Guilford's conceptual framework is particularly valuable for the educator who wants a clear perspective on the range of special aptitudes that ought to be cultivated at school, and who also needs to inventory those that are and those that are not neglected. In all probability, only a few of Guilford's 150 special abilities receive more than just passing attention in any curriculum, even in special ones for the gifted.

A question arises as to how early in a child's life aptitudes become differentiated and measurable. In one of the earliest attempts to assess and cultivate special abilities in children as young as 4 1/2 to 5 1/2, Davis, French, and Lesser (1959) developed the Hunter Aptitude Scales for the Gifted and experimented with them at Hunter College Elementary School in New York City. The tests focused separately on Vocabulary, Number, Reasoning, Science, and Space. When the battery was administered to a sample of 110 children, the average correlation among the subtests was .44, an indication that the five intellectual abilities are related only loosely to each other. A group of 27 preschoolers selected on the basis of high scores on the aptitude tests enrolled in the Hunter College Elementary School and constituted an experimental class. The average IQ for these children was 132. Another preschool class, admitted on the basis of the Stanford–Binet with an average IQ of about 153, served as the control class. Testing on the Thurstone Primary Mental Abilities Test (PMA) was conducted on the experimental and the control groups, and the results generally favored the experimentals on all measures, except Number, despite a 21.1-point difference in IQ favoring the controls. These outcomes demonstrate that IQ and special aptitude scores are fairly independent of each other at the upper extreme of either type of battery.

In the Davis, French, and Lesser (1959) study, efforts were made to provide special emphasis in the five areas in which the experimental class was selected. It was hypothesized that, by matching educational experience to each child's special strengths, there would be an increase in general participation and productivity in the areas in which the children demonstrated exceptional ability. Again, the PMA was administered as a posttest at the end of the year, and again the experimentals outperformed the controls on all but the Number tests. The results add credence to the idea that, within a restricted range in tested intelligence, where IQs are mostly in the upper 2% or 3% of the general distribution, discrepancies of as many as 21 IQ points reveal little about rates and directions of intellectual growth, whereas special ability tests apparently do. Robinson (1977) adds support to the idea that aptitude structures of high-IQ children may be measurable even in the preschool years. In his experiments, children as young as age 2 demonstrated extraordinary special abilities. Some had highly developed verbal skills even before reaching their second birthdays; there were also two- and three-year-olds capable of assembling complex puzzles, drawing maps of their immediate surroundings, and capable of recalling minute details of events they had experienced.

It is therefore apparent that, at high-IQ levels, special aptitudes can be differentiated sharply, perhaps more so than near the middle of the IQ range. This discrepancy is important to consider in characterizing giftedness, because it is meaningless to be talented in general intelligence. The ability to score well on an IQ test is not a productive act comparable, for example, to solving a math problem that has stumped mathematicians for generations or to dealing successfully with pollution in the atmosphere. High potential has to be related to a particular area of productivity or performance that, in turn, is reflected in special aptitudes and reinforced by general intelligence.

Nonintellective facilitators

Conceptually, it is easy to distinguish between intellective and nonintellective factors in human functioning. One denotes the mental powers and processes needed to master or create ideas; the other refers to the social, emotional, and behavioral characteristics that can release or inhibit the full use of a person's abilities. Problems in separating both psychological domains do arise, however, when they have to be assessed. Mental measurement, for example, is accomplished inferentially, through tests of performance, which are always "contaminated" by nonintellective factors.

It may seem possible to determine the level of a child's potential from a score on a cognitive measure, when in reality the score is partially affected by the child's feelings about self, success, the examiner, the test, and the testing situation. It also appears that measures of divergent thinking, which require alternative responses to problems having more than one solution, address different types of abilities than those assessed by convergent thinking measures, which deal with problems having only single solutions. Yet, both instruments could be measuring similar intellective functions, except that one is more comfortable in the hands of an examinee whose *personal tastes* favor playfulness with ideas, a sense of humor, brainstorming, and tinkering with ambiguities, whereas the other type of test is welcomed by a serious-minded, straightforward examinee who prefers to strip a problem of its complexity rather than savor it for a while.

Perhaps the most serious difficulty in determining how personological traits figure in high-level achievement is that nobody can tell which of these attributes are *responsible*, even in part, for human excellence, which are merely *associated* with it, and which are *by-products* of it.

Of all the nonintellective facilitators, none has drawn more attention than motivation to achieve. There is a Yiddish proverb to the effect that a person with determination is more likely to succeed than is one with ability. Renzulli (1978) counts task commitment as one of only three major factors that characterize giftedness, the other two being above-average ability and creativity. There is also research evidence to show that precocity often goes hand in hand with a powerful desire for self-advancement. When Terman's (1925) elementary school sample was evaluated by parents and teachers on 25 traits, the ratings favored the high-IQ children over the controls on each criterion. As might be expected, the greatest discrepancy was on intellectual attributes, followed by volitional, emotional, moral, physical, and social traits, in that order. Similar evidence showing the high-IQ child's striving toward success was noted in a follow-up study with this group five years later (Burks et al., 1930).

High levels of motivation can likewise be found among adults who have achieved renown for their accomplishments. After studying biographical data on 300 geniuses, Cox et al. (1926) concluded that these geniuses distinguished themselves not only through their extraordinary accomplishments but also in three aspects of personality: (a) persistence of motive and effort, (b) confidence in their abilities, and (c) strength of character.

But although motivation is clearly evident in exemplary performance among children and adults, it is by no means the only nonintellective factor. Among others that deserve attention is self-concept, since those who *think* of themselves as gifted will try to *act* as though they were in order to match their projections with their self-perceptions. To some extent, though, the effects are circular: The quality of performance influences the self-image of the performer and the self-image of the performer affects performance. It is therefore important to examine empirical evidence on the relationship between the two. In a large-scale study of 1,050 seventh-graders in four junior high schools, Brookover, Peterson, and Thomas (1962) found a significant correlation between self-concept and achievement (males .42, females .39) when IQ was partialed out (held constant) and a low correlation (.17) between self-concept and IQ when achievement was partialed out. This shows that measures of self-concept and of IQ assess different aspects of human potential. What remains to be determined is whether such a generalization can be made for children who rate at the upper extremes on measures of general and specific abilities.

One cautionary note should be considered in relating self-concept to achievement. Some people who think well of their own abilities tend to "play it safe" and avoid opportunities to prove themselves again and again for fear of failure and the consequent threat to their self-images. Beery (1975) and Covington and Beery (1976) proposed a theory of achievement behavior in which students protect their self-concepts of high ability by exercising little effort to learn. They refuse to submit themselves to a test where the demands are high, to avoid the risk of failure and the implication that their potential is not as high as they think it is. In a study of 360 college freshmen, Covington and Omelich (1979) presented evidence to support the theory that school achievement behavior is affected by feelings of personal competency and efforts to preserve a sense of self-worth. In pressured problem-solving situations, the students tended to give up their pursuit of solutions with the familiar refrain, "nothing ventured, nothing lost." The investigators concluded:

Little wonder that excuses are such a permanent part of the school scene. There emerges from this complex interplay among students, peers, and teachers a "winning" formula when risking failure which is designed to avoid personal humiliation and shame and to minimize teacher punishment: try, or at least *appear* to try, but not too energetically and with excuses always handy. It is difficult to imagine a strategy better calculated to sabotage the pursuit of personal excellence. (p. 178)

Other personal idiosyncrasies play their parts in the fulfillment of potential. Nichols (1966), for example, reported a large-scale follow-up study of National Merit Scholarship Finalists and Scholars who had reached their senior year in college. They were then compared on a number of characteristics with a group of representative college seniors coming from similar socioeconomic backgrounds. The differences were extensive and dramatic. Within the experimental sample there were larger percentages of males, Jews, firstborn, and members of small families; on the other hand, there were smaller percentages of Catholics and blacks. The two groups also differed in their interests and career plans, with the more able students leaning more in the direction of intellectual and artistic activities and away from social activities. Their career choices probably reflected the temper of the times, as they frequently expressed the desire to become scientific researchers, college professors, writers, attorneys, and physicians, while their less able counterparts opted more often for careers as businessmen and as elementary- or secondary-school teachers. However, if such a study were repeated periodically, changes in the labor market might bring about other differences in career choices, and it is conceivable that at times the two groups would resemble each other in their choices.

Self-ratings and assessments by teachers and peers all agreed in characterizing Merit Finalists more frequently than less able students as independent, assertive, idealistic, unconventional, cynical, rebellious, and argumentative. They were less frequently seen as friendly, sociable, easygoing, obliging, cooperative, and submissive. Yet, they were described as more mature, dependable, well-adjusted, and honest than average students. The Merit Finalists tended to be extremely involved in campus political activities, they held more than their share of organizational leadership positions, and they conducted more discussions of political, social, and religious issues with teachers and peers than did the control group. This involvement in idealistic strivings apparently diminished their interest in dating, parties, and socializing with peers. Again, as with career differences, contrasts in personal traits may be a reflection of life on campus in the mid-1960s.

As for mental health status, it seems that studies reporting on such issues refer to individuals who have no pretensions toward immortality. Most of Terman's high-IQ children went on to excel at college and in their subsequent careers and showed signs of better psychosocial development than did members of their group whose promise was never entirely fulfilled (Terman & Oden, 1947, 1959). A more clinically oriented follow-up study of successful college students (Vaillant, 1977) produced similarly encouraging results. Unlike the Terman sample that was originally selected on the basis of high-IQ, Vaillant's 268 male Harvard graduates qualified for the long-range study on account of their apparent emotional stability and academic records as undergraduates. Their tested intelligence was only slightly higher than their classmates'; yet, 61% of them graduated with honors, in contrast to only 26% of their fellow graduates. Also, more than three-quarters of them went on to graduate school, and by the time they reached their middle 40s, their average income and social standing equaled that of a successful businessman or professional, as did those of Terman's group. They also compared favorably with the Terman sample with respect to their representation in *Who's Who in America* and in *American Men of Science*.

However, Witty and Lehman (1930) questioned the relationship of high-IQ and superior mental health on the grounds of psychoanalytic evidence that, according to these researchers, depicts the genius as being often neurally unstable, supersensitive, overresponsive to stimuli, and a marvelously complex and delicately vulnerable organism. Indeed, Gilchrist (1982) cites considerable evidence of emotional disorders among creative scientists, literary figures, artists, and architects. This may be true of the mature genius who is either destined to achieve greatness or has already achieved it. But those who are a cut or two below the genius level and a cut or two above their peers in accomplishment probably rate exceptionally high in mental health.

Among the important traits that tend to be overlooked in precocious children are their mental sets in dealing with problems. These may be regarded as "metalearning" habits or intellectual impulses that are advantageous in the earliest preparation for accomplishment. Metalearning precedes action.

It is a mental pose or stance that enables the learner to tune in to the task ahead with the adaptiveness of a homing pigeon returning to base. Teachers recognize this characteristic as an "intellectual killer instinct" among children who not only keep their wits sharp but have their wits about them at all times, as they focus carefully on the name and rules of the game in which success, even renown, can be won.

In the process of fine-tuning their readiness for success, the potentially gifted realize quickly and clearly that before they initiate problem finding or solving, they should determine in advance whether they are dealing with semantic, symbolic, or figural material. They see the advantages of making preliminary estimates about the parameters within which solutions will be located and beyond which there can only be bizarre or impossible solutions. They have to assume in advance that, in the case of solving differential equations, for example, single, exact, or multiple relevant solutions are expected, not general approximations. They understand that it is helpful to try to reduce data to manageable proportions by eliminating facts and ideas that can only delay or spoil outcomes. They also develop the habit of deferring judgment until all the relevant data are sifted, rather than jumping to hasty solutions. In other words, they are aware of the need to know the road to excellence before testing whether they can make the journey.

All of the metalearning adaptive postures are necessary, though insufficient, for achieving excellence. That is, if metalearning rituals are followed, achievement will depend on whether the student has the requisite kinds and amounts of cognitive power; if they are not, then cognitive power alone cannot mobilize a person toward high-level productivity or performance. Sometimes it is tragic that children with exceptional mental strength, particularly those coming from socially disadvantaged backgrounds, are denigrated for cognitive deficits when in reality the fault is traceable to poor metalearning habits that prevent proper release of potential.

Environmental influences

Human potential cannot flourish in an arid cultural climate; it needs nurturance, urgings, encouragement, and even pressures from a world that cares. The child lives in several worlds, the closest of which are the family, peer group, school, and community, while the remotest are the various economic, social, legal, and political institutions. These environments all help to determine the *kinds* of talent that society is willing to honor as well as the *amount* of investment it is willing to make in cultivating them. Societal conditions are therefore critical in stimulating the gifted child's pursuit of excellence.

Giftedness today is in some ways different from that of preceding or succeeding eras because it is shaped by the special needs and sanctions of a society existing in the last two decades of the twentieth century. Every social structure and every period in history responds differently to human potential, and many individuals earn renown as a result of the special "chemistry" between their talent and the milieu that nurtures it. That milieu is transitory to some extent, but it also reflects long-standing traditions that are often as contradictory as they are pervasive. For example, in America, Laski (1948) detected a social legacy that he called "the quintessence of a secularized Puritanism" (p. 42). This has otherwise been referred to as the "Protestant ethic" (Weber, 1948), but it is applied singularly to the American condition. It extols effort and the belief that success is its inevitable consequence. In a pioneering society, it is praiseworthy to take risks, show courage, innovate and adapt, and even engage in "rugged individualism" to build and maintain a modern society. It takes so much ingenuity and hard work to get the job done that there is hardly much time to cultivate the arts. Indeed, artistic life is a luxury that few can afford when so many shoulders have to be put to the wheel.

Only later – when the pioneering days are over and political, social, and economic institutions are established – can increasing numbers of people allow themselves to turn to the life of the mind. Great political theory and science flourish earliest in the postpioneer years because they are rooted in the necessities of the pioneer period; great drama and music begin to appear much later, also as symbols of hard work and self-perfection in conformance with the Protestant ethic. Thus there is the tradition of the perfectability of human beings and their constant need to prove it through productivity and performance. On the other hand, there is the restraining idea that the precious human attributes of talent and effort should be dedicated to the betterment of the masses and not to self-indulgence through creative arts and literature.

Even though there is a pervasive cultural climate in America affecting all inhabitants, it is transmitted in different ways according to social class and family traditions. Wolf (1966) hypothesized a positive correlation between what he called "process variables" and performance on measures of scholastic ability and suggested that these coefficients are higher than the ones between "status variables" and scholastic performance. Status variables are conventional indices of socioeconomic levels, which, according to Wolf, correlate only about .40 with children's IQ scores. Process variables, on the other hand, refer to various means through which parents encourage and provide opportunities for children to engage in learning experiences outside of school. There are three such variables, each having several specific subcomponents:

1. *Press for Achievement Motivation*
   (a) Nature of the Child's Intellectual Expectations
   (b) Nature of Parents' Intellectual Aspirations for the Child

    (c)   Amount of Information Parents Have Regarding the Child's In-
         tellectual Development
    (d)   Nature of Parental Rewards for the Child's Intellectual Dev-
         elopment

2. *Press for Language Development*
    (a)   Emphasis on Use of Language in Various Situations
    (b)   Opportunities Provided for Enlarging the Child's Vocabulary
    (c)   Emphasis on Correct Usage of Language
    (d)   Quality of Language Models Available in the Home

3. *Conditions for General Learning*
    (a)   Opportunities Provided for the Child to Learn at Home
    (b)   Opportunities for Learning Outside the Home and School
    (c)   Availability of Learning Materials at Home
    (d)   Availability of Books at Home and a Public Library Nearby and
         Parents' Encouragement to Use Them
    (e)   Nature and Amount of Assistance in Learning Provided by the
         Parents

Wolf measured the process variables through a questionnaire administered to mothers of his sample population. Results showed a startlingly high correlation, .69, between mothers' response to the total instrument and the targeted children's Henmon–Nelson IQ scores. An even more impressive coefficient of .80 was obtained in relation to Metropolitan Achievement Test results. In a subsequent replication of this study, Trotman (1977) noted similarly high correlations between the process variables and IQ for white as well as black ninth-graders in a middle-class suburban school system. The studies of Wolf and Trotman focused on children ranging widely in ability, not on the precocious among them.

However, studies of the gifted do not yield consistent results. Most of the available evidence on eminent men and women derives from biographical material relating to their grown-up years (Pressey, 1955; McCurdy, 1960; Goertzel & Goertzel, 1962; Goertzel et al., 1978; Bloom & Sosniak, 1981). All that could be said about children destined for greatness is that they vary widely in their relationships with parents. In some instances, the home provides them with enthusiastic encouragement and opportunities to develop their talents; in other cases, they have to overcome the ill effects of living with "smothering" or dominating mothers, failure-prone fathers, or generally troubled families. From their review of relevant research literature, Colangelo and Dettman (1983) conclude that although there are influences in the "home environment and family relations on the later achievement of high-ability youngsters . . . there is still considerable confusion in terms of what the major family influences are" (p. 25).

In general, therefore, whatever seems *logically* essential in child-rearing practices for the nurturance of giftedness often fails to be confirmed *empirically*. The inconsistency of the picture suggests that perhaps there are no generalizations, except that much depends on the special chemistry between person and parent. For one child, a particular nurturance at home may inspire creative work; for another child, the same parental influence may have an adverse effect, or none at all. This would imply a need to determine what kinds of home environments and childhood individualities constitute the best matches in fostering extraordinary potential in children.

Finally, there are influences of peers and the school curriculum. Empirical evidence shows an association of negative stereotypes with academic brilliance among schoolchildren (Coleman, 1960; Mitchell, 1974; Solano, 1977), provided academic brilliance is combined with other unpopular traits such as lack of interest in sports (Tannenbaum, 1962). Moreover, Coleman (1960) discovered that gifted high school students are less likely to underachieve in school settings where students have relatively positive feelings about scholastic pursuits.

Peer supports can be further reinforced by special educational provisions at school. Daurio (1979) summarizes a considerable amount of research to show that accelerating rapid learners through the conventional curriculum can have a beneficial effect on their achievement at all grade levels. Perhaps the most comprehensive evaluation of special programs for the gifted was reported by Martinson (1961) and involved children in grades 1 through 12 with a mean IQ of 143. The subjects came from rural, semirural, and urban areas in various geographic locations, and nearly all were from the middle and upper socioeconomic classes. All had benefited from some kind of enrichment or acceleration and were matched with control groups on the basis of age, IQ, sex, and social class. A battery of criterion measures contained 16 indicators of how the subjects grew intellectually, emotionally, and socially.

Results were impressive in every way. In comparison with the controls, children exposed to special programs performed better on scholastic achievement tests without penalty to their popularity at school or to the number of friendships they enjoyed. Those who participated in special senior and junior high school programs showed better gains in personal and social maturity than did nonparticipants. It would therefore appear that teachers can make a difference along with the home, the community, and the peer group in helping precocious children fulfill their early promise.

Chance factors

Elements of luck, or chance factors in the environment, are usually ignored in discussions of talent and its fruition. Instead, social scientists focus on influences that are more easily observable, measurable, and perhaps eventually controllable. This bias is understandable, because what is there to say about luck, except that it exists and that it can make the difference between success and failure? Nobody knows what forms it will take or when or how often it will strike. It is treated almost as if it were a supernatural force, inscrutable and therefore outside the pale of science. Yet, Atkinson (1978), a social scientist, seems to ascribe all of human behavior and accomplishment to

two crucial rolls of the dice over which no individual exerts any personal control. These are the accidents of birth and background. One roll of the dice determines an individual's heredity; the other, his formative environment. Race, gender, time and place of birth in human history, a rich cultural heritage or not, the more intimate details of affluence or poverty, sensitive and loving parents and peers, or not, all of them beyond one's own control, have yielded the basic personality: a perspective on the life experience, a set of talents, some capacities for enjoyment and suffering, the potential or not of even making a productive contribution to the community that could be a realistic basis for self-esteem. (p. 221)

In a follow-up study of 24 art students five to six years after their graduation from art school, Getzels (1979) discovered that 8 had abandoned art as a career and 7 were only marginally involved in it. He found that the careers of his subjects were profoundly influenced by what he called "idiosyncratic accidents and exigencies determining each artist's life and achievement" (p. 385). Obviously, whatever information that could be gathered about these subjects as individuals during their years at art school revealed only a little about the prospects for future success in the field. Too much depended on events in the lives of the budding artists that the researcher could not have anticipated.

The existence of chance factors may help to explain why it is easier to predict success at school than at work in the years after graduation. In the school world, the rituals and requirements for success are fairly straightforward. There are few surprise changes in the rules of the game, and the children know who calls the shots along the way. Life in the world of work is far more complex, with surprises happening all the time to boost the chances of some and to distract and discourage others from making it successfully. The unexpected can originate anywhere, in the economy, the social milieu, the workplace, the family, and even within the body itself when there is a sudden change in a person's health status that can affect a career. Therefore, both the knowable and unknowable in a person's self and environment interact in a mutually dependent way: Without intimations of high potential, no amount of good fortune can help the person achieve greatness; conversely, without some experience of good fortune, no amount of potential can be truly realized.

Summary and conclusions

Giftedness is generated by either of two broad categories of ability: (a) skills in *producing* important new ideas or material inventions, or (b) skills in *performing* brilliantly before appreciative audiences or in service to various kinds of clientele who benefit from such services. In one sense this definition is broadly inclusive, embracing a wide range of talents; from another perspective it is restrictive because there is no place in it for rapid learners of existing ideas or for admirers of great performance. It further reserves the label "gifted" only for those with *demonstrated* exceptional abilities, excluding even the young "hopefuls" who show early signs of someday producing or performing with distinction. Children may excel in some meaningful ways, but they usually shine in comparison to their age-mates, rarely by universal adult standards; they should therefore be regarded as *potentially* gifted, not as *manifestly* gifted. Still, those who demonstrate promise in childhood stand a good chance of realizing it as they mature to adulthood, given the right combination of circumstances that allow their talents to incubate.

There are five factors that have to mesh in order for a child to become truly gifted: (a) superior general intellect, (b) distinctive special aptitudes, (c) the right blending of nonintellective traits, (d) a challenging environment, and (e) the smile of good fortune at crucial periods of life. Each of these facilitators is necessary, though not sufficient, for achieving excellence in *any* area of activity. Thus, no combination of four qualifiers is adequate to compensate for the absence or inadequacy of the fifth. And the minimal essentials, or threshold levels, for all five vary with every talent domain. For example, giftedness in theoretical physics requires higher tested intelligence and fewer interpersonal skills than do the social service professions. Obviously, then, no single set of measurement criteria can be equally effective for identifying, say, potential scientists and politicians. Nor is it meaningful to suggest that either the scientist or the politician is the "smarter" of the two because of differences in their general intelligence or in their special aptitudes. The five factors interact in different ways for separate talent domains, but they are *all* represented in some way in *every* form of giftedness.

Conspicuously missing in this discussion of linkages between promise and fulfillment is the concept of creativity. Why not place it alongside general intelligence, special aptitudes, nonintellective facilitators, environmental influences, and chance or luck? The answer is that it is not an additive to these factors but rather is integrated in each of them. In fact, creativity is synonymous with giftedness, which is defined as the potential for becoming an outstanding producer or performer, not just a consumer, spectator, or amateur appreciator of ideas. To the best of our knowledge, creativity (or giftedness) consists of a not yet known combination of general and specific abilities and personality traits associated with high potential that can be realized in a stimulating environment with the help of good fortune. Creativity, like giftedness, is judged by two criteria: the *extent* and *quality* of its innovativeness. Too often, the quality dimension is overlooked in favor of the offbeat and the profuse, and we forget that what is rare is not necessarily valued. Because it denotes rare *and* valued human accomplishment, creativity should be conceptualized as interchangeable with giftedness. For after all, giftedness is reflected in the ability to be an innovator of what is new and treasurable, not just a curator of what is old and treasured.

References

Anastasi, A. (1970). On the formation of psychological traits. *American Psychologist, 25,* 899–910.

Ashby, W. R., & Walker, C. C. (1968). Genius. In P. London & D. Rosenhan (Eds.), *Foundations of abnormal psychology* (pp. 201–25). New York: Holt, Rinehart & Winston.

Atkinson, J. W. (1978). Motivational determinants of intellective performance and cumulative achievement. In J. W. Atkinson & J. O. Raynor (Eds.), *Personality, motivation, and achievement* (pp. 221–242). New York: Wiley.

Beery, R. (1975). Fear of failure in the student experience. *Personnel and Guidance Journal, 54,* 190–203.

Bloom, B. S., & Sosniak, L. A. (1981). Talent development vs. schooling. *Educational Leadership, 39,* 86–94.

Blum-Zorman, R. (1983). Cognitive controls, cognitive styles and mathematical potential among gifted preadolescents. Unpublished doctoral dissertation, Teachers College, Columbia University, New York.

Boring, E. G. (1923). Intelligence as the tests test it. *The New Republic, 34,* 35–36.

Borland, J. H., III (1981). Cognitive controls, cognitive styles, and divergent production among gifted preadolescents. *Dissertation Abstracts International, 42,* 3943A. (University Microfilms No. AAD82–04462)

Brookover, W. G., Peterson, A., & Thomas, S. (1962). *Self-concept of ability and school achievement* (Cooperative Research Project No. 845). East Lansing, Mich.: Office of Research and Publications, Michigan State University.

Burks, G. S., Jensen, D. W., & Terman, L. M. (1930). *The promise of youth: Follow-up studies of a thousand gifted children.* Stanford, Calif.: Stanford University Press.

Carroll, J. B. (1968). Review of the nature of human intelligence by J. P. Guilford. *American Educational Research Journal, 73,* 105–112.

Carter, K. R., & Ormrod, J. E. (1982). Acquisition of formal operations by intellectually gifted children. *Gifted Child Quarterly, 26(3),* 110–115.

Colangelo, N., & Dettman, D. F. (1983). A review of research on parents and families of gifted children. *Exceptional Children, 50,* 20–27.

Coleman, J. S. (1960). The adolescent subculture and academic achievement. *American Journal of Sociology, 65,* 337–346.

Covington, M. V., & Beery, R. (1976). *Self-worth and school learning.* New York: Holt, Rinehart & Winston.

Covington, M. V., & Omelich, C. L. (1979). Effort: The double-edged sword in school achievements. *Journal of Educational Psychology, 71,* 169–182.

Cox, C. M., et al. (1926). *Genetic studies of genius. Vol. 2: The early mental traits of three hundred geniuses.* Stanford, Calif.: Stanford University Press.

Daurio, S. P. (1979). Educational enrichment versus acceleration: A review of the literature. In W. C. George, S. J. Cohn, & C. J. Stanley (Eds.), *Educating the gifted* (pp. 13–63). Baltimore: Johns Hopkins University Press.

Davis, F. B., French, E., & Lesser, G. S. (1959). The identification and classroom behavior of elementary school children gifted in five different mental characteristics. Mimeographed research paper, Hunter College, New York.

Dearborn, W. F., & Rothney, J. (1941). *Predicting the child's development.* Cambridge, Mass.: Science-Art.

Estes, W. K. (1976). Intelligence and cognitive psychology. In L. B. Resnick (Ed.), *The nature of intelligence* (pp. 295–305). Hillsdale, N.J.: Erlbaum.

Feldman, D. H. (1980). *Beyond universals in cognitive development.* Norwood, N.J.: Ablex.

Feldman, D. H. (1984). A follow-up of subjects scoring above 180 IQ in Terman's "Genetic studies of genius." *Exceptional Children, 50,* 518–523.

Gallagher, J. J. (1979). Issues in education for the gifted. In A. H. Passow (Ed.), *The gifted and the talented; Their education and development* (pp. 28–45). The Seventy-eighth Yearbook of the National Society for the Study of Education. Chicago: University of Chicago Press.

Galton, F. (1869). *Hereditary genius*. New York: Macmillan.

Galton, F. (1874). *English men of science, their nature and nurture*. New York: Macmillan.

Getzels, J. W. (1979). From art student to fine artist: Potential problem finding and performance. In A. H. Passow (Ed.), *The gifted and the talented: Their education and development* (pp. 372–387). The Seventy-eighth Yearbook of the National Society for the Study of Education, Part 1. Chicago: University of Chicago Press.

Getzels, J. W., & Csikszentmihalyi, M. (1976). *The creative vision: A longitudinal study of problem finding in art*. New York: Wiley.

Gilchrist, M. B. (1982). Creative talent and academic competence. *Genetic Psychology Monographs, 106*, 261–318.

Goertzel, M. G., & Goertzel, V., Goertzel, T. G. (1978). *300 eminent personalities*. San Francisco: Jossey-Bass.

Goertzel, V., & Goertzel, M. G. (1962). *Cradles of eminence*. Boston: Little, Brown.

Guilford, J. P. (1959). Three faces of intellect. *American Psychologist, 14*, 469–479.

Guilford, J. P. (1967). *The nature of human intelligence*. New York: McGraw-Hill.

Guilford, J. P. (1973). Theories of intelligence. In B. B. Wolman (Ed.), *Handbook of general psychology* (pp. 639–643). Englewood Cliffs, N.J.: Prentice-Hall.

Holmes, B., Lauwerys, J. A., & Russell, C. (1961). Concept of excellence and social change. In G. Z. F. Bereday & J. A. Lauwerys (Eds.), *Concepts of excellence in education*. The Year Book of Education. New York: Harcourt Brace & World.

Honzik, M. P., MacFarlane, J., & Allen, L. (1948). The stability of mental test performance between two and eighteen years. *Journal of Experimental Education, 4*, 309–324.

Horn, J. L., & Knapp, J. R. (1973). On the subjective character of the empirical base of Guilford's structure-of-intellect model. *Psychological Bulletin, 80*, 33–43.

Hughes, H. H., & Converse, H. D. (1962). Characteristics of the gifted: A case for a sequel to Terman's study. *Exceptional Children, 29*, 179–183.

Keating, D. P. (1975). Precocious cognitive development at the level of formal operations. *Child Development, 46*, 276–280.

Laski, H. J. (1948). *The American democracy*. New York: Viking Press.

Laycock, F. (1979). *Gifted children*. Glenview, Ill.: Scott, Foresman.

Lorge, I., & Hollingworth, L. S. (1936). Adult status of highly intelligent children. *Pedagogical Seminary and Journal of Genetic Psychology, 49*, 215–226.

Marland, S. P., Jr. (1971). *Education of the gifted and talented* (2 vols). Washington, D.C.: U.S. Government Printing Office.

Martinson, R. (1961). *Educational programs for gifted pupils*. Sacramento: California State Department of Education.

McCurdy, H. G. (1960). The childhood pattern of genius. *Horizon, 2*, 33–38.

McNemar, Q. (1964). Lost: Our intelligence–Why? *American Psychologist, 19*, 871–882.

Medawar, P. B. (1979). *Advice to a young scientist*. New York: Harper & Row.

Miles, C. C. (1954). Gifted children. In L. Carmichael (Ed.), *Manual of child psychology* (pp. 984–1063). New York: Wiley.

Mitchell, J. O. (1974). Attitudes of adolescents towards mental ability, academic effort and athleticism. Unpublished master's thesis, Department of Sociology, The University of Calgary, Calgary, Alberta.

Nichols, R. C. (1966). The origin and development of talent. *NMSC Research Report, 2* (No. 10). Evanston, Ill.: National Merit Scholarship Corporation.

Oden, M. H. (1968). The fulfillment of promise: 40-year follow-up of the Terman gifted group. *Genetic Psychology Monographs, 77*, 3–93.

Phenix, P. H. (1964). *Realms of meaning*. New York: McGraw-Hill.

Piaget, J. (1952). *The origins of intelligence in children*. New York: International Universities Press.

Piechowski, M. M. (1979). Developmental potential. In N. Colangelo & R. T. Zaffrann (Eds.), *New voices in counseling the gifted* (pp. 25–27). Dubuque, Iowa: Kendall/Hunt.

Pressey, S. L. (1955). Concerning the nature and nurture of genius. *Scientific Monthly, 81,* 123–129.

Renzulli, J. S. (1978). What makes giftedness? Reexamining a definition. *Phi Delta Kappan, 60,* 180–184.

Robinson, H. B. (1977). Current myths concerning gifted children. *Gifted and talented brief No. 5* (pp. 1–11). Ventura, Calif.: National/State Leadership Training Institute.

Roe, A. (1953). *The making of a scientist.* New York: Dodd, Mead.

Sears, P. S. (1979). The Terman studies of genius, 1922–1972. In A. H. Passow (Ed.), *The gifted and the talented: Their education and development* (pp. 75–96). The Seventy-eighth Yearbook of the National Society for the Study of Education. Chicago: University of Chicago Press.

Sears, P. S., & Barbee, A. H. (1977). Career and life satisfaction among Terman's gifted women. In J. C. Stanley, W. C. George, & C. H. Solano (Eds.), *The gifted and the creative: Fifty-year perspective* (pp. 28–65). Baltimore: Johns Hopkins University Press.

Solano, C. H. (1977). Teacher and pupil stereotypes of gifted boys and girls. *Talents and Gifts, 19,* 4–8.

Sontag, L. W., Baker, C. T., & Nelson, V. L. (1958). Mental growth and personality development: A longitudinal study. *Mongraphs of the Society for Research in Child Development, 23* (Whole No. 68).

Spearman, C. E. (1927). *Abilities of man: Their natures and measurement.* New York: Macmillan.

Sternberg, R. J. (1981). A componential theory of intellectual giftedness. *Gifted Child Quarterly, 25,* 86–93.

Tannenbaum, A. J. (1962). *Adolescent attitudes toward academic brilliance. Talented youth project monograph.* New York: Bureau of Publications, Teachers College, Columbia University.

Taylor, C. W., & Ellison, R. L. (1971). All students are now educationally deprived. Paper presented at the Seventeenth International Congress of Applied Psychology, Liège, Belgium.

Terman, L. M. (1924). The physical and mental traits of gifted children. In G. M. Whipple (Ed.), *Report of the society's committee on the education of gifted children* (pp. 157–167). The Twenty-third Yearbook of the National Society for the Study of Education. Bloomington, Ill.: Public School Publishing.

Terman, L. M., & Oden, M. H. (1947). *The gifted child grows up.* Stanford, Calif.: Stanford University Press.

Terman, L. M., & Oden, M. H. (1959). *The gifted group at mid-life.* Stanford, Calif.: Stanford University Press.

Terman, L. M., et al. (1925). *Mental and physical traits of a thousand gifted children.* Stanford, Calif.: Stanford University Press.

Thurstone, L. L. (1947). *Multiple factor analysis: A development and expansion of "The vectors of the mind."* Chicago: University of Chicago Press.

Trotman, F. K. (1977). Race, IQ, and the middle class. *Journal of Educational Psychology, 69,* 266–273.

Vaillant, G. E. (1977). *Adaptation to life.* Boston: Little, Brown.

Vernon, P. E. (1950). *The structure of human abilities.* New York: Wiley.

Voss, J. F. (1976). The nature of the nature of intelligence. In L. B. Resnick (Ed.), *The nature of intelligence* (pp. 307–315). Hillsdale, N.J.: Erlbaum.

Weber, M. (1948). *The Protestant ethic and the spirit of capitalism.* New York: Scribner.

Witty, P. A., & Lehman, H. C. (1930). Instability and genius: Some conflicting opinions. *Journal of Abnormal and Social Psychology, 24,* 486–497.

Wolf, R. (1966). The measurement of environments. In A. Anastasi (Ed.), *Testing problems in perspective* (rev. ed., pp. 491–503). Washington, D.C.: Council on Education.

3 The three-ring conception of giftedness: a developmental model for creative productivity

Joseph S. Renzulli

Outwitted

He drew a circle to shut us out
Heretic, rebel, a thing to flout.
But love and I had the wit to win
We drew a circle that took him in.
Edwin Markham, *Quatrains*

Throughout recorded history and undoubtedly even before records were kept, people have always been interested in men and women who have displayed superior ability. As early as 2200 B.C. the Chinese had developed an elaborate system of competitive examinations to select outstanding persons for government positions (DuBois, 1970), and down through the ages almost every culture has had a special fascination for its most able citizens. Although the areas of performance in which one might be recognized as a "gifted" person are determined by the needs and values of the prevailing culture, scholars and laypersons alike have debated (and continue to debate) the age-old issue of "what makes giftedness."

This chapter will attempt to shed some light on this complex and controversial question by describing a broad range of theoretical issues and research studies that have been associated with the study of gifted and talented persons. Although the information reported here draws heavily on the theoretical and research literature, it is clearly written from the point of view of an educational practitioner who respects both theory and research, but who also has devoted a major amount of his efforts to translating these types of information into what he believes to be defensible identification and programming practices. Those in the position of offering advice to school systems that are faced with the reality of identifying and serving highly able students must also provide the types of underlying research that lend credibility to their advice. Accordingly, this chapter might be considered a theoretical and research rationale for a separate publication that describes a plan for identifying and programming for gifted and talented students (Renzulli, Reis, & Smith, 1981).

The chapter is divided into three sections. The first section deals with several

53

major issues that might best be described as the enduring questions and sources of controversy in a search for the meaning of giftedness and related attempts to define this concept. It is hoped that a discussion of these issues will establish common points of understanding between the writer and the reader and, at the same time, point out certain biases that are unavoidable whenever one deals with a complex and value-laden topic.

The second section will describe a wide range of research studies that support the writer's "three-ring" conception of giftedness. The section will conclude with an explicit definition and a brief review of research studies that have been carried out in school programs using an identification system based on the three-ring concept. The final section will examine a number of questions raised by scholars and practitioners since the time of the original publication (Renzulli, 1978) of this particular approach to a conception of giftedness.

I: Issues in the study of conceptions of giftedness

Purposes and criteria for a definition of giftedness

One of the first and most important issues that should be dealt with in a search for the meaning of giftedness is that there must be a purpose for defining this concept. The goals of science tell us that a primary purpose is to add new knowledge to our understanding about human conditions, but in an applied field of knowledge there is also a practical purpose for defining concepts. Persons who presume to be the writers of definitions should understand the full ramifications of these purposes and recognize the practical and political uses to which their work might be applied. A definition of giftedness is a formal and explicit statement that might eventually become part of official policies or guidelines. Whether or not it is the writer's intent, such statements will undoubtedly be used to direct identification and programming practices, and therefore we must recognize the consequential nature of this purpose and the pivotal role that definitions play in structuring the entire field. Definitions are open to both scholarly and practical scrutiny, and for these reasons it is important that a definition meet the following criteria:

1. It must be based on the best available research about the characteristics of gifted individuals rather than romanticized notions or unsupported opinions.
2. It must provide guidance in the selection and/or development of instruments and procedures that can be used to design defensible identification systems.
3. It must give direction, and be logically related to programming practices such as the selection of materials and instructional methods, the selection and training of teachers, and the determination of procedures whereby programs can be evaluated.
4. It must be capable of generating research studies that will verify or fail to verify the validity of the definition.

In view of the practical purposes for which a definition might be used, it

is necessary to consider any definition in the larger context of overall programming for the target population we are attempting to serve. In other
words, the way in which one views giftedness will be a primary factor in both
constructing a plan for identification and in providing services that are relevant
to the characteristics that brought certain youngsters to our attention in the
first place. If, for example, one identifies giftedness as extremely high mathematical aptitude, then it would seem nothing short of common sense to use
assessment procedures that readily identify potential for superior performance
in this particular area of ability. And it would be equally reasonable to assume
that a program based on this definition and identification procedure should
devote major emphasis to the enhancement of performance in mathematics
and related areas. Similarly, a definition that emphasizes artistic abilities
should point the way toward relatively specific identification and programming
practices. As long as there are differences of opinion among reasonable scholars there will never be a single definition of giftedness, and this is probably
the way that it should be. But one requirement for which all writers of
definitions should be accountable is the necessity of showing a logical relationship between definition on the one hand and recommended identification
and programming practices on the other.

Two kinds of giftedness

A second issue that must be dealt with is that our present efforts to define
giftedness are based on a long history of previous studies dealing with human
abilities. Most of these studies focused mainly on the concept of intelligence
and are briefly discussed here to establish an important point about the process
of defining concepts rather than any attempt to equate intelligence with giftedness. Although a detailed review of these studies is beyond the scope of
the present chapter, a few of the general conclusions from earlier research
are necessary to set the stage for this analysis.[1]

The first conclusion is that intelligence is not a unitary concept, but rather
there are many kinds of intelligence and therefore single definitions cannot
be used to explain this complicated concept. The confusion and inconclu-
siveness about present theories of intelligence has led Sternberg (1984) and
others to develop new models for explaining this complicated concept. Sternberg's "triarchic" theory of human intelligence consists of three subtheories:
a contextual subtheory, which relates intelligence to the external world of the
individual; a two-facet subtheory, which relates intelligence to both the external and internal worlds of the individual; and a componential subtheory,
which relates intelligence to the internal world of the individual. The contextual subtheory defines intelligent behavior in terms of purposive adaptation
to, selection of, and shaping of real-world environments relevant to one's life.
The two-facet subtheory further constrains this definition by regarding as most

relevant to the demonstration of intelligence contextually intelligent behavior that involves either adaptation to novelty or automatization of information processing, or both. The componential subtheory specifies the mental mechanisms responsible for the learning, planning, execution, and evaluation of intelligent behavior. Sternberg explains the interaction among the three subtheories by offering the following examples:

How does the intelligence of a person who is average in the abilities specified by all three theories compare, say, to the intelligence of a person who is high in some abilities but low in others? Or what can one say of the intelligence of a person whose environmental opportunities are so restricted that he or she is unable to adapt to, shape, or select any environment? I am very reluctant to specify any combination rule at all, in that I do not believe that a single index of intelligence is likely to be very useful. In the first case, the two individuals are quite different in their pattern of abilities, and an overall index will hide this fact. In the second case, it may not be possible to obtain any meaningful measurement at all from the person's functioning in his or her environment. Consider, as further examples, the comparison between (a) a person who is very adept at componential functioning, and thus likely to score well on standard IQ tests, but is lacking in insight, or more generally, in the ability to cope well with nonentrenched kinds of tasks or situations, versus (b) a person who is very insightful but not particularly well adept at componential operations. The first individual might come across to people as "smart" but not terribly "creative"; the second individual might come across to people as creative but not terribly smart. Although it might well be possible to obtain some average score on componential abilities and abilities to deal with nonentrenched tasks and situations, such a composite would obscure the critical qualitative differences between the functioning of the two individuals. Or consider a person who is both componentially adept and insightful, but who makes little effort to fit into the environment in which he or she lives. Certainly one would not want to take some overall average that hides the person's academic intelligence (or even brilliance) in a combined index that is reduced because of reduced adaptive skills. The point to be made, then, is that intelligence is not a single thing: It comprises a very wide array of cognitive and other skills. Our goal in theory, research, and measurement ought to be to define what these skills are and learn how best to assess and possibly train them, not to figure out a way to combine them into a single, but possibly meaningless number. (pp. 62–63)

In view of this recent work and numerous earlier cautions about the dangers of trying to describe intelligence through the use of single scores, it seems safe to conclude that this practice has been and always will be questionable. At the very least, attributes of intelligent behavior must be considered within the context of cultural and situational factors. Indeed, some of the most recent examinations have concluded that "[t]he concept of intelligence *cannot* be explicitly defined, not only because of the nature of intelligence but also because of the nature of concepts" (Neisser, 1979, p. 179).

A second conclusion is that there is no ideal way to measure intelligence and therefore we must avoid the typical practice of believing that if we know a person's IQ score, we also know his or her intelligence. Even Terman warned against total reliance on tests: "We must guard against defining intelligence solely in terms of ability to pass the tests of a given intelligence scale" (1921,

p. 131). E. L. Thorndike echoed Terman's concern by stating "to assume that we have measured some general power which resides in [the person being tested] and determines his ability in every variety of intellectual task in its entirety is to fly directly in the face of all that is known about the organization of the intellect" (Thorndike, 1921, p. 126).

The reason I have cited these concerns about the historical difficulty of defining and measuring intelligence is to highlight the even larger problem of isolating a unitary definition of giftedness. At the very least we will always have several conceptions (and therefore definitions) of giftedness; but it will help in this analysis to begin by examining two broad categories that have been dealt with in the research literature. I will refer to the first category as "schoolhouse giftedness" and to the second as "creative–productive giftedness." Before going on to describe each type, I want to emphasize that:

1. Both types are important.
2. There is usually an interaction between the two types.
3. Special programs should make appropriate provisions for encouraging both types of giftedness as well as the numerous occasions when the two types interact with each other.

Schoolhouse giftedness. Schoolhouse giftedness might also be called test-taking or lesson-learning giftedness. It is the kind most easily measured by IQ or other cognitive ability tests, and for this reason it is also the type most often used for selecting students for entrance into special programs. The abilities people display on IQ and aptitude tests are exactly the kinds of abilities most valued in traditional school learning situations. In other words, the games people play on ability tests are similar in nature to games that teachers require in most lesson-learning situations. Research tells us that students who score high on IQ tests are also likely to get high grades in school. Research also has shown that these test-taking and lesson-learning abilities generally remain stable over time. The results of this research should lead us to some very obvious conclusions about schoolhouse giftedness: It exists in varying degrees; it can be identified through standardized assessment techniques; and we should therefore do everything in our power to make appropriate modifications for students who have the ability to cover regular curricular material at advanced rates and levels of understanding. Curriculum compacting (Renzulli, Smith, & Reis, 1982), a procedure used for modifying curricular content to accommodate advanced learners, and other acceleration techniques should represent an essential part of any school program that strives to respect the individual differences that are clearly evident from scores yielded by cognitive ability tests.

Although there is a generally positive correlation between IQ scores and school grades, we should not conclude that test scores are the only factors that contribute to success in school.

Because IQ scores correlate only from .40 to .60 with school grades, they account for only 16–36% of the variance in these indicators of potential. Many youngsters who are moderately below the traditional 3–5% test score cutoff levels for entrance into gifted programs clearly have shown that they can do advanced-level work. Indeed, most of the students in the nation's major universities and 4-year colleges come from the top 20% of the general population (rather than just the top 3–5%) and Jones (1982) reported that a majority of college graduates in every scientific field of study had IQs between 110 and 120. Are we "making sense" when we exclude such students from access to special services? To deny them this opportunity would be analogous to *forbidding* a youngster from trying out for the basketball team because he or she missed a predetermined "cutoff height" by a few inches! Basketball coaches are not foolish enough to establish *inflexible* cutoff heights because they know that such an arbitrary practice would cause them to overlook the talents of youngsters who may overcome slight limitations in inches with other abilities such as drive, speed, teamwork, ball-handling skills, and perhaps even the ability and motivation to outjump taller persons who are trying out for the team. As educators of gifted and talented youth, we can undoubtedly take a few lessons about flexibility from coaches!

Creative–productive giftedness. If scores on IQ tests and other measures of cognitive ability only account for a limited proportion of the common variance with school grades, we can be equally certain that these measures do not tell the whole story when it comes to making predictions about creative–productive giftedness. Before defending this assertion with some research findings, let us briefly review what is meant by this second type of giftedness, the important role that it should play in programming, and, therefore, the reasons we should attempt to assess it in our identification procedures – even if such assessment causes us to look below the top 3–5% on the normal curve of IQ scores.

Creative–productive giftedness describes those aspects of human activity and involvement where a premium is placed on the development of original material and products that are purposefully designed to have an impact on one or more target audiences. Learning situations that are designed to promote creative–productive giftedness emphasize the use and application of information (content) and thinking processes in an integrated, inductive, and real-problem-oriented manner. The role of the student is transformed from that of a learner of prescribed lessons to one in which she or he uses the modus operandi of a firsthand inquirer. This approach is quite different from the development of lesson-learning giftedness that tends to emphasize deductive learning, structured training in the development of thinking processes, and the acquisition, storage, and retrieval of information. In other words, creative–productive giftedness is simply putting one's abilities to work on problems and areas of study that have personal relevance to the student and that can be escalated to appropriately challenging levels of investigative activity. The roles that both students and teachers should play in the pursuit of these problems have been described elsewhere (Renzulli, 1982, 1983).

Why is creative–productive giftedness important enough for us to question the "tidy" and relatively easy approach that traditionally has been used to select students on the basis of test scores? Why do some people want to rock the boat by challenging a conception of giftedness that can be numerically defined by simply giving a test? The answers to these questions are simple and yet very compelling. The research reviewed in the second section of this chapter tells us that there is much more to the making of a gifted person than the abilities revealed on traditional tests of intelligence, aptitude, and achievement. Furthermore, history tells us it has been the creative and productive people of the world, the producers rather than consumers of knowledge, the reconstructionists of thought in all areas of human endeavor, who have become recognized as "truly gifted" individuals. History does not remember persons who merely scored well on IQ tests or those who learned their lessons well.

The purposes of education for the gifted

Implicit in any efforts to define and identify gifted youth is the assumption that we will "do something" to provide various types of specialized learning experiences that show promise of promoting the development of characteristics implicit in the definition. In other words, the *why* question supersedes the *who* and *how* questions. Although there are two generally accepted purposes for providing special education for the gifted, I believe that these two purposes in combination give rise to a third purpose that is intimately related to the definition question.

The first purpose of gifted education[2] is to provide young people with maximum opportunities for self-fulfillment through the development and expression of one or a combination of performance areas where superior potential may be present.

The second purpose is to increase society's supply of persons who will help to solve the problems of contemporary civilization by becoming producers of knowledge and art rather than mere consumers of existing information. Although there may be some arguments for and against both of the above purposes, most people would agree that goals related to self-fulfillment and/or societal contributions are generally consistent with democratic philosophies of education. What is even more important is that the two goals are highly interactive and mutually supportive of each other. In other words, the self-satisfying work of scientists, artists, and leaders in all walks of life usually produces results that might be valuable contributions to society. Carrying this point one step farther, we might even conclude that appropriate kinds of learning experiences can and should be engineered to achieve the twofold goals described above. Keeping in mind the interaction of these two goals, and the priority status of the self-fulfillment goal, it is safe to conclude that supplementary investments of public funds and systematic effort for highly able youth should be expected to produce at least some results geared toward the public good. If, as Gowan (1978) has pointed out, the purpose of gifted programs is to increase the size of society's reservoir of potentially creative and productive adults, then the argument for gifted education programs that focus on creative productivity (rather than lesson-learning giftedness) is a very simple one. If we agree with the goals of gifted education set forth earlier in the chapter, and if we believe that our programs should produce the next generation of leaders, problem solvers, and persons who will make important contributions to the arts and sciences, then does it not make good sense to model our training programs after the modus operandi of these persons rather than after those of the lesson learner? This is especially true because research (as described later in the chapter) tells us that the most efficient lesson learners are not necessarily those persons who go on to make important contributions in the realm of creative productivity. And in this day and age, when knowledge is expanding at almost geometric proportions, it would seem wise to consider a model that focuses on how our most able students access and make use of information rather than merely on how they accumulate and store it.

The gifted and the potentially gifted

A further issue relates to the subtle but very important distinction that exists between the "gifted" and the "potentially gifted." Most of the research reviewed in the second section of this chapter deals with student and adult populations whose members have been judged (by one or more criteria) to be gifted. In most cases, researchers have studied those who have been identified as "being gifted" much more intensively than they have studied persons who were not recognized or selected because of unusual accomplishments. The general approach to the study of gifted persons could easily lead the casual reader to believe that giftedness is a condition that is magically bestowed on a person in much the same way that nature endows us with blue eyes, red hair, or a dark complexion. This position is *not* supported by the research. Rather, what the research clearly and unequivocally tells us is that *giftedness is a condition that can be developed* in some people if an appropriate interaction takes place between a person, his or her environment, and a particular area of human endeavor.

It should be kept in mind that when I describe, in the paragraphs that follow, a certain trait as being a component of giftedness (for example, creativity), I am in no way assuming that one is "born with" this trait, even if one happens to possess a high IQ. Almost all human abilities can be developed, and therefore my intent is to call attention to the potentially gifted (that is to say, those who could "make it" under the right conditions) as well as to those who have been studied because they gained some type of recognition. Implicit in this concept of the potentially gifted, then, is the idea that giftedness emerges or "comes out" at different times and under different circumstances. Without such an approach there would be no hope whatsoever of identifying bright underachievers, students from disadvantaged backgrounds, or any other special population that is not easily identified through traditional testing procedures.

Are people "gifted" or do they display gifted behaviors?

A fifth and final issue underlying the search for a definition of giftedness is more nearly a bias and a hope for at least one major change in the ways we view this area of study. Except for certain functional purposes related mainly to professional focal points (i.e., research, training, legislation) and to ease of expression, I believe that a term such as *the gifted* is counterproductive to educational efforts aimed at identification and programming for certain students in the general school population. Rather, it is my hope that in years ahead we will shift our emphasis from the present concept of "being gifted" (or not being gifted) to a concern about developing *gifted behaviors* in those youngsters who have the highest potential for benefiting from special education services. This slight shift in terminology might appear to be an exercise in heuristic hairsplitting, but I believe that it has significant implications for the entire way we think about the concept of giftedness and the ways in which we structure the field for important research endeavors[3] and effective educational programming.

For too many years we have pretended that we can identify gifted children in an absolute and unequivocal fashion. Many people have been led to believe that certain individuals have been endowed with a golden chromosome that makes them "gifted persons." This belief has further led to the mistaken idea that all we need to do is find the right combination of factors that prove the existence of this chromosome. The further use of such terms as the "truly gifted," the "moderately gifted," and the "borderline gifted" only serve to confound the issue and might result in further misguided searches for silver and bronze chromosomes. This misuse of the concept of giftedness has given rise to a great deal of confusion and controversy about both identification and programming, and the result has been needless squabbling among professionals in the field. Another result has been that so many mixed messages have been sent to educators and the public at large that both groups now have a justifiable skepticism about the credibility of the gifted education establishment and our ability to offer services that are qualitatively different from general education.

Most of the confusion and controversy surrounding the definition of gift-edness can be placed in proper perspective by raising a series of questions that strike right at the heart of key issues related to this area of study. These questions are organized into the following clusters:

1. Are giftedness and high IQ one and the same? And if so, how high does one's IQ need to be before he or she can be considered gifted? If giftedness and high IQ are not the same, what are some of the other characteristics that contribute to the expression of giftedness? Is there any justification for providing selective services for certain students who may fall below a pre-determined IQ cutoff score?

2. Is giftedness an absolute or a relative concept? That is, is a person either gifted or not gifted (the absolute view) or can varying kinds and degrees of gifted behaviors be displayed in certain people, at certain times, and under certain circumstances (the relative view)? Is gifted a static concept (i.e., you have it or you don't have it) or is it a dynamic concept (i.e., it varies both within persons and within learning–performance situations)?

3. What causes only a minuscule number of Thomas Edisons or Langston Hugheses or Isadora Duncans to emerge, whereas millions of others with equal "equipment" and educational advantages (or disadvantages) never rise above mediocrity? Why do some people who have not enjoyed the advantages of special educational opportunities achieve high levels of accomplishment, whereas others who have gone through the best of educational programming opportunities fade into obscurity?

In the section that follows, a series of research studies will be reviewed in an effort to answer these questions. Taken collectively, these research studies are the most powerful argument that can be put forth to policymakers who must render important decisions about the regulations and guidelines that will dictate identification practices in their states or local school districts. An examination of this research clearly tells us that gifted behaviors can be developed in those who are not necessarily individuals who earn the highest scores on standardized tests. The two major implications of this research for identification practices are equally clear.

First, an effective identification system must take into consideration other factors in addition to test scores. Recent research has shown that, in spite of the multiple criterion information gathered in many screening procedures, rigid cutoff scores on IQ or achievement tests are still the main if not the only criterion given *serious* consideration in final selection (Alvino, 1981). When screening information reveals outstanding potential for gifted behav-iors, it is almost always "thrown away" if predetermined cutoff scores are not met. Respect for these other factors means that they must be given equal weight and that we can no longer merely give lip service to nontest criteria; nor can we believe that because tests yield "numbers" they are inherently more valid and objective than other procedures. As Sternberg (1982a) has pointed out, *quantitative* does not necessarily mean *valid*. When it comes to identification, it is far better to have imprecise answers to the right questions than precise answers to the wrong questions.

The second research-based implication will undoubtedly be a major controversy in the field for many years, but it needs to be dealt with if we are ever going to defuse a majority of the criticism that has been justifiably directed at our field. Simply stated, we must reexamine identification procedures that result in a total *pre*selection of certain students and the concomitant implication that these young people are and always will be "gifted." This absolute approach (i.e., you have it or you don't have it) coupled with the almost total reliance on test scores is not only inconsistent with what the research tells us, but almost arrogant in the assumption that we can use a single one-hour segment of a young person's total being to determine if he or she is "gifted."

The alternative to such an absolutist view is that we may have to forgo the "tidy" and comfortable tradition of "knowing" on the first day of school who is gifted and who is not gifted. Rather, our orientation must be redirected toward developing "gifted behaviors" in certain students (not all students), at certain times (not all the time), and under certain circumstances. The trade-off for tidiness and administrative expediency will result in a much more flexible approach to both identification and programming and a system that not only shows a greater respect for the research on gifted and talented people, but one that is both fairer and more acceptable to other educators and to the general public.

II: Research underlying the three-ring conception of giftedness

One way of analyzing the research underlying conceptions of giftedness is to review existing definitions along a continuum ranging from conservative to liberal. *Conservative* and *liberal* are used here not in their political connotations but rather according to the degree of restrictiveness that is used in determining who is eligible for special programs and services.

Restrictiveness can be expressed in two ways. First, a definition can limit the number of specific performance areas that are considered in determining eligibility for special programs. A conservative definition, for example, might limit eligibility to academic performance only and exclude other areas such as music, art, drama, leadership, public speaking, social service, and creative writing. Second, a definition can limit the degree or level of excellence that one must attain by establishing extremely high cutoff points.

At the conservative end of the continuum is Terman's (1926) definition of giftedness as "the top 1% level in general intellectual ability as measured by the Stanford–Binet Intelligence Scale or a comparable instrument" (1926, p. 43).

In this definition, restrictiveness is present in terms of both the type of performance specified (i.e., how well one scores on an intelligence test) and the level of performance one must attain to be considered gifted (top 1%). At the other end of the continuum can be found more liberal definitions, such as the following one by Witty (1958):

There are children whose outstanding potentialities in art, in writing, or in social leadership can be recognized largely by their performance. Hence, we have recommended that the definition of giftedness be expanded and that we consider any child gifted whose performance, in a potentially valuable line of human activity, is consistently remarkable. (p. 62)

Although liberal definitions have the obvious advantage of expanding the conception of giftedness, they also open up two "cans of worms" by introducing a values issue (What are the potentially valuable lines of human activity?) and the age-old problem of subjectivity in measurement.

In recent years the values issue has been largely resolved. There are very few educators who cling tenaciously to a "straight IQ" or purely academic definition of giftedness. "Multiple talent" and "multiple criteria" are almost the bywords of the present-day gifted student movement, and most persons would have little difficulty in accepting a definition that includes almost every area of human activity that manifests itself in a socially useful form of expression.

The problem of subjectivity in measurement is not as easily resolved. As the definition of giftedness is extended beyond those abilities that are clearly reflected in tests of intelligence, achievement, and academic aptitude, it becomes necessary to put less emphasis on precise estimates of performance and potential and more emphasis on the opinions of qualified human judges in making decisions about admission to special programs. The crux of the issue boils down to a simple and yet very important question: How much of a trade-off are we willing to make on the objective–subjective continuum in order to allow recognition of a broader spectrum of human abilities? If some degree of subjectivity cannot be tolerated, then our definition of giftedness and the resulting programs will logically be limited to abilities that can be measured only by objective tests.

The USOE definition

In recent years the following definition set forth by the U.S. Office of Education (Marland, 1972) has grown in popularity, and numerous states and school districts throughout the nation have adopted it for their programs:

Gifted and talented children are those identified by professionally qualified persons who by virtue of outstanding abilities are capable of high performance. These are children who require differentiated educational programs and/or services beyond those normally provided by the regular school program in order to realize their contribution to self and society.

Children capable of high performance include those with demonstrated achievement and/or potential ability in any of the following areas, singly or in combination: (1) general intellectual ability, (2) specific academic aptitude, (3) creative or productive thinking, (4) leadership ability, (5) visual and performing arts, (6) psychomotor ability.

The Office of Education definition has served the very useful purpose of calling attention to a wider variety of abilities that should be included in a definition of giftedness but, at the same time, it has also presented some major problems. The first problem is the failure to include nonintellective (motivational) factors. These factors, which will be discussed in greater detail later in this section, are supported by an overwhelming body of research studies dealing with the accomplishments of gifted and talented persons.

A second and equally important problem relates to the nonparallel nature of the six categories included in the definition. Two of the six categories (specific academic aptitude and visual and performing arts) call attention to fields of human endeavor or general performance areas in which talents and abilities are manifested. The remaining four categories are more nearly processes that can be brought to bear on performance areas. For example, a person can bring the process of creativity to bear on a specific aptitude (e.g., chemistry) or a visual art (e.g., photography). Or the processes of leadership and general intelligence might be applied to a performance area such as choreography or the management of a high school yearbook. In fact, it can be said that processes such as creativity and leadership do not exist apart from a performance area to which they can be applied.

A third problem with the definition is that it tends to be misinterpreted and misused by practitioners. It is not uncommon to find educators developing entire identification systems based on the six USOE categories, and in the process, treating each category as if it is a mutually exclusive entity. What is equally distressing about the USOE definition is that many people "talk a good game" about the six categories but continue to use a relatively high intelligence or aptitude score as a minimum requirement for entrance into a special program. Although both of these problems result from misapplications rather than the definition itself, the definition is not entirely without fault because it fails to give the kind of guidance necessary to avoid such pitfalls.

The three-ring conception of giftedness

Research on creative–productive people has consistently shown that although no single criterion can be used to determine giftedness, persons who have achieved recognition because of their unique accomplishments and creative contributions possess a relatively well-defined set of three interlocking clusters of traits. These clusters consist of above-average, though not necessarily superior, ability, task commitment, and creativity (see Figure 3.1). It is important to point out that no single cluster "makes giftedness." Rather, it is

Figure 3.1 What makes giftedness.

the interaction among the three clusters that research has shown to be the necessary ingredient for creative–productive accomplishment (Renzulli, 1978). This interaction is represented by the shaded portion of Figure 3.1. It is also important to point out that each cluster plays an important role in contributing to the display of gifted behaviors. This point is emphasized because one of the major errors that continues to be made in identification procedures is to overemphasize superior abilities at the expense of the other two clusters of traits.

Well above average ability

Well above average ability can be defined in two ways.

General ability consists of the capacity to process information, to integrate experiences that result in appropriate and adaptive responses in new situations, and the capacity to engage in abstract thinking. Examples of general ability are verbal and numerical reasoning, spatial relations, memory, and word fluency. These abilities are usually measured by tests of general aptitude or intelligence, and are broadly applicable to a variety of traditional learning situations.

Specific abilities consist of the capacity to acquire knowledge, skill, or the ability to perform in one or more activities of a specialized kind and within a restricted range. These abilities are defined in a manner that represents the ways in which human beings express themselves in real-life (i.e., nontest) situations. Examples of specific abilities are chemistry, ballet, mathematics, musical composition, sculpture, and photography. Each specific ability can be further subdivided into even more specific areas (e.g., portrait photography, astrophotography, photo journalism, etc.). Specific abilities in certain areas such as mathematics and chemistry have a strong relationship with general ability and, therefore, some indication of potential in these areas can be determined from tests of general aptitude and intelligence. They can also be measured by achievement tests and tests of specific aptitude. Many specific abilities, however, cannot be easily measured by tests, and, therefore, areas such as the arts must be evaluated through one or more performance-based assessment techniques.

Within this model the term *above-average ability* will be used to describe both general and specific abilities. *Above average* should also be interpreted to mean the upper range of potential within any given area. Although it is difficult to assign numerical values to many specific areas of ability, when I refer to "well above average ability" I clearly have in mind persons who are capable of performance or the potential for performance that is representative of the top 15–20% of any given area of human endeavor.

Although the influence of intelligence, as traditionally measured, quite obviously varies with specific areas of performance, many researchers have found that creative accomplishment is not necessarily a function of measured intelligence. In a review of several research studies dealing with the relationship between academic aptitude tests and professional achievement, Wallach (1976) has concluded that: "Above intermediate score levels, academic skills assessments are found to show so little criterion validity as to be a questionable basis on which to make consequential decisions about students' futures. What the academic tests do predict are the results a person will obtain on other tests of the same kind" (p. 57).

Wallach goes on to point out that academic test scores at the upper ranges – precisely the score levels that are most often used for selecting persons for entrance into special programs – do not necessarily reflect the potential for creative–productive accomplishment. Wallach suggests that test scores be used to screen out persons who score in the lower ranges and that beyond this point decisions should be based on other indicators of potential for superior performance.

Numerous research studies support Wallach's findings that there is a limited relationship between test scores and school grades on the one hand, and real-world accomplishments on the other (Bloom, 1963; Harmon, 1963; Helson & Crutchfield, 1979; Hudson, 1960; Mednick, 1963; Parloff et al., 1968; Richards, Holland, & Lutz, 1967; Wallach & Wing, 1969). In fact, in a study dealing with the prediction of various dimensions of achievement among college students, Holland and Astin (1962) found that "getting good grades in college has little connection with more remote and more socially relevant kinds of achievement; indeed, in some colleges, the higher the student's grades, the less likely it is that he is a person with creative potential. So it seems desirable to extend our criteria of talented performance" (p. 132–133). A study by the American College Testing Program (Munday & Davis, 1974) entitled, "Varieties of Accomplishment After College: Perspectives on the Meaning of Academic Talent," concluded that

the adult accomplishments were found to be uncorrelated with academic talent, including test scores, high school grades, and college grades. However, the adult accomplishments were related to comparable high school nonacademic (extra curricular) accomplishments. This suggests that there are many kinds of talents related to later success which might be identified and nurtured by educational institutions. (p. 2)

The pervasiveness of this general finding is demonstrated by Hoyt (1965), who reviewed 46 studies dealing with the relationship between traditional indications of academic success and postcollege performance in the fields of business, teaching, engineering, medicine, scientific research, and other areas such as the ministry, journalism, government, and miscellaneous professions. From this extensive review, Hoyt concluded that traditional indications of academic success have no more than a very modest correlation with various indicators of success in the adult world and that "There is good reason to believe that academic achievement (knowledge) and other types of educational growth and development are relatively independent of each other" (p. 73).

The recent experimental studies conducted by Sternberg (1981) and Sternberg and Davidson (1982) have added a new dimension to our understanding about the role that intelligence tests should play in making identification decisions. After numerous investigations into the relationship between traditionally measured intelligence and other factors such as problem solving and insightful solutions to complex problems, Sternberg (1982b) concludes that

tests only work for some of the people some of the time – not for all of the people all of the time – and that some of the assumptions we make in our use of tests are, at best, correct only for a segment of the tested population, and at worst, correct for none of it. As a result we fail to identify many gifted individuals for whom the assumptions underlying our use of tests are particularly inadequate. The problem, then, is not only that tests are of limited validity for everyone but that their validity varies across individuals. For some people, tests scores may be quite informative; for others such scores may be worse than useless. Use of test score cutoffs and formulas results in a serious problem of underidentification of gifted children. (p. 157)

The studies raise some basic questions about the use of tests as a major criterion for making selection decisions. The research reported above clearly indicates that vast numbers *and* proportions of our most productive persons are *not* those who scored at the 95th percentile or above on standardized tests of intelligence, nor were they necessarily straight A students who discovered early how to play the lesson-learning game. In other words, more creative–productive persons came from below the 95th percentile than above it, and if such cutoff scores are needed to determine entrance into special programs, we may be guilty of actually discriminating against persons who have the greatest potential for high levels of accomplishment.

The most defensible conclusion about the use of intelligence tests that can be put forward at this time is based on research findings dealing with the "threshold effect." Reviews by Chambers (1969) and Stein (1968) and research by Walberg (1969, 1971) indicate that accomplishments in various fields require minimal levels of intelligence, but that beyond these levels, degrees of attainment are weakly associated with intelligence. In studies of creativity it is generally acknowledged that a fairly high though not exceptional level of intelligence is necessary for high degrees of creative achievement (Barron, 1969; Campbell, 1960; Guilford, 1964, 1967; McNemar, 1964; Vernon, 1967).

Research on the threshold effect indicates that different fields and subject matter areas require varying degrees of intelligence for high-level accomplishment. In mathematics and physics the correlation of measured intelligence with originality in problem solving tends to be positive but quite low. Correlations between intelligence and the rated quality of work by painters, sculptors, and designers is zero or slightly negative (Barron, 1968). Although it is difficult to determine exactly how much measured intelligence is necessary for high levels of creative and productive accomplishment within any given field, there is a consensus among many researchers (Barron, 1969; Bloom, 1963; Cox, 1926; Harmon, 1963; Helson & Crutchfield, 1970; MacKinnon, 1962, 1965; Oden, 1968; Roe, 1952; Terman, 1954) that once the IQ is 120 or higher other variables become increasingly important. These variables are discussed in the paragraphs that follow.

Task commitment

A second cluster of traits that consistently has been found in creative–productive persons is a refined or focused form of motivation known as task commitment. Whereas motivation is usually defined in terms of a general energizing process that triggers responses in organisms, task commitment represents energy brought to bear on a particular problem (task) or specific performance area. The terms that are most frequently used to describe task commitment are perseverance, endurance, hard work, dedicated practice, self-confidence, and a belief in one's ability to carry out important work. In addition to perceptiveness (Albert, 1975) and a better sense for identifying significant problems (Zuckerman, 1979), research on persons of unusual accomplishment has consistently shown that a special fascination for and involvement with the subject matter of one's chosen field "are the almost invariable precursors of original and distinctive work" (Barron, 1969, p. 3). Even in young people whom Bloom and Sosniak (1981) identified as extreme cases of talent development, early evidence of task commitment was present.

Bloom and Sosniak report that "after age 12 our talented individuals spent as much time on their talent field each week as their average peer spent watching television" (p. 94).

The argument for including this nonintellective cluster of traits in a definition of giftedness is nothing short of overwhelming. From popular maxims and autobiographical accounts to hard-core research findings, one of the key ingredients that has characterized the work of gifted persons is their ability to involve themselves totally in a specific problem or area for an extended period of time.

The legacy of both Sir Francis Galton and Lewis Terman clearly indicates that task commitment is an important part of the making of a gifted person. Although Galton was a strong proponent of the hereditary basis for what he called "natural ability," he nevertheless subscribed heavily to the belief that hard work was part and parcel of giftedness:

By natural ability, I mean those qualities of intellect and disposition, which urge and qualify a man to perform acts that lead to reputation. I do not mean capacity without zeal, nor zeal without capacity, nor even a combination of both of them, without an adequate power of doing a great deal of very laborious work. But I mean a nature which, when left to itself, will, urged by an inherent stimulus, climb the path that leads to eminence and has strength to reach the summit – on which, if hindered or thwarted, will fret and strive until the hindrance is overcome, and it is again free to follow its laboring instinct. (Galton, 1869, p. 33, as quoted in Albert, 1975, p. 142)

The monumental studies of Lewis Terman undoubtedly represent the most widely recognized and frequently quoted research on the characteristics of gifted persons. Terman's studies, however, have unintentionally left a mixed legacy because most persons have dwelt (and continue to dwell) on "early Terman" rather than the conclusions he reached *after* several decades of intensive research. As such, it is important to consider the following conclusion that he reached as a result of 30 years of follow-up studies on his initial population:

A detailed analysis was made of the 150 most successful and 150 least successful men among the gifted subjects in an attempt to identify some of the non-intellectual factors that affect life success. . . . Since the less successful subjects do not differ to any extent in intelligence as measured by tests, it is clear that notable achievement calls for more than a high order of intelligence.
 The results [of the follow-up] indicated that personality factors are extremely important determiners of achievement. . . . The four traits on which [the most and least successful groups] differed most widely were *persistence in the accomplishment of ends, integration toward goals, self-confidence, and freedom from inferiority feelings*. In the total picture the greatest contrast between the two groups was in all-round emotional and social adjustment, and in *drive to achieve*. (Terman, 1959, p. 148; italics added)

Although Terman never suggested that task commitment should replace intelligence in our conception of giftedness, he did state that "intellect and achievement are far from perfectly correlated."

Several more recent research studies support the findings of Galton and

Terman and have shown that creative–productive persons are far more task oriented and involved in their work than are people in the general population. Perhaps the best known of these studies is the work of Roe (1952) and MacKinnon (1964, 1965). Roe conducted an intensive study of the characteristics of 64 eminent scientists and found that *all* of her subjects had a high level of commitment to their work. MacKinnon pointed out traits that were important in creative accomplishments: "It is clear that creative architects more often stress their inventiveness, independence and individuality, their *enthusiasm, determination,* and *industry*" (1964, p. 365; italics added).

Extensive reviews of research carried out by Nicholls (1972) and McCurdy (1960) found patterns of characteristics that were consistently similar to the findings reported by Roe and MacKinnon. Although the studies cited thus far used different research procedures and dealt with a variety of populations, there is a striking similarity in their major conclusions. First, academic ability (as traditionally measured by tests or grade point averages) showed limited relationships to creative–productive accomplishment. Second, nonintellectual factors, and especially those related to task commitment, consistently played an important part in the cluster of traits that characterized highly productive people. Although this second cluster of traits is not as easily and objectively identifiable as general cognitive abilities are, these traits are nevertheless a major component of giftedness and should, therefore, be reflected in our definition.

Creativity

The third cluster of traits that characterizes gifted persons consists of factors usually lumped together under the general heading of "creativity." As one reviews the literature in this area, it becomes readily apparent that the words *gifted, genius,* and *eminent creators* or *highly creative persons* are used synonymously. In many of the research projects discussed above, the persons ultimately selected for intensive study were in fact recognized *because* of their creative accomplishments. In MacKinnon's (1964) study, for example, panels of qualified judges (professors of architecture and editors of major American architectural journals) were asked first to nominate and later to rate an initial pool of nominees, using the following dimensions of creativity:

1. Originality of thinking and freshness of approaches to architectural problems.
2. Constructive ingenuity.
3. Ability to set aside established conventions and procedures when appropriate.
4. A flair for devising effective and original fulfillments of the major demands of architecture, namely, technology (firmness), visual form (delight), planning (commodity), and human awareness and social purpose. (p. 360)

When discussing creativity, it is important to consider the problems researchers have encountered in establishing relationships between creativity tests and other more substantial accomplishments. A major issue that has been raised by several investigators deals with whether or not tests of divergent thinking actually measure "true" creativity. Although some validation studies have reported limited relationships between measures of divergent thinking and creative performance criteria (Dellas & Gaier, 1970; Guilford, 1967; Shapiro, 1968; Torrance, 1969) the research evidence for the predictive validity of such tests has been limited. Unfortunately, very few tests have been validated against real-life criteria of creative accomplishment; however, future longitudinal studies using these relatively new instruments might show promise of establishing higher levels of predictive validity. Thus, although divergent thinking is indeed a characteristic of highly creative persons, caution should be exercised in the use and interpretation of tests designed to measure this capacity.

Given the inherent limitations of creativity tests, a number of writers have focused attention on alternative methods for assessing creativity. Among others, Nicholls (1972) suggests that an analysis of creative products is preferable to the trait-based approach in making predictions about creative potential (p. 721), and Wallach (1976) proposes that student self-reports about creative accomplishment are sufficiently accurate to provide a usable source of data.

Although few persons would argue against the importance of including creativity in a definition of giftedness, the conclusions and recommendations discussed above raise the haunting issue of subjectivity in measurement. In view of what the research suggests about the questionable value of more objective measures of divergent thinking, perhaps the time has come for persons in all areas of endeavor to develop more careful procedures for evaluating the products of candidates for special programs.

Discussion and generalizations

The studies reviewed in the preceding sections lend support to a small number of basic generalizations that can be used to develop an operational definition of giftedness. The first of these generalizations is that giftedness consists of an interaction among three clusters of traits – above-average but not necessarily superior general abilities, task commitment, and creativity. Any definition or set of identification procedures that does not give equal attention to all three clusters is simply ignoring the results of the best available research dealing with this topic.

Related to this generalization is the need to make a distinction between traditional indicators of academic proficiency and creative productivity. A sad but true fact is that special programs have favored proficient lesson learners and test takers at the expense of persons who may score somewhat lower on tests but who more than compensate for such scores by having high levels of task commitment and creativity. It is these persons whom research has shown to be those who ultimately make the most creative–productive contributions to their respective fields of endeavor.

A second generalization is that an operational definition should be applicable to all socially useful performance areas. The one thing that the three clusters discussed above have in common is that each can be brought to bear on a multitude of specific performance areas. As was indicated earlier, the interaction or overlap among the clusters "makes giftedness," but giftedness does not exist in a vacuum. Our definition must, therefore, reflect yet another interaction, but in this case it is the interaction between the overlap of the clusters and any performance area to which the overlap might be applied. This interaction is represented by the large arrow in Figure 3.2.

A third and final generalization concerns the types of information that should be used to identify superior performance in specific areas. Although it is a relatively easy task to include specific performance areas in a definition, developing identification procedures that will enable us to recognize specific areas of superior performance is a more difficult problem. Test developers have thus far devoted most of their energy to the development of measures of general ability, and this emphasis is undoubtedly why these tests are relied on so heavily in identification. However, an operational definition should give direction to needed research and development, especially in the ways that these activities relate to instruments and procedures for student selection. A defensible definition can thus become a model that will generate vast amounts of appropriate research in the years ahead.

A definition of gifted behavior

Although no single statement can effectively integrate the many ramifications of the research studies I have described, the following definition of gifted behavior attempts to summarize the major conclusions and generalizations resulting from this review of research:

Gifted behavior consists of behaviors that reflect an interaction among three basic clusters of human traits – these clusters being above average general and/or specific abilities, high levels of task commitment, and high levels of creativity. Gifted and talented children are those possessing or capable of developing this composite set of traits and applying them to any potentially valuable area of human performance. Children who manifest or are capable of developing an interaction among the three clusters require a wide variety of educational opportunities and services that are not ordinarily provided through regular instructional programs.

A graphic representation of this definition is presented in Figure 3.2, and the following "taxonomy" of behavioral manifestations of each cluster is a

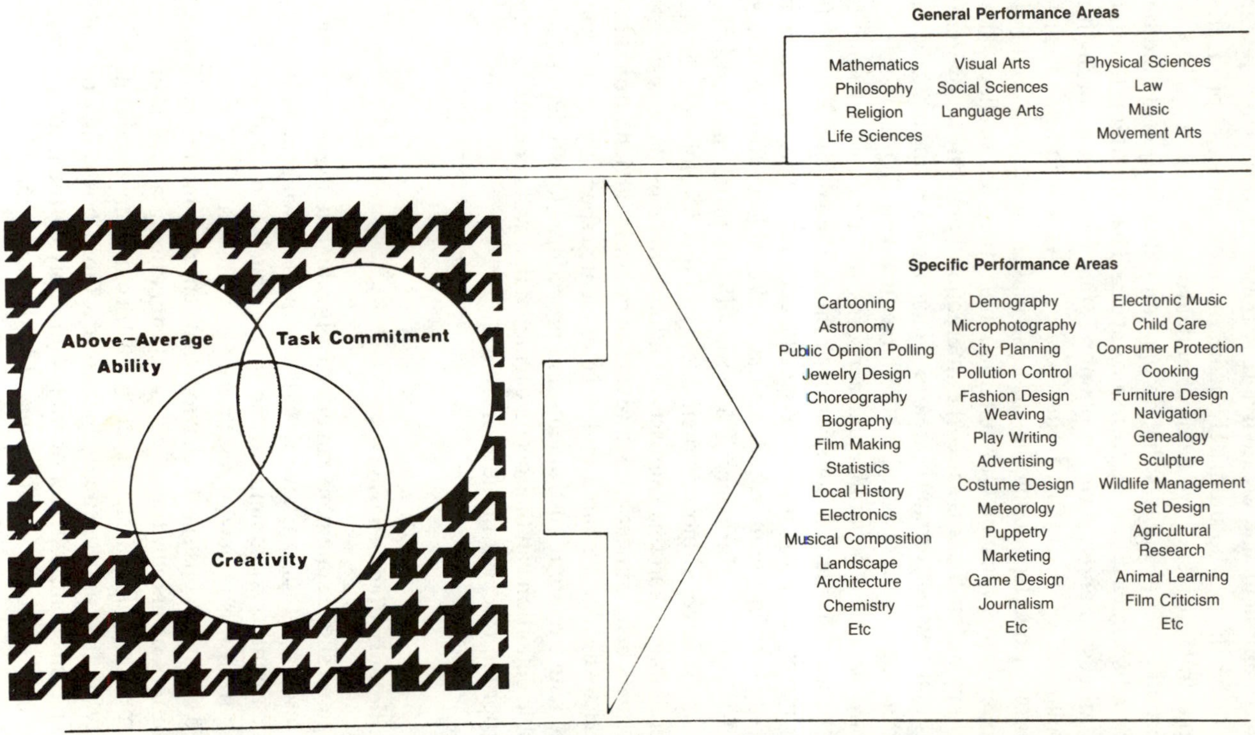

General Performance Areas

Mathematics	Visual Arts	Physical Sciences
Philosophy	Social Sciences	Law
Religion	Language Arts	Music
Life Sciences		Movement Arts

Specific Performance Areas

Cartooning	Demography	Electronic Music
Astronomy	Microphotography	Child Care
Public Opinion Polling	City Planning	Consumer Protection
Jewelry Design	Pollution Control	Cooking
Choreography	Fashion Design	Furniture Design
Biography	Weaving	Navigation
Film Making	Play Writing	Genealogy
Statistics	Advertising	Sculpture
Local History	Costume Design	Wildlife Management
Electronics	Meteorolgy	Set Design
Musical Composition	Puppetry	Agricultural
Landscape	Marketing	Research
Architecture	Game Design	Animal Learning
Chemistry	Journalism	Film Criticism
Etc	Etc	Etc

Above−Average Ability

Task Commitment

Creativity

Figure 3.2 Graphic representation of the definition of giftedness. (The arrow should be read as "brought to bear upon.")

summary of the major concepts and conclusions emanating from the work of the theorists and researchers discussed in the preceding paragraphs:

Well above average ability
General ability:
High levels of abstract thinking, verbal and numerical reasoning, spatial relations, memory, and word fluency.
Adaptation to and the shaping of novel situations encountered in the external environment.
The automatization of information processing; rapid, accurate, and selective retrieval of information.

Specific ability:
The application of various combinations of the above general abilities to one or more specialized areas of knowledge or areas of human performance (e.g., the arts, leadership, administration).
The capacity for acquiring and making appropriate use of advanced amounts of formal knowledge, tacit knowledge, technique, logistics, and strategy in the pursuit of particular problems or the manifestation of specialized areas of performance.
The capacity to sort out relevant and irrelevant information associated with a particular problem or area of study or performance.

Task commitment
The capacity for high levels of interest, enthusiasm, fascination, and involvement in a particular problem, area of study, or form of human expression.
The capacity for perseverance, endurance, determination, hard work, and dedicated practice.
Self-confidence, a strong ego and a belief in one's ability to carry out important work, freedom from inferiority feelings, drive to achieve.
The ability to identify significant problems within specialized areas; the ability to tune in to major channels of communication and new developments within given fields.
Setting high standards for one's work; maintaining an openness to self and external criticism; developing an aesthetic sense of taste, quality, and excellence about one's own work and the work of others.

Creativity
Fluency, flexibility, and originality of thought.
Openness to experience; receptive to that which is new and different (even irrational) in the thoughts, actions, and products of oneself and others.
Curious, speculative, adventurous, and "mentally playful"; willing to take risks in thought and action, even to the point of being uninhibited.
Sensitive to detail, aesthetic characteristics of ideas and things; willing to act on and react to external stimulation and one's own ideas and feelings.

As is always the case with lists of traits such as the above, there is an overlap among individual items, and an interaction between and among the general categories and the specific traits. It is also important to point out that all of the traits need not be present in any given individual or situation to produce a display of gifted behaviors. It is for this reason that the three-ring conception of giftedness emphasizes the interaction among the clusters rather than any single cluster. It is also for this reason that I believe gifted behaviors take place in certain people (not all people), at certain times (not all the time), and under certain circumstances (not all circumstances).

Translating theory and research into a practical plan for identification

The definition of gifted behavior just reported has served as the basis for an identification system entitled the Revolving Door Identification Model (RDIM) (Renzulli, Reis, & Smith, 1981). This model begins with the assumption that we cannot predetermine which students are or are not "gifted." Rather, the model attempts to avoid the strict labeling approach by substituting a somewhat different purpose for special programs that are specifically designed to provide opportunities for advanced-level learning and creativity. Although a detailed description of RDIM is beyond the scope of the present chapter, a brief overview of the system will attempt to illustrate how the underlying theory and research are translated into identification practices. (Renzulli, 1977).

The first step in implementing RDIM is to identify a group of students that will be referred to as the "Talent Pool." This group consists of the top 15–20% of the school population in general ability or any and all specific performance areas that might be considered high priorities in a given school's overall programming efforts. Procedures for forming the Talent Pool are not unlike the usual screening procedures used in more traditional identification systems; however, the major difference is that we do not "throw away" the majority of this group in favor of a finally selected 2% or 3% that is ultimately targeted for services offered by a gifted program. There are three reasons why a Talent Pool of 15–20% is recommended. First and foremost, the research just reviewed tells us that it is from this group we can expect to identify those persons who will ultimately engage in high levels of creative productivity. This research, which has been collectively summarized under the concept of the "threshold effect," has consistently shown that students who possess well above average (but not necessarily superior) ability and who also have the potential for developing task commitment and creativity are the persons who have the highest probability for displaying gifted behaviors. The group unquestionably includes those with the highest IQs, but it is also open to others who show equal potential for creative production.

A second reason for the recommended size of the Talent Pool is that most of the activities typically used in gifted programs that serve only the top 2% or 3% have generally been found to work effectively with this larger group of youngsters. There is no defensible reason why accelerated curriculum or enrichment experiences based on thinking process models such as Bloom's taxonomy (1956) and Guilford's structure-of-intellect (1967) cannot and should not be used with larger groups of students.

A third rationale for Talent Pool size is that, by definition, students working at the 80th or 85th percentile and above are clearly capable of showing high degrees of mastery of the regular curriculum, and therefore these students are prime candidates for curriculum compacting and/or the advanced coverage of regular curricular materials. Curriculum compacting results in making available to these students varying amounts of time that can be more appropriately used for a wide variety of enrichment and acceleration experiences.

Two types of general enrichment are provided for Talent Pool students on a regularly scheduled basis. Type I enrichment consists of general exploratory experiences that are designed to expose students to new topics, ideas, and fields of knowledge not ordinarily covered in the regular curriculum. This type of enrichment is carried out through a variety of procedures such as visiting speakers, field trips, demonstrations, interest development centers, and the use of many different kinds of audiovisual materials. Type I enrichment serves a very special purpose for students in the Talent Pool. Because of their familiarity with the overall programming model, these students are aware that Type I experiences represent *invitations* to more advanced levels of involvement in topics or areas of study that are especially fascinating to an individual (or a small group of students with a common interest). Thus, Talent Pool students self-select those areas in which they may want to pursue a highly intensive research study, creative endeavor, or investigative activity. In the RDIM, we call this process "revolving" from a Type I experience into a Type III activity.

The second category of general enrichment (Type II) consists of methods, materials, and instructional techniques that are specifically designed to develop higher-level thinking processes, research and reference skills, and processes related to personal and social development. Once again, Talent Pool students are encouraged to view Type II enrichment activities as possible sources of motivation for revolving into Type III enrichment. In addition to these two planned types of enrichment, Talent Pool students are also taught how to analyze their own levels of interest and involvement with regular curricular topics and nonschool activities. These interests are also used as possible pathways to Type III enrichment. Classroom teachers are provided with orientation about spotting unusually high levels of interest, and a specific procedure is used to document this information as an early part of the process of revolving students into Type III enrichment.

Type III enrichment consists of individual and/or small group investigations of real problems. The process includes problem finding and focusing, the use of appropriate investigative methodology, and the development of products that are intended to have an impact on a target audience. In this regard, the student assumes the role of a practicing professional (albeit at a somewhat junior level) rather than the traditional student role of lesson learner and exercise doer. The role of the learner becomes one of a firsthand investigator and creative producer, and in this role the student is guided and encouraged to display the kinds of gifted behaviors that have been described earlier in this chapter.

The question that is raised most frequently about RDIM is "What are the specific procedures for 'revolving' a student into advanced-level enrichment experiences?" In other words, how does a student progress from participation in general Talent Pool activities to individual and small group investigations of a more advanced nature? The answer to this important question is based almost entirely on the concept of *action information*. Action information can best be defined as the type of dynamic interactions that take place when a child becomes extremely interested in or excited about a particular topic, area of study, issue, idea, or event that takes place in his school or nonschool environment. The best way to understand this concept is to begin with the second term, *interaction*. An interaction (in learning) takes place when a student comes into contact with and is influenced by a particular person, concept, or piece of knowledge. The influence of the interaction may be relatively limited or it may have a highly positive and extremely motivating influence on the individual. If the influence is strong enough and positive enough to promote further exploration and involvement (in the topic) on the part of the student, then we may say that a dynamic interaction has taken place. For example, if a student is exposed to the topic of solar energy and this exposure provokes an interest in doing more reading on the topic or perhaps in conducting some experiments relating to harnessing power from the sun, we may say that a dynamic interaction has taken place.

An underlying factor in spotting action information and subsequently referring youngsters for possible follow-up activities is that we should attempt to determine if the action information is "productivity oriented." By this we mean that it should relate to a child's desire to pursue a topic farther and more intensively. One of our major goals in providing enrichment for gifted youngsters is to encourage them to engage in investigative activities that will result in the development of a creative product. Thus, a productivity-oriented follow-up experience should focus on a child's desire to *act on* an interest rather than merely to react to the interest. Action information has four key characteristics:

1.   *Action information cannot be gathered at the beginning of a school year by questionnaires, rating scales, or checklists.*

If we attempt to reduce action information to a checklist or rating scale, it will automatically become status information. Certain types of prerecorded status information can certainly give us hints about which children tend to become highly involved in advanced-level projects, research studies, or other creative endeavors. But one of the main goals in this model is to make judgments about revolving children into advanced-level enrichment *at the time* when they express high levels of interest. These types of decisions cannot be made beforehand, and therefore we must keep our identification systems flexible enough to allow students to enter advanced experiences when action information becomes evident. Action information, therefore, always consists of expressions of interests and creativity that are observed *in addition to* prerecorded (i.e., status) information about a child's strengths, interests, and creative ability.

2. *Action information is always something that grows out of the interests of children.*

This characteristic of action information is the single most important concept underlying RDIM. The sincere interests of children should always serve as the point of entry into the special program and the focal point around which we build advanced-level experiences. After a general or specific area of interest has been identified, procedures for determining the strength of the interest and the child's willingness to follow up can be pursued. At this point teachers can begin to assist youngsters with strategies for problem focusing and the development of a plan for investigative activity (see Renzulli, 1983).

3. *Action information is more subjective than status information and is highly dependent on the intuitive thoughts, reactions, and observations of the teacher.*

A great deal of sensitivity and "the art of teaching" are involved in making judgments about action information. This type of information is almost totally dependent on sensitive and insightful teachers who know their studies, trust their own judgments, and are willing to act on such judgments. Although tests have certain obvious value in the status information of RDIM, there are many types of expressions on the part of children that cannot always be determined or verified by testing instruments. It is precisely these types of expressions that we are seeking to spot in the action information dimension of the model, and therefore we should place high value on intuition, subjectivity, and our own personal reactions and judgments.

4. *There is no one "best" situation in which action information can be observed.*

Action information usually occurs in one (or a combination) of three types of learning situations. In some cases unusual levels of interest, excitement, or creativity will be expressed in response to topics covered in the regular curriculum. Another situation where action information may be observed is during the presentation of specially prepared enrichment activities that are purposely designed to provoke high levels of interest or creativity (i.e., Type I and Type II enrichment). The third general category of learning situations where unusual responses on the part of students might be observed is extracurricular activities and the environment in general. In this situation a sustained interest might be sparked by a particular television program, a news event of local or national interest, a hobby or extracurricular activity, or by an interaction the student may have with persons in his or her environment.

The main procedure for gathering action information is observation of the reactions of children to the types of situations described above. The vehicle for documenting and communicating our observations is a form entitled the "Action Information Message." This form is a recording device that will facilitate communication among classroom teachers, resource persons, students, and parents. It has been prepared in the form of a light bulb in order to highlight its role in RDIM. Although this instrument does not yield scores or percentiles, it is the most valid procedure for recording high levels of interest, task commitment, and creativity on the part of a student or small group.

When an Action Information Message is transmitted, a series of relatively specific procedures are enacted that usually (but not always) result in one or more students revolving into advanced-level enrichment and/or acceleration experiences. These procedures have been described elsewhere (see Reis & Cellerino, 1983; Reis & Hebert, in press; Renzulli, 1982, 1983; Renzulli, Reis, & Smith, 1981, chapter V).

I believe that action information is the one feature about this model that makes it different from most other approaches to identification and programming. This use of a second level of identification helps us to avoid all of the problems associated with total preselection decisions and, at the same time, helps us to respect the concept of differentiated giftedness (i.e., gifted youngsters are as different from one another as they are from the population in general). It is easy to see how action information helps to respect concepts such as individualized assessment, self-chosen performances, freedom of expression, and the involvement of persons who might be better qualified to determine the degree of quality or potential for quality that is implicit in samples of performance displayed by varying youngsters.

As has been indicated above, this approach avoids the essentially unresolvable question about whether or not a child is "gifted." Rather, the focus is placed on providing opportunities and creating situations within which students can display gifted behaviors. The display of such behaviors will not be automatic! Teachers, mentors, and resource persons must provide the kinds of materials, resources, encouragement, and feedback that will result in the escalation of any given type of student involvement to higher and higher levels of scholarship and creative productivity. Indeed, task commitment and creativity and the display of other kinds of gifted behaviors are viewed as the objectives or outcomes of special programs rather than as predetermining conditions for entrance into this most advanced level of enrichment within the overall programming model.

As is always the case in such situations, the quality of behaviors displayed in connection with any particular aspect of one's work will exist along a continuum, and the determination about whether or not certain activities qualify as "gifted behaviors" will largely be a judgmental issue that takes into consideration several factors, not the least of which is the age of the child pursuing a particular topic. We cannot guarantee gifted behaviors on the part of any given youngster who is working on a particular problem or area of study, but we can guarantee making opportunities for such study available and we can at least strive to provide resources that increase the possibility of advanced-level expressions of behavior.

Research on school programs using the three-ring conception of giftedness

Although RDIM is a relatively new system for identification and programming, its effectiveness has been documented by a series of research studies and field tests in schools with widely varying socioeconomic levels and program organizational patterns. Using a population of 1,162 students in grades one through six in 11 school districts, Reis and Renzulli (1982) examined several variables related to the effectiveness of RDIM. Talent Pools in each district and at each grade level were divided into two groups. Group A consisted of students who scored in the top 5% on standardized tests of intelligence and achievement. Group B consisted of students who scored from 10 to 15 percentile points below the top 5%. Both groups participated equally in all program activities.

An instrument entitled the Student Product Assessment Form (SPAF) was used to compare the quality of products from each group. This instrument provides individual ratings for eight specific qualitative characteristics of products and seven factors related to overall product quality. The validity and reliability of the SPAF were established through a year-long series of studies (Reis, 1981) that yielded reliability coefficients as high as .98. A double-blind method of product coding was used so that judges did not know group membership (i.e., A or B) when evaluating individual products. A two-way analysis of variance indicated that there were no significant differences between Group A and Group B with respect to the quality of students' products. These findings are offered as a verification of the three-ring conception of giftedness underlying RDIM and as support for the effectiveness of the model in serving a group somewhat larger than the traditional top 5%. The findings are, of course, open to other interpretations that must be explored through further research. For example, the products completed by students may not have required the manifestation of particular attributes on which the two groups differed. This interpretation would undoubtedly raise the issue of the validity of qualitative analyses of student products and the establishment of cause–effect relationships between psychological characteristics and the behavioral manifestations of such characteristics. Similarly, in spite of the high degree of construct validity and reliability that was established for the Student Product Assessment Form, the instrument may not be sensitive enough to detect differences in the manifestations of the three rings, or the behaviors that are more nearly a function of the personality and environmental factors in which the three rings are embedded. As is always the case with the study of complex human behaviors, a point is reached where empirical verification gives way to theoretically biased interpretations. Although agreement among various theorists is difficult to achieve, we are nevertheless duty bound to explore different interpretations and to at least pursue verification through additional research studies.

Questionnaires and interviews were used to examine several other factors related to overall program effectiveness. Data obtained from classroom and special program teachers, parents, and Talent Pool students indicated that attitudes toward this identification system were highly positive. Many classroom teachers reported that their high level of involvement in the program had favorably influenced their teaching practices. Parents whose children had been placed previously in traditional programs for the gifted did not differ in their opinions about the Revolving Door Program from parents whose children had been identified as gifted under the expanded Revolving Door criteria. And resource teachers – many of whom had been involved previously in traditional programs for the gifted – overwhelmingly preferred the Revolving Door identification procedure to the traditional reliance on test scores alone. In fact, several resource teachers said they would resign or request transfers to regular classrooms if their school systems did not continue to use RDIM.

Additional research (Delisle & Renzulli, 1982) examined academic self-concept and locus of control. This study established the importance of non-intellective factors in creative production and verified earlier research related to the three-ring conception of giftedness. Using a stepwise multiple regression technique to study the correlates of creative production, Gubbins (1982) found that above-average ability is a necessary but not sufficient condition for high-level productivity. The roles of task and time commitment and the importance of student interests were verified. Several factors related to improved productivity were identified. A study of student, parent, and classroom teachers' attitudes toward RDIM (Delisle, Reis, & Gubbins, 1981) revealed support for this approach and a high degree of cooperation among all persons involved in the implementation of an RDIM program. A comprehensive study of administrators' attitudes toward programs based on RDIM was conducted by Cooper (1983). The findings indicated that although the programs had not been integrated into the school curriculum as thoroughly as had been anticipated, the model was effective in serving Talent Pool students, helped to minimize attitudes of elitism, and promoted a "radiation of excellence" (Ward,

1961) throughout the buildings in which the model was implemented. A detailed technical report (Renzulli, 1984) describing studies dealing with all aspects of the RDIM system is available from the Bureau of Educational Research at the University of Connecticut.

III: Discussion about the three rings

Since the original publication of the three-ring conception of giftedness (Renzulli, 1977), a number of questions have been raised about the overall model and the interrelationships between and among the three rings. In this section, I will use the most frequently asked questions as an outline for a discussion that will, I hope, clarify some of the concerns raised by persons who have expressed interest (both positive and negative) in this particular approach to the conception of giftedness.

Are there additional clusters of abilities that should be added to the three-ring conception of giftedness?

One of the most frequent reactions to this work has been the suggestion that the three clusters of traits portrayed in the model do not adequately account for the development of gifted behaviors. An extensive examination of the research on human abilities has led me to an interesting conclusion about this question and has resulted in a modification of the original model. This modification is represented figurally by the houndstooth background in which the three rings are now imbedded (see Figure 3.1).

The major conclusion is that the interaction among the original three rings is still the most important feature leading to the display of gifted behaviors. There are, however, a host of other factors that must be taken into account in our efforts to explain what causes some persons to display gifted behaviors at certain times and under certain circumstances. I have grouped these factors into the two traditional dimensions of studies about human beings commonly referred to as personality and environment. The research[4] clearly shows that each of the factors listed in Table 3.1 plays varying roles in the manifestation of gifted behaviors. What is even more important is the interaction between the two categories and among the numerous factors listed in each column (In fact, a houndstooth pattern was selected over an earlier checkerboard design in an effort to convey this interaction.) When we consider the almost limitless number of combinations between and among the factors listed in Table 3.1, it is easy to realize why so much confusion has existed about the definition of giftedness.

Each of the factors is obviously a complex entity in and of itself and could undoubtedly be subdivided into numerous component parts. The factor of socioeconomic status, for example, accounts for such things as prenatal care

Table 3.1. *Personality and environmental factors influencing giftedness*

Personality factors	Environmental factors
Perception of self	Socioeconomic status
Courage	Parental personalities
Character	Education of parents
Intuition	Stimulation of childhood interests
Charm or charisma	Family position
Need for achievement	Formal education
Ego strength	Role model availability
Energy	Physical illness and/or well-being
Sense of destiny	Chance factors (financial inheritance, death,
Personal attractiveness[a]	living near an art museum, divorce, etc.)
	Zeitgeist

[a]Although personal attractiveness is undoubtedly a physical characteristic, the ways in which others react to one's physical being are quite obviously important determinants in the development of personality.

and nutrition, educational opportunities, and even things such as "occupational inheritance." Werts (1968) found, for example, that there is a clear tendency for college students to gravitate toward the occupation of their fathers. On the personality side of the ledger, MacKinnon (1965) found that in studies of highly effective individuals it was discovered time and time again that persons of the most extraordinary effectiveness had life histories marked by severe frustrations, deprivations, and traumatic experiences. Findings such as these help to highlight the complexity of the problem. The advantages of high socioeconomic status, a favorable educational background, and early life experiences that do not include hardship, frustration, or disappointment may lead to a productive career for some individuals, but for others it may very well eliminate the kinds of frustration that might become the "trigger" to a more positive application of one's abilities.[5]

An analysis of the role that personality and environment play in the development of gifted behaviors is beyond the scope of this chapter, and in many ways for school persons who are charged with the responsibilities of identifying and developing gifted behaviors, they are beyond the realm of our *direct* influence. Each of the factors above shares one or a combination of two characteristics. First, most of the personality factors are long-term developmental traits or traits that in some cases are genetically determined. Although the school can play an important role in developing things like courage and need for achievement, it is highly unrealistic to believe that we can shoulder the major responsibility for overall personality formation. Second, many factors such as socioeconomic status, parental personalities, and family position are chance factors that children must take as givens when they are born and that educators must take as givens when young people walk through the schoolhouse door. We can't tell a child to be the firstborn or to have parents who stress achievement! It is for these reasons that I have concentrated my efforts on the three sets of clusters set forth in the original model. Of course, certain aspects of the original three clusters are also chance factors, but a large amount of research clearly has shown that creativity and task commitment are in fact modifiable and can be influenced in a highly positive fashion by purposeful kinds of educational experiences (Reis & Renzulli, 1982). And although the jury is still out on the issue of how much of one's ability is influenced by heredity and how much by environment, I think it is safe to conclude that abilities (both general and specific) can be influenced to varying degrees by the best kinds of learning experiences.

Are the three rings constant?

Most educators and psychologists would agree that the above-average-ability ring represents a generally stable or constant set of characteristics. In other words, if an individual shows high ability in a certain area such as mathematics, it is almost undeniable that mathematical ability was present in the months and years preceding a "judgment day" (i.e., a day when identification procedures took place) and that these abilities will also tend to remain high in the months and years following any given identification event. In view of the types of assessment procedures most readily available and economically administered, it is easy to see why this type of giftedness has been so popular in making decisions about entrance into special programs. Educators always feel more comfortable and confident with traits that can be reliably and objectively measured, and the "comfort" engendered by the use of such tests often causes them to ignore or only pay lip service to the other two clusters of traits.

In our identification model (Renzulli et al., 1981), we have used above-average ability as the major criterion for identifying a group of students who are referred to as the Talent Pool. This group generally consists of the top 15–20% of the general school population. Test scores, teacher ratings, and other forms of "status information" (i.e., information that can be gathered and analyzed at a fixed point in time) are of practical value in making certain kinds of first-level decisions about accessibility to some of the general services that should be provided by a special program. This procedure guarantees admission to those students who earn the highest scores on cognitive ability tests. Primary among the services provided to Talent Pool students are procedures for making appropriate modifications in the regular curriculum in areas where advanced levels of ability can be clearly documented. It is nothing short of common sense to adjust the curriculum in those areas where high levels of proficiency are shown. Indeed, advanced coverage of traditional material and accelerated courses should be the "regular curriculum" for youngsters with high ability in one or more school subjects.

The task commitment and creativity clusters are a different story! These traits are not either present or absent in the same permanent fashion as pointed out in our mathematics example above. Equally important is the fact that we cannot assess them by the highly objective and quantifiable means that characterize test score assessment of traditional cognitive abilities. We simply cannot put a percentile on the value of a creative idea, nor can we assign a standard score to the amount of effort and energy that a student might be willing to devote to a highly demanding task. Creativity and task commitment "come and go" as a function of the various types of situations in which certain individuals become involved.

There are three things that we know for certain about the creativity and task commitment clusters. First, the clusters are variable rather than permanent. Although there may be a tendency for some individuals to "hatch" more creative ideas than others and to have greater reservoirs of energy that promote more frequent and intensive involvement in situations, a person is not either creative or not creative in the same way that one has high ability in mathematics or musical composition. Almost all studies of highly accomplished individuals clearly indicate that their work is characterized by peaks and valleys of both creativity and task commitment. One simply cannot (and probably should not) operate at maximum levels of output in these two areas on a constant basis. Even Thomas Edison, who is still acknowledged to be the world's record holder of original patents, did not have a creative idea for a new invention every waking moment of his life. And the most productive persons have consistently reported "fallow" periods and even experiences of "burnout" following long and sustained encounters with the manifestation of their talents.

The second thing we know about task commitment and creativity is that they can be developed through appropriate stimulation and training. We also know that because of variations in interest and receptivity, some people are more influenced by certain situations than others. The important point, however, is that we cannot predetermine which individuals will respond most favorably to a particular type of stimulation experience. Through general interest assessment techniques and a wide variety of stimulus variation we can, however, increase the probability of generating a greater number of creative ideas and increased manifestations of task commitment in Talent Pool students. In our identification model, the ways in which students *react* to planned and unplanned stimulation experiences has been termed "action information." This type of information constitutes the second level of identification and is used to make decisions about which students might revolve into more individualized and advanced kinds of learning activities. The important distinction between status and action information is that the latter type cannot be gathered before students have been selected for entrance into a special program. Giftedness, or at least the beginnings of situations in which gifted behaviors might be displayed and developed, is in the *responses* of individuals rather than in the stimulus events. This second-level identification procedure is, therefore, part and parcel of the general enrichment experiences that are provided for Talent Pool students, and is based on the concept of *situational testing* that has been described in the theoretical literature on test and measurements (Freeman, 1962, pp. 538–54).

Finally, the third thing we know about creativity and task commitment is that these two clusters almost always stimulate each other. A person gets a creative idea; the idea is encouraged and reinforced by oneself and/or others. The person decides to "do something" with the idea and thus his or her commitment to the task begins to emerge. Similarly, a large commitment to solving a particular problem will frequently trigger the process of creative problem solving. In this latter case we have a situation that has undoubtedly given rise to the old adage "necessity is the mother of invention."

This final point is especially important for effective programming. Students participating in a gifted program should be patently aware of opportunities to follow through on creative ideas and commitments that have been stimulated in areas of particular interest. Similarly, persons responsible for special programming should be knowledgeable about strategies for reinforcing, nurturing, and providing appropriate resources to students at those times when creativity and/or task commitment are displayed.

Are the rings of equal size?

In the original publication of the three-ring conception of giftedness, I stated that the clusters must be viewed as "equal partners" in contributing to the display of gifted behaviors. I would like to modify this position slightly, but will first set forth an obvious conclusion about lesson-learning giftedness. I have no doubt that the higher one's level of traditionally measured cognitive ability, the better equipped he or she will be to perform in most traditional (lesson) learning situations. As was indicated earlier, the abilities that enable persons to perform well on intelligence and achievement tests are the same kinds of thinking processes called for in most traditional learning situations, and therefore the above-average ability cluster is a predominant influence in lesson-learning giftedness.

When it comes to creative–productive giftedness, however, I believe that an interaction among all three clusters is necessary for high-level performance. This is not to say that all clusters must be of equal size or that the size of the clusters remains constant throughout the pursuit of creative–productive endeavors. For example, task commitment may be minimal or even absent at the inception of a very large and robust creative idea; and the energy and enthusiasm for pursuing the idea may never be as large as the idea itself. Similarly, there are undoubtedly cases in which an extremely creative idea and a large amount of task commitment will overcome somewhat lesser amounts of traditionally measured ability. Such a combination may even cause a person to increase her or his ability by gaining the technical proficiency needed to see an idea through to fruition. Because we cannot assign numerical values to the creativity and task commitment clusters, empirical verification of this interpretation of the three rings is impossible. But case studies based on the experience of creative–productive individuals and research that has been carried out on programs using this model (Reis, 1981) clearly indicate that larger clusters do in fact compensate for somewhat decreased size on one or both of the other two areas. The important point, however, is that all three rings must be present and interacting to some degree in order for high levels of productivity to emerge.

Summary: What makes giftedness?

In recent years we have seen a resurgence of interest in all aspects of the study of giftedness and related efforts to provide special educational services for this often neglected segment of our school population. A healthy aspect of this renewed interest has been the emergence of new and innovative theories to explain the concept and a greater variety of research studies that show promise of giving us better insights and more defensible approaches to both identification and programming. Conflicting theoretical explanations abound and various interpretations of research findings add an element of excitement and challenge that can only result in greater understanding of the concept in the years ahead. So long as the concept itself is viewed from the vantage points of different subcultures within the general population and differing societal values, we can be assured that there will always be a wholesome variety of answers to the age-old question: What makes giftedness? These differences in interpretation are indeed a salient and positive characteristic of any field that attempts to further our understanding of the human condition.

In this chapter, I have attempted to provide a framework that draws upon the best available research about gifted and talented individuals. I have also reviewed research offered in support of the validity of the three-ring conception of giftedness. The conception and definition presented in this chapter have been developed from a decidedly educational perspective because I believe that efforts to define this concept must be relevant to the persons who will be most influenced by this type of work. I also believe that conceptual explanations and definitions must point the way toward practices that are economical, realistic, and defensible in terms of an organized body of underlying research and follow-up validation studies. These kinds of information can be brought forward to decision makers who raise questions about *why* particular identification and programming models are being suggested by persons who are interested in serving gifted youth.

The task of providing better services to our most promising young people can't wait until theorists and researchers produce an unassailable ultimate truth, because such truths probably do not exist. But the needs and opportunities to improve educational services for these young people exist in countless classrooms every day of the week. The best conclusions I can reach at the present time are presented above, although I also believe that we must continue the search for greater understanding of this concept which is so crucial to the further advancement of civilization. Perhaps the following quotation by Arnold Gesell best summarizes the state of the art: "Our present day knowledge of the child's mind is comparable to a fifteenth century map of the world – a mixture of truth and error. Vast areas remain to be explored. There are scattered islands of solid dependable facts, uncoordinated with unknown continents."

Notes

1 Persons interested in a succinct examination of problems associated with defining intelligence are advised to review "The Concept of Intelligence" (Neisser, 1979).

2 The term *gifted education* will be used in substitution for the more technically accurate but somewhat awkward term *education of the gifted*.

3 For example, most of the research on the "gifted" that has been carried out to date has used high-IQ populations. If one disagrees (even slightly) with the notion that giftedness and high IQ are synonymous, then these research studies must be reexamined. These studies may tell us a great deal about the characteristics, and so on, of high-IQ individuals, but are they necessarily studies of the gifted?

4 Literally hundreds of research studies have been carried out on the factors listed. For persons interested in an economical summary of personality and environmental influences on the development of gifted behaviors, I would recommend the following: D. K. Simonton (1978); B. T. Eiduson and L. Beckman (1973).

5 I am reminded of the well-known quote by Dylan Thomas: "There's only one thing that's worse than having an unhappy childhood, and that's having a too-happy childhood."

References

Albert, R. S. (1975). Toward a behavioral definition of genius. *American Psychologist, 30*,140–151.

Alvino, J. (1981). National survey of identification practices in gifted and talented education. *Exceptional Children, 48*, 124–132.

Barron, F. (1968). *Creativity and personal freedom.* New York: Van Nostrand.

Barron, F. (1969). *Creative person and creative process.* New York: Holt, Rinehart & Winston.

Bloom, B. S. (Ed.). (1956). *Taxonomy of educational objectives: Handbook 1. Cognitive domain.* New York: McKay.

Bloom, B. S. (1963). Report on creativity research by the examiner's office of the University of

Chicago. In C. W. Taylor & F. Barron (Eds.), *Scientific creativity: Its recognition and development*. New York: Wiley.

Bloom, B. S., & Sosniak, L. A. (1981). Talent development vs. schooling. *Educational Leadership, 38*, 86–94.

Campbell, D. T. (1960). Blind variation and selective retention in creative thought as in other knowledge processes. *Psychological Review, 67*, 380–400.

Chambers, J. A. (1969). A multidimensional theory of creativity. *Psychological Reports, 25*, 779–799.

Cooper, C. (1983). *Administrators' attitudes towards gifted programs based on enrichment Triad/ Revolving Door Identification Model: Case studies in decision-making*. Unpublished doctoral dissertation, University of Connecticut, Storrs.

Cox, C. M. (1926). *Genetic studies of genius: Vol. 2. The early mental traits of three hundred geniuses*. Stanford, Calif.: Stanford University Press.

Delisle, J. R., Reis, S. M., & Gubbins, E. J. (1981). The revolving door identification model and programming model. *Exceptional Children, 48*, 152–156.

Delisle, J. R., & Renzulli, J. S. (1982). The revolving door identification and programming model: Correlates of creative production. *Gifted Child Quarterly, 26*, 89–95.

Dellas, M., & Gaier, E. L. (1970). Identification of creativity: The individual. *Psychological Bulletin, 73*, 55–73.

DuBois, P. H. (1970). *A history of psychological testing*. Boston: Allyn & Bacon.

Eiduson, B. T. & Beckman, L. (1973). *Science as a career choice: Theoretical and empirical studies*. New York: Russell Sage Foundation.

Freeman, F. S. (1962). *Theory and practice of psychological testing*. New York: Holt, Rinehart & Winston.

Gowan, J. C. (1978, July 25). Paper presented at the University of Connecticut, Storrs.

Gubbins, J. (1982). *Revolving door identification model: Characteristics of talent pool students*. Unpublished doctoral dissertation, University of Connecticut, Storrs.

Guilford, J. P. (1964). Some new looks at the nature of creative processes. In M. Fredrickson & H. Gilliksen (Eds.), *Contributions to mathematical psychology*. New York: Holt, Rinehart & Winston.

Guilford, J. P. (1967). *The nature of human intelligence*. New York: McGraw-Hill.

Harmon, L. R. (1963). The development of a criterion of scientific competence. In C.W. Taylor & F. Barron (Eds), *Scientific creativity: Its recognition and development*. New York: Wiley.

Helson, R. & Crutchfield, R. S. (1970). Mathematicians: The creative researcher and the average Ph.D. *Journal of Consulting and Clinical Psychology, 34*, 250–257.

Holland, J. L., & Astin, A. W. (1962). The prediction of the academic, artistic, scientific and social achievement of undergraduates of superior scholastic aptitude. *Journal of Educational Psychology, 53*, 182–183.

Hoyt, D. P. (1965) *The relationship between college grades and adult achievement: A review of the literature* (Research Report No. 7). Iowa City: American College Testing Program.

Hudson, L. (1960). Degree class and attainment in scientific research. *British Journal of Psychology, 51*, 67–73.

Jones, J. (1982). The gifted student at university. *Gifted International, 1*, 49–65.

MacKinnon, D. W. (1962). The nature and nurture of creative talent. *American Psychologist, 17*, 484–495.

MacKinnon, D. W. (1964). The creativity of architects. In C. W. Taylor (Ed.), *Widening horizons in creativity*. New York: Wiley.

MacKinnon, D. W. (1965). Personality and the realization of creative potential. *American Psychologist, 20*, 273–281.

Marland, S. P. (1972). *Education of the gifted and talented: Report to the Congress of the United States by the U.S. Commissioner of Education*. Washington, D.C.: U.S. Government Printing Office.

McCurdy, H. G. (1960). The childhood pattern of genius. *Horizon, 2*, 33–38.

McNemar, Q. (1964). Lost: Our intelligence? Why? *American Psychologist, 19,* 871–882.

Mednick, M. T. (1963). Research creativity in psychology graduate students. *Journal of Consulting Psychology, 27,* 265–266.

Munday, L. A., & Davis, J. C. (1974). *Varieties of accomplishment after college: Perspectives on the meaning of academic talent.* (Research Report No. 62). Iowa City: American College Testing Program.

Neisser, U. (1979). The concept of intelligence. In R. J. Sternberg & D. K. Detterman (Eds.) *Human Intelligence* (pp. 179–189). Norwood, N.J.: Ablex.

Nicholls, J. C. (1972). Creativity in the person who will never produce anything original and useful: The concept of creativity as a normally distributed trait. *American Psychologist, 27,* 717–727.

Oden, M. H. (1968). The fulfillment of promise: 40-year follow-up of the Terman gifted group. *Genetic Psychology Monograph, 77,* 3–93.

Parloff, M. B., Datta, L., Kleman, M., & Handlon, J. H. (1968). Personality characteristics which differentiate creative male adolescents and adults. *Journal of Personality, 36,* 528–552.

Reis, S. M. (1981). *An analysis of the productivity of gifted students participating in programs using the revolving door identification model.* Unpublished doctoral dissertation, University of Connecticut, Storrs.

Reis, S. M., & Cellerino, M. B. (1983). Guiding gifted students through independent study. *Teaching Exceptional Children, 15,* 136–141.

Reis, S. M., & Hebert, T. (in press). Creating practicing professionals in gifted programs: Encouraging students to become young historians. *Instructor.*

Reis, S. M., & Renzulli, J. S. (1982). A research report on the revolving door identification model: A case for the broadened conception of giftedness. *Phi Delta Kappan, 63,* 619–620.

Renzulli, J. S. (1977). *The enrichment triad model: A guide for developing defensible programs for the gifted and talented.* Mansfield Center, Conn.: Creative Learning Press.

Renzulli, J. S. (1978). What makes giftedness? Reexamining a definition. *Phi Delta Kappan, 60,* 180–184, 261.

Renzulli, J. S. (1982). What makes a problem real: Stalking the illusive meaning of qualitative differences in gifted education. *Gifted Child Quarterly, 26*(4), 148–156.

Renzulli, J. S. (1983). Guiding the gifted in the pursuit of real problems: The transformed role of the teacher. *The Journal of Creative Behavior, 17* (1), 49–59.

Renzulli, J. S. (1984). *Technical report of research studies related to the revolving door identification model* (rev. ed.). Bureau of Educational Research, University of Connecticut, Storrs.

Renzulli, J. S., Reis, S. M., & Smith, L. H. (1981). *The revolving door identification model.* Mansfield Center, Conn.: Creative Learning Press.

Renzulli, J. S., Smith, L. H., & Reis, S. M. (1982). Curriculum compacting: An essential strategy for working with gifted students. *The Elementary School Journal, 82,* 185–194.

Richards, J. M., Jr., Holland, J. L., & Lutz, S. W. (1967). Prediction of student accomplishment in college. *Journal of Educational Psychology, 58,* 343–355.

Roe, A. (1952). *The making of a scientist.* New York: Dodd, Mead.

Shapiro, R. J. (1968). Creative research scientists. *Psychologia Africana* (Suppl. 4).

Simonton, D. K. (1978). History and the eminent person. *Gifted Child Quarterly, 22,* 187–195.

Stein, M. I. (1968). Creativity. In E. Borgatta & W. W. Lambert (Eds.), *Handbook of personality theory and research.* Chicago: Rand McNally.

Sternberg, R. J. (1981). Intelligence and nonentrenchment. *Journal of Educational Psychology, 73,* 1–16.

Sternberg, R. J. (1982a). Paper presented at the Annual Connecticut Update Conference, New Haven.

Sternberg, R. J. (1982b). Lies we live by: Misapplication of tests in identifying the gifted. *Gifted Child Quarterly 26*(4), 157–161.

Sternberg, R. J. (1984). Toward a triarchic theory of human intelligence. *Behavioral and Brain Sciences 7*(2), 269–316.

Sternberg, R. J. & Davidson, J. E. (1982, June). The mind of the puzzler. *Psychology Today*, *16*, 37–44.

Terman, L. M., et al. (1926). *Genetic studies of genius: Mental and physical traits of a thousand gifted children*. 2nd ed. Stanford, Calif.: Stanford University Press.

Terman, L. M. (1954). The discovery and encouragement of exceptional talent. *American Psychologist*, *9*, 221–230.

Terman, L. M., & Oden, M. H. (1959). *Genetic studies of genius: The gifted group at mid-life*. Stanford, Calif.: Stanford University Press.

Thorndike, E. L. (1921). Intelligence and its measurement, *Journal of Educational Psychology*, *12*, 124–127.

Torrance, E. P. (1969). Prediction of adult creative achievement among high school seniors. *Gifted Child Quarterly*, *13*, 223–229.

Vernon, P. E. (1967). Psychological studies of creativity. *Journal of Child Psychology and Psychiatry*, *8*, 153–164.

Walberg, H. J. (1969). A portrait of the artist and scientist as young men. *Exceptional Children*, *35*, 5–12.

Walberg, H. J. (1971). Varieties of adolescent creativity and the high school environment. *Exceptional Children*, *38*, 111–116.

Wallach, M. A. (1976). Tests tell us little about talent. *American Scientist*, *64*, 57–63.

Wallach, M. A. & Wing, C. W., Jr. (1969). *The talented students: A validation of the creativity-intelligence distinction*. New York: Holt, Rinehart & Winston.

Ward, V. (1961). *Educating the gifted: An axiomatic approach*. Westerville, Ohio: Merrill.

Werts, C. E. (1968). Paternal influence on career choice. *Journal of Counseling Psychology*, *15*, 48–52.

Witty, P. A. (1958). Who are the gifted? In N. B. Henry (Ed.), *Education of the gifted*. Fifty-seventh Yearbook of the National Society for the Study of Education, Part 2. Chicago: University of Chicago Press.

Zuckerman, H. (1979). The scientific elite: Nobel laureates' mutual influences. In R. S. Albert (Ed.), *Genius and eminence*, pp. 241–252. Elmsford, N.Y.: Pergamon Press.

4 The educational definition of giftedness and its policy implications

James J. Gallagher and Richard D. Courtright

Recent reviews and critiques of the American educational system have highlighted the special problems of those students who are advanced in their intellectual and academic abilities. Once again, as in the early 1960s, we are concerned, as a society, about excellence – about whether our best and brightest are being challenged to use their outstanding potential (Coleman & Selby, 1983; Hunt, 1983; National Commission on Excellence, 1983). One of the more dramatic rhetorical flourishes on this topic came from the report of the National Commission on Excellence in Education:

If an unfriendly foreign power had attempted to impose on America the mediocre educational performance that exists today, we might well have viewed it as an act of war. As it stands, we have allowed this to happen to ourselves. We have even squandered the gains in student achievement made in the wake of the Sputnik challenge. Moreover, we have dismantled essential support systems which helped make those gains possible. We have, in effect, been committing an act of unthinking, unilateral educational disarmament. (p. 5)

Such concerns have, in turn, placed the spotlight on how the schools try to find those students with outstanding academic aptitude and how this concept of giftedness is defined.

It is the purpose of this chapter to explore the issues surrounding the *educational definition of the gifted* and how this definition, conceptually and operationally, fits other definitions of giftedness that have been developed for other purposes and other times.

It will be the position of the authors of this chapter that one term, *gifted*, has been used to describe two different constructs. These constructs, although overlapping, emerge from different traditions and have a number of subtle differences that create confusion and contradiction. One of these constructs stems from a century of investigations of social scientists on individual differences, while the other construct stems from educational practice and the need for schools to design special educational programs for students who possess abilities and performance far in excess of their age-mates.

93

Individual differences

The study of individual differences in children has focused on two major problems: the assessment of individual development and the exploration of mental operations – how the brain works.

The documentation of characteristics such as height, weight, or IQ scores provides an example of assessment objectives. A person is "normal" or "abnormal" as his or her characteristics are compared with the performance of others of similar age or other characteristics.

The emphasis is on the individual mental operations and their development. In one sense, giftedness can be perceived as representing unusual or abnormal development – *oversensitivity*, in the words of Dabrowski (1964). A child or adult can be measured in the abilities to draw implications from, or transform, symbolic systems, even though that particular skill was of minimal usage in a particular society. With this approach, one could try to catalog the full range of mental processes apart from societal requirements or interest.

There has also been an increasing interest in mental processes such as *memory*, *association*, *classification*, *reasoning*, and *evaluation*. This interest has spawned many laboratory experiments that have been designed to answer questions such as, "How do we remember?" and "What is the mechanism through which we cluster items together into concepts?" and, of course, "Why do some children perform much better or much worse in these functions?"

Academic advancement

The approaches used by the education community include many of the methods and tools originally designed to measure individual differences, such as IQ tests. These measures were supposed to find students who perform in an outstanding fashion, *or who could perform in an outstanding fashion,* in our educational systems. This approach brought the school environment into the construct, along with the individual's abilities. This approach also presents a societal view of what content or skills are important to learn in school.

It has been a common observation that a country's educational system mirrors its society. The virtues and the problems of each society appear to manifest themselves in the rules about who gets educated, under what type of environment, by whom, and for how long. Our educational definition of giftedness should and does say a great deal about society's current views on those questions.

Although the two approaches, individual differences and academic advancement, yield clearly overlapping categories of giftedness, it is easy to see that there would be some youngsters who would appear superior in one of these categories but not in the other. For example, a youngster with great talent for manipulation and organization of forms or shapes might be termed "gifted" in terms of individual differences but not by the school whose interests and programs do not recognize that talent. Another student could, by full use of motivation and desire to learn, be considered to be "gifted" from an academic perspective but be considered only "superior" by those testing mental operations.

Giftedness through measurement of individual differences

The early pursuit of giftedness was the province of philosophers and introspective scholars. Plato stated that the task of society was to "compel the best nature" to learn that its achievements might serve to common good (Bronowski, 1973). But it was not until the end of the 19th century that the scientific study of individual differences was pursued. Contributors of this period were many; however, we shall confine our comments to three giants, each of whom made significant contributions to the final portrait: Galton, Binet, and Terman.

Sir Francis Galton carried out the first known research on the topic of high intellectual ability. His concept of the nature of giftedness lay in his designation of genius as the extreme of the "deviation from the average" in achievement of "eminence." In his work, *Hereditary Genius* (1883), Galton traced familial relationships of those who had achieved eminence in 19th-century England. He concluded: "Hence, we arrive at the undeniable, but unexpected conclusion, that eminently gifted men are raised as much above mediocrity as idiots are depressed below it; a fact that is calculated to considerably enlarge our ideas of the enormous differences of intellectual gifts between man and man." (p. 36).

Galton's purpose was to illustrate the connection between inherited natural ability on the one hand and the genius-level performance on the other. Hence *performance* was the determining factor of the identification of the gifted individual.

Alfred Binet (with his colleague Theophile Simon) sought to develop the first test to measure the innate intellectual abilities of children (Binet & Simon, 1976) to determine which children would most benefit from instruction. Though never specifically establishing a definition of giftedness, from the time of his first tests Binet proposed that mental tests should be complex, measuring the variety of processes that constitute the sum total of the higher mental processes. "Comprehension, invention, direction, and criticism – intelligence is contained in these four words" (Binet, 1909).

Binet did not, however, believe this ability to be immutably fixed by heredity. He admonished those who with "brutal pessimism" believed there was nothing to be gained by the education and training of those with low intellectual capacity (Binet, 1909). He wrote: "With practice, enthusiasm, and especially with method one can succeed in increasing one's attention, memory, and judgment, and in becoming literally more intelligent than before; and this progress will go until one reaches one's limit" (p. 143).

To Binet, intelligence comprised the ability to take in information from the environment and process it; and, further, this ability was quantifiable by comparing the individual's performance in processing the information to others of the same and different chronological ages.

The third influential scientist was Lewis Terman, who developed and used the Stanford–Binet scale to identify a large sample of California school children who scored at the top 1% of the test. This longitudinal study, which followed these high-IQ children for over half a century, is the source of the notion that "Intelligence is what an intelligence test measures" and became, though an intellectual tautology, the operational definition of giftedness for 40 years (Terman & Oden, 1947, 1959).

These three, Galton, Binet, and Terman, set out to assess the cognitive abilities of individuals based on their performance of certain mental processes and functions. Subsequent work has modified the concept of what skills should be measured in assessing intelligence. Guilford (1967), for example, has proposed *structure-of-intellect* as a theoretical model, which expanded the specification of mental products and operations to many more than are typically assessed in an intelligence test.

During more recent times, there have been three rather distinctly different strategies that have been generated to help understand the construct of intelligence. Each strategy has tried to answer an important question regarding the construct. The first set of models tries to answer the question "How do children develop and mature intellectually?" Piaget and Binet are noteworthy in trying to devise instruments and develop theory to answer that question.

The second question is "What are the individual competencies that constitute intelligence?" Thurstone, Guilford, and Wechsler might be counted as key figures in the group that tries to develop models or instruments to answer that question. The third strategy asks, "Precisely how does a human being solve problems or store memories or maintain an appropriate attention set?" This attempt to explain human information processing has many current followers including Campione, Brown, Estes, Zeaman, Ellis, and so on. A comprehensive volume, *Handbook of Human Intelligence*, provides a detailed review of these strategies (Sternberg, 1982).

This movement, focusing on information processing, emerged strongly in the 1960s and 1970s in psychological research. Psychologists wished to pursue the mechanisms, the cognitive processes, by which intellectual operations occurred. How do we store and retrieve information; what factors determine the clustering of concepts; how are new ideas generated? The growing computer industry with its obvious analogies to mental operations encouraged attention to the nature of mental operations as well (Newell & Simon, 1972).

Through the development of a more precise understanding of how the brain functions, a gradually evolving change in the educational view of giftedness is also emerging.

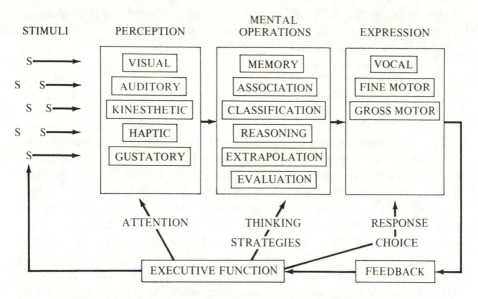

Figure 4.1. Information-processing model.

It is possible to identify and study six different mental operations: *memory*, *association*, *classification*, *reasoning*, *evaluation*, and *executive function*. Figure 4.1 provides a schematic model of information processing that includes perception, mental operations, expression, a feedback mechanism, and an executive function that controls attention, mental strategies, and response choice. We will focus here on the mental operations and the executive function.

Memory involves the storage of information, in both short-term memory (STM) and long-term memory (LTM). It is the function of this process to store information in a complex system so that information, facts, groups, categories, or classes of data are available for scan or search to find a response to the question at hand.

Association is the fundamental mental operation in which facts and ideas from memory and/or experience are subsequently linked, or associated, through the analysis of their attributes. These attributes may include properties, functions, or conceptual elements. It is through the process of association, for example, that the child applies the knowledge of the method of tying his shoelaces to tying the string onto his kite.

Classification deals with the capacity to group objects, ideas, or data according to some criterion. This operation requires a higher level of abstracting ability on the part of the individual as she or he must abstract critical elements of the objects or ideas involved in order to form new linkages that are more than memory and more than simple linkages. The identification of a chair, sofa, or table as furniture is an economical way of grouping many perceptually diverse elements.

Reasoning is the set of rules and strategies by which an individual can generate new knowledge by logical organization of existing information. For example, the knowledge that

> Tom is taller than Sam
> and Sam is taller than Jim

yields a new piece of information:

> ∴ Tom is taller than Jim

The reasoning process may be used to obtain a solution to a problem (e.g., the value of the hypotenuse of a right triangle). It is the mental operation that enables the individual to apply a strategy (the Pythagorean theorem) to solve for the conclusion. This type of problem solution derived through logical thinking is an example of *convergent thinking*, which was shown by Guilford (1967) to represent one type of mental ability most often measured on standardized tests of intelligence. Another kind of thinking operation proposed by Guilford is *divergent thinking* (e.g., what would happen if the oceans rose 10 feet?), which is seldom found in instruments used to generate IQ scores. Though less obviously a form of reasoning, it should also be included here since the same intellectual operation applies. The reasoning process can be extrapolated as follows: "If the oceans rose 10 feet, and New York City is at sea level, *then* New York City would be underwater." Divergent thinking, which places a value on many different answers, merely asks the respondent to go through the logical reasoning process a number of times (Gallagher, Aschner, & Jenne, 1968).

Evaluation is the process of applying a criterion or establishing a continuum of value, and then comparing a given element against that criterion or continuum. In this way we can determine the merit of a fact in a relative or an absolute quantity ("six is greater than five"; "six is not equal to five") or quality ("this play is better than her first"; "that book has no plot!")

However, there is one additional element of cognition to add to the information processing model, which is not present in any of Guilford's dimensions – the executive function. The *executive function* is the cognitive process that deals with choice. The process controls the selection between stimuli, strategies, or modes of expression. It is the mental function that determines what the individual will pay attention to, how the individual will process new information, and how the individual will express the results of the internal processing. The executive function mediates the synthesis of information both simultaneously and successively, acting as a gatekeeper for the control of the flow of information processing.

In terms of intellectual development, therefore, giftedness can be defined as superior or precocious performance in these six operations. Analyses of verbal classroom interactions of gifted students across content fields of language arts, science, and social studies have indicated a high correlation between the dimensions of memory, convergent thinking, divergent thinking, and evaluative thinking as they operate in the classroom (Gallagher et al., 1968). It seems that high intellectual performance will require the efficient use of all of these major mental operations, working in complex combinations with one another.

Interestingly enough, some of the insights into superior mental functioning have come from the careful analysis of the thinking of mentally retarded individuals. Theoretical models of memory by Ellis (1978) and attention by Zeaman (1978) clearly owe their development to work with citizens with mental retardation. Campione and Brown (1979) summarized the literature on the nature of intelligence in mentally retarded children and concluded that the critical skill in which the mentally retarded individuals were deficient was the ability to generalize or classify. They commented: "We characterize the retarded as showing neither spontaneous invention or generation of strategies nor generalization following training." (p. 149).

Campione and Brown believed that these limitations represent generalization failures, and they placed heavy emphasis on the role of "metacognitive" processes, which refers to the subject's awareness of his own cognitive operations. They believe that the failure of the mentally retarded individual to generalize from one task to another is based on two factors:

1. They must detect the similarity of the two tasks in terms of the processing demands; and they must
2. Modify the rehearsal strategy to fit the new situation more closely. (p. 155)

It is precisely these characteristics that youngsters whom we call gifted have in abundance – the ability to generalize and the ability to make rapid transfer of information from one situation to another appropriately.

There appears to be some evidence to suggest that there is a type of mirror-image pattern of cognitive development with retarded and gifted children showing opposing patterns of relative strengths and weaknesses in their test profiles in measures of mental development (Gallagher & Lucito, 1960).

Basis for individual intellectual superiority

Since the time of Galton, the role that heredity plays in giftedness has been well accepted. The evidence from twin and sibling studies (Plomin, DeFries, & McClearn, 1980), as well as the impressive evidence of early precociousness, has seemed definitive. The portrait of Mozart, composing music at age 4, challenges any environmentalist to produce a set of experiences or training that would allow a typical 4-year-old to emulate such performance.

In most instances, high ability in one of the mental operations is clearly linked to high ability in all of them, and so a question remains: How does one obtain extraordinary facility in the use of these intellectual operations? Recent attention in neurology has been given to the presence of many neurotransmitters – neurochemical substances that facilitate the transmission of impulses across nerve fibers. It seems reasonable to suggest that one mechanism that could be operating in genetic transmission of ability is an increased capability to produce certain types or levels of neurochemicals that would facilitate such transmission. Yet there is also reason to believe that experience, or the increased amount of relevant stored information to be drawn upon, also plays a critical role in later performance (Purpura, Gallagher, & Tjossem, 1981).

There is also some reason to believe in the powerful influence of an interaction effect between heredity and environment, that certain positive environmental factors can enhance the superior abilities inherited by a child, producing outstanding performance. Bloom (1982), in his study of world-class performers in music, athletics, or mathematics, has stressed the importance of early identification or perception of high ability by the "significant others" in the child's life. Such a perception appears to cause the adults to provide more opportunities to develop the child's talent. The child's own belief in his or her abilities becomes part of the pattern of motivation for the high accomplishment that follows, and that high accomplishment leads to more self-confidence, and so on.

The great scientific debates over how environment and heredity contribute to intelligence are generally not about the nature of the model itself, which expressed in simple form is

Intelligence = Heredity × Environment × (Heredity × Environment Interaction)

Such opposing theoreticians as Hunt (1961) and Jensen (1969) are really quarreling over the *relative variance* that is contributed to the final product, and not the basic model. Recent research would suggest that the interaction factor may be of much greater importance than was previously considered (Sameroff & Chandler, 1975).

Educational definition – academically advanced

It is the recognition of the role played by the surrounding social forces in developing intellectual abilities that has led to a somewhat different view of intelligence in educational circles. As noted earlier in this chapter, the educational definition of giftedness has changed with the times and with educational philosophy. The earlier definitions focused on superior personal (individual difference) characteristics with little attention to the specific environmental conditions or restrictions created by the schools.

A gifted child is one whose performance is consistently remarkable in any potentially valuable area. (Witty, 1940)

The gifted are defined as those who possess a superior nervous system characterized by the potential to perform tasks requiring a comparatively high degree of intellectual abstraction or creative imagination. (Sumption & Luecking, 1960)

Gifted children are those individuals from kindergarten through high school age who show unusual promise in some socially useful area and whose talents might be stimulated. (DeHaan & Havighurst, 1957)

All such definitions, of course, leave for someone else to decide, on some operational level, how the terms *remarkable, superior, unusual promise*, and the like, get translated into some specific quantitative statement, a process that must take place if a student is to be determined *eligible* for some school program for gifted students. Much of the educational activity on defining gifted children emerged from the need to determine eligibility, a task made necessary by the requirements for obtaining special state funds by local school districts.

The current educational view, which is clearly different from earlier attempts at measuring individual differences noted in the preceding paragraphs, is well represented by a definition that was used in federal legislation for the gifted and talented in 1971 and has since become known as the Marland definition (Marland, 1972):

Gifted and talented children are those identified by professionally qualified persons who by virtue of outstanding abilities are capable of high performance. These are children who require differentiated educational programs and/or services beyond those normally provided by the regular school programs in order to realize their contribution to self and society.

Children capable of high performance include those with demonstrated achievement and/or potential ability in any of the following areas, singly or in combination: (1) general intellectual ability, (2) specific academic aptitude, (3) creative or productive thinking, (4) leadership ability, (5) visual and performing arts, (6) psychomotor ability.

The Marland definition was adopted in federal legislation in P.L. 93-380 (Special Projects Act). The sixth category, psychomotor ability, was dropped in subsequent federal legislation. Surveys by Karnes and Collins (1980) and Gallagher, Weiss, Oglesby, and Thomas (1983) showed that more than two-thirds of the states had legislation, or working guidelines, that supported a definition of giftedness similar to this federal legislation (Gifted and Talented Children's Education Act of 1978).

This definition had a number of important elements to it that both reflected and shaped the schools' approach to gifted and talented children. It identifies gifted children as those "capable of high performance." In other words, the student need not be currently manifesting outstanding performance but need merely indicate an aptitude for such performance.

The children "require differentiated . . . programs . . . in order to realize their contribution to self and society." In this instance, there is a recognition that even with the presence of a strong general education program in the schools, something special would still be needed to meet the intellectual needs of these students. Therefore, gifted and talented programs are not seen as merely compensating for a less than adequate general education program.

Furthermore, the specific mention of five areas – "general intellectual ability, specific academic aptitude, creative or productive thinking, leadership ability, and visual and performing arts" – appeared to be a reaction to an earlier tendency for the schools, in the 1940s and 1950s, to settle for a very narrow definition, stressing only traditional scholarly behavior in standard subjects such as English or mathematics.

The schools are especially interested, however, in those children who show aptitudes that link directly with societally important topics such as the sciences or mathematics. Other mental abilities in dimensions such as art receive much less attention.

The schools also have to base their program, not on individual students, but on the particular combination of students who are available for education. Decisions on educational organization are often made on the basis of those group characteristics rather than on individual abilities. A youngster of moderately high aptitude might stand out dramatically in a group of slow-learning or developmentally delayed students and might require some special educational adaptations. If this same student of moderately high ability was in a school where there were a large number of students of similar aptitudes, he or she would probably require less of a special educational experience. Thus, the need to find and label gifted youngsters and provide special services for them would be either reduced or enhanced as determined by the nature of the local student population!

Does a student get labeled "gifted" as a function of his or her performance in one or more of Marland's areas or by being extraordinarily able at the processing of information as represented by Figure 4.1? The Marland approach is the educational point of view; the second is the psychological model.

Galton's assessment of eminence directly relates to the educational definition of giftedness as traditionally viewed by schools, focusing as it does on *performance* in society (eminence) as the key factor. Students must demonstrate their giftedness (academic superiority) through the attainment of eminence in the classroom as reflected by grades and test scores. Here, the emphasis of defining giftedness lies in the product.

From a research standpoint, it should be possible to define giftedness as the high-level processing of information that brings to bear the components of metacognition in a highly effective manner. Within each domain of the discrete categorizations of educational processes of giftedness, these components of metacognition can be found. The Binet–Terman approach to the evaluation of cognitive abilities would be used to identify those whose performance is far above the norm through tests.

These two parallel definitions, while usually implicitly clear to those practicing within one domain or the other, cause no small amount of confusion to most of society, because others fail to infer the differences inherent in the distinct purposes of the two realms. The school setting is where confusion about the purpose of the programs and identification procedures for the gifted in the schools may generate anxiety, mistrust, and consternation regarding the proposed purpose of the program for "gifted students." It is in this area that the clarification of the two definitions is most important to professionals, parents, and society in general.

The strange case of creativity in educational circles. One of the strangest results of the current educational definition of "giftedness" is the separation of the concept of creativity from intellectual superiority. One finds peculiar results from studies that report low correlations between "giftedness" and creativity (Getzels & Jackson, 1962). On the surface, it would seem clear that creativity should be the highest manifestation of intellectual performance, not separate from it. The only basis for separation of these dual manifestations of intellectual growth would be the assumption that American school systems value only memory and convergent thinking abilities, but not the originality or unique problem-solving operations related to what we traditionally consider as creativity.

Educators such as Torrance (1979) have stressed the importance of including mental operations not traditionally found in the operational definition of giftedness or in the school curriculum. Using Guilford's structure of intellect as a model, Torrance built tests of creative thinking that stressed

> Fluency – The production of many ideas
> Originality – The uniqueness of ideas
> Elaboration – The extension of ideas
> Flexibility – Modifiability of ideas

As Torrance said: "It also seems obvious that the rational and logical processes involved in intelligence tests are called into play in the process of creative thinking, especially in evaluating alternatives, making decisions, and the like" (p. 361).

The study of creative persons, as opposed to the study of the creative process or factorial studies of creativity, has often focused on the personality or life-style of the creative person (MacKinnon, 1978). The consistent findings that the creative person has less commitment to social norms and a stronger self-image suggest that the key to creative production may rest less in particular cognitive skills and more in motivational patterns and life-styles.

Social pressures on definition

One of the most recent attempts to create an educational definition that includes a specific social component has been provided by Renzulli (1979):

Giftedness consists of an interaction among three basic clusters of human traits – these clusters being above average general abilities, high levels of task commitment, and high levels of creativity. Gifted and talented children are those possessing or capable of developing this composite set of traits and applying them to any potential valuable area of human performance. . . . Children who manifest or who are capable of developing an interaction among the three clusters require a wide variety of educational opportunities and services that are not ordinarily provided through regular instructional program (p. 23).

Renzulli stresses performance over aptitude and requires some manifest evidence, beyond student performance on tests of individual differences, before he is willing to call a child gifted.

Cultural differences and educational concept of giftedness. Yet, educators are only too painfully aware that even the expanding educational concept of giftedness, from IQ score to academic productivity to creativity, has left untouched a large number of students – culturally different, gifted children. In no other instance does our concern for accurate operational definitions have more profound, far-reaching effects.

Terman's longitudinal study of the gifted (Terman & Oden, 1947) ended the stereotype of the 94-pound, four-eyed weakling – but left untouched many students of high potential from subcultures of our society. Native Americans, Hispanics, and blacks have often been bypassed, overlooked, and ignored in the quest to identify and provide special educational programs for gifted children. If, as Marland has stated, our gifted children are our most neglected natural resource, then these may be the neglected of the neglected. The conspicuously limited participation in gifted programs by minority students raises the question about the tools we are using for our operational definitions (Baldwin, Gear, & Lucito, 1979; Bernal, 1979).

When our tools yield findings that violate our own sense of values or assumptions, they are viewed with some suspicion. When girls fail to qualify for advanced programs in mathematics and few black children reach eligibility standards for gifted programs, then questions are raised about the validity of the tools emphasized in such decision making (Fox, 1977). One such question is whether the basic assumptions of the intelligence tests have been met (Algozzine & Ysseldyke, 1983): "An underlying assumption in psychological and educational assessment is that the acculturation of the person being assessed is comparable to, although not necessarily identical with, that of the people upon whom the test was standardized" (p. 139).

We have used three different strategies to try to meet the issue of cultural differences as it would affect the educational definition. (a) We can modify the standards for giftedness, (b) we can seek new instruments that are more culture-fair, or (c) we can include other criteria beyond standardized test scores for the operational definition.

Mercer & Lewis (1977) continue to employ test instruments for identification, but also use a complex set of social factors to adjust the actual test score to a presumed truer measure of potential: the System of Multicultural Pluralistic Assessment (SOMPA). Thus, a child in an unfavorable environmental setting could have an IQ score adjusted from 110 to 130 by the process of readjusting the reference groups so that the child is compared against children from his or her own sociocultural setting.

Others have tried to introduce different tests or subtests that more adequately measured minority children (Bernal, 1974; Bruch, 1971). Tests of nonverbal abilities such as the Raven Progressive Matrices and the Davis–Eels Test have not proven helpful, and the search for a measure untainted by prior experience is now largely agreed to be futile.

The third method includes self-report scales, such as the *Biographical Inventory of Creativity* (BIC) and such teacher rating scales as the Renzulli et al. (1976) and the Multidimensional Screening Device (MDSD) by Kranz (1978). Obviously, which students will be called "gifted" may vary substantially, depending on the set of indicators in use.

All of these efforts to force equality of numbers among variables of sex, race, income level, and the like have in common an important flaw. They are trying to isolate the individual from his or her cultural surroundings and influences. As Newland (1976) explains:

In certain portions of our society there are no inherent demands nurturant to the acquisition of a broad experience base for ultimate symbol acquisition. Many of the "disadvantaged" are so reared. True, they generalize and acquire symbols, but their motivation is generally born more of immediate social needs than of a response to the nurturance of the kind of "inherent intellectual inquiry" that has been suggested, and as a result the symbols they acquire are of limited utility in the broad social scene. The school's role in compensating for this is particularly important with respect to the "disadvantaged" and especially the gifted among them. (p. 16)

If this is true, then we will have to decide to what extent pure performance will be used as a definition of giftedness, which would rule out many culturally different students, because performance inevitably rests, in part, on experience. We will have to decide whether certain special indicators will be accepted as measures of potential or aptitude that will choose those students whose experiences have been different from those of the middle-class students, broadly defined. The variety of compromises now being used in American education in identification of the gifted is well represented in the following example.

A sample operational definition. There must be some way to translate these general statements into some operational standards for educational systems. This is true particularly when the state will pay additional attention because of funds made available for gifted programs. The local schools, in order to become eligible for such special funds, must identify bona fide gifted students.

An example of how one state, North Carolina, carried out that task is shown in Table 4.1 (N.C. Department of Public Instruction, 1984). A student can achieve credit toward a label of "gifted" through four separate sources.

Table 4.1. *North Carolina guidelines for identification as academically gifted* (1984)

Category	Score range	Weighted value[a]
Achievement test data	96th–99th %ile	8
	93–95	7
	89–92	6
	85–88	5
	77–84	4
Intelligence quotion data	96th–99th %ile	5
	93–95	4
	89–92	3
	85–88	2
	77–84	1
Academic grades data	A or 96–99 or Superior	5
	B or 93–95 or Very Good	4
	C or 89–92 or Average	3
Teacher recommendation data	Most outstanding of the group	5
	Superior	4
	Above average	3
	Average	2
	Below average	1

[a]Maximum number of points = 23, and 19 points are needed to identify subject as gifted.

1. *Standardized achievement test score.* The results on a standardized achievement test will yield a maximum weighted score of 8 for performance above the 95th percentile.
2. *Intellectual assessment.* An individual or group test of mental ability can yield a weighted score of 5 for a performance at or above a percentile rank of 95.
3. *Teacher recommendations.* One of several checklists or behavioral scales is used by professional personnel to assess characteristics of ability to learn, motivation, creativity, and leadership. Most use a Likert-style scale, rating whether the behavior ranges from "always" to "never."
4. *Academic grades.* The grade average for the previous year is calculated and can yield a weighted score of 5 for the highest grades.

A total of 19 out of a possible 23 points collected through these four dimensions can earn the child a title of "gifted" and make him or her eligible for special educational services. There are a number of issues to be noted about this process. Students of extraordinary ability, as measured by instruments stressing intellectual aptitude, can be kept from the label of "gifted" in the schools if they have not performed well on academic measures, or if teachers do not like them or don't observe their talents.

The multidimensional approach can prevent some students, such as minority children, from being overlooked through the sole use of intellectual

Table 4.2. *Two different concepts of giftedness*

Discipline	Individual differences	School performance and assessment
Mental abilities considered	Full range available	Range limited to societally important predictors of academic success
Measuring instruments	Batteries of instruments touching all domains	Norm performance instruments on school related variables
Ecological influence	Independent of ecological factors	Dependent on school and cultural environment
Purpose of measurement	Discovery of the nature of cognitive processes	Placement in proper educational environment
Possible label	*Gifted*	*Academically advanced*

ability tests. It also provides many opportunities for the current educational styles and the instructional status quo to be influential through the use of criteria such as grades, teacher ratings, and achievement tests.

The emphasis in this process of academic advancement is on traditional academic abilities so that the offbeat, the unusual, and the unique thinker might well be ignored. Edison and Einstein might well be two obvious examples of "nongifted" students with these criteria in effect.

Where next?

If the authors have been correct in their proposition that there are two different constructs masquerading under one term – *gifted* – then what is to be done? The first step, we believe, would be to encourage a full understanding of these two separate perspectives and their implications. Table 4.2 provides a summary statement of the differences between the two constructs.

In terms of the mental abilities to be considered, the schools can be counted on to focus on abilities that have clear relevance to their perceived purposes and objectives, whereas the social scientists, anxious to catalog the full range of mental abilities, will pursue a much broader scope of abilities to be considered.

The measuring instruments utilized in each of the two approaches will also reflect the above difference. The school will limit itself to academic aptitude measures (i.e., CAT or IQ tests) and subjective ratings. The scientist studying individual differences will be developing other tasks and tests to try to measure a broader range of abilities.

The influence of ecological factors will be of minimal interest to those pursuing individual differences, except as such skills emerge out of social interactions and experiences. The emphasis is on the individual and where he or she fits in the distribution of that particular characteristic. On the other hand, the particular group the child is in school with may have an unusually important role to play in whether he or she may be called "gifted."

The problem of the relativistic nature of the educational approach is that if the definition of "giftedness" is to be different from one community to another, because of the differing presses and needs of communities and school systems across the country, then what is to become of such a concept? What is the use of a concept of giftedness that is different in San Diego from what it is in Chicago, with both being different from Miami? It would be an odd taxonomy for butterflies that would define them in terms of the flowers they approach rather than their own essential characteristics.

Finally, the purposes for paying attention to these youngsters are different. The social scientists seek insight into human abilities and their development. The educator is looking for reliable and defensible ways for placing the proper children in the most appropriate educational setting. Given these differences, it is no wonder that the uses of the term *gifted* become a source of occasional confusion and controversy.

How does this conceptualization fit into other formulations? There would seem to be a link between the dichotomy proposed in Table 4.2 and the triarchic theory proposed by Sternberg (1984), in which he suggests three separate dimensions of intelligence.

a. Adaptation to real-world environments.
b. The automatization of information processing and adaptation to novelty.
c. Information processing – learning how to do things, planning what to do, and doing it.

The School Performance and Assessment area in Table 4.2 seems to fit the adaptation to the real-world component, whereas the individual differences concept fits into Sternberg's component focusing on information processing.

Renzulli, in Chapter 3 of this book, similarly uses the School Performance and Assessment domain as his criterion for giftedness. The combination of creativity, intellectual aptitude, and motivation will likely yield elevated school performance. The concept of the gifted underachiever is a peculiar one worthy of special notice regarding these two different concepts of giftedness. The gifted underachiever is a child with high measured ability in the Individual Differences domain and poor or mediocre performance in the School Performance and Assessment domain (Whitmore, 1980). One must accept both of these concepts of giftedness in order to think about underachievement as an entity, a condition accepted by almost any teacher or educator.

It is important that neither of these concepts totally replace or eliminate the other. An exclusive emphasis on the academically talented student would cause us to ignore those developing human abilities that should be called on more adequately by the school and the culture. One has only to think of the domain of *social intelligence*, where measures might presumably identify individuals of high sensitivity to others' feelings and the capabilities for reaching solutions to conflict without violence. Although neither the schools nor the culture are currently attempting to nurture such abilities in a systematic fashion, the continued study of these dimensions may well eventually yield a change in current educational practice.

On the other hand, an exclusive emphasis on individual differences might result in an extensive body of information about mental abilities based heavily on isolated laboratory performances, and we would not have a chance to see how those abilities are expressed in the variety of social and cultural environments that the developing child must experience.

What is probably required are *two* terms. *Gifted* would perhaps be reserved for extraordinarily rapid development in these channels of individual differences as described by Guilford, for example; the term *academically advanced* would be reserved for students needing special educational attention. This division of terms would serve another useful purpose because of the tendency of local school systems to want to broaden the definition to include a much larger sample of students than is typically identified under the term *gifted*. While *gifted* is rarely seen to include more than 5% of the population on a given characteristic, school systems often wish to organize instructional programs for high aptitude students that would include 10%, 15%, or 20% of the student body. It often makes more educational sense to group them in this form and number.

In some fashion, we must come to grips with these two different views, because so many of our identification and program goals must necessarily follow from the constructs we accept. Our tasks would be made easier if we could reach a professional consensus on the differential terminology suggested here.

References

Algozzine, B., & Ysseldyke, J. (1983). Learning disabilities as a subset of school failure: The oversophistication of a concept. *Exceptional Children, 50*, 242–246.

Baldwin, A., Gear, G., & Lucito, L. (Eds.). (1979). *Educational planning for the gifted*. Reston, Va.: The Council for Exceptional Children.

Bernal, E. (1974). Gifted Mexican-American children: An ethnoscientific perspective. *California Journal of Educational Research, 25*, 261–273.

Bernal, E. (1979). The education of the culturally different gifted. In A. H. Passow (Ed.), *The gifted and the talented: Their education and development*. The Seventy-eighth Yearbook of the National Society for the Study of Education, Part I. Chicago: University of Chicago Press.

Binet, E. (1909). *Les idées modernes sur les enfants*. Paris: E. Flemanarion.

Binet, A., & Simon, T. (1976). The development of intelligence in the child. In W. Dennis & M. W. Dennis (Eds.), *The intellectually gifted* (pp. 13–16). New York: Grune & Stratton.

Bloom, B. (1982). The role of gifts and markers in the development of talent. *Exceptional Children, 48,* 510–522.

Bronowski, J. (1973). *The ascent of man.* Boston: Little, Brown.

Bruch, C. (1971). Modification of procedures for identification of the disadvantaged. *Gifted Child Quarterly, 15,* 267–272.

Campione, J., & Brown, A. (1979). Toward a theory of intelligence: Contributions from research with retarded children. In R. Sternberg & D. Delterman (Eds.), *Human intelligence.* Norwood, N.J.: Ablex.

Coleman, W., Jr., & Selby, C. (1983). *Educating Americans for the 21st century.* Washington D.C.: National Science Board Commission on Precollege Education in Mathematics, Science, and Technology.

Dabrowski, K. (1964). *Positive disintegration.* Boston: Little, Brown.

DeHaan, R., & Havighurst, R. (1957). *Educating gifted children.* Chicago: University of Chicago Press.

Ellis, N. (1978). Do the mentally retarded have poor memory? *Intelligence, 2,* 41–54.

Fox, L. (1977). *Changing times and the education of gifted girls.* Paper presented at the Second World Conference for Gifted and Talented Children, San Francisco.

Gallagher, J., Aschner, M., & Jenne, W. (1967). *Productive thinking of gifted children in classroom interaction* (CEC Research Monograph Series B5). Arlington, Va.: Council for Exceptional Children.

Gallagher, J., & Lucito, L. (1960). Intellectual patterns of gifted compared with average and retarded. *Peabody Journal of Education, 38,* 131–136.

Gallagher, J., Weiss, P., Oglesby, K., & Thomas, T. (1983). *The status of gifted/talented education: United States survey of needs, practices, and policies.* Los Angeles: National/State Leadership Training Institute of the Gifted and Talented.

Galton, F. (1883). *Hereditary genius.* London: Macmillan. (Original work published 1869)

Getzels, J. W., & Jackson, P. W. (1962). *Creativity and intelligence: Explorations with gifted children.* New York: Wiley.

Guilford, J. P. (1967). Creativity: Yesterday, today, tomorrow. *Journal of Creative Behavior, 1,* 3–14.

Hunt, J. (1961). *Intelligence and experience.* New York: Ronald Press.

Hunt, J., Jr. (1983). *Action for excellence.* Denver, Colo.: Education Commission of the States, Task Force on Education for Economic Growth.

Jensen, A. (1969). How much can we boost IQ and scholastic achievement? *Harvard Educational Review, 39,* 1–123.

Karnes, F., & Collins, E. (1980). *Handbook of instructional resources and references for teaching the gifted.* Boston: Allyn & Bacon.

Kranz, B. (1978). *Multi-dimensional screening device (MDSD) for the identification of gifted/talented children* (Bureau of Educational Research and Services Publication No. 9). Grand Forks: University of North Dakota.

MacKinnon, D. (1978). The nature and nurture of creative talent. *American Psychologist, 17,* 484–495.

Marland, S. (1972). *Education of the gifted and talented.* Report to the Congress of the United States by the U.S. Commissioner of Education. Washington, D.C.: U.S. Government Printing Office.

Mercer, J., & Lewis, J. (1977). *System of multicultural pluralistic assessment (SOMPA).* New York: The Psychological Corporation.

National Commission on Excellence in Education. (1983). *A nation at risk: The imperative for educational reform* (A report to the Nation and the Secretary of Education). Washington, D.C.: U.S. Government Printing Office.

Newell, A., & Simon, H. (1972). *Human problem solving.* Englewood Cliffs, N.J.: Prentice-Hall.

Newland, T. (1976). *The gifted in socio-educational perspective.* Englewood Cliffs, N.J.: Prentice-Hall.

Newland, T. (1976). *The gifted in socio-educational perspective*. Englewood Cliffs, N.J.: Prentice-Hall.

North Carolina State Department of Public Instruction. (1984). *Rules governing programs and services for children with special needs*. Raleigh, N.C.: North Carolina State Department of Public Instruction.

Plomin, R., DeFries, J., & McClearn, G. (1980). *Behavioral genetics: A primer*. San Francisco: Freeman.

Purpura, D., Gallagher, J., & Tjossem, T. (1981). *Mental retardation: An evaluation and assessment of the state of the science*. Washington, D.C.: National Institute for Child Health and Human Development.

Renzulli, J. (1979). *What makes giftedness?* Los Angeles: National/State Leadership Training Institute on the Gifted and the Talented.

Renzulli, J., Smith, L., White, A., Callahan, C., & Hartman, R. (1976). *Scales for rating the behavioral characteristics of superior students*. Mansfield Center, Conn.: Creative Learning Press.

Sameroff, A., & Chandler, M. (1975). Reproductive risk and the continuum of caretaking casualty. In F. Horowitz (Ed.), *Review of Child Development Research* (Vol. 4, pp. 187–244). Chicago: University of Chicago Press.

Sternberg, R. (Ed.). (1982). *Handbook of human intelligence*. Cambridge University Press.

Sternberg, R. J. (1984). Toward a triarchic theory of human intelligence. *Behavioral and Brain Sciences*, 7(2), 264–316.

Sumption, M., & Luecking, E. (1960). *Education of the gifted*. New York: Roland Press.

Terman, L., & Oden, M. (1947). *Genetic studies of genius: Vol. 4. The gifted child grows up*. Stanford, Calif.: Stanford University Press.

Terman, L., & Oden, M. (1959). *Genetic studies of genius: Vol. 5. The gifted group at mid-life*. Stanford, Calif.: Stanford University Press.

Torrance, E. (1979). Unique needs of the creative child and adult. In A. Passow (Ed.), *The gifted and the talented: Their education and development*. The Seventy-eighth Yearbook of the National Society for the Study of Education (pp. 352–371). Chicago: University of Chicago Press.

Whitmore, J. (1980). *Giftedness, conflict, and underachievement*. Boston: Allyn & Bacon.

Witty, P. (1940). *Intelligence: Its nature and nurture*. The Thirty-ninth Yearbook of the National Society for the Study of Education, Part II (pp. 401–409). Bloomington, Il.: Public School Publishing.

Zeaman, D. (1978). Some relatives of general intelligence and selective attention. *Intelligence*, 2, 55–73.

5 A conception of giftedness

John F. Feldhusen

Giftedness in a child or adolescent consists of psychological and physical predisposition for superior learning and performance in the formative years and high-level achievement or performance in adulthood. The latter may, of course, come early in the life of a gifted person. Because predisposition requires nurturing opportunities, chance may play a large role in the development of giftedness. The school and the family are major nurturing agencies, and both may fail to meet the demands of the task.

Giftedness in all fields is linked to the pursuit of high-level goals, to striving for excellence, and to the creation of new ideas or products. Thus, it would seem that creative ability should be a conceptual component of giftedness. But perhaps it is a mere tautology to assert that giftedness involves creativity. In reality, creativity may simply be the end product of talent development. For the present, creativity or divergent thinking tests offer no compelling evidence of validity links to creative production in adulthood. Thus, a conception of creativity as cognitive abilities measured by tests should not be a part of our conception of giftedness. However, the work of MacKinnon (1978) and others leads us to believe that motivational and self-concept aspects of creativity, acquired in childhood, may be primogenitors of creative production or performance in adulthood.

Our composite conception of giftedness then includes (a) general intellectual ability, (b) positive self-concept, (c) achievement motivation, and (d) talent. This is not to say that these are the only components. Surely the gifted adult is a composite, fully functioning individual whose entire physical and psychological being interacts with his or her milieu to yield creative productivity. This is Gruber's (1982) basic approach to the study of giftedness: the creatively productive adult as a total system. However, in focusing on these four aspects we are asserting that they constitute "principal components." It is also to say that, for the present, we can conceptualize a large part of giftedness within these four dimensions.

General intellectual ability, even as fractionated into macro- or microlevel factors, is nevertheless the general underpinning of giftedness. It facilitates the acquisition of knowledge and it supports formal-operational thinking.

Necessary levels of general intellectual ability vary from field to field or discipline to discipline. For some, disciplines such as pure mathematics or theoretical physics, the necessary levels are very high. New conceptions of intelligence and its trainability are emerging from the work of Sternberg and others. However, for the present, we agree with Horn's (1978) assertion that "the concept of intelligence is used to designate an innately determined quality, a potential that will become manifest as a function of normal maturation" (p. 108). However, with this said, it must be added that no known tests measure innate intelligence. All intelligence tests measure ability as reflected in learned behavior.

Nevertheless, currently available tests of intelligence do provide reliable indices that can be used in estimating giftedness. But there are no known criterion levels of performance that are universal across fields, nor are differentiated criteria available for particular fields. The criteria used in programs for the gifted reflect tremendous diversity in IQ levels required for admission. One common practice is to suggest that the IQ should be two standard deviations above the mean, or approximately 130, but this, too, is simply an arbitrary decision. For the present, we believe that programs for the gifted should recognize the IQ as one valuable index along with other test scores, ratings, and observations and should make professional judgments concerning the potential giftedness or talent of youth.

The second component of giftedness is talent. It is more difficult to assess. For many fields, performance or product assessment is essential. This is certainly true of talent in the arts, but it is equally true for such talent areas as electronics, playwriting, fashion design, and journalism. Some components of talent may be assessed with such instruments as the Differential Aptitude Tests or the Primary Mental Abilities Test. Generally, however, there is considerable faith that adult experts in a field can assess performance or products and determine the level of talent in youthful aspirants.

Assessments of talent via performance or products can best be implemented in programs for the gifted by creating opportunities for program "tryouts." Candidates for art classes in the Saturday program for able youth at Purdue University (Feldhusen & Sokol, 1982) must present themselves for a tryout class in which they are assigned a drawing task, their performance is observed and evaluated while they are drawing, and their products are later evaluated by staff in art education. The evaluation of talent continues once they enter classes. At the end of each semester their work is graded (rated) and the information can be used to predict future talent potential for each student.

Talent for mathematics and science seems to be quite well predicted by the mathematics score of the Scholastic Aptitude Test (SAT) (Benbow & Stanley, 1983). The verbal score is also useful in assessing talent for the study of literature, composition, and related fields. Ratings from several of the *Scales for Rating the Behavioral Characteristics of Superior Students* (Renzulli et al.,

1976) can also be useful in talent identification. The art scale, for example, is yet another measure used to identify talent in the Purdue Saturday program. The best combination might often be a retrospective rating of performance, observations, and rating of ongoing performance, some test scores, and/or product evaluations. Talent is complex, and it probably requires multiple assessments to secure valid and reliable indices of its level in a potentially gifted youth.

Self-concept can be assessed, but as a measure of typical, not maximum, performance we can scarcely use it as an index for admission to a program for gifted youth. Programs for gifted youth may, however, recognize the central role of self-concept in the gifted and strive to help gifted youth clarify and enhance their views and understanding of self. In the program for gifted youth at Wayne Township in Indianapolis, Indiana, counselors meet once a week with junior high school students in small group sessions to discuss personal, interpersonal, and educational problems encountered by students of high ability. The counselors endeavor to help the students clarify their values, achieve insight regarding human behavior, and understand themselves better. Although no specific effort is made to help the students raise their self-concepts, it is nevertheless assumed that a more realistic view of self among the gifted should lead to a higher or more positive self-concept.

Gifted youth should especially grow in the view of self as competent and capable of developing new ideas, new inventions, new performances, new products. This conception of self can best be achieved through early opportunities to undertake projects or to prepare for performances that are well above grade or age level. That is to say that gifted youth need to carry out studies, projects, and learning activities and to exhibit their precocity to significant audiences. Such experiences can have a powerful effect on the self-concept in convincing gifted youth that they have prodigious talent. Thus, self-concept is enhanced. Schools can provide these opportunities and teachers can be the guides, catalysts, mentors, or stimulators who evoke such precocity in gifted youth.

Motivation to achieve is also an essential ingredient in giftedness. It begins to show itself as early as the first grade in school. We can be alert to the child who exhibits high-level, task-involved motivation. Children who possess high-level general ability, specific talents, and manifest achievement motivation are indeed prime candidates for services in programs for the gifted. Their intensity of interest, drive, or achievement orientation is often clearly visible to teachers and gifted program leaders. Their energy seems boundless. They are involved in countless activities. They read voraciously. In short, they are often paragons of productive activity.

For highly able youth who do not yet exhibit such high-level achievement motivation, it should be a goal of gifted program services to evoke and develop achievement orientation and motivation. Bloom (1982a) found that demanding mentors or teachers can serve as the motivating stimuli for gifted youth. He (Bloom, 1981) also found that parents often play such a stimulating role. The Goertzels (1978) also confirmed in their biographical analyses of giftedness that mentors and parents play a significant role in evoking motivation to achieve in gifted youth. Finally, it seems likely that gifted youth thrive on association with other gifted youth because they stimulate or motivate one another. Many workers in the field of gifted education report observing the phenomenon of interpersonal stimulation among the gifted. They share ideas and ambitions at a level appropriate to their talents and thereby evoke appropriately high-level learning and performance activities.

Supporting literature and conceptions

Insights concerning the nature of giftedness and talent come in part from the study of biographies and autobiographies of highly gifted and eminent adults. The following people who represent diverse types of achievement in art, science, politics, and education were studied carefully for signs of the special talents, aptitudes, or abilities that might have emerged early in their lives and thus have been harbingers of giftedness (Feldhusen, 1982).

Anna Brito	Thomas Jefferson	Lewis Terman
Rachel Carson	Martin Luther King, Jr.	Kurt Vonnegut
Charles Darwin	Abraham Lincoln	George Washington
Albert Einstein	Amedeo Modigliani	Jessamyn West
Mohandas Gandhi	Wolfgang Mozart	Tennessee Williams
Ernest Hemingway	Georgia O'Keeffe	Frank Lloyd Wright
Eric Hoffer	Lewis Sullivan	

The results of that analysis yielded the following signs:

1. Early mastery of knowledge or techniques in a field or art form.
2. Signs of high-level intelligence, reasoning ability, or memory in early childhood.
3. High energy level, drive, commitment or devotion to study or work as a young person.
4. Intense independence, preference for working alone, individualism.
5. A sense (self-concept) of creative power and an internal locus of control.
6. Stimulated by association with other gifted youth or adults.
7. Heightened reactions to details, patterns, and/or other phenomena in the physical world.
8. Profit from access to accelerated artistic or intellectual experiences.

From a similar set of biographical analyses and from experimentation with creative activities, Amabile (1983) has also derived a conception of the components of creative giftedness. She suggest that they are (a) domain-relevant skills, (b) creativity-relevant skills, and (c) task motivation. Domain-relevant skills include the knowledge, technical skills, and special talents, unique to the area of gifted performance, that must be acquired as antecedents of high-level performance. Creativity skills include cognitive and work styles as well as knowledge of the heuristics for generating new ideas. Task motivation is a set of intrinsic interests and drives that stimulate and sustain interest to pursue creative tasks.

By tradition, giftedness has been defined as ability or aptitude, with a strong implication that it is an inherited and stable set of characteristics (Tannenbaum, 1983). Furthermore, it is assumed that test scores are the best indices of giftedness. A child who exhibits precocity in designing an experiment or writing a story is unlikely to gain admission to a program for the gifted without presenting appropriate test scores. The test scores alone, without real behavioral evidence, will often be accepted as the essential criteria of giftedness. Once identified as gifted by test scores, the child may languish or show little precocious behavior, but teachers and parents will continue to proclaim the child's giftedness.

Giftedness is also viewed as a very general condition. Programs for gifted and talented youth typically seek to identify "all-purpose" gifted children, and then they offer a common or general program of studies for all the youth in the program. As a part of the process of identification, a set of test scores and ratings representing ability, achievement, creativity, motivation, leadership, and the like are combined to yield a composite index of giftedness. The combination often reflects a selection process based on Renzulli's three-ring concept of giftedness (1979).

In contrast to the general view of giftedness, the Study of Mathematically Precocious Youth (SMPY) (Stanley, 1979) has pioneered an assessment–identification process that uses high, offgrade testing with the Scholastic Aptitude Test administered in seventh or eighth grade. Offgrade testing is used because tests at grade level often are too easy for gifted youth, have too low a ceiling, and thus do not assess ability reliably. This identification process in SMPY assesses giftedness in relation to the two major SAT abilities, verbal and mathematical. The concept of general, all-purpose giftedness gives way to a concept of giftedness as representing specialized talent. Because the SAT is influenced by learning opportunities, it may represent a combination of general aptitude and specific academic achievement.

Creativity

The role of creative capacities in giftedness remains quite uncertain. Attacks on divergent thinking tests as representing creativity have appeared often. Nicholls's (1972) review of research in this area suggested that researchers should avoid equating divergent thinking and creativity, and they should concentrate more efforts on real-world creativity. Torrance (1979), however, presented a very positive view of the role of creativity in conceptions of giftedness. He listed tests, rating scales, and observation procedures that he claimed would provide valid and reliable bases for assessment of creative capacity. The Torrance Tests of Creative Thinking were, of course, a prominent part of the list. He especially emphasized a need for multiple assessments. From his own review of research on creativity tests and a review of several longitudinal studies in particular, Torrance concluded that creativity tests administered in high school predict high-level creative achievement in adulthood.

Tannenbaum (1983) also reviewed the research on creativity testing and the relationship between creativity and intelligence. He concluded, first of all, that there is no research base for the conception of a threshold level of intelligence (e.g., 120) in relation to creative productivity, although several researchers have pronounced such a concept. Second, he concluded that IQ and divergent thinking are only partly distinguishable. There is some overlap and some independence. Finally, he concluded that creativity or divergent thinking tests are of uncertain value in discerning talents that other tests might overlook.

Gruber (1982) also concluded that the psychometric approach has failed to provide reliable or valid indices of the creativity construct. He says, "There is hardly a shred of evidence that scores on [creativity tests] correlate with real creative performance in any line of human endeavor" (p. 17). Gruber goes on to extol the merits of his systems approach to the study of creativity in the lives of eminently creative people. In this developmentally oriented analysis, Gruber and his associates have studied the processes by which early gifts develop into later creativity.

Feldman (1982) also addressed the problem of defining creativity. His definition stresses the concept of creativity as an extension of knowledge: "In its most powerful form creativity is the extension of a body of knowledge, beyond the structural borders that preceded its appearance. Thus, creativity in the sense of major new contribution is built out of mastery of a field or domain." (p. 40)

The measurement of creative capacity or divergent thinking in youth seems to be a questionable psychometric value and probably adds little or nothing to the identification of giftedness. The work of MacKinnon (1978) and Gruber (1982) as well as the excellent review by Michael (1977) leave no doubt that creative capacity is an emerging construct in the lives of children who are destined to become creatively productive adults. However, the creativity construct in childhood may simply be a collection of personality functions such as introversion, intuition, autonomy, individualism, flexibility, open-mindedness, alertness, and sensitivity.

Knowledge or information

The role of knowledge, learning, or specific achievement in relation to giftedness is very little explored, but our general faith is that gifted and talented youth should receive tutelage of some kind and should become knowledgeable in some discipline or area of study as a prelude to creative achievement. Sternberg (1981) for example, says that gifted individuals have a much deeper and broader knowledge base than average individuals. Further, he notes that as the knowledge base grows, the stored information increasingly helps the individual to increase the knowledge base. That is to say that knowledge begets knowledge.

MacKinnon (1978), too, noted in his samples of creative architects, scientists, inventors, mathematicians, artists, and writers that they had a wide range of information at their command. He noted, however, that the information they possessed may readily enter into new combinations because of their large information base and their fluency in combining ideas (p. 180).

Feldman (1982) also noted that creative giftedness usually represents achievement at advanced levels in a specific discipline or artistic domain. He speaks of creative production as the extension of knowledge, a view, artistic interpretation, or style, or a scientific advancement to new understandings. Gagne and Dick (1983), in reviewing aptitude–treatment interaction studies, also concluded that the most powerful variables related to high achievement are intelligence and accumulated knowledge. What a student already knows has a profound effect on future learning. Thus, it seems likely that superior knowledge, achievement, skills, and understanding must be or become a part of the gifted person's accoutrements.

Motivation

We have no doubt that motivational factors are involved in giftedness. Terman and Oden (1959) recognized the role of motivation in their sample of gifted people and especially in the 150 who had been highly successful in life. They did not differ significantly in intelligence from 150 people in their sample who were unsuccessful, but they did differ significantly in personality and motivational patterns. "Persistence in the accomplishment of ends," "drive to achieve," and "integration toward goals" were three uniquely relevant characteristics.

Nicholls (1983) has proposed that youth may derive achievement motivation from task involvement in learning or performance situations. That is, they may have a deep intrinsic interest that propels their motivation. However, Bloom (1982b) found that a sense of competitiveness may also be at the heart of motivation of productively gifted individuals.

Feldman (1979) also discussed the nature of motivation, especially in the very highly gifted. He noted that prodigious or high-level achievement in childhood is a reflection of the powerful interests and motivation of gifted youth. "Perhaps the most striking quality in the children in our study as well as other cases is the *passion* with which excellence is pursued. Commitment and tenacity and joy in achievement are perhaps the best signs that a coincidence has occurred among child, field and moment in evolutionary time" (p. 351).

Spence and Helmreich (1983) have recently published an extensive review of the literature on achievement-related motives and behavior. They begin by asserting that "ambition and drive to achieve excellence are widely recognized as crucial ingredients in successful attainment" (p. 10). They define achievement as follows: "Achievement is task-oriented behavior that allows the individual's performance to be evaluated according to some internally or externally imposed criterion, that involves the individual in competing with others, or that otherwise involves some standard of excellence" (p. 12). Spence and Helmreich (1983) concluded that we are not yet sure of how intrapersonal competitiveness and rewards function in motivation, although there are signs that they interact with intrinsic motivators to produce negative effects.

Nicholls (1983) has been developing a theoretical integration of achievement motivation, particularly as motivation relates to achievement in schools. He distinguishes three types of motivators: (a) extrinsic involvement or rewards, (b) ego-involvement, and (c) task involvement. In extrinsic motivation, learning is pursued in order to get an external payoff. In ego involvement, the learner does not value learning but is instead preoccupied with looking able or good. Finally, in task involvement, the student shows full interest in the task to be learned or performed and no interest in self-aggrandizement or the external payoff.

In task involvement, learning is more inherently valuable, meaningful, or satisfying, and attention is focused on the task and the strategies needed to master it rather than on the self. In ego involvement, on the other hand, learning is a means to the end of looking smart or avoiding looking stupid, and attention is focused on the self (p. 214).

Nicholls concludes that task involvement is clearly the preferred mode of motivation because it leads to superior learning and higher satisfaction on the part of the learner with his or her accomplishments. It also seems clear that the intrinsic motivation of task involvement is characteristic of gifted and talented learners. Signs of task involvements are then likely to be signs of giftedness. Gifted youth may more safely adopt task-involved motivational approaches because they are less likely than average- or low-ability youth to look weak or stupid in learning or performance situations. Children who exhibit deep task involvement are manifesting a major sign of giftedness.

Self-concept

The self-concepts of gifted youth are studied chiefly in terms of whether they are high or low in relation to average youth. Several researchers, notably Ketcham and Snyder (1977) and Ringness (1961), both of whom worked with elementary-level children, have found the self-concepts of gifted children to be higher than the self-concepts of average-ability children. Anastaziow (1964) found a positive correlation between reading ability and self-concept. Feldhusen and Kolloff (1981) and Kolloff (1983) reviewed the research and theoretical literature in this area. They concluded that although there is some mixed evidence, it appears that gifted youth have higher self-concepts than youth of average ability.

Theoretically, highly competent individuals ought to perceive themselves as superior in ability. Terman and Oden (1959) noted that their gifted sample were highly self-confident and free from inferiority feelings. MacKinnon (1978) also described his sample of creative architects as basically self-accepting, confident of themselves, able to be their gifted selves and to pursue their own ideals. Perhaps the fundamental ingredients of appropriate self-concept in gifted individuals are accurate perception of self as gifted or talented and perception of self as capable of creative or innovative endeavors. These perceptions should interact with motivational states to drive the gifted individual to study and to creative endeavors.

Self as perceived by the gifted probably exerts a dynamic force in the development of giftedness. Self-concept is a set of perceptions, interpretations, and evaluations of self and one's own talents, abilities, and liabilities. Shavelson, Hubner, and Stanton (1976) reviewed self-concept research extensively. They concluded that conceptions of self are formed through experience and interpretations of experience. Some experiences are perceived as successes, others as failures. Success and failure may be attributed to one's own capacities or weaknesses as well as to external events and individuals. Gifted youth should experience more frequent and higher-level successes and increasingly perceive those successes as a function of their own abilities and efforts. Of course, it is also possible that parents and teachers of gifted youth impose high expectations on them and in turn evoke high performance expectations in gifted youth themselves. Then it is possible that relatively high-level successes may still be perceived as falling short of expectations.

In a later review and research effort, Shavelson and Bolus (1982) hypothesized and partially confirmed that self-concept has seven major features or aspects: organization, multifacetedness, hierarchical structure, stability, increasing multifacetedness as the individual develops, descriptive and evaluative dimensions, and distinctness from other psychological constructs such as motivation and intelligence. Clearly, self-concept is complex, and in the gifted it is probably highly complex.

Self-concept exerts a dynamic force on the life and development of an individual. Self-concept and behavior reflect each other. Gifted youth must come to see themselves as highly competent, knowledgeable, and capable of producing new ideas, products, or performances. The self-confidence of the gifted is and should be congruent with their competence.

Feldhusen (1984b) proposed that self-concept in the gifted increasingly becomes a clear view and understanding of one's own talents and abilities, a sense of one's social and affective relationships with other high-ability youth, adolescents, or adults. It is also a sense of satisfaction with self, with one's abilities, and with one's performances. Thus, the gifted and talented should achieve a positive sense of strength in viewing self (p. 7).

General intelligence

Intelligence is possibly a general condition, but several researchers propose that it is multifaceted (Guilford, 1967) or componential (Sternberg, 1981). Horn (1976, 1978) criticized the Guilford structure of intellect as really failing to substantiate the independence of factors in the model, but the Sternberg componential model is gaining acceptance as an information-processing approach to the conception of intelligence. Of course, it should also be noted that Guilford (1968) described the structure of intellect as an information-processing model. He asserted that the content and product dimensions are both relevant to information, and the operations refer directly to the processing of that information.

Sternberg (1981) views all of the components of intelligence as information processes or metacomponents. Metacomponents are higher-order cognitive control processes. Gifted individuals, he asserts, excel in the following six components.

1. Decision as to just what the problems are that need to be solved.
2. Selection of lower order components of problem solving.
3. Selection of strategies for solving problems.
4. Selection of representations for information.
5. Decisions regarding allocation of componential resources in problem solving.
6. Solution monitoring in problem solving.

He goes on to describe performance components, which are processes used to execute what the metacomponents plan:

1. *Inference* is detecting relations between objects.
2. *Mapping* is relating aspects of one domain to another.
3. *Application* is predicting on the basis of perceived maps.
4. *Comparison* involves the examination of a prediction in relation to alternative predictions.
5. *Justification* is a process of verifying options.
6. *Response* is communicating a solution.

Sternberg, Ketron, and Powell (1982) say that they are also optimistic that componential approaches can be used to train, modify, or improve intelligence. They particularly stress the possible modifiability of the metacognitive components to make people "truly more intelligent." Garber and Heber (1982) reported some of the most dramatic but controversial data concerning the improvement of intelligence in children, but their methods were not based on Sternberg's approach.

In addition to the Sternberg componential view and the Guilford structure of intellect model, the Cattell (1971) theory of crystallized and fluid intelligence has been pervasive in the development of conceptions of intelligence. Gagne and Dick (1983) equate crystallized intelligence with accumulated knowledge, and intellectual ability with fluid intelligence. Horn (1976) describes crystallized intelligence as "Awareness of concepts and terms . . . as measured in general information tests" (p. 445). Fluid intelligence is described as "Facility in reasoning, particularly in figural and non-word symbolic materials." Horn goes on to list the more pervasive abilities that have been viewed as parts of or related to intelligence: verbal fluency, verbal productive thinking, visualization and field independence, memory, and auditory abilities.

From this review of conceptions of intelligence, we conclude that current theoretical views of intelligence as componential or multifaceted probably reflect best the complexity of the phenomenon and make difficult the selection of instruments or procedures to assess it. In any event, it seems likely that superior general intelligence or ability is a large part of giftedness. Both fluid and crystallized aspects are probably essential to high-level intellectual functioning and verbal fluency, and visualization and auditory abilities are probably relevant aspects of intelligence for particular cognitive tasks. For the present, while our conceptions of intelligence are being clarified, there is nevertheless no way of specifying necessary levels or thresholds for any of the components in defining giftedness, but relatively high intelligence seems to be most promising.

Special talents

A part of the review of intelligence has focused on factors, components, or parts of general intelligence. Some of these components may constitute or be parts of the clusters of special ability we call talent. In 1951, the Youth Development Commission of Quincy, Illinois, initiated a project to discover and help youngsters who had special needs. One of the products of that project, a book titled *Identifying Students with Special Needs* (DeHaan and Kough, 1956), presented a comprehensive system for identifying students who were (a) physically handicapped; (b) emotionally, socially, or educationally maladjusted; or (c) gifted and talented. It is the last of the three, gifted and talented, which is our concern. Ten talent or ability areas were delineated: (1) intellectual, (2) scientific, (3) leadership, (4) creative, (5) artistic, (6) writing, (7) dramatic, (8) musical, (9) mechanical, and (10) physical. In a companion publication, *Helping Students with Special Needs* (Kough and DeHaan, 1957), the same authors presented methods and materials for nurturing talent in these youth. A subsequent publication, *Educating Gifted Children*, by DeHaan and Havighurst (1957), offered an extended discussion of the concept of talents and their nurturance.

The work of Havighurst, Kough, and DeHaan undoubtedly influenced the authors of the Marland report (1972), who proposed the following definition of giftedness:

Gifted and talented children are those identified by professionally qualified persons who by virtue of outstanding abilities are capable of high performance. These are children who require differentiated educational programs and services beyond those normally provided by the regular school program in order to realize their contribution to self and society.

Children capable of high performance include those with demonstrated achievement and/or potential ability in any of the following areas, singly or in combination: (1) general intellectual ability, (2) specific academic aptitude, (3) creative or productive thinking, (4) leadership ability, (5) visual and performing arts, (6) psychomotor ability.

This definition is clearly one that focuses on talent areas.

Talents represent clusters of ability or aptitude related to particular areas of human endeavor. Undoubtedly, they are complex and involve factors or components of the type discussed earlier under the heading of intelligence. Talents are clearly related to established disciplines, arts, or professions. Tannenbaum (1983) proposed four types or bases of talent. He speaks first of *scarcity* talents. These are talents that society needs to make life safer, easier, or healthier, such as a Jonas Salk to save us from polio, an Abraham Lincoln to save the Union, or a Martin Luther King, Jr., to end segregation. Second, there are *surplus* talents. These are the talents that beautify the world: Picasso, Pavlova, Bach, Mozart, and Emily Dickinson. They, too, strive for excellence, but we do not demand or need their talents in the sense that we need scarcity talents. *Quota* talents are those specialized, high-level abilities we need to function well as a society: physicians, political leaders, teachers, engineers, lawyers, commercial artists, and business executives. Finally, there are *anomalous* talents, which may have practical value and/or provide amusement but do not have the need or demand function described for the three talent categories just described. These are such limited talents as marksmanship, trapeze artistry, gourmet cooking, or proficiency in auto repair.

Renzulli et al. (1976) have developed a conception of talent or areas of giftedness that has been translated into the *Scales for Rating the Behavioral Characteristics of Superior Students*. These scales are widely used in identifying gifted and talented students. They cover the following areas: (a) learning, (b) motivation, (c) creativity, (d) leadership, (e) art, (f) music, (g) drama, (h) precision in communication (i) expressiveness in communication, and (j) aptitude for planning. Although several of these scales, such as motivation and creativity, may not represent typical talent domains, the authors nevertheless argue that they focus on specified abilities and behaviors. Renzulli is, of course, also renowned for his three-ring conception of giftedness (1979) which, in a broader sense, portrays three general areas of functioning: (a) above-average ability, (b) creativity, and (c) task commitment. He suggests that giftedness is really an interaction among the three factors and that the three clusters can be brought to bear on or in specific talent areas. Approximately 40 such talent areas are presented in his discussion ranging from cartooning, filmmaking, and pollution control to costume design, wildlife management, and playwriting.

Feldhusen (1984a) has proposed a school-based conception of talent areas that relates talent to curriculum domains:

1. Academic–intellectual
   A. Science   D. Social studies
   B. Mathematics   E. Language
   C. English   F. Computers

2. Artistic–creative
   A. Dance   D. Graphic
   B. Music   E. Sculpture
   C. Drama   F. Photography

3. Vocational areas
   A. Home economics   C. Agriculture
   B. Industrial arts   D. Business

Obviously, within any of these domains there would be many subcategories of talent. Under science, there could be talent in chemical engineering, biology, or physics. Dance talent could be manifested in ballet, square dancing, or musical comedy. Talent in agriculture might be seen in farm managers, fertilizer specialists, or agricultural forecasting.

MacKinnon (1978) also discussed the problem of talent. In fact, he devotes an entire chapter of his book *In Search of Human Effectiveness* to this topic. He reports an intensive search through the psychological literature, which revealed few references to the term. He noted that there is a movement away from the narrow intellectual meaning of talent toward a conception that combines superior aptitude and motivational forces. MacKinnon offers the following definition of talent: "A complex of traits which qualify one for superior performance in some occupation, or more typically, some profession" (p. 23).

This definition, he asserts, is associated with a necessity for nurturance and the development of talent through educational experiences. Aptitude and ability are more unitary traits, he says. Talent is molar.

In their recent research on the development of talent, Bloom and Sosniak (1981) identified the three domains of art, psychomotor capacity, and cognitive ability as their major areas of talent and the following occupations as specific talents: concert pianists, sculptors, swimmers, tennis players, mathematicians, and research neurologists. They concluded that talent development places emphasis on learning in a particular field and on learning as an individual experience. They go on to say that talented individuals "lived and breathed their talent development" (p. 92). Clearly, *talent* is seen or conceptualized as a psychological entity to be identified and nurtured. Although there is no taxonomy of talents or system of talents classification that is widely accepted, talent is recognized as the set of aptitudes and abilities that predispose an individual to superior performance or achievement.

Conclusion

Giftedness is a combination of general ability, special talents, self-concept, and motivation that predisposes the gifted individual to learn, to achieve, to strive for excellence. Youth who possess the ingredients of giftedness set lofty goals for themselves (Flack, 1983) and they work hard to attain them. High general ability without special talents, achievement motivation, and appropriately high self-concept will not lead to creative production or high-level performance in maturity. Signs of general ability and talent may be used as identification criteria for admission to gifted programs, but it is exceedingly difficult to set defensible criterion levels. Self-concepts and motivation can be assessed and, if high, can be used as corroborative evidence of giftedness. However, for youth who have high indices of general ability and talent, but lower achievement motivation and self-concepts, admission should not be denied. A major purpose of programs and services for gifted youth should be to help them develop realistic views of self and high achievement motivation.

References

Amabile, T. M. (1983). *The social psychology of creativity*. New York: Springer-Verlag.

Anastasiow, N. S. (1964). A report of self concept of the very gifted. *Gifted Child Quarterly*, 8, 177–178.

Benbow, C. P., & Stanley, J. C. (1983) *Academic precocity*. Baltimore: Johns Hopkins University Press.

Bloom, B. S. (1982a). The master teachers. *Phi Delta Kappan*, 63, 664–668, 715.

Bloom, B. S. (1982b). The role of gifts and markers in the development of talent. *Exceptional Children*, 48, 510–522.

Bloom, B. S., & Sosniak, L. A. (1981). Talent development. *Educational Leadership*, 39, 86–94.

Cattell, R. B. (1971). *Abilities: Their structure, growth and action*. Boston: Houghton Mifflin.

DeHaan, R. F., & Kough, J. (1956). *Identifying students with special needs*. Chicago: Science Research Associates.

DeHaan, R. F., & Havighurst, R. J. (1957). *Educating gifted children*. Chicago: University of Chicago Press.

Feldhusen, J. F. (1982). Multi-resource programing for the gifted and talented. Paper presented at the Annual Convention of the American Psychological Association, Washington, D. C.

Feldhusen, J. F. (1984a). Policies and procedures for the development of defensible programs for the gifted. In C. J. Maker (Ed.), *Defensible program for the gifted*. Rockvillle, Md.: Aspen.

Feldhusen, J. F. (1984b). The pursuit of excellence in gifted education. In J. F. Feldhusen (Ed.), *Toward excellence in gifted education* (pp. 1–16). Denver, Colo.: Love.

Feldhusen, J. F., & Kolloff, M. B. (1981). Me: A self-concept scale for gifted students. *Perceptual and Motor Skills*, 53, 319–323.

Feldhusen, J. F., & Sokol, L. (1982). Extra-school programming to meet the needs of gifted youth: Super Saturday. *Gifted Child Quarterly, 26*, 51–56.

Feldman, D. (1979). The mysterious case of extreme giftedness. In A. H. Passow (Ed.), *The gifted and the talented: Their education and development*. The Seventy-eighth Yearbook of the National Society for the Study of Education (pp. 335–351). Chicago: University of Chicago Press.

Feldman, D. H. (1982). A developmental framework for research with gifted children. In D. H. Feldman (Ed.), *Developmental approaches to giftedness and creativity* (pp. 31–45). San Francisco: Jossey-Bass.

Flack, J. D. (1983). Profiles of giftedness: An investigation of the development, interests and attitudes of ten highly gifted adolescents. Unpublished doctoral dissertation, Purdue University, West Lafayette, Ind.

Gagne, R. M., & Dick, W. (1983). Instructional psychology. *Annual Review of Psychology, 34*, 261–295.

Garber, H., & Heber, R. (1982). Modification of predicted cognitive development in high-risk children through early intervention. In D. K. Detterman & R. J. Sternberg (Eds.), *How and how much can intelligence be increased* (pp. 121–137). Norwood, N.J.: Ablex.

Goertzel, M. G., Goertzel, V., & Goertzel, T. G. (1978). *300 eminent personalities*. San Francisco: Jossey-Bass.

Gruber, H. (1982). Giftedness: Speculations from a biographical perspective. In D. H. Feldman (Ed.), *Developmental approaches to giftedness and creativity* (pp. 47–60). San Francisco: Jossey-Bass.

Guilford, J. P. (1967). *The nature of human intelligence*. New York: McGraw-Hill.

Guilford, J. P. (1968). *Intelligence, creativity and their educational implications*. San Diego: Robert R. Knapp.

Horn, J. L. (1976). Human abilities: A review of research and theory in the early 1970s. *Annual Review of Psychology, 27*, 437–485.

Horn, J. L. (1978). The nature and development of human abilities. In R. T. Osborne, C. E. Noble, & N. Weyl (Eds.), *Human variation: The biopsychology of age, race, and sex* (pp. 107–136). New York: Academic Press.

Ketcham, R., & Snyder, R. T. (1977). Self-attitudes of the intellectually and socially advantaged student: normative study of the Piers-Harris children's self-concept scale. *Psychological Reports, 40*, 111–116.

Kolloff, M. B. (1983). The effects of an enrichment program on the self-concepts and creative thinking abilities of gifted and creative elementary students. Unpublished doctoral dissertation, Purdue University, West Lafayette, Ind.

Kough, J., & DeHaan, R. F. (1957). *Helping students with special needs*. Chicago: Science Research Associates.

MacKinnon, D. W. (1978). *In search of human effectiveness*. Buffalo: Creative Education Foundation.

Marland, S. P. (1972). *Education of the gifted and talented*. Report to the Congress of the United States by the U.S. Commissioner of Education. Washington, D.C.: U.S. Government Printing Office.

Michael, W. B. (1977). Cognitive and affective components of creativity in mathematics and the physical sciences. In J. C. Stanley, W. C. George, & C. H. Solano (Eds.), *The gifted and the creative* (pp. 141–172). Baltimore: Johns Hopkins University Press.

Nicholls, J. G. (1972). Creativity in the person who will never produce anything original and useful. *American Psychologist, 27*, 717–727.

Nicholls, J. G. (1983). Conceptions of ability and achievement motivation: A theory and its implications for education. In S. G. Paris, G. M. Olson, & H. W. Stevenson (Eds.), *Learning and motivation in the classroom* (pp. 211–237). Hillsdale, N.J.: Erlbaum.

Renzulli, J. S. (1979). *What makes giftedness: A reexamination of the definition of the gifted and talented*. Los Angeles: National/State Leadership Training Institute on the Gifted and the Talented.

Renzulli, J. S., & Smith, L. H., White, A. J., Callahan, C. J., & Hartman, R. K. (1976). *Scales for rating the behavioral characteristics of superior students*. Mansfield Center, Conn.: Creative Learning Press.

Ringness, T. A. (1961). Self concept of children of low, average, and high intelligence. *American Journal of Mental Deficiency*, *65*, 453–461.

Shavelson, R. J., & Bolus, R. (1982). Self-concept: The interplay of theory and methods. *Journal of Educational Psychology*, *74*, 3–17.

Shavelson, R. J., Hubner, J. J., & Stanton, J. C. (1976). Self-concept: Validation of construct interpretations. *Review of Educational Research*, *46*, 407–441.

Spence, J. T., & Helmreich, R. L. (1983). Achievement-related motives and behavior. In J. T. Spence (Ed.), *Achievement and achievement motives: Psychological and sociological approaches* (pp. 10–74). San Francisco: Freeman.

Stanley, J. C. (1979). The study and facilitation of talent for mathematics. In A. H. Passow (Ed.). *The gifted and the talented: Their education and development*. The Seventy-eighth Yearbook of the National Society for the Study of Education (pp. 169–185). Chicago: University of Chicago Press.

Sternberg, R. J. (1981). A componential theory of intellectual giftedness. *Gifted Child Quarterly*, *25*, 86–93.

Sternberg, R. J., Ketron, J. L., & Powell, J. S. (1982). Componential approaches to the training of intelligent performances. In D. K. Detterman & R. J. Sternberg (Eds.), *How and how much can intelligence be increased* (pp. 155–172). Norwood, N.J.: Ablex.

Tannenbaum, A. J. (1983). *Gifted children: psychological and educational perspectives*. New York: Macmillan.

Terman, L. M., & Oden, M. H. (1959). *The gifted group at mid-life*. Stanford: Stanford University Press.

Torrance, E. P. (1979). Unique needs of the creative child and adult. In A. H. Passow (Ed.), *The gifted and the talented: Their education and development* (pp. 352–371). The Seventy-eighth Yearbook of the National Society for the Study of Education. Chicago: University of Chicago Press.

6   Giftedness: coalescence, context, conflict, and commitment

Patricia Haensly, Cecil R. Reynolds, and William R. Nash

Attempts to define giftedness have ranged from the early conceptions of genius as a form of madness, through eminence as a reflection of socially valued productivity, to the educationally oriented focus on potential as indicated by characteristics or traits predictive of future accomplishment (Reynolds & Birch, 1977). Typically, the label of eminence has been reserved for intellectual ability expressed in prominent responses that are defined by the demands of a particular time and society; however, eminence was also accorded for achievements whose origin was more creative than intellectual and for the many expressions of aesthetically appreciated talents. In each case, eminence resulted from recognition and approval of contemporaries, or of historians and observers who had access to the artifacts, the permanent deposits of achievement. Somewhat the same position regarding eminence has been taken by Albert (1975) in his behavioral definition of genius. The implications of these limitations (definition and observation) are that evolving recognition and understanding of giftedness, intellectual prowess, and creative genius has always been dependent on the limited *and* limiting perspective of fallible definers and interpreters, as well as on the presence of observers who could, would, and did record the achievements. One might view this situation as the age-old question of whether a falling tree makes a sound in a forest when no one is present to hear it, but one might also view it as a Type II statistical error. What has been hypothesized in the past regarding the eminence of humankind reflects the level of *precision of knowledge* held by the observers, the *value* they placed on specific achievements, and, finally, the availability of knowing and valuing *observers*. Thus, for example, we know little of the ability of prehistoric society or of devalued members of society; and accomplishments within specific domains of human functioning, such as the affective domain, have been neglected. The following elaboration provides examples of the expansion of viewpoint that gradually took place as knowledge of the constructs of intelligence and creativity evolved.

During the historical development of the concept of intelligence, there often was little distinction made between insanity and the lack of intelligence, that is, mental retardation. Though Esquirol published a treatise early in the 19th

128

century in which he distinguished between mental retardation and insanity, and implied that intelligence was not an all-or-none proposition but a matter of degree of mental functioning, confusion remained. Even today giftedness and creativity are sometimes associated with schizophrenia or viewed as manifested with this condition (Eysenck, 1983; Karlsson, 1970). In the opening remarks to his 1980 volume, Prentky quotes Schopenhauer in his statement that "Genius is closer to madness than to ordinary intelligence." Schopenhauer goes on to compare gifted intellectuals with "lunatics." Remarkably, Prentky credits Schopenhauer in his remarks as having "poignant insight." Anecdotal evidence is then cited to support the relationship between genius and psychosis, according to Prentky (1980, p. 1), an oft-noted phenomenon. Such a view is contrary to contemporary knowledge in the field. Despite popular conceptions, gifted individuals are more likely to be taller, more attractive, and physically and emotionally healthier than their peers, and to have fewer behavior problems as children or adolescents (cf. Hildreth, 1938; Ludwig & Cullinan, 1984; Mensh, 1950; Reynolds & Bradley, 1983). Giftedness is a healthy "condition" as well as a dynamic one. It is also, unquestionably, related to intelligence, both biological and psychological (cf. Reynolds, 1981). A high level of intelligence appears to be a necessary but insufficient condition for giftedness to occur. This, too, has stirred controversy.

As philosophers and scientists alike wrestled with the concept of intelligence, they alternately attributed its origin to natural tendencies (heredity), or to the effect of the environment (nurture), or to both. Galton's survey of the family trees of the most eminent men in English history, science, and letters paralleled the biological research of his cousin Charles Darwin, who held that intelligence is an inherited characteristic that enables the species to adapt in order to survive. Yet, Itard (1932) had also demonstrated that environment affects basic human functions such as language. Stemming from these perspectives, by the beginning of the 20th century, Binet and Simon (1905) had developed an instrument designed to assist educators in distinguishing between those individuals who could not learn due to *inherited* or acquired biological deficiencies and those who could learn, but might not, due to a deficient *environment* – a lack of opportunity or motivation. The prominent concern throughout this historical development of understanding regarding intelligence was focused on the extremes – the very deficient and the eminent or very gifted.

Contemporary views continue to reflect similar issues. The early view of Jensen (1969), that more than 80% of the variation in intelligence is due to heredity, was primarily based on long-standing familial studies of the inheritance of IQ in twins and siblings. This view has since been tempered by more recent genetic studies of large populations and of twins, especially those reared apart, studies conducted with greater sophistication and consistency than in the early years of psychological research. The newer studies suggest that perhaps as little as 50% of the variation in observed intelligence is due to heredity (Plomin & DeFries, 1980). Some early intervention studies involving families, as well as cross-racial adoption studies by Scarr-Salapatek and Weinberg (1976), have reaffirmed the tremendous potential for intellectual development in an environment that provides depth and breadth of experience for the infant and young child. Further, the developmental theories of Piaget, Bruner, Kagan, and others, and recent information-processing theories have focused attention on the process rather than the origin of intelligence, although both are clearly of some import. The response of educators to these conflicting views on origin of intelligence has been an eclectic attempt to fill whatever void existed for environment by creating the best possible setting for intellectual processes to occur.

The fact that each of these views has had its advocates from the time of early Greek philosophers, such as Plato, to present-day psychologists and/or educators suggests: (a) Nature and nurture continue to be as inseparable now as in prescientific time; (b) definition-searchers *impose* their own perspective on a multifaceted term in order to retrieve an individually meaningful description; (c) past and present educational programming has often relied on accurate prediction of future performance through identification of measurable characteristics; and (d) deepened understanding of the genesis and development of giftedness may require that we retain a multifaceted perspective instead of forcing giftedness into a conceptual box in order to simplify dealing with it. The intent of this chapter is to provide such a multifaceted perspective, a prism, as it were, through which giftedness may be viewed as an ever-widening magnificent possibility rather than a sharply defined and limited trait. It is fitting that a concept such as giftedness should be approached in this enigmatic fashion, through an inductive rather than a deductive process, yet pursuing a holistic synthesis rather than a particulate analysis.

What are the premises on which this holistic synthesis will be based? The premises we have established focus on (a) the multidimensional or dynamic possibilities of human responses, (b) the immense variety of abilities that are available for any single response, and (c) the intricate combination of abilities and attitude that qualitatively differentiates gifted responses from the ordinary.

In keeping with the above assumptions, a meaningful definition of giftedness must first and foremost reflect the dynamic nature of the human response to specific and varied settings. Giftedness, then, implies an ability to adjust a response to a situation or setting in a way that will produce a maximal outcome, with the adjustment defined and shaped by the individual. This kind of response, dynamic in nature, unpredictable from a prior repertoire or population of responses, contrasts with the static, predictable, and limited responses of nongifted behavior. The dynamic response is not limited, as stated, to the expected; it can take a variety of forms ranging from self-adaptation or accommodation to the setting, through direct modification of the setting itself, to a considered, planful exiting from the setting. For example, mankind has devised portable environments in order to explore space (accommodation); pioneers cleared land, erected fortifications, and built railroads to create livable space (modification); and emigrants left despotically governed countries to search for the freedom to live differently. Sternberg (1984) expresses a similar view regarding setting in his contextual subtheory of the triarchic theory of intelligence.

The second premise, perhaps most closely allied to past conceptions or definitions, is that giftedness encompasses a wide variety of abilities, talents, or propensities. This variety contributes not only to the many possible responses available to individuals as a group, but also to the many possible responses available to any single individual. Thus, within our human population there exist individuals who have shown outstanding abilities: to consider, formulate, and communicate such seemingly abstract dimensions as existence, energy, mass, and interstellar space; to assemble language in a meaningful way, from philosophical treatises to poetry; to discover processes such as pasteurization, immunization, and healing through antibiotics; to engineer such feats as the San Francisco bridge, multistory buildings that respond to earth movement, and space shuttles; to elicit harmonious and moving sound from the gut and steel fibers of a violin or from the human vocal cords; to combine texture, space, and color to produce works of art; to perform psychomotor feats of agility, grace, and/or endurance; to govern with brilliant rationale or with charisma; and to nurture and support the human spirit. All of these abilities and others have raised mankind above a mediocrity of existence because many gifted individuals functioned well, expressing their ability with a high degree of excellence in a way that others were influenced by it.

This variety of possible responses, however, often is multiply expressed within individuals. Leonardo da Vinci was not only a superb artist but also a remarkable engineer, anatomist, and scientist whose discoveries provided great advantages in these latter areas. Although it may seem an oversimplification to discuss "variety of abilities," the possibility that gifted individuals often have access to numerous abilities in a lifetime is an important consideration, both for self-development and in our nurturing responsibilities for others. The realization of multiple ability-options in individuals who are gifted will result in a greater flexibility regarding career options. Further, it is conceivable that divergence in abilities may include type of mental processing, and that the variety of final outcomes in any situation or setting will only be limited by the types of processing an individual uses in that setting. As further stated by Sternberg (1983, p. 203), intelligence is "characterized as the 'metacomponential' ability to use a set of performance components over a wide range of tasks."

The third premise, and perhaps the most salient in *present* conceptualizations, is that giftedness goes beyond the variety of abilities or degree of talent available to an individual; further, that it only occurs when ability, setting, and internal dynamic direction come together in a synergistic type of reaction whose outcome is expressed or communicated in some manner. Giftedness, in this sense, is a uniting of the following abilities:

> To see possibilities where others do not
> To act upon those possibilities in an extraordinary way or with extraordinary skill
> To maintain sufficient intensity to overcome obstacles over a sufficient duration of time
> To produce a response (material or physical)
> To share the outcome of the process with society in some temporal or permanent way.

Just as the concept of intelligence, when considered in a global sense, cannot be limited to a reflection of the relative placements of individuals within the normal distribution or normal curve for any single characteristic, or for limited groups of characteristics, neither can the concept of giftedness. We propose that a meaningful definition of giftedness must take into account what and how abilities have productively come together (coalescence); the type of setting that elicits expression of those abilities (context); the opposing forces that generate a divergence of expression (conflict); and the quality, intensity, and duration of that expression (commitment).

Giftedness in this sense is not something that can be neatly measured. It is a pervasive potential, yet it must complete itself to exist. It must be recognized as influential through its imprint on society in general or a portion thereof. One might say it can almost be considered "a way." When applied to living individuals, especially the child, giftedness must always be considered as in the process of becoming, and, to become, it must come full circle to convey to others in society in an influential way what originally was seen as a possibility that others did not see. The emphasis, in the final analysis, must be on communication and on influence; and the extent and sphere of influence will vary with the level of process and target audience.

This implies that educators must be much more open to the potential of their students and less judgmental – "how can I know if I have the ability if I've never tried myself?" Identification must open doors rather than shut them (Renzulli, Reis, & Smith, 1981), with emphasis on reducing Type II errors. Assessment instruments must be sought and developed that permit many alternative ways of bringing forth (emitting rather than eliciting) the creative response as well as the intelligent response, and identify processing, as well as products, of the response. In identification more attention should also be given to products developed in settings other than the academic, where attention and motivation are maximized, and where the child has selected and designed the task and, undoubtedly, is using a preferred style of functioning.

Why is such a definition important? The rationale is twofold. Although static definitions are more "comfortable" because they allow us to characterize or pigeonhole information, they also are self-limiting in scope, tending to suggest labels and unidimensional provisions. Static definitions tend to generate packaged, programmatic approaches for the education of the gifted, clearly abusing the crucial concept of an operational definition. Again, although this is "comfortable" because it makes teaching manageable, and selection of students convenient, it is limiting because coalescence, context, conflict, and commitment will never be exactly the same for any two students or groups of students. Good educators, teachers and planners alike, must forever be adjusting their sights, and it is unfair to suggest that education of the gifted can or should be any different.

By contrast, the dynamic nature of the suggested definition relates the process, and the content on which the process acts, to situational demands. Giftedness does not demand any preset arrangement of process and content; in any particular setting, the process used may vary depending on available ability, as well as either obvious or obscure factors related to the situation. Keeping this perspective foremost frees us from preformed, limiting expectations, both of the individual and for the situation. For example, although the invention of the wheel was a creative breakthrough (an act of creative genius) in prehistoric times, it was the attachment of the wheel to a chair in later times that was the expression of "gifted" insight. Further, the process becomes an act of individual genius by the way in which an individual perceives the conflicting demands of any task and then responds to those demands; task demands may mesh more specifically and efficaciously with the styles of some learners and doers than with the styles of others. Whereas the beautiful paintings of indolent, lush island life could arise from the brush and palette of Gauguin, an El Greco's response to that setting might never have been made, yet both were gifted artists. It took the specific perception and style of Dickens to immortalize an era of English history that might have been obliterated by the pens of others. Finally, the dynamic definition takes into account the variable nature of gifted responses due to variation in the attentive time required by different tasks. Though undoubtedly preceded by considerable incubation time, the idea of the benzene ring configuration took form in a flash. On the other hand, responding to the idea that emotional needs of the dying and their loved ones require special psychological approaches (Kübler-Ross, 1981) had to be pursued and developed over a long span of Elisabeth Kübler-Ross's life before it could take a stable, long-lasting, high-quality form (Haensly & Roberts, 1983).

Thus, the proposed definition of giftedness demands a variety of educational provisions. Although specific process and content abilities may be exhibited spontaneously and/or identified through various psychological measurements (tests), the abilities we have proposed as intrinsic to giftedness are more likely to require direct training or extensive nurturance. Undoubtedly, many of the most eminent of individuals have spontaneously exhibited these intrinsic abilities, and probably early in life. Yet, for a vast number of individuals who have gifted potential, a significant effort may have to be expended to develop and nurture that potential. "To see possibilities where others do not" requires an environment that promotes and rewards curiosity, asking questions, searching the strange and unusual, insistence on dissecting further, daring to be different, testing known limits – a Torrance checklist, as it were (Torrance, 1970). "To act . . . with extraordinary skill" requires not only academic skills, accelerated as is necessary (Stanley, 1976), but also training and direction in research skills, creative problem solving, and other thinking processes – as in Renzulli's Type II enrichment (Renzulli, 1977). "To maintain sufficient intensity" must be nurtured through early insistence and allowance of independence by parents and teachers; again, Torrance (1970) describes the early training in persistence and the ability to endure hardship and delay gratification, exhibited by Japanese children, as a step toward creative productivity. "To produce a response" and "To share the outcome" can only come about to the degree and level of giftedness we are discussing through allowing and insisting that students seek and communicate real answers to real problems in real settings. Students must be permitted to engage the real world with their developing skills in order to note and pursue relevance in their studies (see Haensly & Roberts, 1983, and Renzulli, 1982).

A more detailed examination of the components of the proposed multi-faceted definition of giftedness – coalescence, context, conflict, and commitment – should further clarify the perspective we have adopted. It should be kept in mind that, in each case, although the component is associated with the response the individual makes, we view this response as determined and shaped by the individual, not by external forces, which only provide the opportunity for response. We have adopted a developmental perspective regarding the directive role of the individual in his or her actions, rather than the contrasting view that the individual is a passive participant whose responses are determined by environmental stimuli or cues and increased or decreased in frequency and persistence by particular reinforcement schedules. At the same time, however, we recognize the role of cues, associated through past experience, in eliciting responses or hierarchies of responses, and the role of reinforcement, or lack of it, in altering the likelihood of repeated responses. The view we have adopted focuses on the individual as a seeker of information about the universe and of interaction with its elements, directing him- or herself to an ever more complex understanding of those elements. Before we begin to discuss each component of our definition, some further comment on the role of intelligence seems appropriate.

The role of intelligence in giftedness

To discuss intelligence intelligently also requires a definition and one derived from a theory of intelligence. Here we will invoke Reynolds's (1981) distinction between biological intelligence and psychological intelligence. Biological intelligence is described as the general physiological efficiency of the central nervous system and resembles Head's (1926) early conceptualization of psychological vigilance and Halstead's (1947) *Power* (P) factor of intelligence. Biological intelligence, barring trauma or extremes of environmental conditions, is primarily, though not completely, genetically determined. A high level of biological intelligence is prerequisite to giftedness but is not enough. Biological intelligence is the primary determinant of one's level of information-processing ability, that is, how well and how quickly information can be gathered, decoded, encoded, and transformed. Efficiency in this process offers greater opportunity to search out alternative responses and mentally test hypotheses regarding those responses. Fluency has been shown on many occasions to be related to creativity as well as to other ability factors such as language skill.

It is tempting to define giftedness in terms of biological intelligence. However, complex as biological intelligence is, it is too simple to account for giftedness. The relationship between biological intelligence and giftedness is analogous to the relationship between reliability and validity in measurement theory. Just as reliability forms a foundation that makes validity possible, biological intelligence makes giftedness possible but does not ensure that it will occur. With the exception of that well-known theoretical anomaly, the idiot savant, we know of no gifted acts performed on a sustained basis by anyone with a relatively low level of biological intelligence.

Psychological intelligence, primarily determined by environment, though not entirely, and almost certainly in the presence of a genetic template (again in the absence of trauma or severe extremes of environmental conditions) may be more responsible for the manifestation of giftedness. And, indeed, to exist, as per our definition, giftedness must be manifest. Psychological intelligence is more directly related to the form, the content, and the method of manipulation in information processing, the latter perhaps best described at present through simultaneous and successive cognitive processes. Psychological intelligence is how biological intelligence is used in intelligent action. Personality and cognitive style are certainly influential in the process and may well be a subcomponent of psychological intelligence (e.g., see Eysenck & Eysenck, 1985). It is through psychological intelligence that giftedness will come into being and through which it will be expressed, provided that sufficient biological intelligence is available. Giftedness as we will now discuss it is unquestionably a product of the interaction of these broad components of intelligence, but is seen as more directly related to psychological intelligence as it interacts daily with its environs. A complete discussion of each of these aspects of giftedness is a chapter unto itself, but let us now at least sketch our essential understanding of those factors we have chosen to emphasize.

Coalescence

Although abilities such as verbal reasoning, language, mathematical, and spatial, or such talents as artistic, musical, and psychomotor provide the basis for the most familiar classification and assessment of giftedness, they are only the obvious expressions of differences in giftedness. The heart of these differences in expression lies in the manner of mental processing that an individual uses most proficiently, that is, an analytic, sequential versus a holistic, simultaneous type of processing of information or stimuli. In fact, the quality of some of the above abilities, such as mathematical and musical, often depends on the complementary use of both types of processing. Torrance and Reynolds (1978) have indicated that individuals exhibit different styles of learning and processing information, not only through their preference but also through the efficiency with which they use one or the other style and in knowing when to employ primarily one style or the other. The attempt to assess differences in preferences for information-processing styles in this way has resulted in an instrument, Your Style of Learning and Thinking, available both for adults (Torrance et al., 1977) and for children (Reynolds, Kaltsounis, & Torrance, 1979).

We propose that giftedness may stem from both a metacognitive as well as a metacreative awareness of the appropriate time to apply one or the other type of processing, and in what mixture or proportions to apply them. Meta-awareness would refer not only to the timing within the problem-solving sequence, but also to the type of stimuli and information on which action is being taken. Productively gifted individuals are those, tutored or untutored, who use both processes but who focus the appropriate process on the stimuli in such a way and at such a point in the sequence that optimal use of both the left and right cerebral hemispheres occurs (Roeder, Haensly & Edlind, 1982).

Elements of the extraordinary response, the kind of response that has been the mark of historically eminent individuals as well as of contemporary gifted, reflect the meta-awareness aspect. Exemplars of these elements would include foresight, planfulness, reflectiveness, insight, executive ability, and what might most descriptively be termed "stick-to-itiveness."

Foresight refers to an ever present alertness to possibilities and a receptiveness to "the possible" in *any* situation. In the discovery of the Americas by European explorers, cities rose and fell, depending on the foresight of individuals who saw possibilities in natural resources and marketing routes. Jules Verne was not just an author but a scientist who saw the possibilities of travel through yet unknown dimensions. The description of the structure of DNA, a molecule with "novel features which are of considerable biological interest," by Watson and Crick in 1953 laid the foundation for remarkable discoveries linking biology, chemistry, physics, and genetics (Watson & Crick, 1953, p. 737). Watson and Crick were receptive to "the possibilities" of their strange ladderlike model of the vital chemical DNA.

Planfulness requires an analysis of the situation and a definition of the problem. Getzels (1975) emphasizes that the quality of solution to any problem depends on this element, that is, on a statement of the problem in such a way that the most appropriate process is cued to be used for solution. This type of awareness can be available to even the young gifted child as expressed by one of the children in the Roeder et al. (1982) study: "First I get a picture in my mind. Then I break the task into steps and think of questions that would get better answers. Some kids go ahead without planning steps." This child had not been taught this sequence – he had learned it from his own experiences.

The contrast between reflectiveness and impulsiveness in response to problem solving has often been documented (Baron, 1981, 1982; Messick, 1976). There must be a time for incubation of ideas to take place, and reflectiveness initiates that incubation period. Individuals who do not allow for this step or recognize its importance seldom experience the next component of extraordinary response, that is, insight, nor do they take advantage of their biological efficiency in generating many possible solutions during this time. The manner in which insight may occur in the gifted, focusing on relevant information while setting aside the irrelevant, has been described by Sternberg and Davidson (1983). Insight, according to Sternberg and Davidson, involves the psychological processes of encoding, combination, and comparison, each applied to information in a selective manner. Selective encoding gives precedence to certain pieces of new information, ignoring, at least for the moment, those pieces that are less pertinent to the problem at hand. Although much information may be scanned, only the pieces that directly impinge on the problem are selected for the second process, that of combination, in which insight again selects the most appropriate combination of information pieces. The third process, selective comparison, depends on insight to direct the search through stored or old information in order to find that which will best illuminate the new information and can be appropriately used in the problem solution. Efficiency of mental processing, reflective of biological intelligence as described earlier in this chapter, will be characteristic of all three of these processes in the gifted. Again, such an approach suggests a meta-awareness in which the gifted individual deliberately or intuitively focuses on information that will yield the most productive solution from the many potential solutions.

Without executive ability or the knowledge of how, when, and where to

implement ideas, ideas remain simply just that – mental associations temporarily available only to the individual who created them or within whom
the specific stimuli and responses may have uniquely come together. The
gifted individual can take these associations and give them some communicable and tangible form. Thus, the unique idea takes shape in a way such
that others can participate in the extraordinary response. To this ability to
carry out an idea must of course be added the persistence ("stick-to-itiveness")
to test the idea, accommodate or make adjustments, educate the audience
for whom the idea is communicated, and, most importantly, support the idea
until it has found acceptance (Haensly & Roberts, 1983).

As can be seen from this list of elements, there must be a constant balance
between convergence and divergence and between analysis and synthesis, in
order for giftedness to be present according to the definition we have proposed. Giftedness may even be present when individuals are limited to singular
areas of extraordinary response, and we must allow this opportunity, although
it indeed seems anomalous to certain other pronouncements. However, extreme talent that is manifest and communicated to others must represent a
form of giftedness. For example, the young man who has, for his entire span
of life, done little but persistently sculpt animals that elicit great aesthetic
appreciation, from materials whose possibilities were often foreseen only by
him, has had to balance planning and execution with divergent uses of material
to produce unique products of beauty that are appreciated by others for their
richness and uniqueness of expression and thus valued highly (Harper, 1983).
This 26-year-old man has not been able to develop other mental capacities
beyond that of a 6-year-old; no other evidence of biological intelligence seems
apparent, yet some type of encoding, combination, and comparison has taken
place.

The necessity of communication of ideas cannot be underestimated. Gowan's comments (1979) on this point are particularly relevant, stating that the
creative idea evokes only an emotion of pleasure to the creator until it takes
a form through which it can be communicated to others in society. In this
respect, the generation of ideas through artificial stimulants or natural processes (no matter how unique, all-encompassing, or insightful the ideas are)
cannot be classified as the giftedness of extraordinary response unless those
ideas take a tangible, communicable form. A scientist who does not communicate his findings to other members of the scientific community, no matter
how brilliant the work may be, has not completed the work, will not influence
or be appreciated by others, and will not receive recognition – indeed, in the
present publish-or-perish world of the major universities able to support top-
notch science, this individual will soon become unemployed or an adminis-
trator (we shall resist commenting on the worse evil in this case). An act of
giftedness, as with science, is not complete until it is communicated to one's

peers; communication in this instance may well be a moral and social re-quirement (e.g., see Reynolds et al., 1984, chap. 7).

Thus, the extraordinary response is a product of the coalescence of abilities internally directed in response to a setting. Conceivably, such coalescence is not unlike the biological coming together of cellular elements: For life to occur, the elements must not only be present in the correct quantitative balance but must have come together in an appropriate sequence of processes, uniquely directed by the DNA, without which the elements remain inanimate. Individuals who exhibit giftedness purposely and uniquely bring to bear on a problem or situation different types of mental processing, expressible through a variety of content areas, directed in a way that is qualitatively and quan-titatively unique within (different from) the majority of responses given to that problem.

Context

The quality and eventual worth of any response must inevitably be determined in relation to the particular set of situational factors within which that response is given, that is, the context. An individual who sings exquisitely beautiful operatic arias may receive much attention on the floor of the New York Stock Exchange but will not be likely to be noted for her brilliant financial selling and buying (nor likely to find this behavior tolerated for any length of time). A highly skilled analysis of anthropological data may assist social scientists in the interpretation of the relationship of matriarchal societies to independ-ence in young males, but it may be of little value in solving the nutritional problems of that society. A philosophical treatise may be an eloquent and stimulating force for patriotic fervor, but it may not provide a convincing diplomatic appeal between forces about to make war. And, in each of these cases, the response may never receive recognition because the audience to which it is communicated is not the appropriate recipient. The context has not been correctly assessed by these individuals and the "potentially brilliant" response must await a better executive plan. Sometimes we ask and answer the wrong question. Knowing just what questions to ask is a problem of context and is crucial to developing a gifted response.

In addition, it might be assumed that, as a mark of an extraordinary re-sponse, not only must the context be specifically appropriate for the response, but the response must also have generalizability. The staying power of the type of response that has earned the label of extraordinary or eminent depends on its applicability to times and places that go beyond the original setting that elicited the response. The extraordinariness of McClintock's discovery of "jumping genes" lies in the fact that this mechanism not only correctly and creatively described the original biological setting (context), but that the description had a global dimension; that is, the context could be extended in a variety of ways over a range of settings, yet the description could retain its integrity and have a lasting impact for society. Thus, flash-in-the-pan responses, which may seem temporarily brilliant but are limited to the eliciting setting and a moment in time, do not possess the characteristics of extraordinary or gifted responses as we have defined them.

The reverse situation must also be considered, that is, when individuals contribute insightful and remarkable responses within the appropriate context, extensive responses that have generalizability, yet do not receive recognition because their responses required a mesh with numerous others in order to achieve meaning (cf. Merton, 1961; Albert, 1975). The remarkable breakthrough of Watson and Crick was built on the work of numerous others; Rosalind Franklin's X-ray photograph of crystalline DNA had direct effect on their structural hypothesis. Many other discoveries in a wide range of content have been made possible because of the sustained contributions of others. Not all gifted responses, then, receive recognition, and many individuals must take satisfaction from the personal realization of their contributions or remain frustrated.

This is not to say, however, that many extraordinary responses have not had to wait for some later time, place, and audience in order to receive recognition. Giftedness lies in the determination to persist with a response that the individual has deemed appropriate to the context, but which others have not yet recognized because of their own limited foresight or limited insight into the real problem, that is, they didn't recognize the real question. In these cases, even though the original planfulness and executive ability have nurtured a unique response appropriate to the context, the belief in the integrity of the response is limited to the doer until such times as it can be recognized by others.

Response to context, in this sense, is an integral part of giftedness. The ability to envision the widest possible scope within which to match individually peculiar talents to a task, that is, to see options not seen by others (or by the general "others"), and then to be able to focus precisely on the peculiar demands of the task (again, perhaps, not seen by others), are a part of the gifted response to context. And, finally, integrity demands that the response to context must be able to exhibit some type of permanency and worth beyond and separate from the individual. The Socratic dialogue and philosophy continue to exert an influence on the thinking of today's scholars.

Conflict

Although coalescence and context would appear to be describing forces flowing together in a perfect match of abilities and task, timing, and momentum, gifted responses do not emerge without encountering obstacles. However, the definition of intelligent behavior suggests that obstacles are characteristically a positive force, contributing both to accurate definition of the problem (an external force) and to the motivation or the drive to solve that is experienced by highly intelligent beings (an internal force). Research in developmental psychology (Arend, Gove, & Sroufe, 1979) verifies that young children who do not avoid problem situations but attempt to solve them are later more advanced in their cognitive development. Obstacles or conflict seem to serve as a honing tool, shaping the response to meet task demands and encompass contextual options more creatively, yet more precisely.

As an external force, conflict serves to shape and define the response in several ways. First of all, conflict often occurs when the common, traditional response to a situation seems to be the only acceptable one. This type of conflict can serve as a yardstick for the comparison of all other possible responses that the circumstances may elicit. For example, the size of a conventional airplane that can take off and land from a given space traditionally was dependent upon the length of runway that could be provided. Limited runway spaces prompted the use of catapults on ships, horizontal rotors on helicopters, and rocket-propelled space ships; stretching the length of runway had seemed the only option to the traditional approach, yet the gifted responses came as a result of redefinition of the problem.

A second way in which conflict acts as a positive force may be related to the Piagetian concept of adaptation and equilibration (Haensly, Chissom, & Nash, 1978). The cognitive dissonance that arises when new information is being assimilated serves as a cue to reformulation of one's mental schema. It might be described as "idea-nudging," in which, because the pieces of information no longer fit, a schema must be adjusted to accommodate. Individuals who cannot or will not see the pieces as incompatible (dissonant) continue to respond according to an inappropriate plan. The extraordinary response is often formulated because the gifted individual is more sensitive to inconsistencies and inaccuracies of the schema than are others. In fact, attempts to minimize diversity in the educational setting may be counterproductive.

Creative thinking through brainstorming can also be enhanced by bouncing ideas off the obstacles. Although many wild and fanciful ideas may arise in a situation where individuals are attempting to enlarge the positive possibilities, the presence of an outstanding obstacle seems to add an entirely new dimension to the idea search. The hierarchy of ideas can thus be extensively expanded.

As an internal force, conflict seems to serve in a motivating fashion. Examination of the biographies of eminent artists, inventors, and thinkers reveals again that obstacles, especially in one's personal life, seem to act as a forge molding the intent of these individuals, intensifying their activities, and driving them to achieve beyond their own or others' wildest dreams. Those who have made it despite all odds, responding to the impossible, have an intrinsic and unique gift.

Further, our experience in education of the gifted repeatedly indicates that gifted youth respond to challenges. When challenge is lacking, apathy ensues and there is an increasing failure to use one's potential gifts and talents. On the other hand, things that "can't be accomplished" become goals – the mountain must be scaled, the solution must be determined, the art form must be established, the cure must be discovered, the pinnacle must be reached.

Major advances in science often follow this model. Conflict in science, the incompatibility of theories that seem to explain the same phenomena, gives rise to crucial experiments (defined relatively and not absolutely as in a true Baconian sense). Crucial experiments occur as a direct result of conflict and result, often, in a new way of viewing our world, that is, in the creation of new paradigms. Conflict thus forces a creative response producing what Kuhn (1962) refers to as paradigmatic shifts and true scientific revolutions. The only other response is stagnation, yet without the perception of conflict, and its catalytic action, the gifted response would have little opportunity to occur or to be recognized when it did. Conflict also gives rise to the transformation of the original issues into something new, largely through the design of the crucial experiment, which is itself elegant and a gifted response (e.g., see Brown & Reynolds, 1984).

Commitment

Commitment, alluded to earlier as persistence or "stick-to-itiveness," is a necessary personal component of the extraordinary response. The tendency to view this characteristic as "single-mindedness" distracts from the perspective that commitment is a dedication to an idea, topic, or principle (Haensly, Shiver, & Fulbright, 1980). It is in no way a tunnel-vision type of approach, that is, a mental blocking or refusal to see alternatives. Commitment constantly seeks breakthroughs and more fruitful, alternative paths to developing the idea, topic, or principle, yet consistently seeks to promote the nuclear idea. This type of commitment not only acts as a catalytic force to ensure that an idea will take tangible form, but also serves to retain the integrity of the idea until it finds an accepting and acceptable audience.

How long must this dedication persist to qualify as commitment and dedication, or be labeled as folly? Some successfully productive individuals spend long years developing and promoting a singular effort (Haensly & Roberts, 1983). A 1983 Nobel Prize winner for medicine, Barbara McClintock, devoted a lifetime to research and study before achieving recognition. The acceptance of the ideas and products of many gifted individuals did not occur until years and even generations after their lifetime. Perhaps folly is a label limited in use only for the critics of an idea. Individuals with commitment, who see their ideas and products as having integrity and great worth, tend to believe that society will eventually "catch up" or come to understand that worth; however, even if society does not, these individuals seem to have sufficient confidence to continue to affirm their own contribution.

Commitment also appears to permit the individual to deal rationally with obstacles. As pointed out, obstacles may be viewed as defining and expanding forces for extraordinary responses rather than as barriers to completion. In the use of the rational approach, individuals must sufficiently free themselves from their creations (whether they be ideas, inventions, or artistic endeavors) to view objectively weaknesses and limitations. Such an examination may then suggest alterations – to either self, or product, or targeted audience – that will move the creation closer toward recognition and acceptance (Haensly & Roberts, 1983). Such commitment in no way denies the basic integrity of the creation but, in fact, reiterates its intrinsic worth.

The flash of insight or the design of a crucial experiment does not come from a passing familiarity with a problem or a conflict. Rather, it is far more likely to stem from a long-term commitment to the resolution of some precisely identified problem. Science is accomplished almost never through a single piece of research but rather through the accumulation of much research in the context of the work of other gifted scientists who made the new work possible. Commitment to a problem is as crucial to science as is the crucial experiment. Without commitment, we would never reach the point of being able to design the necessary research to forge ahead and resolve or recast conflict.

A special case of gestalten

Perhaps the best way to clarify the definition of giftedness that we have proposed – one that revolves around coalescence, context, conflict, and commitment – is to give an example of giftedness in an individual who has been able to bring these components together in a special and unique way. Our example concerns John Hall, a man who is an outstanding inventor and problem solver, who has an international reputation for such things as designing underground settings to contain nuclear bomb explosions and oil well blowouts, and troubleshooting large water-project dam failures. We base our description on a talk he gave about his life and work to an advanced doctoral seminar on creative thinking (Hall, 1983).

Hall could easily have been considered a disadvantaged child by today's standards. By the time he had reached second grade, he had been forced out of the school setting by misinformed individuals with power, who viewed his condition of extremely crossed eyes as potentially "marking" or damaging to the local banker's unborn child. In addition, his visual condition, which also included uncorrected nearsightedness, had prevented him from learning to read by actual letter perception; nevertheless, he did his best to remember letters and words by their general form or shape. His parents chose from limited options to place John in an Indian reservation school, where his companion students were mainly adults and older boys who were being taught the working words of the English language. Because Hall spoke Spanish, as well as English, he was able to assist the teacher in this task. His education was a serendipitous experience, gained by alert attention to the words and acts of wisdom of these unschooled people who were "at one" with their surroundings. It was also attained through his constant companionship with his father, an inventor who had descended from a line of inventors; his father taught him inventiveness and (in Hall's words) salesmanship – of self and of ideas.

By the time Hall was 12, he was working as a man in the oil fields. In reflecting on his experiences, Hall seems never to have considered his surroundings as lacking in opportunity. He consistently saw possibilities in his working associates and learned from them as from the most advanced scholars. He states that he constantly looked for giftedness in people, but it appears that what he really did was to stay alert and sensitive to the possibilities of every stimulus in his environment. By constantly trying to visualize what was happening, he saw opportunities and ways to solve problems that others overlooked. His capacity for imagery seems to have been enhanced by his nontraditional education.

At about the age of 13, he was finally fitted with glasses and taught himself to read. After a month, he was reading everything he could find, including the adventure stories of Jack London. He entered an essay contest on the perils of smoking and won because, as he said, he was aggressive enough to interview people for information, whereas the losers hadn't been so enterprising. Hall was never afraid to talk to people, to appear "dumb," to ask questions, to make mistakes, to attempt to satisfy an insatiable curiosity. His freedom from inhibition to seek answers was one of his most outstanding character-assets, an asset that permitted him to sell himself and his ideas to receptive and nonreceptive audiences alike. His father's educational gift, the knowledge of how to do this, included a systematic approach of "plan, operate, review, plan again, and repeat until perfection is attained," an approach often reiterated by Hall. The other part of that salesmanship skill had to do with communication with both his peers and his "betters." Hall has made both of these a part of his philosophy of life.

Hall's fantastic memory and ability to see connections – to generalize from past experiences to new settings – has contributed to the extraordinary way in which he has resolved problems throughout his life. He recalls distinctly an incident when he was about 7, hunting rattlesnakes on the desert with Indian friends; he had placed his jackknife between the expansion joints of the railroad track for safekeeping. When he tried to retrieve the knife after a train had passed by, he found that the joint that had become heated had closed in on the knife; yet when the joint cooled, his knife came out easily. This stored experience, relating to the principle of material expansion under heat, became the nucleus of an effective solution for containing underground nuclear explosions. Even the act of having a dentist repair a filling prompted Hall to recall from childhood how people drilled a hole in the end of a windshield crack to prevent the fracture from spreading; this memory recalled was the basis for a new alloy for a dental repair material that would not need constant replacement because of fracturing. But Hall didn't just *think* about this connection – he immediately acted on it and within weeks the new alloy was developed, although it took dentists more than two years to accept it. His idea had become a reality to be shared with society.

Hall's commitment is illustrated by an amazing production of ideas and also by his attitude toward risk taking. He emphasized that you must go at problems in every possible way you can think of, and, above all, you must not fear to fail. In fact, he points out that you must enjoy succeeding – if you consider each small step a victory, you can be reinforced a thousand times over in every project. Hall believes in taking joy in each of those steps!

In this remarkable individual, energized by a demanding drive to seek out questions as well as answers, problems as well as solutions, a wealth of possible cognitive and personal abilities has been brought to bear on the settings within which he has found himself. Hall seems to have thrived on the conflict that others with more traditional orientation have directed toward him. His answer to critics that "this is *not* a theory, this is an idea!" reflects the direction that his responses to problems seem to take – practical solutions to be shared with society.

Hall exhibits all of the factors we have discussed in a way that is astonishing to observe. His mind works with great rapidity and efficiently so, identifying the crucial elements of a problem long before others and processing elements of that problem in sequence until a final simultaneous synthesis appears. Hall is able to manipulate quickly many proposed solutions to conflict, projecting their impact on the problem at hand, discarding faulty perceptions and solutions, and keeping the most promising for continued evaluations. During this time he seems preoccupied as he commits himself to the task at hand. He has a gift for communication as well, one that takes a visual form in many cases as he creates for his listener an image of just what the solution is to be. His language is replete with words that carry strong imaging value and allow you to see what he is proposing. His ability to communicate his ideas so clearly has certainly increased his success in getting others to accept his work and produce the products associated with them. Hall works in the context of large-scale problems that involve tremendous financial and human risk in their solution. Yet, he has gained the confidence of corporation presidents and engineers throughout the world because of his demonstrated success that has come through an innate ability to process information efficiently. He has learned how to define the information, visibly integrating successive and simultaneous processing, identifying the conflict and being stimulated by it, knowing the context of his work and seeking shelter as well as inspiration from the work of others, and by a commitment to problems, following each to completion. Hall indeed is a special case of gestalten!

As stated by MacKinnon (1983, p. 127), regarding highly effective individuals, "To summarize what . . . strikes me most forcibly . . . it is their openness to experience, and the fact that they . . . are seeking to tolerate and to bind increasingly large quantities of tension as they strive for a creative solution to ever more difficult problems . . . which they set for themselves."

References

Albert, R. S. (1975). Toward a behavioral definition of genius. *American Psychologist, 30*, 140–151.

Arend, R., Gove, F. L., & Sroufe, L. A. (1979). Continuity of individual adaptation from infancy to kindergarten: A predictive study of ego-resiliency and curiosity in preschoolers. *Child Development, 50*, 950–959.

Baron, J. (1981). Reflective thinking as a goal of education. *Intelligence, 5*, 291–309.

Baron, J. (1982). Personality and intelligence. In R. J. Sternberg (Ed.), *Handbook of human intelligence*. Cambridge University Press.

Binet, A., & Simon, Th. (1905). Methodes nouvelles pour le diagnostic du niveau intellectuel des anormaux. *Année psychologique, 11*, 191–244.

Brown, R. T., & Reynolds, C. R. (1984). Crucial experiments in psychology. In R. Corsini (Ed.), *Wiley encyclopedia of psychology*. New York: Wiley.

Eysenck, H. J. (1983). The roots of creativity: Cognitive ability or personality trait? *Roeper Review, 5*(4), 10–12.

Eysenck, H. J., & Eysenck, M. (1985). *Personality and individual differences: A natural science approach*. New York: Plenum.

Getzels, J. W. (1975). Problem finding and the inventiveness of solutions. *Journal of Creative Behavior, 9*, 12–18.

Gowan, J. C. (1979). The production of creativity through right hemisphere imagery. *Journal of Creative Behavior, 13*, 39–51.

Haensly, P. A., Chissom, B., & Nash, W. R. (1978). Dissonance and information in equilibration to formal operations. *Perceptual and Motor Skills, 47*, 1159–1170.

Haensly, P. A., & Roberts, N. M. (1983). The professional productive process and its implications for gifted studies. *Gifted Child Quarterly, 27*(1), 9–12.

Haensly, P. A., Shiver, D., & Fulbright, M. (1980). Task commitment as the productive determiner in giftedness. *Roeper Review, 3*, 21–24.

Hall, J. (1983, April). My life and work (videotape). Talk given to a doctoral seminar on creative thinking, Texas A&M University, College Station.

Halstead, W. C. (1947). *Brain and intelligence*. Chicago: University of Chicago Press.

Harper, T. (1983, October 4). Celebrated sculptor can't even read (Associated Press writer, Boulder, Colorado). *Bryan–College Station Eagle*, page 1C.

Head, H. (1926). *Aphasia and kindred disorders of speech*. New York: Macmillan.

Hildreth, G. (1938). Characteristics of young gifted children. *Journal of Genetic Psychology, 53*, 287–311.

Itard, J. (1932). *The wild boy of Aveyron*. New York: Appleton-Century-Crofts. (Original work published 1894)

Jensen, A. R. (1969). How much can we boost IQ and scholastic achievement? *Harvard Educational Review, 39,* 1–123.

Karlsson, J. L. (1970). Genetic association of giftedness and creativity with schizophrenia. *Hereditas, 66*(2), 177–182.

Kübler-Ross, E. (1981). *Living with death and dying.* New York: Macmillan.

Kuhn, T. S. (1962). *The structure of scientific revolutions.* Chicago: University of Chicago Press.

Ludwig, G., & Cullinan, D. (1984). Behavior problems of gifted and nongifted elementary school boys and girls. *Gifted Child Quarterly, 28,* 37–39.

MacKinnon, D. W. (1983). The highly effective individual. In R. S. Albert (Ed.), *Genius and eminence. The social psychology of creativity and exceptional achievement.* Elmsford, N.Y.: Pergamon Press.

Mensh, I. (1950). Rorschach study of the gifted child. *Exceptional Children, 17,* 114–119.

Merton, R. K. (1961). Singletons and multiples in scientific discovery. *Proceedings of the American Philosophical Society, 105,* 470–486.

Messick, S. B. (1976). Reflection-impulsivity: A review. *Psychological Bulletin, 83,* 1026–1052.

Plomin, R., & Defries, J. C. (1980). Genetics and intelligence: Recent data. *Intelligence, 4,* 15–24.

Prentky, R. A. (1980). *Creativity and psychopathology: A neurocognitive perspective.* New York: Praeger.

Renzulli, J. S. (1977). *The enrichment triad model.* Mansfield Center, Conn.: Creative Learning Press.

Renzulli, J. S. (1982). What makes a problem real: Stalking the illusive meaning of qualitative differences in gifted education. *Gifted Child Quarterly, 26,* 147–156.

Renzulli, J. S., Reis, S.M., & Smith, L. H. (1981). *The revolving door identification model.* Mansfield Center, Conn.: Creative Learning Press.

Reynolds, C. R. (1981). The neuropsychological basis of intelligence. In G. W. Hynd & J. W. Obrzut (Eds.), *Neuropsychological assessment and the school age child: Issues and procedures.* New York: Grune & Stratton.

Reynolds, C. R., & Bradley, M. (1983). Emotional stability of intellectually superior children versus nongifted peers as estimated by chronic anxiety levels. *School Psychology Review, 12,* 190–194.

Reynolds, C. R., Gutkin, T. B., Elliott, S., & Witt, J. C. (1984). *School psychology: Essentials of theory and practice.* New York: Wiley.

Reynolds, C. R., Kaltsounis, W., & Torrance, E. P. (1979). A children's form of "Your Style of Learning and Thinking": Preliminary norms and technical data. *Gifted Child Quarterly, 23,* 757–767.

Reynolds, M. C., & Birch, J. W. (1977). *Teaching exceptional children in all America's schools.* Reston, Va: The Council for Exceptional Children.

Roeder, C., Haensley, P. A., & Edlind, E. P. (1982). The productive gifted child: The "secret" ingredients [Summary]. *Convention Abstracts. National Association for Gifted Children.*

Scarr-Salapatek, S., & Weinberg, R. A. (1976). I.Q. test performance of black children adopted by white families. *American Psychologist, 31,* 726–739.

Stanley, J. C. (1976). The case for extreme educational acceleration of intellectually brilliant youths. *Gifted Child Quarterly, 20*(1), 66–75.

Sternberg, R. J. (1983). Componential theory and componential analysis: Is there a Neisser alternative? *Cognition, 15,* 199–206.

Sternberg, R. J. (1984). Toward a triarchic theory of human intelligence. *Behavioral and Brain Sciences, 7*(2), 269–316.

Sternberg, R. J., & Davidson, J. E. (1983). Insight in the gifted. *Educational Psychologist, 18*(1), 51–57.

Torrance, E. (1970). *Encouraging creativity in the classroom.* Dubuque, Iowa: Brown.

Torrance, E. P., & Reynolds, C. R. (1978). Images of the future of gifted adolescents: Effects of alienation and specialized cerebral functioning. In J. C. Gowan, J. Khatena, & E. P.

Torrance (Eds.), *Educating the ablest*. Itaska, Ill: Peacock. (Reprinted from *Gifted Child Quarterly*, *22*, 40–54)

Torrance, E. P., Reynolds, C. R., Riegel, R. T., & Ball, O. E. (1977). Your Style of Learning and Thinking, Forms A and B: Preliminary norms, abbreviated technical notes, scoring keys, and selected references. *Gifted Child Quarterly*, *21*, 563–573.

Watson, J. D. & Crick, F. H. C. (1953). Molecular structure of nucleic acids. *Nature*, *171*, 737–738.

Part III

Explicit-theoretical approaches: cognitive theory

7 A conception of giftedness designed to promote research

Nancy Ewald Jackson and Earl C. Butterfield

Most twentieth century conceptions of giftedness (e.g., Renzulli, 1978; Tannenbaum, 1983; Terman, 1925) share three related assumptions. First, to be gifted is to create excellent socially valued products. Second, because children are unlikely to produce creative work that meets absolute standards of excellence and social importance, childhood giftedness is the potential for adult productivity. Third, even though a child's potential for adult productivity cannot be measured well, it is assumed that adult giftedness can be predicted with some accuracy from childhood performance, because measurable traits related to giftedness, such as general intelligence, are moderately stable from childhood to adulthood.

Despite widespread acceptance of the assumptions that giftedness shows itself in the production of socially valued work, that it can be defined during childhood only as potential, and that the estimation of potential for adult productivity is feasible, there is great variation in the childhood markers of giftedness chosen by different theorists. Some theorists have relied on a single index to identify gifted children. Terman (1925) and Hollingworth (1942) chose general intelligence as measured by the Stanford–Binet. As an alternative to general intelligence, Getzels and Jackson (1962) emphasized performance on tests of divergent thinking ability. Davidson and Sternberg (1983) have proposed that performance of children on batteries of paper-and-pencil insight problems may reveal the operation of cognitive processes similar to those used by adults in the production of creative insights.

Other theorists have combined diverse criteria into multidimensional conceptions of child giftedness. Renzulli (1978) defines as gifted those children who have at least moderately high general intelligence, exceptional degrees of task commitment, and creativity. Tannenbaum (1983, p. 87) proposes that "giftedness in children . . . denotes their potential for becoming critically acclaimed performers or exemplary producers of ideas in spheres of activity

Preparation of this paper was supported in part by NIH grant HD 16241 to the second author. We thank Wendy Conklin Roedell for her constructive comments on a preliminary draft.

151

that enhance the moral, physical, social, intellectual, or aesthetic life of humanity." He regards the emergence of giftedness as dependent on the convergence of general and specific abilities, nonintellective factors such as dedication to a chosen field, appropriate environmental stimulation, and chance.

The foregoing conceptions have considerable merit for certain purposes. For example, a broad-based, culturally relevant definition such as Tannenbaum's provides bench marks against which to judge ourselves, our schools, and our society. We ourselves would use such conceptions if, for example, we were setting long-term goals for an educational system. However, current conceptions of giftedness create unnecessary obstacles to its study in children, and they sharply limit opportunity to integrate the study of giftedness into broader study of developmental and individual differences in cognition. Our purpose is to foster research, especially research in cognition, by supplementing rather than supplanting others' conceptions.

In the next two sections of this chapter, we shall discuss some of the limits of current conceptions of giftedness and propose as an alternative that giftedness be defined primarily as an attribute of performance rather than of persons. A review of studies that fall within the scope of our definition follows. This review is divided into five parts, each devoted to a different theoretical perspective on gifted performance. The chapter closes with a summary of current knowledge about gifted performance and suggestions for future research.

Limits of current conceptions

We began developing our own conception of giftedness by considering the implications for research of current conceptions. Tannenbaum's was especially valuable for this purpose, because it highlights the role of sociocultural contexts in defining giftedness, the difficulty of predicting adult giftedness from any set of child and environmental characteristics, and the diversity of individual, cultural, and chance factors that contribute to giftedness as it is usually defined. The explicit breadth of Tannenbaum's definition makes apparent the limitations of all definitions based on the concept of potential for culturally valued productivity.

One salient point is the difficulty of integrating all of the contributors to giftedness identified by Tannenbaum into a conception that might guide research. Some of the contributors lie within the psychology of individual differences in cognition and personality; others are in the province of those who study how characteristics of school programs and social environments influence development; and still others are in the domain of sociological, anthropological, or philosophical studies of cultural norms and values. To use such a panoply of concepts as a guide for research would require a presently unachievable synthesis of different levels of analysis, perspectives, and scientific disciplines.

Any definition of childhood giftedness that is based on potential for adult productivity is inherently problematic as a guide to the study of children. Despite the moderate stability of IQ-test scores and the possible stability of personality and environmental factors that might predict giftedness, there are many children whose adult performance will never fulfill their early promise. Similarly, there are many undeniably gifted adults whose childhood performance did not mark them as candidates for eminence. Consequently, educators or researchers working with children defined as gifted according to any measures of potential are inevitably working with many children who will not as adults produce excellent socially valued products. Moreover, such educators and researchers are necessarily missing opportunities to nurture or study children whose adult performance will mark them as gifted. Only by abandoning the notion of potential can we avoid the investigative imprecision it creates. Benton (1962, 1970) has argued this point fully as it applies to identifying mentally retarded children.

Another undesirable consequence of all conceptions of giftedness based on the idea of potential for socially valued productivity is the exclusion of some interesting groups of children from studies of the gifted. Current conceptions of giftedness offer no guidance to researchers interested in educationally or theoretically important activities that some children do extremely well but that are not predictors of adult achievement. Extraordinarily early attainment of advanced reading ability is one such activity. Precocious reading ability is not a reliable predictor of any form of adult giftedness. Reading is not a particularly creative activity, and there is little social value to being an exceptionally able reader as either a child or an adult. Nonetheless, first-grade children who have been reading fluently for several years have an immediate need for the kind of differentiated programming that is the essence of gifted education. If we define giftedness in a way that excludes research with such children, we cut off the possibility of generating an empirical base to guide their instruction.

Adopting any conception of giftedness that requires that only creative and socially important abilities be studied places awkward, even unacceptable limits on researchers who wish to understand the nature of giftedness in children. Many tasks that yield important measures of individual differences in intellectual ability have no apparent social utility, and they involve absorption rather than creation of knowledge. It is difficult enough to find tasks that are sufficiently well understood to allow strong inferences about cognitive processes; finding tasks that are both well understood and directly relevant to some aspect of children's everyday classroom performance is more difficult still. If we impose on ourselves the further requirement that the tasks we study be demonstrably related to creative excellence in adulthood, we place unacceptably narrow constraints on the scope of our work.

Davidson and Sternberg (1983) have tried to meet this challenge in their studies of gifted children's performance on insight problems, and we applaud their effort. But we must note that they have not sought to establish an empirical link between children's insightfulness and their adult productivity. We share Sternberg's (1984) belief that the ability to learn new kinds of skills and concepts may be central to the development of giftedness across the life-span. However, this assumption cannot be verified without long-term, prospective longitudinal research. Such research is not justified until the nature of performance on tasks such as those studied by Davidson and Sternberg has been clarified by intensive analytic studies. In the meantime, it would be a serious mistake to exclude from research on giftedness the broad array of other learning, memory, and problem-solving tasks that have contributed to understandings of children's cognition. We gain enormous advantage when we tie our work with the gifted to the large body of previous research on developmental and individual differences in cognition. We are unwilling to define away that advantage.

Conceptions and studies of giftedness should contribute to theories of individual differences among all children, but few discussions of giftedness mention this possibility. One reasonable way to further this goal would be to test hypotheses about the gifted derived from what we know about differences between retarded and average children or between children who perform poorly and children who perform adequately on some task such as learning to read. An argument against this approach is that the mechanisms that distinguish gifted from average performers may ultimately prove to be quite different from those that distinguish average from poor performers. This argument assumes that gifted children may be qualitatively different from their peers in ways that cannot be predicted from our knowledge of how other subgroups of children differ from one another. But this assumption can be affirmed or refuted only by working from a view of giftedness that is integrated into a broad conception of individual differences.

Giftedness as excellent performance

For purposes of fostering cognitive research on giftedness, the most troublesome aspect of current conceptions is the assumption of long-term stability. Stripping this assumption away to achieve a more useful conception for research leads to a focus on gifted performances rather than gifted persons. We would prefer to discard entirely the labeling of children as "gifted" or "not gifted." Such labels imply the existence of a trait, "giftedness," that is stable across situations and over long periods of time. Believing as we do that the assumption of stability of giftedness in children is both unjustified by current evidence and counterproductive for guiding new research, we would like to write only about gifted performance. However, this perspective is awkward to maintain consistently in reviewing a literature that often focuses on gifted individuals. Thus, we content ourselves with the following definition: Gifted performances are instances of excellent performance on any task that has practical value or theoretical interest. A gifted child is one who demonstrates excellent performance on any task of practical value or theoretical interest. We intend the term *performance* to be construed broadly and dynamically. Thus, learning a new skill with unusual speed or ease would qualify as an instance of gifted performance. Our definition, which is similar in some respects to a conception proposed many years ago by Paul Witty (1940, 1951), does not preclude the possibility of gifted performance throughout a lifetime, but it does not require it either. It makes investigation of long-term stability of performance an option of the researcher who studies giftedness, rather than an obligation inherent in the definition of the subject matter.

By including in our definition any activity having practical value or theoretical interest, we deliberately expand the range of behaviors that can be called gifted. Our own interest is in behaviors that involve intellectual reasoning and are relevant to doing well in school, but we see no reason to exclude from our definition skills that are predominately physical, artistic, or interpersonal.

Defining gifted performance as broadly as we have done raises the question of whether any common processes underlie all instances of giftedness. We believe that the paucity of available data requires that this question be left open. Beginning with a broad definition should facilitate the eventual determination of boundaries within which a common process explanation of giftedness will apply.

By emphasizing the diversity of gifted performances, we intend to make the distinction between general intellectual giftedness and specific talents (Tannenbaum, 1983) into a dimension of study rather than letting it remain a basis for sorting children into assumedly different categories. One of the most interesting questions that can be asked about any instance of gifted performance is "To what extent is the child's performance on this task related to his or her performance on other, more or less similar, tasks?" Our definition includes the behavior of children who perform exceptionally well only in a single intellectual, artistic, or other realm as well as the behavior of all-around prodigies. We include even the most extreme cases of specialized talent, namely, the talents of individuals called idiot savants, who are profoundly limited in most of their behavior but who have a single, narrowly circumscribed flair for musical performance, feats of memory, drawing, or mental arithmetic (Hill, 1978). There are dramatic differences between the performances of idiot savants and those of normal (i.e., not intellectually retarded or neurologically impaired) prodigies, but there are similarities, too, and we will not consider any theory of giftedness to be complete until it accounts for both the similarities and the differences among all subgroups of children with some exceptional ability.

By our definition, excellent intelligence-test performance is, in itself, an instance of giftedness, because intelligence tests are composed of tasks having practical value and theoretical interest. Many of the items on intelligence tests are sufficiently similar to everyday school problems to be called practically valuable, and the contributions of psychometric researchers to cognitive psychology (e.g., Carroll, 1982) show that intelligence-test performance is theoretically interesting. Nonetheless, our own preference is to deemphasize the importance of studying intelligence-test performance and to focus on performances that are more readily amenable to process analysis.

Recent studies of developmental and individual differences in cognition include many process analyses of how younger and older or retarded and average children differ in their performance on a broad array of reasoning and memory tasks. We know not only that older and brighter children perform better on these tasks, but also which process components of performance are responsible for the overall performance differences. For example, older and brighter children perform better on many memory tasks because they spontaneously use effective strategies such as mentally clustering the to-be-remembered items into logical groupings. When young or retarded children are taught to use effective strategies such as clustering, their performance on the target task improves dramatically. Analysis of the process components of cognitive performance differences is not just a scientifically interesting exercise. The results of these analyses often provide models for instructional techniques that can be used in the classroom.

There is a small but growing literature devoted to the process analysis of gifted performance on problems that have also been used in studies of average and poor performers. Such performances include mathematical, verbal, and scientific reasoning (Butterfield et al., 1985; Ferretti & Butterfield, 1983; Holzman, Pellegrino, & Glaser, 1982), reading (Healy, 1982; Jackson & Biemiller, 1985; Jackson & Cleland, 1984), playing games such as chess (Chi, 1978), and feats of memory or mastery of highly structured bodies of knowledge (Chi, in press). By using the same well-analyzed tasks in the study of giftedness that have been used in the study of deficient performance, investigators can draw on vital research traditions and on perspectives that have immediate relevance for the development of classroom instructional techniques.

It could be objected that advocating the use of procedures that have been developed for the study of average and retarded performance might needlessly restrict techniques for studying gifted performance. That is surely not our intent. Earlier, we applauded Sternberg and Davidson for their development of new procedures for examining insight, and we would applaud any other innovative approach that clarifies gifted performance. However, we feel that such new approaches should be treated as additions to, not substitutes for, older approaches to the study of individual differences. When a topic has not been studied extensively, and giftedness has not been, more rapid progress can be made by borrowing technology and theory from related fields of inquiry than by starting from scratch. At best, starting from scratch means reinventing earlier inventions by other investigators. Typically, it means developing un-refined procedures for doing grossly what refined versions of earlier inventions do precisely and elegantly. Too often, it means muddying the waters by mucking around. When a new area has been mined with the methods and conceptions of related and more mature areas of investigation, the hard work of developing new methods can be spent on problems that have been shown to require them.

We know that early investigators of mentally retarded people thought that the retarded are qualitatively different from normal people and that the study of the deficient intellectual performance of mentally retarded persons requires new techniques. Nevertheless, techniques were borrowed from the study of normal people, and they were used until their application revealed particular needs for new techniques. After those new techniques were developed for use with retarded people, they were used as well in the study of average performance by normal individuals. Despite many years of intense study, there is no evidence that unique principles are required to account for the behavior of the mentally retarded. We suggest that this story will be repeated as gifted performance is studied more fully.

Studies of gifted performance by children

Feldman (1982) has claimed that "we know almost every detail imaginable about children who receive IQ scores above 130 and below 160 on standard tests." We agree with Feldman's implication that more studies are needed of other sorts of gifted children, such as those with particular intellectual or artistic abilities. But our review of the literature says that little more is known about the cognitive processes of children with IQs between 130 and 160 than about other sorts of gifted children. Nowhere near enough is known to ensure the effective planning of special programs for children whose performance is markedly superior to the average in any realm.

Newland (1976) listed characteristics believed to be typical of intellectually gifted children:

> Fundmentally, the gifted are particularly capable of quick and generally accurate generalization . . . .
> [Individuals differ and the gifted are superior in] the speed with which they acquire symbols of the same order of complexity . . . and the *degree* of

abstractness of symbols they can learn . . . and the complexity of the relationships among symbols which they can deduce. . . .
    While it is not psychologically their special forte, bright persons manifest a
disconcerting superior intellectual adhesiveness (memory).

Although Newland does not give any evidence in support of this description,
it is consistent with the small empirical literature on the gifted and with what
we have learned from working with gifted children and their teachers. It is
especially striking that Newland's description specifies no distinction between
average and gifted children that has not been specified by others as a distinction between retarded and average children. Furthermore, the intellectual
performances of older and younger children have been found to differ on
these same dimensions. No emergent or qualitative differences are apparent
in Newland's description of the superiority of gifted to average children. The
distinctions proposed by Newland are entirely consistent with models of gifted
performance that could be extrapolated from existing general models of developmental and individual differences in cognition.

   In the paragraphs that follow, we shall describe, evaluate, and interpret
studies of gifted performance and gifted children. Each of five sections will
be devoted to discussion of a particular perspective on the nature of the
processes that may be responsible for differences between gifted and average
performances. Within each section, we shall summarize the studies that fall
within that perspective, discuss the extent to which the performance of younger
gifted children is similar to that of older children of average ability, and
consider whether differences between gifted and average performers are similar to those between average and deficient performers. Whenever the literature allows it, we shall discuss the issue of generality versus specificity in
superiority of performance. Throughout, we shall highlight methodological
limits that need to be overcome in future studies of average as compared with
gifted performance.

Studies from a Piagetian perspective

Most of the approaches to the study of gifted children's cognition that we
shall describe in the following sections are very new and represent theoretical
perspectives that dominate most of the current research in cognition and
cognitive development (Brown et al., 1983; Siegler & Richards, 1982). However, we shall begin our review with a selection of studies from an older and,
perhaps, more familiar perspective on cognitive development. All of these
studies focused on the extent to which the performance of gifted (typically,
high-IQ) children on Piagetian tests of logical–mathematical reasoning ability
was different from, or more advanced than, the performance of average
children.

   The results of the Piagetian studies were expected to have both theoretical and practical implications. Studying gifted children was a convenient way to test Piaget's hypotheses about the universality of a fixed sequence and relatively constant rate of development and about the uniformity of children's performance across different types of problems. Educators concerned about appropriate programs for gifted children looked to these studies for information about whether it was reasonable to expect children who have earned high scores on general intelligence tests to solve logical–mathematical problems in the same way an average older child would. Should the gifted be expected to reason in exceptionally mature ways or to perform much like other children their own age?

Some investigators have concluded that children with high IQ scores do not progress through Piaget's major stages at an unusually rapid pace. Brown (1973) found that high-IQ 4-year-olds did not differ significantly from average-IQ 4-year-olds in performance on measures of conservation of number or continuous quantity. The gifted 4-year-olds performed significantly less well than average-IQ 6-year-olds or retarded 8-year-olds. Similarly, Webb (1974) found that 6- to 11-year-olds with extremely high scores (above 160) on the Slosson Intelligence Scale were not substantially advanced in their performance on measures of formal-operational reasoning, although they did do consistently well on concrete-operational tasks.

Other investigators have found that gifted children do progress through the major Piagetian stages at an unusually rapid pace. Keating (1975) found that a group of 11-year-old boys selected for high ability in mathematics and high scores on the Raven Progressive Matrices intelligence test surpassed average 13-year-old boys in performance on both concrete- and formal-operational reasoning tasks. Krinsky et al. (1977) administered the Concept Assessment Kit standard test of conservation to 34 children, aged 3 to 6 years, who were enrolled in a preschool/kindergarten for the gifted. These children, who had been selected for their school on the basis of multiple measures of intellectual and academic ability, performed on the various conservation tasks at levels typical of children two years older.

Although these studies have not provided a consistent answer to the question of what kinds of logical–mathematical reasoning ability might be expected from gifted children, there is a pattern in the data. The criteria used to select gifted groups were different in the studies in which gifted children have not been found to be substantially advanced in performance on Piagetian reasoning tasks and those in which advancement has been found. In the Brown and the Webb studies, the index of giftedness was performance on intelligence tests (the Stanford–Binet and the Slosson) that emphasize verbal knowledge and verbal reasoning ability. Verbal ability is only moderately related to performance on Piagetian measures, and it is likely that the absence of precocious Piagetian reasoning by the children in the Brown and Webb samples is the result of having picked the "wrong" gifted children. In contrast, the gifted children in the Keating and Krinsky et al. studies were selected on the basis of performance on less verbally oriented tests. The children in the Krinsky et al. study had the additional advantage of exposure to a preschool–kindergarten program that included advanced lessons in science and mathematics. This fact is important because many investigators have found that performance on Piagetian measures is influenced by a child's educational experience. (See Jackson, 1979, for further discussion of these and related issues.)

The possible relationship between the way giftedness is defined and the nature of a gifted child's performance on Piagetian tasks is dramatically evident in Feldman's (1980) case studies of two 8-year-old chess prodigies and a 10-year-old composer. Each of these boys exhibited remarkably mature abstract reasoning ability within his own domain of expertise, but the three all performed within age-appropriate limits on various concrete- and formal-operational reasoning tasks. The children's advanced performance in their own areas of expertise may have been facilitated by the intensive instruction they had received within those domains.

The foregoing studies show that there is great variability in the extent to which gifted children demonstrate precocity in Piagetian reasoning. Although systematic evidence on this point is not available, it seems that the more precocious reasoners are those whose giftedness has been defined in terms of multiple criteria that include a substantial perceptual–logical reasoning component. Specific educational experiences may also contribute to the acceleration of gifted children's progression through the Piagetian stages (Feldman, 1980; Krinsky et al., 1977). Finally, it appears that a child's precocity in reasoning may be limited to a narrowly defined area of expertise (Feldman, 1980).

The studies of gifted children's performance on Piagetian tasks raise several issues that will recur throughout our review:

Is the performance of gifted children similar to that of older average children or is their problem-solving a special, more effective version of what other children their age are doing? In the mental retardation literature, a similar issue has been more or less resolved by a large number of studies that have demonstrated that performance of mentally retarded individuals and that of children with more circumscribed intellectual deficiencies is highly similar to that of younger normal individuals. A deficient individual's profile of intellectual strengths and weaknesses may be somewhat different from those of average children, but the description of cognitive deficiency as cognitive delay is sufficiently accurate to make a delay model a useful guide for research with deficient individuals. In the following sections of this chapter, we shall consider the extent to which the mirror image of this conceptualization – the description of giftedness as developmental precocity – is also consistent with the literature.

The related issue of evenness versus unevenness in cognitive development will also recur in other contexts. For example, one of the perspectives we shall consider, the knowledge perspective, suggests that a child's reasoning abilities may be highly uneven across different content domains, with the quality of reasoning in any domain determined by the extent and organization of a child's knowledge of that domain. Other perspectives stress the importance of relatively general-purpose strategies that should enhance performance even in content areas a child does not know well.

The limitations of the Piagetian studies provide a useful context for considering the advantages of more recent approaches to the study of gifted children's cognition. Piaget's theory has been widely criticized for its failure to specify empirically testable links between overt performance and the hypothesized internal representation of reality that supposedly determines children's performance on logical–mathematical reasoning tasks. Knowing that a child has passed or failed a particular Piagetian task tells one nothing about the specific processes that might be responsible for that performance. The observed performance is consistent with many different process explanations in addition to Piaget's own. Without more extensive data about the components of performance, Piaget's assertion that logical reasoning is dependent on the structure of a child's representation (i.e., internal knowledge) of reality is untestable.

Untestable theories do not advance our understanding of the processes that underlie developmental and individual differences in cognitive performance. Furthermore, such theories do not provide any guidance for those who wish to provide instruction that will facilitate children's progress to more advanced levels of performance. The theoretical perspectives represented in the following sections provide more testable, and therefore more useful, hypotheses about the cognitive processes responsible for gifted performance.

Cognitive efficiency

One currently popular set of process explanations of developmental and individual differences in cognition stresses the critical role of a few elementary cognitive processes in determining even the most complex intelligent behavior. These theories emphasize the fact that people differ in how rapidly and automatically they can perform simple tasks that involve the identification and recall of familiar stimuli, such as letters and numbers. Individuals who are slow to identify incoming information (i.e., to retrieve from long-term memory the stored information that gives the current input its meaning) or who need to devote their full attention to this task may not have enough attentional capacity left over for performing the higher-level, integrative components of a complex task. For example, a poor reader may have to devote most of his or her limited attentional capacity to such low-level aspects of the reading process as identifying individual letters or words, leaving little attention free for the higher-order synthesis and comprehension of text (Perfetti & Lesgold, 1981).

Efficiency theorists also note that individuals differ in the speed with which they can process information that is all within the focus of their current attention. The hypothetical "place" where information currently being attended to is stored and manipulated is called "working memory." Working memory has a limited capacity. Efficient use of that capacity is necessary for the solution of complex problems that require simultaneous attention to and integration of many different elements.

Individual differences in cognitive efficiency are not generally regarded to be either fixed, or constant, across different kinds of problems. We all become more efficient and automatic in our information processing as we master the elements of a new skill such as driving a car or as we become more familiar with the contents of a new domain of knowledge such as a foreign language. Some efficiency theorists emphasize the existence of general, perhaps to some extent innate, differences in the efficiency with which people process general categories of perceptual input such as linguistic or visual–spatial information. Other theorists stress the importance of an individual's familiarity with a particular content domain and type of problem for determining how efficiently the person will respond. What all theorists working from this perspective do share is a conviction that performance on a broad range of complex intellectual tasks can be explained in terms of elementary cognitive processes that are evident in performance on very simple reaction time tasks (Cooper & Regan, 1982).

There is evidence suggesting that intellectually gifted children may have more efficient memory processes than do average children. Some of the evidence comes from recognition–memory problems in which children were shown a set of digits and then asked whether a subsequently displayed digit was or was not a member of the original set. In general, people participating in experiments of this kind respond more slowly as the number of digits in the display set increases. Imagine that you yourself are a subject in such an experiment. As you stare at a computer screen, a sequence of digits such as 7, 2, 5, 8, 1 flashes on the screen. Just after this sequence disappears, you are shown a single digit, perhaps 8, and asked to indicate whether that digit was or was not one of the set you saw earlier. If you are typical of subjects in such experiments, it should take you a bit longer to respond "yes" to the digit 8 than to one of the digits closer to the beginning of the series you were shown. Subjects in these experiments act as if they form a mental representation of the original display in short-term memory, and then scan that representation sequentially when the digit targeted for recognition is presented. High-IQ children are less affected by increases in memory set size than are average-IQ children (Keating & Bobbitt, 1978; McCauley et al., 1976). High-IQ children attain an adult memory scanning rate by the time they are 9 years old, but average-IQ children do not attain this degree of efficiency until sometime between the ages of 13 and 17 years (Keating & Bobbitt, 1978).

High-IQ children also surpass other children their age in the speed with which they retrieve familiar semantic information from long-term memory. Studies of this aspect of processing efficiency often involve comparing the speed with which subjects make "same" judgments about physically identical pairs of stimuli (e.g., *AA*) to the speed of making judgments based on name identity (e.g., *Aa*). People generally require more time to make name- than physical-identity judgments, and this extra time is interpreted as an index of how long it takes to retrieve name information (one form of semantic information) from long-term memory. Keating and Bobbitt found that high-IQ 9-, 13-, and 17-year-olds performed this kind of letter–name retrieval faster than average-IQ groups of the same ages. Peck and Borkowski (1983) obtained similar results in a study of 7- and 8-year-olds.

An association between giftedness and cognitive efficiency has been found in at least one other gifted group besides school-age, high-IQ children. Jackson and Myers (1982) administered a letter naming speed task to children enrolled in a preschool program for the intellectually and academically gifted. All of the children in the study could name letters accurately, yet they varied greatly in their ability to read words. Performance on the letter naming speed task was moderately associated with precocious reading achievement. Moreover, the results of a 6-month longitudinal study suggested that rapid letter naming was a predictor, not a consequence, of reading achievement.

As we have noted above, children whose short- and long-term memory processes are more efficient should have more working memory capacity available for solving complex problems. The small amount of evidence available to date is not entirely consistent with this hypothesis (Butterfield et al., 1985; Globerson, 1983; Holzman et al., 1982, 1983). Testing hypotheses about memory capacity requires great care because capacity can only be inferred from memory performance, and many factors beside capacity, such as the use of mnemonic strategies, can affect performance. However, we do know it would be unwise to attribute any apparent differences in the effective working memory capacities of gifted and average performers to structurally fixed differences in capacity. No good evidence for such differences has been found in studies comparing younger and older children, average and retarded children, or average and gifted children (Globerson, 1983; Siegler & Richards, 1982).

In summary, several studies suggest that intellectually and academically gifted children are highly efficient in the use of both short- and long-term memory processes. It can be argued that these processes contribute importantly to quality, as well as speed, of performance on tasks as diverse as short-term memory and reasoning problems and reading comprehension (Cooper & Regan, 1982). However, a conclusion that the gifted are fundamentally distinguished by the efficiency of their memory processes can*not* be drawn from the available data. Associations between memory efficiency measures and indices of giftedness tend to be modest, and may be just one indication of an overall faster rate of responding by the gifted, rather than speed of memory per se. Moreover, for the studies mentioned above, there is no way of knowing whether the efficiency of performance on the memory tasks should be attributed to a general efficiency of the gifted groups' memory processes or to the gifted children's greater familiarity with the letter and number stimuli used. Finally, there is no evidence that efficiency is the sole, or even the most salient, attribute of gifted performance. Precisely the same conclusions can be drawn from the literature comparing average and retarded children (Campione, Brown, & Ferrara, 1982).

The data on memory capacity and memory efficiency are generally, but not entirely, consistent with a model stating that the processes differentiating gifted from average performers are the same as those differentiating older from younger children (Globerson, 1983; Keating & Bobbitt, 1978). The issue of parallelism between developmental and individual differences in efficiency is especially difficult to resolve because of the methodological problems inherent in the study of processing speed and capacity (Cooper & Regan, 1982; Siegler & Richards, 1982).

None of the studies reviewed above suggest any qualitative difference in the basic short- and long-term memory processes of gifted and average children. Even though gifted children may scan information in short-term memory more rapidly than average children do, they use the same serial scanning strategy. Finally, none of the data address the issue of whether the efficient memory processes of gifted children are general across all types of information or specific to certain domains.

Knowledge

Some investigators have suggested that gifted performance results from possession of more and better-organized knowledge rather than from greater processing capacity or proficiency (Chi, 1976; Holzman et al., 1982, 1983). Thus, Holzman et al. (1982) argued that "poor performance on a test of inductive reasoning may not necessarily signify inadequate reasoning processes, *per se*, but might also indicate a poor command of basic facts to be reasoned about" (p. 371).

There are no systematic data about the extent to which gifted children possess richer knowledge bases than average children. Rather, the studies we have assembled in this section represent three separate lines of research. The three sets of studies differ from one another in the types of gifted performance studied, the way in which giftedness was defined, and the kinds of behavior from which knowledge of a content area has been inferred.

The first set of studies involves comparisons of gifted and average children's performance on inductive reasoning problems. Inductive reasoning problems such as analogies (wolf : dog :: lion : - - - -) and series completions (3 9 4 16 5 - -) appear frequently on tests of general intelligence. Performance on these problems tends to be strongly related to performance on other measures of verbal ability (Butterfield et al., 1985). Cognitive psychologists have studied inductive reasoning problems intensively because the elements of the problems can be varied systematically. By observing how accurately or rapidly people solve problems with different classes of constituent elements and different kinds of relations among the elements, investigators have been able to develop models of the cognitive processes involved in problem solution. Models of inductive reasoning specify the extent to which different components of a problem contribute to its being easier or more difficult than other problems within the same general class. Typically, these models also specify the extent to which individual differences in speed or accuracy of performance can be attributed to the various components.

In the studies of inductive reasoning reviewed below, gifted performers were selected on the basis of IQ scores or enrollment in a special program for the academically gifted. However, the only aspect of the children's knowledge of interest to these investigators was knowledge of the problem content areas (arithmetical and letter series relations) tapped by the reasoning problems being studied. Content knowledge was inferred from the children's patterns of success and failure on problems with different knowledge requirements. In two of the studies (Holzman et al., 1982, 1983), amount of content knowledge was also estimated from performance on a mathematics achievement test.

Holzman et al. (1982, 1983) have reported two studies of the inductive reasoning performance of gifted and average children and adults. One study examined performance on numerical analogies of the form "2 : 4 :: 9 : 11 :: 15 : - -" (Holzman et al., 1982), and another examined performance on numerical series problems such as "45 36 44 36 43 36 . . ." (Holzman et al., 1983). Problems of both sorts were constructed so their solution depended on knowledge of addition, subtraction, division, or multiplication. The performance of gifted children remained relatively accurate across problems involving all four types of arithmetic operations, but average children had greater difficulty with some types of operations than with others. This group difference, in combination with failure to observe performance differences attributable to memory capacity, led the investigators to conclude that "factual information directly taught in school has critical discriminative power for a task purportedly designed to measure abstract reasoning ability" (1982, p. 371). The implication is that instruction might compensate for the difference between average and gifted performers.

It is not entirely clear that the differences observed in either of the Holzman et al. studies should be attributed to knowledge of arithmetic operations rather than the effective capacity of working memory. One could also think of the computational operations in the more difficult types of arithmetic operations as placing especially heavy demands on working memory (Butterfield et al., 1985). One reason that Holzman et al. emphasized knowledge rather than memory processes as the source of gifted performance is that both their series and analogy problems varied in ways other than type of arithmetic operation; these variations were specifically designed differentially to tax working memory. The difference in performance between gifted and average children was not significantly greater for problems with high memory demand than for those with low memory demand.

In their studies of problems involving letter rather than number series, Butterfield et al. (1985) used a theoretical model of series performance different from the one used by Holzman et al. (1983). The Butterfield et al. model permits separate predictions about the roles of knowledge and working memory factors in accounting for series performance and is useful in clarifying the ambiguities in the Holzman et al. data. The model provides separate assessments of the influence of children's knowledge about possible patterns of serial (alphabetical) relations among letters and the influence of the number and difficulty of the operations that must be manipulated in working memory to solve a problem.

In order to determine the extent to which the superior performance of gifted children could be attributed to knowledge of letter series relations or working memory load, we administered to 128 gifted children the 96 letter series problems that had been administered to 128 average children by Butterfield et al. (in press). The children in both studies ranged in age from 7 to 12 years. Gifted children correctly completed 86% of the problems, whereas average children correctly completed only 37%. Correlational analyses performed separately for data from average and gifted children showed that knowledge and memory processes contributed comparably to the two groups' performance. That is, gifted and average children used knowledge and memory processes in the same ways to solve the letter series, but gifted children had more knowledge and more effective memory processes. These are among the most direct data on the question of whether average and gifted children solve problems in the same ways. When solving letter series problems, they do. These data also suggest that Holzman et al. failed to find differences in memory effectiveness in their numerical series study only because the theoretical model they used to interpret performance provides too indirect an index of the memory demands of a series.

A second set of studies of the relationship between knowledge and gifted performance illustrates the usefulness of defining giftedness broadly as performance. Studies of idiot savants, a group rarely considered by those who study the gifted, have sometimes included attempts to determine the nature of the knowledge underlying their impressive specialized talents (Hill, 1978). One such study is especially interesting because it provides information that makes it possible to compare the knowledge of a group of savants with that of other gifted children.

Young children who are markedly deficient in their cognitive and linguistic abilities and who show signs of neurological impairment occasionally display a talent that has been called "hyperlexia" (Healy, 1982; Huttenlocher & Huttenlocher, 1973). Hyperlexic children begin reading, often obsessively, at preschool age. They rapidly develop the ability to decode (read aloud) words and passages with meanings that are well beyond their limited ability to comprehend either spoken or written language. By elementary school age, hyperlexic children may score at the upper elementary or high school levels on measures of decoding ability, even though their comprehension ability remains rudimentary (Healy, 1982).

Because the decoding skill of hyperlexic children, like the specialized talents of other kinds of idiot savants, seems so inconsistent with their limited cognitive and linguistic ability, it has frequently been assumed that this skill is based on inflexible rote memory for a large body of "sight" words. However, Healy (1982) has shown that these children are well able to decode phonetically regular pseudowords. The children cannot possibly have recognized the pseudowords as familiar wholes. Therefore, their ability to pronounce these words indicates they they must have acquired some representation of grapheme–phoneme correspondence rules.

Although precocious knowledge of decoding rules may seem difficult to reconcile with severe deficiency in verbal ability, the data from hyperlexic readers are perfectly consistent with findings from a study of a large group of normal (i.e., not neurologically impaired or cognitively deficient) precocious readers of kindergarten age (Jackson & Cleland, 1984). As a group, these children are advanced in their ability to comprehend as well as to decode text, and comprehension may be their greatest strength. However, analysis of individual differences in precocious readers' skill patterns reveals the existence of a separate ability to use decoding rules in reading phonetically regular real and pseudowords. Unlike individual differences in comprehension, this decoding rule use factor is not related to verbal ability. Thus, although normal precocious readers and hyperlexic readers differ greatly in the scope and utility of their gifts, the two groups do appear to share similar knowledge of decoding rules. This commonality makes the achievements of hyperlexic readers seem less mysterious and suggests that further comparisons of idiot savants with normal gifted individuals might help us disentangle the components and origins of gifted performance.

In the studies described thus far in this section, investigators have made indirect inferences about the knowledge of gifted and average performers from observing their reasoning or reading performance. The third set of studies focuses directly on the systematic description of children's knowledge. These studies are also unusual in their focus on giftedness defined by performance within a narrow, explicit content area.

More than any other investigator's work, that of Michelene Chi illustrates that one can focus on gifted performances as distinct from gifted children.

For example, in her studies of chess expertise, Chi (1978, 1981) showed that it is possible to reverse the usual developmental pattern of adults performing better than children on memory problems. Her approach was to compare memory of expert and novice chess players for chessboard positions. The critical wrinkle in her design was that her expert players were children and her novice players were adults. Her child experts showed substantially better recall for chess position than her adult novices, even though her adults recalled lists of digits better than did her child experts. She interprets this finding as evidence that domain-specific knowledge influences memory over and above general, age-related memory strategies. This is a reasonable conclusion, but it would be stronger if Chi had made additional comparisons to verify a specific causal link between knowledge and recall performance. (See Butterfield, Siladi, & Belmont, 1980, for a fuller treatment of the methodological requirements of such comparative investigations.)

Other investigations by Chi (in press; Chi & Koeske, 1983) also make the point that knowledge differences may underlie average versus gifted performance differences that are usually attributed to greater effective memory capacity or to the use of more effective strategies. The role of general memory and problem-solving strategies in gifted performance will be considered at length in the next section of our review. Chi (in press) has argued that although strategy use may determine performance on memory tasks, it is domain knowledge that is responsible for strategy use. By systematically assessing children's knowledge of dinosaurs, Chi was able to show, both within and between subjects, that categorical clustering strategies were more likely to be used when children possessed more knowledge. Categorical clustering results in greater recall than does use of some other strategies. Chi's interpretation is that knowledge may always be more important than possession of appropriate mnemonic strategies. This is too broad a conclusion, since the particular mnemonic strategy she examined cannot be employed by children who do not possess the taxonomic categories necessary for clustering, and not all strategies depend centrally on such knowledge. Nevertheless, these data are the strongest available suggesting that knowledge base can influence intellectual performance. (See Chi, Glaser, & Rees, 1982, for a full discussion of the difficulties of assessing children's knowledge for research purposes.)

In summary, the few studies available to date suggest that a child's knowledge of a content domain may be one important determinant of whether that child demonstrates gifted performance on memory or reasoning problems that tap that knowledge. Unfortunately, these studies do not address the equally interesting question of how some children have managed to acquire rich and extensive knowledge while others, with similar opportunities, have not (Sternberg, 1984). However, one important aspect of this literature is that it suggests that the acquisition of extensive and well-organized knowledge within a particular domain can enable even young children to equal or surpass their elders' performance within that domain. Perhaps there are no general limits to the reasoning ability of young children, simply limits on the amount of knowledge they have acquired in the domains tapped by the problems we pose for them. Similarly, differences in accumulated knowledge may account for a substantial proportion of the differences we observe in the reasoning abilities of retarded, average, and gifted children. Research is needed that will compare the adequacy of a knowledge-based account of developmental and individual differences in intellectual performance with competing accounts emphasizing processing components such as cognitive efficiency, strategy use, and metacognitive functions. Summaries of studies involving the last two classes of components follow.

Strategy use

A great diversity of strategies is used spontaneously by older and better problem solvers, and individuals who use them perform better than those who do not. Some of these strategies (e.g., rehearsal and categorical clustering) seem inherently specific to particular kinds of problems (e.g., verbal recall), although they may be applicable to a broad range of problem content domains (Brown, Campione, & Barclay, 1979; Butterfield et al., 1980). Other strategies (e.g., forming visual images or verbal summaries of problem elements) have the potential for effective application across different problem contents (e.g., verbal or mathematical problems) and different problem types (e.g., free recall, reasoning, and reading comprehension).

When it was first discovered that young children and mentally retarded people seldom use effective problem-solving strategies, it was suggested that they lacked whatever cognitive machinery might be required to employ strategies. However, considerable analytic and instructional research has shown that this is not correct. Rather, both young and mentally deficient people can be led quickly by cognitive instruction to employ adult strategies (e.g., Borkowski & Cavanaugh, 1979). The inference that has been drawn is that young children are production deficient, that is, they do not produce strategies spontaneously but can use them with great effectiveness when instructed to do so.

If differences between average and gifted performance reflect processing differences similar to those that underlie differences between the performance of retarded and average individuals or younger and older individuals, we would expect gifted children to employ spontaneously those strategies that are typically used only by older children or adults. Unfortunately, there have been surprisingly few investigations of gifted children's strategic repertoires. The literature with which we are familiar includes studies of memory and of problem-solving strategies. Findings vary from one study to another with regard to whether gifted children (a) use strategies more often than do average children, (b) use strategies that are the same as those of average children, or (c) use strategies characteristic of older children.

Geis and Corriher (1977) compared the performance of average and moderately high-IQ third- and fifth-graders on several multi-trial free recall tasks. The high-IQ children showed both better recall and more extensive use of organizational strategies on all tasks. Robinson and Kingsley (1977) obtained similar results in a study of average and gifted second- and fourth-graders on multi-trial free recall. At both grade levels, the gifted groups showed better recall and more consistent use of a sequential organization strategy. The extent to which this strategy was used was moderately related ($r = .37$) to individual differences in recall accuracy. Although Robinson and Kingsley's gifted groups were more effective strategy users, the younger gifted group did not use exactly the same strategy as the two older groups. Regardless of ability level, the younger children organized their recall on a word-by-word basis, but the two older groups organized their recall by groups of words.

Not all investigators have found more strategic behavior in gifted than in average children. Peck and Borkowski (1983) reported a study of gifted and average children's memory strategies. These investigators employed two procedures that allowed them to assess the extent to which children clustered items categorically as a way of facilitating recall. Comparisons of 7- and 8-year-old average and gifted children revealed no strategic differences. This failure to observe differences may reflect the fact that all of the subjects were below the age or intellectual maturity level at which these tasks would elicit memory strategies from any children.

Ferretti and Butterfield (1983) used balance-scale problems to study strategy use by retarded, average, and gifted children. These problems involve a horizontal beam attached to a central fulcrum, as in a playground seesaw. The two ends of the beam are braced so it will not tilt, and weights are placed on both sides of the beam. The child's task is to predict which end of the beam will go down when the braces are removed. Variants of the problem involve different amounts of weight placed at different distances from the fulcrum.

Ferretti and Butterfield (1983) patterned their versions of the balance-scale problem set after Siegler (1976), who developed procedures for determining the rules that children use to solve these problems. Although it is possible to view these rules as knowledge of physical laws, they are also strategies, because they guide the encoding and manipulation of information to yield problem solutions. Siegler (1976) has shown that four rules form a developmental progression in that some are acquired before others and the ones acquired earlier allow correct solution to fewer balance-scale problems. Using the rule "multiply weight by distance for each side and compare the two values" will generate correct solutions for all possible variants of the problem. However, use of this advanced rule is rare among children and far from universal among adults.

Ferretti and Butterfield (1983) compared the rule classifications earned by 38 retarded, 115 average, and 119 gifted children on a comprehensive assessment test. The distribution of rule classifications differed across the three intelligence levels. Most retarded children were classed as using the lowest rule, most average children as using the middle two rules, and most gifted children as using the most advanced rule. Except that no retarded children used the most advanced rule, some children at each intelligence level were classed at each of the four rule levels. These data indicate strategic differences as a function of intelligence, but they do not suggest qualitative strategic differences between gifted and nongifted children. The gifted children were more likely to use strategies characteristic of older average children.

There remains a need for many more investigations of the extent to which gifted children do or do not use memory and problem-solving strategies different from those used by average and retarded children. So far, the evidence is insufficient to indicate the circumstances in which gifted children use (perhaps more effectively) the same strategies as other children their age and the circumstances in which they use strategies characteristic of older children. The inconsistency of the evidence is reminiscent of the data on Piagetian task performance presented in a preceding section of this review. It would be useful to determine how differences in strategy use by gifted and average children are related to particular age levels, educational experiences, individual differences in knowledge of the problem domain, criteria for defining giftedness, and specific properties of the tasks and strategies being studied. At present, it appears that differences in strategy use between gifted and average children are similar to those between average and retarded children. There is no evidence that gifted children use unique, qualitatively different memory or problem-solving strategies.

Metacognition

The term *metacognition* was coined in 1971 by Flavell, who later defined it as "knowledge or cognition that takes as its object or regulates any aspect of cognitive endeavor" (1978, p. 4). Interest in metacognition grew from observations that young and intellectually deficient individuals frequently behave as if they are unaware of the strategic requirements of the problems they face or of ways in which they might monitor and manage their own behavior for effective problem solution (Butterfield & Belmont, 1977). Metacognition may be domain-specific and therefore contribute to unevenness in performance across different content areas (Brown et al., 1983; Chi, 1981). However, most theorists working from this perspective (e.g., Butterfield & Belmont, 1977;

Sternberg, 1984) have emphasized that these broadly useful superordinate processes may play a central role in determining the quality of an individual's problem solving in many different contexts.

Hypotheses about the role of metacognition as a determinant of individual differences in intelligent behavior have appeared only recently in the developmental and comparative literatures. Nonetheless, quite a few studies already have been done to test, or have been interpreted in terms of, the possibility that metacognitive factors are central to gifted performance. We begin with research reports that include metacognitive explanations of their findings and then we turn to studies designed specifically to test hypotheses about metacognitive processes.

The inductive reasoning studies mentioned above (Butterfield et al., in press; Holzman et al., 1982, 1983) were guided by theories that emphasize the role of higher-order processes that select and guide the use of lower-order processes. Such higher-order processes can be called metacognitive, and the fact that gifted children performed better than average children in the studies of Butterfield et al. and Holzman et al. is sufficient reason to suggest that the results obtained might be due to metacognitive factors. However, no metacognitive measures or manipulations were included in these investigations, and in their reports, both sets of investigators offered other explanations that might account for all of the superior performance of their gifted subjects.

Studies of exceptionally precocious young readers suggest slightly more strongly that superior metacognitive skills may contribute to the performance of gifted children. The progress made by most young readers in learning to comprehend text seems to be limited by the efficiency with which they execute lower-order processes such as identifying individual letters and words (Lesgold & Curtis, 1981; Perfetti & Roth, 1981), but the comprehension of very precocious readers does not seem to be limited by lower-order processes. Thus, Jackson and Biemiller (1985) found that although kindergarten readers named individual letters much more slowly than either second- or third-graders and read individual words at the same speed as did second-graders, both their average performance on a standard test of comprehension and their text reading speed were at the third-grade level. As noted in our discussion of other findings from the same sample (Jackson & Cleland, 1984), some of the children were exceptionally advanced in their word decoding skills. Nonetheless, the pattern of the group's average performance on different reading tasks suggests that the precocious readers were somehow using higher-order, text-level processes to fill in the gaps in their lower-order skills. Unfortunately, the extent to which effective text-level processing was attributable to precocious readers' advanced verbal knowledge or to the exceptionally effective application of that knowledge (i.e., metacognitive processing) cannot be determined.

Turning to studies that have tested metacognitive hypotheses directly, we note that the literature on average and retarded children has employed three different procedures. Some investigators have employed interviews to assess children's introspective access to their metacognitive understandings and have tried to relate those understandings to performance. Others have used the extent to which instructed strategies transfer to uninstructed tasks as an indication of the extent of children's metacognition (Campione et al., 1982). The idea is that transfer depends on recognizing relations between what one has been taught and how effectively one performs and on recognizing similarities among the processing requirements of training and transfer tasks. Such recognition is assumed to be a metacognitive matter. Yet other investigators have tried to teach metacognitive understandings and then have examined the extent to which these teachings facilitate subsequent learning and transfer. All three of these approaches have been used in the study of gifted children.

Peck and Borkowski (1983) interviewed children about several aspects of metacognition. They asked children questions designed to elicit information about their (a) understanding of the efficacy of elaborative learning strategies, (b) planfulness in preparing for a memory test, (c) appreciation of the value of systematic searches when faced with a difficult memory retrieval problem, and (d) understanding of the relative ease of gist recall as compared to rote recall. Peck and Borkowski also assessed (e) children's accuracy at estimating how well they had recalled recently learned material, (f) how fully they appreciated the extent to which being interested in something facilitates learning about it, and (g) a composite score reflecting all of the above factors. Comparisons of 7- and 8-year-old gifted and average children showed that the gifted exceeded the average on six of the seven measures. The force of these findings is diminished by the fact that only one of many possible within-group correlations between metacognition and cognitive performance was significant. This lack of relationship between interview assessments and performance is typical of this kind of research with average and retarded children, too, and probably results from a combination of knotty methodological and conceptual difficulties, the solutions to which are not yet clear (Brown et al., 1983; Cavanaugh & Perlmutter, 1982). Fortunately, there are other approaches to the study of metacognition.

Ferretti and Butterfield (1983) selected retarded, average, and gifted children so that they all used the simplest of four rules that children eventually master for solving balance-scale and other formal-operational problems (Siegler, 1976). Using a mastery criterion, the investigators then taught all children the three higher rules in their normal order of acquisition. Following mastery of each higher rule, Ferretti and Butterfield administered an unprompted transfer test. This test required the child to transfer the rule that had been mastered in the context of physical manipulation of a real balance scale to the solution of pencil-and-paper balance-scale problems. Children who did not transfer were then prompted to use what they had learned during training.

Children who still failed to transfer were given further instruction and prompts. These procedures allowed scaling of the ease with which retarded, average, and gifted children could be taught the higher strategies and the ease with which they could be induced to transfer newly acquired strategies.

Even though the strategy instruction employed teaching techniques that minimize individual differences in rate of learning, the gifted children mastered all three higher strategies more readily than did the average children, who learned them more readily than did the retarded children. The conclusion is that filling in even minimal instructional gaps is done more readily by more intelligent children. Theoretically, the processes employed in filling in instructional gaps are metacognitive (Campione et al., 1982). Ferretti and Butterfield (1983) also found that both gifted and average children transferred more readily than did retarded children, but no differences were observed in ease of transfer between normal and gifted children. Because ease of transfer is determined, in part, by similarity among the training and transfer tests, it cannot be concluded that average children transfer all newly acquired material as readily as do gifted children. If the training and transfer tasks in Ferretti and Butterfield's study had been less similar, the gifted children may have transferred more readily than the average children.

Davidson and Sternberg (1983) reported four studies of gifted and average children's performance on logical–mathematical problems of insight, which they hypothesized has three aspects: selective encoding (sifting out relevant from irrelevant information); selective combination (combining selectively encoded information to form a relevant whole); and selective comparison (relating newly acquired information to information acquired in the past). Sternberg (1984) describes these selective processes as basic components of knowledge acquisition and does not consider them to be among the metacognitive aspects of his model of intelligence. This classification seems appropriate to us for certain simple sorts of selective encoding, combination, and comparison. However, Davidson and Sternberg's insight problems were designed to make use of the selective processes nonobvious and difficult. In such circumstances, selectively encoding, combining, or comparing information involves processes that we would call metacognitive. For example, selecting the facts relevant to solution of an arithmetic word problem from a paragraph that includes several misleading pieces of irrelevant information would seem to require that the problem solver (a) decide what kind of answer is required and what facts are needed to compute such an answer; (b) search the paragraph, sorting out the relevant and irrelevant cues; (c) evaluate the match between the information required and that selectively encoded as relevant; (d) if necessary, repeat the search process with revised criteria for selectively encoding or ignoring information; and (e) compute an answer and evaluate its adequacy. Such disciplined self-management of the problem-solving process is one key aspect of metacognition. In an experiment on selective encoding, Davidson and Sternberg found that gifted children spontaneously selected relevant information from story problems containing both relevant and irrelevant facts, but that average children needed cues to use the relevant information. A closely related experiment involved selective comparison (the transfer and application of relevant information from a prior context). When no prior example was given, the performance of gifted and average children on the criterion problems was similar, indicating that performance on these problems was not sensitive to some unidentified problem-solving skills in which the gifted might have been superior. However, mere exposure to a relevant prior example maximally improved the performance of the gifted children, but the average children profited increasingly from prior examples as more explicit information about the relevance of these examples was supplied. When the relevance of the prior examples was made fully explicit, the performance of the average children was as accurate as that of the gifted children without any relevance prompts. These two experiments show that gifted children require less prompting to identify information that is relevant to solving a novel problem. In the experiment on selective encoding, the relevant information was a part of the problem to be solved. In the experiment on selective comparison, the relevant information was part of a prior example. In both cases, the selective processes can be described as metacognitive.

There are marked similarities between Davidson and Sternberg's (1983) experiment on selective comparison and the experiment by Ferretti and Butterfield (1983). Both experiments concern conditions necessary to promote transfer, a key test of metacognitive ability. Both used prompts graded from general to explicit. Both showed that more intelligent children require less specific prompts to transfer. Both justify the inference that more intelligent children employ metacognitive knowledge more readily than do less intelligent children.

Davidson and Sternberg (1983) report another experiment in which they attempted to inculcate insight in average and gifted children. The inculcating instruction improved the problem-solving performance of both gifted and average children, and it improved the scores of both groups equally. The fact that Davidson and Sternberg's "insight" instruction did not diminish performance differences between average and gifted children indicates that the instruction did not convey what (or *only* what) the gifted children were doing without instruction that the average children were not. Had the uninstructed gifted children been employing selective encoding, selective combination, and selective comparison consistently and with maximum effectiveness, they would not have benefited from the instruction. Because they did benefit, the conclusion is that Davidson and Sternberg's instruction tells us how to foster insight, but it does not tell us how gifted children differ from average children (cf. Butterfield et al., 1980). Apparently they do not differ in the sense of using optimally without instruction all of the processes affected by Davidson and Sternberg's comprehensive training program.

One possibility that should be evaluated with more analytic instructional experimentation is that gifted children use some of the three selective processes spontaneously in some of the appropriate situations, but not all of them on all tasks. It might also be fruitful to develop procedures for determining whether a particular child is using a particular selective process, since it may be that different gifted children employ different aspects of what Davidson and Sternberg (1983) would call insight and we would call metacognition.

In summary, the rapidly growing new literature on metacognition and giftedness suggests that superordinate processes regulating task analysis and self-management of problem-solving behavior may be important components differentiating gifted from average performance. Findings contrasting the performance of gifted and average children have been consistent with findings contrasting the performance of average and retarded children. To our knowledge, direct comparisons of metacognitive differences between gifted and average children with those between younger and older children have not yet been made. Extrapolating from studies of retarded children, we predict that gifted children's metacognitive processes may be similar to those of older average children, but that gifted children will be found to be more extremely advanced in metacognitive processes than in other components of their intellectual performance. Children whose gifted performance is restricted to a narrow domain may show superior metacognition only within that domain (Chi, 1981; in press), but it remains to be determined whether such children might be able to apply their metacognitive skills more broadly, given reasonable opportunities to do so.

A conclusion that gifted performers are primarily and fundamentally distinguished by superior metacognitive processes is not justified by the studies available to date. However, there is an encouraging similarity between the findings of the metacognition studies and those of a much older and larger, although less analytically precise, literature – studies of aptitude–treatment interactions in classroom learning (Snow & Yalow, 1982). The most consistent finding in that literature has been that academic performance differences between more and less intelligent students are most strongly evident in programs that require students to organize their own learning and fill in instructional gaps. This is just what we would predict from the literature on metacognition and giftedness, and the new literature shows promise of identifying the particular cognitive processes that intelligent children use to succeed in structured learning situations.

Summary

At the beginning of our review of the empirical literature on cognitive processing in the gifted, we suggested that we do not yet have a full picture of the special characteristics of gifted performance or gifted children. Many critical questions do remain to be answered, but the studies summarized above have given us some important preliminary insights into the nature of giftedness.

Perhaps the most striking aspect of the literature we have reviewed is the consistency of the empirical findings from studies of gifted performance and gifted children with intuitive descriptions of giftedness (Newland, 1976) and with the literatures on the normative developmental sequence (Brown et al., 1983), differences between average and retarded children (Campione et al., 1982), and aptitude–treatment interactions in the classroom (Snow & Yalow, 1982).

None of the results of the studies we have reviewed suggest the need to postulate new kinds of cognitive processes to explain giftedness. Gifted performance appears to be explainable in the same terms as average and deficient performance. We acknowledge that it is difficult to find unique, qualitatively different processes when one's studies are designed primarily to detect variation in the use of familiar processes. Perhaps unique attributes of cognitive processing in the gifted will eventually be identified in studies specifically designed to focus on attributes hypothesized to be central to giftedness. However, those studies in our review that came closest to that approach (Chi, 1981; Davidson & Sternberg, 1983) did not reveal any phenomena that could not be interpreted in the context of general theories of individual and developmental differences. Gifted performance is different from ordinary performance, but it does not appear to be different in any way that would justify the creation of separate cognitive theories of giftedness.

Directions for future research

Although there does not seem to be any more mystery about gifted than about average or retarded performance, our understanding of giftedness is limited by the general boundaries of current scientific knowledge about the relative contributions of cognitive efficiency, knowledge, strategies, and metacognition to cognitive performance. We do not know whether (or in what contexts) some of these processing components are more important than others, how the developmental origins of each might differ, or how the components interact with one another during problem solution. Resolution of any of these theoretical issues will have important educational implications.

One of many possible examples of the practical implications of theoretical questions about the processing components of giftedness arises from the inconsistencies in the literature on strategy use by the gifted and in the related Piagetian literature. Gifted children sometimes appear to use more developmentally advanced and effective strategies than average children do (e.g., Ferretti & Butterfield, 1983; Keating, 1975), but this superiority is not consistent across all types of problems, strategies, or gifted children. On the other hand, the studies that have been done to date suggest that the gifted are consistently superior in the ability to learn new strategies and to apply them appropriately (Davidson & Sternberg, 1983; Ferretti & Butterfield, 1983). This pattern of findings suggests that a child's potential for success in a program requiring the use of sophisticated problem-solving strategies, such as an advanced physics class, might be determined more accurately by a screening process that focused on the child's ability to learn the new strategies than by a process focused on assessment of the child's current strategic repertoire. Vygotsky's concept of the "zone of proximal development," which is the object of much interest among educators working with intellectually deficient groups (Campione et al., 1982), might be equally relevant to the identification and enhancement of giftedness. However, further research is needed to verify our tentative preliminary conclusions about strategy use and strategy learning in the gifted.

Another issue with practical relevance for the education of the gifted is the question of how domain-specific knowledge and more general strategic and metacognitive processes each contribute to the development of a child's ability to apply previous learning to new problems, synthesize information from different domains, and solve new kinds of problems. Currently, many curricula for the gifted focus on the development of general-purpose problem-solving skills (Glaser, 1984; Tannenbaum, 1983). However, to our knowledge, no attempts have been made to determine whether the long-term goal of teaching a child to be a consistently effective and creative problem solver might be better met by programs that devoted substantial blocks of time to the transmission of domain-specific knowledge and only a little time to teaching children how to apply, interpret, integrate, and evaluate that knowledge. If our preliminary conclusions from the cognitive literature are correct, the superior metacognitive skills of gifted children should enable them to profit very rapidly from minimal instruction in general problem-solving skills. Theory-based instructional research is sorely needed to establish just what balance of domain knowledge versus strategic and metacognitive instruction might be optimal. Quite probably, the best mix of instruction would vary according to the age and abilities of the children being taught, the knowledge domains involved, and the exact nature of the criteria used to define instructional success.

Better understanding of the process components of giftedness will also yield practical benefits of a sort rarely considered in the literature on giftedness. When we have identified more precisely the cognitive processing parameters that result in gifted performance, we will be in a position to foster giftedness in children who have not previously demonstrated such excellence. A model of instruction based on thorough understanding of how gifted and ordinary performance differ is likely to provide an excellent general model for differentiated education. As we have tried to show in this chapter, we who study the gifted can learn much from working within a conception of giftedness that permits us to take advantage of what is known about the cognitive characteristics of other groups of children. Working within such a conception also helps us to fulfill our responsibility to promote the integration of our own findings into that larger body of knowledge and to contribute to the better education of all children.

References

Benton, A. L. (1962). The concept of pseudofeeblemindedness. In E. P. Tropp & P. Himelstein (Eds.), *Readings on the exceptional child: Research and theory* (pp. 82–95). New York: Appleton-Century-Crofts.

Benton, A. L. (1970). Interactive determinants of mental deficiency. In H. C. Haywood (Ed.), *Social-cultural aspects of mental retardation* (pp. 661–671). New York: Appleton-Century-Crofts.

Borkowski, J. G., & Cavanaugh, J. C. (1979). Maintenance and generalization of skills and strategies by the retarded. In N. R. Ellis (Ed.), *Handbook of mental deficiency, psychological theory and research* (2nd ed., pp. 569–618). Hillsdale, N.J.: Erlbaum.

Brown, A. L. (1973). Conservation of number and continuous quantity in normal, bright, and retarded children. *Child Development, 44,* 376–397.

Brown, A. L., Bransford, J. D., Ferrara, R. A., & Campione, J. C. (1983). Learning, remembering, and understanding. In J. H. Flavell & E. M. Markman (Eds.), *Handbook of child psychology* (4th ed.). *Cognitive development* (Vol. 3, pp. 77–166). New York: Wiley.

Brown, A. L., Campione, J. C., & Barclay, C. R. (1979). Training self-checking routines for estimating test readiness: Generalization from list learning to prose recall. *Child Development, 50,* 501–512.

Butterfield, E. C., & Belmont, J. M. (1977). Assessing and improving the executive cognitive functions of mentally retarded people. In I. Bialer & M. Sternlicht (Eds.), *The psychology of mental retardation: Issues and approaches* (pp. 277–318). New York: Psychological Dimensions.

Butterfield, E. C., Nielsen, D., Tangen, K. L., & Richardson, M. B. (1985). Theoretically based psychometric measures of inductive reasoning. In S. Embretson (Ed.), *Test design: Contributions from psychology, education, and psychometrics* (pp. 77–147). New York: Academic Press.

Butterfield, E. C., Siladi, D., & Belmont, J. M. (1980). Validating theories of intelligence. In H. W. Reese & L. P. Lipsitt (Eds.), *Advances in child development and behavior* (Vol. 15, pp. 95–162). New York: Academic Press.

Butterfield, E. C., Wambold, C., & Belmont, J. M. (1973). On the theory and practice of improving short-term memory. *American Journal of Mental Deficiency, 77,* 654–669.

Campione, J. C., Brown, A. L., & Ferrara, R. A. (1982). Mental retardation and intelligence. In R. J. Sternberg (Ed.), *Handbook of human intelligence* (pp. 372–490). Cambridge University Press.

Carroll, J. B. (1982). The measurement of intelligence. In R. J. Sternberg (Ed.), *Handbook of human intelligence* (pp. 29–120). Cambridge University Press.

Cavanaugh, J. C., & Perlmutter, M. (1982). Metamemory: A critical examination. *Child Development, 53,* 11–28.

Chi, M. T. H. (1976). Short-term memory limitations in children: Capacity or processing deficits? *Memory and Cognition, 4,* 559–572.

Chi, M. T. H. (1978). Knowledge structures and memory development. In R. S. Siegler (Ed.), *Children's thinking: What develops?* (pp. 73–96). Hillsdale, N.J.: Erlbaum.

Chi, M. T. H. (1981). Knowledge development and memory performance. In M. Friedman,

J. P. Das, & N. O'Connor (Eds.), *Intelligence and learning* (pp. 221–231). New York: Plenum.

Chi, M. T. H. (in press). Interactive roles of knowledge and strategies in the development of organized sorting and recall. In S. Chipman, J. Segal, & R. Glaser (Eds.), *Thinking and learning skills: Current research and open questions* (Vol. 2). Hillsdale, N.J.: Erlbaum.

Chi, M. T. H., Glaser, R., & Rees, E. (1982). Expertise in problem solving. In R. J. Sternberg (Ed.), *Advances in the psychology of human intelligence* (Vol. 1, pp. 7–75). Hillsdale, N.J.: Erlbaum.

Chi, M. T. H., & Koeske, R. D. (1983). Network representation of a child's dinosaur knowledge. *Developmental Psychology, 19*, 29–39.

Cooper, L. A., & Regan, D. T. (1982). Attention, perception, and intelligence. In R. J. Sternberg (Ed.), *Handbook of human intelligence* (pp. 123–169). Cambridge University Press.

Davidson, J. E., & Sternberg, R. J. (1983, April). *The role of insight in intellectual giftedness.* Paper presented at the biennial meeting of the Society for Research in Child Development, Detroit.

Feldman, D. H. (1980). *Beyond universals in cognitive development.* Norwood, N.J.: Ablex.

Feldman, D. H. (1982). *Developmental approaches to giftedness and creativity* (New Directions for Child Development Series). San Francisco: Jossey-Bass.

Ferretti, R. P., & Butterfield, E. C. (1983, March). *Testing the logic of instructional studies.* Paper presented at the Gatlinburg Conference on Mental Retardation/Developmental Disabilities, Gatlinburg, Tenn.

Flavell, J. H. (1978). Metacognitive development. In J. H. Scandura & C. J. Brainerd (Eds.), *Structural process theories of complex human behavior.* Alphen a.d. Rijn, The Netherlands: Sijthoff & Noordhoff.

Geis, M. F., & Corriher, S. E. (1977, March). *Memory and organizational processes in high-IQ children.* Paper presented at the biennial meeting of the Society of Research in Child Development, New Orleans.

Getzels, J. W., & Jackson, P. W. (1962). *Creativity and intelligence: Explorations with gifted students.* New York: Wiley.

Glaser, R. (1984). Education and thinking: The role of knowledge. *American Psychologist, 39*, 93–104.

Globerson, T. (1983). Mental capacity and cognitive functioning: Developmental and social class differences. *Developmental Psychology, 19*, 225–230.

Healy, J. (1982). The enigma of hyperlexia. *Reading Research Quarterly, 17*, 319–338.

Hill, A. L. (1978). Savants: Mentally retarded individuals with special skills. In N. R. Ellis (Ed.), *International review of research in mental retardation* (Vol. 9, pp. 277–298). New York: Academic Press.

Hollingworth, L. S. (1942). *Children above 180 IQ Stanford–Binet.* New York: World Book.

Holzman, T. G., Pellegrino, J. W., & Glaser, R. (1982). Cognitive dimensions of numerical rule induction. *Journal of Educational Psychology, 74*, 360–373.

Holzman, T. G., Pellegrino, J. W., & Glaser, R. (1983). Cognitive variables in series completion. *Journal of Educational Psychology, 75*, 603–618.

Huttenlocher, P. R., & Huttenlocher, J. (1973). A study of children with hyperlexia. *Neurology, 23*, 1107–1116.

Jackson, N. E. (1979, March). *Passing the individual differences test: A cram course for developmental psychologists.* Paper presented at the biennial meeting of the Society for Research in Child Development, San Francisco. (ERIC Document Reproduction Service No. ED 174358)

Jackson, N. E., & Biemiller, A. J. (1985). Letter, word, and text reading times of precocious and average readers. *Child Development, 56*, 196–206.

Jackson, N. E., & Cleland, L. N. (1984, April). *The structure of precocious reading ability.* Paper presented at the annual convention of the American Educational Research Association, New Orleans. (ERIC Document Reproduction Service No. ED 24752)

Jackson, N. E. & Myers, M. G. (1982) Letter naming time, digit span, and precocious reading achievement. *Intelligence, 6*, 311–329.

Keating, D. P. (1975). Precocious cognitive development at the level of formal operations. *Child Development, 46*, 276–280.

Keating, D. P., & Bobbitt, B. L. (1978). Individual and developmental differences in cognitive processing components of mental ability. *Child Development, 49*, 155–167.

Krinsky, S. G., Sjursen, F., Krinsky, R., Jackson, N. E., & Robinson, H. B. (1977). *Conservation in intellectually advanced children of preschool age: Levels of performance and relation to other intellectual and academic abilities*. Unpublished manuscript, University of Washington Child Development Research Group, Seattle.

Lesgold, A. M., & Curtis, M. E. (1981). Learning to read words efficiently. In A. M. Lesgold & C. A. Perfetti (Eds.), *Interactive processes in reading* (pp. 329–350). Hillsdale, N.J.: Erlbaum.

McCauley, C., Kellas, G., Dugas, J., & DeVillis, R. F. (1976). Effects of serial rehearsal training on memory search. *Journal of Educational Psychology, 68*, 474–481.

Newland, T. E. (1976). *The gifted in socio-educational perspective*. Englewood Cliffs, N.J.: Prentice-Hall.

Peck, V. A., & Borkowski, J. G. (1983, April). *The emergence of strategic behavior in the gifted*. Paper presented at the biennial meeting of the Society for Research in Child Development, Detroit.

Perfetti, C. A., & Lesgold, A. M. (1981). Interactive processes in reading: Where do we stand? In A. M. Lesgold & C. A. Perfetti (Eds.), *Interactive processes in reading* (pp. 387–407). Hillsdale, N.J.: Erlbaum.

Perfetti, C., & Roth, S. F. (1981). Some of the interactive processes in reading and their role in reading skill. In A. M. Lesgold & C. A. Perfetti (Eds.), *Interactive processes in reading* (pp. 269–298). Hillsdale, N.J.: Erlbaum.

Renzulli, J. S. (1978). What makes giftedness? Reexamining a definition. *Phi Delta Kappan, 60*, 180–184, 261.

Robinson, J. A., & Kingsley, M E. (1977). Memory and intelligence: Age and ability differences in strategies and organization of recall. *Intelligence, 1*, 318–330.

Siegler, R. S. (1976). Three aspects of cognitive development. *Cognitive Psychology, 8*, 481–520.

Siegler, R. S., & Richards, D. D. (1982). The development of intelligence. In R. J. Sternberg (Ed.), *Handbook of human intelligence* (pp. 897–971). Cambridge University Press.

Snow, R. E., & Yalow, E. (1982). Education and intelligence. In R. J. Sternberg (Ed.), *Handbook of human intelligence* (pp. 493–585). Cambridge University Press.

Sternberg, R. J. (1984). Toward a triarchic theory of human intelligence. *Behavioral and Brain Sciences, 7* (2), 269–316.

Tannenbaum, A. J. (1983). *Gifted children: Psychological and educational perspectives*. New York: Macmillan.

Terman, L. M. (1925). *Genetic studies of genius: Vol. 1. Mental and physical traits of a thousand gifted children*. Stanford, Calif.: Stanford University Press.

Webb, R. (1974). Concrete and formal operations in very bright 6- to 11-year-olds. *Human Development, 17*, 292–300.

Witty, P. (1940). Some considerations in the education of gifted children. *Educational Administration and Supervision, 26*, 512–521.

Witty, P. (1951). *The gifted child*. Lexington, Mass: Heath.

8   Causes and consequences of metamemory in gifted children

John G. Borkowski and Virginia A. Peck

So numerous are the intellectual gifts that differentiate gifted and regular children that an attempt to find an area of "weakness" or even average development in the gifted is no easy undertaking. It is almost self-evident to state that gifted children know more about the world around them and learn new information with seeming ease (cf. Tannenbaum, 1983). Less obvious are the theoretical difficulties posed by the embarrassment of intellectual riches in the gifted: With so many genetic and environmental advantages, how can unequivocal causes for their learning and problem-solving proficiencies be isolated? A somewhat similar problem has hindered theoretical advancement at the opposite end of the intellectual spectrum for nearly three decades: Retarded children suffer so many deficits – in attention, perception, memory, and cognition – that it is difficult, if not impossible, to pinpoint a cause, or set of causes, for any instance of poor performance (Detterman, 1979). This interpretive dilemma is particularly acute when the search is for the causes of retarded behavior from a life-span perspective, featuring a combination of historical, biological, social, and psychological variables (Borkowski, Reid, & Kurtz, 1984).

From a complex, interactive view of reality, how can specific causes and consequences of important achievements in the lives of gifted children be unraveled and understood, especially when research must address multifaceted, intellectual skills? The thrust of this chapter is aimed at unraveling the causes and consequences of an intellectual skill common to young gifted children: a greater awareness about how minds operate and function. Our approach to understanding giftedness centers on a developmental process known to influence learning and memory performance in normal children – knowledge about memory states and processes, or metamemory (Flavell & Wellman, 1977). The aims of this chapter are to describe the empirical and theoretical consequences we ascribed to metamemory in gifted children; to

The writing of this paper was supported by NIH Grant #HD-17648. The second author was supported by an NIH Training Grant (HD-07184) during the duration of the research projects. A version of the chapter was presented at the annual meeting of the Society for Research in Child Development, Detroit, April 1983.

observe how metamemory influences the emergence of strategic, purposeful behaviors; and to speculate about the origins of this unique attribute of giftedness.

First, we will sketch the Campione–Brown (1978) model of intelligence and assess the state of existing knowledge about gifted children from the framework of this model. In point of fact, much of the literature we will review deals with high-IQ or high-verbal children rather than gifted children per se. Future research will need to delineate more carefully the respective roles of intelligence, past achievement, and creative thinking as functional components of gifted performance; for the moment, such distinctions are all but impossible to draw in the existing literature on giftedness.

The major portion of the chapter describes a longitudinal study of gifted and regular children over a two-year period (from ages 7–8 to 9–10), focusing on the importance of metamemory as a setting condition for the emergence of strategic behaviors. In the research to be described, gifted and regular children were observed before the onset of differences in their use of strategies on laboratory learning and memory tasks. At that time, however, the groups differed along a number of other dimensions of intelligence: knowledge about the world, perceptual skills, and metacognition. These components, singly or in combination, have the potential of fostering the emergence of differences in strategic skills for gifted and regular children. The intent was to contrast these factors against one another in the prediction of strategic behaviors on transfer tests. The design of the study enabled us to "assist" the educational environment in producing strategic behaviors, providing children various amounts of training on strategies appropriate for a variety of different learning and memory tasks. At the conclusion of the study, we measured performance on several tasks, assessing the extent of strategy differences due to giftedness and determining the most plausible reason for these differences. This sequence of arranged and natural events, embedded in a theoretical approach that features the importance of metacognition, provided a context in which to understand how gifted children's rich knowledge about their own mental operations sets the stage for the emergence of learning strategies.

In the final section of this chapter, we provide a theoretical interpretation of how metamemory may be linked to the development of strategies and skills in gifted children and suggest connections between their early environmental experiences and corresponding metamemory development, especially the role played by parental recognition of perceptual-memory "gifts" and the subsequent provision of enriching activities.

A model of giftedness

Early studies of giftedness were generally descriptive in nature. Gifted children are faster than average children at mastering oddity learning tasks (Brown,

1970), superior to average children on paired-associate learning (Jensen, 1963), and more organized in their approach to free recall problems (Geis & Corriher, 1977; Wachs, 1969). Although findings such as these were informative about performance differences of gifted and normal samples, these early studies about the nature and consequences of giftedness were not conducive to theoretical integration and advancement for several reasons: (a) Each project focused on an isolated aspect of learning or cognition, usually studying a single, momentary process and its influence on performance. The past history of each child in the two samples was generally ignored, as were other concomitant intellectual processes. (b) Past research provided only a narrowly framed description of how gifted children perform on idiosyncratic tasks; limited theoretical accounts were given about why performance variability occurs in gifted children. Systematic information was not gathered about individual differences, both between and within groups, in terms of the processes assumed to underlie cognitive development in the gifted. The narrowness of research designs and restricted perspectives about the reasons for cognitive-intellectual variability have led to a dearth of theory about the nature of giftedness.

The time is ripe for theoretical advancements about cognition and intelligence in gifted children and adolescents because of important developments in the parent area of information processing. For instance, more comprehensive, multiple-component theories of intelligence seem to provide a more adequate account of individual differences in normal and handicapped people across a wide range of tasks (e.g., Campione & Brown, 1978; Horn, 1978; Sternberg, 1982). These theories differ in the extent to which they focus on factors (e.g., fluid vs. crystallized intelligence), components (e.g., mapping or inferring), or higher-level metacomponents (e.g., monitoring or revising strategies). The present study utilized the broad framework provided by the Campione–Brown (1978) perspective on key factors underlying intelligence. This model sketches an interactive theory of intelligence with two hierarchical levels, reflecting both elementary and higher-order systems of information processing, storage, and retrieval.

In the Campione–Brown (1978) model, the function of the elementary or architectural level is to register and respond to sensory input. The speed of information processing and retrieval provides an index of operating *efficiency*. The higher-order level, or *executive*, has three key components: (a) a content-oriented knowledge base consisting of existing semantic networks and schema structures; (b) a dynamic processing component consisting of rules and strategies for learning and problem solving; and (c) a metacognitive component, which informs and regulates cognitive strategies.

The Campione–Brown model provides a useful framework for understanding the sources of individual differences on learning, memory, and problem-solving tasks. The speed and efficiency by which information is processed is critical for all other aspects of the processing system, especially the automatic processing of information. In addition, executive skills, involving the knowledge base, metacognition, and control processes, are important components of deliberate problem-solving on complex tasks. The question now addressed is how existing data on giftedness might be reinterpreted and understood from the perspective of both the architectural and executive systems.

Perceptual efficiency and giftedness

The architectural system can be defined by reference to properties of the sensory register and of short-term memory (cf. Atkinson & Shiffrin, 1968): durability or relative permanence of information; capacity or the number of slots in memory; and efficiency or the ease of storing and accessing information. Of these, evidence points to perceptual efficiency as the property of the architectural system most closely linked to differences in intellectual ability and age (Campione & Brown, 1978).

There are a number of possible ways to measure perceptual efficiency, including memory span and search (or scanning) speed. For instance, Cohen and Sandberg (1977) found that IQ scores correlated with measures of primary memory in young adolescents varying in intelligence. More specifically, the recall of auditorily presented nine-digit lists showed reliable correlations between IQ and accuracy for the most recently presented items (i.e., those in primary memory). In contrast, no relationship was found between IQ and earlier-presented items, those contained in the more active secondary memory system, which is influenced by rehearsal and other forms of strategic behavior. From a different operational base, Dempster (1981) concluded that the speed with which items are identified represents a major source of variance in ability and age differences in memory span. From another definitional perspective of "speeded" performance, high-ability groups are superior to low-ability groups in accessing and manipulating information in short-term memory (Hunt, Frost, & Lunneborg, 1973). High-verbal college students (i.e., those with high WPCT scores) manipulated information more rapidly in memory than low-verbal students. That is, the slope of reaction time functions for low-verbal individuals was steeper than for high-verbal individuals. Along this same line, Keating and Bobbitt (1978) found that higher-IQ children were consistently faster than average children on a memory scanning task and that more intelligent children were less affected by set size. Spiegel and Bryant (1978) suggested that the speed of processing information not only may be a correlate of IQ but might directly contribute to it. That is, processing efficiency could lead to superior intelligence, as displayed on IQ tests and learning tasks.

Research with gifted populations focusing on decoding processes also suggests differences in perceptual efficiency. Decoding and retrieving highly learned information in long-term memory has been found by Hunt and his colleagues to differentiate high-verbal from low-verbal students (Hunt et al., 1973; Hunt, Lunneborg, & Lewis, 1975). Using the semantic–physical identity task developed by Posner (cf. Posner et al., 1969), high-verbal students accessed overlearned material in long-term memory more rapidly than did low-verbal students (Hunt et al., 1973). In this task, a subject is shown two letters having the same name but different visual codes (*Aa*), or two letters having the same name and the same physical characteristics (*AA*). The subject's task is to identify whether the letters are the "same" or "different" when embedded among obviously incorrect or different letter pairs. Differences among response times to semantic and physical identity pairs reflects the time it takes to retrieve names of letters from long-term memory. Results indicated that low-verbal students had higher name identity minus physical identity scores, reflecting slower decoding processes, than did high-verbal students.

These findings were generalized to other stimuli and tasks in a study by Goldberg, Schwartz, and Stewart (1977). These investigators found that college students with high verbal ability were faster than college students with average verbal ability in making taxonomic category matches, as in *deer* and *elk*, and homophone identity matches, as in *deer* and *dear* (Goldberg et al., 1977). Both tasks are considered to be indicative of long-term retrieval efficiency. High-verbal students were also faster on making physical identity matches.

More recently, Ford and Keating (1981) focused on long-term memory in persons differing in age and ability. They explored two possible sources of variance in long-term retrieval in fourth-graders, eighth-graders, and college students: retrieval processing efficiency (speed) and semantic organization (a measure of strategy use). Retrieval efficiency from long-term memory was highly related to intellectual ability, especially verbal fluency, in children but not in adults. In contrast, measures of semantic organization or strategy use were unrelated to ability at all ages. In summary, a sizable body of data leads to a straightforward conclusion about the importance of the architectural system in understanding individual differences in intelligence: speed or efficiency in both encoding and decoding processes differentiates gifted from regular children.

Executive functioning and giftedness

In the Campione and Brown (1978) model, the general knowledge base, strategic behaviors, and metacognitive knowledge (and processes) are important components of the executive system. They add considerably to the prediction of individual differences in process and performance variability, especially in contrasts of normal and retarded children on memory and problem-solving tasks (Borkowski et al., 1984). We reflect now on how these components differentiate gifted and regular children.

General knowledge

Various theorists emphasize the knowledge base as an important component of intelligence (cf. Chi, in press; Wechsler, 1958). Since general knowledge is reflected in composite IQ scores, gifted children by definition have a superior knowledge base, at least in restricted domains such as vocabulary, general information, and math. From Horn's (1978) perspective, they probably are superior in the amount of crystallized, acculturated knowledge.

According to Ornstein and Corsale (1979), effective processing of new information is due in part to the compatibility of incoming information with existing knowledge. Similarly, Bransford, Franks, Morris, and Stein (1979) suggest that encoding quality depends partially on the integration of new knowledge and preexisting knowledge. Chi (1978) argues cogently that important developmental differences are often the result of increased knowledge about the task and about appropriate task-specific rules, rather than basic memory strategies. Clearly, general and domain-specific knowledge distinguishes school-age gifted children from their peers, giving the gifted a decided learning advantage.

Strategic behavior

Several studies have analyzed the strategic behavior of average- and high-ability children on recall and information-processing tasks. Robinson and Kingsley (1977) assessed accuracy and its underlying organizational structure on a 10-item list of unrelated words presented eight times in various random orders; a brief recall period followed each presentation. Second- and fourth-grade children with superior ability consistently recalled more words than did their average-ability peers. The level of recall for superior younger children was equivalent to that for older children of average ability. In addition, children with superior abilities showed greater organizational skill than did children of average ability, regardless of grade. When the children were asked about the strategy they had applied to remember the materials, average fourth-grade children reported using a more sophisticated recall strategy than did second-grade children of both ability levels. Robinson and Kingsley concluded that average children were as capable of formulating an appropriate strategy as were gifted children, but not as capable of executing it. Similarly, Keating and Bobbitt (1978) found that all subjects utilized a serial and exhaustive search strategy on a Sternberg memory scanning task, regardless of age and ability levels. The intelligent children, however, used the strategy more effectively, as evidenced by the fact that they were faster on the task, independent of the number of items in the set.

McCauley, Kellas, Dugas, and DeVillis (1976) trained a covert rehearsal strategy for use on a Sternberg recognition–memory task. Faster reaction times and faster rates of memory search were found for high-IQ fifth- and sixth-grade children. All children used the experimenter-trained rehearsal strategy and all children rehearsed equally often. Average-IQ children, however, tended to use the strategy primarily as an aid to storage, whereas gifted children tended to use the strategy to elaborate and associate "connections" between items. McCauley et al. (1976) concluded that the reaction time differences may have resulted from the greater depth to which target set items were processed (cf. Craik & Lockhart, 1972).

In summary, research on strategic behavior and giftedness has been inconclusive. Several authors have contended that individual differences in memory performance for children in the superior range of intelligence are characterized by the efficient use of strategies rather than the kinds of strategies used (Keating & Bobbitt, 1978; McCauley et al., 1976; Robinson & Kingsley, 1977). In addition, others have suggested that processing efficiency accounts for differences in cognitive performance more than does knowledge about or use of strategies (Cohen & Sandberg, 1977, 1980; Dempster, 1981). It should be noted that both of these interpretations generally rest on research that has failed to contrast perceptual efficiency and strategy use in the same design and on multiple tasks.

Metacognition

Several theorists have contended that metacognition (a person's awareness of his or her own cognitive machinery) is a vital component of intelligence (Brown, 1978; Flavell, 1978). Metacognitive knowledge is assumed to be crucial in the selection and implementation of problem-solving strategies, lower-level control processes, and higher-order executive routines. Metamemory, a subcomponent of metacognition, has gained increasing recognition in the literature on cognitive development (cf. Paris & Lindauer, 1982). This form of self-knowledge about the memory system's operations, capacities, and limitations underlies important aspects of efficient information processing (Borkowski, 1985). Generally, the more accurately children understand their own memory processes, the more likely they will be to use this knowledge in understanding the value of newly acquired strategies, thus incorporating their representations into long-term memory.

Geis and Corriher (1977) examined the memory knowledge of gifted and regular children using four metamemory questions adapted from the questionnaire developed by Kreutzer, Leonard, and Flavell (1975). The only significant finding was that a greater number of higher-IQ-than-average-IQ third-graders were able to explain why related words would be easier to remember than would be unrelated words. No other study has extensively analyzed metacognition in gifted and regular samples, even though the metacognitive component of the executive system may be important in understanding the emergence of strategic skills in gifted children (Borkowski & Kurtz, 1984).

Three generalizations can be drawn from research with gifted and regular children with respect to two key systems in the Campione and Brown model – efficiency of processing and executive functioning. First, gifted children seem faster at storing and accessing information in memory, especially when deeper levels of processing are required. Second, there is a trend in various accounts of intelligence to emphasize perceptual efficiency more than strategic behavior, as the major defining characteristic of gifted children. Third, few studies have contrasted multiple components of intelligence in order to determine their relative impact on learning processes in gifted and regular children. It is against this background that we assessed the importance of metamemory as a determinant of learning skills in gifted versus regular children.

The purpose of the two studies to be described was to advance our understanding of the intellectual development of gifted children and to isolate components of intelligence that contribute to their learning proficiencies. Experiment 1 was exploratory in nature – designed to identify major information-processing differences between gifted and regular children within the framework of the Campione–Brown (1978) model. Experiment 2 was a training study that focused on the emergence of strategic behavior in gifted and regular children, providing a context in which to contrast perceptual efficiency and metamemory as potential sources of individual differences in strategy maintenance and generalization.

Experiment 1: multiple components of intelligence

Research with gifted children has generally concentrated on a single component of intelligence, perceptual efficiency. Studies that have examined other components, such as strategic behavior, have often done so using perceptual efficiency tasks. We initially assessed gifted and regular children on a wide variety of achievement, perception, learning, and cognitive tasks. In Experiment 1, 78 gifted and regular children, ages 7 to 8, were selected from special programs in the Bellevue, Washington, school system.

The placement of children in the gifted group had been based on three criteria: full scale Wechsler Intelligence Scale for Children – Revised (WISC-R); combined scores on the reading comprehension and the math concepts subtests of the Stanford Achievement Test; and teacher evaluations of giftedness. The latter measure was a 20-question, 5-point scale assessing creativity, motivation, problem solving, and general knowledge. All of the gifted children scored in the superior range on the full-scale WISC-R and above the 98th percentile on either one or both of the Stanford Achievement subtests. In addition, they scored consistently high on the teacher evaluation scale. The gifted children were participating in a special enrichment program (1 hour per day, 5 days a week), designed to challenge and to stimulate their cognitive abilities. However, most children had been in the program less than 1 year.

A battery of eight tests was administered during three testing sessions. Perceptual efficiency was assessed by means of three tasks: Posner letter-matching (Posner & Mitchell, 1967), reaction time, and word-span tests. General knowledge was measured by the vocabulary and information subtests of the WISC-R. Metamemory indices were obtained in an extensive interview battery that assessed children's knowledge about memory states and processes (see Cavanaugh & Borkowski, 1980, or Kurtz et al., 1983, for details about items on the metamemory test). Finally, direct measures of strategy use were assessed on two memory tasks: sort–recall readiness and alphabet search. The former permitted a direct assessment of organizational behavior, whereas the latter assessed systematic retrieval strategies.

The analyses of the eight tests of the efficiency and executive systems confirmed many of our hypotheses, with gifted children enjoying a wide advantage over the regular children on most tasks. For instance, performance on the Posner letter-matching task suggested that gifted children were faster than regular children in accessing information from long-term memory. Also, gifted children were capable of storing and maintaining significantly more words than regular children in memory, as evidenced by differences on the word-span tests. These data are consistent with the prevalent hypothesis emerging from past research, stressing perceptual efficiency as a fundamental characteristic of giftedness Not surprisingly, they were also superior on the information and vocabulary tests, reflecting greater general knowledge about the world.

One of the more interesting and novel findings was the substantial difference between the gifted and regular samples on measures of metamemorial knowledge. Gifted children reported a greater number of strategies for retrieving information. They were more aware that the type of retrieval test (strict recall vs. gist recall) would influence performance. They knew that embedding to-be-remembered words in a story would aid in recall. They realized that an interest in the topic under study was an important determinant of ease of learning. In summary, gifted children were not only more capable of processing information efficiently and rapidly but also were superior to regular children in metamemorial knowledge and general knowledge.

In striking contrast was the data on strategy use. Spontaneous invention of appropriate strategies failed to differentiate the processing style of gifted and regular children on the two laboratory tests of learning and memory. This provocative finding suggested that gifted children, despite their meta-cognitive advantages, did not differ from regular children in strategic behavior or recall accuracy on tasks appropriate for their age levels. This anomaly served as the springboard for testing these same children one year later for strategy use on a variety of tasks following varying degrees of instruction.

Experiment 2: metamemory and the emergence of strategic behavior

The emergence of strategic behavior in gifted and regular children was analyzed in Experiment 2 following the training and transfer of multiple strategies.
The major hypothesis of this study centered on a contrast of differences in
strategy transfer in the sample of gifted and regular children who had been
tested a year previously on a variety of tests of the efficiency and executive
systems.

We assumed that gifted and regular children would be differentially affected
by the extent of training. Given extensive strategy training, all children should
perform equally well on maintenance and generalization tests. Differences in
performance due to giftedness were predicted following minimal strategy
training. That is, children with superior metamemories should be in a better
position to understand the full importance of the strategy even though it was
embedded in incomplete instructions. Finally, the quality of metamemory
should be related to the natural emergence of strategic behavior on a task
where no strategy training was provided.

Although this experiment focused on the importance of metamemory for
effective strategy use, it allowed for tests of competing explanations of strategy
transfer. As noted earlier, most models of giftedness feature processing efficiency, rather than strategic behavior, in the account of individual differences
surrounding cognitive performance (Cohen & Sandberg, 1977; Cohen & Sandberg, 1980; Dempster, 1981). The plausibility of the dominant account of
giftedness was tested by contrasting perceptual efficiency and metamemory
in terms of the strength of their relationships with learning proficiency. Does
metamemory predict strategy transfer better than perceptual efficiency?

Children from Session 1 (Experiment 1) were randomly assigned to experimental and control conditions. Those children in the experimental condition received varying degrees of strategy training on paired-associate and
sort–recall readiness tasks. Children in the control condition were administered the same tasks without benefit of strategy instructions. The major events
that transpired during the subsequent six sessions can be found in Table 8.1.

An elaboration strategy was taught following the administration of the
paired-associate task in Session 2 and again prior to its administration in
Session 3; this task was associated with complete or maximum training of the
elaboration strategy. Children were taught to execute four steps in producing
the elaboration strategy: (a) thinking about a possible relationship between
two items and verbalizing that relationship; (b) learning to form a "why"
question; (c) performing a semantic analysis of the items (i.e., What do I
know about each of these items?); and (d) forming a reason that explains the
relationship. All children were presented a new paired-associate list in Session
4 (the maintenance test), and a near-generalization test involving three-picture
sets in Session 5. Both accuracy and strategy use measures were obtained

Table 8.1. *Research design for Experiment 2*

Session 1	Session 2	Session 3
Pretest Posner task Vocab. (WISC)	Training of the paired-associate task (control groups received no instructions)	Training prior to the paired-associate task
Sort–recall task Alphabet search task Pretest metamemory	Sort–recall task (without training)	Training after the sort–recall task No training on the alphabet search task
Session 4 (Strategy maintenance – no training)	**Session 5** (Strategy generalization)	**Session 6**
Paired-assoc. test Sort–recall test Alphabet search test	Triad test (generalization of the paired-associate strategy) Cog. cuing test (generalization of the sorting strategy) Alphabet search (no training)	Posttest metamemory Posttest Posner task Far-generalization tests

during the maintenance and generalization tests. A far-generalization task was presented in Session 6; each child was asked how he or she might teach another child to remember city–state pairs.

The sort–recall readiness task was used to implement the minimal strategy training condition. Following the third administration of the sort–recall task in Session 3, children in the training condition received a brief explanation about how to use a clustering-rehearsal strategy, appropriate for the sorting task. A maintenance test was presented in Session 4, and a near generalization test (cognitive cuing) in Session 5; the cognitive cuing task required children to place picture cards in a file box that had category instances on the top of each container (cf. Borkowski et al., 1983). The far-generalization task presented in Session 6 consisted of 12 cards, with one sentence on each, describing the characteristics of a fictitious animal. The child was asked how he or she might teach another child to learn the story about the animal; the cards were clusterable into groups of four sentences each. For all administrations of the sort–recall readiness and the cognitive-cuing tasks, separate measures of input and output strategies as well as recall performance were recorded.

In Sessions 3, 4, and 5, an alphabet search task was given without strategy training. Output strategies and recall were again obtained for all administrations of this task. A posttest metamemory battery and a posttest letter-matching task were administered in Session 6. The interval between each session (2 to 5) was approximately 2 weeks; a 5-month interval separated Sessions 5 and 6. The focus of our interpretation of the findings centered on the three types of training and on metamemory–strategy use relationships.

Perhaps the most interesting results were found in the analyses of the relationships between metamemory and the emergence of strategic behavior. On the well-trained paired-associate task, children learned to use the elaboration strategy effectively, irrespective of ability level. The elaboration strategy was so well learned that decisions were not required for strategy implementation; the strategy was automatically employed on the maintenance test by all children. Hence, it is not surprising that metamemory was minimally involved in tests of strategy maintenance and near generalization (as shown by the absence of metamemory–strategy use correlations on the well-trained paired-associate task). Furthermore, gifted and regular children did not differ in strategy use on this task.

On the far-generalization test of the elaboration strategy, however, gifted children showed superior strategy scores. Here, metamemory was significantly correlated with strategy use, with the correlation remaining significant when perceptual efficiency and verbal IQ were partialed out. In contrast, no consistent relationships between perceptual efficiency and strategy use were found; such relationships might be expected if speed of encoding and decoding are implicated in a wide range of perceptual, learning, and memory tasks. In summary, gifted children adjusted the experimenter-generated elaboration strategy on the far-generalization test in the face of changing task demands. The correlations with metamemory suggest a reliance by the gifted children on advanced metamemorial knowledge, in order to extend the strategy to a new task especially when it had surface dissimilarity with the training task.

The influence of metamemorial awareness and executive processes on strategy transfer was more pronounced following minimal strategy training. As can be seen in Figure 8.1, gifted and regular children in Sessions 1, 2, and 3, prior to the introduction of the clustering strategy, used an unsophisticated rehearsal strategy to aid recall. However, significant differences in the use of organization emerged following minimal strategy training. As hypothesized, gifted children realized the effectiveness of the strategy and applied it appropriately even without the aid of complete and explicit instructions. As Figure 8.1 reveals, gifted children had significantly higher strategy scores than regular children during Session 4. It should be noted that strategy differences in Session 4 were paralleled by recall differences. Most importantly, significant metamemory–strategy use correlations obtained during Session 4 (the maintenance test) suggested that gifted children engaged in more metacognitive–executive processing than did regular children. In addition, metamemory correlated with strategy transfer on the far-generalization task. As with the maximally trained strategy, gifted children were more successful in implementing the minimally trained strategy in the face of new task demands. Furthermore, the metamemory–strategy use correlations at transfer remained

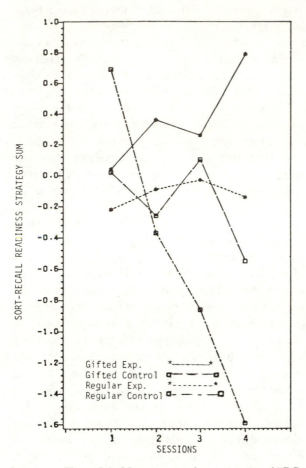

Figure 8.1. Mean *z* scores for strategy use (ARC scores) for gifted and regular experimental and control children on the sort–recall readiness task in Sessions 1, 2, 3, and 4.

significant when perceptual efficiency and IQ were partialed out; the converse was not found for measures of perceptual efficiency. These findings suggest that, given minimal training, metamemory is a more plausible account of strategy transfer than perceptual efficiency.

The next set of analyses center on the untrained, alphabet search task. Do gifted children develop strategies on their own, following repeated experiences with a task? We suspected an indirect effect on the untrained task: that is, strategy training on the other two tasks might prompt the development of an appropriate strategy for the untrained search task. Inspection of the data for the experimental and control conditions failed to confirm our expectation – at least not until the final session. As can be seen in Figure 8.2, all children initially applied an inefficient search strategy. As the task was presented a

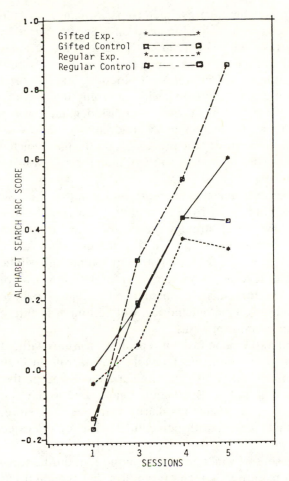

Figure 8.2. Mean ARC scores for gifted and regular experimental and control children on the alphabet search task in sessions 1, 3, 4, and 5.

second, third, and fourth time, the form of the strategy improved, as did recall, although the most appropriate retrieval strategy – an exhaustive search through the alphabet – was not extensively used. It is important to note that gifted experimental children finally developed a highly systematic search strategy on the final test session. In addition, recall was superior for gifted children during the last test of the alphabet search strategy (Session 5).

All of the data presented thus far find interpretation within metamemory theory. This theory provides a set of useful concepts to explain the emergence of strategic behaviors in gifted children. Metamemory is especially applicable in understanding how experimenter-generated strategies were put to use in new learning contexts. When a strategy applied to a task was well trained and automatic, metamemory was minimally related to performance variability, except on far-transfer tests where ability-related differences in strategy use were also found. In contrast, when children received incomplete strategy training, metamemory predicted strategy use and recall differences on both maintenance and generalization tests. Children with superior metamemories generally retained the trained strategy, applied it without prompting on transfer tasks, and modified the strategy to meet changes in task demands on far-generalization tests. In contrast, low-metamemory children were not as sophisticated in their use of these executive-type processes. On the uninstructed task, metamemory was eventually related to strategy monitoring following repeated learning opportunities.

The consistent correlations between metamemory and strategy use that emerged on all tasks can be considered from several perspectives. When a strategy is highly available, lower-level, strategy-specific metamemory will be only weakly related to performance variability. In this situation, knowledge about higher-level, executive processes useful for strategy monitoring will be related to performance; lower-level, strategy-specific information will be of little value in achieving good performance. It should be noted that we believe gifted children, with their advanced metamemories, will be found, in future research, to possess superior monitoring skills.

When children are presented the same task on repeated occasions without the benefit of clear strategy instruction, metamemory plays a role in both strategy acquisition and deployment. Children with superior metacognitive knowledge are more likely to fill in the "instructional gaps" and to develop appropriate strategies as they gain greater familiarity with the task. Here, metamemory plays the dominant role, with perceptual efficiency relegated less explanatory status.

There are a number of reasons why metamemory is important during strategy acquisition. For one, a mature metamemory implies that the child has had numerous past encounters with strategic-based learning. These experiences can then be drawn upon to prompt reflections about modifying a new strategy to meet current task demands or to round out incomplete instructions. In addition, a child with a rich metamemory will monitor the newly created strategy more actively than a child with an immature metamemory, resulting in strategy modifications across trials. Finally, when children receive minimal strategy training, metamemorial knowledge helps the child form hypotheses about other potential strategies or to seek out additional information about the task that might aid further strategy development. It is for these reasons that gifted children with their superior metamemories retain acquired strategies, apply them without prompting on transfer tests, and modify strategies appropriately to meet changing task demands in a manner different from their nongifted peers.

Conclusions: comparisons of components

The interpretations we have thus far developed lead us to believe that there is a critical level, or threshold, of metamemorial knowledge above which strategy transfer is more likely to occur. As Sternberg (1980) contends, metacomponential knowledge may be a limiting aspect in the intelligence system. When an individual is introduced to a novel task, or when vague strategy information is presented about a complex task, a child's metacomponential processing capacity may be exceeded, with strategy use appearing quite unsophisticated. Consider the implementation of the minimally trained organizational strategy in Experiment 2: When confronted with a new strategy, with few essential details, the child who possessed impoverished metamemorial knowledge was generally unable to utilize ("understand") the instructions because of the unavailability of relevant metamemorial information. That is, mature knowledge about the attributes necessary for specific strategy implementation was missing (cf. Pressley, Borkowski, & O'Sullivan, 1985). More importantly, the child may have failed to realize that information about when, where, and how to deploy the strategy was not included in the instructions. Such insights are necessary if the child is to "perfect" an incomplete strategy.

One additional point needs consideration in emphasizing the theoretical connection between metamemory and giftedness: General world knowledge as well as metamemorial knowledge differentiates gifted from regular children. Perhaps knowledge about the to-be-learned materials or other aspects of domain-specific knowledge were responsible for the effects we ascribed to metamemory. Although general knowledge is an important component of intelligence (Bransford et al., 1979; Ornstein & Corsale, 1979), its influence was minimized in the present study in two ways: (a) by presenting novel tasks not previously confronted by the children, and (b) by presenting stimulus items (letters or pictures) that were highly familiar. Levels of world knowledge will most likely contribute to performance on tasks in which the concepts needed to solve the problem are more difficult and complex than those employed in the present study.

Although Experiment 1 revealed that speed of processing information differentiated gifted from regular children, it was only weakly correlated with strategy transfer and recall accuracy in Experiment 2. The minor role we attribute to efficiency might well be related to the fact that the memory tasks prompted deliberate, controlled processing as opposed to effortless, automatic processing as required by most speeded tasks (cf. Sternberg, 1981). Efficiency will probably contribute to performance variability on tasks in which the processing demands are simple and in which well-learned, domain-specific knowledge is accessed automatically.

Adequate theories of cognition and intelligence in gifted children seem to require metacognition, as well as perceptual efficiency, in order to explain performance differences across a wide range of tasks and settings. Even more interesting is the potential causal role played by perceptual efficiency in the development of a gifted child's knowledge about mind. We conclude by speculating about this relationship.

Although we have contrasted the efficiency and executive systems in our research to date, we believe there are causal relationships linking the development of the two systems, especially during the preschool years. Parents likely observe the efficiency of their child's information-processing system very early in life. It is unlikely to go undetected if a child shows a keen ability to size up the environment, is attentive to novelty, displays a good short-term memory, and has fast response times accompanied by accurate judgments. On observing these characteristics of perceptual efficiency, parents likely respond with greater intellectual stimulation, including game playing and early encouragement to take on challenging tasks and puzzles. Attention to these stimulating activities requires the child to become more deliberate, effortful, and strategic.

Emerging from this enriched environmental context – originally prompted by signs of perceptual efficiency – the gifted preschool child gains the metacognitive advantages that we observed at ages 7 and 8, and that probably are present as early as 3 or 4. As we have seen, it is from these metacognitive states that planful, strategic behaviors emerge to help the child confront the challenges of new task demands. When viewed from this perspective, perceptual efficiency, perhaps the earliest hallmark of giftedness, becomes a distal cause of controlled processing, with metacognition the more proximal cause.

What is clear from our research on strategy transfer is that the components that underlie cognition and intelligence in gifted children are complicated and multifaceted. The threads that bind the causes and consequences of the efficiency and executive system, and their interactions across the major stages of development, demand careful unraveling. An increased use of multidimensional, longitudinal, and observational research will likely prove valuable in addressing the complexities of intelligence in gifted children. It seems only right that the search for the salient features of giftedness will challenge the limits of extant theory and methodology.

References

Atkinson, R. C., & Shiffrin, R. M. (1968). Human memory: A proposed system and its control processes. In K. W. Spence & J. T. Spence (Eds.), *The psychology of learning and motivation*. New York: Academic Press.

Borkowski, J. G. (1985). Signs of intelligence: Strategy generalization and metacognition. In S. Yussen (Ed.), *The development of reflection in children*. New York: Academic Press.

Borkowski, J. G., & Kurtz, B. (1984). Metacognition and special children. In B. Gholson & T. Rosenthal (Eds.), *Applications of cognitive development theory*. New York: Academic Press.

Borkowski, J. G., Peck, V., Reid, M. K., & Kurtz, B. (1983). Impulsivity and strategy transfer: Metamemory as mediator. *Child Development, 54,* 459–473.

Borkowski, J. G., Reid, M. K., & Kurtz, B. (1984). Metacognition and retardation: Paradigmatic, theoretical, and applied perspectives. In C. McCauley & P. Brooks (Eds.), *Learning and cognition in the mentally retarded*. Hillsdale, N.J.: Erlbaum.

Bransford, J. C., Franks, J. J., Morris, C. D., & Stein, B. S. (1979). Some general constraints on learning and memory research. In L. S. Cermak & F. I. M. Craik (Eds.), *Levels of processing in human memory*. Hillsdale, N.J.: Erlbaum.

Brown, A. L. (1970). Subject and experimental variables in the oddity learning of normal and retarded children. *American Journal of Mental Deficiency, 75,* 142–151.

Brown, A. L. (1978). Knowing when, where, and how to remember: A problem of metacognition. In R. Glaser (Eds.), *Advances in instructional psychology* (Vol. 1). Hillsdale, N.J.: Erlbaum.

Campione, J. C., & Brown, A. L. (1978). Toward a theory of intelligence: Contributions from research with retarded children. *Intelligence, 2,* 279–304.

Cavanaugh, J. C., & Borkowski, J. G. (1980). Searching for the metamemory–memory connection: A developmental study. *Developmental Psychology, 16,* 441–453.

Chi, M. T. H. (1978). Knowledge structures and memory development. In R. Siegler (Ed.), *Children's thinking: What develops?* Hillsdale, N.J.: Erlbaum.

Chi, M. T. H. (In press). Representing knowledge and meta-knowledge: Implications for interpreting metamemory research. In R. H. Kluwe & F. E. Weinert (Eds.), *Metacognition, motivation, and learning*. Hillsdale, N.J.: Erlbaum.

Clark, H. H., & Chase, W. G. (1972). On the process of comparing sentences against pictures. *Cognitive Psychology, 9,* 534–554.

Cohen, R. L., & Sandberg, T. (1977). Relation between intelligence and short-term memory. *Cognitive Psychology, 9,* 534–554.

Cohen, R. L., & Sandberg, T. (1980). Intelligence and short-term memory: A clandestine relationship. *Intelligence, 4,* 319–331.

Craik, F. & Lockhart, R. (1972). Levels of processing: A framework for memory research. *Journal of Verbal Learning and Verbal Behavior, 11,* 671–684.

Dempster, F. N. (1981). Memory span: Sources of individual and developmental differences. *Psychological Bulletin, 89,* 63–100.

Detterman, D. K. (1979). Memory in the mentally retarded. In N. Ellis (Ed.), *Handbook of mental deficiency: Psychological theory and research* (2nd ed.). Hillsdale, N.J.: Erlbaum.

Flavell, J. H. (1978). Metacognitive development. In J. M. Scandura & C. J. Brainerd (Eds.), *Structural process theories of complex human behavior*. Alphen a.d. Rijn, The Netherlands: Sijthoff and Noordhoff.

Flavell, J. H., & Wellman, H. M. (1977). Metamemory. In R. Kail & J. Hagen (Eds.), *Perspectives on the development of memory and cognition*. Hillsdale, N.J.: Erlbaum.

Ford, M. E., & Keating, D. P. (1981). Developmental and individual differences in long-term memory retrieval: Process and organization. *Child Development, 52,* 234–241.

Geis, M. F., & Corriher, S. E. (1977). Memory and organizational processes in high-IQ children. Paper presented at the biennial meeting of the Society for Research in Child Development, March. New Orleans.

Goldberg, R. A., Schwartz, S., & Stewart, M. (1977). Individual differences in cognitive processes. *Journal of Educational Psychology, 69,* 9–14.

Harris, G. J., & Fleer, P. B. (1974). High speed memory scanning in mental retardates: Evidence for a central processing deficit. *Journal of Experimental Child Psychology, 17,* 452–459.

Horn, J. (1978). The nature and development of intellectual abilities. In R. Osborne, C. Noble, & N. Weyl (Eds.), *Human variation: The biopsychology of age, race, and sex*. New York: Academic Press.

Hunt, E. (1978). Mechanics of verbal ability. *Psychological Review, 85,* 109–130.

Hunt, E., Frost, N., & Lunneborg, C. (1973). Individual differences in cognition: A new approach to intelligence. In G. Bower (Ed.), *The psychology of learning and motivation,* Vol. 7. New York: Academic Press.

Hunt, E., Lunneborg, C., & Lewis, J. (1975). What does it mean to be high verbal? *Cognitive Psychology, 7,* 194–227.

Jensen, A. (1963). Learning ability in retarded, average, and gifted children. *Merrill-Palmer Quarterly, 9,* 123–140.

Keating, D. P., & Bobbitt, B. L. (1978). Individual and developmental differences in cognitive processing components of mental ability. *Child Development, 49,* 155–167.

Kreutzer, M. A., Leonard, C., & Flavell, J. H. (1975). An interview study of children's knowledge about memory. *Monographs of the Society for Research in Child Development, 40* (1, Serial No. 159).

Kurtz, B. E., Reid, M. K., Borkowski, J. G., & Cavanaugh, J. C. (1982). On the reliability and validity of children's metamemory. *Bulletin of the Psychonomic Society, 19,* 137–140.

McCauley, C., Kellas, G., Dugas, J., & DeVillis, R. F. (1976). Effects of serial rehearsal training on memory search. *Journal of Educational Psychology, 68,* 474–481.

Ornstein, P. A., & Corsale, K. (1979). Organizational factors in children's memory. In C. R. Puff (Ed.), *Memory organization and structure.* New York: Academic Press.

Paris, S. G., & Lindauer, B. K., (1982). The development of cognitive skills during childhood. In B. W. Wohran (Ed.), *Handbook of developmental psychology.* Englewood Cliffs, N. J.: Prentice-Hall.

Posner, M.I., Boies, S. J., Eichelman, W. H., & Taylor, R. L. (1969). Retention of visual and name codes of single letters. *Journal of Experimental Psychology, 79,* 1–16.

Posner, M. I., & Mitchell, R. F. (1967). Chronometric analysis of classification. *Psychological Review, 74,* 392–409.

Pressley, M., Borkowski, J. G., & O'Sullivan, J. T. (1985). Children's metamemory and the teaching of memory strategies. In D. L. Forrest-Pressley, D. MacKinnon, & T. G. Waller (Eds.), *Metacognition, cognition, and human performance.* San Diego: Academic Press.

Robinson, J. A., & Kingsley, M. E. (1977). Memory and intelligence: Age and ability differences in strategies and organization of recall. *Intelligence, 1,* 318–330.

Spiegel, M. R., & Bryant, N. E. (1978). Is speed of information processing related to intelligence and achievement? *Journal of Educational Psychology, 70,* 904–910.

Sternberg, R. J. (1980). Sketch of a componential subtheory of human intelligence. *Behavioral and Brain Sciences, 3,* 573–614.

Sternberg, R. J. (1981). The evolution of theories of intelligence. *Intelligence, 5,* 209–230.

Sternberg, R. J. (1982). A componential approach to intellectual development. In R. J. Sternberg (Ed.), *Advances in the psychology of human intelligence* (pp. 413–463). Hillsdale, N.J.: Erlbaum.

Tannenbaum, A. J. (1983). *Gifted children.* New York: Macmillan.

Wachs, T. D. (1969). Free-recall learning in children as a function of chronological age, intelligence, and motivational orientation. *Child Development, 40,* 577–589.

Wechsler, D. (1958). *The measurement and appraisal of adult intelligence.* Baltimore: Williams & Wilkins.

9   The role of insight in giftedness

Janet E. Davidson

Almost everyone would agree that some individuals are more intellectually "gifted" than are others. Similarly, almost everyone recognizes the potentially great contributions that gifted individuals can make to the societies in which they live. Few people agree, however, on just what giftedness is.

In order fully to understand and develop the talents of gifted individuals, it is necessary to know (a) what giftedness consists of and (b) how giftedness can be identified. In addressing these issues, this chapter considers why some people are more intellectually gifted than others. It presents a subtheory of intellectual giftedness that takes into account individuals' insight abilities and the contribution these abilities make to intelligent behavior. However, no attempt will be made to provide a comprehensive theory of individual differences in intelligence. Although research will be presented in support of the view that insight abilities represent an important part of the story of individual differences in intelligence, it should be noted that insight abilities do not represent the whole story. Certainly, other psychological abilities and functions constitute additional parts of the story as well (see, e.g., Carroll, 1976; Hunt, 1978; Sternberg, 1981).

Before considering the nature of insight and its role in intellectual giftedness, it would be helpful to consider two major views regarding the nature and measurement of intelligence. These two views (which of course are not the only ones) are the psychometric and information-processing views. (For a further discussion of alternative views of intelligence, see Sternberg, 1982.)

According to the psychometric view, intelligence is conceived as comprising some set of latent mental abilities. Measurements are usually accomplished through the use of IQ tests consisting of a variety of timed tasks, such as analogies and spatial visualizations. Then, latent mental abilities are identified through the statistical method of factor analysis, which reduces a matrix of correlations between scores on the mental abilities tests to a smaller number of alleged latent sources of individual differences. For example, some individuals might be seen as superior to other individuals in their level of general

Preparation of this chapter was supported by a grant from the Spencer Foundation.

intelligence (Spearman, 1927) or in their levels of major mental abilities such as reasoning, verbal comprehension, or spatial visualization (Thurstone, 1938).

Information-processing views of intelligence arose in large part in response to the perceived failure of psychometric theorists to specify the underlying processes that constitute intelligent behavior. There are many information-processing views of intelligence: Different theorists examine different aspects of information processing. For example, Hunt (1978; Hunt, Davidson, & Lansman, 1981) has emphasized the role of speed of access to information in long-term memory in intelligent performance. In his earlier work, Sternberg (1977) viewed intelligent performance as attributable primarily to componential abilities. What is common to all information-processing views, however, is their emphasis on understanding intelligence in terms of underlying dynamic mental processes. The subtheory presented in this chapter is an example of an information-processing view; it emphasizes processes in insightful thinking.

Why use the study of insight abilities as a preferred entrée for examining intellectual giftedness? At least two bases exist for this preference.

First, significant and exceptional intellectual accomplishments – for example, major scientific discoveries, new and important inventions, and new and significant understandings of major literary, philosophical, and similar works – almost always involve major intellectual insights. The thinkers' gifts seem directly to lie in their insight abilities, rather than in their IQ-like abilities or in their mere abilities to process information rapidly. Indeed, it is now well known that some intellectually gifted individuals, such as Einstein and Watson, did not test particularly highly on IQ tests, for whatever reasons. Moreover, whereas truly intelligent individuals may have several major intellectual insights in their lifetimes, less intelligent individuals may have no (or very few) major intellectual insights in their lifetimes. Therefore, insight abilities seem to provide an important source of individual differences in intelligence.

Second, it is possible, in studying insight, to study problems in a wide variety of content domains. Insight is not a skill limited to any one particular domain. One need not, for example, discriminate against verbally talented individuals by concentrating only on mathematical problems, or to discriminate against the mathematically oriented by studying only verbal problems. Similarly, one need not discriminate against individuals with restricted educational opportunities by concentrating only on tasks that require large amounts of prior knowledge. Indeed, it seems important to show that a general theory of intellectual giftedness does extend beyond any one content domain. If one's goal is to avoid pitfalls of past theory and measurement, insight seems to provide a theoretically sound basis for understanding intelligent performance. But what do we know about insight itself? What is it, and how can insight ability be measured?

Conventional views of insight fall into two basic groups – the "special-process" views and the "nothing-special" views. Consider each of these views.

According to special-process views, insight is a process that differs in kind from other kinds of information processes. These views are most often associated with the Gestalt psychologists and their successors (e.g., Köhler, 1927; Maier, 1930; Wertheimer, 1959). Among these views are the ideas that insight results from extended unconscious leaps in thinking or flashes of inspiration, that it results from greatly accelerated mental processing, and that it is due to a short-circuiting of normal reasoning processes (see Perkins, 1981). In other words, the special abilities needed to solve insight problems are thought to be different from the more conventional abilities required to solve problems of the kinds found on intelligence and creativity tests. For example, Burke and Maier (1965) used a "hat rack" problem to study the relationship between problem solving and intelligence.

In the hat rack problem, the individual is required to build a structure, sufficiently stable to support a man's overcoat, using only two sticks and a C-clamp. The opening of the clamp is wide enough so that the two sticks can be inserted and held together securely when the clamp is tightened. Participants in the experiment are placed in a small room, and are asked to build a hat rack in the center of the room.

When people's ability to solve the hat rack problem was correlated with Verbal and Mathematical scores on the Scholastic Aptitude Test as well as with scores on tests of creativity, personality, and interests, the correlations were all trivial. In other words, whether or not people had the insight needed to solve the hat rack problem was unrelated to their scores on standardized tests. (In order to solve the hat rack problem, subjects have to see the relevance of the floor and ceiling of the room. The hat rack is formed by clamping the sticks together and wedging them between the floor and ceiling.) Burke and Maier concluded that the abilities needed to solve insight problems (such as the hat rack problem) may be different from the abilities required to solve problems of the kinds found, for example, on IQ tests. But they also conceded that other interpretations of their data were possible. Their study is of limited value, however: They used only one insight problem, and scored the responses only in terms of "right" or "wrong."

Although the special-process views are intuitively appealing, they seem to have at least three problematical aspects. First, they do not really pin down what insight is. Calling insight an "unconscious leap in thinking" or a "short-circuiting of normal reasoning" leaves insight pretty much as a "black box" of unknown contents. Even were one of these theories correct, just what insight is would still need to be identified. Second, the bulk of the evidence in support of these views is anecdotal rather than experimental, and for each piece of anecdotal evidence to support one of these views, there is at least one corresponding piece of evidence to refute it (Perkins, 1981). Finally, the positions are probably not specified enough, as they stand, to permit empirical test. As a result, it is not clear that the positions are even falsifiable.

In contrast to the "special-process" views, the "nothing-special" views propose that insight is merely an extension of ordinary processes of perceiving, recognizing, learning, and conceiving. Past failures to identify any special process of insight are attributed to the fact that there is no special process of insight (Perkins, 1981). Insights, according to the nothing-special views, are merely significant products of ordinary processes. For example, in a particularly ingenious set of experiments, Weisberg and Alba (1981) asked subjects to solve "classical" insight problems such as the "nine-dot" problem. In the nine-dot problem, people are given a 3 × 3 array of 9 equally spaced dots and are asked to connect the 9 dots with 4 straight lines without lifting pencil from paper. What was unique about Weisberg and Alba's design was that subjects were actually given the insight needed to solve the problem. (Subjects were told that the problem could be solved only by drawing the lines beyond the boundaries formed by the dots.) Weisberg and Alba found that even after they were given the insight, subjects still had considerable difficulty in solving the "insight" problem. They interpreted their results as suggesting that insight problems may not be insight problems at all. Instead, they argued, such problems may measure largely problem-specific prior knowledge.

The above example illustrates how arguments for the nothing-special views are arguments by default (because insight processes have not been identified, they have no independent existence). After repeated failures to identify a construct empirically, one can easily be tempted to ascribe the failure to the nonexistence of the construct. However, recent research (Davidson & Sternberg, 1982; Sternberg & Davidson, 1982) indicates that a main reason psychologists (and others) have had so much difficulty in isolating insight is that it involves not one process but three separate but related psychological processes. This chapter proposes that these three basic cognitive processes, when performed in novel and imaginative ways, form the basis for insightful thinking:

1. *Selective encoding*. Insight occurs in encoding when one sees in a stimulus, or set of stimuli, one or more things that have been nonobvious to oneself, to others, or to both. Significant problems generally present an individual with large amounts of information, only some of which is relevant to problem solution. An insight of selective encoding involves sorting out information that is relevant from information that is irrelevant for one's purposes.

One could cite many examples of selective encoding in real-world performance. Doctors are usually presented with a large amount of information regarding a patient's background and symptoms: An insightful doctor is able to sift out those facts that are relevant for diagnosis and treatment. The facts connected with a crime are often both numerous and confusing: An insightful detective is able to decide which of many potential clues are relevant to tracking down the perpetrator of the crime. Similarly, more insightful scientists seem better able than less insightful scientists to recognize what is important in their data. The less insightful scientists seem almost to evaluate their findings with a uniform distribution of weights. Sir Alexander Fleming's discovery of penicillin is a famous example of a selective encoding insight in science. Fleming had been attempting to grow bacteria, but his culture was spoiled by a certain kind of mold that inhibited bacterial growth. An ordinary scientist, not realizing the relevance of this occurrence, might have considered the experiment a failure. Fleming, however, noticed that what had started off as a mundane experiment had become a monumental one: He had discovered a way of killing bacteria via a mold named penicillin.

2. *Selective combination.* Insight occurs in combination when one puts together seemingly unrelated elements of a problem situation in a way that has been nonobvious to oneself, to others, or to both. The elements are all there and easy to see: The problem is how to combine them.

There are numerous examples of how selective combination insights operate in real-world situations. For instance, an insightful doctor is able to figure out how to combine information about various isolated symptoms in order to diagnose a given medical problem. An insightful detective is able to put together relevant clues in order to pinpoint the perpetrator of a crime. Similarly, many insightful scientists are able to fit their findings together into a coherent package or story. Less insightful scientists often seem not to realize how their various findings are related. They present their findings as isolated facts, rather than as part of a finely woven story about the phenomenon under investigation. Also, Darwin's formulation of the theory of evolution seems to have involved primarily an insight of selective combination. He had all of the facts for a long time: What Darwin finally discovered was how to put the facts together to form a coherent theory.

3. *Selective comparison.* Insight occurs in comparison when one discovers a nonobvious relationship between new information and information acquired in the past. It is here that analogies, metaphors, and models are used to solve problems: An insightful person realizes that new information is similar to old information in certain ways (and dissimilar to it in other ways), and then uses this information better to understand the newly acquired information.

One could cite any number of examples of selective comparison insights in operation. For instance, an insightful doctor may consider a previous patient whose symptoms resembled those of a present patient. The diagnosis relevant in the earlier case might well be relevant in the present case. An insightful detective often draws on his or her experience in order to solve a crime. The detective may bring to mind a previous case in which the clues fit into a similar pattern, and then use this case as a guideline for solving the newly committed crime. Similarly, many insightful scientists are able to relate their new work to previous work that has been conducted in the field. They have a sense of where their work fits into the current scientific picture, and of just what its contribution is to ongoing scientific research. Less insightful scientists often do not seem to know how their research is related to past research, and they may do their work without a clear understanding of why it is, or is not, worth doing. Kekulé's discovery of the structure of the benzene ring is a famous example of a selective comparison insight. Kekulé had a dream in which a snake curled back on itself and caught its own tail. When he awoke, Kekulé realized that the image of the curled snake was a metaphor for the structure he had been trying to decipher.

In sum, these three processes form the basis for a theory of insightful information processing. To the extent that there is a commonality in the three kinds of processes, it appears to be in the importance of selection to each kind. In encoding, one is selecting elements to encode from the often numerous possible elements that constitute the problem situation; the trick is to select the right elements. In combination, an individual is selecting one of many possible ways in which elements of information can be combined or integrated; the trick is to select the right way of combining the elements in a given situation. In comparison, an individual is selecting one (or more) of numerous possible old elements of information to which to relate new information. There are any number of relations that might be drawn; the trick is to select the right comparison or comparisons to make for one's purposes. It should be noted that not every instance of selective encoding, selective combination, or selective comparison is an instance of an insight: The products of these operations are referred to as "insights" when the cues in a given problem or situation are encoded, combined, or compared in nonstandard and novel ways.

This three-process theory of insightful information processing leads us to a subtheory of what it is that makes for individual differences in intelligence. According to the proposed subtheory, intelligence is in part a function of insight abilities. Some individuals are better able to have insights than are other individuals; this difference is related to differences in intelligence.

Individual differences in insight abilities may extend beyond quantitative differences in people's abilities to have each of the three kinds of insights. There may be qualitative differences in styles of insightful thinking that derive from a combination of ability in and preference for each of the three kinds of insights. Consider, for example, the scientist looking for ideas for experiments. Scientists have different preferred modes for coming up with ideas. These preferred modes may relate to the three kinds of insights. A scientist who peruses through journal articles in search of ideas for experiments might be one who prefers selective encoding as his means of coming up with ideas: He or she scans voluminous amounts of information, looking for something that will touch off experimental ideas. A scientist who likes to take existing theories and facts and see how they might fit together might be viewed as a selective combiner. A scientist who seeks analogies to phenomena outside his immediate field of endeavor, or who seeks any kind of physical model to explain scientific results, might be viewed as a selective comparer. The point to be made is that insightful people need not be particularly adept at attaining all three kinds of insights. They may prefer one or two of the kinds of insights as the means by which they achieve important discoveries. We have tested the quantitative aspects of the theory of individual differences in some research looking at fairly mundane kinds of insights. The subtheory of individual differences in intelligence provided an excellent account of the data from experiments that involved testing New Haven–area adults on mathematical word problems requiring various mixtures of the three kinds of insights (Davidson & Sternberg, 1982; Sternberg & Davidson, 1982). Consider some examples of the insight problems that were used in this research:

1. If you have black socks and brown socks in your drawer, mixed in the ratio of 4 to 5, how many socks will you have to take out to make sure of having a pair the same color?
2. Suppose you and I have the same amount of money. How much money must I give you so that you have ten dollars more than I?
3. Water lilies double in area every 24 hours. At the beginning of the summer there is one water lily on the lake. It takes 60 days for the lake to become covered with water lilies. On what day is the lake half covered?

Of these particular problems, the first emphasizes selective encoding, the second emphasizes selective combination, and the third emphasizes both selective encoding and selective combination. Selective comparison was measured by training subjects on sample problems that were similar to a few complex problems in the test booklet. Subjects could solve the test items only if they saw the connection between these items and the related sample problems. Some of the more interesting results from this research were that (a) some subjects have considerable difficulty knowing when to apply each of the three kinds of insights; (b) some subjects' use of selective comparison can be facilitated by certain instructional sets, and impeded by others; (c) the ability to apply all three kinds of insights is highly correlated with scores on a general intelligence test (roughly at the level of .6); and (d) higher-IQ subjects are slower, not faster, than lower-IQ subjects in analyzing the problems and applying the insights. However, it should be emphasized that this research provides only preliminary data regarding the empirical validity of the proposed subtheory.

The goal of a subsequent set of studies (Davidson & Sternberg, 1984) was to examine each of the three insight processes – selective encoding, selective combination, and selective comparison – in depth, and to look at the contribution each of these processes makes to individual differences in intelligence. These studies extended previous research in four ways. First, individuals in these studies were preselected so as to be of either high or average intelligence. By preselecting subjects on the basis of their intelligence, it was possible to monitor more closely the relationship between insight skills and intelligence. Second, unlike most studies of insight, the subjects in these studies were fourth- , fifth- , and sixth-grade children rather than adults. Using a different population of subjects made it possible to test the generality of the subtheory. Third, convergent–discriminant validation of the mathematical insight problems was tested by comparing performance on these problems with performance on other problems, some of which tapped the same insight processes and some of which did not. Of particular interest was the comparison between performance on the mathematical insight problems and performance on verbal insight problems. These two types of problems were thought to be different measures of the same psychological constructs. Finally, each of the three kinds of insight processes was isolated in subjects' performance. The isolation of these processes was accomplished by manipulating the amount of information available to the subjects. In particular, subjects received the insight problems either with or without cuing of one of the three kinds of insights. It was predicted that the highly intelligent children would spontaneously produce the insights required to solve the insight problems; therefore, they would profit very little from cuing of the insights. In contrast, it was believed that the children of average intelligence would have difficulty producing the required insights and, therefore, would benefit from the cuing.

Study 1: Convergent–discriminant validation

This study had two purposes. One purpose was to provide operational measures of each of the three kinds of insights through two different task vehicles – verbal insight problems and mathematical insight problems. It was hoped that the two task vehicles would provide converging operations on the psychological constructs, thereby freeing them from task specificity. The second purpose of this study was to determine whether performance on the two types of insight problems showed the predicted pattern of convergent–discriminant validation. In particular, it was expected that performance on the insight problems (a) would be better for intellectually gifted children than for children with average intellectual skills, and (b) would correlate highly with problems that differ in content from the mathematical and verbal problems but that tap some of the same insight processes. It was also predicted that performance on the insight problems would correlate next most highly with performance on inductive problems, which require the subject to go beyond the information given, and least highly with performance on deductive problems, which provide all information needed for solution.

Method

Subjects were 86 students (grades four to six) in an upper-middle-class suburban school district. Forty of the subjects had been identified by the school system as intellectually gifted on the bases of IQ test scores, Torrance creativity test scores (Torrance, 1974), class performance, achievement test scores, and teacher recommendations. These gifted children had an average score of 127 on the group-administered IQ test, with a range of scores of 109 to 148. The other 46 subjects had been indentified as having average intellectual skills. The mean IQ test score for this group was 107, with a range of scores of 84 to 128. Subjects were approximately equally divided between the sexes.

Five tests were administered in this study. All of the tests were given in booklet form and none of the problems made heavy demands on subjects' prior knowledge.

The first test consisted of 15 mathematical insight problems that were compiled from a number of puzzle books. These problems were similar to ones used in previous research (Davidson & Sternberg, 1982; Sternberg & Davidson, 1982) and they were equally divided with respect to their emphasis on selective encoding, selective combination, and selective comparison.

The second test consisted of 20 verbal insight problems that required subjects to define unknown words in various verbal contexts. For example, consider the following problem: "It was 6:30 P.M. and my QUETZ had just run out of ink. I hurried to the store to buy another one, but I was too late. The store was closed." In this case, subjects had to figure out what QUETZ meant, based on information in the problem. Like the mathematical problems, some of the verbal insight problems emphasized selective encoding, some emphasized selective combination, and others emphasized selective comparison.

The third test consisted of 10 short mystery stories. In these mysteries, subjects had to use selective encoding, selective combination, and selective comparison, as well as other processes, to figure out how a detective knew the identity of the perpetrators of various crimes.

The fourth test consisted of 15 inductive reasoning problems, Letter Sets, from the Kit of Reference Tests for Cognitive Factors (French, Ekstrom, & Price, 1963). In this test, subjects were presented with five sets of letters – for example, NOPQ DEFL ABCD HIJK UVWX – and were asked to choose the set of letters that was based on a rule different from the rule used as basis for the other four sets.

Finally, subjects were given 15 deductive reasoning problems, Nonsense Syllogisms, which were also taken from the Kit of Reference Tests for Cognitive Factors. In this test, subjects were presented a problem such as "All trees are fish. All fish are horses. Therefore, all trees are horses," and were asked to indicate whether the conclusion was logically valid or not.

Intellectual level (between subjects) was crossed with problems measuring the three types of insights (within subjects). The dependent variables in this study were the numbers of correctly solved mathematical insight problems and verbal insight problems. The independent variables were (a) intellectual level, and (b) performance on the reference tests (mysteries, inductive reasoning, deductive reasoning, and IQ).

Table 9.1. *Correlations of the insight measures with the reference tests*

Reference tests	Insight measures[a]	
	Math	Verbal
Deductive test	.43***	.40***
Inductive test	.53***	.52***
Mysteries	.55***	.53***
IQ test	.55***	.72***
Math–verbal insight measures	.65***	

[a]*** $p < .001$

Subjects were tested in groups of from 10 to 25 members. Testing took place in two sessions. During the first session, subjects were given the mathematical insight problems followed by the verbal insight problems. During the second session, subjects were given the mysteries, then the inductive reasoning test, and, finally, the deductive reasoning test. Subjects were asked to do their best to solve each problem and to show their work on each problem. Subjects were given as much time as they needed to solve the problems.

Results

As predicted, the subjects with high intellectual ability did better than the subjects with average intellectual ability on both the mathematical and verbal insight problems. The respective mean numbers of mathematical problems correct (out of 15 possible) were 8.45 for the highly intelligent children (with a standard deviation of 2.82 and a range of 3 to 13) and 5.36 for the children of average intelligence (with a standard deviation of 1.95 and a range of 2 to 10). The difference between the two means was statistically significant. The respective mean numbers of verbal problems correct (out of 20 possible) were 15.69 for the highly intelligent children (with a standard deviation of 2.77 and a range of 6.5 to 19.5) and 9.71 for the children of average intellectual ability (with a standard deviation of 2.31 and a range of 4 to 16). The difference between these two means was also significant. Correlations of performance on the mathematical and verbal insight problems with performance on the reference tests are shown in Table 9.1.

Although the differences between correlations were not significant, the correlations seemed at least to fall into the expected pattern. The lowest correlation was between the insight problems and the deductive reasoning test, which does not require one to go beyond the information given. Intermediate correlations were obtained between the two kinds of insight problems and the mysteries and the inductive reasoning test. The highest correlation was obtained between the mathematical insight problems and the verbal insight problems, despite surface-structural differences between these two types of problems. The mathematical and verbal insight measures were also significantly correlated with a standard measure of intelligence that had been administered by the schools.

The results from this study indicate that highly intelligent children perform better than children of average intelligence on both mathematical and verbal insight problems. The external validity of the insight measures was also established. The two types of insight measures were highly correlated (a) with each other, and (b) with other measures used to assess intellectual ability. The insight measures were less highly correlated with deductive reasoning.

Study 2: Selective encoding

The purpose of this study was to examine the process of selective encoding in some detail. In particular, the study attempted to show that (a) problems asserted to measure selective encoding do in fact measure this skill; (b) when the selective encoding component is removed from these problems, they become less potent predictors of intelligence; and that (c) selective encoding is an important factor in intelligent performance.

Method

Subjects were 78 of the students that participated in Study 1. Thirty-nine of these subjects had been identified as intellectually gifted and 39 had been identified as having average intellectual skills. Because of absenteeism, Studies 2 through 4 had fewer subjects than did Study 1.

Subjects received two booklets containing 12 problems each. One of the booklets was presented in cued form and the other booklet was presented without cues. Six of the problems in each booklet were selective encoding problems; they contained both relevant and irrelevant information. When these problems were cued, the solution-relevant parts were underlined. For example, the following problem was either given in normal form, or with the relevant information highlighted, as shown: "A farmer buys 100 animals for $100. *Cows are $10 each*, sheep are $3 each, and pigs are 50 cents each. *How much did he pay for 5 cows?*" The other six problems in each booklet contained only relevant information and involved insights of selective combination. These problems were designated as "nonselective" encoding problems for the purpose of this study. When the nonselective encoding problems were presented in cued form, the entire problem was underlined.

Intellectual level was crossed with level of cuing (cuing vs. no cuing) and type of problem (selective encoding vs. nonselective encoding). The independent variables were (a) intellectual level (between subjects), (b) level of cuing (within subjects), and (c) type of problem (within subjects). The dependent variables were number of selective encoding problems and number of nonselective encoding problems correctly solved in the cued and noncued conditions. The nonselective encoding problems were included in this study in order to show that any improvement in cued performance resulted specifically from cuing the selective encoding insight rather than from the cuing manipulation in general.

Subjects received the two test conditions in a counterbalanced order. In other words, half of the subjects received the cued problems followed by the noncued problems, and half of the subjects received the noncued problems followed by the cued problems. Which booklet was or was not cued was also counterbalanced. In other words, one booklet was given with cues to half of the subjects, and the same booklet was presented without cues to the other subjects.

In the noncued condition, subjects were given the following instructions: "When you read each problem, try to figure out which information is important and which is irrelevant. If you know which information is important and which information is misleading, you will find that many of the problems are easy to solve. Sometimes you will need only a small part of the information in a problem. Other times you will need all of the information. Please do your best to solve each problem and show all of your work." In the cued condition, the instructions were: "You will find that words in each problem are underlined. Underlined words tell you that the information is important for solving the problem. Words that are not underlined are irrelevant to the problem and can be misleading. Focus only on the underlined information and do not concentrate on words that are not underlined. Sometimes an entire problem is underlined. This tells you that everything is important. Please do your best to solve each problem and show all of your work." Subjects were given as much time as they needed to solve the problems.

Results

There were five major predictions regarding the results.

First, it was predicted that highly intelligent children would perform better on the insight problems than would children of average intelligence. This prediction was confirmed, with respective mean insight scores (out of 24 possible) of 16.32 and 9.77. The difference in performance between the two groups of subjects was significant.

Second, it was predicted that performance on the cued problems would be better than performance on the noncued problems. This prediction was also confirmed. Mean scores were 7.26 for cued problems and 5.79 for noncued problems (out of 12 possible). An analysis of variance indicated that there was a significant difference in performance between the cued and noncued conditions.

Third, it was predicted that, overall, performance would be better on the selective encoding problems than on the nonselective encoding problems. The reason for this prediction is as follows. For problems that were noncued, there need not be a difference between means for encoding and nonencoding problems. However, for cued problems, performance should be better on the encoding problems because the cuing selects out that subset of information that is relevant for problem solution. Because all information is relevant in the nonencoding problems, cuing does not provide the insight needed to solve these problems. Thus, there should be a main effect of selective encoding due to the facilitation of performance by cuing only for the encoding, but not the nonencoding, problems. This prediction was confirmed. Mean scores were 6.84 for encoding problems and 6.21 for nonencoding problems (out of 12 possible).

Fourth, it was predicted that there would be a significant cuing-by-encoding interaction. Indeed, the last main-effect prediction was a derivative of this predicted interaction, namely, that cuing would help for encoding, but not for nonencoding problems. If the cued information did genuinely facilitate selective encoding, then this interaction should be significant. This prediction was also confirmed. Means were 2.99 for noncued nonencoding problems, 3.22 for cued nonencoding problems, 2.80 for noncued encoding problems, and 4.04 for cued encoding problems (all out of 6 possible).

Fifth, and finally, it was predicted that there would be a significant triple interaction among the effects of intellectual level, cuing, and encoding. Such an interaction would occur if there were a greater facilitation by cuing for children of average intelligence than for highly intelligent children, and if this facilitation were greater for encoding than for nonencoding problems. In other words, according to the proposed subtheory of intelligence, the highly intelligent children would spontaneously select relevant information from the selective encoding problems; providing the cuing would be of little help to them. Children of average intelligence, however, would have difficulty in producing the proper insight. Thus, providing them with the insight of selective encoding should be quite helpful. This prediction, too, was confirmed: There was a significant Intellectual Level × Cuing × Encoding interaction. Examination of the eight relevant means confirmed that the interaction resulted from the predicted pattern of results. In this study, and in the ones that follow, differential performance of the highly intelligent children and the children of average intelligence was not due to ceiling effects, which did not occur in any of the studies.

To conclude, the results of this study were wholly consistent with the five major predictions. The results thus supported the proposed role of selective encoding as critical to solution of insight problems, and as an important factor in individual differences in intelligence.

Study 3: Selective combination

This study was similar to Study 2, with the exception that the focus of study was the selective combination insight rather than the selective encoding insight. In particular, the study attempted to show that (a) problems asserted to measure selective combination do in fact measure this skill; (b) when the selective combination component is removed from these problems, they become less potent predictors of intelligence; and that (c) selective combination is an important factor in individual differences in intelligence.

Method

Subjects were 70 of the students that participated in Studies 1 and 2. Half of these subjects had been identified as intellectually gifted, and half had been identified as having average intellectual skills.

Two booklets were used in this study, with each booklet containing eight selective combination problems. In these problems, more than one piece of information had to be combined or integrated for problem solution. One of the booklets was presented in cued form and the other booklet was presented without cues. Consider an example of a problem and how it was cued:

There are five people sitting in a row at a dinner party.

Scott is seated at one end of the row.

Ziggy is seated next to Matt.

Joshua is not sitting next to Matt or Scott.

Only one person is sitting next to Walter.

Who is sitting next to Walter?

In its uncued form, the problem was presented just as above. In its cued form, a diagram appeared directly below the problem. This diagram consisted of five rectangles placed one immediately horizontally adjacent to the next. The name *Scott* was written in the farmost left rectangle. The subject was thereby shown how to organize the relations among the terms of the problem, and was given a clue as to the location of one individual at the table. It should be noted that not all of the cued problems involved diagrams. Some of the problems were cued with a list of steps that the subject needed to complete in order to obtain the correct solution.

Intellectual level was crossed with level of cuing (cuing vs. no cuing). The independent variables were intellectual level (between subjects) and level of cuing (within subjects). The dependent variables were the number of problems correctly solved in the cued and noncued conditions.

Subjects received the two test conditions in a counterbalanced order. In other words, half of the subjects received the cued problems followed by the uncued problems, and half of the subjects received the uncued problems followed by the cued problems. Which booklet was or was not cued was also counterbalanced. In the uncued condition, subjects were told to do their best on each problem and to show all of their work. In the cued condition, the subjects were given the following instructions: "Below each problem, you will see a chart or a set of steps. These clues will help you solve the problem. Try to complete the chart or steps before you answer the question. Please do your best on each problem and show all of your work." Subjects were given as much time as they needed to solve the problems.

Results

There were three main predictions for this study. First, it was predicted that the highly intelligent children would perform better on the insight problems than would the children of average intelligence. This prediction was confirmed, with respective mean insight scores (out of 16 possible) of 13.00 and 8.31 for the highly intelligent subjects and the subjects of average intelligence. The difference in performance between the two groups of subjects was significant. Second, it was predicted that performance on the cued problems would be superior to performance on the noncued problems. This prediction was also confirmed. Mean scores were 5.82 on the cued problems and 4.84 on the noncued problems (out of 8 possible). Finally, it was predicted that there would be a significant Intellectual Level × Cuing interaction, with the subjects of average intelligence profiting more from the cuing than the highly intelligent subjects. This prediction, too, was confirmed. Relevant means for the highly intelligent subjects were 6.56 on the noncued problems, and 6.44 on the cued problems. Relevant means for the subjects of average intelligence were 3.11 on the noncued problems, and 5.20 on the cued problems (all out of 8 possible). As in Study 2, the children of average intellectual ability profited more from receiving the insight than did the highly intelligent children. The highly intelligent children spontaneously used selective combination in solving the insight problems.

In sum, this study supports the proposed subtheory of individual differences in intelligence. In particular, selective combination appears to play an important role in solving certain insight problems. Moreover, it appears to be a primary source of difficulty for children of average intelligence but not for highly intelligent children.

Study 4: Selective comparison

The purpose of the final study was to assess the role of selective comparison in insightful problem solving. This study was parallel to Studies 2 and 3 in intent and in most aspects of execution. The major difference was that, in this study, there were four conditions of item cuing in a between-subjects design.

Subjects were 80 of the students that participated in Study 1. Forty of these subjects had been identified as intellectually gifted and 40 had been identified as having average intellectual skills. Ten highly intelligent subjects and ten children of average intelligence were each assigned to one of four experimental conditions.

One test booklet containing 12 problems was administered in this study. There were also two worked-out example problems preceding the test problems. Six of the test problems in the booklet were extremely difficult and it was believed that they could only be solved if the subjects had learned similar examples; these problems were designated as "comparison" problems. Three of these six problems required the same solution procedure as the first example in the tests' instructions, and the other three problems were based on the same solution procedure as the second example in the instructions. For instance, one of the examples was: "You are flipping a fair coin. So far it has come up heads 10 times and tails 1 time. What are the chances that it will come up tails the next time that you flip the coin?" One test problem corresponding to this example was: "There are an equal number of red, white, and blue gum balls in a penny gum machine. Sandy spent 6 pennies last week and got 5 red gum balls and 1 white one. What are the chances that if she puts in one penny today she will get a red gum ball?" The other six problems in the booklet were selective encoding and selective combination problems, and were thus designated as "noncomparison" problems for the purpose of this study. The noncomparison problems were not similar to either of the examples in the tests' instructions.

Intellectual level was crossed with level of precuing and type of problem (selective comparison vs. noncomparison). The independent variables were (a) intellectual level (between subjects), (b) level of precuing (between subjects), and (c) type of problem (within subjects). The dependent variables were number of selective comparison problems and number of noncomparison problems correctly solved. There were four levels of precuing in this study:

Condition 1 (control): Subjects received the test problems with no precuing (i.e., prior problems of analogous structure).

Condition 2: Subjects received the test problems with precuing. No explicit mention was made of the fact that the solution procedures used in the sample problems could be used in some of the test problems.

Condition 3: Subjects received the test problems with precuing. Explicit mention was made of the fact that the solution procedures used in the sample problems could be used in some of the test problems. Subjects were not told which sample problems were related to which test problems, however.

Condition 4: Subjects received the test problems with precuing. They were not only explicitly told that the solution procedures used in the sample problems could be used in some of the test problems, but they were also told which sample problems were related to which test problems.

The successive amounts of precuing were used in an attempt to isolate several possible loci of selective comparison insights: having available prior information that can be used in current problem solving (Condition 2 vs. Condition 1); recognizing that prior information can be used in current problem solving (Condition 3 vs. Condition 2); knowing exactly what prior information is relevant for each particular problem that needs to be solved (Condition 4 vs. Condition 3).

With the exception of the subjects in Condition 1, subjects received two different example problems before receiving the test booklet. After subjects read the example problems, the nature of the problems was explained to them, and they were given a detailed explanation of how to solve each example. After everyone understood the example problems, subjects received the test booklet. (Subjects in Condition 1 received the test booklet without the examples.) Subjects in Conditions 1 and 2 did not receive special instructions about the test problems. Subjects in Condition 3 were told that the examples were relevant to the solution of some of the test problems. Subjects in Condition 4 were told that the examples were relevant to the solution of some of the test problems, and were explicitly told which examples were relevant for which problems. All subjects were told to do their best on each problem and to show all of their work. Subjects were given as much time as they needed to solve the problems.

Results

There were five major predictions regarding the results.

First, it was predicted that the highly intelligent children would perform better than the children of average intelligence. This prediction was confirmed, with respective mean scores (out of 12 possible) of 7.7 and 4.99 for the highly intelligent children and the children of average intellectual ability. The difference in performance between the two groups of subjects was significant.

Second, it was predicted that some of the problems would become easier as more selective comparison information was provided to the subjects. This prediction was also confirmed. Mean scores (out of 12 possible) were 4.45 for Condition 1, 5.78 for Condition 2, 7.30 for Condition 3, and 7.85 for Condition 4. The difference in performance between the four conditions was significant.

Third, it was predicted that, overall, the comparison problems, for which the precuing manipulation would be expected to provide facilitation, would be easier than the noncomparison problems, for which the precuing manip-

Table 9.2. *Mean number of correctly solved problems, as a function of condition, problem type, and intellectual level*

	Comparison problems		Noncomparison problems	
	High intelligence	Average intelligence	High intelligence	Average intelligence
Condition 1	1.70	1.30	3.90	2.00
Condition 2	4.60	1.55	3.30	2.10
Condition 3	4.70	3.50	3.90	2.50
Condition 4	4.80	4.80	3.90	2.20

ulation would be expected to provide no facilitation. Again the prediction was confirmed: Respective means were 3.37 for comparison problems and 2.60 for noncomparison problems (out of 6 possible). The difference in performance on the comparison and noncomparison problems was significant.

Fourth, it was predicted that there would be a significant interaction between the effects of condition and comparison. The last main effect was a derivative of this predicted interaction, namely, that the comparison problems would become easier as more selective comparison information was provided to the subjects, but the noncomparison problems would not become easier. This prediction, too, was confirmed. In Condition 1, means were 1.5 for comparison problems and 2.95 for noncomparison problems; in Condition 2, means were 3.08 for comparison problems and 2.70 for noncomparison problems; in Condition 3, means were 4.1 for comparison problems and 3.2 for noncomparison problems; in Condition 4, means were 4.8 for comparison problems and 3.05 for noncomparison problems (all out of 6 possible). The Condition × Comparison interaction was significant.

Fifth, and finally, it was predicted that there would be a significant triple interaction among the effects of intellectual level, condition, and comparison. Such an interaction would follow if there were a greater facilitation by successive amounts of relevance information for children of average intelligence than for highly intelligent children, and if this facilitation were greater for comparison than for noncomparison problems. The prediction of a significant Intellectual Level × Condition × Comparison interaction was confirmed. Examination of the 16 relevant means confirmed that the interaction resulted from the predicted pattern of results.

The relevant means are shown in Table 9.2. Note that on the comparison problems, the highly intelligent subjects benefited only from the receipt of examples. Relevance information seemed to have little or no effect on their performance. However, when no prior examples were given, the performance of the highly intelligent subjects and the less intelligent subjects was similar on the comparison problems, indicating that performance was due to selective comparison rather than to some unidentified problem-solving skills in which the highly intelligent subjects might have been superior. Unlike the highly intelligent children, the children of average intelligence benefited incrementally on the comparison problems as each further amount of information was given to them. When the relevance of the examples was made fully explicit, the children of average intelligence performed as well as the highly intelligent children performed without any relevance information.

In sum, this study supports the proposed subtheory of individual differences in intelligence. In particular, selective comparison appears to play an important role in solving insight problems. Moreover, it appears to be an important factor in distinguishing highly intelligent individuals from less intelligent individuals. Highly intelligent subjects seem to perform spontaneously the selective comparison that less intelligent subjects perform only when prompted.

Implications of results of studies

The results from the four studies support both the three-process theory of insightful information processing and the subtheory of individual differences in intelligence. Selective encoding, selective combination, and selective comparison were found to play an important role in the solution of insight problems, and in individual differences in intelligent behavior. The results from this study replicate and extend the findings from previous research using adults (Davidson & Sternberg, 1982; Sternberg & Davidson, 1982).

In particular, Study 1 showed that highly intelligent children perform better than less intelligent children on mathematical and verbal insight problems. The convergent–discriminant validity of the insight measures was established by showing that (a) performance on the mathematical insight problems was highly correlated with performance on the verbal insight problems, (b) performance on both types of problems was highly correlated with performance on standard measures of intellectual ability, and that (c) performance on both types of problems was less highly correlated with performance on problems that did not require subjects to go beyond the information given. Study 2 isolated the process of selective encoding and demonstrated that highly intelligent children spontaneously select and apply relevant information from insight problems, whereas children of average intelligence need cues to use the relevant information. Study 3 isolated the process of selective combination and showed that highly intelligent children spontaneously combine and integrate relevant information. In contrast, less intelligent children need cues to guide them in the combination of information. Finally, Study 4 isolated the process of selective comparison and demonstrated that highly intelligent children spontaneously apply relevant examples when solving insight problems. Children of average intelligence, on the other hand, need fairly explicit instructions before they benefit from prior information.

It should be emphasized that there are limitations to these findings on insight abilities and their role in individual differences in intelligence. First, the kinds of problems studied certainly did not involve major insights. The three-process theory of insight needs to be tested on more consequential kinds of insight problems before any strong conclusions can be drawn. Second, IQ and reasoning tests served as external criteria. In order fully to examine the role that insight abilities play in intelligent behavior, significant creative and intellectual accomplishments should also be used as external criteria. Finally, it is not clear whether the three kinds of insight constitute three distinct sources of individual differences, or, rather, fewer sources by virtue of their derivation from some "higher-order" insight ability. This question remains open to empirical determination of its answer.

Despite the above-mentioned limitations, it is believed that the approach used in this study provides an important supplement to alternative psychometric and information-processing approaches to understanding and assessing individual differences in intelligence.

First, the approach presented in this chapter differs from many psychometric and information-processing approaches in starting with a theory and proceeding to task selection, rather than the other way around. Factor theories of intelligence have traditionally been derived as a function of the tasks selected. One starts with a standard battery of conventional psychometric tests, and then proceeds to factor analyze them in one way or another, and to rotate the obtained factors. Information-processing theorists have often started either with the standard psychometric tasks or the standard information-processing tasks and then developed theoretical accounts on the basis of performance on these tasks. The advantage of such an approach is that one starts with tasks that are "time-honored" and whose properties are well known. The disadvantage is that the possibility for discovering new knowledge about individual differences in intelligence may be restricted. The approach presented in this chapter extends previous approaches by examining "nonentrenched" performance in a "nonentrenched" way.

Second, the proposed approach does not use the kinds of low-level information-processing tasks that characterize much experimental–psychological research on intelligence. For example, tasks involving speed at naming letters of the alphabet provide one basis for differentiating levels of intelligence. However, there seems also to be a need for the use of information-processing tasks that examine higher-order differences in intelligence. Insight problems provide one method of understanding and assessing higher-order processes that distinguish highly original thinkers from more ordinary ones.

Third, the proposed approach avoids the extreme emphasis on speed that characterizes many psychometric and information-processing assessments of intellectual abilities. Despite the many fine features of reaction time or speeded responses, in general, as dependent variables, they seem to need supplementation when one's goal is to understand or assess individual differences in intelligent behavior. Whereas almost all measures of intelligence emphasize highly speeded performance, major intellectual products tend to be produced over days, weeks, months, or years (but certainly not seconds).

Finally, the measurement of insight skills can take place in the absence of items that make heavy demands on prior knowledge. Therefore, it is possible to study individual differences in thinking skills, without having to control for individual differences in prior knowledge.

The present research also contributes to our knowledge about insight. In contrast to the "special-process" views of insight, the results from the present study indicate that performance on insight problems is highly related to intelligence. These results also indicate that there is more than one cognitive process that forms the basis for insightful performance. The reason that Perkins (1981) and other proponents of the "nothing-special" views have not found any commonality across all of the various insights they have studied may stem from the fact that insight is not simply one process that works for all cases. Providing one kind of insight for subjects may not be sufficient for problem solution if other kinds of insights are also needed.

The proposed approach may also help us understand puzzling results from other studies. For example, in the Weisberg–Alba study mentioned near the beginning of the chapter, providing subjects with the insight assumed to be necessary to solve the nine-dot problem did not automatically make the problem easy for them. From the present point of view, this may be because solution of the problem requires a selective combination insight (how to combine the four lines) as well as the selective encoding insight (the lines can go outside the periphery of the dots) that the investigators gave the subjects. In other words, it would have been necessary to provide two insights, not just one, to render the problem easily soluble by the subjects. Similarly, Maier's hat rack problem is so difficult because it involves not just one insight but multiple insights. A selective encoding insight is needed to recognize the relevance of the floor and the ceiling. A further selective encoding insight is needed in those versions of the problem that have multiple task-irrelevant objects strewn around the room. A selective combination insight is needed to see how to combine the elements – floor, ceiling, two rods, and the C-clamp – into a hat rack. And a selective comparison insight may be needed to recognize that hats can hang from objects that look like a C-clamp, even if they are not, in fact, C-clamps. The point to be made, then, is that analysis of traditional insight problems through the theory presented in this chapter makes clear just why people have traditionally found them to be so difficult to solve.

In conclusion, this chapter proposes that insight abilities provide a useful approach to understanding and assessing individual differences in intelligence. This new approach to the study of individual differences in intelligence and to the study of insight provides a useful complement to previously tested approaches.

References

Burke, R. J., & Maier, N. R. F. (1965). Attempts to predict success on an insight problem. *Psychological Reports, 17*, 303–310.

Carroll, J. B. (1976). Psychometric tests as cognitive tasks: A new structure of intellect. In L. B. Resnick (Ed.), *The nature of intelligence* (pp. 27–56). Hillsdale, N.J.: Erlbaum.

Davidson, J. E., & Sternberg, R. J. (1982, November). Insights about insight. Paper presented at the annual meeting of the Psychonomic Society, Minneapolis.

Davidson, J. E., & Sternberg, R. J. (1984). The role of insight in intellectual giftedness. *Gifted Child Quarterly, 28*, 58–64.

French, J. W., Ekstrom, R. B., & Price, I. A. (1963). *Kit of reference tests for cognitive factors.* Princeton, N.J.: Educational Testing Service.

Hunt, E. (1978). Mechanics of verbal ability. *Psychological Review, 85*, 109–130.

Hunt, E., Davidson, J. E., & Lansman, M. (1981). Individual differences in long-term memory access. *Memory and Cognition, 9*, 599–608.

Köhler, W. (1927). *The mentality of apes* (2nd ed.). New York: Harcourt Brace.

Maier, N. R. F. (1930). Reasoning in humans: I. On direction. *Journal of Comparative Psychology, 12* 115–143.

Perkins, D. (1981). *The mind's best work.* Cambridge, Mass.: Harvard University Press.

Spearman, C. (1927). *The abilities of man.* New York: Macmillan.

Sternberg, R. J. (1977). *Intelligence, information processing, and analogical reasoning: The componential analysis of human abilities.* Hillsdale, N.J.: Erlbaum.

Sternberg, R. J. (1981). Intelligence and nonentrenchment. *Journal of Educational Psychology, 73*, 1–16.

Sternberg, R. J. (Ed.). (1982). *Handbook of human intelligence.* Cambridge University Press.

Sternberg, R. J., & Davidson, J. E. (1982, June). The mind of the puzzler. *Psychology Today*, pp. 37–44.

Thurstone, L. L. (1938). *Primary mental abilities.* Chicago: University of Chicago Press.

Torrance, E. P. (1974). *The Torrance Tests of Creative Thinking: Norms-technical manual.* Bensenville, Ill.: Scholastic Testing Service.

Weisberg, R. W., & Alba, J. W. (1981). An examination of the alleged role of "fixation" in the solution of several "insight" problems. *Journal of Experimental Psychology: General, 110*, 169–192.

Wertheimer, M. (1959). *Productive thinking.* New York: Harper & Row.

10   A triarchic theory of intellectual giftedness

Robert J. Sternberg

In this chapter, I describe a new "triarchic" theory of intellectual giftedness. The theory is "triarchic" in the sense that it comprises three subtheories that serve as the governing bases for understanding extraordinary intelligence. The theory is believed to go beyond many previous theories in its scope, and to answer a broader array of questions about giftedness than has been answered in the past by single theories.

The triarchic theory comprises three subtheories. The first subtheory relates intelligence to the internal world of the individual, specifying the mental mechanisms that lead to more and less intelligent behavior. This subtheory specifies three kinds of information-processing components that are instrumental in (a) learning how to do things, (b) planning what things to do and how to do them, and (c) actually doing the things. The second subtheory specifies those points along the continuum of one's experience with tasks or situations that most critically involve the use of intelligence. In particular, the account emphasizes the roles of novelty and of automatization in exceptional intelligence. The third subtheory relates intelligence to the external world of the individual, specifying three classes of acts – environmental adaptation, selection, and shaping – that characterize intelligent behavior in the everyday world.

The three subtheories in combination provide a rather broad basis for characterizing the nature of extraordinarily intelligent behavior in the world, and for specifying the kinds of tasks that are more and less appropriate for the measurement of intellectual giftedness. The componential subtheory specifies the potential set of *mental mechanisms* that underlie exceptionally intelligent behavior, regardless of the particular behavioral contents. It addresses the question of how behaviors are intelligent in any given setting. The experiential subtheory specifies the relation between exceptional intelligence as exhibited on a task or in a situation, on the one hand, and *amount of experience*

A full account of the triarchic theory of human intelligence can be found in Sternberg (1985). Preparation of this article was supported by the Spencer Foundation. Requests for reprints should be sent to Robert J. Sternberg, Department of Psychology, Yale University, Box 11A Yale Station, New Haven, Connecticut 06520.

223

with the task or situation, on the other. It addresses the question of when behaviors are intelligent for a given individual. The contextual subtheory specifies the potential set of *contents* for behaviors that can be characterized as exceptionally intelligent. It addresses the question of what behaviors are intelligent for whom, and where these behaviors are intelligent.

The first subtheory is universal: Although individuals may differ in what mental mechanisms they apply to a given task or situation, the potential set of mental mechanisms underlying intelligence is viewed to be the same across all individuals and sociocultural settings. The second subtheory is relativistic only with respect to the points at which novelty and automatization are relevant for a given individual. But the relevance of the two facets to exceptional intelligence is perceived to be universal. The third subtheory is "relativistic" with respect to both individuals and the sociocultural settings in which they live. What constitutes an exceptionally intelligent act may differ from one person to another. Thus, the vehicles by which one might wish to measure intelligence (test contents, modes of presentation, formats for test items, etc.) will probably need to differ across sociocultural groups, and possibly even within such groups; but the underlying mechanisms to be measured, and their functions in dealing with novelty and in becoming automatized, do not differ across individuals or groups.

The triarchic theory of intellectual giftedness is a special case of a more general triarchic theory of human intelligence (Sternberg, 1985). The triarchic theory is not the first tripartite theory, either of intelligence or of intellectual giftedness. In the realm of intelligence, for example, Guilford (1967) has proposed that intelligence can be understood in terms of three facets – operations, contents, and products – that can provide a comprehensive basis for characterizing the kinds of items traditionally used to measure intelligence. For another example, Cattell (1971) has proposed a "triadic" theory of intelligence, according to which there are three kinds of abilities: general capacities, which are general factors deriving from brain functioning that extend across all cognitive performances; provincials, which are local organizations of behavioral factors relating to sensorimotor capacities; and agencies, which are primary (group) factors that take shape largely from cultural and general learning. In the realm of giftedness, Renzulli (1978) has proposed that three elements combine to serve as a basis for giftedness: above-average ability, unusual task commitment, and unusual creativity. The triarchic theory proposed here draws on elements of these tripartite theories, but is quite different in focus and scope.

A componential subtheory of intellectual giftedness

A theory of exceptional intelligence ought to specify the mechanisms by which intelligent performance is generated. The purpose of this section is to specify the mechanisms proposed by the triarchic theory. An earlier version of this subtheory was presented in more detail in Sternberg (1981a).

What is a component?

A component is an elementary information process that operates on internal representations of objects or symbols (Sternberg, 1977, 1980; see also Newell & Simon, 1972). The component may translate a sensory input into a conceptual representation, transform one conceptual representation into another, or translate a conceptual representation into a motor output. What is considered elementary enough to be labeled a component depends on the desired level of theorizing. Just as factors can be split into successively finer subfactors, so components can be split into successively finer subcomponents. Thus, no claim is made that any of the components referred to here are elementary at all levels of analysis. Rather, they are elementary at a convenient level of analysis. The same caveat applies to the proposed typology of components. Other typologies could doubtless be proposed that would serve this or other theoretical purposes as well or better. The particular typology proposed, however, has proved to be convenient in at least certain theoretical and experimental contexts.

Kinds of components

Components perform (at least) three kinds of functions. *Metacomponents* are higher-order processes used in planning, monitoring, and decision making in task performance. *Performance components* are processes used in the execution of a task. *Knowledge-acquisition components* are processes used in learning new things. It is essential to understand the nature of these components, because they form the mental bases for adapting to, shaping, and selecting environments, for dealing with novel kinds of tasks and situations, and for automatizing performance. In this section, I will consider measurement issues simultaneously with the consideration of each of the kinds of components.

Metacomponents. Metacomponents are specific realizations of control processes that are sometimes collectively (and loosely) referred to as the "executive" or the "homunculus" (although, as discussed later in the chapter, they lose their executive character during automatic processing). I have identified seven metacomponents that I believe are quite prevalent in intellectual functioning.

1. Decision as to just what the problem is that needs to be solved.
2. Selection of lower-order components.
3. Selection of one or more representations or organizations for information.
4. Selection of a strategy for combining lower-order components.
5. Decision regarding allocation of attentional resources.
6. Solution monitoring.
7. Sensitivity to external feedback.

An example of the importance of metacomponents in exceptional intelligence can be seen in the role of resource allocation in test performance, as well as in everyday tasks. It is often assumed that exceptional intelligence is associated with sheer speed of thought (e.g., Jensen, 1982). But the metacomponential point of view would emphasize the role of speed allocation, rather than sheer speed, in thinking and behaving. Thus, this point of view can predict the many kinds of situations in which slower, rather than faster, thinking and behaving, is positively associated with higher levels of intelligence (see Sternberg, 1982a, for examples and further development of this argument).

Performance components. Performance components are used in the execution of various strategies for task performance. Although the number of possible performance components is quite large, many probably apply only to small or uninteresting subsets of tasks, and hence deserve little attention.

Performance components tend to organize themselves into stages of task solution that seem to be fairly general across tasks. These stages include (a) encoding of stimuli, (b) combination of or comparison between stimuli, and (c) response. In the analogies task, for example, I have separated encoding and response components (each of which may be viewed as constituting its own stage) and inference, mapping, application, comparison, and justification components (each of which requires some kind of comparison between stimuli). Why is it important to decompose global performance on intellectual tasks and tests into its underlying performance components? I believe there are several reasons.

First, studies of mental test performance have shown that one set of performance components, the performance components of inductive reasoning – such as inferring relations between terms, mapping relations between relations, and applying old relations to new situations – are quite general across test formats typically found in intelligence tests. Sternberg and Gardner (1983) showed that high correlations (with magnitudes as high as .7 and .8) can be obtained between component scores and performance on psychometric tests of inductive reasoning, and high correlations are also obtained between corresponding component scores on the various inductive tasks. Thus, at least these performance components seem to be quite generalizable across both cognitive tasks of theoretical interest and psychometric tests of practical (and for many, theoretical) interest.

Second, decomposition of task performance into performance components is important because there is evidence that different components behave in various ways. Consider syllogistic reasoning tasks, for example. Some of the components of syllogistic reasoning operate on a linguistic representation, others on a spatial representation (Sternberg & Weil, 1980). Overall scores on syllogistic reasoning tests, whether expressed in terms of latencies or errors, are therefore confounded with respect to the linguistic and spatial abilities involved. An individual could achieve a given score through different combinations of componential efficacies, and even through the use of different strategies. For example, Sternberg and Weil (1980) found that untrained subjects spontaneously use at least four different strategies for solving linear syllogisms. To the extent one wishes to understand the cognitive bases of task performance, componential decomposition of task performance is desirable and even necessary.

Separation of performance components becomes especially important for purposes of diagnosis and remediation. Consider, for example, the possibility of a very bright person who does poorly on tests of abstract reasoning ability. It may be that the person is a very good reasoner, but has a perceptual difficulty that leads to poor encoding of the terms of the problem. Because encoding is necessary for reasoning about the problem terms as encoded, the overall score is reduced not by faulty reasoning, but by faulty encoding of the terms of the problem. Decomposition of scores into performance components enables one to separate out, say, reasoning difficulties from perceptual difficulties. For purposes of remediation, such separation is essential. Different remediation programs would be indicated for people who perform poorly on reasoning items because of reasoning, on the one hand, or perceptual processing, on the other.

Finally, componential decomposition can be important if the individual's problem is not in the components at all, but rather in the strategy for combining them. A person might be able to execute the performance components quite well, but still do poorly on a task because of nonoptimal strategies for combining the components. By modeling the examinee's task performance, it is possible to determine whether the person's difficulty is in the performance components, per se, or rather in the way the person combines those performance components.

Knowledge-acquisition components. Knowledge-acquisition components are processes used in gaining new knowledge. It is proposed that three components are relevant to acquisition of declarative and procedural knowledge in virtually all domains of knowledge.

1. *Selective encoding.* Selective encoding involves sifting out relevant from irrelevant information. When new information is presented in natural contexts, relevant information for one's given purposes is embedded in the midst of large amounts of purpose-irrelevant information. A critical task for the learner is that of sifting the "wheat from the chaff": recognizing just what information among all the pieces of information presented is relevant for one's purposes.

2. *Selective combination.* Selective combination involves combining selectively encoded information in such a way as to form an integrated, plausible whole. Simply sifting out relevant from irrelevant information is not enough to generate a new knowledge structure: One must know how to combine the pieces of information into an internally connected whole.

3. *Selective comparison.* Selective comparison involves relating newly acquired information to information acquired in the past. Deciding what information to encode and how to combine it does not occur in a vacuum. Rather, encoding and combination of new knowledge are guided by retrieval of old information. New information will be all but useless if it cannot somehow be related to old knowledge so as to form an externally connected whole.

We have assessed the role of knowledge-acquisition components in intelligence through the study of vocabulary learning. There is reason to believe that vocabulary is such a good measure of intelligence because it measures, albeit indirectly, children's ability to acquire information in context (Jensen, 1980; Sternberg & Powell, 1983; Werner & Kaplan, 1952). Most vocabulary is learned in everyday contexts rather than through direct instruction. Thus, new words are usually encountered for the first time (and subsequently) in textbooks, novels, newspapers, lectures, and the like. More intelligent people are better able to use surrounding context to figure out the words' meanings. As the years go by, the better decontextualizers acquire the larger vocabularies. Because so much of one's learning (including learning beside vocabulary) is contextually determined, the ability to use context to add to one's knowledge base is an important skill in intelligent behavior. We have attempted to measure these skills directly by presenting high school children with paragraphs written at a level well below their grade level (Sternberg & Powell, 1983). Embedded within the paragraphs are one or more unknown words. The children's task is to use the surrounding context to figure out the meanings of the unknown words. Our theory of task performance attempts to specify exactly how children accomplish this decontextualization. We found high correlations between the predictions of the theory, which specifies the cues people use in decontextualizing word meanings (e.g., spatial cues, temporal cues, class membership cues, and the like) and the actual ease with which people can figure out word meanings. Correlations between predicted and observed values were .92 for literary passages, .74 for newspaper passages, .85 for science passages, and .77 for history passages. Note that in this testing paradigm, differential effects of past achievements are reduced by using reading passages that are easy for everyone, but target vocabulary words that are unknown to everyone. We have found that the quality of children's definitions of the unknown words is highly correlated with overall verbal intelligence, reading comprehension, and vocabulary test scores (about .6 in each case). Thus, one can measure an important aspect of intelligence – knowledge acquistion – directly and without heavy reliance upon past achievement.

An experiential subtheory of intellectual giftedness

The experiential subtheory proposes that a task measures "intelligence" to the extent that it requires either or both of two skills (the nature of which will be specified in greater detail in the next section): the ability to deal with novel kinds of task and situational demands, and the ability to automatize information processing. These two abilities apply to the interaction between individuals, on the one hand, and tasks or situations, on the other, precisely at those points when the relation between the individual and the task or situation is most rapidly changing. It is this fast rate of change that makes these two points (or regions) of experience most relevant for assessing intelligence. Consider each of these abilities in turn.

Ability to deal with novel task and situational demands

Novel tasks. The idea that intelligence involves the ability to deal with novel task demands is itself far from novel. Sternberg (1982b) has suggested, in fact, that exceptional intelligence is best measured by tasks that are "nonentrenched" in the sense of requiring information processing of kinds outside people's ordinary experience. The task may be nonentrenched in the kinds of operations it requires, or in the concepts it requires the subjects to use. On this view, then, intelligence involves

not merely the ability to learn and reason with new concepts but the ability to learn and reason with new kinds of concepts. Intelligence is not so much a person's ability to learn or think within conceptual systems that the person has already become familiar with as it is his or her ability to learn and think within new conceptual systems, which can then be brought to bear upon already existing knowledge structures. (Sternberg, 1981b, p. 4)

It is important to note that the usefulness of a task in measuring intelligence is not a linear function of task novelty. The task that is presented should be novel, but not totally outside the individual's past experience (Raaheim, 1974). If the task is too novel, then the individual will not have any cognitive structures to bring to bear on it, and as a result, the task will simply be outside of the individual's range of comprehension. Calculus, for example, would be a highly novel field of endeavor for most five-year-olds. But the calculus tasks would be so far outside their range of experience that such tasks would be worthless for the assessment of exceptional intelligence in five-year-olds. In Piagetian (1972) terms, the task should primarily require accommodation, but must require some assimilation as well.

Novel situations. The notion that exceptional intelligence is particularly aptly measured in situations that require adaptation to new and challenging environmental demands inheres both in experts' and laypersons' notions of the nature of intelligence (Intelligence and Its Measurement, 1921; Sternberg et al., 1981). The idea is that a person's intelligence is best shown not in run-of-the-mill situations that are encountered regularly in everyday life, but rather in extraordinary situations that challenge the individual's ability to cope with the environment to which he or she must adapt. Almost everyone knows someone (perhaps oneself) who performs extremely well when confronted with tasks presented in a familiar milieu but who falls apart when similar or even identical tasks are presented in an unfamiliar milieu. For example, a person who performs well in his or her everyday environment might find it difficult to function in a foreign country, even one that is similar in many respects to the home environment. In general, some people can perform exceptionally well, but only under situational circumstances that are highly favorable to their getting their work done. When the environment is less supportive, their efficacy is greatly reduced.

Essentially the same constraints that apply to task novelty apply to situational novelty as well. Too much novelty can render the situation nondiagnostic of intellectual level. Moreover, there may exist situations in which no one could function effectively (perhaps as epitomized by the situation confronted by the protagonist in Sartre's *No Exit*).

Measurement of the ability to deal with novelty

I have attempted directly to measure individuals' skills in dealing with novel tasks using two different paradigms of research and measurements. (As I have not yet attempted directly to measure automatization, I will discuss only the issue of novelty here.) The first paradigm involved novelty primarily in task *comprehension*. The second paradigm involved novelty primarily in task *solution*.

The first paradigm involved presenting individuals with variants of a "concept projection" task. Consider just one (of four) variants that were used (Sternberg, 1982b). Individuals were presented with a description of the color of an object in the present day and in the year 2000. The description could be either physical–a green dot or a blue dot – or verbal – one of four color words, namely, *green, blue, grue,* or *bleen*. An object was defined as green if it appeared physically green both in the present and in the year 2000. An object was defined as blue if it appeared physically blue both in the present and in the year 2000. An object was defined as grue if it appeared physically green in the present but physically blue in the year 2000 (i.e., it appeared physically green until the year 2000 and physically blue thereafter). An object was defined as bleen if it appeared physically blue in the present but physically green in the year 2000 (i.e., it appeared physically blue until the year 2000 and physically green thereafter). (The terminology is based on Goodman, 1955.)

Because each of the two descriptions (one in the present and one in the year 2000) could take one of either two physical forms or four verbal forms, there were 36 (6 × 6) different item types. The individual's task was to describe the object in the year 2000. If the given description for the year 2000 was a physical one, the subject had to indicate the correct verbal description of the object; if the given description for the year 2000 was a verbal one, the subject had to indicate the correct physical description of the object. There were always three answer choices from which the subject had to choose the correct one. There were many complexities in the task that cannot be described here but that rendered the problems quite challenging for the subjects. For example, certain types of items presented inconsistencies, and other types presented information that was only partially valid.

Performance on the task was modeled via an information-processing model of task performance. The model accounted for an average of 92% of the variance in the response-time data (averaged over five variants of the task and five sets of subjects). The median correlation between task performance and scores on a battery of inductive reasoning tests (taken from standard intelligence measures) was − .62 (with the correlation negative because response times were being correlated with numbers correct on the reasoning tests). Most important, however, was that when individual processing-component scores were correlated with the reasoning measures, it was precisely those components that measured ability to deal with novelty (e.g., time spent in switching from one conceptual system to another, and time spent in recognizing physical transformations from one time period to another) that correlated with the induction tests. The results therefore suggested that it was ability to deal with novelty, rather than more conventional aspects of test performance, that were critical to measuring subjects' reasoning skills.

The second type of novel task involved "insight" problems of the kinds found in puzzle books available in any bookstore. Consider some examples of the insight problems we used (Sternberg & Davidson, 1983):

1. If you have black socks and brown socks in your drawer, mixed in the ratio of 4 to 5, how many socks will you have to take out to make sure of having a pair the same color?
2. Water lilies double in area every 24 hours. At the beginning of the summer there is one water lily on a lake. It takes 60 days for the lake to become covered with water lilies. On what day is the lake half covered?

We theorized that three kinds of insights are involved in problems such as these. These kinds of insights are special cases of knowledge-acquisition components in which the usual heuristics for knowledge acquisition do not work. The first kind of insight, *selective encoding*, involves recognizing those elements of a problem that are relevant for task solution, and those elements that are not. For example, Fleming's discovery of penicillin involved an insight of selective encoding, in that Fleming recognized that the mold that had ruined his experiment had done so by killing off the bacteria in a petri dish. Thus was born the first of the modern antibiotics through a selective encoding of information that would have escaped the large majority of scientists. The second kind of sight, *selective combination*, involves figuring out how to combine information that has been selectively encoded. Such information can typically be combined in many ways, only one of which is optimal. For example, Darwin's formulation of the theory of evolution hinged on his recognizing how the multitudinous facts he and others had collected about species could be combined to yield an account of the transition between species over the course of time. The third kind of insight, *selective comparison*, involves figuring out how new information can be related to old information. For example, Kekulé's discovery of the structure of the benzene ring hinged on his recognizing that a dream he had had of a snake reaching back and biting its tail provided the basis for the geometric structure of the ring.

We used these problems to test our theory of insight (Davidson & Sternberg, 1984). The main question we addressed was whether we could isolate selective encoding, selective combination, and selective comparison in subjects' performance. We were in fact able to isolate all three processes by manipulating the amount of information given to subjects solving problems. In particular, subjects would receive the insight problems either with or without precuing by one of the three kinds of insights. Providing subjects with each of the three kinds of insights substantially improved performance, especially for less able subjects who were less likely to have the insights on their own.

We also sought to determine whether the ability to deal with these novel problems provided a good measure of intelligence. Note that the novelty in these problems is not in understanding the instructions (which are straightforward – namely, to solve the problems), but rather in coming up with a strategy for task solution. Although some of the problems can be solved by conventional algorithms, the problems typically could be solved more easily by shortcuts or heuristics that are not standardly taught in mathematics classes. Solution of problems such as these requires a fair amount of insight, but very little in the way of prior mathematical knowledge. And performance on such problems is correlated about .6 to .7 with IQ. Thus, insight problems measure something related, but not identical to, what IQ tests measure. What they add to IQ test measurement, however, would seem to be an important part of intelligence, broadly defined.

Ability to automatize information processing

Many kinds of tasks requiring complex information processing seem so intricate that it is a wonder we can perform them at all. Consider reading, for example. The number and complexity of operations involved in reading are staggering, and what is more staggering is the rate at which these operations are performed. Performance of tasks as complex as reading would seem to be possible only because a substantial proportion of the operations required in reading are automatized and thus require minimal mental effort. Deficiencies in reading have been theorized to result in large part from failures in automatization of operations that in normal readers have been automatized (LaBerge & Samuels, 1974; Sternberg & Wagner, 1982).

The proposal being made here is that complex verbal, mathematical, and other tasks can feasibly be executed only because many of the operations involved in their performance have been automatized. Failure to automatize such operations, whether fully or in part, results in a breakdown of information processing and hence less intelligent task performance. Intellectual operations that can be performed smoothly and automatically by more intelligent individuals are performed only haltingly and under conscious control by less intelligent individuals. In sum, gifted individuals can automatize information processing unusually efficiently and effectively.

Relationship between abilities to deal with novelty and to automatize processing

For many (but probably not all) kinds of tasks, the ability to deal with novelty and to automatize information processing may occur along an experiential continuum. When one first encounters a task or kind of situation, ability to deal with novelty comes into play. The more intelligent person will be more rapidly and fully able to cope with the novel demands being made on him or her. Moreover, the fewer the resources that need to be devoted to processing the novelty of a given task or situation, the more the resources that are left over to automatize performance; conversely, more efficient automatization of performance leaves over additional processing resources for dealing with novel tasks and situations. As a result, novelty and automatization trade off with each other, and the more efficient the individual is at the one, the more the resources that are left over for the other. As experience with the kind of task or situation increases, novelty decreases, and the task or situation will become less apt in its measurement of intelligence from the standpoint of processing of novelty. However, after some amount of practice with the task or in the situation, automatization skills may come into play, in which case the task will start to become a more apt measure of automatization skills.

Implications for task selection

The proposed subtheory carries with it certain implications for the selection of tasks to measure exceptionally high intelligence. In particular, one wishes to select tasks that involve some blend of automatized behaviors and behaviors in response to novelty. This blending is probably best achieved within test items, but may also be achieved by items that specialize in measuring either the one skill or the other. The blending may be achieved by presenting subjects with a novel task, and then giving them enough practice with the task so that performance becomes differentially automatized (across subjects) over the length of the practice period. Such a task will thereby measure both response to novelty and degree of automatization, although at different times during the course of testing.

The experiential view suggests one reason why it is so exceedingly difficult to compare levels of intelligence fairly across members of different sociocultural groups. Even if a given test requires the same components of performance for members of the various groups, it is extremely unlikely to be equivalent for the groups in terms of its novelty and the degree to which performance has been automatized prior to the examinees' taking the test. Consider, for example, the by now well-known finding that nonverbal reasoning tests, such as the Raven Progressive Matrices or the Cattell Culture Fair Test of g, actually show greater differences between members of different sociocultural groups than do the verbal tests they were designed to replace (Jensen, 1982). The nonverbal tests, contrary to the claims that have often been made for them, are *not* culture-fair (and they are certainly not culture-free). Individuals who have been brought up in a test-taking culture are likely to have had much more experience with these kinds of items than are individuals not brought up in such a culture. Thus, the items will be less novel and performance on them more automatized for members of the standard U.S. culture than for its nonmembers. Even if the processes of solution are the same, the degrees of novelty and automatization will be different, and hence the tests will not be measuring the same skills across populations. As useful as the tests may be for within-group comparisons, between-group comparisons may be deceptive and unfair. A fair comparison between groups would require comparable degrees of novelty and automatization in test items as well as comparable processes and strategies.

In sum, it has been proposed that behavior is exceptionally intelligent when it involves unusual efficacy in either or both of two sets of skills: adaptation to novelty and automatization of performance. This proposal has been used to explain why so many tasks seem to measure "intelligence" in greater or lesser degree. Most importantly, the subtheory provides an a priori specification of what a task or situation must measure in order to assess intelligence. It is distinctive in that it is not linked to any arbitrary choice of tasks or situations. These follow from the subtheory, rather than the other way around.

A contextualist subtheory of intellectual giftedness

Contextual definition of exceptional intelligence

I view exceptional intelligence in context as consisting of *purposive adaptation to, shaping of, and selection of real-world environments relevant to one's life.* Consider just what this definition means.

Relevance. First, I define intelligence in terms of behavior in real-world environments that are relevant to one's life. The intelligence of an African pygmy could not be legitimately assessed by placing the pygmy into a North American culture and using North American tests, unless it were relevant to the test of the pygmy for survival in a North American culture and one wished to assess the pygmy's intelligence for this culture (as, for example, if the pygmy happened to live in our culture and had to adapt to it). Similarly, a North American's intelligence could not be legitimately assessed in terms of his or her adaptation to pygmy society unless adaptation to that society were relevant to the person's life.

An implication of this view is that exceptional intelligence cannot be fully understood outside a sociocultural context, and it may in fact differ for a given individual from one culture to the next. Our most intelligent individuals might come out much less intelligent in another culture, and some of our less intelligent individuals might come out more intelligent.

Purposiveness. Second, intelligence is purposive. It is directed toward goals, however vague or subconscious those goals may be.

Adaptation. Third, intelligence is adaptive. Indeed, definitions of intelligence have traditionally viewed it in terms of adaptation to one's environment (see, e.g., Intelligence and Its Measurement, 1921). Typically, individuals attempt to *adapt* to the environment in which they find themselves. Adaptation consists of trying to achieve a good fit between oneself and one's environment. Such a fit will be obtainable in greater or lesser degree. But if the degree of fit is below what one considers satisfactory for one's life, then the adaptive route may be viewed, at a higher level, as maladaptive. For example, a partner in a marriage may find him- or herself unable to attain satisfaction within the marriage; or an employee of a business concern may find his or her values so different from those of the employer that a satisfactory fit does not seem possible; or one may find the situation one is in to be morally reprehensible (as in Nazi Germany). In such instances, adaptation to the present environment presents an unviable alternative to the individual, and the individual is obliged to try something other than adaptation to the given environment.

Thus, it is perhaps incorrect simply to equate exceptional intelligence with exceptional adaptation to the environment.

Shaping. Fourth, intelligence involves shaping of the environment. Environmental *shaping* is used when one's attempts to adapt to the given environment fail. In this case, one attempts to reshape one's environment so as to increase the fit between oneself and the environment. The marital partner may attempt to restructure the marriage; the employee may try to convince his or her employer to see or do things differently; the citizen may try to change the government, through either violent or nonviolent means. In each case, however, the individual attempts to change the environment so as to increase his or her fit to the (new) environment, rather than merely attempting to adapt to what is already there.

What this means is that there may be no one set of behaviors that is "intelligent" for everyone, in that people can adjust to their environments in different ways. Whereas the components of intelligent behavior are very likely universal, their use in the construction of environmentally appropriate behavior is likely to vary not only across groups but across individuals.

What does seem to be common among people mastering their environments is the ability to capitalize on strengths and to compensate for weaknesses (see Cronbach & Snow, 1977). Unusually successful people are able not only to adapt well to their environments, but actually to modify the environments they are in so as to maximize the goodness of fit between the environment and their adaptive skills.

Consider, for example, the "stars" in any given field of endeavor. What is it that distinguishes such persons from all the rest? Of course, this question, as phrased, is broad enough to be the topic of a book and, indeed, many books have been written on the topic. But for present purposes, the distinguishing characteristics to which I would like to call attention are (a) at least one extraordinarily well-developed skill, and (b) an extraordinary ability to capitalize on the skill or skills in their work. For example, generate a short list of "stars" in your own field. Chances are that the stars do not seem to share any one ability, as traditionally defined, but rather share a tendency toward having some set of extraordinary talents that they make the most of in their work. In my own list, for example, are included a person with extraordinary spatial visualization skills (if anyone can visualize in four dimensions, he can!), a person with a talent for coming up with almost incredibly counterintuitive findings that are of great theoretical importance, and a person who has an extraordinary sense of where the field is going, and repeatedly tends to be just one step ahead of it so as perfectly to time the publication of his work for maximum impact. These three particular persons (and others on my list) share little in terms of what sets them apart, aside from at least one extraordinary talent on which they capitalize fully in their work. Although they are also highly intelligent in the traditional sense, so are many others who never reach their heights of accomplishment.

Because what is adaptive differs at least somewhat, both across people and across situations, the present view suggests that exceptional intelligence is not quite the same thing for different people and for different situations. The higher-order skills of capitalization and compensation may be the same, but what is capitalized on and what is compensated for will vary. The differences across people and situations extend beyond different life paths within a given culture.

Selection. Fifth, intelligence involves active selection of environments. When adaptation is not possible or desirable, and when shaping fails, the individual may attempt to *select* an alternative environment with which he or she is able, or potentially able, to attain a better contextual fit. In essence, the person recognizes that attempts to succeed within the given environment have not worked, and that attempts to mold that environment to be suitable for one's values, abilities, or interests have also not worked; it is time to move out of the environment altogether and to find a new one that better suits oneself. For example, the partner may leave the marriage; the employee may seek another job; the resident of Nazi Germany may attempt to emigrate. Under these circumstances, the individual considers the alternative environments available to him or her, and attempts to select that environment, within the constraints of feasibility, with which he or she will attain maximal fit. But sometimes this option is infeasible. For example, members of certain religions may view themselves as utterly committed to their marriage, or an individual may decide to stay in the marriage on account of children, despite its lack of appeal; or the employee may not be able to attain another job, either for lack of positions, lack of qualifications, or both; or the individual wishing to leave a country may find him- or herself lacking the resources or permission to leave that country.

Consider how environmental selection can operate in career choice of gifted individuals. A rather poignant set of real-world examples is provided by Feldman's (1982) account of *Whatever Happened to the Quiz Kids?* The Quiz Kids were selected first for the radio show, and later the television show of the same name, for a number of intellectual and personal traits. But existing records suggest all or almost all of them had exceptionally high IQs, typically well over 140 and in some cases in excess of 200. Yet, one cannot help be struck by how much less distinguished their later lives have been than their earlier lives, in many cases, even by their own standards. There are undoubtedly any number of reasons for this lesser later success, including regression effects. But what is striking in biography after biography is that the ones who were most successful were those who found what they were good at and were interested in, and then pursued it relentlessly. The less successful ones had difficulty in finding any one thing that interested them, and in a number of cases, floundered while trying to find a niche for themselves.

Measurement of contextually directed intelligence

We have made several attempts to measure intelligence as it applies to real-world contexts. I will describe here two of these approaches.

One approach we have taken to understanding intelligence as it operates in the everyday world is that, underlying successful performance in many real-world tasks, is a set of judgmental skills based on tacit understandings of a kind that is never explicitly taught and in many instances never even verbalized. Interviews with prominent business executives and academic psychologists – the two populations that served as the bases for our initial studies – revealed a striking level of agreement that a major factor underlying success in each occupation is a knowledge and understanding of the ins and outs of the occupation. These ins and outs are generally things one learns on the job rather than in any preparatory academic or other work. To measure potential for occupational success, therefore, one might wish to go beyond conventional ability and achievement tests to the measurement of an individual's under-standings of and judgments using the hidden agenda of his or her field of endeavor.

In particular, we have found three kinds of tacit understandings to be particularly important for success, namely, understandings regarding man-aging (a) oneself, (b) others, and (c) one's career (Wagner & Sternberg, 1985). These understandings and the judgments based on them were measured by items drawing on decisions of the kinds one typically has to make in the everyday world of one's occupation. Separate questionnaires were constructed for the business executives and academic psychologists. For example, one item on each questionnaire presented the situation of a relatively inexperi-enced person in the field who had to decide what tasks were more and less important to be done within a short period of time. Subjects rated the priorities of the various tasks. Another item presented various criteria that could be used in judging the success of an executive or an academic psychologist, and subjects had to rate how important each criterion was. Yet another item presented various considerations in deciding what projects to work on; sub-jects had to decide how important each of the various considerations was in deciding on which project to work. Subjects receiving the psychology ques-tionnaire were a national sample of university psychology faculty and graduate students, as well as a sample of Yale undergraduates; subjects receiving the business questionnaire were national samples of business executives and busi-ness graduate students, executives at a local bank, and a sample of Yale undergraduates. Scores on the questionnaires were correlated at about the .4 level with measures of success among members of each occupation, such as, for academics, the number of articles published in a year or published rating of the university with which one is affiliated, and, for the business executives, merit salary increases and performance ratings. The subscale most highly correlated with successful performance was that for managing one's career. Moreover, at least for the undergraduates, performance on the two questionnaires was uncorrelated with scores on a standard verbal reasoning test, indicating that the obtained correlations with external measures of success were not merely obtained via a measure that was nothing more than a proxy for IQ.

A second approach we have used in measuring intelligence in the everyday world is based on the notion that intelligence can be measured with some accuracy by the degree of resemblance between a person's behavior and the behavior of the "ideally" intelligent individual (see Neisser, 1979). Sternberg, Conway, Ketron, and Bernstein (1981) had a group of individuals rate the extent to which each of 250 behaviors characterized their own behavioral repertoires. A second group of individuals rated the extent to which each of the 250 behaviors characterized the behavioral repertoire of an "ideally intelligent" person.

The behaviors that were rated had previously been listed by entirely different individuals as characterizing either "intelligent" or "unintelligent" persons. The intelligent behaviors were shown (by factor analysis) to fall into three general classes: problem-solving ability (e.g., "reasons logically and well," "identifies connections among ideas," and "sees all aspects of a problem"); verbal ability (e.g., "speaks clearly and articulately," "is verbally fluent," and "reads with high comprehension"); and social competence (e.g., "accepts others for what they are," "admits mistakes," and "displays interest in the world at large"). No attempt was made to classify the unintelligent behaviors, as they were not the objects of interest in the study.

We computed the correlation between each person's self-description and the description of the ideally intelligent person (as provided by the second group of individuals). The correlation provided a measure of the degree of resemblance between a real individual and the "ideally intelligent" individual. The claim was that this degree of resemblance is itself a measure of intelligence. The facts bore out this claim: The correlation between the resemblance measure and scores on a standard IQ test was .52, confirming that the measure did provide an index of intelligence as it is often operationally defined.

People's conceptions of intelligence can be used not only to predict their own scores on standard psychometric intelligence tests, but also to predict how people will evaluate the intelligence of others. We presented subjects with descriptions of persons in terms of the various intelligent and unintelligent behaviors that had been generated in our initial data collection. The subjects were asked to rate the intelligence of each described person on a 1 to 9 scale. We then attempted to predict people's ratings on the basis of the weights our theory assigned to each behavior in each description of a person. The correlation between predicted and observed ratings was .96. In making their ratings, people weighted the two more academic factors – problem solving and verbal abilities – more heavily than social competence ability, but all three factors received significant weightings in people's judgments.

Conclusions

I have proposed in this article a description of a triarchic theory of intellectual giftedness. The theory comprises three subtheories: a componential subtheory, which relates intelligence to the internal world of the individual; an experiential subtheory, which relates intelligence to both the external and internal worlds of the individual; and a contextual subtheory, which relates intelligence to the external world of the individual. The componential subtheory specifies the mental mechanisms responsible for the planning, execution, and evaluation of intelligent behavior. The experiential subtheory further constrains this definition by regarding as most relevant to the demonstration of intelligence behavior involving either adjustment to novelty or automatization of information processing, or both. The contextual subtheory defines intelligent behavior as that involving purposive adaptation to, selection of, and shaping of real-world environments relevant to one's life.

The theory has clear implications for the evaluation of intellectual giftedness. First, one should test people on behavior that is relevant to, or predictive of, contextually appropriate behavior in their real-world environments. But not every contextually appropriate behavior is equally informative with respect to individual differences in intelligence (e.g., eating). Hence, one should assess behaviors in response to novelty or in the development of automatization. But even here, not all behaviors are equally informative: Response to novelty, for example, would seem to have more to do with intelligence if it involves solving a new kind of complex problem, such as learning calculus, than if it involves solving a new kind of simple problem, such as what to do if a staple falls out of a set of collated pages. Hence, the behaviors most relevant to evaluation are those that more heavily involve components and particularly metacomponents of intelligence. In sum, all three subtheories of the triarchic theory are relevant to the formulation of an evaluation or assessment battery for measuring exceptional intelligence.

An important issue concerns the combination rule for the abilities specified by the three subtheories. How does the intelligence of a person who is average in the abilities specified by all three subtheories compare, say, to the intelligence of a person who is gifted in some abilities but low in others? Or what can one say of the intelligence of a person whose environmental opportunities are so restricted that he or she is unable to adapt to, shape, or select any environment? I am very reluctant to specify any combination rule at all, in that I do not believe a single index of intelligence is likely to be very useful. Different individuals may be intellectually gifted through different patterns of abilities. In the first case, the two individuals are quite different in their pattern of abilities, and an overall index will hide this fact. In the second case, it may not be possible to obtain any meaningful measurement at all from the person's functioning in his or her environment. Consider, as further examples, the comparison between (a) a person who is very adept at componential functioning, and thus likely to score well on standard IQ tests, but who is lacking in insight or, more generally, in the ability to cope well with nonentrenched kinds of tasks or situations, versus (b) a person who is very insightful but not particularly well adept at componential operations. The first individual might come across to people as "smart" but not terribly "creative"; the second individual might come across to people as creative but not terribly smart. Although it might well be possible to obtain some average score on componential abilities and abilities to deal with nonentrenched tasks and situations, such a composite would obscure the critical qualitative differences between the functioning of the two individuals. Or consider a person who is both componentially adept and insightful, but who makes little effort to fit into the environment in which he or she lives. Certainly one would not want to take some overall average that hides the person's academic intelligence (or even brilliance) in a combined index that is reduced because of reduced adaptive skills. The point to be made, then, is that intelligence is not a single thing: It comprises a very wide array of cognitive and other skills. Our goal in theory, research, and measurement ought to be to define what these skills are and learn how best to assess and possibly train them, not to figure out a way to combine them into a single but possibly meaningless number.

Although the triarchic theory consists of three subtheories, the subtheories are interrelated. For example, the ability to deal with novelty results from the application of certain metacomponents, performance components, and knowledge-acquisition components to novel material; automatization of information processing occurs when certain ones of these kinds of components come to be processed outside conscious control. Similarly, intelligence in context is a function of componential activities, although individuals who are skilled in applying components in everyday contexts may not be the same ones as those who are skilled in applying components in more academic contexts. Moreover, important aspects of intelligence in context are the abilities to handle novelty and to automatize information processing. Indeed, in one's life, much of one's ability to cope is precisely a result of one's ability to deal with situations quite dissimilar to any situations previously encountered. A person might be gifted in any of the aspects covered by the subtheories, but not so in putting together these various aspects. Again, such a notion argues for a plurality of kinds of giftedness. In short, then, the three subtheories need to be considered collectively as well as individually in order to understand intelligent functioning.

To conclude, the triarchic theory implies a notion of intellectual giftedness that is quite a bit broader than usual conceptions, even those that take into account creativity and motivation as well as intelligence (e.g., Renzulli, 1978). But the present theory has in common with broad conceptions of giftedness, such as Renzulli's and Tannenbaum's (1983), the idea that far from being a unidimensional attribute, giftedness can be attained in any of a number of ways. Indeed, these ways may differ not only from one group to another, but from one person to another. Giftedness, like intelligence, is not quite the same thing from one person to another. If we are to optimize our utilization of giftedness as a national resource, we will have to take into account the multiplicity of forms in which it can be found.

References

Cattell, R. B. (1971). *Abilities: Their structure, growth and action*. Boston: Houghton Mifflin.

Cronbach, L. J., & Snow, R. E. (1977). *Aptitudes and instructional methods*. New York: Irvington.

Davidson, J. E., & Sternberg, R. J. (1984). The role of insight in intellectual giftedness. *Gifted Child Quarterly, 28*, 58–64.

Feldman, R. D. (1982). *Whatever happened to the Quiz Kids?* Chicago: Chicago Review Press.

Goodman, N. (1955). *Fact, fiction, and forecast*. Cambridge, Mass.: Harvard University Press.

Guilford, J. P. (1967). *The nature of human intelligence*. New York: McGraw-Hill.

Intelligence and its measurement. A symposium. (1921). *Journal of Educational Psychology, 12*, 123–147, 195–216, 271–275.

Jensen, A. R. (1980). *Bias in mental testing*. New York: Free Press.

Jensen, A. R. (1982). Reaction time and psychometric g. In H. J. Eysenck (Ed.), *A model for intelligence*. Heidelberg: Springer-Verlag.

LaBerge, D., & Samuels, J. (1974). Toward a theory of automatic information processing in reading. *Cognitive Psychology, 6*, 293–323.

Neisser, U. (1979). The concept of intelligence. *Intelligence, 3*, 217–227.

Newell, A., & Simon, H. (1972). *Human problem solving*. Englewood Cliffs, N.J.: Prentice-Hall.

Piaget, J. (1972). *The psychology of intelligence*. Totowa, N.J.: Littlefield, Adams.

Raaheim, K. (1974). *Problem solving and intelligence*. Oslo: Universitetsforlaget.

Renzulli, J. S. (1978). What makes giftedness? Reexamining a definition. *Phi Delta Kappan, 60*, 180–183.

Sternberg, R. J. (1977). *Intelligence, information processing, and analogical reasoning: The componential analysis of human abilities*. Hillsdale, N.J.: Erlbaum.

Sternberg, R. J. (1980). Sketch of a componential subtheory of human intelligence. *Behavioral and Brain Sciences, 3*, 573–584.

Sternberg, R. J. (1981a). A componential theory of intellectual giftedness. *Gifted Child Quarterly, 25*, 86–93.

Sternberg, R. J. (1981b). Intelligence and nonentrenchment. *Journal of Educational Psychology, 73*, 1–16.

Sternberg, R. J. (1982a). Lies we live by: Misapplication of tests in identifying the gifted. *Gifted Child Quarterly, 26*, 157–161.

Sternberg, R. J. (1982b). Nonentrenchment in the assessment of intellectual giftedness. *Gifted Child Quarterly, 26*, 63–67.

Sternberg, R. J. (1985). *Beyond IQ: A triarchic theory of human intelligence*. Cambridge University Press.

Sternberg, R. J., Conway, B. E., Ketron, J. L., & Bernstein, M. (1981). People's conceptions of intelligence. *Journal of Personality and Social Psychology, 41*, 37–55.

Sternberg, R. J., & Davidson, J. E. (1983). Insight in the gifted. *Educational Psychologist, 18*, 51–57.

Sternberg, R. J., & Gardner, M. K. (1983). Unities in inductive reasoning. *Journal of Experimental Psychology: General, 112*, 80–116.

Sternberg, R. J., & Powell, J. S. (1983). Comprehending verbal comprehension. *American Psychologist, 38*, 878–893.

Sternberg, R. J., & Wagner, R. K. (1982, July). Automatization failure in learning disabilities. *Topics in learning and learning disabilities, 2*, 1–11.

Sternberg, R. J., & Weil, E. M. (1980). An aptitude-strategy interaction in linear syllogistic reasoning. *Journal of Educational Psychology, 72*, 226–234.

Tannenbaum, A. J. (1983). *Gifted children. Psychological and educational perspectives*. New York: Macmillan.

Wagner, R. K., & Sternberg, R. J. (1985). Practical intelligence in real world pursuits: The role of tacit knowledge. *Journal of Personality and Social Psychology, 49*, 436–458.

Werner, H., & Kaplan, E. (1952). The acquisition of word meanings: A developmental study. *Monographs of the Society for Research in Child Development* (No. 51).

Part IV

Explicit-theoretical approaches: developmental theory

11   The self-construction of the extraordinary

Howard E. Gruber

Different kinds of gifts

There are gifts and there are gifts. The concept of gift is complex and ambiguous. There are the gifts of Lady Bountiful and Lady Luck, neither of which reflect much credit on the recipient. And there are white elephants and Trojan horses, neither of which do the recipient much good. H. G. Wells was often preoccupied with the deceptive gifts, ones that are of no use because they cannot be properly inserted into the social fabric: In "The Country of the Blind," the sighted person who wanders into that strange land finds he cannot dominate the inhabitants because they have found a coherent set of adaptations to their blindness (Wells, 1911); Wells's Invisible Man aspires to use his extraordinary power of disappearing by turning to a career of crime, but he fails because he comes up against a tough and resilient organization – the world as it is (Wells, 1897).

The kind of gift that interests me is the kind that can be transformed by its possessor into effective creative work for the aesthetic enrichment of human experience, for the improvement of our understanding of the world, or for the betterment of the human condition and of our prospects for survival as a species. In previous essays I have examined with some skepticism the hypothesis of a relationship of necessity and/or sufficiency between early giftedness and adult creativity.

In the present chapter I hope to continue that examination. I hope also to give some account of this process of creative work, and to make some suggestions about how we might begin to think of its origins in childhood and adolescence.

I thank Dr. Doris B. Wallace for her helpful suggestions during the preparation of this essay.

An evolving-systems approach to creative work provides the underlying theoretical framework for this chapter. It has been described in Gruber (1980) and in a chapter by Doris B. Wallace, "The Problem of Giftedness and the Construction of a Creative Life," in F. D. Horowitz and M. O'Brien (Eds.), *The Gifted and the Talented: A Developmental Perspective* (1985). The evolving-systems approach will be more fully presented in a volume now in preparation: Doris B. Wallace and Howard E. Gruber (Eds.), *Creative People at Work: Twelve Cognitive Case Studies*.

247

The main body of my argument is carried by four points. First, the concept of "gift" depends for its meaning on establishing some connection between the property labeled "gift" and the development of an extraordinary adult. Because this connection has been quite difficult to establish empirically, an important research strategy is to identify extraordinary human beings and work backward to the processes and conditions that gave rise to them. Second, the main force in the development of an extraordinary person is that individual's own activity and interests. Third, the meaning and value of any particular kind of extraordinariness depends on the historical and social circumstances in which it appears. Fourth, our best hope for understanding the development of human extraordinariness is to study closely the lives of creative people. This entails radical changes in empirical methods, especially a greatly increased emphasis on the case-study method.

Altogether, I object to the a prioristic, all too easy assumption that gifts preexist and are somewhere out there remaining only to be given to their recipients. Rather, I believe that the qualities of human extraordinariness are striven for and constructed. Usually I avoid the word *gift* and prefer to speak of *human extraordinariness*. But this is sometimes a clumsy phrase. Moreover, since I grant that a common interest unites the authors of this volume and other discussions of giftedness – an interest in what human beings are like when they are at their best – I will sometimes, concede a point and say *giftedness* for short.

Naturally, everyone interested in maximizing the realization of the human potential will be interested in the transformation of childhood gifts into adult creative work. In my own research I have been mainly concerned with understanding how such extraordinary adults do their work (Gruber, 1980, 1981). It seems self-evident that such an understanding is necessary for understanding the *transformation, early gifts to creativity* – from now on I will abbreviate that phrase as *T(G to C)*.

But even if we could be there to record every millisecond of it, we could not read off what we want to know directly from a moving picture of the creative life. All developmental processes are constructions of the scientific imagination.

In part, my emphasis on beginning with clear-cut cases of creative lives is a heuristic and methodological one: then at least we are studying the genuine article, and we can with some confidence in the pertinence of our efforts press our research as far back in the developmental history as possible. But in part my emphasis on approaching the study of giftedness through the study of creativity is intended to raise a question about the value of the concept of giftedness. *Only* if we can construct a plausible picture of *T(G to C)* is the concept of giftedness useful. If we neglect the outcome of an extraordinary developmental process, the whole investigation may be built on sand. What could it possibly mean for someone to be gifted if it does not imply something about the later course of development?

Of course, we already know that the relation between giftedness and creativity is an elusive one. Some, probably most, precocious or extraordinary children do not become creative adults. And some, possible many, adults who do creative work were not, on the available evidence, precocious or exceptional children. So research starting at the childhood end of *T(G to C)* and working forward in time is bound to produce many errors of both kinds.

Starting at the other end has as its main risk the tendency to draw too long a bow, in trying to infer remote origins from later conduct. But if we avoid this pitfall, when we study a creative life known to us through adult performance we cannot fail to be examining a phenomenon that is some part of the *T(G to C)*.

Although our ability to predict a creative life from early performance is, to say the least, limited, there are certain distinctions we recognize easily among adults. For example, although it brings me up short, I understand what is meant by "B is more brilliant but C is the more creative." Speaking of adults, we might describe one person as gifted or talented and another as creative or productive. In other words, we have intuitive ways of distinguishing between the conception of ability at a high level and the conception of what the person does with it.

It has always seemed to me that Thomas Huxley was more brilliant and versatile than Darwin. Certainly, any fellowship awards committee comparing young Huxley's plans when setting out on the voyage of the *Rattlesnake* (Huxley, 1935) with young Darwin's plans when setting out on the voyage of the *Beagle* (Darwin, 1934) – both wrote them down in a page or so – would have given first place to Huxley and put Darwin on the waiting list.

Both men, of course, led highly creative lives. Yet we have no question as to which one transformed biology and humanity's image of itself. When Huxley finally heard about the theory of evolution through natural selection, he exclaimed, "Why didn't I think of that?" He might well ask, and so might we. Even if our answers can be only speculative, of one thing we can be reasonably sure, it was not Darwin's greater brilliance that made the difference.

My belief is that Darwin and Huxley had fundamentally different views of science and of nature, and that for the task at hand, waiting for someone to take it up, young Darwin's vague and open receptiveness was a better beginning than young Huxley's hard-edge analytic objectivism, bordering on an early form of positivism. It is a pity that cognitive psychology has provided us with so little guidance as to the relationships among such broad ideologies or points of view and the conduct of a creative life.

The best discussion I know of this openness of Darwin's is "Beyond Anthropocentrism," by Elisa Campbell (1983), a student of English literature.

In *Darwin on Man* I stressed the importance of point of view as against mere problem-solving ability, and even included a chapter called "A Family Weltanschauung." But I did not hit on this particular aspect of cognitive style, which is also captured in Evelyn Fox Keller's recent biography of Barbara McClintock, "A Feeling for the Organism" (1983).

If we want to understand the transformation of early gifts into later creative work, it might be helpful to compare individuals who are very good at something with others who are extraordinary – the merely gifted versus the extraordinary. At least then we would know that we were comparing people who can all do the kind of work being considered, and do it very well. There are possible flaws in this line of reasoning, but the comparison could hardly fail to be instructive. Do they employ the same processes? If not, what are the differences? If so, then what does account for the disparity in level of achievement?

In most domains it is well nigh impossible to make meaningful comparisons of this kind. But the world of chess has a highly developed system for rating the strength of each player. This permitted the Dutch psychologist DeGroot, himself a chess player with an expert rating, to compare the play of 6 grandmasters, 4 masters, and 12 who were rated either expert or second-class players (DeGroot, 1965).

They were all at least excellent, the weaker players having won a number of regional and national tournaments. Presenting each player with a series of chess positions to pursue, DeGroot elicited loud-thinking protocols. In one set of comparisons between 5 grandmasters and 5 experts, there was no question about it: The play of the former was far superior to that of the latter. But, astonishingly, DeGroot could detect no fundamental differences in the processes employed by the two groups.

Then what makes the difference?

Although the main aim of DeGroot's rich work is to understand the cognitive processes involved in high-level chess, when it comes to answering this question, over and over he puts major emphasis on matters of motivation and character. The grand master has lived the game with a greater passion, and has gone through at least one period of youthful chess monomania. As a result, he simply knows more chess: He has a richer knowledge base to draw on, and has it more readily accessible to him. This makes him both faster and more powerful. But this deeper knowledge of the game is the fruit of thousands of hours of play and study. If the grand master has a greater gift than the master, it is not a photographic memory or other magic, but is rather the *Sitzfleisch* and passion necessary to spend those hours.

DeGroot's picture of the development of chess champions may help to explain the high frequency of excellent chess players in certain populations, such as Russian Jews, in which culturally sustained attitudes lead often to early exposure, encouragement, and, above all, taking the game very seriously. (When I was a child, but by no means a chess prodigy, I was the only person permitted to play chess with my Uncle Sam, an expert. He had a bad heart, and any more serious challenge was considered dangerous to his life.) But we need not suppose that the emergence of such patterns necessarily depends on long-established ethnic or family traditions. In Indianapolis, Robert Cotter, a fifth-grade science teacher in an inner-city elementary school, organized a chess club for the students. A chess team emerged, disciplined and hardworking, willing to lose again and again in tournaments, and go back again. Three years later this all-black team won the U.S. national elementary school championship. In one year, 4 of their players were ranked nationally among the best 50 players under the age of 13. As one child put it, "It was the only sport here" (*New York Times*, May 10, 1983, p. 16).

DeGroot cites approvingly and at length a study of young composers by Bahlke, in which biographical evidence lent support to the

"rational" view, contradictive to such "irrational" conceptions as an effortless "growth" toward mastership, inborn genius, unanalyzable, miraculous inspiration, magical intuition, and so on. He showed the prime importance of the factor of self-organization both in the developing composer's creative production proper and in his antecedent learning processes. Here, too, a very strong long-term motivation towards self-development in the field in question leads to a rapid accumulation of fertile, differentiated "experience." Instrumental, even indispensable, are the self-organized work and intensive training of the composer's early years. Even to an unparalleled genius like Mozart, it was by no means the gods who presented him with the gift of composing: he too had to acquire his system of creative methods bit by bit. (DeGroot, p. 348)

Recently one of my students analyzed two series of string quartets composed by Mozart, the first in 1773 when he was 17 years old and the second, begun after a lapse of 9 years, from 1782 to 1785 (Leresche, 1984). Both series were immediately preceded by the appearance of string quartets by Haydn, and both owed much musically to him. The first series are imitative, well schooled, formal, and a little dull. The second series – richer, more subtle, and more flowing – was begun shortly after Mozart made his personal discovery of Bach, whose music he then studied with ardor.

Mozart dedicated the 1782–85 quartets to Haydn, and wrote to his friend and master a letter openly acknowledging his debt, avowing that Haydn was "the father, the guide, and the friend" of these pieces, Mozart's "sons," whom he commends to Haydn for protection. Thus, like other young men leaving adolescence behind, when Mozart had grown musically independent of his older model, and had the time to assimilate other influences into forms that were more and more "Mozartish," then he could acknowledge his origins with gratitude.

This incident is of interest to us because it shows development on two time-scales (within the earlier series, i.e., within a 2-month period of work, and between the two series, i.e., over a 12-year period). It shows also the way in which a creative person assimilates external influences to increasingly personal structures, and the differences between a gifted youth and a mature composer. Finally, it shows how these changes come about through the work the person does.

If we are looking for an agent with the transformative power required for *T(G to C)*, we should look at the process of the creative work itself. Through being creative we become creative. Through struggle we become capable of struggle. Why does the first sound like a tautology, the second not? They are the same!

The time it takes to think

"By thinking on it continually." This was Isaac Newton's reply to the question of how he had discovered the law of universal gravitation (Westfall, 1980, p. 110).

We are tempted to see the achievement of the creative person as miraculous, in part because we do not take account of the extraordinary amount of effort and time that goes into the work itself and also into the self-constructive activity that makes the work possible. This is an understandable failing. Thinking is such a private activity. Even when recorded traces are left, as in scientific notebooks or artists' sketches, it takes almost Herculean labors of interpretation to relate these traces to the finished product. Moreover, as I have shown in a study of insights remembered, the creative person in his retrospective accounts necessarily telescopes events drastically (Gruber, 1980).

Nevertheless, if we want a picture of the growth of creative work, that is, *T(G to C)*, we need some idea of the actual time it takes to think creatively and also of the time and effort necessary to effectuate an important change in the equipment the creative person brings to the work. We can get some idea of the first point by looking at creative lives. The second point is probably more amenable to experimental investigation.

There is no more reliable fact in the study of creative lives than this: Important creative achievements result from prolonged work, from protracted and repeated encounters of the creative person with the task he or she has undertaken. Consider a few examples, some of which are dealt with in greater detail elsewhere in this chapter.

William Gilbert, preeminent pioneer of the experimental method, and founding father of the study of electricity and magnetism, worked 18 years to produce *De Magnete* (Gilbert, 1600), at the age of 60.

John Milton conceived of a first provisional plan for his masterwork in 1640. He resumed work on it in 1658 and finished *Paradise Lost* (1665) 7 years later, at the age of 66 (Milton, 1665).

Isaac Newton, in his "annus mirabilis" (actually, the two years 1665–1666) began the work in mathematics, optics, and mechanics and gravitation that became the part of his lifework for which he is still almost worshiped. In spite of Newton's faulty recollections in old age, modern studies of the manuscripts show that it really took him the next 20 years to move from these preliminary sketches to *Principia Mathematica* (Newton, 1685–1687), which he wrote and published over a 2-year period, when he was 45 years old.

Charles Darwin became a professional naturalist during the 5-year voyage of the *Beagle*, began the search for a workable theory of evolution soon after returning home, and in about 1 1/2 year's work fashioned the outlines of the theory of evolution. Twenty-one years later he wrote and published *On the Origin of Species* (Darwin, 1859), at the age of 50.

Sigmund Freud, from boyhood interested in dreams, made the decisive turn away from somatic medicine when he went to Paris to study with Charcot at the age of 30. Ten years later, in 1891, he began the work that led to his founding masterwork, *The Interpretation of Dreams* (1899) when he was 43 years old (Freud, 1899).

Even the seeming counter-examples of astonishing early achievements display this character of prolonged work. Einstein was only 26 in 1905, and that year he wrote and published six finished articles, each of them fundamental, two of them expounding the theory of special relativity. But he had been thinking about the issues for some 10 years. In 1895 at the age of 16, he had written a paper, "On the Examination of the State of Aether in a Magnetic Field," which he sent to an uncle in Belgium, but which was never published. The same year, he conceived of his now celebrated thought-experiment: What would happen if the observer ran after a light wave with the same velocity as the light itself? In the intervening years leading up to 1905, he continued to think about related questions in an increasingly sophisticated way (Pais, 1982, pp. 130–132; Miller, 1981, pp. 123–135).

Mozart's precocity as a performer and composer is not in question, but, as we have seen, this is not to say that his adolescent compositions were highly creative.

When I was writing *Darwin on Man* (Gruber, 1981), at one point I faced a very specific problem. There were several important early notebook entries that could not be reliably dated: Had such and such a thought occurred to Darwin in 1835 or 1836? Or this other idea in 1836 to 1837? On the basis of the evidence available to me, and a hard-won feel for the subject, I made my best guesses, and am glad to say that they have been confirmed by subsequent research (Sulloway, 1982). But the more important point is this: From the point of view of the psychology of thinking as it stood then (and now too, I fear), the decision as to dates made absolutely no difference. For my purposes, to reconstruct the major episodes in a thought process, *accurate knowledge of sequence was enough*. But we have very little information about *rate*, nor even any good reason, explicitly stated within a theoretical framework, why we should seek it. We have some picture of the rapid, intuitive, percept-like processes that take up to a few seconds; we have a rather different picture of the tactical and strategic exploitation of means and ends in problem-solving episodes that take 10 minutes to an hour; and we have still another picture of the much slower processes, like the growth of the self-concept or the evolution of purpose, that takes years and decades. But we do not have any theoretical apparatus for distinguishing problem-solving processes on the 1-hour time scale from those on the 1-year time scale.

For example, in forming a plausible and correct impression of such widely cited "moments" of insight as Poincaré's celebrated account of mathematical thinking (1952), it is important to insist that this occurred in seven distinct episodes in different places over a period of several months, and not in one blinding flash as he stepped onto a bus (Gruber, 1981). But suppose it had been days rather than months: How would that affect our understanding of Poincaré's thinking? Or suppose Darwin had first been struck by some ornithological anomaly in 1835 rather than 1836? In either case, the "remainder" of the thought process (that is, most of it) in question took many more months, and our present-day cognitive theories cannot distinguish between 1 and 15 months.

Insofar as it takes time to develop the kind of collegial relationships necessary for mutual aid, it might be important to know that Darwin became a convinced evolutionist in 1836, after certain important contacts with the ornithologist John Gould. Placing the event in 1835 (the *Beagle* voyage coming to an end) would make Darwin's thought a much lonelier, unaided process. Similarly, insofar as level of aspiration and estimate of self-worth are important in making great plans, the timing of events may matter. Darwin's undertaking a cosmic resynthesis of all biological knowledge *after* receiving an enthusiastic welcome and respectful recognition upon his return from the voyage is different from choosing the same task *before* this boost.

But notice, this argument of the preceding paragraph makes no cognitivist claim about the time it takes to think. It deals rather with some ideas about the construction of social relations and of the self, and of their import for creative work. Cognitive psychology, at this point in its history, is still almost indifferent to time.

This indifference emerges dramatically when we consider the time scale of the typical laboratory experiment as compared with the time that goes into training and practice in real creative lives. The differences lie in the range between 1 and 4 orders of magnitude – between tenfold and ten thousand fold. Anyone who thinks we can simply extrapolate from one scale to another should read *Powers of Ten* (Morrison and Morrison, 1982). So should everyone else. In other words, the great mass of experimentally gained knowledge may be very little pertinent to the study of creative lives.

The gulf, however, may not be unbridgeable. We cannot and would not want to reenact a creative life in the laboratory. But we can fairly easily scale up an experiment from about 1 hour to 100 hours per subject, and when we do this we begin to see profound transformations in the function being studied. Of course, such large methodological changes do not come free. Important compensatory changes, in the number of subjects and in the degree of standardization desired, must be permitted in the design. But we still have investigations that we can recognize as bona fide controlled experimentation.

At the biographical level, I do not know many good examples describing this sort of concentration of effort – ranging from the very persistent to the monomaniacal – except in the fields of athletics and the performing arts. Detailed accounts would make for rather dry reading. But Freeman Dyson's account of an adolescent summer spent teaching himself calculus is a good case in point (Dyson, 1979). If interest in this subject grows, we will be able to accumulate a better picture of the process of concentration itself and of the social and familial supports it both requires and engenders.

The shape of a creative life

In the context of a volume of giftedness it is difficult to shake off the stereotyped idea of a "normal" sequence for a creative life: precocity in childhood, early commitment and achievement, single-minded pursuit of creative goals, a lifetime of elaboration of these beginnings, eventual decline.

But a little consideration of a few cases will show how little grasp this schema gives us of the shapes of creative lives. Albert Einstein was not precocious, did not learn to speak until about 3. William James was a lost soul until about the age of 30, when his reading of the French philosopher Renouvier helped him to shake off a prolonged crisis of will (Perry, 1948, p. 121). Neither Isaac Newton nor Bertrand Russell (each an author of a *Principia Mathematica*) was particularly "single"-minded. Each had "sidelines" that began early and took up something like half or more of his lifetime – in Newton's case, religion and alchemy, in Russell's, pacifism. Russell wrote his *Foundations of Mathematical Philosophy* while in Brixton prison for his antiwar activity during World War I.

Studies such as Lehman's *Age and Achievement* (1953) provide a different path into the discussion of the shape of a creative life. The field of mathematics is widely mentioned as proof par excellence of the importance of an earlier achievement for the later career. But one of England's most distinguished mathematicians, G. H. Hardy, himself quite an elitist, in his provocative book *A Mathematician's Apology* (1941), claimed that he had not reached the height of his powers or done his best work until his 40s.

A careful reading of the main source of information, Lehman's work, shows how weak is the support of this stereotype. Lehman took his data from Cajori's *History of Mathematics*. He plotted the total number of contributions against age of first important contributions to mathematics for 444 mathematicians. Lehman concluded, "Mathematicians will be interested to know that the correlation ratio between these two variables is − .61, which means that the earlier the age of beginning, the greater the total number of contributions" (Lehman, 1953, p. 185).

As every graduate student knows, a correlation of .61 accounts for only about one-third of the variance. Moreover, Lehman's scatterplot suggests that a small number of cases accounts for most if not all of the correlation. Eliminating about 5 extreme cases from each end of the scatterplot would reduce the correlation to almost zero. Much the same could be said for Lehman's scatter plots of the same variables for chemists and physicists.

It should be added that people who start late and therefore make only one or two important contributions actually provide evidence *against* the early-start stereotype under discussion. There are in Lehman's scatterplot 6 mathematicians who "began" past the age of 70 and made only one significant contribution to mathematics. Pumped uncritically into the scatterplot, they account for much of the correlation, and seem to add credibility to the stereotype. Yet their lives testify against it.

Still, something is probably gained by the knowledge that there is some low correlation between the age of beginning and number of contributions. It might conceivably mean that an "innate" gift that finds early expression will continue to do so. On the other hand, it might reflect the way in which a person shapes himself and the road he will take. In psychological development as in embryological, first steps in one direction are fateful for whatever is to follow. This is the meaning of Maruyama's phrase "initial kick" in systems that can evolve in different directions, in his paper with the wonderful title "The Second Cybernetics: Deviation-amplifying Mutual Causal Processes" (Maruyama, 1963). It is also the meaning intended by Robert Frost's poem "The Road Not Taken."

The emphasis on quantitative analysis in studies of age of achievement leads to some peculiar omissions. A case in point is John Milton. To examine the age of achievement in literature, Lehman compiled a table of the 16 most prolific contributors to English literature, again arguing for the relation between age of first contribution and total number of contributions. It is certainly a good list, headed by Shakespeare and also including Dryden, Bulwer-Lytton, Shelley, and Defoe. But Milton's name is missing. Presumably, had he not spent so much time in politics, he would have been more prolific in poetry. My encyclopedia says, "Had Milton died in 1640, when he was in his thirty-second year, and had his literary remains been then collected, he would have been remembered as one of the best Latinists of his generation and one of the most exquisite of minor English poets" (Masson, 1911).

This article goes on to give one of the best short accounts I know of a creative life in which different enterprises take center stage at different times. Masson explains the functional relationship among such waxings and wanings, defending Milton against those who feel he "deserted" literature for politics.

Not so, says Masson, his pamphlets *are* great literature, and moreover, without this 20-year interlude he would not have formed of his life the "true poem" necessary for him to write *Paradise Lost*.

More dramatically, his greatest work, *Paradise Lost*, would never have been written had Milton (Cromwell's champion and secretary for foreign affairs) not escaped the scaffold at the Royalist Restoration after Cromwell was deposed and executed in 1658. Milton had begun work on *Paradise Lost* in about 1640, put it aside and resumed it in 1658, and finished it in 1665 when he was 66 years old.

Although Milton's masterwork was written in his later life, he was hardly a late bloomer. The poetry he wrote before the age of 40 stands as part of the treasure of English literature. His contemporary, John Locke, however, first studied and practiced medicine, and then participated vigorously in political life as secretary to the earl of Shaftesbury. Only in 1666, when he was 34 years old, did he write a significant philosophical piece (the *Essay Concerning Toleration*). It was not until 4 years later, and then almost by chance, that he found the road that led him eventually to his masterwork, the *Essay Concerning Human Understanding* (Locke, 1959), which appeared in 1690 when he was 58 years old.

In a good English tradition, Locke did much of his philosophical thinking and writing, including the *Essay*, while on the run from the British government. He spent the years 1683–1689 in Holland, and there completed the *Essay*. This work should be considered one of the founding documents of cognitive psychology, but the unity of its author's life would not stand well with today's exponents of a bloodless, depoliticized, decontextualized cognitive science. Locke was as much concerned with the political philosophy of human freedom as he was with the way people think and get knowledge when they are free. It is, incidentally, a gross distortion of the history of ideas to shrug off Locke as an exponent of the passive receptive mind entailed in the metaphor of the tabula rasa. That was only his way of saying that ideas are not inborn but come through active experience. Another metaphor he employs for the getting of knowledge captures the spirit of his intellect more aptly: The knower is a hunter, a falconer who sends his bird out to the hunt, to bring back the prey of truth ("Epistle to the Reader," with which the *Essay* opens).

Another figure who found his way rather late is Sigmund Freud. There are few if any indications of very early precocity in his biographies. There was at least one moment of early revolutionary activity: At the age of 7 or 8 he deliberately urinated in his parents' bedroom (Jones, 1953, vol. 1, p. 16). And there is one account of early recognition: In a casual encounter, Freud's father exclaimed to a child who was arguing with his father, "My Sigmund's little toe is cleverer than my head, but he would never dare to contradict me!" (Jones, 1953, vol. 1, p. 19).

It does seem that sometime between the ages of 8 and 10 young Freud was "turned on" to the life of the mind–beginning the interest in language, literature, and antiquities that eventually made him not only a great psychologist but a great writer. As is well known, his early medical studies took him in the direction of neurology and pharmacology, in which fields he made promising research starts. It was not until 1885 (age 29) that he made his fateful visit to Paris and worked with Charcot for 6 months. Ten years later, after a complex gestation, he began to write the work that may be his most important (he thought so), *The Interpretation of Dreams* (1899), finished and published when he was 43.

Freud's life brings home the point that a person leading a creative life need not crash the scene like Gangbusters. Some great figures find their way slowly. Freud put it well: "The voice of the intellect is a quiet one, but in the end it will be heard." His life also demonstrates great integrative powers. His deep knowledge of language and the classics formed a preeminent part of his psychoanalytic theorizing. His neurological training played a vital, if sub-rosa, part in his psychological thought (Sulloway, 1979).

I hope the reader understands by now that I am not questioning the occurrence of precocity, early achievement, and single-mindedness in creative lives. Of course they occur in some cases, and sometimes even all three of them together. But I am questioning both their necessity and sufficiency for the evolution of a creative life, and also their aptness, when taken together, as a syndrome for characterizing the typical course of creative growth.

Much of our discussion up to this point has centered around questions of time – the time that goes into practice, the time needed to create a great work, and the age of achievement. All these are separable but connected issues. The different sorts of evidence I have assembled are meant to show that the time required is long. Perhaps this is the true meaning of the expression "Ars longa, vita brevis." This disparity exacts of the creative person that he mobilize himself for his tasks. Any discussion of *T(G to C)* must deal with that process of self-mobilization.

Self-mobilization and the feeling of specialness

"I am different, let this not upset you." I was in graduate school when I first knew these words of Paracelsus, and I relished them. Ten years and a war earlier, as an undergraduate, when I first studied the psychology of thinking by listening to Solomon Asch lecture from the typescript of Max Wertheimer's *Productive Thinking* (1959), Paracelsus would have seemed strange to me. We learned to approach creative thinking as nothing but problem solving, albeit informed by the sensitive grasp of structural change inherent in *Gestalttheorie*. The proper and productive attitude toward the problem confronting the thinker was "task-oriented," and heaven forbid an errant "ego-oriented excursion." What could be more reasonable, it seemed then: If you want to think well, surrender yourself to the task, become engrossed in it, respond to the structural requirements of the situation. If we had thought of creativity as a characteristic of a person, we would have thought of it as the capacity for just such task absorption.

There is a small historical paradox here. It was the Lewinian offshoot of *Gestalttheorie* that fostered the distinction between task- and ego-motivation (also known as intrinsic and extrinsic motivation, although there are different shades of meaning involved). Yet is was the same Lewinian ethos that produced and vigorously pursued the fruitful concept of *level of aspiration* (Lewin, 1935), which gave rise to an interesting experimental literature. It should have provided the hint necessary to see that in real life, attacking the most difficult tasks requires the highest level of aspiration, and consequently puts stressful demands on the ego system.

History aside, it seems to me now that we will never have an adequate theory of creative work unless we come to understand exactly how the creative person moves back and forth between these two attitudes, both *surrendering* himself or herself to the requirements of the task and *mobilizing* every personal resource to surmount its difficulties. For we are not speaking of tasks that present themselves politely, visiting card in hand, but of life goals that the creative person shapes and assumes, a set of special requirements few others feel. We are speaking also of estimates of one's own powers that lead the creative person to attack the almost impossible, the formerly undreamed-of, the question of questions.

To the person doing creative work, once on the road, such choices need not feel at all like arrogance. He or she is not a stumblebum. It is part of the métier to have some grasp of the historical situation and a realistic estimate of available personal resources, in short, the self and world knowledge necessary to move purposefully and effectively in a direction.

The development of a self-concept adequate for creative work must include:

1. A grasp of the disparity between the actual and the possible, and the visionary spirit necessary to treat the latter as more real than the former – to *dwell* in the world of the possible.
2. A sense of special mission; a will to commit enormous energies and all the time necessary, a lifetime, to the chosen task.
3. A sense of daring, a high level of aspiration – *The Courage to Create*, in Rollo May's words (1975).

If the creative person does not knowingly set high and difficult goals, then we would have to think of him as moving blindly toward his achievements. There are potentially a few such examples to consider. At least two of Darwin's contemporaries, Algernon Wells and Patrick Matthews, hit on the idea of natural selection. But they were not interested in exploiting it, did not see its importance, did not think of themselves as special individuals trying to transform humanity's image of itself and its origins. So the name you recognize is Charles Darwin – and, of course, Alfred Russel Wallace, who was also *consciously* searching for a theory of evolution.

I have assembled a few examples of clear expressions of this sense of specialness and high purpose. They occur at different moments in the life history and illuminate different aspects of the construction of self in the creative person.

Newton, in a famous remark, said, "If I have seen further it is by standing on the sholders [sic] of giants." Since he said it in connection with a dispute over priorities, one of several, with Robert Hooke, Manuel (1979) has suggested that it was Newton's not so subtle way of casting aspersions on his physically crooked and dwarfed rival. With or without the note of spite, it was a less than modest remark. Newton certainly did not think of himself as a pygmy on the shoulders of giants (although that was probably the original form of the metaphor). His high level of aspiration is reflected in a less disputatious remark: In the first two books of *Principia*, he wrote, he had "laid down the principles of philosophy. . . . It remains, that from the same principles, I now demonstrate the frame of the System of the World," (book 3 of *Principia*, cited in Andrade, p. 83).

Darwin, too, left no doubt as to the cosmicality of his aspirations. One example will have to do. A few months after he began his first notebook on evolution, he wrote a summary of the progress he had made. I select, from a context that is mainly "task-oriented" and focused on the specific tasks of constructing an evolutionary biology, a few phrases that suggest Darwin's level of aspiration:[1]

> "Before attraction of gravity discovered it might have been said . . ." (B-notebook, p. 196, Darwin manuscripts in Cambridge University Library). Here follows an analogy between his own and Newton's tasks.
> " . . . My theory very distinct from Lamarck's" (B-notebook, p. 214). This is one of several passages where he compares himself with his precursor and rival.
> "The grand question which every naturalist ought to have before him when dissecting a whale, or classifying a mite, a fungus or an infusorian is What are the Laws of Life?" (B-notebook, p. 229). Darwin knew only too well that this was not the attitude of his contemporaries.

Darwin made those remarks in a notebook written in his late 20s. But he kept the same spirit throughout his life. For example, in 1856 (aged 47) he wrote to a colleague, "I have lately been especially attending to Geograph [ical] and Distrib [ution], and most splendid sport it is, – a grand game of chess with the world for a Board" (letter to Charles Bunbury, April 21, 1856).

Freud, in several places, likened himself to Copernicus and Darwin in revolutionizing man's image of his place in the world: His planet was not at the center of the universe, his species was not at the pinnacle of creation, and his rational mind was not in control of itself: a Miltonic triple dethronement and 5-century revolt of the angels against the order of heaven, with Freud himself leading Satan's legions into the 20th century.

Einstein, whom we rightly know as a modest man, in 1905 wrote to his friend Conrad Habicht, "I promise you four papers ... the first ... deals with radiation and the energy characteristics of light and is very revolutionary." He goes on to describe the other papers, the last of which is the first article on the special theory of relativity (Miller, 1981; Pais, 1982).

Whichever of the six (not four) fundamental papers he wrote in 1905 was the more revolutionary does not concern us, only the evident fact that he did not mind the role, that he saw himself as the person whose thinking would transform physics.

I do not mean to suggest with these examples that these people were all arrogant or immodest or unduly preoccupied with the greatness of their goals. On the contrary, they managed very well to *harmonize* their personal needs and the historical requirements of the situations that confronted them. Nor do I mean to suggest that they had similar personalities. With regard to the ego-needs under discussion, they each handled matters very differently. In his priority disputes with Hooke and others, Newton was bitter and fierce, and then sometimes willing to back down a bit, but still leaving much rancor. Darwin avoided a potential dispute with Wallace by asking a group of distinguished scientists (all of them his friends) to mediate, and as I have written elsewhere (Gruber, 1981), they did so quite satisfactorily for all concerned. Freud worked more closely with others, and simply threw them out of his circle as need be to maintain unity, always a great blow to those father-figure followers. Einstein may have been a bit above it all. If Darwin was the most human of this lot, Einstein was the most saintly.

Conclusion

The issues I have been raising here are not arbitrary or idiosyncratic intrusions in a discussion of human extraordinariness that otherwise has a clear rationale to justify it. They are necessary considerations.

If the concept of giftedness is to be taken seriously, a gift must have as its consequence some connection with extraordinary achievement.

If the transformation of a gift into a creative achievement is to be understood, the end point of the process must be studied as an integral part of improving our concept of giftedness.

If the creative person is identified by his unique achievements, scientific method must be adapted to fit it for the study of unique events, or the project must be abandoned as standing beyond science.

If creative achievements are rare and unique because they are difficult, complex, and improbable, then they must take time in their construction.

If protracted purposeful work is essential to creative achievement, the creative person must be capable of it, having not only the skills of his métier but also the sense of purpose, ego strength, and other personal resources necessary to sustain the effort.

If creative achievement depends on such combinations of purpose, self-mobilization, and skills, then the study of creative work requires the study of such unique personological configurations in action.

The shaping of a creative life is not an a priori gift but a process of self-construction.

Note

1 All citations from the Darwin manuscript are based on my own reading of them in the Manuscript Room of the Cambridge University Library with the help of my collaborator, Paul H. Barrett. These quotations can also be found in *Darwin on Man* (Gruber, 1981).

References

Andrade, E. N. Da C. *Isaac Newton*. (1950) London: Max Parrish.

Campbell, E. K. (1983). Beyond anthropocentrism. *Journal of the History of the Behavioral Sciences, 19*, 54–67.

Darwin, C. R. (1859). *On the origin of species*. London: John Murray.

Darwin, C. R. (1934). *The Beagle diary*. Edited by Nora Barlow. Cambridge University Press.

DeGroot, A.D. (1965). *Thought and choice in chess*. The Hague: Mouton.

Dyson, Freeman (1979). *Disturbing the universe*. New York: Harper & Row.

Freud, S. (1899). *The interpretation of dreams*.

Gilbert, W. (1958). *De Magnete*. New York: Dover. (Original work published 1600.)

Gruber, H. E. (1979). On the relation between "Aha experiences" and the construction of ideas. *History of Science, 19*, 41–59.

Gruber, H. E. (1980). "And the bush was not consumed." The evolving systems approach to creative work. (pp. 269–299). In S. Modgil and C. Modgil (Eds.), *Toward a theory of psychological development*. Windsor, England: NFER Press.

Gruber, H. E. (1981). *Darwin on man: a psychological study of scientific creativity* (2nd ed.). Chicago: University of Chicago Press. (First published in 1974.)

Gruber, H. E. (1985). Giftedness and morality: creativity and human survival. In F. D. Horowitz and M. O'Brien (Eds.), *The gifted and the talented: A developmental perspective* pp. 301–330. Washington, D.C.: American Psychological Association.

Hardy, G. H. (1941). *A mathematician's apology*. Cambridge University Press.

Huxley, T. H. (1935). *The diary of the voyage of H.M.S. Rattlesnake*. Edited by Julian Huxley. London: Chatto & Windus.

Jones, E. (1953-57). *The life and work of Sigmund Freud (3 vols.)*. New York: Basic Books.

Keller, E. F. (1983). *A feeling for the organism: the life and work of Barbara McClintock*. San Francisco: Freeman.

Lehman, H. C. (1953). *Age and achievement*. Princeton, N.J.: Princeton University Press.

Leresche, K. (1984). Approche cognitive d'un créateur: W. A. Mozart. Unpublished student paper, University of Geneva.

Lewin, K. (1935). *Dynamic theory of personality*. New York: McGraw-Hill.

Locke, J. (1959). *An essay concerning human understanding* (2 vols.). New York: Dover. (Original work published 1690.)

Manuel, F. E. (1979). *A portrait of Isaac Newton*. Washington D.C.: New Republic Books. (Original work published 1968 by Harvard University Press.)

Maruyama, M. (1963). The second cybernetics: deviation amplifying mutual causal processes. *American Scientist 51*, 164–179, 250–256.

Masson, D. (1911). John Milton. *Encyclopedia Britannica* (11th ed.), *18*, 490.

May, R. (1975). *The courage to create*. New York: Norton.

Miller, A. I. (1981). *Albert Einstein's special theory of relativity, emergence (1905) and early interpretation*. Reading, Mass.: Addison-Wesley.

Milton, J. (1665). *Paradise lost*.

Morrison, P., Morrison, P., and the office of Charles and Ray Eames (1982). *Powers of ten*. New York: Scientific American Books.

The New York Times, May 10, 1983, p. 16.

Newton, I. (1685–1687). *Principia Mathematica*.

Pais, A. (1982). *"Subtle is the Lord..." The science and life of Albert Einstein*. New York: Oxford University Press (Clarendon Press).

Perry, R. B. (1948) *The thought and character of William James* (briefer version). Cambridge, Harvard University Press.

Poincaré, H. (1952). *Science and method*. New York: Dover. (Original work written and published 1908, many years after the famous mathematical insight it describes.)

Russell, B. (1919). *The foundations of mathematical philosophy*.

Sulloway, F. J. (1979). *Freud, biologist of the mind: Beyond the psychoanalytic legend*. New York: Basic Books.

Sulloway, F. J. (1982). Darwin's conversion: The Beagle voyage and its aftermath. *Journal of the History of Biology, 15*, 325–396.

Wallace, D. B. (1985). The problem of giftedness and the construction of a creative life. In F. D. Horowitz and M. O'Brien (Eds.), *The gifted and the talented: a developmental perspective*, pp. 361–385. Washington, D. C.: American Psychological Association.

Wells, H. G. (1911). *The country of the blind and other stories*. London: Nelson.

Wells, H. G. (1897). *The Invisible Man: a grotesque romance*. London: Pearson.

Wertheimer, M. (1959). *Productive thinking* (enlarged ed.) New York: Harper & Row. (First published 1945.)

Westfall, R. S. (1980). Newton's marvellous years of discovery and their aftermath: Myth versus manuscript. *Isis, 71*, 109–121.

12   Culture, time, and the development of talent

Mihaly Csikszentmihalyi and Rick E. Robinson

The literature on giftedness gives the impression that most authors conceive of talent (*talent, giftedness,* and *prodigious performance* will be used interchangeably) as a stable trait that belongs to a person. Although some writers have warned us not "to view giftedness as an absolute concept – something that exists in and of itself, without relation to anything else" (Renzulli, 1980, p. 4), most people consider giftedness as an objective fact, something you either have or don't have, like green eyes or a mole on the nose. Our 20 years of research with mature artists and other creative individuals suggests a different view, which might be summarized as follows:

1. Talent cannot be observed except against the background of well-specified cultural expectations. Hence, it cannot be a personal trait or attribute but rather is a relationship between culturally defined opportunities for action and personal skills or capacities to act.
2. Talent cannot be a stable trait, because individual capacity for action changes over the life-span, and cultural demands for performance change both over the life-span and over time within each domain of performance. Thus, it cannot be assumed that a 5-year-old prodigy will be considered outstanding as a teenager or adult. (Artificially restricted definitions of talent based purely on test performance, such as an IQ score, are a partial exception to this rule.)

These two points may seem to have only obscure, ivory-tower academic interest. But their implications have a rather substantial bearing on what we think giftedness is, how we measure it, and what predictions we think are warranted by our measurements. The remainder of this chapter will attempt to explicate these implications as suggested by our longitudinal studies of gifted individuals struggling to develop their talents in the real world.

The researches referred to in this article were supported by the Spencer Foundation (longitudinal study of artists) and by an SSRC grant to study gifted mathematics students.

264

The sociocultural constitution of giftedness

Investigators in the field of giftedness occasionally remark that, whereas there are young prodigies in music, chess, foreign languages, sports, or mathematics, there are no child prodigies in the realms of morality, altruism, politics – or even art and poetry. This fact is interpreted to mean that children are able to develop precocious skills in music, math, and the like, but not in morality.

An entirely different interpretation is also possible. We do not see early talent in morality, not because children lack the appropriate skills, but because what we mean by morality has never been as clearly articulated as, say, what we mean by mathematics. Without a clear definition, we have no criteria for recognizing in young children the behaviors that might develop into outstanding moral ability. It is not simply that we are lacking the right test or scale, but that, when dealing with domains that have not been fully and consensually defined by society, we do not even have a good grasp of what it is we are looking for. More than 20 years ago, in their exploration of creativity, Getzels and Jackson (1962) suggested that "psychosocial excellence" was as important a skill as outstanding intellectual ability was, and they began to investigate the characteristics of highly moral teenagers. But when, last year, Howard Gruber, of the Committee on Giftedness of the Social Science Research Council, organized a symposium on moral giftedness at Yale University, it was as if every participant had to rethink and redefine the concept of morality from ground zero. Instead of fostering a greater consensus, the intervening twenty years seem to have served only to increase confusion about the nature of morality.

Musical or mathematical talent can be easily recognized, because Western culture long ago developed a fairly clear and unanimous agreement as to what these domains are. Equally important, for every well-defined domain there is a well-elaborated set of criteria that permits specification of what constitutes excellence at any of a number of points in the life-span. Thus, accuracy and excellence in those domains is easy to assess. Those trained in the field have the means to recognize superior performance at once. Consequently, an outstanding performance can label the performer as having a "gift," which can then be reinforced and nurtured through a series of increasingly demanding challenges that the medium (music, mathematics, swimming, etc.) presents. Domains that are less clearly defined also lack the articulated series of challenges and criteria for evaluation. Therefore, it becomes exceedingly difficult to identify the precursors of excellence and those who may possess them. Furthermore, those who do possess potentials in such domains are given none of the systematic support necessary to refine and develop potentials into abilities commensurate with the needs of society and demands of the domain.

The reification of giftedness

The quintessence of a talent that has been quantified in light of its societal definition is the one measured by the IQ score. The IQ was developed as a measure of performance in Western academic institutions, and for the sake of the argument, its effectiveness in such settings might be granted. But it is important to realize that intelligence as defined by the IQ did not exist before Binet invented it. Therefore, the whole argument about the relative contributions of nature and nurture to intelligence is meaningless. Intelligence refers to patterns of thought evolved by culture and recognized by society. It cannot exist outside its social context. Of course, like all human behavior, it is mediated by the biochemical processes of the nervous system. But to locate intelligence within the brain is to reify a phenomenon that manifests itself only in interaction. The IQ refers to a peculiar process adapted to its peculiar environment – the Western academic bureaucracy – just as skill in chess is a mental process adapted to the particular setting of the chess game. A superior IQ or a high chess ranking indicate the ability to function exceptionally well within the rules of the appropriate social system. It takes a bit of magical thinking to believe that these abilities have any value beyond the school or the tournament. Outside their social context, they retain only the attraction of whatever stands out because of its scarcity – much like a rare postage stamp or an unusual stone.

The precise measurement of the IQ makes it possible for scholars and educators to ask such questions as: What proportion of the population is truly gifted? Is it 3% or 5%? There are two meanings such questions can have, what we might call a *naturalistic* meaning and an *attributional* meaning (Brannigan, 1981). The naturalistic assumption is that giftedness is a natural fact, and therefore the number of gifted children can be counted, as one might count white herons or panda bears. If this is the sense in which people are asking the question, the question is meaningless. The attributional assumption recognizes that giftedness is not an objective fact but a result jointly constituted by social expectations and individual abilities. From this perspective it is obvious that the question "What proportion of the population is gifted?" means "What proportion of the population have we agreed to call gifted?"

In other words, no objective criterion "out there" will ever reveal how many gifted children there are. The collectivity as a whole must make up its mind where to draw the line. One can argue that any child who can move, see, speak, and think is gifted – after all, how rare such skills are in the empty vastness of the galaxies! And if we reflect on what small proportion of these gifts are developed in the schools or used by the culture, we realize what an enormous task it is to help unfold the basic giftedness of our normal children. On the other hand, one might argue that giftedness is more properly reserved as a title for those boys and girls who show truly exceptional performance in some important domain – the "prodigies" whose skills are perhaps one in a million, or one in 10 million. And there is nothing wrong in claiming that the gifted constitute 5% of the population either, as long as we admit that this figure is not the result of any scientific deduction, but the outcome of a purely pragmatic consensus.

Then there are vast areas of human action in which precise quantifications, or even comparisons, are either difficult or impossible. Variations in ability certainly exist in these areas, but they have not been conceptualized in terms amenable to quantification. It is easy to find out in what percentile one ranks in terms of the IQ scale. It is easy to ascertain that someone is the 14th best tennis player in the world, or someone else the 6th ranked mathematician in his age group. But who is the best mother? Or the 5th most honest politician?

The fact that we can detect talent in chess but not in moral behavior does not mean that chess is more important than morality. Nor does it mean that it is a superior talent. It simply means that, being a rational activity conceived by humans, anything that happens in chess can be completely encompassed by the mind, and ability in it can be accurately measured – whereas morality will evade quantification until the culture evolves a general enough consensus about its nature.

It is in fact equally plausible to advance an opposite claim: that the activities in which prodigious performance can be easily detected are by definition relatively trivial. What makes giftedness so exciting in these domains is not the value of the performance but its clearly measurable extraordinariness. Precocious talent in these fields shares with the feats chronicled in *The Guinness Book of World Records* an appeal to our propensity to respond to the improbable – be it freak or genius.

It is more likely that neither of these claims is completely the case. Still, it is important to keep in mind that precision in measurement is not tantamount to significance or value. The IQ score, the GRE test, or mathematical ranking may be reliable and exact, but precision says nothing about the individual or social value of what is being measured. What remains to be elucidated through the study of the constitution of domains are the sociocultural factors, as well as factors intrinsic to the domains, that determine the degree to which any given domain is clearly defined and talent within it correspondingly quantifiable. But how valuable the domains themselves are must be assessed in light of a general theory of social priorities.

Variations within the domains

The cultural expectations that make the expression of talent possible differ not only from one domain to another, as between poetry and physics, but also within the same one over time. For instance, it was much easier to recognize artistic talent in the Renaissance than it is in the present, because at that time a child who could draw lifelike pictures had something important to contribute to the art of the time. Giotto's gift was supposedly recognized by the Pope's envoy who was riding by the pasture where the young shepherd was sketching his lambs using a flat rock and a bit of charcoal. Most of the artists whose lives Vasari describes were noted at an early age for their skill at reproducing likeness. By contrast, during the height of abstract expressionism in the 1950s and 1960s, drawing lifelike pictures no longer constituted a valuable talent. Spontaneity and emotionality were considered the key elements in the production of good art. Young people who had these qualities were thought to have talent by the gatekeepers of the domain – the art teachers, gallery owners, curators, critics, and collectors. Then, during the following decades, painting returned to much more controlled styles, such as a hard-edge and photo-realism. The qualities that had identified promising abstract expressionists were no longer in demand.

Children with graphic talents for rendering natural forms, or for evoking emotions through their drawing, certainly still exist. Indeed, such children's art is encouraged as a charming expression of spontaneity and innocence by parents, by progressive educators, and by producers of UNICEF Christmas cards. But these talents are no longer considered relevant to mature artistic performance by the gatekeepers of the domain – if anything, they are believed to be detrimental. We see, then, that as the nature of the domain changes over time, the selection criteria for young talent vary accordingly. Because of the interactive and socioculturally constituted nature of talent, as its social definition changes, so does its manifestation – children who in a previous era would have been thought gifted no longer stand out, and others who would not have been noticed now appear to have talent.

How many talents?

The sociocultural constitution of giftedness also provides a relevant perspective on the debate as to whether talent is a unitary gift or whether there are multiple "talents." It has been recognized for a long time that the reduction of giftedness to a unitary dimension is completely arbitrary. Some writers have also taken the next step by admitting that the number of distinct talents we wish to recognize (like the level at which we wish to set the threshold of giftedness) is purely a matter of convention and convenience. There being no "natural" talents, their number and kind depend entirely on distinctions we are willing to make. For example, Paul Torrance wrote as follows:

It is quite clear that there is a variety of kinds of giftedness that should be cultivated and are not ordinarily cultivated without special efforts. It is clear that if we establish a level on some single measure of giftedness, we eliminate many extremely gifted individuals on other measure of giftedness. It is also clear that intelligence may increase or decrease, at least in terms of available methods of assessing it, depending on a variety of physical and psychological factors both within the individual and within his environment. (Torrance, 1965, p.49)

Recently, Feldman (1980) has focused our attention on the existence of different *domains* in which giftedness manifests itself, and has pointed out that, whereas some domains seem to be universal, others are more dependent on the culture or on a restricted subset of performances within it. Howard Gardner's (1983) latest book describes *multiple intelligences,* each potentially resulting in one of seven relatively independent basic talents. Which of these "raw intelligences," if any, a child develops depends on differences in neurological organization that make the child more sensitive to a particular range of stimuli and better able to function within it at a superior level.

These departures from previous orthodoxy point to the direction in which the field is likely to be moving in the future. Yet even these progressive concepts appear to be rooted in a somewhat naturalistic view of giftedness because they conceive of domains as being either more or less dependent on culture. But from an attributional perspective, every domain of thought is entirely constituted by culture, and at the same time entirely dependent on individual physiology. To think of thought as an "interaction" is misleading because it suggests that the two components act separately, that thinking is a combination of discrete biological and cultural factors (Freedman, 1980). In actuality, every act of thought, every symbolic connection, is shaped simultaneously by endogenous biological patterns and by exogenous cultural patterns. It is, of course, possible to alter the content of, or the process of, thought by modifying either template separately. But when a child's thinking is changed through the cultural template, the resulting thought is no more dependent on culture than it was before. The biological processes that make thought possible are just as essential as they ever were. And vice versa: Culture shapes even the most universal, the most basic, conceptual domains.

Perhaps a thought experiment will help clarify these points. Let us suppose that somewhere in the world a new game is invented and given the name of *mo.* (Johann Huizinga, the Dutch cultural historian, has argued that most of the hallowed human institutions – such as science, religion, warfare, the law, poetry – were originally games and only later became serious and binding; thus, the example is not altogether trivial.) To play *mo* well, one must recognize fine spatial and color distinctions, one must be very agile, and one must have a high tolerance for alcohol. With time, the game of *mo* becomes very popular among the cultural elite, and good players are in great demand. But few people possess all the skills necessary to excel in the game, so extensive searches for *mo* prodigies are instituted. The question is, will they find them? As the reader will probably agree, it is logically certain that young *mo* geniuses will indeed be found. It could not be otherwise: Because people differ in spatial perception, agility, and tolerance for alcohol, it follows that there must be a small number of individuals who will be relatively outstanding in all the three skills. This concludes the thought experiment. Now comes the interpretation of its results: Should we conclude that talent in *mo* was caused by physiological factors? Certainly, because all the component skills depend on demonstrably neurological processes. Or should we say that talent in *mo* is culturally constituted? Certainly, because the combination of physiological skills was meaningless before the game was invented.

It would be too facile to resolve this paradox by saying that talent in *mo* is the result of an interaction between individual skills and cultural rules. It is more a question of codevelopment in which latent potentials are shaped by expectations that in turn were made possible by the existence of biological potentials. It is idle to try separating these two components in the genesis of talent.

Implications of the sociocultural model

These considerations suggest that to reify talent as some kind of preformed gift that exists within the child is a mistake. The homuncular view of giftedness does not fit the facts. It is not that the child's talent reveals itself and is recognized by society. It is closer to the truth to say that the possibility to reveal talent is provided by the cultural environment, and that it is this possibility that the "talented" child recognizes.

The clearest practical implication of this perspective is that ideas about identifying gifted children need to be reformulated. Early identification and accurate prediction (the acid test of any identification paradigm) have been the goal toward which much giftedness research has been working. Yet that entire endeavor is predicated on an assumption of giftedness as a stable, intra-individual trait. Recognizing that giftedness is socioculturally constituted means it would be premature to dismiss as infertile the domains where precocity is not now evident (such as morality). Further, we must realize that, as the domain changes through history or across the life-span in response to shifting sociocultural demands, what constitutes an expression of giftedness will also change. Delisle and Renzulli's (1980) "revolving door" model of programming is one approach that already takes this notion into account during the school years.

In addition, a skillful marriage of this attributional perspective with the concepts advanced by Feldman (1980) and Gardner (1983) suggests profitable new directions to explore. On the one hand, we need to know more about multiple intelligences or the potential skills that children possess but that go unrecognized and undeveloped because we are blind to their existence. On the other hand, we must know more about the organization of the domains in which talent manifests itself, because it is what we expect of a chess player, pianist, artist, mathematician, or *mo* player that defines what will constitute talent.

And, what is perhaps most important, we might ask ourselves what it would take to *create* talent in domains that are important to our survival, such as nurturance, wisdom, or frugality. Perhaps all it would take is agreement on the criteria of performance, and then – as if by magic – talent will reveal itself.

The temporal constitution of giftedness

Because the great majority of research in the field of giftedness consists of cross-sectional studies of children, it is easy to fall into the habit of thinking that the "gifted child" is a permanent entity. Such children may grow and develop, may even lose their gift, but basically it is assumed that gifted children studied at 5 and 10 years of age will retain their relative superiority over time, unaffected by qualitative transformations.

Even longitudinal studies (Terman, 1925; Oden, 1968) seem to assume that the passage of time is simply something akin to friction in mechanics, a variable that slowly decreases the predictive power of an early diagnosis of talent. Even when it is recognized that developmental stages in the human life-span introduce qualitative transformations, as in the recent article by Mönks and Ferguson (1983), the authors describe the gifted teenager as a static entity moving through the vicissitudes of adolescence, rather than as a person who may change ways of thinking, wishing, and acting beyond recognition – and hence who may also cease to be gifted by the original diagnostic criterion.

The point is that, if we agree talent depends on social attributions rather than on a naturalistic trait locked in the child's physiology, then it follows that talent should be thought of not as a stable characteristic but as a dynamic quality dependent on changes within the individual and within the environment.

Below, we examine four developmental vectors that express this dynamic: the psychosocial, the cognitive-developmental, the domain, and the field. Although we explicate each separately, it should be borne in mind that movement along each is concurrent with movement along the rest, and that all four are complexly interdependent.

Giftedness through the life-span

A child of 10, born with an exceptional sensitivity to sounds, might enjoy developing his "talent" in music under the guidance of his parents and teachers. In the preadolescent years, as some developmental psychologists have observed, the main challenge confronting a child is to find out whether he can act with competence, whether he can master increasingly complex tasks (Erikson, 1963; Havighurst, 1951). So for the preteen boy, practicing the piano happens to coincide with a possible resolution of this central developmental task. He can throw all his energies into playing music.

After puberty, our little pianist turns into a person with new impulses, new desires, and with a different conception of self related to different experiences and social expectations. He is, to all intents and purposes, an entirely different organization of psychic energy. If we are to follow the Eriksonian map of psychosocial development, we would say that the need to establish his identity becomes the boy's main concern. According to Havighurst, the boy will be mostly concerned to establish his autonomy from the family. In either case, it is easy to see that for the teenage boy to play the piano might now conflict with his developmental task: He might feel that he cannot find his identity or establish his autonomy as long as he continues to devote all his energies to what his parents expect of him. Yet, without constant practice, he cannot fulfill his promise. A great number of talented youngsters presumably succumb to the reorganization of psychic energy ushered in at adolescence.

Similar changes in priority await the growing boy a few years later. The issue of intimacy, of developing close and stable relations with another person, is the salient task for most people in late adolescence. It is a task that is both a challenge and a new opportunity. Those who respond to it may find their old goals reshuffled once more. Practicing the piano may become meaningless compared with a date.

Another reorganization of motives awaits the growing man when he begins to establish a family of his own. We might, with Erikson, call this the crisis of generativity. It involves choices about where to allocate one's psychic energy in terms of replicating one's identity over time. The basic choice is whether to put the most effort into replicating one's *genes* or one's *memes;* that is, whether to raise offspring or to pass on ideas; whether to transmit the information contained within one's biological structure or that contained within one's memory. The Romans used the saying, *libri aut liberi* "books or children" to indicate the dilemma. Of course, there are many examples, headed by that redoubtable patriarch J. S. Bach, of men and women who left both children and works of genius to an appreciative posterity. But by and large it is true that many adults who have succeeded in keeping their talent intact up to their twenties feel they must choose between *libri* and *liberi*. In our studies, we found that promising artists who decide to continue in fine arts as adults tend to marry less often and have fewer children than their colleagues who opt out of their domain of giftedness to pursue more secure careers. This is especially true of women, for whom the competition between bearing (and rearing) children and dedication to art is more acute than for men. Many artists who have placed their talent on a back burner admit that family responsibilities had to take precedence; just as many others confess they simply had to give up marriage and children because their talent exerted an uncompromising attraction.

Although these conflicts have long been recognized, it has been generally assumed that real genius perseveres despite all the upheavals of the life cycle. "Talent will out" is the common opinion; those who are distracted from its relentless unfolding are obviously the weak and the less gifted. But, of course, we do not know if this is indeed the case. Perhaps it is the most talented people, the ones most sensitive to the possibilities of existence, who drop out of the single-minded pursuit necessary to maintain excellence in a domain of giftedness. In a trivially circular sense it is true, by definition, that the most talented are those who persevere. We do not know, however, whether this is also true in an empirical sense – nor is there a way we can see how this proposition could be tested.

Identity, intimacy, generativity: In our culture, these are themes that offer the typical person a chance to restructure his or her self around new goals. They are themes that tend to emerge in a sequence, at predictable times along the life cycle, at the confluence of maturational changes and social expectations. How do they affect the development of the once gifted youngster? Under what conditions will talent emerge untouched from the crisis, and when will it be transformed beyond recognition or abandoned?

Of course, there are also myriad unpredictable events and accidents, some private, some historical, that will affect the development of talent. An illness, the death of a parent, an economic depression, or a sudden epiphany might either reaffirm the young person in his or her goal or change the direction of life forever. At this point, there is no way to take the impact of these random events into account. But the universal regularities of the life cycle, with the dynamic interaction of its psychosocial phases, presents a set of predictable conditions that can be related to the unfolding of talent. In fact, unless such relations are established, it is difficult to see how an early diagnosis of giftedness can have any prognostic value.

Giftedness and cognitive development

Superimposed on the sequence of changes in goal structure at different stages of life are transition points between cognitive stages. The development of thought, as Piaget has shown, does not consist of a simple quantitative increase in the content of knowledge or the ability to reason. It proceeds, rather, by discontinuous reorganizations in the way we think. As Carter and Ormrod (1982) have shown, gifted children (or at least children with IQs above 130) pass through the same sequence of transformation in thinking strategies as normal children do, but faster; at age 13, the average gifted child thinks in terms of formal operations, whereas the average normal child 2 years later is still combining concrete and formal operations in his thought.

The qualitative transitions in thought processes introduce another source of unpredictability in the development of giftedness. Passing from sensorimotor learning to concrete operations, or from concrete to abstract thought, it appears that the growing child might lose the edge of superiority he or she had at the previous stage. Excellence at the concrete-operational stages in no way guarantees excellence at the stage of formal operations.

Jeanne Bamberger (1982), for example, interprets the large dropout rate of talented musicians in adolescence as due to an inability on their part to continue to excel after the transition to formal thought. A child prodigy in music need not operate at the abstract level; superior sensorimotor skills can mark him or her as a genius. But by adolescence, teachers and the critical public begin to expect from the budding genius a sensitivity to the formal relationships in the music he or she plays. According to Bamberger, many brilliant performers must face the realization that the superior skills that served so well at the previous stage do not necessarily allow them to meet the new set of expectations. Presumably, the opposite pattern obtains as well. "Late blooming" may occur when a child who is not particularly good at the sensorimotor or concrete-operational level enters the stage of formal thinking and finds himself at home there.

The complexities of interdependence among the different lines of development begin to be apparent when we note that the main stage in the reorganization of personal goals – that of identity formation and search for autonomy – overlaps in time with the period during which most young people grapple with the transition from concrete- to formal-operational thought. Clearly, then, this is a phase of life in which genius might either vanish or shine with a renewed light. Of course, there might be transitions in cognitive development other than the ones included in the Piagetian canon, and hence other predictable turning points in the trajectory of talent. As cognitive psychology continues its explorations, its finding will have to be constantly integrated with our understanding of what happens to giftedness through the life-span.

Another way to look at time-related changes in the requirements for thought is by adopting the *presented problem-solving* versus the *discovered problem-finding* model of the creative process. This model highlights the fact that when we measure superior performance in children with the IQ or with practically any other test, we are measuring ability to solve problems that are presented. However, superior adult performance in a creative domain requires the ability to formulate new problems on one's own. The skill needed to solve problems appears to be of an entirely different order from the one necessary to discover problems; hence, predictions based on the former may have little bearing on later outcomes (Getzels, 1964). Anyone teaching graduate students suspects, for example, that the indicators of problem-solving ability such as GPA, SAT, and GRE scores, performance on tests and the like are all rather poor at predicting which student will be able to propose an original dissertation. Dropouts from doctoral programs are often brilliant problem-solvers who all through their academic careers were rewarded for their cognitive skills; confronted for the first time with the tasks of formulating a problem of their own, however, they become paralyzed – while candidates far less promising on traditional measures succeed in discovering a worthwhile thesis.

Among artists, for example, it is clear that the ability to find problems is more essential for success than the ability to solve them (Getzels & Csikszentmihalyi, 1976). In our current follow-up study, IQ tests and problem-solving ability measures taken 20 years ago bear no relationship, or a slightly negative one, to current artistic recognition. However, the tendency to approach unstructured tasks with a discovery orientation, and the ability to formulate new problems where none were posed, are still good predictors of success 20 years later.

At this point, we know next to nothing about why and how a child may get stuck at the stage of concrete operations, or never be able to formulate a novel problem. Unless we learn more, a cross-sectional assessment of talent in childhood will remain a useless indicator of achievements to come.

Changing requirements of the domain

The stages of cognitive development discussed above presumably apply to everyone – at least for people growing up in the rationalistic environment of Western culture. But in addition to such more or less "universal" sequences, each domain in which talent can be shown has its own sequences of expected levels of performance, and some of these may require reorganizations of skills that will suddenly inhibit the further development of talent or spur it to new heights.

In mathematics, for instance, the introduction of geometry as a subject at about the first year in high school opens up new opportunities and calls for spatial skills that are apparently based on structures of the brain different from the ones previous computational skills had relied on (Franco & Sperry, 1977). This shift in challenges can overwhelm some formerly talented youngsters and allow others to shine for the first time. In general, however, it is probably the case that a change in cognitive demands at a new stage in the domain is more likely to dampen outstanding performance than to enhance it, for the simple reason that the youngsters who were not performing at the top in a previous stage are usually no longer in contention for "gifted" status by the time that status and its attendant support change in ways that might benefit them. In highly competitive domains, such as music, math, or sports, the way down is always much broader than the way up; year by year, it becomes more difficult to catch up, and dropping out becomes increasingly easy.

For psychosocial and cognitive development, theorists such as Erikson,

Havighurst, and Piaget have provided models of sequences of development that are valuable heuristics for understanding the order and organization of those vectors. For the domain, which at first may seem more arbitrary than coherently ordered, a model familiar to most researchers in giftedness exemplifies a general order across domains: Bloom's *Taxonomy of Educational Objectives* (Bloom et al., 1956). Given that the taxonomy was derived through the analysis of responses to thousands of different tests and test items, refocusing it on domains rather than on individual abilities is a justifiable and possibly more appropriate use of the taxonomy.

Looking at domains in terms of the taxonomy makes it possible to specify transition points where talent is likely to falter or to bloom (with apologies for the pun). Individuals who distinguish themselves by their rapid acquisition and comprehension of knowledge, and facile application of that knowledge to real problems (the first three major levels of the taxonomy) may belie their talent when it comes to analyzing, synthesizing, and evaluating (the three highest levels). Conversely, an individual who has mastered the three lowest levels at a more conventional pace, thus never being identified as "gifted" may find in the higher levels the perfect medium for expressing exceptional ability. Werner von Braun, who developed the principles of rocket propulsion, failed ninth-grade algebra. Yet, we must assume that he eventually mastered the basics of that domain, even if with less than flying colors, before he was able to achieve his masterful solution to the problem and put humanity on the path to the moon and stars. Albert Einstein, as a teenager, failed the admission exams in science at the Zurich Polytechnic.

A distinction similar to the one that involves Bloom's taxonomy has been drawn by Susanne Langer in her discussion of genius and talent. Langer considers talent to be technical mastery and genius to be "the power of conception." Bloom's taxonomy is clearly a further specification of these general definitions. Langer illustrates the implications of this distinction quite clearly when she writes:

Precocity [in talent] is commonly taken for a sign of genius; and every year the concert stage, the radio, the screen, and sometimes even the picture gallery hail as an undoubted genius some truly amazing child, whose talent overcomes the difficulties of technique as a deer takes the pasture bars, and sometimes that child grows up to set the art world afire . . . but far more often its adult life proves to be that of a good professional artist without special distinction. . . . But it is a mistake to think genius is complete from the beginning. . . . Genius, indeed, sometimes appears only with maturity, as in Van Gogh, whose early pictures are undistinguished, and grows and deepens from work to work, like Beethoven's, Shakespeare's, or Cézanne's, long after technical mastery has reached its height. (Langer, 1953, pp. 408–409)

Although it is obvious that technical knowledge will vary from domain to domain, it is less obvious, but probably true, that the higher-order operations – analysis, synthesis, and evaluation – will also vary significantly across domains. Thus, the abilities that facilitate these operations in, say, music, may have no relation to the same operations in physical chemistry. This is, of course, implied in Gardner's concept of multiple intelligences.

Descending once more from the ivory tower, we might point out a practical implication of the distinctions drawn in this section. It has been shown that more rapid cognitive development and technical mastery is one dimension that differentiates "gifted" from "normal" children. This may be termed the quantitative differential. We have also argued that giftedness may manifest itself after certain levels are mastered at a conventional rate on both of these vectors. This type of differentiation is not a matter of rate but of changes in process – a qualitative differential. Quantitative versus qualitative is the basis of the "enrichment" versus "acceleration" debate in curriculum design for the gifted. By considering qualitative and quantitative progression as attributes of the same dimensions, it becomes clear that programming is not a matter of "either/or." Rather, the gifted child builds one upon the other, and programming should be a matter of providing both and modulating their emphasis as the individual develops and changes. The implications for identification should be abundantly clear.

For instance, children placed in a gifted program by virtue of their rapid progress through the early levels of domains may not measure up to the requirements when the quantitative differential ceases to be the primary means of distinguishing the more from the less able. Conversely, as Delisle and Renzulli (1980) have pointed out, the "pool" of potential participants must be kept large and open, so that those who do not distinguish themselves along purely quantitative lines have the opportunity to foster and develop the more qualitative aspects of their abilities when progress through the domain brings them to the point of efficient mastery so as to utilize fully their superior skills at the higher levels. Finally, when higher-order qualitative processes become prerequisites of further progress within a domain, further opportunities arise for assessing the newly emerging skills of students both in and out of the program. Specific domains may differ in terms of when critical shifts in demands for performance occur. If both the domain and the individual involved in it undergo significant changes at these points – as we argue they must – it makes sense for the program and its identification apparatus to undergo a similar reorganization.

Significant work might be done to identify which domains have common abilities necessary for mastery of different levels. As the levels of the taxonomy are worked through for each new domain, the relationship of mastery in one domain to mastery in another also could be ascertained. There are clear parallels between transitions in this hierarchy and those in the other dimensions of our model. An obviously interesting one is the connection between concrete operations, presented problem solving, and the lowest orders of a domain and that of the transition to higher orders, formal operations, and discovered problem solving.

Finally, it should be apparent from the earlier discussion that some domains are much more stable than others. These tend to be the ones that are clearly defined and thus more amenable to precise measurement. What constitutes a great performance in running has not changed since the first Olympic games almost 3 millennia ago, and the criteria in math, music, or chess are almost as hallowed. In a *closed* domain, constructed by humans according to rational principles, requirements are likely to remain stable because the symbolic system is largely autonomous and self-contained – it need not respond to changes in the rest of the culture. Western music or math evolve in terms of their own intrinsic logic, to a large extent regardless of what happens elsewhere. There is no clear link between the transition to non-Euclidean geometry, or to 12-tone music, and any changes outside the domain of math or of music. These transitions were the outcome of dissatisfaction with symbolic formulations within the specific fields and owed very little to social, political, or technological events or to progress in other symbolic media.

To put it another way, we can draw upon Saussure's (1959) distinction between *langue,* the abstract, synchronic semiotic system of language, and *parole,* or the concrete everyday speech of language users. *Langue* is a closed system with its own rules and internal logic; speech, although rooted in language, is a more open system, more responsive to sociocultural influences. Music is an analogous symbolic system. Popular music may shift in response to historical change, but the semiotics of music remain a relatively closed system that sets the parameters within which the popular variations occur. Criteria of excellence in closed domains will tend to be consistent over time.

By contrast, the plastic arts are relatively more open systems without the set language and rules that music is ultimately based on. Open domains interact more with whatever happens outside their own province. Their boundaries are more permeable. Art and poetry are relatively less autonomous than music and math; to be effective, they must stay in touch with what is happening in the rest of the world. The poetry of Rupert Brooke idealizing war lost much of its point after he was killed in a conflict that revealed its sordid meaninglessness, whereas Picasso's *Guernica* owes its success in great part to the fact that it expresses the revulsion we have come to feel in the face of war. Criteria of excellence in open domains are bound to change more often and more drastically than in closed domains, because their parameters are less predictable.

Shifting requirements of the field

If by "domain" we mean a culturally structured pattern of opportunities for action, requiring a distinctive set of sensorimotor and cognitive skills – in short, a symbolic system such as music, mathematics, or athletics – we may designate by "field" the social organization of a domain. A field includes all the statuses pertinent to the domain; it specifies the habitual patterns of behavior – or roles – expected from persons who occupy the various statuses. The field of art includes the statuses and attendant roles of art student, teacher, museum visitor, collector, critic, speculator, historian, as well as that of the creative artist.

We like to believe that the gifted are immune to societal pressure – that the jargon of status and role is not relevant in their case. But it takes only the briefest glimpse at the struggles gifted people must undergo in real life to realize how deep the effects of social expectations are on the development of their talent. And to the extent that these expectations change at different stages of the progress within a field, some previously gifted persons will not be able to continue in the role, whereas others might flourish.

A good example involves the transition between the status of art student to that of an independent fine artist. In our culture (at least in the 1960s, when our study was conducted), many young people who were good at drawing entered art school because they were attracted to the artist's role: the bohemian life-style of the solitary, independent, unconventional genius without material concerns. Fine-arts students who internalized this role were rewarded in art school. They received better grades and stood higher in the opinion of their teachers. Many possibly talented young artists dropped out of the field at this stage because they felt uncomfortable in the expected role.

As the young artist began to move out of his student status and tried to establish himself as a practicing artist, an entirely new set of role requirements, often diametrically opposed to the previous ones, came into effect. To be recognized as an artist in our present culture, a young person has to turn from being a withdrawn, introspective loner into becoming a gregarious self-promoter who can attract the attention of the gatekeepers of the field and who can negotiate advantageous terms with gallery owners and collectors. To make it as an artist, he must learn to banter with businessmen, flatter dowagers, and impress foundations. Many talented young persons succumb to these unexpected challenges that strain the adaptive capacity of even the most flexible among them (Getzels & Csikszentmihalyi, 1976, pp. 184–208). Of course, in other societies, at different times, the artists' status will require other behaviors, other compromises. In contemporary socialist countries, for example, the artist's role is much less individualistic and unconventional from the very beginning; hence, the later adaptation to the requirements of a collectivistic bureaucracy are less discontinuous.

Similar adjustments are required in other fields. For instance, when a young singer or instrumentalist becomes good enough to enter auditions and competitions, an entirely new set of demands enters the picture, and even the most promising musical talent may be cut short by the pressures of public performance. Later on, one might have to learn to politic and to ingratiate oneself with those who control good singing parts or prizes at competitions, and the gifted musician may discover he has no gifts for that.

The demand for mathematical talent in society influences the way it is taught in school. The resultant competitive pressures can take a heavy toll even among the best students. In our current study of gifted high school mathematicians, girls especially express a distaste for the weekly contests that pit students against each other to determine their relative standing as "mathletes." Typically, if a girl displaces a boy from one of the highest ranks, the other boys will sympathize with their demoted colleague and ostracize the successful girl. But also, many of the boys who are good at math and enjoy working at it are unable to cope with the requirements surrounding their status. Later on, of course, the demands will change again – first in college, then in graduate school, then in the professional roles. The competition remains, although in a less obvious form; many new considerations will also enter the picture. For instance, the number of scholarships available in college, the state of the job market, will deter some talented persons or attract others to the field.

The implications of these shifts for the identification of talent are that one must take into account carefully the role requirements of the next status before making predictions on the basis of success in a previous one. For instance, success in school is a rather poor predictor of success in many of the real-world settings in which gifted people usually perform. This for at least two reasons: first, because the academic incentive system is typically extrinsically motivated (e.g., grades), whereas genuine creative performance relies on intrinsic motivation and may be hindered by extrinsic rewards (Amabile, 1983). Hence talented children who perform well in the school system often become lost after graduation when the extrinsic reward structure can no longer guide their performance. Second, academic institutions emphasize and reward problem solving, whereas talented performance after school depends heavily on problem finding (Getzels and Csikszentmihalyi, 1976). Therefore, one might conclude that a child who is exceptionally well adapted to the social system of the school and excels therein is *ipso facto* less likely to be well adapted to the requirements of a creative role, especially in fields like art, literature, and basic sciences, where extrinsic rewards might be arbitrary, and problem finding is at a premium.

The crossing paths of development

Figure 12.1 summarizes what we have said so far about the temporal constitution of giftedness. The lowest of the four steplike lines represents the major psychosocial transitions in the life cycle. Erikson's eight stages were used in this illustration, but the number of transitions depends on how fine an analysis

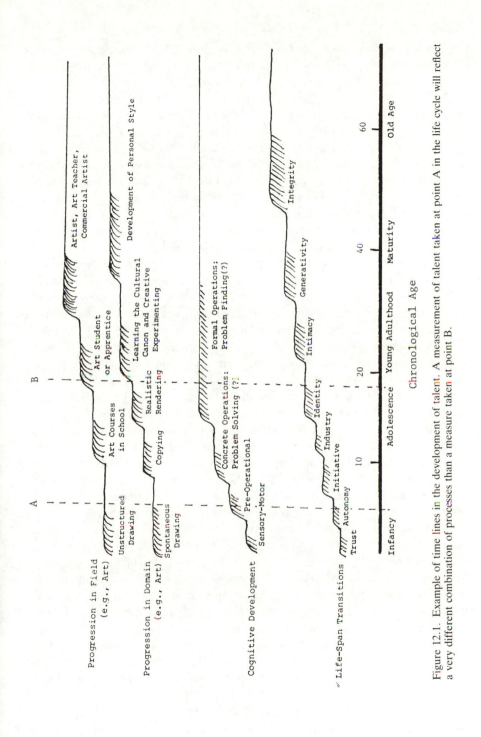

Figure 12.1. Example of time lines in the development of talent. A measurement of talent taken at point A in the life cycle will reflect a very different combination of processes than a measure taken at point B.

is required. For example, Mönks and Ferguson (1983) consider as many as six "transformations in behavioral patterns" during adolescence: attachment, friendship, sexuality, achievement, autonomy, and identity.

The second line from the bottom illustrates major changes in cognitive development. Here the traditional Piagetian transitions are indicated, plus the problem solving–problem finding dimension is alluded to, although as yet there is no evidence about the chronology of that transition. Here again, of course, more refined distinctions in the developmental sequence are possible.

Whereas the two lower lines refer to sequences common to most people in our culture, the two upper lines will vary by domain and by field. In this illustration, the domain of the figurative arts was used as an example. Transition points along these two lines are even more approximate than on the lower ones; they are based on experience rather than rigorous data. To identify clearly the stages at which domains require restructuring of performance is one of the challenges for giftedness research. If we want to be able to give informed help to the gifted and to assist their development, it seems we ought to identify such transitions and understand their dynamics. For example, if we compare a gifted child at around age 5 (line A in Figure 12.1) and then in his late teens (line B), it is clear that the youngster will be in different developmental stages on all four time lines. And if we chose the same two time points for a different youngster with different abilities in a different domain, the cross sections would be different yet again. The challenges will be qualitatively different and so will the resources one needs to draw on. The traits that make the child gifted at A may not be of much use to the young person at B. If the assumption of giftedness as a stable "trait" is maintained, the parent, teacher, or counselor who knows what help A needs to maintain his gifts may well be far off the mark when it comes to helping B.

In the study of gifted high school mathematicians mentioned in the previous section, we met an intriguing problem. When teachers were asked to rate students on "performance as compared to what you see as their potential," almost all of the freshmen were rated at or near their potential, whereas seniors were rated bimodally – half at or near, half "far below." Is this due to sheer difference in ability? It does not seem to be so: The students who live up to their potential are no different on a number of standardized measures of mathematical ability from the students who are not using their talents. Is it due to the *Sturm und Drang* of adolescence? Possibly; the achieving students see getting into a good college as the central current problem of their lives. The underachievers tend to say things such as "figuring out where I am and where I'm going," or "trying to make peace with mother and at least start talking to my father before I leave for college." Is it due to changing interests as new domains are opened up? Possibly; although they are taking the same courses, achievers spend over twice as much time thinking about mathematics as the nonachievers do. Is the difference due to increasingly difficult demands within the domain of mathematics? Again, possibly; trigonometry and calculus are certainly more demanding in an absolute sense, and seniors perceive math work as more challenging than do freshmen. Finally, we must consider the possibility that the whole concept of living up to one's potential is an artifact of the teacher's differential perception of freshmen versus seniors. Teachers have a set of preconceptions as to what constitutes the "proper" progression through a high-powered math program. Students who adapt to these expectations, who fulfill their "proper" role, may be seen as the achievers, whereas those who calculate and integrate to the tune of a different drummer are rated as nonachievers. It is also true that teachers cannot tell whether a freshman does or does not live up to his or her potential; for freshmen, aptitude and achievement are synonymous. Only later in high school is it possible not to live up to one's potential.

Our intuition at this point, though, is that no one of these possibilities gives the full answer for every student. Rather, the relative contribution of each dimension may differ greatly in explaining why each youth did or did not use his or her gift. Of course, only a longitudinal study could answer the questions completely.

To maintain her or his talent over the life-span, a person has to integrate more and more complex experiences in consciousness and behavior. A child prodigy who fails to grow along the four vectors of complexification becomes an increasingly pathetic example of unfulfilled promise. At what age does the unfolding of giftedness stop? There does not seem to be a definite end to its growth. Verdi, who was considered to have talent early in life, composed *Falstaff* when he was nearly 80 years old, and the joy and beauty in that work is like nothing he had ever written before.

Those working with children who are able to perform at exceptional levels in some domain are understandably eager to recognize and to encourage what truly seems to be a precious gift – a rare and enviable possession. It is a natural reaction that we share. But valuing exceptional performance should not lead to blind worship or specious pleading. It is not necessary to subscribe to the naturalistic fallacy, to a position that reifies a process constituted jointly by cultural expectations and by individual abilities.

By reifying giftedness as "scientific fact," one might gain short-term respectability and financial support. But we shall certainly sacrifice long-term growth in understanding. For talent is not the expression of a personal trait but the fulfillment of a cultural potential; it is not just a cognitive process but the focusing of the whole of consciousness on a task; it is not a gift one has to hold on to forever, because changes in the growing person's priorities, and changes in the demands of the domain and of the field, often turn gold into ashes and ashes into gold. To pretend otherwise only serves to obscure reality and prevents a conceptual grasp of the phenomenon.

The directions for research suggested in this chapter may seem circuitous and difficult to follow. They include assuming a perspective alien to those trained in a purely cognitive approach. Yet it is liberating to realize that giftedness is a much more flexible potential than the naturalistic approach asserts it to be, and that in the last resort it is up to us to decide what talents are and how much giftedness there shall be.

References

Amabile, T. M. (1983). *The social psychology of creativity*. New York: Springer-Verlag.

Bamberger, J. (1982). Growing up prodigies: The midlife crisis. *New Directions for Child Development, 17,* 61–78,

Bloom, B. S., Englehart, M. D., Furst, E. D., Hill, W. H., & Graghwohl, D. R. (1956). *Taxonomy of eductional objectives: Handbook I. Cognitive domain*. New York: Makay.

Brannigan, A. (1981). *The social basis of scientitic discoveries*. Cambridge University Press.

Carter, K. R., & Ormrod, J. E. (1982). Acquisition of formal operations by intellectually gifted children. *Gifted Child Quarterly, 26*(3), 110–15.

Delisle, J. R., & Renzulli, J. S. (1980). The revolving door identification and programming model: Correlates of creative production. *Gifted Child Quarterly, 26*(2), 89–95.

Erikson, E. H. (1963). *Childhood and society* (2nd ed.). New York: Norton.

Feldman, D.H. (1980). *Beyond universals in cognitive development*. Norwood, N. J. Ablex.

Franco, L., & Sperry, R. W. (1977). Hemisphere localization for cognitive processing of geometry. *Neuropsychologia, 15,* 107–14.

Freedman, D. G. (1980). The social and the biological: A necessary unity. *Zygon, 15*(2), 117–31.

Gardner H. (1983). *Frames of mind*. New York: Basic Books.

Getzels, J. W. (1964). Creative thinking, problem solving, and instruction. In E. R. Hilgard (Ed.), *Theories of learning and instruction* (pp. 240–267). The Sixty-third Yearbook of the National Society of the Study of Education, Part 1, Chicago: University of Chicago Press.

Getzels, J. W., & Cskiszentmihalyi, M. (1976). *The creative vision: A longitudinal study of problem finding in art*. New York: Wiley.

Getzels, J. W., & Jackson, P. W. (1962). *Creativity and intelligence; explorations with gifted students*. New York: Wiley.

Havighurst, R. J. (1951). *Developmental tasks and education*. New York: Longhmans.

Langer, S. K. (1953). *Feeling and form: A theory of art*. New York: Scribner.

Mönks, F. J., & Ferguson, T. J. (1983). Gifted adolescents: An analysis of their psychosocial development. *Journal of Youth and Adolescence, 12*(1), 1–18.

Oden, M. (1968). The fulfillment of promise: 40-years follow-up of the Terman gifted group. *Genetic Psychology Monographs, 77,* 3–93.

Renzulli, J. S. (1980). Will the gifted child movement be alive and well in 1990? *Gifted Child Quarterly, 24*(1), 3–9.

Saussure, F. de. (1959). *Course in general linguistics*. New York: Philosophical Library.

Terman, L. M. (1925). *Genetic studies of genius: Vol. 1. Mental and physical traits of a thousand gifted children*. Stanford, Calif.: Stanford University Press.

Torrance, E. P. (1965). *Gifted children in the classroom*. New York: MacMillan, Quoted in W. S. Barge & J. S. Renzulli (Eds.) (1975). *Psychology and education of the gifted* (2nd ed, pp. 48–55). New York: Wiley.

13   Giftedness as a developmentalist sees it

David Henry Feldman with the assistance of
Ann C. Benjamin

Introduction

The developmentalist challenge to the field of giftedness is, to my mind, the most significant one in its 70-year history. The creativity movement of the 1950s paved the way for defining giftedness as something beyond IQ. It did not, however, question the assumptions of the psychometric tradition itself (Feldman, 1974, 1980a; Wallach, 1971). Developmentalist approaches, I believe, do this as well. They share with the creativity research movement the belief that IQ, despite its intended generality, is a remarkably confining and limited notion of intellectual giftedness. Beyond this, however, they question the long-held assumption that giftedness is a stable trait of the individual and see it, in contrast, as a complex interaction of human qualities, cultural responses, and traditions of excellence in specific domains.

This chapter presents my point of view about giftedness. As is clear from the title, my perspective is "developmental," and I will discuss in some detail what is meant by this term. In some respects my developmental view is shared by others who call themselves developmentalists, but to some extent it is distinctively my own. Therefore, I will endeavor to highlight those features that developmental viewpoints share, as well as to explain exactly how it is that this developmentalist sees giftedness. If there is reason for assembling a collection such as this it is, of course, that such distinctive viewpoints exist.

Also, I will describe some of the empirical work that has guided and been guided by my particular point of view. This research is as different in style and technique from traditional research on gifted children as are the meanings of key terms in the two approaches. Indeed, much of my research is not with gifted children at all. Rather, the focus has been on transition mechanisms that account for movement from one stage of development to the next. A key assumption of my point of view is that if we understand development, we will begin to understand giftedness, and vice versa.

Developmentalists of two sorts: micro and macro

A developmentalist, to my way of thinking, is an investigator who takes the problem of significant change or transformation as the major focus of his or her work. The size of the changes a developmentalist is interested in can vary from small, relatively local changes to total transformation and reorganization of the organism's psychic apparatus. Indeed, a major issue in the study of development centers around the "learning versus development" debate (e.g., Bereiter, 1982; Brown, 1980; Feldman, 1982b). Piaget has been perhaps the most energetic spokesman for the importance of the distinction between development and learning:

Development, according to Piaget (1972), is the reorganization of the child's entire mental apparatus, an event that occurs roughly three times in the course of growing up. These major reorganizations are believed to take place in all children in all cultures over all historical periods and mark plateaus in the reasoning processes. In contrast to development – the process of achieving and then transforming these qualitatively distinct systems of reasoning – Piaget argued that learning was the accumulation of discrete bits of information such as cardinal numbers or vocabulary words. Development, Piaget said, sets the limits on and specifies the qualities of learning; while learning can be influenced by the environment (i.e., by education), development cannot be. (Feldman, 1982b, p. 26)

Developmentalists, then, consider how best to conceptualize change and ask questions about how much change constitutes a developmental shift. Those who concentrate on relatively small changes often have their theoretical roots in the experimental tradition of learning theory. Those who believe that major, qualitative reorganization must occur before one speaks of development are typically identified with the stage-developmental Piagetian school (Overton, 1983).

There are a number of ways that the study of change can be organized, and these, too, tend to differ depending on one's definition of development. Those who are most interested in small increments of change tend to organize their findings in terms of quantitative increases over time in the particular function in question. For example, the number and variety of word–meaning associations that a child has increases monotonically as the child gets older, up to a certain age, at which point it begins to level off (Estes, 1970). Those who look for more across-the-board changes tend to organize these into various hierarchical systems, typically "stage" theories of one sort or another.

Despite these differences, however, most developmental frameworks share distinctive qualities that, at the same time, separate them from more traditional psychometric points of view.

First, developmentalists tend to emphasize *processes* of intellectual functioning, rather than underlying traits of various kinds and sizes. Second, developmentalists chart *sequences of stages* or levels of mastery in preference to attempting the measurement of general ability. Finally, stage developmentalists in particular have recently begun to see giftedness as *domain-specific* (Feldman, 1980a, 1982a). *Stage* developmentalists are, of course, those who see the issue of major change as somehow best represented in a concept of stage.

Although it is true that stage-developmental views (mine, in particular) exemplify the combination of the three features just described perhaps more than others, all three can be found to some degree in any point of view that carries the label "developmental."

These three features, as expressed in stage-developmental views, may imply substantial change in the field of giftedness; in fact, they could lead to a reconceptualization of the basic concepts used to define the field. In particular, the meanings of talent, giftedness, creativity, and genius may be altered in very significant ways. In the passage reproduced below, I have tried to give a sense of how terms now used in the field might take on new meanings.

Talent from a cognitive-developmental perspective is the potential for constructive interaction with various aspects of the world of experience. Talent of varying degrees does not suggest necessarily that there are fundamentally different developmental processes involved in realizing potential, only that individuals may and do vary in the activities they pursue, the interests they have, etc. That one person becomes a mathematician and another a weaver is due neither to ambient factors in the utilization of general ability, as psychometric theory would tend to imply, nor is it due to reinforcement contingencies in the environment (a behavioral framework); it is due to the continuous interaction of an individual with various potentials and a world with various possibilities. If these processes of interaction lead to high level performance, then it is appropriate to speak of giftedness. To show mastery of advanced topological concepts such as Thom's catastrophe theory is to exhibit a gift for mathematical reasoning, whereas the production of oriental rugs represents giftedness in weaving. Mathematical reasoning and weaving may both involve general conceptual processes, but this is not the issue; giftedness is seen as domain specific in the view presented here.

If the processes of development manifest themselves not only in the mastery of a challenging domain but in reorganization of the structure of that domain as well, we are witnessing signs of creativity. For Piaget, Cantor's invention of set theory is an example of reorganization. Thus, giftedness represents mastery of existing forms, while creativity implies the construction of new forms, or at least novel interpretations of existing forms. Most reorganizations make relatively minor changes in the structure of a domain: microsurgery, for example, uses advanced technology but does not fundamentally change the surgeon's role. On those extremely rare occasions when an entire domain is fundamentally reorganized, we are approaching the realm of genius. Copernicus' recasting of the physical world, Darwin's of the biological world, Freud's of the emotional, and Piaget's of the intellectual worlds; these are examples of genius of a very high order. Fundamentally, however, there is believed to be continuity in the developmental processes responsible for all degrees of utilization of potential. (Feldman, 1983, pp. 1–3)

Historically, developmental psychologists of the more quantitative sort have had little interest in the study of giftedness; their aim has been to look for the most elemental and common processes of change, without reference to variations across individuals. Indeed, individual variation has been seen within this tradition as a source of error (Cronbach, 1957; Feldman, 1980a, 1980b; Sternberg, 1981, 1983). Neither have developmentalists of the broader, qualitative-shift variety had much interest in giftedness, perhaps because Piaget himself had little concern about the topic (Feldman, 1983). They, too, have tended to focus on common areas of universal change.

Recently, however, both "micro" and "macro" developmentalists have begun to direct some of their efforts to giftedness. Although it is hardly a widespread movement, an increasing number of developmental psychologists are becoming involved in this area, as indeed the present volume attests.

Nonuniversal developmental domains

To show how developmentalists have extended their models to incorporate extraordinary progress in a domain and thereby to approach issues of giftedness, it is necessary to introduce the notion of *nonuniversal developmental domains* (Feldman, 1974, 1980a, 1980b). The basic idea of nonuniversals is that developmental psychology has somewhat shortsightedly focused its attention on universal changes in children's behavior. In recognizing this both macro- and micro-oriented developmentalists have begun focusing on nonuniversal domains.

For those developmentalists who are are of the information-processing or cognitive-science persuasion, a common set of core abilities or cognitive functions is implicated in all intellectual performance, gifted and nongifted alike. Thus, the more micro developmentalists see giftedness as a function of utilizing one or a combination of these core abilities to master a specific domain such as chess or physics (Larkin et al., 1980; Siegler, 1978, 1981; Simon & Chase, 1973; Sternberg, 1979). A chess master, for example, is said to have many more items in his or her memory than does a novice or average player. The master also has established appropriate patterns among these elements and is able to select the more appropriate sequence of moves because there are simply more to choose from. Yet, in spite of the fact that the core abilities are presumed to be common ones, it is acknowledged that not everyone has the memory capability of a chess master. There are some disputes about why one person would have 10,000 patterns in memory, and another only 100, but the fact remains that few people do have such a large capacity. Therefore, most people either do not have it or have not developed it. In either case, we are dealing with a situation that is not universal, at least from the point of view of performance. Some individuals have used their capabilities to become highly expert at chess. They may not have been able to use these same abilities for another purpose equally well.

The field of chess itself (and it is, of course, only one example) is indisputably not a universal achievement. Most people do not play chess at all, and those who do often play at a low level. Few are rated as tournament players, and only a tiny fraction of these become masters. Why some individuals are better players than others is obviously a question that relates to the topic of giftedness.

Cognitive scientists are working to make more explicit the cognitive processes and functions that distinguish a novice from an expert in several domains. At this time, however, cognitive scientists seem to emphasize time and effort as the most critical variables in achievement (Simon & Chase, 1973). Theoretically, it is possible for anyone to master the domain at the level of expert, although it may typically take 10 years to travel from novice to master (Hayes, 1981). Although an uplifting point of view in some respects, it does not seem to square with the experience of master teachers (John Collins, personal communication). Some players, no matter how many years they play, and no matter how hard they try, just do not seem to get much better.

A recent example, although drawn from the world of music rather than chess, illustrates this point as well. After listening to Mi Dori, the 11-year-old Chinese violinist, play Paganini's First Violin Concerto, Irvin Rosen, Principal Violinist of the Philadelphia Orchestra's second violin section, said: "I was so overcome by what she did in rehearsal . . . . If I practiced three thousand years, I couldn't play like that. None of us could" (Witty, 1984, p. 79). Putting in the requisite time and effort may be necessary, it seems, but not sufficient for truly extraordinary achievement (Feldman, 1980a; Gardner, 1983).

Another group, more macro-oriented (myself included), has also been attempting to understand how extraordinary achievement differs from more ordinary performance. In contrast to more micro-oriented colleagues, our focus has been on the unique capabilities of specific individuals, as well as on the unique demands made by various fields of endeavor (Feldman, 1982a). A number of individuals are working along these lines, and several are represented in this volume (e.g., Bamberger, Csikszentmihalyi, Gardner, Gruber).

The most familiar work in this tradition has been done by Howard Gruber (Gruber, 1980b, 1981). For a number of years he has studied the development of Charles Darwin's thinking prior to and including the time when the theory of evolution through natural selection was fashioned. For Gruber, choosing an extreme case like Darwin removes any question of "real" giftedness. Gruber argues that Darwin went through a protracted, laborious developmental process to achieve his unique set of insights. He contends that this process is fundamentally similar to the process of general cognitive-developmental change described by Piaget and his coworkers (Gruber, 1981).

In the case of Darwin, we find an even clearer example of achievement in a domain that itself is not mastered by all individuals. Here, as with the cognitive-science or micro approach, universal and nonuniversal aspects of a field or a person's mastery of it are combined in an attempt to explain giftedness. Thus, it is true that both approaches – cognitive science and cognitive developmental – highlight aspects of achieving expert performance that seem to be developmental but are clearly not universal. Attention to nonuniversal domains is a major and, I believe, critical shift in the direction of developmental psychology. Certainly, it has made the study of giftedness and creativity much more feasible from any developmental perspective (Feldman, 1982a).

The explicit or implicit introduction of nonuniversals, then, is the key to the recent tendency for both information-processing and cognitive-developmental psychologists to become more interested in problems of giftedness. Whether it turns out to be a more accurate explanation of giftedness to use certain universal cognitive functions for a specific purpose, such as learning to play chess, or to combine certain distinctive talents, capabilities, and personal qualities with a universal set of developmental changes, or perhaps both, is less important than the fact that an interplay of universal and nonuniversal processes is implicated.

Transition processes

The basic premise of my point of view about giftedness is that there is much to be learned about becoming a master in a given domain by studying the *mechanisms of transition* both within that field and in general. Much of the work by others up to this point has been studying universal transition mechanisms, that is, mechanisms that account for movement from one general cognitive-developmental stage to the next. More recently, I have extended these studies into nonuniversal domains for the specific purpose of illuminating these transition mechanisms further. In particular, my work has focused on transitions between stages in the drawing of simple geographic maps (Feldman, 1971, 1980a, 1980b; Snyder & Feldman, 1977, 1980, 1984).

The work that my colleagues and I have done on map drawing is, as is true of the research on transitions in universal domains, not directly related to giftedness. With very different techniques, I have also studied child prodigies as they master various specific fields such as music or chess (Feldman, 1979, 1980a, 1983, in press). Again, however, the focus has been on processes of transformation and change.

The studies of transition mechanisms in the domain of map drawing, although not directly related to giftedness, have nonetheless yielded some fascinating bits of information about how one moves from less to more sophisticated mastery within any domain of knowledge, universal or nonuniversal. The results of these studies must be taken with some reasonable restraint because there are numerous methodological problems in doing this kind of work. I will not go into these problems in great detail here, but suffice it to say that at this point, our results are suggestive and of heuristic value, but should not be taken as decisive evidence bearing on the points to be discussed. More generally, one of the disadvantages of the broad-gauged approach I have taken is that it leaves many methodological questions unanswered and lacks statistical verification so central in much psychological research. Nonetheless, it seems worthwhile to pursue these lines of inquiry as a guide to future efforts. Therefore, the discussion to follow should be taken as provisional, based on data, to be sure, but not data analyzed in traditional ways or subject to traditional statistical verification (Feldman, Snyder, & Goldsmith, 1984).

Basically, we believe that anyone who performs well must go through a process of mastery, a process marked by a sequence of major mental reorganizations of the subject matter or field in question. This seems to be true of a novice at chess, a child mastering Piaget's conversation problems, and the scientist working at the frontiers of knowledge. Perhaps the central idea of my view of giftedness is that it can best be comprehended within a framework of both broader and more specific stage transitions.

For the average person, the number of stages or levels that he or she will master in a given domain is obviously fewer than for the "gifted" individual. Another way of approaching the issue is to think of certain domains as being less likely to be selected for mastery than others; in so doing, "giftedness" might be revealed not only by the number of levels one achieves, but also by the domain within which an individual chooses to pursue mastery.

Why some individuals elect certain more difficult domains to pursue, and reach more advanced levels of them than others, remains unanswered, although Howard Gardner has suggested some intriguing possibilities (Gardner, 1983; also this volume). Holding a developmental view, however, I would not accept that one individual has spent more time than another working within a domain as the sole reason for differential performance, nor would I accept that the use of various cognitive processes such as memory or attention account for differences in performance, although differences in performance no doubt reflect differential utilization of cognitive processes. The search for explanation, in contrast, moves to a much broader level, one that includes: qualities of the individual; propensities such as talents and personality differences; characteristics of the context within which an individual pursues mastery; characteristics of those who are critical influences on the process such as parents, teachers, and peers; and the state of development of all the various fields that might be mastered at a given moment in time. The combination of all of these possible areas of influence makes up the overall field of study.

Now, I grant that this expansion of inquiry brings with it many problems, not the least of which is to comprehend the various components of achievement and how they might interact (Fischer, 1981). Yet, it seems justifiable to take this broad approach when the problem to be addressed concerns extraordinary achievement. The search for an explanation must go beyond individual characteristics; there have been too many examples of equally or even more gifted individuals not doing what their seemingly less gifted peers have done, to leave the search at the boundary of the individual's psyche. Whatever form such explanations eventually take, they will need to incorporate the individual, those who influence the individual, the social, cultural, and institutional context within which an individual is working, and, in all likelihood, historical and even evolutionary forces that impact on the environment during the period of time that an individual is developing.

To put these matters somewhat differently, the point of view I am trying to convey sees the following kinds of questions as necessary: How does an individual find a field or domain within which to pursue mastery? Under what conditions are the possibilities for utilizing one's potential optimized? How critical is it that an individual be exposed to and allowed to begin working in a domain at an early age? Do fields develop themselves over time, and if so, how do these developmental changes interact with and affect those who might aspire to master them? When one sees seemingly uncanny mastery of a difficult domain, as is the case with child prodigies, what are the interacting forces that might produce such extraordinary performance? How critical are catalytic forces, such as parents and teachers, or more static ones, such as technologies and books, on bringing forth the possibilities for an individual's pursuit and mastery of a given field?

The work that like-minded colleagues and I have been doing in the area of giftedness and creativity is intended to establish generalizations such as these at a fairly holistic level. We see previous efforts as being either too broad and all-encompassing on the one hand, or too precise and limited on the other. The idea of a single metric such as IQ or a creativity test score encompassing the many qualities of giftedness and the many forms in which individuals can produce creative works seems in need of differentiating and sharpening if understanding of giftedness is to be furthered. Yet, we find that the works of our more mechanistically oriented colleagues (those who associate themselves with information-processing or cognitive-science perspectives) seem too focused on the specifics of performance and miss most of what might be encompassed by the idea of giftedness (Feldman, 1979, 1982a).

It is a difficult task to try to conceptualize concepts and variables to be tested at this "intermediate," or broader level of generality. There is also a paradoxical quality to the enterprise. This quality consists of the overall aim of the work, which is to broaden and increase the variety of forms in which giftedness and creativity are recognized on the one hand, while arguing for concepts more specific than IQ and overall creativity scores as the best means for achieving that goal on the other. It almost sounds as if we have been trying to make giftedness broader by making it more specific, a paradox if ever there was one. Yet, in a sense, this is precisely what we are trying to do. Rather than saying that a person is overall more gifted or more creative than another person, we are trying to suggest that a person is likely to exhibit giftedness in only one or a small number of domains (Gardner & Feldman, 1984). With a broad definition, such as IQ, the field is left open for giftedness to manifest itself in many ways, but there is no set of concepts, categories, or variables that helps direct attention to more specific aspects (although see Sternberg, 1981).

For the information processor, the problem is virtually the opposite. Because some people perform better than others in almost every field imaginable, it becomes a more or less arbitrary decision which fields to study. The reasons for studying one field versus another field, indeed, seem to have more to do with the requirements of a research paradigm, or with technical issues such as the possibility of performance being simulated on a computer, than with the inherent interest of the domains in which giftedness manifests itself. In any case, the question of giftedness as a possible reason for differences in achievement is rarely addressed. The term used for much of the research that might be of interest in this field is "expert systems." The emphasis, then, is more on aspects of performance that can be systematically identified as utilizing common cognitive processes such as attention, memory, or pattern recognition (Larkin, 1980; Siegler, 1978, 1981; Simon & Chase, 1973).

However, Howard Gruber's work on the development of Charles Darwin's thought aims to capture aspects of the creative process at a broader level of analysis. Perhaps the most widely known of these ideas is Gruber's notion of "networks of enterprise" (Gruber, 1981). Gruber emphasizes that creative work is done by purposeful human beings, organizing their efforts and orchestrating a life's work. To focus only on the object of transformation itself (in Darwin's case, the theory of evolution) may obscure its place in a larger set of activities. Gruber argues that Darwin maintained an amazingly complex set of interrelated activities, the overall organization of which can only be comprehended by seeing them in the context of a career or a lifetime. Somewhat similar points have been made about creative individuals by Brewster Ghiselin (1952). He suggests that the truly creative person is able to "concentrate a life" around certain deeply held goals and aims.

The only concept that I am aware of at a similar level of generality in the psychometric tradition of giftedness is the idea of the *underachiever*. This term has found its way into common use, and it refers to a student who is not performing up to his or her capability. A corresponding term, *overachiever*, is also used, but with less conviction. Both terms rest on the premise that it is possible to know what a person's capability is (generally based on IQ test performance) and to predict what a student's performance should be. If achievement is substantially less than would be predicted by IQ, the student may be given the label *"underachiever."* The reverse might also be done, but this is less frequently the case.

These terms, although at the appropriate level of generality, focus on a person's living up to or failing to live up to certain assumed expectations. That ability can be measured by a standardized test, and that the results predict future performance is accepted by psychometricians without questioning the underlying assumptions of such an approach; therefore, everyone's achievement is expected to fall on the mark, above it, or below it. Interestingly, there is no term for achieving just what is predicted. In other words, there is really no way to win in this system. One does less than one is supposed to do; one does more than one is supposed to do (bringing with it the suspicion of an overzealous and compulsive need to do well); or one does what one is predicted to do (which brings with it no great surprise or delight). Thus, although the ideas of over- and underachievement are broad enough to be comparable to developmental concepts of giftedness, they are nonetheless as confined and confining as the psychometric definition of giftedness itself (Thorndike, 1963).

Also, psychometric attempts to identify and measure giftedness and creativity were complicated by concomitant attempts to "raise IQ" or to teach creativity (see Jensen, 1969; Wallach, 1971). The psychometric approach thus invalidated its own belief concerning the nature of traits:

Since a trait approach to creativity assumes that the traits to be measured will express themselves under most existing environmental conditions, it follows by definition that such traits should not be easily influenced by environmental change.... If they *are* easily influenced, they probably are not traits; because training is unlikely to affect them significantly . . . such programs fail when they succeed and succeed when they fail. (Feldman, 1974, p. 52)

Map drawing

Our research has been guided by Piaget's equilibration model, the most comprehensive account to date of how a child moves from stage to stage or level to level. Essentially, our work has attempted to refine and extend Piaget's formulation, with particular emphasis on changes in the child's set of cognitive structures over time at a much more detailed level than is found in Piaget. For Piaget, there are two fundamental processes that account for all such transformations; assimilation and accommodation. These complementary processes cause cognitive structures to be extended, strengthened, and ultimately transformed. *Assimilation* means to use existing, stable modes of organization, such as categories or hierarchies, to organize information as it enters the cognitive system. *Accommodation*, the reciprocal process, means to extend or otherwise change existing structures to more accurately and adequately represent and process incoming information. There are also a number of more subtle processes described by Piaget that have to do with how and under what conditions various kinds of assimilation and accommodations take place (cf. Piaget, 1975).

Piaget and Inhelder (1948/1967) studied map drawing as perhaps the richest source of information about the development of children's spatial–logical interaction structures. Based on this work, they proposed a six-stage sequence from primitive to sophisticated map drawing; this sequence has also been used, with some modifications, in the research I am about to describe. In addition to those qualities that interested Piaget and Inhelder, map drawing was chosen for study because it could be analyzed into its component skills in a relatively clear and precise manner without losing the overall quality of the task (Snyder & Feldman, 1977; Snyder, Feldman, & LaRossa, 1976).

Obviously, as with most other research, we do not get every feature of the problem we are working on with one set of studies. Our work is intended to shed light on one critical aspect of developmental transitions – the appearance of novel ideas in an evolving system – in the belief that whatever explanation may be ultimately given for giftedness, new ideas and the ability to move to more advanced levels of a domain will be important parts of it.

In using map drawing as our experimental task, we have found that it is possible to characterize the child's overall system for representing geographic space in terms of both its level of sophistication and its transition characteristics. For example, in collaboration with Samuel Snyder, I have found that there are six phases that occur between each of the developmental stages of map drawing as originally described by Piaget and Inhelder (Snyder & Feldman, 1980, 1984). Using an elaborate diagnostic procedure, we were able to determine, with reasonable accuracy, where in a transition cycle a given child is. By estimating the overall or the modal stage of the system, calculating the amount of variability among stages in the system, and determining the system's direction of movement (forward, backward, or stable), we can predict reasonably well what the system will do next. This allows us to determine quite accurately where a child's system for drawing maps is going as it is transformed through stages in a highly detailed manner.

All of our research on map drawing to date has been with unselected samples of children. It would be our presumption that children labeled "gifted" in various ways would show no fundamental deviations from the system as described, but might move at varying rates through the defined states for that domain. On the other hand, it may turn out that talent of one sort or another may influence the characteristics of the system and thereby change the model as well. Needless to say, empirical research is needed. Giftedness from this viewpoint can manifest itself in at least three ways: In can mean *faster* movement through the stages of mastery of a domain; it can mean movement to more *advanced* levels that very few reach; and it can mean *deeper* understandings of each of the levels reached. For a small number of individuals, it may mean all three things.

Another line of work we have pursued has been at a much more molecular level. It is also concerned with transitions in map drawing, but here we have been concerned not with the overall characteristics of the system, but rather with some critical details. Most relevant for our purposes here is the study of novelties. It is, of course, a central problem for the study of giftedness and creativity to deal with new ideas or qualitatively advanced ways of doing things. In the research we have done, the novelties are not new in the sense that they qualify as previously unknown contributions to a field of knowledge. Still, they do qualify as just this sort of advance or breakthrough for the individual experiencing them. Creativity in this sense is a natural aspect of development. Each individual constructs a language, a number system, a model of musical understanding and production, a symbol system for drawing, including map drawing, and the like (Gardner, 1983).

The distinction among creative works, then, is one that applies not at the individual level, but rather at the level of social significance. As Piaget has noted, to realize for the first time that a physical transformation of an object does not necessarily change its quantity (the classic conservation situation) can be a profoundly moving experience (Piaget, 1971). Yet, of course, every individual has precisely this experience sometime along the way toward developing concrete operations, to use Piaget's terminology. And so we study novelty or breakthroughs in a predictable sequence within a known domain, not because we believe that creativity of all sorts is the same but rather because we hope that certain fundamental processes of transformation and change are common to all creative advances (Gruber, 1980a, 1980b). To identify and investigate these change processes has been the central purpose of my work. To assume that there are common change processes, however, does not imply that *all aspects* of change are common (cf. Feldman, 1980a, Gruber, 1980a, 1980b). The key is to establish those things that are common to mastery of all domains and those things that are perhaps unique to a single domain.

Without going into technical details, we have defined a novelty in a child's map-drawing system as the emergence of a particular capability that functions at a developmental stage unprecedented for that child in that domain. In map drawing, for example, where there are six defined stages of development; to be able to represent objects from a 90-degree perspective for the first time represents a novel solution for that child. Because our studies have been longitudinal in nature, we have been able to follow our subjects long enough to be reasonably well assured that when a capability appears such as the one I have just described, it is appearing for the first time.

The overall thrust of the research program has been to study the conditions under which novelties tend to appear in the child's map-drawing systems. By being able to examine the system both before, at the time of, and following the appearance of a novelty, we have been able to find some regularities about novelties that in turn suggest future lines of inquiry focused more directly on giftedness.

More often than not, a novelty does seem to have some qualities that may reflect a psychological sense of "breakthrough." A novelty tends to be not a simple movement forward of a skill, but rather a "leap" from somewhere out of the middle of the child's map-drawing system to a much more advanced level. More frequently than with other of the child's skills, the skill that is to become a novelty advances two or even three developmental stages in order to move to a place of singular expertise for the child. Within the map-drawing system, it takes an average of more than a year for a set of skills to move a single development stage, so the acceleration of movement for a novelty is really quite striking when it happens.

We have also learned that, subsequent to the appearance of a novelty, there is a tendency for it to revert or move back into the center of the system. In other words, a skill that has reached Stage 5 to become a novelty, may revert to Stage 3 by the time of the next testing. In other words, a novelty is not a very stable achievement, at least not initially. This finding suggests that a novelty may be best described as *part* of the creative process but not itself a true creative act. A novelty, as we have defined it in the context of the map drawing research, is probably more akin to a glimpse for the individual of a major qualitative advance in capability than it is such an advance itself. It is often reported in anecdotal accounts by creative individuals that they have had such foreshadowing experiences, which then seem almost to pull them along toward an eventual solution or construction that remains stable (Feldman, 1974, 1980a; Ghiselin, 1952; Gruber, 1981).

It is often asked whether these novelties are simply caused by chance fluctuations in a child's map-drawing system. This is of course always a possibility; however, the pattern of movements and identities of elements that become novelties suggests otherwise. Although one could perhaps explain the emergence of an element from the middle of a system as chance governed, the fact that the *same elements* tend to become novelties militates against chance (Feldman, Snyder, & Goldsmith, 1984). The fact that, after emerging, elements that were novelties tended to revert back to the more stable center of the system at a rate much greater than chance also suggests that we are not dealing with random fluctuation.

Another of our findings reinforces the interpretation of a novelty as systematic variation. We have found that novelties seem to exert a "pulling" effect on the rest of the child's map-drawing system. By pulling, we mean that elements associated with the novel element tend to advance more rapidly than the rest of the system. In other words, if the novel element is "perspective from 90 degrees" of buildings, then the child's representation of other objects shows advances in perspective as well, although not as dramatically as the novel element itself. This pattern of effects seems to suggest that the novelty has a kind of energizing effect on the system, catalyzing conceptual progress in a certain area, not simply in the novel skill itself. Then, once having served this catalytic function, the novel element itself reverts to an earlier level. The role of novelties in transitions, therefore, seems to be one of energizing and catalyzing a broader system-wide change.

Our work with novelties is about general properties of an evolving system for representing geographic space. It does not attempt to address issues of giftedness and creativity directly. We do not know, for example, if some individuals produce a greater number of novelties than others, or if novelties do or do not function differently for children who seem to have a "gift" for working in a domain.

We have also not addressed the environmental conditions that accompany the various changes we have observed in children's map-drawing systems. Clearly, there is much to be done if the general developmental model we are using is to impact directly on questions about giftedness and creativity. Although map drawing is not a field in which giftedness is taken very seriously, this was not always the case. As late as the 1920s, prodigies in geography (and specifically map drawing) were included in works about such children (Baumgarten, 1930; see also Thrower, 1972). Although this is an intriguing link between giftedness and map drawing, our purposes here require only that we focus attention on transitions in development. At this point, we don't claim to have shown anything specific about the nature of giftedness or about how creativity in the more exalted sense happens. Instead, our purpose has been to show how studies of transition processes can inform and provide a context for addressing such issues. Without question, the work is at a very early stage, one that must be substantially moved forward if the claims of relevance to giftedness and creativity of developmental views are to be put to empirical test.

Studies of child prodigies

Since the prodigies studies have been or will be described elsewhere, I will not go into detail about them here (Feldman, 1979, 1980a, 1983, in press). A few points about what I have learned are in order, however. These are necessary, it seems, to provide the reader with enough information to see how the prodigy contradicts widely held notions of giftedness.

The prodigy has been a subject of awe and wonder for centuries, but actually, few studies have been done on the topic (Barlow, 1952). To my knowledge, only two major works exist, both published more then 50 years ago and originally in German (Baumgarten, 1930; Revesz, 1925/1975). Historically, prodigies were thought to be a sign or portent sent by the gods to signal some major change in the established order (Barlow, 1952; Feldman, 1980a; *Webster's Third New International Dictionary*, 1971). Although hardly a scientific explanation, this belief reveals that prodigies have long been assigned special status among human variations. A prodigy was, as *Webster's* says, "something out of the usual course of nature." As fascinating as the prodigy has always been, however, scientists in general and psychologists in particular seem to have given the prodigy a wide berth. For the most part, science has virtually ignored the prodigy; this, to me, is amazing in itself and has led directly to the research I have undertaken.

Why the prodigy has been so totally ignored in this country, where there has been such a tradition of studying "giftedness," is mystifying to me. Although I have not been able to answer this question or resolve this dilemma to my own satisfaction, I suspect that the psychometric tradition itself may have something to do with it. When all children are placed along a single continuum of intellectual capacity, the prodigy is presumed to be simply a very gifted child, perhaps with an IQ above 150 or so (Hollingworth, 1942; Feldman, 1979). To me, however, prodigiousness seemed so discrepant from the traditional concept of "giftedness as high IQ" that I was led to construct my current position about giftedness, which is in part intended to question that tradition itself.

I think of a prodigy as a child who is able to perform at or near the level of an adult professional in an intellectually demanding field. This definition modifies the definition I proposed in 1979. At that time, I defined a prodigy as a child who, *before the age of 10*, performed at an adult professional level. Subsequently, I have found this definition too restrictive, since prodigies do not appear in several fields where we tend to expect them (most notably math and visual arts) until after age 10. In any case, it should be obvious that the definitions used are provisional and that as the phenomenon becomes better described our ability to sharpen and clarify distinctions will improve.

In general, I have found that prodigies show orderly movement through various levels of mastery of their domains, just as others do, but at a much faster rate. In this sense, then, the process of mastery seems similar to what one would expect of anyone attempting to become better at doing something; it is a process common to all who attempt to master the knowledge of a given domain. Most of the assumptions of cognitive-developmental theory hold for the prodigy, as they do for other children, but there is a *hastening* of *transition* from stage to stage within a particular domain. Although there seem to be some broad developmental constraints in how far ahead a prodigy can go in a field (a chess player has never become a master before the age of 12, for example), the range of possible levels achieved is sufficiently great to allow for wide differences among individuals. There may well be other, more qualitative differences between prodigies and other children, but this is difficult to say. What makes the prodigy seem so different from others is the uneven quality of his or her developmental profile. The prodigy, as Baumgarten (1930) noted many years ago, exhibits a mixture of childlike and adultlike qualities.

The description of the prodigy does not, however, address the issue of how it is possible for a prodigy to occur at all. To address this question, I would like to introduce a process I have called "co-incidence." Basically, this idea "relocates" the existence of prodigiousness from inside the child (perhaps wired into the brain or nervous system, as is commonly thought) to an evolving system of interactions. That is, I believe that a prodigy is better seen as the dynamic intersection of a set of forces, only one of which is the child's talent, brain, or whatever. A continuing, near perfect coordination of precisely the right sets of forces produces and sustains prodigious behavior. These forces include the child's family, peers, teachers, and mentors, as well as cultural and historical factors. Perhaps most critically, a field or domain must also exist that, in its own history and development, is matched to the talents, proclivities, sensibilities, and purposes of a given individual at a given time in a given locale.

In addition to the forces themselves, there seems to be a kind of calculus of variations that seeks a constant, stable, continuing coordination among these forces. Sustaining this most complex coordination is dependent on timing, duration, pace, sequence, stress, and integration of experience into an overall plan. Especially critical for the successful coordination of co-incident forces is the optimal marshaling and deployment of resources over time. In trying to visualize a near perfect coordination in co-incidence, I have sometimes thought of it as a ballet of great subtlety, or perhaps as a system like the ones that transfer genetic code, a kind of cosmic DNA/RNA of psychological messages and orders.

The processes by which prodigies' talents develop, I believe, are the same processes that underlie all developmental change. When we hear that a volcano has erupted or that an earthquake has occurred, we are given the opportunity to learn about the nature of the earth. When we predict that there will be an eclipse of the sun, it allows us to test our knowledge of planetary movement. When a piece of pottery is found in a place and with a date much older than seemed possible, it challenges us to reorganize our ideas about the origins and history of human cultures. Freud taught us that disordered and disturbed behavior is often a more extreme playing-out of the same emotional conflicts that are part of the human condition. And prodigies teach us that extreme instances of intellectual achievement are caused by the same forces and explained by the same principles as more common achievements. These forces and principles, however, are very different from those postulated by psychometrics. Rather than emphasize unchanging general (or even specific) capabilities or talents, the developmentalist directs attention to common change processes and common principles that account for the expression of potential. That prodigies represent extreme cases of talent both psychometric and developmental views would acknowledge. The developmental view differs in its emphasis on what happens to facilitate the expression of potential and the extraordinary delicateness of the processes of mastery of any challenging domain.

It should also be noted that I depart from the traditional notion of prodigy when I interpret the prodigy developmentally. That traditional definition labels the prodigy as something out of the usual course of nature. The appearance of a prodigy was traditionally interpreted as some kind of a sign or portent that signaled some important cosmic change. It meant that the balance of things was somehow about to be disturbed, and the prodigy carried a hint about what the impending change might be. To the contrary, I am claiming that the appearance and development of prodigies in various fields is a function of the same sets of forces that lead to the appearance and development of any other human potential. It is an assumption of my view that through these common, natural, cultural, and educational processes, an unbelievable range of human capabilities is possible. Yet it is also true of my view of the prodigy that *change* of an important sort is portended by his or her appearance. But not change of the world order. The prodigy, it seems to me, represents a natural laboratory for the study of developmental change processes because his gifts are typically very pure and his movement through levels of mastery so accelerated. I also would like to think the prodigy portends another kind of change, a change in our way of viewing giftedness.

I take it for granted, then, that in the natural course of events, human organisms appear with capabilities that in strength and quality far exceed those of others of the same age. The time of appearance and subsequent development of these abilities is earlier and on a steeper trajectory than is typically the case, but not fundamentally different in kind, at least not with respect to certain processes of developmental change. Prodigies possess a familiar, if unusual, ability or abilities, but at an unusually young age. The combination of a relatively rare capability (for example, an understanding of some aspects of mathematics or music) by a relative newcomer makes the person really quite extraordinary. We may be impressed with the virtuosity of any really good mathematician, but we are stunned when we see these same capabilities appearing in a child.

Coincidence, the framework that is used to try to comprehend how a prodigy happens, is based on the belief that a prodigy, although without question an extraordinarily talented child, nonetheless requires the existence and coordination of numerous other conditions for potential prodigiousness to become actualized. Just what these conditions are and how they work is the main focus of a book-length treatment of prodigies now in progress (Feldman, in press). Admittedly, this framework is very general and inclusive; this is quite intentional in that I believe that to do otherwise, at this point, would be to constrain unduly what can be observed of prodigiousness and to restrict what sorts of explanatory concepts might be proposed. Given that the phenomenon itself has received so little research attention, I have also adopted naturalistic observation techniques, more similar to those used by anthropologists or ethologists than those used in the psychological research tradition.

To my mind, the idea of coincidence (or something very much like it) will ultimately supplant psychometrics as the framework within which we will try to understand and enhance human excellence.

Conclusion

In this chapter, I have presented a developmental point of view that seems to offer promise for approaching some unanswered questions about giftedness and creativity. In contrast to some of my developmentally oriented colleagues who have focused on relatively molecular aspects of performance in various domains, I have tried to present a view that is relatively holistic and that attempts to characterize the overall system as it undergoes transformation and change.

A developmentalist, then, sees giftedness best represented as *movement through the stages or levels of a domain* that leads to performance superior to that of most others. The rate at which these levels are mastered can be thought of as one aspect of giftedness. Another concerns the depth of mastery of each stage, while yet another concerns the ways in which mastery of each level can be done in individual or unique ways. The central idea is that it is useful to think of all development, including extraordinarily gifted development, as in some sense characterized by sequential transformation of overall systems. This idea is fundamental to my point of view.

A second and related point is that giftedness takes many forms, and these forms may occur relatively independently from other forms (Gardner, 1983; Gardner & Feldman, 1984). The work with child prodigies, for example, has shown that children can advance rapidly in a specific field such as chess or music without necessarily advancing in such dramatic fashion in any other domain. From this and other evidence, it appears to me that giftedness is relatively *domain specific* in the ways that it becomes expressed. In contrast to the psychometric tradition, which sees giftedness as an overall intellectual quality, I see it as a set of relatively specific capabilities in relatively specific domains. This is not to say that individuals who have broad intellectual capabilities do not exist (cf. Feldman, 1984; Hollingworth, 1942). The point is rather that it is unwise to limit notions of giftedness to such individuals because they represent only a small fraction of the possible forms that giftedness might take. Furthermore, *performance* is virtually always domain specific, and it is, after all, performance or achievement that gives the gift whatever legitimacy it may attain.

The third general feature of my developmental view is that it conceives of giftedness as achieved through a *coordination of forces*, only some of which are individual qualities and characteristics. In addition to whatever qualities the individual possesses, both intellectual and personal, my view of giftedness requires that the child be seen in the context of his or her social environment, culture, historical period, and specific domain. I see domains of knowledge themselves as having developmental histories that intersect or coincide with individual proclivities and talents at various points in time while not connecting with them at others; this is an idea Piaget was intrigued by but was unable to pursue (Bringuier, 1980; Piaget, 1971). Giftedness, then, is the outcome of a sustained coordination among sets of intersecting forces, including historical and cultural as well as social and individual qualities and characteristics.

To some extent, this view is concordant with with that of Tannenbaum (1983; also this volume) as well. To the delicate coordination of forces that go into giftedness, I have given the label "co-incidence." Co-incidence draws attention to the need for relatively broad concepts to complement the more molecular and detailed observations of our mechanistically oriented colleagues in cognitive science.

I said earlier that developmental frameworks pose the most significant challenge to the field of research on giftedness since the field began with the work of Lewis Terman and others during the early years of the century. In a sense, the challenge is as much to ourselves as it is to the field. The next decade or so will show if developmental approaches will raise important new questions and lead to the gathering of significant new information about giftedness and creativity. Clearly, that task has barely begun.

References

Barlow, F. (1952). *Mental prodigies*. Westport, Conn.: Greenwood Press.

Baumgarten, F. (1930). *Wunderkinder psychologische Untersuchungen*. Leipzig: Johann Ambrosius Barth.

Bereiter, C. (1982). Structures, doctrines, and polemical ghosts: A response to Feldman. *Educational Researcher, 11*, 22–25.

Bringuier, J. C. (1980). *Conversations with Jean Piaget*. Chicago: University of Chicago Press.

Brown, A. (1980). Learning and development: The problems of compatibility, access and induction. *Human Development, 25*, 89–115.

Collins, J. (1980). Personal communication.

Cronbach, L. J. (1957). The two disciplines of scientific psychology. *American Psychologist, 12*, 671–684.

Estes, W. K. (1970). *Learning theory and mental development*. New York: Academic Press.

Feldman, D. H. (1971). Map understanding as a possible crystallizer of cognitive structures. *American Educational Research Journal, 8*, 485–501.

Feldman, D. H (1974) . Universal to unique: A developmental view of creativity and education. In S. Rosner & L. Abt (Eds.), *Essays in creativity*. Cronton-on-Hudson, N.Y.: North River Press.

Feldman, D. H. (1979). The mysterious case of extreme giftedness. In A. H. Passow (Ed.), *The gifted and the talented: Their education and development*. The Seventy-eighth Yearbook of the National Society for the Study of Education. Chicago: University of Chicago Press.

Feldman, D H. (1980a). *Beyond universals in cognitive development*. Norwood N.J.: Ablex.

Feldman, D. H. (1980b). Stage and sequence: Getting to the next level. *The Genetic Epistemologist, 9*, 1–6.

Feldman, D. H. (1981). Beyond universals: Toward a developmental psychology of education. *Educational Researcher, 10*, 21–31.

Feldman, D.H. (Ed.). (1982a). *Developmental approaches to giftedness and creativity*. San Francisco: Jossey-Bass.

Feldman, D. H. (1982b). A rejoinder to Bereiter. *Educational Researcher*, *11*, 26–27.

Feldman, D. H. (1983). Piaget on giftendess – a very short essay. *The Genetic Epistemologist*, *12*, 1–10.

Feldman, D. H. (1984). A follow-up of subjects scoring above 180 IQ in Terman's "Genetic studies of genius." *Exceptional Children*, *50*, 518-523.

Feldman, D. H. (in press). *Nature's gambit: The mystery and meaning of the child prodigy*. New York: Basic Books.

Feldman, D. H., Snyder, S. S., & Goldsmith, L. T. (1984). *An exploratory study of novelties in development*. Unpublished manuscript.

Fischer, K. W. (1981). The last straw for Piagetian stages? A review of *Beyond universals in cognitive development*. *Contemporary Psychology*, *26*, 338–339.

Gardner, H. (1983). *Frames of mind*. New York: Basic Books.

Gardner, H., & Feldman, D. H. (1984). *The monitoring of intellectual propensities in early childhood*. A proposal submitted to the Spencer Foundation, Chicago.

Ghiselin, B. (1952). *The creative process*. New York: Mentor.

Gruber, H. E. (1980a) Afterword. In D. H. Feldman, *Beyond universals in cognitive development*. Norwood, N.J.: Ablex.

Gruber, H. E. (1980b). "And the bush was not consumed": The evolving systems approach to creativity. In S. Modgil & C. Modgil (Eds.). *Toward a theory of psychological development*. Windsor, England: NFER Press.

Gruber, H. E. (1981). *Darwin on man: A psychological study of scientific creativity* (2nd ed.). Chicago: University of Chicago Press.

Hayes, J. (1981). *The complete problem solver*. Philadelphia: Franklin Institute Press.

Hollingworth, L. (1942). *Children above 180 IQ Stanford–Binet*. New York: World Book.

Jensen, A. (1969). How much can we boost IQ and scholastic achievement? *Harvard Educational Review*, *39*, 1–123.

Larkin, J., McDermott, J., Simon, D. P., & Simon, H. A. (1980). Models of competence in solving physics problems. *Cognitive Science*, *4*, 317–345.

Overton, W. F. (1983). World views and their influence on psychological theory and research. Kuhn–Lakatos–Laudan. In H. W. Reese (Ed.), *Advances in child development and behavior* (Vol. 18). New York: Academic Press.

Piaget, J. (1971). The theory of stages in cognitive development. In D. Green, M. Lord, & G. Flamer (Eds,), *Measurement and Piaget*. New York: McGraw-Hill.

Piaget, J. (1972). Intellectual evolution from adolescence to adulthood. *Human Development*, *15*, 1–12.

Piaget, J. (1975). *The development of thought: Equilibration of cognitive structures*. New York: Viking.

Piaget, J., & Inhelder, B. (1948/1967). *The child's conception of space*. New York: Norton.

Revesz, G. (1925/1975). *The psychology of a musical prodigy*. Freeport, N.Y.: Books for Libraries Press.

Siegler, R. S. (Ed.). (1978). *Children's thinking: What develops?* New York: Wiley.

Siegler, R. S. (1981). Developmental sequences within and between concepts. *Monographs of the Society for Research in Child Development*, *46*(2, Serial No. 189).

Simon, H., & Chase, W. G. (1973). Skill in chess. *American Scientist*, *61*, 364–403.

Synder, S. S., & Feldman, D. H. (1977). Internal and external influences on cognitive development change. *Child Development*, *48*, 937–943.

Snyder, S. S., & Feldman, D. H. (1980). Individual developmental transitions: A film metaphor. In D. H. Feldman, *Beyond universals in cognitive development*. Norwood, N.J.: Ablex.

Snyder, S. S., & Feldman, D. H. (1984). Phases of transition in cognitive development: Evidence from the domain of spatial representation. *Child Development*, *55*, 981–989.

Snyder, S. S., Feldman, D. H., & LaRossa, C. (1976). A manual for the administration of scoring of a Piaget-based map drawing exercise. In O. Johnson (Ed.), *Test and measurements in child development: A handbook* (Vol. 2). San Francisco: Jossey-Bass.

Sternberg, R. J. (1979). The nature of mental abilities. *American Psychologist, 34*, 214–230.

Sternberg, R. J. (1979). Intelligence and nonentrenchment. *Journal of Educational Psychology, 73*, 1–16.

Sternberg, R. J. (1983). Components of human intelligence. *Cognition, 15*, 1–48.

Tannenbaum, A. J. (1983). *Gifted children*. New York: Macmillan.

Thorndike, R. L. (1963). *The concepts of over and underachievement*. New York: Teachers College.

Thrower, N. (1972). *Maps and man*. Englewood Cliffs, N.J.: Prentice-Hall.

Wallach, M. A. (1971). *The creativity-intelligence distinction*. New York: General Learning Press.

Witty, S. (1984, January). Beyond great expectations. *GEO Magazine*, 76–87.

14 The crystallizing experience: discovering an intellectual gift

Joseph Walters and Howard Gardner

Introduction

According to standard mathematical history, Evariste Galois (1811–1832) was initially tutored at home by his mother and entered the public school at the age of 11. Because his unpredictable disposition and stubborn attitude precluded any formal success as a student, he had to make the personal discovery of the world of mathematics on his own. Quite by chance he came across a geometry textbook written by Legendre: "The book aroused his enthusiasm; it was not a textbook written by some hack, but the work of art composed by a creative mathematician. A single reading sufficed to reveal the whole structure of elementary geometry with a crystal clarity to the fascinated boy. He had mastered it" (Bell, 1965, p. 364).

Galois next turned to algebra and, finding no suitable textbook, began studying the works of Abel, Legrange, and Gauss in the original. After high school, Galois twice failed the entrance examination for the Polytechnique Institute in Paris (presumably for reasons other than mathematical ability); he was killed in a duel at the age of 21. Up to the day of his death he pursued mathematics on his own. His collected papers, many of them published posthumously, served as the basis for a new field of mathematics now called "Galois Theory."

Composer Claude Debussy (1862–1918) began his formal study of music at the Conservatory in Paris at the age of 9, and by 14 he had won the prize for piano. During these first years he did not show any interest in composition and in fact he hated his harmony class. This changed, however, when he began studying music theory with the young instructor Lavignac:

Lavignac introduced Debussy to the music of Wagner. We read in the memoirs of [a fellow student] that one winter evening, after class time, the score was set out on the

Acknowledgments: The research reported in this paper was supported by grants from the Social Science Research Council and the Bernard van Leer Foundation of The Hague. We are grateful to the teachers who willingly gave of their time, and to Mara Krechevsky, Robert Sternberg, and Janet Davidson, who gave many helpful comments on earlier drafts.

piano of the Overture to Tannhauser, the work which had recently created a notorious scandal at the Paris Opera. Here is [Debussy] confronted for the first time with the work of the composer who was soon to exert the most powerful influence on his creative life. The experience was overwhelming.

The young professor and his eager pupil became so absorbed in the novel Wagnerian harmonies that they forgot all sense of time. When they eventually decided to leave they found themselves locked in and were obliged to grope their way out, arm in arm, down the rickety stairs and the dark corridors of the crumbling scholastic building. (Lockspeiser, 1962, p. 32)

As an apprentice porcelain decorator, Pierre-Auguste Renoir (1841–1919) demonstrated a facility with a paintbrush that earned him an adult's wages at the age of 12. Despite this useful technical proficiency, he showed little interest in or sensitivity to the aesthetic qualities of the visual arts. During his apprentice years he made regular trips to the Louvre to sketch the masterworks, but only with the intention of using these sketches in designing porcelain.

One day during his apprenticeship he had this experience:

He made a momentous discovery, the sixteenth-century Fontaine des Innocents. "I stopped spell-bound," he said afterward. He gave up the idea of lunch in a restaurant, and instead bought some sausage at a nearby shop and returned to the fountain. He walked round and round it slowly, studying the group of statues from every angle. From that moment he felt a particular affinity with the sculptor Jean Goujon; his work possessed everything he loved: grace, solidity, and elegance, with the feeling of living flesh. "Goujon knew how to make drapery cling to figures. Until then I hadn't realized how drapery brings out the form." (Hanson, 1968, p. 15)

These three events – each crucial to the life of a particular creative individual – share a number of common features. In each case, the individual discovered an important and hitherto unappreciated aspect of a particular field of endeavor. In reading Legendre, Galois chanced upon a world of mathematical discovery, filled with challenges. Through Wagner's opera, Debussy came to realize the creative potential of composition in contrast to musical performance. Renoir's experience at the Fontaine des Innocents crystallized a notion of the power of sculpture to transcend the limited world of decoration.

The three anecdotes also share the fact that each event occurred in relative isolation, either apart from or prior to formal instruction. Galois read Legendre outside mathematics class. Debussy's discovery of Wagner occurred only shortly after his first systematic study of composition. Renoir began art instruction when he was 18, several years after his experience at the Fontaine. In each case, these young individuals brought certain expectations, skills, or predispositions to the three events, something apparently not acquired through previous experiences with the domains, as if they had been "prepared" for those domains in some special way.

Following the work of our colleague David Feldman (1980), we will designate these unusual encounters between a developing person and a particular field of endeavor as "crystallizing experiences." As we define them, such experiences involve remarkable and memorable contact between a person with unusual talent or potential and the materials of the field in which that talent will be manifested. As illustrated in our three examples, these crystallizing experiences may appear in advance of formal training. In any case, their dramatic nature focuses the attention of the individual on a specific kind of material, experience, or problem. Moreover, the individual is motivated to revisit these occasions for the indefinite future and to reshape his self-concept on the basis of these experiences.

Our interest in the existence and structure of these so-called crystallizing experiences has grown out of the theory of human intelligence called multiple intelligences theory (hereafter MI theory). According to this view (see Gardner, 1983, for a detailed discussion), all normal individuals are capable of at least seven independent forms of intellectual accomplishment: linguistic, musical, logical–mathematical, spatial, bodily-kinesthetic, interpersonal, and intrapersonal. Initially, these intelligences exist as biological potentials; they are manifest in the opening years of life as the capacities to process certain kinds of information (e.g., patterned sounds) in certain kinds of ways (e.g., pitch analysis, phonological analysis). When the individual becomes capable of symbolic behavior, the intelligences are manifested in the deployment of various symbol systems (like natural language, drawing, map making, religious customs, and the like). Still later in development, the intelligences form the core capacities involved in all cultural roles, ranging from parenting to toolmaking to the practice of science.

Under normal or reasonably enriched conditions, a human being can be expected to become involved with or achieve some measure of competence in each of these intellectual realms. Ultimate achievements, however, will vary greatly across individuals and across specific intelligences or groups of intelligences. One source of variance is probably genetic proclivity, but the earliness of exposure to a field and the amount of practice and training clearly make equally decisive contributions. One may achieve high skill in music through strong biological heritage (autistic children), through intensive training (the Suzuki method) and, most happily, through the epigenetic interaction of these features, as in the case of Mozart (cf. Gardner, 1982).

This overall framework, which we have only briefly sketched here, provides the motivation for our exploration of crystallizing experiences, as well as a structure for our model of giftedness. To illustrate, consider an individual with a rather uneven profile of intelligences, so that he possesses strong potential in domain x but only modest potential in domains y and z. Because of the accidents of parental interests or community concerns, that individual, as a child, receives little exposure to the activities of area x and is consigned to spend much time in the activities of domains y and z. It is possible that the individual will eventually acquire significant skills in y or z, or, less happily, that he will fail despite his efforts and will lose motivation altogether. It is also possible that through a chance occurrence he will come into contact with materials (e.g., certain symbol systems, trained persons, engaging puzzles, etc.) that activate latent skills of his previously underutilized intelligence, x. Here is the setting for a crystallizing experience that, in the extreme circumstance, will change the individual's major activities of life as well as the way in which he thinks about himself.

A crystallizing experience, then, is the overt reaction of an individual to some quality or feature of a domain: the reaction yields an immediate but also a long-term change in that individual's concept of the domain, his performance in it, and his view of himself. We restrict the term *crystallizing experience* to those experiences that exhibit the set of symptoms just described. Of course, it is not possible to identify a crystallizing experience at the moment of its occurrence. Only retrospectively, after the individual's behavior in the postcrystallizing period has been observed, is it possible to single out an experience as having crystallized ensuing activities.

In our view, crystallizing experiences can take various forms. For example, some crystallizing experiences, which we term "initial," occur early in life and signal a general affinity between an individual and some large-scale domain in his culture: An example would be Galois's discovery of the excitement involved in mathematical proof. Other crystallizing experiences, which we term "refining," occur well after an individual has undergone an initial attraction to a domain. In these refining cases, an individual discovers a particular instrument, style, or approach within a field to which he or she is especially attuned. Both the Renoir and the Debussy episodes might be thought of as refining crystallizing experiences.

The theory of multiple intelligences does not prescribe the existence or the importance of crystallizing experiences. But it does suggest that such experiences may well occur across a variety of domains and it provides an explanation for why they may exert powerful, long-term effects on the individual. It is consistent with the theory that many (if not most) individuals will experience the affective phase of such experiences; however, unless an individual is "at promise" within a particular intelligence or domain, it is unlikely that the experiences will have a lasting effect and result in ultimate redefinition of self. In short, then, crystallizing experiences are neither necessary nor sufficient for ultimate achievement within the field; yet at the same time, they are a useful construct for explaining how certain talented individuals may first discover their area of giftedness and then proceed to achieve excellence within the field. Our present investigation of the construct of crystallizing experiences thus helps to assess the utility of multiple intelligences and brings that theory into contact with such broader issues as the nature of giftedness and the achievement of talent.

Several empirical questions can be asked of the construct of crystallizing experiences. One set of questions concerns the commonness of such experiences: for example, are they typical or quite atypical? And if they are typical, are they restricted to those with intellectual gifts or are they found throughout the population? Another set of questions concerns the possible explanations for such crystallizing experiences: Why do they occur, how do they occur, and what are their consequences?

Finally, a set of questions arises from the perspective of multiple intelligences. We are interested in determining how crystallizing experiences may differ across the various intelligences; for instance, do they appear in childhood in all domains or are they found at different points in different domains? We hypothesize that there may be "initial crystallizing experiences" that occur when a young child (or novice to the domain) makes his first genuine contact with that domain: These contrast with later-occurring "refining crystallizing experiences" that help the individual discover his or her own particular métier within an intellectual domain. In the present chapter, we undertake an empirical investigation of the phenomenon of crystallizing experiences and then offer our own thoughts about why this singular kind of event may unfold in the manner that it does.

Of course, there are other possible approaches to the issue of crystallizing experiences. One is to challenge the legitimacy of these reports. For example, to researchers who believe that the differences in achievements are due primarily to the amount of training received (cf. Bloom, 1982), the crystallizing experiences, as in the vignettes of Galois or Renoir, might be treated as anomalies, exaggerations, or retrospective justifications or rationalizations. On this view, the example taken from Debussy begs the question of talent versus training, because here the crystallizing experience appears after a considerable amount of training.

To illustrate this point, we can contrast the multiple intelligences (MI) perspective with a strict training theory. According to the training explanation, highly talented children like Mozart are anomalies. One cannot diagnose talent in a child until he has received a reasonable amount of training; and even then, what appear in the child's behaviors are manifestations not of inborn "talent" or "gift" but rather of the effectiveness of a particular set of training experiences. On the MI view, on the other hand, gifted children are anticipated – children with a high degree of "raw" or unmediated intelligence in a specific field should under certain circumstances demonstrate evidence of that intelligence even before they are engaged in any kind of training regimen. In contrast to the training account, MI predicts a small but measurable number of such gifted children in each of the fields identified.

It is possible to subscribe to a combination of these points of view as well. For example, one might insist on the need for many years of training even in those cases where there is an initial, and perhaps inborn, proclivity to excel in an intellectual domain (cf. Hayes, 1981). In fact, in detailing the basic "intelligences," MI theory is careful to distinguish between the "raw" or unmediated intelligence that predominates in children; the marshaling of that intelligence to various symbol systems, as evidenced in older children; and the adoption of a much more specific and focused domain of expertise by the adolescent or young adult. Development from the "raw" intelligence to the focused domain of expertise is as much a function of training as a function of the raw intelligence. In this way, MI theory describes a lengthy gestation period for the development of even the most brilliant adult from the initial crystallizing experience to the level of mature performance in the domain.

With our own approach to crystallizing experiences and these alternative views as a background, we undertook an empirical investigation designed to assess the commonness of crystallizing experiences and to cull information on the ways in which they may occur. We used two sources of data in our study. First, we reviewed the biographical and autobiographical literature in the three aforementioned domains: mathematics, music, and the visual arts. A total of 25 people in these three fields were chosen and the available biographical materials were reviewed for each subject. We recorded the experiences that we considered as crystallizing, as well as any other evidence documenting a subject's unusual talent as a child. Finally, any information about the nature of talents outside the domain, including success or failure in school or other areas, were noted as well.

The second part of the study involved interviews with teachers of especially talented students in the same three areas. We asked these teachers how they recognized talent in their students, how the students performed during lessons, and whether or not they were cognizant of crystallizing experiences in their students or in their own personal histories. The results from the interviews are presented in the second part of the chapter.

It is important to indicate how we regard these data. In our view, we have secured support for the notion of crystallizing experiences as a relatively common phenomenon among talented contributors in certain fields. On the other hand, we do not consider this review as decisive confirmation of our orientation or our conclusions, for several reasons. First, the subjects were not selected in a random fashion; how can any study of giftedness in musicians fail to consider Mozart, for instance? Second, because of their retrospective nature, biographies lack the objectivity of an "on-line" longitudinal account of development. Finally, our analysis of the biographical materials is interpretive because of inevitable incompleteness in these reports.

In sum, our work here is presented as a preliminary investigation of the construct of crystallizing experiences derived from the theory of multiple intelligences. Our purpose is not to confirm or disconfirm the theory with these results; in that sense, the construct of crystallizing experience is not a critical variable within the theory. Instead, we look upon this work as an exploration of the theory of multiple intelligences through one particular manifestation. We feel that these findings may provide important insights into the nature of giftedness.

The biographies

Musicians

Our study indicates that 10 of the 11 distinguished musical composers and performers included in this review were either very talented as children or demonstrated crystallizing experiences. Table 14.1 indicates that three subjects who were recognized as talented while still young did not have crystallizing experiences: Mozart, Beethoven, and Mendelssohn announced their talent very early, but the crystallizing of that talent occurred without fanfare or self-recognition.

Mozart and Beethoven came from musical families and their total immersion in the world of music can be attributed to the efforts of others; but this is not always the case. For example, Mendelssohn's parents provided the opportunity for private music lessons, but they had him tutored in other subjects as well. Later he studied law at the university and pursued music only as a sideline. Indeed, for the affluent and privileged Mendelssohn-Bartoldy family, musicianship and the life of the stage were considered degrading.

Rubinstein also came from a nonmusical family. He announced his talent in what might be considered a crystallizing experience at the age of three, when the family purchased a piano:

The drawing room became my paradise. . . . Half in fun, half in earnest, I learned to know the keys by their names and with my back to the piano I would call the notes of any chord, even the most dissonant one. From then on it became mere "child's play" to master the intricacies of the keyboard, and I was soon to play any . . . tune that caught my ear. (Rubinstein, 1973, p. 4)

The family recognized the extraordinary talent of their son and obtained an audition with Joseph Joachim, a renowned 19th-century musician, who guided his career and obtained patron support for him. It appears, then, that childhood talent, as exemplified by Mendelssohn and Rubinstein, can be recognized even by parents who are untrained in music.

The crystallizing experiences that appear in the biographies of the musicians are of two distinct types. First, there are the earliest experiences with music: experiences that reveal a "raw talent." For instance, Menuhin's reaction at age 3 to the violin sound of Louis Persinger or Stravinsky's response to Glinka's orchestra both fall into this category. The anecdote reported in the Rubinstein quotation might also be considered as an illustration, although it does not have the same sense of immediate insight. Finally, Wagner's reaction as a teenager to the singing of *Fidelio* can be included in this category as

Table 14.1. *The musicians*

Joseph Haydn, 1732–1809, Austria
> *Childhood talent*: Talent did not appear during childhood. Sang in the Vienna Boys'
> Choir
> *Crystallizing experience*: None reported.

Wolfgang Amadeus Mozart, 1756–1791, Austria
> *Childhood talent*: First composition at 5 years. First symphony at 9. First opera at
> 13.
> *Crystallizing experience*: None reported.

Ludwig van Beethoven, 1770–1827, Germany
> *Childhood talent*: Concert at 9. Assistant organist at 14. Began study of composition
> with Haydn at 22.
> *Crystallizing experience*: None reported.

Felix Mendelssohn, 1809–1847, Germany
> *Childhood talent*: Debut at 9. Began studying composition at 10. Mastered counter-
> point and figured bass at age 12.
> *Crystallizing experience*: None reported.

Richard Wagner, 1813–1883, Germany
> *Childhood talent*: Talent did not appear during childhood.
> *Crystallizing experience*: As an adolescent, he heard a famous singer in *Fidelio* and
> was greatly moved. He wrote the singer a letter in which he dedicated his life to
> music, delivered it to her hotel room, and then "ran out into the street, quite mad"
> (Wagner, 1911, p. 44).

Gustav Mahler, 1860–1911, Czechoslovakia
> *Childhood talent*: Played the concertina at 4. At 15, auditioned for Julius Epstein,
> who sent him immediately to the Conservatory in Vienna where he was described
> as "the new Schubert."
> *Crystallizing experience*: None reported.

Claude Debussy, 1862–1918, France
> *Childhood talent*: Entered Conservatoire at age 9. Won the prize for piano at
> age 14.
> *Crystallizing experience*: Transcribing the opera *Tannhauser* described in the
> Introduction.

Igor Stravinsky, 1882–1971, Russia
> *Childhood talent*: Talent did not appear during childhood.
> *Crystallizing experience*: As a child, he attended the theater weekly, and notes that
> he was greatly moved by the "sound of Glinka's orchestra and the compositions of
> Tchaikovsky" (White, 1966, p. 23).
> Although he was generally uninterested in the skills of composition as a college stu-
> dent, his eventual career as a composer was fixed in his mind during his 5-year ap-
> prenticeship with Rimski-Korsakov.

Arthur Rubinstein, 1887–1982, Poland
> *Childhood talent*: Auditioned for the violinist Joseph Joachim at the age of 3. Be-
> gan lessons with Joachim at 10 and gave his first concert the next year.
> *Crystallizing experience*: Rubinstein reports that when the family purchased a piano,
> "the drawing room became my paradise." He learned to play by ear and to name
> the notes in dissonant chords within a matter of months.

Table 14.1. (*cont.*)

Yehudi Menuhin, 1916–, United States
>   *Childhood talent*: Debut at the age of 9.
>   *Crystallizing experience*: He was taken to concerts of the San Francisco Symphony
>   regularly when he was 3 years old. Upon hearing the sound of the orchestra, and in
>   particular Louis Persinger's violin, he said, "I asked for a violin for my fourth birth-
>   day, and Louis Persinger to teach me to play it" (Menuhin, 1977, p. 22). He got
>   both.

Pierre Boulez, 1926–, France
>   *Childhood talent*: Talent did not appear during childhood.
>   *Crystallizing experience*: At the age of 19, when studying composition, he heard for
>   the first time the music of Messaien and recognized the 12-tone style as a new lan-
>   guage, "a revelation."

---

well, even though he was appreciably older. These experiences suggest the minds of these musicians were "prepared" in some way for the experience of hearing the violin, the orchestra, or the voice.

Such responses to musical sound are not restricted to a few isolated examples. In the interview portion of our study, a violin teacher reported a similar response in her selection of the violin as the preferred instrument when she was around 6 years old:

I always knew it was the violin: I was always satisfied with the violin, and I never wanted to play a bigger instrument. Now part of that is a physical identification since I am a rather small person and it would have been hard for me to cope with a viola or cello. But some of it is identification with sound.

I think that striking the keys of the piano is a very mechanical process. The piano is colder and the violin warmer. I had in my mind this very warm and very beautiful sound. When I began to play the violin and it was in my hands, I could feel a lot more direct control for the sound. I think that appealed to me.

[How old were you at the time?] About 6 or 7.

A second type of crystallizing experience occurs later in development and presupposes an individual who is already attuned to the area of music. In this particular case, the "refining crystallizing experience" guides the individual to that area of the musical domain in which his strongest talents or deepest inclinations may lie. In the cases we studied, individuals who were already musically inclined discovered that composition – or a certain kind of composition – was the appropriate form of involvement in music. The experience of Debussy in transcribing the opera of Wagner (reported in the Introduction) and the reaction of Stravinsky to harmony and counterpoint are good examples of this form of crystallizing experience. In each case, the crystallizing experience involves the recognition of the complexities of composition. The reaction is not that of the "initiating experience" of early youth, in which the "raw intelligence" encounters the domain itself for the first time. Rather, one sees at work a more mature problem-solving faculty that perceives subtle distinctions or potentials in the materials of the domain. This "refining experience" also served as a revelation to the artist, but in a way that is more sophisticated than the earlier "initiating" experience.

As a young adult, Pierre Boulez recognized in the music of Messiaen a "new language": "Here was the music of our time, a language with unlimited possibilities. No other language was possible. It was the most radical revolution since Monteverdi, for all the familiar patterns were now abolished. With it music moved out of the world of Newton and into the world of Einstein" (Peyser, 1976, pp. 25–26). Boulez had been trained in standard analyses of harmony and counterpoint, but his understanding of these dimensions changed when he heard Messiaen's compositions. In this case, we see the reaction of the relatively mature artist to the most serious and profound deliberations of the art form. According to our analysis, these insights reflect not the "raw intelligence" or even the manipulation of the symbol system, but rather the skills important to a domain or subdomain of the adult culture.

It appears, then, that all crystallizing experiences are not the same; instead, they reflect the level of development in the artist (or scientist). The developmental gap between the young Menuhin and the mature Boulez provides a picture of a spectrum of experiences that range from first contacts in childhood – the more dramatic crystallizing experiences of the untrained but extremely talented individual – to the more mature decisions and reflections of young adult artists and scientists.

On several counts, Haydn emerges as an anomaly. He did not attend the Conservatory, he received no individual training, and he was never an accomplished performer. Haydn sang in the Vienna Boys' Choir as a child, but during that time he received no systematic instruction. His talent for musical composition developed over a period of many years through self-guided methods, and, indeed, at the time he was 50, his younger brother Michael was considered by contemporaries as a far better composer. However, unlike Michael, Franz Joseph continued to develop, greatly influenced Mozart, and ended up as one of the titans of composition.

In sum, the musicians are characterized by talented childhoods, some crystallizing experiences that occur at different points during development, and relatively little self-instruction, especially in the realm of performance. There are important similarities as well as significant differences to be found in the analysis of the domain of mathematics.

Mathematicians

An early beginning proves even more important in the area of mathematics than it is in music. In almost every case, our subjects made important, seminal contributions to the field of mathematics before they were 30 years old. This appears to lend credence to the contention that "mathematics is a young man's game." Also, six out of the eight mathematicians were legitimate child-hood prodigies; and this list does not include G. H. Hardy, who was an outstanding high school student, and David Hilbert, who consistently received "Excellent" in mathematics. Table 14.2 also documents the five instances of crystallizing experiences in this group.

A brief review of the mathematicians who demonstrated talent during child-hood underscores that in mathematics the accomplishments of these subjects far surpass those of even the most gifted high school students. Gauss derived important principles of prime numbers at the age of 15, and Poincaré's genius for mathematics was a matter of public record even before he took the ad-missions test for the Polytechnique Institute. Wiener's school career speaks for itself: BA at 14 and PhD at 18. Von Neumann was considered a genius by everyone who knew him. Eugene Wigner, a Nobel laureate in physics, was a good childhood friend who said: "Particularly from having known Jansci von Neumann [as a child], I realized what the difference was between a first-rate mathematician and someone [like me]" (Heims, 1980, p. 43). We may conclude that marked talent during the childhood years is fairly commonplace among mathematicians, just as it is among musicians.

Mathematics proves quite different from music, however, with respect to the role that self-training can play. Although highly unusual in music – Haydn alone fell into this category – self-training is almost commonplace in math-ematics. Galois and Ramanujan were almost entirely self-trained, and, to a lesser extent, most of the other mathematicians taught themselves a significant part of their field. Furthermore, one of our interviewees, a university math-ematician, asserted that "all the masters taught themselves mathematics." Of course, it is possible that self-training is more difficult in contemporary math-ematics, where there is so much material to be mastered before original contributions are possible. It is also possible that self-training is found only in those areas marked by the fewest conventional constraints (the frontiers of mathematics, writing, jazz, etc.), simply because the conventional con-straints can be learned only through rigorous formal training (e.g., perform-ance of classical music, mastery of law, medicine, or laboratory science). At any rate, the distinction is fairly robust in the subjects reviewed here under mathematics and music.

Both Galois and Ramanujan serve as excellent illustrations of the role of a crystallizing experience in the developing career of a mathematician. In both cases, initial contact with the field came in the course of reading a mathematics textbook on one's own. Galois read Legendre, whereas Ra-manujan read a text of a substantially different sort.

Born to a poor family in India, Ramanujan showed his facility with numbers and interest in mathematics in elementary school. His obsessive devotion to mathematics, however, made him a poor student overall. He failed to com-plete even 1 year at the university, though he had received a scholarship for

Table 14.2. *The mathematicians*

Carl Friedrich Gauss, 1777–1855, Germany

    Childhood talent: Original mathematics produced at the age of 15 when he derived certain principles regarding the laws of prime numbers.

    Crystallizing experience: During his first year at the university, Gauss discovered a method for constructing a 17-sided polygon with only Euclidean tools. He announced the discovery proudly in the advance notices in a mathematics journal, saying it was "a discovery [with] special interest" because it made a significant advance upon the work of Euclid. If there had been any doubt in his mind about his eventual career as a mathematician, it was removed with this discovery" (Hall, 1970, pp. 21–24).

Evariste Galois, 1811–1832, France

    Childhood talent: Self-taught in mathematics. Original publications beginning at age 17.

    Crystallizing experience: Reading the geometry textbook of Legendre, cited in the Introduction.

Henri Poincaré, 1854–1912, France

    Childhood talent: His talent appeared during adolescence when he won a mathematics context without taking notes during lectures. In the examination for the Polytechnique his examiner suspended the examination for an hour in order to construct an especially difficult question for Poincaré. He answered it correctly and received the highest grade.

    Crystallizing experience: None reported.

David Hilbert, 1862–1943, Germany

    Childhood talent: Hilbert received outstanding grades in mathematics during school but was not a prodigy along the lines of Gauss or Poincaré. He stated later that he did not concentrate on mathematics during his school years because he "always knew he would do that later" (Reid, 1970, p. 7).

    Crystallizing experience: After an uninspired dissertation, he spent several years traveling and studying with mathematicians like Klein, Poincaré, and Hermite. He made no major contribution until at the age of 27 he published the solution to Gordan's problem; in this proof, he demonstrated that a solution was impossible. Although first criticized by the establishment as "unearthly," this technique was shortly accepted by the mathematical community and secured Hilbert's position as a leader (Reid, pp. 28–28).

G. H. Hardy, 1877–1947, England

    Childhood talent: Although an outstanding student throughout school, Hardy was not a child prodigy.

    Crystallizing experience: He did well in school mathematics without developing any "passion" for the subject. When he began study at the university with Professor Love, however, he said, "I learned for the first time what mathematics really meant. From that time onwards, I was on my way to becoming a real mathematician with sound mathematical ambitions and a genuine passion for mathematics" (Hardy, 1967, p. 24).

Srinivasa Ramanujan, 1887–1920, India

    Childhood talent: Ramanujan was almost entirely self-educated. He never finished the first year at the university, and yet when he sent some of his original work to

Table 14.2. (*cont.*)

Hardy in England, his genius was immediately recognized and Hardy obtained a
fellowship for him to work and study at Cambridge.
Crystallizing experience: Reading the tutorial manual, Carr's *Synopsis of Pure Mathematics*, described in this chapter.

Norbert Wiener, 1894–1964, United States
Childhood talent: Tutored by his father, he graduated from high school at age 10,
and from Tufts College at 14. He obtained a PhD from Harvard by the age of 18.
Crystallizing experience: None reported.

John von Neumann, 1903–1957, Hungary
Childhood talent: Tutored in mathematics through high school, he published original work at the age of 16. He won a nationwide mathematics contest at 18. By 22
he had obtained two doctorates.
Crystallizing experience: None reported.

his mathematical skills. Leaving the university, he took up a job as a clerk
and continued his mathematical research on his own, publishing several papers
and receiving some encouragement from local mathematicians. At the age of
25, he wrote a letter to the English mathematician G. H. Hardy, in which he
announced several of his discoveries. Hardy was so impressed with the originality and insight of the work that he secured a scholarship for Ramanujan
at Cambridge, and they collaborated there until Ramanujan's death at the
age of 32. Ramanujan was the first Indian elected to the Royal Academy,
receiving that accolade at the age of 28.

Ramanujan's crystallizing experience occurred while reading a mathematics
textbook:

It was in 1903 on a momentous day for Ramanujan, that a friend of his secured for
him the loan of a copy of Carr's *Synopsis of Pure Mathematics*. Through the new
world thus opened to him, Ramanujan went ranging with delight. It was this book
that awakened his genius. He set himself to establish the formulae given therein. As
he was without the aid of other books, each solution was a piece of research so far
as he was concerned.

He first devised some methods for constructing magic squares. Then he branched
off to Geometry, where he took up the squaring of the circle and succeeded so far as
to get a result for the length of the equilateral circumference of the earth which differed
from the true length only by a few feet. He [then] turned his attention to Algebra
where he obtained several new series. (Seshu Aiyar, & Ramachandra Rao, 1927,
p. xii)

These feats are even more remarkable when considered in the light of the
text that Ramanujan was working with. G. H. Hardy noted:

I suppose that the book is substantially a summary of Carr's coaching notes. If you
were a pupil of Carr, you worked through the appropriate sections of the *Synopsis*.
It contains the enunciations of 6165 theorems, systematically and quite scientifically
arranged, with proofs that are often little more than cross-references and are decidedly
the least interesting part of the book. All this is exaggerated in Ramanujan's famous

notebooks (which contain practically no proofs at all), and any student of the note-books can see that Ramanujan's ideal of presentation had been copied from Carr's. (Hardy, 1940, p. 7)

Ramanujan's experiences with Carr's text prove relevant to our discussion in two ways. First, despite its unusual pedagogical style and a minimum of explanation, this book revealed to Ramanujan the world of mathematics; his intellect filled in the gaps. Second, the book had a profound impact on the manner in which Ramanujan pursued the field as an adult. In other words, Ramanujan was crystallized to mathematics via Carr's *Synopsis* and can be said to have been stunted by it as well.

Hardy's own crystallizing experience was as different from Ramanujan's as was his cultural background and schooling. Whereas Ramanujan was self-educated in a small village in India, Hardy was thoroughly trained in the English public school system. Although an excellent mathematics student throughout school, he did not develop a passionate devotion to the subject until he worked with a particular professor at Cambridge. That experience crystallized his sense of the subject matter as well as his view of himself as a "real mathematician with sound mathematical ambitions" (Hardy, 1967, pp. 23–24).

In contrast to Galois, Ramanujan, and Hardy, the crystallizing experiences of Hilbert and Gauss were manifested in significant mathematical discoveries made during early adulthood. Gauss discovered the construction of the 17-sided polygon, a major contribution to the geometry of Euclid. In announcing the discovery, Gauss stated with evident pride the significance of his achievement within the context of mathematics. At the age of 25, Hilbert published the proof demonstrating that the solution to Gordan's problem was impossible. This proof raised a considerable stir in the mathematical community at the time, and later, when the proof was demonstrated to be correct, Hilbert's concept of himself as a mathematician, as well as his reputation within the field, was firmly established.

The aforementioned relationship of crystallizing experience to developmental level reappears in mathematics. The earlier "initiating" crystallizing experiences ushered in the rapid development of certain talented subjects, in which they reached adult levels at an early age (Galois and Ramanujan; Rubinstein and Menuhin). With the older children and young adults, on the other hand, the "refining" crystallizing experiences reflect an interaction between an already blossoming talent and certain more subtle, but crucial, distinctions within the domain (Debussy and Boulez; Gauss and Hilbert). In some cases, a prodigious talent together with a highly supportive initial environment removes the opportunity (or the need) for a crystallizing experience in childhood (Mozart; Wiener). One finds examples of autodidacts in mathematics as well as music (Haydn; Galois and Ramanujan).

Finally, in both domains, the nature and extent of crystallizing experiences appears closely related to the environment in which the talented child is raised.

Crystallizing experiences prove more likely in those environments in which the domain is not stressed or where it is underutilized – Ramanujan and Galois serve as illustrations. But Hardy and Debussy suggest a more complex explanation. In these two cases, the domain was thoroughly supported in childhood – Hardy in the English public schools and Debussy at the Conservatoire – and consequently the crystallizing experiences occurred closer to adulthood, as the subjects developed new insights into their respective domains. For instance, Debussy's crystallizing reaction to the scandalous music of Wagner was in part a response to the conservative and perhaps uncreative atmosphere that permeated his theory and composition instruction. Finally, those environments that provided strong, immediate experiences in the domain from an early age (Wiener, Mendelssohn, Mozart) were least likely to produce crystallizing experiences.

Visual artists

The pattern of childhood talent and crystallizing experiences that cuts across the domains of music and mathematics does not recur in the domain of the visual arts. As seen in Table 14.3, there are only two talented children, Rembrandt and Turner, and there are only two clear-cut crystallizing experiences, Renoir and Klee. Consequently, whereas the evidence from music and mathematics provided support for the notion of crystallizing experiences, the evidence from the visual arts causes us to reconsider the pervasiveness of this phenomenon.

Turning first to the question of early talent, there are no child prodigies; the closest contenders were Rembrandt and Turner, who had acquired substantial reputations by their early 20s. Second, both candidate crystallizing experiences occurred in early adulthood to subjects who had already defined themselves as practitioners in the field. In a sense, Renoir at the Fontaine des Innocents and Paul Klee experiencing the beauty of nature in an aquarium in Naples are reminiscent of Debussy or Hardy: young adults making a refined discrimination in their chosen field. Only if we broaden the concept of crystallizing experiences to a more general experience – such as working with fellow artists or viewing the masters in a gallery – can a greater number of visual artists be included. For instance, Cézanne, Miro, and Cassatt all found inspiration for their own work in these ways.

One possible reason for this distinction between the visual arts and the other two domains arises from the following: It is much more likely for an artist to take up the career during young adulthood than for a musician or mathematician. Van Gogh and Matisse come to mind as examples. In our interviews with teachers (discussed in detail in the next section), we asked a distinguished and extremely knowledgeable college mathematics professor if he knew of any students who entered the mathematics program after a career

Table 14.3. *The visual artists*

Rembrandt van Rijn, 1606–1669, Netherlands

    Childhood talent: Rembrandt came from a modest background and turned down an opportunity to study at the university in order to pursue a career in art. After a 4-year apprenticeship, he established his own shop at the age of 19 and began giving art lessons. Constantine Huygens, a scholar visiting Leyden, described Rembrandt at this time as having great promise even though his "teachers were insignificant" (Brown, 1911, pp. 59–60).

    Crystallizing experience: None reported.

J. M. W. Turner, 1775–1851, England

    Childhood talent: As a schoolboy, Turner gained a reputation as someone who would rather draw than work. He began study at the Royal Academy at age 14 and finished at 18. He immediately took on commissions and was exhibited at the Royal Academy at the age of 22; he was elected ARA at 24.

    Crystallizing experience: None reported.

Paul Cézanne, 1839–1906, France

    Childhood talent: Talent did not appear during childhood.

    Crystallizing experiences: None reported.

Pierre-Auguste Renoir, 1841–1919, Paris

    Childhood talent: His facility with the paintbrush earned him a full adult wage while an apprentice porcelain decorator.

    Crystallizing experience: He found a beauty in the statue at the Fontaine des Innocents in Paris that he had not anticipated in his consideration of art as an aesthetic rather than decorative medium (cited in the Introduction).

Mary Cassatt, 1844–1926, United States

    Childhood talent: Talent did not appear until adulthood.

    Crystallizing experience: None reported.

Paul Klee, 1879–1940, Switzerland

    Childhood talent: Talent did not appear until early adulthood.

    Crystallizing experience: He studied art briefly at the Academy in Munich, after which he began a tour of Italy. In Naples he visited the aquarium, where he found that "the silent creativeness of Nature challenged man's fantasy to indulge in as much freedom" (Haftman, 1954, p. 30). This experience, when combined with his careful observation of the galleries of Florence and Rome, caused him to give up the formal study of art and return instead to his home in Switzerland. There he spent the next 10 years experimenting.

Jean Miro, 1893–1983, Spain

    Childhood talent: Talent did not appear until early adulthood.

    Crystallizing experience: None reported.

---

in another field. He answered, "It probably happened twice in the history of mathematics. I really don't know of any examples of that." We asked the same question of the director at a college of art. His response was quite different:

In this school this year we only took 23 students out of high school in the whole student body of about 600 students. We tend to have older students. It is a tough school to get into out of high school, simply because if we let them in they flounder

...[Do you find people who quit a job in order to come to school for art training?] Yes, all the time. One of my staff members was an attorney. He is now an artist. He was in his 30s or early 40s and he made a complete turnaround. It took him a long time of real struggle to get anywhere. But now he is an artist of real merit.

From one perspective, it might appear that our view of crystallizing experiences is invalidated by these findings from the visual arts. Yet, paradoxically, these findings reinforce a principal tenet of MI theory. Our survey suggests that rather than development occurring in a parallel fashion in every domain, an experience critical in certain domains – for example, the early emergence of the talented mathematician or the musician – proves relatively unimportant in another cultural domain, the visual arts. Just why this is so is difficult to say. It may be that these three domains are viewed in a particular way by Western culture and may, in fact, be viewed differently by other cultures. For example, in Bali it might turn out that the visual arts are heavily stressed in early life, and that consequently there are more crystallizing experiences and more examples of prodigious behavior in that domain. It is also possible to imagine a society in which logical–mathematical precocity is of no relevance, or even actively discouraged, in which case one would not expect to find rapid development in that domain.

Another quite different explanation suggests that the mental processes involved in the visual arts develop at a different rate and hence are less susceptible to the one-time crystallizing experiences than are the quickly developing and more digitalized processes entailed in other domains. Mathematics and music, for example, are both more self-contained, more likely to develop in relative isolation from the real world, and relatively digital and notational. In contrast, according to this analysis, the visual arts relate from the first to the external world, and are not in any sense self-contained; also, digital or notational processes do not play any role in the visual arts, which inherently entail continuous and analog symbol systems (Goodman, 1968).

The interviews

The information and insights obtained from the biographical literature provided one important and useful perspective on the phenomenon of crystallizing experiences. As a source of data, however, the biographies have several significant shortcomings. First, biographies are often derived from the reminiscences of the subject and the subject's friends after a successful career. The biographies also restrict our exploration in that they provide no opportunity for cross-examination. It was for these reasons, then, that we supplemented the investigation of biographies with interviews of master teachers in these three domains. We hoped that intensive conversations with master teachers would provide an important supplement (and perhaps a needed corrective) to information culled from the genre of written biography.

During the interviews, we posed a large set of questions. We sampled broadly for two reasons: (a) our interest in the issues surrounding the discovery and development of talent in general; (b) our desire not to focus directly on crystallizing experiences. (As will become evident, we succeeded quite well in masking our goal of eliciting crystallizing experiences from these teachers!) Among the questions we posed were whether or not teachers perceived some of their students as more talented than others; if they could recognize that talent quickly and easily; what skills co-occurred with the talent in question; and, of course, whether or not the teachers had observed or been informed of any crystallizing experiences.

The subjects of the interviews were teachers who had worked with gifted students. The music and art teachers were affiliated with private schools or colleges for music and art. The two teachers of mathematics were professors at a university. The interviews lasted about 1 hour; they were tape-recorded and the tapes were later transcribed. The quotations reported here are taken from those tapes with only minor editing to improve continuity. Because the teachers responded to the interviews with a frank honesty, even when the questions concerned their own development, we will refer to them only through their specialties: violin, cello, piano, photography, number theory, and topology.

Crystallizing experiences

The teachers did not report crystallizing experiences on the part of their students. Although this finding was unanticipated, we can offer an explanation in retrospect. In the biographies, crystallizing experiences were most frequent in precisely those cases where there was little or no teaching or where there was an early discovery of the domain before teachers had been contacted. Even in cases where crystallizing experiences occurred relatively late, the individuals were frequently alone and engaged in self-instruction when it happened. It may also be that individuals themselves do not recognize a crystallizing experience fully at the time it happens; only in retrospect do individuals become aware of it. Finally, crystallizing experiences are by their nature intensely personal and private: adolescent students may be reluctant to share these with others, even trusted parents and teachers.

Although the teachers did not observe crystallizing experiences in their students, most reported them in discussing the development of their own careers:

Photographer: When I was growing up I had very little exposure to art; we visited the Metropolitan Museum maybe once. Then, in the Navy, I was lying in my bunk reading the book *Lust for Life*, the novelization of Van Gogh's life, and I noticed that the pictures in the back were in the Museum of Modern Art in New York, and since we were in dry dock in the Brooklyn Naval Yard at the time, I jumped up and went to see them.

I remember that day like yesterday – the weather, the people on the street. I guess you could say it was an "epiphany." When I left the Navy, I tried to get a job as a guard in an art museum because I had been a payroll guard in the Navy.

Topologist: My father was an interesting person mathematically. He had a great deal of facility, although he was no mathematician. He had worked out for himself a number of interesting "tricks" and I can give you an example of one. You would write a number and he would write after it immediately another number. When you added the two, the answer was divisible by 37. I remember him doing this kind of trick and being very impressed by it and being very curious about how it could work. I was attracted to this because it was a completely unposed problem, not a problem in a book. He did this trick, and he didn't have any training – how did he figure it out?

I think that kind of experience was probably very important to me at the time.

These two experiences are quite different in terms of drama and immediacy. And yet they share a common quality – they serve as a reference point in the individual's perception of his development as an artist or mathematician. For the photographer, the situation involved the first contact with the world of art. Its impact was quite immediate and profound, and we might suppose that he was "prepared" in some way for this experience. In the second case, what was crystallized was the topologist's appreciation of mathematics as a field of inquiry. As a field, mathematics contains many problems that have no solution; problems posed in texts, on the other hand, inevitably do have solutions and their study is not representative of the highest and most creative aspects of the field.

The teachers also discussed a phenomenon that might also be interpreted along "crystallizing" lines – choosing the instrument in the domain (e.g., violin, photography, or topology). We found that the teachers described this choice as if it were "predetermined" in some way – as if they had to discover the instrument most appropriate for them. This suggests that talent may be tuned not only to a domain but, more specifically, to a particular approach within that domain. For example:

Violinist: I have found that it is not just enough to be musical; there has to be some orientation toward the actual physical process of playing around *that* particular instrument. For example, when I started music, I wanted to play the flute. But then my idea changed around 6 or 7. My mother said that I would begin the piano, but by that time I wanted to play the violin, but she insisted on the piano as a "basis." It was very clear to me as a child that I was not primarily interested in piano even though I learned it easily and well. I really wanted to play the violin, and through my subsequent study it was that way: I *knew* the violin was . . . me.

We would listen to the radio, we heard classical music. . . . I had in my mind this very warm and very beautiful violin sound. When I began to play the violin and it was in my hands, I could feel a lot more directly the control of the sound. I think that appealed to me.

It is quite the opposite for other people. I have a friend who is a wonderful pianist; she is very talented. She took up the cello and she told me that she could never play in tune on the cello. She is the despair of her cello teacher. She is a wonderfully talented pianist, and yet somehow she didn't click with the cello. She liked it and she wished she could do well on it, but it just didn't suit her.

Pianist: It often happens that somebody is extremely talented on the violin and starts on the piano, for instance, and does very poorly. Some of my colleagues have told me that they have done that.

I personally encourage the children to start a general education in music with the rhythms of dance and playing with different kinds of instruments of very simple types. So they have a chance after a year maybe of that to decide with their teacher which instrument is best. They play those simple recorders and pitch pipes and drums and string instruments and keyboard instruments. They may gravitate toward one of them. That is the more natural way.

Similarly, in art school, students are exposed to a vast array of media, from oils to watercolor to goldsmithing to videotape:

Photographer: Just as I talk I remember a student who came here to be sculptor, and then went down to the photography department, just to learn enough photographic technique to photograph his sculpture, and he found that he really was a *photographer*! It happens all the time. [Art school] is a smorgasbord and you have to find how you operate and then find the medium that is most appropriate.... Film, photography, woodworking, printmaking, every kind of sculpture you can imagine – it is not just a coincidence that art schools are the places that people go to become artists.

These early experiences at "choosing an instrument" can be considered fine-tuning in the domain – finding a niche within the field; in this case, the teacher serves as an important aid in this search for the instrument. In fact, the teachers report that an important part of the job is to provide the right kinds of experiences that help their students choose wisely. At the same time, however, several of these experiences sound very much like "crystallizations" in themselves. In these cases, the teacher does not play an important role. Both Yehudi Menuhin and the violinist in our interviews reported that the sound of the violin was different for them as young children, before any formal instruction. In these cases, hearing the violin crystallizes the sense of the individual as a musician at a time antecedent to formal training. We consider these types of revelations to be legitimate examples of crystallizing experiences.

These examples of choosing an instrument recall our distinction between initiating crystallizing experiences and refining experiences. That is, the choice of the instrument does not serve to crystallize the youngster to the domain per se, but rather to the way in which that child will enter the domain. So, it is a crystallizing experience at the time that we usually find the initiating experiences, but it has more of the flavor of the refining experiences generally found later on.

The issue of talent

As a part of our interest in crystallizing experiences, we talked to teachers about how they judged the talents of their students – what specific things made some students special, how quickly could the teachers make such a distinction, what specifically marked the differences among students, and so on. We were particularly interested in determining whether the teachers would report simply that children *are* talented, or whether such differences were merely a matter of hours of practice.

The answers prove quite instructive. On the one hand, the teachers described, quite articulately, differences among their students that may be attributed to differences in talent. At the same time, those teachers often denied outright that there was such a quality that operated independent of their teaching. For example:

Violinist: You can notice the very great musical feeling sometimes from the very beginning. A student can play a little Bach duet, just beautifully, with such grace and taste and [still] be quite elementary [in terms of technique]. I heard a tape recently of an 8-year-old girl who plays so beautifully, so musically. Now, she is not particularly advanced for 8 years old by our standards today, but in her playing there is such a feeling of her whole being; and just so free, and such expression in it, that I thought on hearing the tape, "Hmm, this is a remarkable child."

Photographer: Some of those ways of being in the world seem somehow more nutritious and salubrious to us than others. Those are the people we think of as having talent. And they have some of the characteristics of being clear, and vulnerable, and graceful in a potent way. I suppose that is really the magic that you are talking about [with respect to "talent"]. I don't know where it comes from.

Topologist: [In talking about a former student] He was very, very bright. Throughout his period here as a graduate student we regularly recognized his grasp of things. He was always ahead of the other graduate students.

[Question: Are there things in mathematics that are untaught or unteachable?] I don't know what it is and I wish I could tell what it is that makes someone good at mathematics. It is very hard to *teach* somebody mathematics when you don't know how to start. When you do mathematics, you rather naturally "see" certain kinds of relationships and you don't have to be told what they are, and you get the drift. And when you get somebody [in class] who doesn't see the world that way, it is extremely difficult. I can't figure out why it is that I can't *explain* to them why 2 + 2 is 4!

At the same time, the teachers also said:

Cellist: I think that one of the most important things is cultivating a love of music in the young person. If you start them very young and train and develop them slowly, then you have the time to set up the technique but at the same time to develop the love of playing and the love of music, and that in the long run will make for a child who wants to play well . . . who will develop a musical soul from that.

Number theorist: [Question: In mathematics, what can't be taught?] *Anything* can be taught! The difference is strictly in terms of motivation. To be a mathematician you have to "do math" 16 hours a day.

These quotations suggest two different perspectives on eventual success in a domain – a special quality, aptitude, or predilection in the learner versus a disciplined motivation derived in part from well-managed teaching. The two views were not stated as contending points of view; instead, they constituted an inconsistency within a single point of view. That is, we found several teachers who reported both perspectives in the same interview. Of course, the two perspectives are not logically contradictory; success in a field could result from a combination of natural aptitude and good teaching. However, the teachers did not appear to embrace this compromise position and maintained instead either one pole or the other. Since a primary goal of the interviews was to determine how teachers conceptualize the notion of "talent" in their students, we must consider this result in some detail.

There is an explanation for the apparent inconsistency in the teachers' point of view. Good teachers have a high investment in the act of teaching and in its role in the process of the development of the mature artist or mathematician. They believe – they *must* believe – that teaching makes a difference. At the same time, however, they actively seek out those students who display unique qualities or talents within the field, even before the instruction has begun. This is equally important to the teaching process: for one thing, students with these special qualities are more likely to achieve success, but perhaps more importantly, they are more likely to continue the development of their talent over a longer period of time. The teachers, and perhaps especially those in music, consider the time they spend in instruction as an investment in a particular student, and they are very careful to select those students who will not squander that investment. They make this choice on the basis of motivation and aptitude. Consequently, the teachers can discuss aptitude in detail and they can articulate specific skills and behaviors that they look for as indicators of aptitude. These concerns lead to the paradoxical situation where the teacher can, on the one hand, claim that anything can be taught to anyone who is properly motivated, while at the same time actively seeking out certain kinds of students to receive that teaching.

In choosing students, the teachers look for several very specific traits that in their experience are related to eventual success. For instance, the number theorist described one such attribute he had observed in successful mathematicians:

Number theorist: Yet another interesting trait is "artful dodging." Some people, when they run into a problem, persistently remain there even if they are getting no closer to a solution. This is counterproductive. Others, if they are "artful dodgers," know enough to try something else, or to drop the problem, or to contrive the skill that they lack. This is much more adaptive and productive.

And the cellist who described the need for "love of playing" earlier, also looked for the following skills in young children:

Cellist: The talented generally have strong, flexible fingers. This is a real key to the whole of playing. The child has to be strong enough to push the string down, but at the same time the hand is still flexible so that you can get a beautiful sound. I can just tell when a student comes in, in the first month of lessons, I can tell by the feel of their hand whether it is going to be easy or hard for them.

The music teachers also mentioned the ability to handle different kinds of problems (e.g., key, rhythm, fingering) at the same time, as well as the ability to process information quickly (especially in sight-reading). The mathematicians mentioned the ability to identify and focus on one particular quality of a problem. So, even as they talked in general terms about "lyricism" or "insightfulness" or "vulnerability," the teachers also talked about specific skills like intonation, craft, and problem solving. It does not appear that "talent" as described by these teachers resides strictly in either the mysterious intangibles, nor does it reside in the technical faculties. Rather, talent comprises both factors and perhaps they cannot and should not be separated.

Motivation is yet another feature to which teachers pay careful attention – the love of playing in a young musician, or the desire to "do mathematics 16 hours a day." To some degree, motivation is outside the direct control of the teachers and so they are very careful to evaluate motivation in their students; but at the same time, they feel that motivation can be instilled and to this degree they can affect it. In contrast, talent as defined in our culture is entirely outside the control of the teachers, and again, this probably is responsible in part for the unenthusiastic response of the teachers to the construct "talent."

Although teachers claim it is important to have motivation, and that this is within the students' (if not the teachers') control, the theory of multiple intelligences suggests a different perspective. Specifically, turning the usual formula on its head, we propose that individuals are, or become, motivated to the extent that they have some facility within a particular domain. That is, a talented mathematician would be more likely to do "mathematics 16 hours a day" because of a basic understanding of the domain and the intriguing problems that it presents than the person who does not have that talent and does not understand the domain in that way. Motivation then would be the consequence of talent rather than the explanation of it.

In sum, then, the teachers described differences among their students along several lines. They articulated general differences – the love of playing, the insightfulness, the vulnerability; and they talked about specific skills and attributes that contributed to this success, such as flexible fingers, facility with manipulating symbols, rapid processing of information, and so on. This is quite compatible with the incidence of childhood talent found in the biographies and the specific skills displayed by those subjects when they were children. Taken together, the two sources of data provide a more complete picture of the early development of talented children.

When asked specifically about this talent, however, the teachers responded in two nearly contradictory ways. Although they described differences among their students, they often denied that these differences were independent of teaching and insisted instead that they were the product of external factors such as "motivation." This response was quite unexpected because there is nothing similar in the biographical literature. We interpret it as a reflection of an educational philosophy that emphasizes the potential of each student rather than the constraints posed by limitations in talent.

Concluding remarks

It is important to indicate certain limits intrinsic to our study. To begin with, there are limitations in theory. Although the perspective of multiple intelligences can, loosely speaking, be considered a theory, it clearly lacks axioms, postulates, a set of testable hypotheses, and other paraphernalia of a theory in the hard sciences. By the same token, the construct of crystallizing experiences does not follow in any lock-step fashion from the treatment of giftedness in MI theory. As we have seen, there are individuals of indisputable achievement who lack crystallizing experiences, and without a doubt there are other individuals who experience some, or even all, of the features of a crystallizing experience without achieving notable success in any domain. What lends our study urgency is the need for a construct that is consistent with the major assertions of MI theory and that at the same time helps to explain, if sometimes in a post hoc fashion, major findings concerning the genesis and realization of talent. It is in this spirit that we have formulated our construct of crystallizing experiences and examined it in the light of biographical and interview testimony. To the extent that the construct has proved its utility (and we believe it has), it is now opportune to initiate more systematic studies, which would include control groups, and perhaps experimental manipulations as well.

With these caveats in mind, we offer the following summary of our findings. In the biographies, we found that crystallizing experiences do occur frequently, but that there are noticeable and probably important differences across individuals and across domains. For one thing, the nature of a crystallizing experience depends on the age of the subject. The experiences of younger subjects are closely related to unmediated or "raw" intelligence; we called these "initiating crystallizing experiences." The anecdote from Galois in the introduction illustrates this; Menuhin provides another example. With older children and young adults, the crystallizing experience reflects a mediated contact with the domain, in which some training in the materials of the domain is presupposed – Debussy's reaction to Wagner or Hardy's response to his Cambridge mathematics professor illustrate what we have called "refining crystallizing experiences."

Our results also suggest that crystallizing experiences differ across domains as well. They are more prevalent in mathematics and music than in the visual arts, for instance. Perhaps in the visual arts individuals are "crystallized" over a longer period of time, through repeated visits to museums, for instance. In that case, the memorable experience of Renoir stands as an exception and the more gradual development of Cézanne as the rule. Or it may be that visual artists are less willing to share their experiences with teachers and appreciate the crystallizing experience only in retrospect.

The domains also differed with respect to the early appearance of talent. Music and mathematics were both characterized by a large number of talented children, whereas the visual arts were not. Similarly, music and mathematics appear to require disciplined training during childhood, whereas the visual arts do not. We have considered the possibility that these differences may reflect contrasting cultural values about the various domains (e.g., early mathematics being valued more than early visual art in our culture), but they may also reflect the differences intrinsic to the domain (the degree to which the domain is cut off from others and can be negotiated in a manner independent of real-world experiences).

Some of these findings from the biographies were affirmed by our interviews with the teachers: the requirement of early training or learning in mathematics and music but not the visual arts; the personal experiences of the teachers in discovering their own talents; the manner in which training keeps pace with the general move from "raw" intelligence to mediated intelligence. However, other points emerged during the interviews that did not appear in the biographies. For instance, the teachers spoke a great deal about motivation in contrast to talent. This perspective can be seen as either a challenge to the theory of multiple intelligences, or, as we have described previously, a call for supplementary data. Also, aside from the choice of the particular instrument, the teachers reported no observations of crystallizing experiences in their students, although they did report them from their personal development. We have offered several retrospective explanations for this apparent discrepancy.

How, then, does our perspective fare in accounting for the phenomenon of crystallizing experiences? Our analysis strongly suggests that crystallizing experiences are a genuine phenomenon, although one that is not immune to differences across domains. It would be difficult to maintain that these experiences are accidental or artifactual, because this implies that they should occur in the same fashion and with the same frequency across domains and across developmental levels. Second, it appears that the crystallizing experience is a fragile phenomenon that occurs principally when circumstances combine inborn talent, self-teaching, and proper exposure to a set of materials in a particular way. Finally, in those circumstances where there is a strong predisposition to excel with a given material, and where there are some but not exceptional opportunities, crystallizing experiences are most likely to occur.

For the purposes of this chapter, we have stressed the kinds of experiences that may befall individuals of indisputable talent and that help to set them on their life course. In conclusion, we would like to raise the question about whether crystallizing experiences are indeed just a purview of the most gifted, or whether they may occur in more mundane ways with individuals who are closer to the norm. The present study casts no light on this question. Still, it would seem to be good pedagogy – if not just good common sense – to treat all children as if they have the potential for crystallizing experiences, and to expose them at an early age to materials that may motivate them to explore a domain. It may turn out that there are far more "gifted" children than could have been anticipated from the unplanned encounters that until now have been the chief locus for crystallizing experiences.

References

Bell, E. (1965). *Men of mathematics*, New York: Simon & Schuster.
Bloom, B. (1982). The role of gifts and markers in the development of talent. *Exceptional Children, 48*, 510–522.
Brown, G. (1911). *Rembrandt: A study of his life and work*. New York: Scribner.
Feldman, D. (1980). *Beyond universals in cognitive development*. Norwood, N.J.: Ablex.
Gardner, H. (1982). Giftedness: A biological perspective. In D. Feldman (Ed.), *Developmental approaches to giftedness and creativity*. (*New Directions for Child Development, 17*), pp. 47–60.
Gardner, H. (1983). *Frames of mind*. New York: Basic Books.
Goodman, N. (1968). *Languages of art*. Indianapolis: Bobbs-Merrill.
Haftman, W. (1954). *The mind and work of Paul Klee*. New York: Praeger.
Hall, T. (1970). *Carl Friedrich Gauss*. Cambridge, Mass.: MIT Press.
Hanson, L. (1968). *Renoir: The man, the painter, and his world*. New York: Dodd, Mead.
Hardy, G. (1940). *Ramanujan*. Cambridge University Press.
Hardy, G. (1967). *A mathematician's apology*. Cambridge University Press.
Hayes, J. (1981). *The complete problem solver*. Philadelphia: Franklin Institute Press.
Heims, S. (1980). *John von Neumann and Norbert Wiener*. Cambridge, Mass.: MIT Press.
Lockspeiser, E. (1962). *Debussy: His life and mind*. London: Cassell.
Menuhin, Y. (1977). *Unfinished journey*. New York: Knopf.
Peyser, J. (1976). *Boulez*. New York: Schirmer.
Reid, C. (1970). *Hilbert*. New York: Springer-Verlag.
Rubinstein, A. (1973). *My young years*. New York: Knopf.
Seshu Aiyar, P., and Ramachandra Rao, R. (1927). Srinivasa Ramanujan. An obituary republished in G. Hardy, P. Seshu Aiyar, & B. Wilson (Eds.), *The collected papers of Srinivasa Ramanujan*. Cambridge University Press.
Wagner, R. (1911). *My life*. New York: Dodd, Mead.
White, E. (1966). *Stravinsky*. Berkeley, Calif.: University of California Press.

15 The achievement of eminence: a model based on a longitudinal study of exceptionally gifted boys and their families

Robert S. Albert and Mark A. Runco

Giftedness and the family: basic orientation and assumptions

Although the attainment of high eminence is rare and difficult to explain scientifically, both its life history and its behavioral makeup are broadly definable (Albert, 1969, 1971, 1975). Without getting into the specific personal and interpersonal factors involved, we have assumed all along that the attainment of eminence involves the gifted child's family in a number of ways – as product, as experience, as canalization, and as the outcome of the family values and emphases involved in its expression. We should say at the outset that we view the processes of canalization and expression as being both biological and experiential in nature.

When examined in some detail, most eminent persons appear to be highly intelligent and specifically gifted, yet it has been something of a disappointment over the years that fewer than expected of Terman's original sample of gifted children have attained eminent careers. Exactly why is difficult to say. But, if anything, this result speaks of the limits that high, even gifted, IQs alone can achieve, and it should warn us from taking too simple and too cognitive a view of giftedness itself. We believe it warns us against explaining achievement only in terms of cognitive variables without putting personality variables and family processes in the picture. As we now know from Oden's (1968) pioneer follow-up of Terman's subjects and Berrington's (1974) incisive psychoanalytic study of British prime ministers, very complicated early family experiences are involved in a gifted person's achievements – experiences that range from the quality and educational thrust of one's parents to the unexpected tragedy of early childhood parental bereavement. For these reasons – the unpredictable power of the IQ in eminence and the few but strong hints of powerful, noncognitive early family experiences and values in the achievement of eminence – we focus our own research as much on our subjects' parents as on the subjects themselves.

It is a pleasure to thank the Robert Sterling Clark Foundation and the John D. and Catherine T. MacArthur Foundation publicly for their financial support through grants to Robert S. Albert; to thank Professor Julian Stanley for his generous encouragement, and to thank Dr. Kevin Marjoribanks for sharing his Family Environment Inventory.

Believing that it is out of personal dispositions and early experiences that families' parent–child values and emphases will have evolved, we have developed the following set of explicit assumptions about how families work over time. From these assumptions, we have developed a set of operations that we anticipate will allow us eventually to trace out the more salient family histories and processes of influence.

Our basic assumptions are the following.

1. At high levels of cognitive ability *and* talent, especially at the level of giftedness, it is not necessary to separate intelligence and creative behavior. They share a number of attributes and perform in similar ways within the person and his or her interactions with the environment. Each is necessary for eminence; neither alone leads to much. We discuss this in more detail later in the chapter.

2. In order for gifted persons to achieve a recognizably high level of eminence, there must be a transformation of their early giftedness into a set of appropriate values, drives, and skills or abilities that permits them to engage in highly important and/or unusual work within a career that is significant to others as well as to them. Put simply, one usually does not attain eminence without influencing and impressing people in a position to understand and judge the results (Albert, 1975; Zuckerman, 1977).

3. The transformation of gifted creativeness into eminence-producing ability and effort begins initially within one's family of origin but becomes steadily refined through one's formal and informal education as well as one's early career efforts (Roe, 1952). In terms of these three assumptions alone we believe that it takes a great deal of maintained effort within the context of family, school, and career on the part of a highly gifted young person ever to be in a position to achieve eminence. Without long-term effort it is likely that the giftedness will lie fallow and become relatively unproductive in even the most inviting of careers.

4. The fourth assumption involves the "goodness of fit" between giftedness and career demands. These early efforts are directed – often deliberately – by family experiences and values as well as later by the young person's parallel educational and career opportunities. The three – family, education, and career, in this order – offer successive *informing opportunities* in which the gifted person acquires the necessary skills and tests realistically their relevance to early aspirations and career goals. Put simply, one must be able to meet the experiential demands peculiar to his or her career choice. Without this testing one can never know or appreciate, much less experience, the appropriateness and fit of one's giftedness to real-world opportunities that have their own demand qualities. For this reason, we speak of both the family and one's early career choices as experience-selecting agents in the development of one's giftedness. Both family and career choices demand and generate drives to be something specific and often special; under these conditions, they canalize a child's early giftedness, skills, and efforts into progressively better-fitting abilities, styles, and areas of interest. For example, a quiet, introverted 18-year-old with a SAT math score of 760, a verbal score of 420, and an IQ of 156 is much more likely to feel cognitively and functionally at home in a mathematically based field than as a stand-up comic.

5. The experience-producing and experience-selecting attributes of a family reside mainly in the socioeconomic status, personalities, and values of its members, especially those of the parents and grandparents. This assumption tells us two things: First, what parents and children *do* has simultaneous motivating and canalizing consequences (Yarrow & Peterson, 1976). Just as giftedness itself is experience-producing and, to a lesser degree depending on the level or extent of the giftedness, has specific experience-selecting properties, so do participants' personalities and values selectively motivate them toward certain behaviors. Second, this giftedness has a developmental history itself because it is the consequence of early parental expectations and experiences. Because of this history, gifted individuals are *not* wide-open to non-specific training and interventions. For maximization of giftedness, there must be a "fitting" between what the giftedness is about (e.g., sports, music, and people) and the extraneous training and interventions (Albert, 1978; Bloom, 1982; Feldman, 1980; Stanley, 1974). Over time – a relatively short time with exceptional giftedness – the giftedness becomes more formal and irreversible, that is, canalized. The sixth assumption speaks to this.

6. Outside of the work of psychoanalysis, the dynamic, historical nature of families is not well understood, but we can say that it is an active implicit history enacted by all family members, and thus influences the history and development of each member. It is important to keep in mind that many of the parents' motivations and values regarding themselves and their children come from their own development and experience and that most of the important early parent–child interactions will be prompted and shaped by these motivations and values. For this reason our project has attempted to tap these histories in two ways: in terms of their contemporary personality configurations through the *California Psychological Inventory* (CPI), a paper-and-pencil measure of personality, and in terms of their family presses through the *Majoribanks Family Press Inventory*, an open-ended questionnaire centering on six important family presses or emphases. The six presses are Activity, Achievement, Intellectuality, Independence, and Mother's and Father's Involvements with the subject. These, too, are historical in nature. Therefore, we are interested in operationalizing them in the present, and in understanding something of their origins. An excellent example of the role and power of such family presses and history in the achievement of many members of a family is given by Poland (1978) in her description of the Longfords of Eng-

land, in which both parents and all six children have attained remarkably productive careers.

For this reason, we are investigating another set of operations. This set consists of two other interviews. The initial one is with both parents together. It focuses on parents and grandparents. It is concerned with demographics and the Majoribanks Family Press Inventory. It is open-ended, although answers have been coded.

The second interview is a standardized open-ended individual interview with each parent alone. The focus of the first parents-together interview is on the families' origin, what they want educationally and vocationally for the child, and what they specifically do toward achieving these goals. The focus of the second interview is into parents' early history – educationally and intrafamily. It inquires into focal experiences and relationships. This interview also seeks to understand something of why and how each parent has come to press for the particular experiences now highly valued and actively sought for the subject. It attempts to understand something of the early critical psychology and experiences of each parent, coming to see them as persons with their own distinctive histories. It starts with the fact that, at one time, each parent was the same age as his or her children.

7. Last, we make a specific assumption about giftedness in relation to the family. We look upon it as an *organizer* in the biological and interpersonal senses. It focuses and mobilizes much of the surrounding social environment as well as "directs" the development of the gifted individual. According to its particular nature and saliency, giftedness itself selects and discourages simultaneously many of the experiences that parents and child undertake together. Giftedness in its most general meaning implies exceptionality and, like the family, it is experience-producing and experience-selecting (see Scarr & McCartney, 1983). And because they function in somewhat similar manners, families and giftedness often become aligned with one another. Only where the fit between them is close and realistic do we believe that a favorable developmental start has been made toward a significant and satisfactory career (for example, Feynman, 1974; Wiener, 1958). Where the fit is somewhat faulty, overinvested, out of step and/or basically unrealistic, we believe the future development of giftedness to eminence or even a satisfactory career is at risk and the gifted child is not likely to achieve as easily or as significantly as he might have when the family and giftedness are in conjunction. Several careers come to mind as examples. William James's is interesting for illustrating the point that often a highly successful career is not necessarily the ultimate or most satisfying one available to a gifted person. James was a successful college teacher, psychologist, and physician before he became what he had for years secretly aspired to be – a philosopher (see Strout, 1968, for details of his early family life and career "choices"). Freud also "went through" several careers before settling into the development of psychoanalysis (Jones, 1957).

At minimum, we can say that exceptionality of any sort focuses the attention, the interest, and the important behaviors of participants. This is one source of the biological and environmental canalization and expression of intelligence that Scarr-Salapatek (1975) describes so well.

Because of their rather distinctive natures, we believe that the two types of giftedness under study (exceptionally high-IQ and high math–science abilities) will stimulate and be stimulated by significantly different parental personalities, family presses, and later career choices and experiences. If exceptionality is an organizer, then we believe it follows that these two types of exceptional giftedness are and will remain for a number of years extraordinarily powerful organizers in the development and life experiences of our subjects. Over time, we expect to see significant family differences between the two samples as well as progressively distinct patterns of creative behavior, educational experiences, and career choices for each sample.

Creative behavior and its sources

Because we are not only interested in distinguishing between two types of exceptional giftedness but also in ascertaining whether or not one type more readily leads to significant creative behavior, it is important for us to keep in mind that cognitive giftedness and creative behavior have a number of similarities. They are not completely independent of one another developmentally but, more than anything else, represent application to different existential goals. We have assumed that creative behavior is not a distinct form of intelligent behavior; it is intelligence in action. This is not to say that unless one is being creative, one is not intelligent, but we propose that there is no such thing as unintelligent creativity, and perhaps no uncreative intelligence, although at very low points, this is likely the case. Because IQ is so tightly linked to learning it is often thought that our intelligence is primarily learning ability. But this is not so. As we will describe, it is extremely problem-oriented; it is cognitive behavior directed at finding and/or solving problems.

When we delve into the lives of eminent persons, we see that their intelligence becomes more creative in some area(s) through the application of their intelligence to selected problems – problems yet undiscovered, problems not taken seriously by others, or problems that have been inadequately solved by others. A common theme in the achievement of eminence is that "others" have not performed adequately. Implied in a person's long-term creative behavior is his or her belief that others' efforts were somehow lacking and perhaps not good enough. Creative behavior is thus in part oppositional and disapproving; and in attempting to be creative, the individual is stating a preference for one approach, another solution, or one resolution over others. It seems fair to state that in participating in creative behavior, an individual is to some extent experiencing discontent and disapproval. To be oppositional and discontented is the opposite of being passive and contented, the inner state of the less creative (MacKinnon, 1978). It seems, therefore, that long-term creative behavior is among other things a sublimation of pervasive negative feelings. These feelings are not necessarily aggressive or destructive (McClelland, 1962), although they can be or might once have been, but are feelings that are unaccepting and, to some degree, rejecting. We should note that the criticism can be of oneself as well as of others. Often it is both. In a general way, regardless of how abstract the particular problem or medium, creative behavior must always carry an implied criticism of some person or approach.

Therefore, we should find among the traits characterizing persons who are creative that they are discontented and rejecting of some aspect of the status quo, critical, and perhaps even envious, of others. This is all negative, affective, and fairly consistent with Freud's view of the origins of creativity. But one might ask whether or not there are any positive traits and motivations involved in creative behavior. For an understanding of these, we need to turn to the literature of psychology rather than to that of psychiatry. Psychologists interested in creative behavior are usually more interested in the conscious personality and cognitive characteristics of creative persons than in their unconscious personal and emotional histories. It is important to keep in mind that this is not because the disciplines simply disagree as much as it is because they are and have been interested in different levels of the creative person. Whereas Freud sought the answer to *why* people are creative (in their developmental and very early family histories) and sought clues in their affective histories, social scientists have been more inclined to deal with the contemporary problematic demands and efforts at problem finding and problem solving (e.g., Getzels and Csikszentmihalyi, 1976). In a more cognitive approach (e.g., Winner, 1982), social scientists view the creative person more as an information processor, or problem finder and problem solver, than as a person resolving unconscious personality conflicts. Whereas dynamic psychology and psychiatry view creativity primarily as an *intrapersonal* effort, social scientists have traditionally viewed it as more deliberate, social, and rational, with creativity more under the control of reality-oriented (secondary) cognitive processes than the product of irrational primary processes.

One reason for this difference in emphasis lies in the nature of the research, particularly the subjects studied. Psychoanalysis originated in a late–19th-century Romanticism in which artists were looked on as the epitome of the creative person. This was also an era during which many artists presented themselves to the public as florid, passionate bohemians rather than craftsmen (Becker, 1978). Psychoanalysis was an early effort to make "rational" such colorful behavior; its own history has been to link creative behavior inextricably to artistic behavior, primarily creative writing, leaving psychologists and other social scientists to study other forms of creative behavior, especially the sciences. However, when one looks at creative science over centuries, one appreciates the stimulating power and structure inherent in scientific theories and *their* histories (Kuhn, 1962; Merton, 1969). Scientists' creative behavior is a response as much to problems as to the more personal motivations depicted by psychoanalysis and dynamic psychology. Yet, common to the two approaches is the individual's discontent and sensitivity to perceived inadequacies. Taken together, the approaches add up to a mixture of specific facilitating personality traits, high cognitive ability, and sensitivity to significant problems. One's personality furnishes the discontent or oppositional behavior, the feelings of dissatisfaction with the status quo and the wish or need "to do it better." To appreciate this individual quality, recall that not all persons within the same discipline respond creatively to the same potentially challenging problems.

A good example of this selectivity is the difference in response to the 1960s civil rights problems shown by Keniston's *Young Radicals* (1968), who took the issues personally and applied themselves to them, and his group *The Uncommitted* (1965), consisting of equally bright college students who were unable to involve themselves in the civil rights movement. The differences between the two groups lay more in their personal histories, not in their cognitive abilities, and is seen in the capacity of "Young Radicals" to direct their energies to problems that existed independent of themselves. "The Uncommitted" appear caught in a web of unresolved intrafamily battles and conflicting relationships. More recently, Perkins (1981) demonstrates in *The Mind's Best Work* that although creative persons do have talent, their creativity is not solely a result of this talent but is a function of their values and beliefs. The values he describes are the theoretical (as contrasted to the pragmatic or conventional) and the importance of demonstrating one's own originality, knowing, and independence. Perkins describes creative individuals as holding as a central concern a belief in doing what can be done as opposed to passive acceptance. As he reads them, Perkins, like others before him – especially MacKinnon – believes that creative persons are mainly creative because of what they believe in and what they value, that they *make* themselves creative and strive to remain so. In this sense, Freud and his followers are right: The core to creative behavior is less in *how* you do something and more concerned with *why* you do it. Regardless of the level at which it originates, it appears that conflict as dissatisfaction inspires and guides our creative potential rather than "causes" it.

Another critical trait shared by most creative persons is independence. Independence is confidence in action. Because one cannot be independent and out of control and under the sway of impulses, we must not confuse independence with impulsiveness or foolhardiness. The creative person's independence shows itself most clearly in situations with challenge, replete with ambiguity and puzzling complexity. It is generally held that these situations are first met in early childhood when we are learning about ourselves and acquiring the "tools" to meet and resolve puzzling situations. Thus, independence is acquired and practiced early amid the family. The families facilitating this development – where we have data – appear to value and stress these early efforts at independence, and this comes through to the child as clear ethical–moral standards, respect, and tolerance for early errors and mistakes (Baumrind, 1971). In such families, to err not only is to be human but is the result of special expectations and recurrent opportunities.

Thus, we find over years of research that the creative individual is usually highly intelligent, significantly self-sufficient, independent, introverted, dominant, and involved and sober when engaging in his or her interests. All noticeably creative persons are productive in some area or way and both intelligent and intellectual. That is, they have more than average cognitive ability and they like to think about problems and issues. Moreover, they see themselves as inventive, independent, determined, industrious, enthusiastic, and responsible to their own high standards, and often try to solve problems in somewhat individualistic manners. When asked if they are creative, they would probably answer yes.

Independence thus appears to be a prime personality disposition for creative performance, and for this reason we look specifically at families' independence training. There are typically several significant differences between the families of creative children and the families of less creative but effective children. Among these are (a) differences in the type of relationship that exists between parents and child, (b) differences in the role models, and (c) differences in the amount of anxiety a child grows up to feel and function with. Let us explore these.

Families of creative children generally evidence unusual features (Albert, 1971, 1980a, 1980b). For example, such families tend to experience a high rate of parental loss. Often, the father is much older than the mother and the child an only child, or if he is not, then probably the oldest. The families of effective children, on the other hand, tend to fit a more conventional pattern of a nuclear family, with the parents existing together and being close in age; moreover, the child is generally part of a bigger family. The relationship of the effective child to his parents is usually a loving one, in which the process of socialization unfolds in a rather typical manner. This relationship, being harmonious, allows for a strong binding identification with the parents. Father–son relationships are especially tolerable and harmonious, compared with those of the families of creative children.

In the families of creative children, there is a tendency of one or both parents to select the child as special. This often puts an extra responsibility on the child. His or her interpersonal relationship within the family tend to be laced with high expectations and some conflict. The parents themselves often do not get along, and this, too, affects the level of conflict experienced. The creative child typically has more hostility to contend with than the equally bright but less creative child.

As just mentioned, due to the differences in the family the identification models tend to be different. Effective children tend to choose as models people who are immediate in their lives. These models are often competent and effective but are rarely highly creative. Because of the frequent intrafamily conflict or indifference felt in the families of the creative, or the previously mentioned absence of one parent, creative children often have as their models persons they do not even know – some sort of hero. Moreover, they tend to choose a greater variety of models than effective children do.

Neither family would fit Baumrind's (1971) description of permissive parents. In accordance with their goals of socialization and concern for the child, the parents of effective children are authoritative; in the sense that the parents of creative children have great expectations for the child, they, too, are authoritative. But we feel that their child-rearing goals are different, though their general style – authoritative – is not. It appears to be primarily the degree of intrafamily stress experienced and the type of child each family emphasizes that carry most of the developmental differences, not the degree of early giftedness or talent. This being so, we expect to find systematic differences in the personalities of parents of more creative subjects and those of less creative ones. Further, the parents of the more creative gifted subjects should place less emphasis on "good" social skills, on their concern for conventional achievement, and on conformity itself. That almost all of our own subjects' parents are themselves gifted is to be expected, so it will be in their personalities and family values that the parents should differ. For this reason, we stress the parental personalities and family environments that these gifted subjects are surrounded by and must come to terms with.

The creative personality profile: the essentials

Because we are interested in tracing the development of creative ability over the years, it is important that we have clear evidence of the personality traits that support and facilitate this ability. Creative persons from adolescence through adulthood are remarkably identifiable insofar as their psychological traits and dispositions are concerned.

As we have suggested, creativity is a blend of processes and values that motivate and infuse behavior, selective attitudes, and personality traits. Still, even with the necessary personality and giftedness, not everyone can be creative. The historical times and the opportunities afforded by one's culture determine and to some extent predetermine what one can do. More precisely, cultural factors set limits on one's creativity. Whether deliberately or not, the creative person is always selecting from the available possibilities or problems what to do and what to invest himself or herself in. And it is in this sense that education is important in showing what the state of the art is in a variety of fields. Just as important, education shows what remains to be done – what is possible among a *finite* number of opportunities.

Note that when individuals involve themselves in this process of challenge and selection, they are also specifically defining themselves as artists, computer programmers, businessmen, scientists, or whatever. This selection and involvement is an existential act. One's selection of a career and one's attempts in it to be creative are tantamount to assuming responsibility and attempting a special, often highly personalized, purpose and identity within this endeavor. We can say that in trying to be creative, individuals are also attempting to define themselves as particular kinds of people and to express themselves in a highly personal manner. In terms of autobiographies and biographies, it appears that truly creative persons rarely, if ever, stumble easily upon their careers. Career-long creativity is too selective and too purposeful simply to occur. Its difficulty and rarity go against the common idea that it is more a function of personal abandonments and impulsivity. Creativity is made up of a particular sensitivity and an orientation to problems, each of which controls our visions of self and opportunity. Together they permit – even require – that creative individuals have very personally determined, and at times perhaps even idiosyncratic, encounters with their environments and their self-images. So important to this enterprise is having the requisite cognitive capacity, and so powerful are one's early identifications and socializations in framing cognitive skills, that only a few persons have the "right stuff" to show this creative potential consistently and significantly. Exceptional creativity, when it is present as a special capacity of an individual, shows up in *active* problem-finding and problem-solving efforts, as well as in the feelings of high responsibility and sensitivity to some pertinent aspect of one's career.

Nonetheless, at any one time, some cultures and the potential careers within them are more supportive and opportune for creativity than in other times and other cultures (Simonton, 1978). This is an aspect of creative behavior to which Galton (1869) alluded when he discussed the different frequencies of genius among different nationalities, and to some extent it is one that Kuhn (1962) has tried to explain among the sciences and their episodic breakthroughs and redefinitions. Within the physical sciences in which Nobel Prizes are awarded, Zuckerman (1977) has teased out some of the special educative processes of candidate selection and professional socialization that occur among laureates and prospective laureates-to-be. To summarize, not all gifted persons can be highly creative; only a small proportion working in any particular field can be and are noticeably creative. This selectivity is a function of undergoing early sensitizing preparations that become crystallized in a rather specific type of personality, that is, what we speak of as a creative personality (Cattell, 1971; MacKinnon, 1978; Roe, 1952; Winner, 1982; Winnicott, 1976).

One of the most accurate and succinct descriptions of this profile, we believe, has been given by Donald MacKinnon. In the following, we will summarize his and others' general research findings and try to show how some of our data from subjects' and their parents' CPI scores might fit this personality profile.

In whatever manner they are studied, through biographical inventories or clinical evaluation, we find that creative individuals are highly individualized in the sense that various personality theorists use the term. They show their individuality in their high capacity to pick up, retain, and keep available for application the results of their own experiences. Part of this facility is a function of their higher than average intelligence, and part is because as a group, in whatever field we observe them, they show a lack of psychological repression and suppression as psychological defenses. They are relatively *open to their experiences, impulses, and imagery*, mainly because they tend not to deny or overcontrol them. Maslow (1959) has made somewhat the same point about those relatively rare persons that he believes are self-actualized. One critical consequence of this lack of rigid psychological defenses, especially of repression, is that more ideas and feelings are available to them as stimuli and working materials for their creativity. We suggested earlier that creativity is at one level a responsiveness to tension, to a feeling that something is not right or as good as it can or should be. A lack of repression is important in allowing one to become aware of these discordant feelings. But it goes further. A lack of repression also makes available to the creative person more imagery and information to work with and helps in regard to their divergent thinking (Mednick, 1962; Runco & Albert, 1984). This is not a wild, disorganized array of images or scraps of information, but as Kubie (1958) has argued, a selective but nonetheless largely associative fund of information. Creative people know a great deal about their area of interest and, moreover, they are regularly using and adding to it. Thus, as MacKinnon and others have described them, creative persons do two things at once and do them quite well. They are alert and can concentrate their energies and attention, while also being able to shift their energies and attention in search of more appropriate or missing parts. This dual capacity gives the creative person a wide access to possibilities within both his or her own fund of knowledge and from the environment (Wild, 1965). This openness to experience in turn accounts for the "ah-ha!" experience or moment of sudden illumination creative persons often describe (Winner, 1982). If worked with long enough, the pieces eventually fall into place.

Another trait of creative persons often mentioned is their capacity to express both masculine and feminine aspects to their personalities. This, of course, does not mean that creative men or women are more homosexual than less creative persons, but rather that they usually have a broader range of interests and, equally importantly, that they are motivated by a wider array of feelings than their less creative counterparts. Once again, we can see how an aspect of the creative personality predisposes an individual to a larger source of stimulation (inspiration) and wider possibilities for divergent thinking than might otherwise be the case. Sexual identity is a matter of early identifications, and it makes sense that creative persons as children often have a greater diversity of identification models (Getzels & Jackson, 1962). From more models of each sex, it follows that some of the selective interests and behaviors of both will become integrated in the developing personality of the creative person, and that this wider emotional and informational base can later act as an emotional and cognitive resource when the creative person tries to solve problems or perform in the arts. This array of identification models also seems to be involved in the creative person's greater flexibility in selecting "unconventional" career goals, as well as in acquiring the means of achieving them.

Running through the above personality characteristic of a relative lack of repression is the parallel ability to use internal imagery and environmental cues, described as a preference for and an ability to deal with complexity (Barron, 1963, 1968). Creative persons also appear to be less interested in the small details or "facts" of a problem, and much more interested in their theoretical implications and ultimate meaning. In the main, creative persons are speculative and "philosophical." They value problems and broad principles over the here and now, more conventional, more pragmatic applications of technique and knowledge. Thus, in the realm of values, one finds among creative persons of both sexes a strong preference for dealing with theoretical issues and problems and an interest in and drive toward the aesthetic or elegant solution or experience. On this, artists and scientists agree: The two predominant values of creative persons repeatedly reported over the years have been theoretical and aesthetic, showing up in late adolescence and early adulthood (Hall & MacKinnon, 1969; Stanley, Keating, & Fox, 1974). Together with their preference for complexity, their high evaluation of the theoretical and aesthetic aspects of a problem further predisposes them to perceive and pursue their interests in a rather highly personalized manner, although not necessarily in a *deliberately* idiosyncratic or nonconforming manner.

As MacKinnon points out, creative individuals' behavior is usually dictated by their own values (independence) rather than by others' (conformity). Yet, in areas of life that are not central to their creative problems and interests, these people can be just as conventional as the next person. It is primarily in those areas in which one takes a deep personal interest and has staked a salient aspect of one's identity that the more individualized and "creative" components of one's personality are engaged and expressed. For these reasons such opportunities tend to be highly motivating, and in order to be resolved satisfactorily, they require the special kind of behavior and efforts we often describe as creative.

At the minimum, we are describing a person who is less concerned with social conformity and more interested than most persons in correcting or completing an otherwise unsatisfactory state of affairs. This demand quality is a joint product of the creative person's personality and his historical and cultural time and place, for no one, to our knowledge, has ever invented a problem area or the basic ingredients of a solution to it without awareness or recourse to others' efforts. This implies a dual sensitivity to, and an independence from, others – the twofold capacity of being aware of but not enthralled by others or their work.

Intelligence

Because our interests are focused on cognitively gifted subjects rather than those who are artistically or physically talented, it behooves us to say a few words about how we conceptualize cognitive giftedness, and how this is related to selected family variables.

To a large extent, one of the main goals of our project is to determine the involvement and predictive power of exceptionally high IQs and exceptionally high preadolescent mathematical-science reasoning abilities in the attainment of early eminence. Therefore, we have deliberately taken a very conservative, traditional stance regarding intelligence (IQ) as cognitive behavior; it has been very conservatively operationalized through our use of widespread measures of cognitive ability, scores on the Stanford–Binet or the Wechsler Intelligence Scale for Children-Revised (WISC-R) intelligence tests, or scores on the Scholastic Aptitude Test (SAT) math and verbal tests. Our sample selection has been restricted to these measures.

All humans have some intelligence; it is this capacity that underlies their ability to adjust to the new and to use appropriately the old. We view intelligence as more than learning ability. It is also the general ability to adapt to and manipulate the environment effectively and efficiently. Obviously this view is too broad for any one test to measure. However, an important implication is that the individual has initiative as to when and how he operates on the environment: He actively responds to the environment, and in the process organizes *and* synthesizes the results of his operations. Just as the individual is active in these person–environment interactions, he actively develops new or revised principles of informational organization and operations, much as Hollingworth (1942) described for her exceptionally gifted subjects. It is assumed that these abilities are highly individualized but measurable, so that an array of same-aged persons would show different modes and degrees of adaptation and learning.

There are at least three broadly pervasive components to intelligent behavior. Together they make up the basic underlying capacity of an individual's learning ability *and* problem solving. We should stress that we clearly see creative behavior as one manifestation of intelligence as problem solving, although over the years, psychometrically high levels of intelligence and creativeness have been found to be generally psychometrically distinct, with very low, often negative correlations between scores (Runco & Albert, 1984b).

In order to be succinct, let us present now a working definition of intelligence.

Intelligence is a set of aptitudes that together make up an individual's general ability to adapt to and manipulate his or her environment effectively and efficiently. It is assumed in the definition that the individual has the power of initiating cognitive interactions with the environment, searching as well as responding to it; and that intelligence is not merely passive absorption or rote learning, that is, the passive acquisition of whatever is "out there" external to him, attendable and reinforced. Intelligence, as suggested by Piaget (1952), is a set of active biological functions always searching for the "best" fit, namely, the most efficient, economical, and integrated fit of information and experience that is accessible to the individual with information already internalized, assimilated, and more or less organized. Cognition operates and develops according to Piaget's basic principles of accommodation and assimilation. There are three sources of intellectual or cognitive drives. These are the degree of assimilation and the degree of organization of the internalized material, and the degree of "fit," relevance, or appropriateness, of this material to the goals undertaken by the individual. Like Piaget, we believe there is a sizable but hitherto undetermined degree of biological "prepackaging" of the modes of operation and of the sequence, the speed, the range, and the complexity of these operations. Thus, no two persons are likely to have the same kind or degree of intelligence, although because of the nature of our measures of intelligence, they may have the same measured intelligence. Clearly, it is primarily because of the limits of our technical measures *and* the canalizations of cultures that persons appear as similar or alike cognitively as often as they do; the more measures one uses and the more different persons' cultures are, the more different cognitively and intelligently they will be.

The major components of intelligent behavior appear to be: (a) learning ability, that is, capacity and strategies; (b) two broad reasoning abilities – problem-finding and problem-solving abilities; and (c) the conservation of energy, psychologically and physically.

Learning ability is discriminable in terms of its altitude or abstractness, the range or variety of materials one can learn, and the speed or quickness at which materials are learned (Thorndike, 1926). These characteristics determine the variety and abstractness of materials that persons can learn. Aptitudes such as verbal, mathematical, mechanical, social, and the like are involved. They give the individual resources and tools with which further to interact and operate on the environment (Gardner, 1982). The second component – reasoning ability – is seen clearly in an individual's ability to find and/or respond to problems. Reasoning ability is the capacity to respond to cognitive discontinuity or tensions, and it leads to and often raises questions (which need not be conscious or verbalizable). Problem finding, behaviorally, is also problem *feeling* in terms of the tension one experiences, and it is the active basis to what is generally termed curiosity or the search for answers and resolution. The psychological bridge between problem finding and problem solving is the felt need to reduce and/or resolve one's curiosity about oneself and some aspects of the environment. To put it briefly, the human brain responds to differences (tension) and seeks similarities (assimilation). When it succeeds, there are new accommodations and homeostasis.

Therefore, another subset of intelligent behavior linked biologically and psychologically to the problematic aspects of the environment is reasoning or problem solving. Problem solving often leads to answers that result in the resolution of tensions, and concludes often in an active reorganization of parts of previously learned (accommodated) information. At the minimum, problem solving is the application of learning ability to a present problem; naturally, problem solving can therefore range from the simplest rote applications to extensive, complicated reasoning, or transformations of previous cognitive organizations. Further, problem solving in turn may result in a new or better solution to a specific more or less mechanical here–now problem or to a change in world perspective, for example, the difference between how to bunt a fast ball to the general theory of relativity. We conceptualize that where individuals possess more than adequate cognitive abilities, the differences among them in the nature of their problem solving will be a function of different motivations, values, and their sensitivity to problems–variables that we believe are the products of early family experiences and socializations.

Synchronized with the above two cognitive aptitudes – learning and problem finding and solving – is a broad biological process that is also evident in intelligent behavior. This is the conservation or selective allocation of energy expenditure in learning and problem-oriented operations. Although it appears to be an inherent attribute, this conservation is probably not an offshoot of these operations. It is an active, metacognitive countering of disorganization and chaos. (There are sloppy as well as efficient learners.) This conservation attempts to minimize entropy and is observed in the style or strategy and the procedures used, such as mass versus spaced learning, reflective versus impulsive modes, repression versus intellectualization. The conservation of energy results in and is often spoken of as one's "cognitive style." It is often observed in the elegance, the degree of relevance, and the "originality" or distinctiveness of the learning–problem solving operations, especially in regard to those related, although not limited to problem-oriented behavior. It seems to us that there is an implicit difference in the demands on one's abilities between learning and problem-oriented operations, with the latter using or incorporating more of the results of learning and demanding greater efforts of orientation and accommodation.

So far, we have not included creative behavior in the above model. This is not an oversight but recognition that intelligent behavior is often creative. Both – so-called intelligent behavior and creative behavior – require that there be a relevant, "good" fit between the task or problem undertaken and the solution achieved; something is resolved in an effective and efficient manner. Some aspects of intelligent behavior as we have defined it necessarily will be creative, relevant, and better fitting than what would be achieved through the rote or forced application of earlier learned material, and some aspects of creative behavior, most likely attempts to solve problems with novel or deliberately "designed" responses, also will have to be relevant rather than simply novel or distinctive if they are to work effectively and efficiently. For otherwise, creativity might be novel but irrelevant – or at best a random lucky hit – if it were not intelligent and guided, which would also conserve energy. To paraphrase what has been said before, one can be original and not be either creative or intelligent, but one must be intelligent and original in order to be creative (MacKinnon, 1978). This relation between intelligent and creative behaviors leads us to believe that there are two basic types or ways to be creative, depending not on the product or type of problem undertaken but on the process: (a) through the *power* of one's intellection, specifically, one "sees," "understands," and applies more information than most people; and (b) through the development of infrequent, intuitive, *somewhat* divergent responses, whose correlations to the problem are not always obvious or conventional to most persons, but may be novel. For obvious reasons such responses are likely to occur infrequently, although not necessarily uniquely.

As is evident, there is more overlap between these two types of creative behavior than there are differences. The core of behavior that is intelligent and creative is satisfaction – of the environmental demands responded to and with oneself in how they have been met. The prototypical experience to both is child's play (Freud, 1980; Piaget, 1951). It promotes selective satisfactions and their connections. It does not do them justice, conceptionally or operationally, to speak of divergent or of convergent processes as making up respectively the basic types of creative and noncreative cognitions, for not only do they share much – learning, reasoning, and organizing processes – but, at the least, they are complementary; each represents two types of potentially intelligent, "creative" behavior.

Giftedness and sample selection

Gibson and Chennells (1976) have suggested that different definitions of giftedness prevail within different societies. Perhaps this is how it should be, because different societies have applied giftedness to different purposes and in different areas of life, for instance, the Chinese imperial civil service (Laycock, 1979). It is not, however, all diversity. What is strikingly consistent among the variety of definitions of giftedness is the emphasis, whether explicit or implied, on early formal learning ability. By "formal," we mean a school or educational system set up for the "best" instruction of a society's youth in terms of generally abstract topics. Such systems have an implicit logical and developmental progression to them. Most often, it is the speed and efficiency with which the intellectually gifted child goes through this system that identifies the child as gifted and a candidate for further psychological testing. For example, the U.S. Department of Education defines the "gifted and talented" as:

Children capable of high performance include those with the demonstrated achievement and/or potential ability in any of the following areas, singly or in combination: 1. General intellectual ability. 2. Specific academic aptitude. 3. Creative or productive thinking. 4. Leadership ability. 5. Visual and performing arts. 6. Psychomotor ability. (Subcommittee on Education, 1972, p. 2)

Notice that the first three areas – intellectual ability, academic aptitude, and creative and productive thinking – are the areas of early giftedness most commonly used and tested for among children in the United States. It is within these three areas that, over the past half century, we have done most of the testing of children for giftedness. It is in the cognitive domain that we believe giftedness is to be most likely, most important, and most clearly demonstrated. Moreover, the most successful areas for operationally defining giftedness have been the domains of general intellectual ability and specific aptitude. Because these two cognitive domains are usually significantly and positively correlated (Brody & Brody, 1976), if we measure one area accurately, we will have good psychometric prediction of the child's potential performance in the other areas. Note here that most state education departments use an IQ of approximately 130 as their operational definition of giftedness (e.g., California, Hawaii). This is some guarantee of better than average academic performance, although not of much else. An IQ of 130 is not as high as Terman's sample of gifted children (minimum IQ of 140), but it is used by most states and appears to be the consensual operational definition of intellectual giftedness among researchers and educational experts. Depending on whether the Stanford–Binet or the Wechsler Intelligence Scale for Children is used, an IQ of 130 will place the child within the upper 2% or 3% of a random school population (Sattler, 1982).

However, just as important as knowing that an IQ of 130 defines academic giftedness is knowing what level of IQ predicts *lifetime* high achievement. Unfortunately, this is less clear or empirically certain if a particular IQ – for example an IQ of 130 or 140 – does represent the necessary IQ level for the ultimate payoff – high adult achievement. Three studies that do throw some light on this issue (Cox, 1926; Roe, 1952; Walberg, Rasher, & Hase, 1978) suggest that although the range of estimated IQs among clearly eminent persons in a variety of fields is rather broad, the median IQ is extremely high (approximately an IQ of 160) and the lower limit may be approximately an IQ of 145 for most fields. It appears that individuals who end up known in history as highly productive achievers in those fields requiring extensive formal schooling are likely to have an IQ of at least 145.

Because we are interested in testing this prediction, we have deliberately sought out young, preeminent subjects who are well within the range of cognitive giftedness that others have found characteristic of persons of noticeable achievement in a variety of fields (e.g., Chaunsey & Hilton, 1965). More specifically, we have assumed that a necessary but not sufficient IQ for the achievement of eminence in a nonmathematical science area of adult achievement will be approximately 150, and that an equivalently high SAT math score will be necessary but not sufficient for later eminence in a mathematically scientific area.

Recent empirical research

It is for this reason that one of the samples in our ongoing longitudinal research – 28 exceptionally high-IQ boys and their parents – was selected with a minimum IQ of 150 but without other equally notable gifts. Both Cox (1926) and Terman (1954) have stated that "the genius who achieves highest eminence is one whom intelligence tests would have identified as gifted in childhood." Our own research hence relies on standardized tests, but it should be emphasized that our work is in part designed to evaluate the predictive power of the tests themselves. Also, we do not presume that tested intelligence is the salient factor in real-world achievement. Still, an IQ of 150 places this sample well within the upper 99th percentile, with an approximate frequency of 1 in 1,000 randomly selected children (Laycock, 1979). As there is no way of estimating the frequency of a Leonardo, a Darwin, a Freud, or a Homer, the best one can say is that because there has been only one of each of these persons in Western recorded history, the frequency of such achievements is very much less than 1 in 1,000, and perhaps 1 in the billions of persons living over the last thousand years. This rarity suggests not only that the intellectual giftedness of such persons is rare, but that other infrequent factors must be involved in their outstanding achievement. Our second sample – 26 mathematical-science gifted boys – was drawn on the basis of their high rank in the Study of Mathematically Precocious Youth (Keating, 1976; Stanley et al., 1974). These subjects are among the top 40 participants in 1976, ranked according to a composite score based on their SAT (math and verbal) and six other tests of mathematical aptitude and reasoning given them earlier by the Study of Mathematically Precocious Youth. Their mean SAT math score was 635 at age 12.

It is with these two samples, including their families, that we hope to observe over at least a decade in order to uncover how two different types of cognitive giftedness (each operating at approximately the same level of infrequency) develop within family and school environments, and eventually become highly productive and achieving individuals. Our major research goals are understanding the impact that different types of giftedness may have within families and education, and how different types of interpersonal relationships, family histories, and values may facilitate or inhibit productive development (Albert, 1975, 1978, 1980c). In the final analysis, the longitudinal outcome will be determined according to the subjects' (a) ability to select and engage in productive careers; (b) level of attained eminence or likely eminence in early adulthood, in terms of selected empirical indices (Albert, 1975); (c) psychological well-being; and lastly, (d) career satisfaction.

Looking briefly at our findings to date, our primary measure of personality traits was the California Psychological Inventory (CPI) (Gough, 1957), a measure chosen because it is suitable for a large range of ages and has been used previously to identify "creative personalities" (e.g., Hall & MacKinnon, 1969; Helson, 1983; Helson & Crutchfield, 1970; MacKinnon, 1978; Parloff & Datta, 1965; Parloff et al., 1968). Our CPI results have indicated that the exceptionally high-IQ children have higher scores than the high math-science children on the scales related to social skills (e.g., Sociability, Social Presence, Good Impression); this is consistent with common images of these types of giftedness. The math-science individual is usually seen as less socially interested and adroit than nonmathematically gifted individuals (Cattell, 1963, 1971; Eiduson, 1962; Roe, 1952). We should point out that all 18 CPI scale scores of *both* samples are higher and more mature than a randomly selected sample of average eighth-grade boys (Keating, 1976), a finding that agrees with Terman's observation that the gifted child is psychologically and physically healthier, more robust, and more confident than nongifted children.

Turning next to the parents, the CPI scores of the parents also are significantly different in the two samples, and the childrens' profiles seem to resemble more the mothers' than the fathers'. We have found that the fathers of exceptionally high-IQ children were significantly higher than their wives on only one scale (Psychological-Mindedness). On the other hand, the fathers of high math-science children were significantly higher than their wives on six of the scales (e.g., Dominance, Self-Acceptance, Intellectual Efficiency). Comparing the parents of the two samples, the parents of the exceptionally high-IQ children present themselves on the CPI as more sociable, socially confident, and self-controlled and accepting. There is, however, a definite and important tendency for the math-science parents to be more interested than the parents of the high-IQ children in achievement through independence rather than through conformance.

Compared with the CPIs of persons with established "real-life" creativity reported in Barron (1968) and MacKinnon (1978), our two groups of fathers resemble each other more than either resembles groups of creative architects and writers. They do, however, appear somewhat similar to these two groups of creative men in terms of their relatively high scores for Achievement-through-Independence, Psychological-Mindedness, Flexibility, and Femininity – traits previously found positively related to real-life creativeness. Now, assuming that our male subjects do eventually identify more with their fathers, one can see the potentially facilitative impact that their fathers' personalities could have on their gifted sons' development into creative adults. Moreover, these CPI results could account for that first transition of giftedness into creativity necessary for the achievement of eminence later in life (Albert, 1980b, 1980c).

Comparing the mothers' CPI scores with the creative and less creative women mathematicians of Barron (1968), we find somewhat unexpectedly that the CPI scores of the mothers of the exceptionally high-IQ boys resemble those of creative mathematicians more than do the CPI scores of the mothers of the gifted math-science boys. In fact, the group these mothers most resemble are the Mensa females reported by Southern and Plant (1968). Of course, many of these mothers would probably qualify for Mensa membership (which is open to males and females who score on an adult IQ test at or above the 98th percentile).

We have also begun to assess intrafamily similarities on the CPI. A possible outgrowth of parent–child similarity has to do with the antecedents of high creative potential. Most theories of creativity suggest one of two personality sources of creativity: intrafamily personality "conflict," or early identification with someone, be it a parent or hero, who already has the requisite personality traits for creative behavior. Although there is little empirical evidence for either hypothesis, we take the dynamic view that personality *dissimilarity* between parents and between parents and child is more allied to personality individuation, and that this in turn will be linked to noticeably high creative potential, given sufficient intelligence and talent and extrafamily opportunities. Thus, although we have already seen that there is considerable CPI similarity among both samples of children and either of their parents, we expect that in the long run it is parental CPI *dissimilarity* that will be more related to subjects' creativity scores. The reason for this assumption is that parental dissimilarity constitutes an early experience of *complexity* necessary for the development of creative potential (Albert, 1978). Parental dissimilarity may be the early problem or complexity that the child needs to solve or resolve as a prerequisite to problem-solving skills.

There is some evidence for this. Parents' CPI similarities and their sons' creativity scores are negatively related in 7 of the 8 statistically significant instances for the math-science boys. The scale with the most consistent negative correlation to young creative potential is Capacity for Status – an index of ambitiousness and status seeking. Where there is significantly low similarity between parents on this scale, there is high creative potential among exceptionally high-IQ boys' Biographical Inventory of Creativity (BIC) (Schaefer, 1970) scores and their total divergent thinking test (Wallach & Kogan, 1965) scores. The same negative relationship also holds for the math-science boys' divergent thinking test scores. Other significant negative correlations are exceptionally high-IQ boys' BIC scores and low parental CPI similarity on the Tolerance, Communality, and Achievement-through-Independence scales. Parental similarity on the Tolerance scale also correlates negatively and significantly with exceptionally high-IQ sons' total divergent thinking test scores. Among the math-science sons, BIC scores are negatively correlated with parental similarity on Achievement-through-Conformance, but positively with parental similarity on the Socialization and Psychological-Mindedness scales. These correlations suggest that at age 12 a gifted boy's creative potential is not yet tightly linked to personality, either his own or his parents', but may be more a function of the boy's exceptional cognitive giftedness. Still, these correlations are interesting, more as an indication of possible developments than as a statement of present relationships between parental personality and creativity.

We should point out that these correlations are in line with a general (and we believe important) finding occurring in our other analysis: the math-science boys' creativity and cognitive scores are generally less linked to their own and their parents' personalities and values, whereas the creative potential of the exceptionally high-IQ boys appears at age 12 to be somewhat more related to their own and their parents' personalities and values. When both samples are considered, the relationships between their CPI and creative potential go against the belief that a child's early years are critically formative in his personality and creative capacity. Our subjects, gifted as they are at age 12, appear still open to influence and growth; there is still "openness" to their personalities and their creative potential. In this regard, our early assumption that there remains much more time and opportunity for further cognitive and personality growth appears substantiated.

Turning now to general family "environment," we have utilized the Marjoribanks Family Environment Interview. This is a semistructured interview that has demonstrated its utility in the work of Marjoribanks (1972, 1974) and is also presented in its entirety (Marjoribanks, 1979). For statistical purposes, this interview can be divided into factors, or "environmental presses." In our research, these are presses for Achievement, Activity, Intellectuality, Independence, Mother-Involvement, and Father-Involvement. Briefly summarizing, we have found that the two samples differ significantly in terms of their family environments. More importantly, we have found highly significant (canonical) correlations between the Marjoribanks presses and the divergent thinking test scores, BIC, and tested "intelligence" (IQ or achievement test) for the exceptionally high-IQ group. The environmental presses were *not* related to the cognitive test scores in the high math-science group. Overall, then, these correlations reinforce our hypothesis that the exceptionally high-IQ boys are more influenced by their family than are the math-science boys. This is true on the level of environmental presses – a behavioral measure – and on the more implicit level of the CPI.

Similar results come from our research focused on intrafamily cognitive similarities. Simply stated, we have found strong (canonical) correlations between the divergent thinking test scores of these subjects and their parents'. Significant Pearsonian correlations were also found between subjects and mothers, and subjects and fathers, for both figural and verbal tests. There were, consistent with the aforementioned findings, some notable differences between the exceptionally high-IQ group and the high math-science group, with the former subjects having divergent thinking scores more strongly related to their parents' than those of the latter.

Although these correlational analyses do *not* indicate a causal relationship, the divergent thinking correlations, such as the CPI and family environmental results, suggest that the exceptionally high-IQ boys are more sensitive to and influenced by the personalities, behavioral activities, and cognitive abilities of their parents.

Overview and conclusions

In its earliest form our research was conceived as a study of incipient genius, genius being defined as one person's extraordinary productivity and impact within an identifiable field of human interest and active endeavor (Albert, 1975). This vague and ambitious aim has been drastically modified over the years by both our initial findings and a growing awareness of the limitations to such a focus. In part, we have the difficulty of defining and operationalizing basic terms, but also, now we have a clearer realization of our main interests. That is, What is giftedness? What does exceptional cognitive giftedness do to families, and they to it? And what does such exceptional giftedness lead to in early adulthood? In the process of setting up the empirical portion of our research, as distinct from the conceptual (Albert, 1969, 1971, 1975, 1978, 1980a, 1980b, 1980c), it has become evident that a much less glorious and a much more pragmatic goal was called for. "Genius," no matter how defined or operationalized, would always retain its mystical and philosophical aura; it would always suggest the supranatural and preternatural even though an operational definition was possible in terms of genius's infrequency of oc-

currence, its behavioral manifestations, and its observed and traceable influence in the lives and occupations of many (see Albert, 1975). Furthermore,
the idea of genius can throw one off the track; worse yet, it would imbue our
research with more than a hint of hubris and uncalled-for exaggeration. Finally, it might be most unkind to the mothers, the fathers, and the teachers
of the exceptionally gifted boys, as well as to themselves.

It is becoming clear at the halfway mark of our project that none of the
participants lives an effortless, genius-inspired life. All of the parents are
somewhat at bay, busy, hard at work doing what most parents do, and all of
the adolescents are developing and changing as most adolescents do. As bright
as they are, these parents and boys are very human. Several boys may cultivate
remarkable careers (just how many and in what exactly, it is still too early
to tell), but it is already evident that they and the rest of their cohorts will
do it with hard work, faith in the future, and a healthy degree of openness
to freshly appearing opportunities. None seem "destined." Because of this,
we have reaffirmed our original interest in the entire families. It is within
them that these efforts first appeared to become merged with individual ambition and childish opportunity.

So much for where we stand. What lies ahead? We are doing additional
analyses and research that include comparisons of our findings from the exceptionally gifted with less gifted and nongifted subjects and their families.
For example, we are in the process of comparing different levels of giftedness
of boys and girls with each other and with their parents regarding their attitudes of independence. Also, we are attempting to relate these attitudes to
subjects' divergent thinking and cognitive abilities. Further, we are looking
at *children's* perceptions of their family environments and how these may be
related to different levels of giftedness and divergent thinking. This is just a
small portion of our own work. Clearly there is much left to study in the area
of giftedness and genius. Amen.

References

Albert, R. S. (1969). The concept of genius and its implications for the study of creativity and
    giftedness. In R. S. Albert (Ed.), *Genius and eminence: The social psychology of creativity
    and exceptional achievement* (pp. 6–18). New York: Oxford University Press (Pergamon
    Press), 1983.
Albert, R. S. (1971). Cognitive development and parental loss among the gifted, the exceptionally
    gifted and the creative. *Psychological Reports, 29,* 19–26.
Albert, R. S. (1975). Toward a behavioral definition of genius. In R. S. Albert (Ed.), *Genius
    and eminence: The social psychology of creativity and exceptional achievement* (pp. 59–72).
    New York: Oxford University Press (Pergamon Press), 1983.
Albert, R. S. (1978). Observations and suggestions regarding giftedness, familial influence and
    the achievement of eminence. *Gifted Child Quarterly, 22,* 201–211.
Albert, R. S. (1980a). Family positions and the attainment of eminence: A study of special family
    positions and special family experiences. In R. S. Albert (Ed.), *Genius and eminence: The*

social psychology of creativity and exceptional achievement (pp. 141–154). New York: Oxford University Press (Pergamon Press), 1983.

Albert, R. S. (1980b). Exceptional creativity and achievement. In R. S. Albert (Ed.), *Genius and eminence: The social psychology of creativity and exceptional achievement* (pp. 19–35). New York: Oxford University Press (Pergamon Press), 1983.

Albert, R. S. (1980c). Exceptionally gifted boys and their parents. *Gifted Child Quarterly, 24,* 174–179.

Barron, F. (1963). The needs for order and disorder as motivation in creative activity. In C. W. Taylor & F. Barron (Eds.), *Scientific creativity: Its recognition and development* (pp. 153–160). New York: Wiley.

Barron, F. (1968). *Creativity and personal freedom.* New York: Van Nostrand.

Baumrind, D. (1971). Current practices of parental authority. *Developmental Psychology Monograph, 4*(4), 1–103.

Becker, G. (1978). The mad genius controversy. In R. S. Albert (Ed.), *Genius and eminence: The social psychology of creativity and exceptional achievement* (pp. 36–39). New York: Oxford University Press (Pergamon Press), 1983.

Berrington, H. (1974). Prime Ministers and the search for love. In R. S. Albert (Ed.), *Genius and eminence: The social psychology of creativity and exceptional achievement* (pp. 358–373). New York: Oxford University Press (Pergamon Press), 1983.

Bloom, B. S. (1982). The role of gifts and markers in the development of talent. *Exceptional Children, 48*(6), 510–522.

Brody, E. B., & Brody, N. (1976). *Intelligence: Nature, determinants, and consequences.* New York: Academic Press.

Cattell, R. B. (1963). The personality and motivation of the researcher from measurements of contemporaries and from biography. In C. W. Taylor & F. Barron (Eds.), *Scientific creativity: Its recognition and development* (pp. 119–131). New York: Wiley.

Cattell, R. B. (1971). *Abilities: Their structure, growth and action.* Boston: Houghton Mifflin.

Chaunsey, H., & Hilton, T. L. (1965). Aptitude tests for the gifted. In R. S. Albert (Ed.), *Genius and eminence: The social psychology of creativity and exceptional achievement* (pp. 85–98). New York: Oxford University Press (Pergamon Press), 1983.

Cox, C. M. (1926). *Genetic studies of genius. Vol. 2: The early mental traits of three hundred geniuses.* Stanford: Stanford University Press.

Eiduson, B. I. (1962). *Scientists: Their psychological world.* New York: Basic Books.

Feldman, D. H. (1980). *Beyond universals in cognitive development.* Norwood, N.J.: Ablex.

Feldman, D. H. (1982). A developmental framework for research with gifted children. In D. H. Feldman (Ed.), *Developmental approaches to giftedness and creativity* (pp. 31–45). San Francisco: Jossey-Bass.

Feynman, R. (1974). An interview with Nobel Prize winner Richard Feynman. *Engineering and Science, 37*(4), 10–13, 22–25.

Freud, S. (1908). The relation of the poet to day-dreaming (pp. 173–183). In *Collected Papers* (Vol. 4). London: Hogarth Press, 1948.

Galton, F. (1869). *Hereditary genius.* New York: Macmillan.

Gardner, H. (1982). Giftedness: Speculations from a biological perspective. In D. H. Feldman (Ed.), *Developmental approaches to giftedness and creativity* (pp. 47–60). San Francisco: Jossey-Bass.

Getzels, J. W., & Csikszentmihalyi, M. (1976). *The creative vision: A longitudinal study of problem finding in art.* New York: Wiley.

Getzels, J. W., & Jackson, P. W. (1962). *Creativity and intelligence: Explorations with gifted students.* New York: Wiley.

Gibson, J., & Chennells, P. (1976). *Gifted children: Looking to their future.* London: Latimer New Dimensions.

Gough, H. G. (1957). *Manual for the California Psychological Inventory.* Palo Alto, Calif.: Consulting Psychologists Press.

Hall, W. B., & MacKinnon, D. W. (1969). Personality inventories as predictors of creativity among architects. *Journal of Applied Psychology, 53*(4), 322–326.

Helson, R. (1983). Creative mathematicians. In R. S. Albert (Ed.), *Genius and eminence: The social psychology of creativity and exceptional achievement* (pp. 311–330). New York: Oxford University Press (Pergamon Press), 1983.

Helson, R., & Crutchfield, R. S. (1970). Mathematicians: The creative researcher and the average Ph.D. *Journal of Consulting and Clinical Psychology, 34,* 250–257.

Hollingworth, L. (1942). *Children above 180 IQ Stanford-Binet.* New York: World Book.

Jones, E. (1957). *The life and work of Sigmund Freud* (Vol. 3). New York: Basic Books.

Kagan, J., & Moss, H. A. (1962). *Birth to maturity: A study in psychological development.* New York: Wiley.

Keating, D. P. (Ed.) (1976). *Intellectual talent: Research and development.* Baltimore: Johns Hopkins University Press.

Keniston, K. (1965). *The uncommitted.* New York: Dell (Delta Books).

Keniston, K. (1968). *Young radicals.* New York: Harcourt Brace Jovanovich.

Kubie, L. S. (1958). *Neurotic distortion of the creative process.* Lawrence: University of Kansas Press.

Kuhn, T. S. (1962). *The structure of scientific revolutions.* Chicago: University of Chicago Press.

Laycock, F. (1979). *Gifted children.* Glenview, Ill: Scott, Foresman.

McClelland, D. C. (1962). The calculated risk: An aspect of scientific performance. In C. W. Taylor & F. Barron (Eds.), *Scientific creativity: Its recognition and development* (pp. 184–192). New York: Wiley.

MacKinnon, D. W. (1960). The highly effective individual. In R. S. Albert (Ed.), *Genius and eminence: The social psychology of creativity and exceptional achievement* (pp. 114–127). New York: Oxford University Press (Pergamon Press), 1983.

MacKinnon, D. W. (1978). *In search of human effectiveness.* Buffalo: Creative Education Foundation.

Marjoribanks, K. (1972). Environment, social class and mental abilities. *Journal of Educational Psychology, 63,* 103–109.

Marjoribanks, K. (1974). Another view of the relation of environment to mental abilities. *Journal of Educational Psychology, 66,* 460–463.

Marjoribanks, K. (1979). *Families and their learning environments.* Boston: Routledge & Kegan Paul.

Maslow, A. H. (1959). Creativity in self-actualizing people. In H. H. Anderson (Ed.), *Creativity and its cultivation.* New York: Harper & Row.

Mednick, S. A. (1962). The associative basis of the creative process. *Psychological Review, 69,* 220–232.

Merton, R. K. (1969). Behavior patterns of scientists. In R. S. Albert (Ed.), *Genius and eminence: The social psychology of creativity and exceptional achievement* (pp. 253–261). New York: Oxford University Press (Pergamon), 1983.

Milgram, R. M., Milgram, N., & Landau, E. (1974). *Identification of gifted children in Israel: A theoretical and empirical investigation.* (Technical research report). Tel-Aviv University, Ramat-Avit, Israel.

Oden, M. (1968). The fulfillment of promise: 40-year follow-up of the Terman gifted group. In R. S. Albert (Ed.), *Genius and eminence: The social psychology of creativity and exceptional achievement* (pp. 203–213). New York: Oxford University Press (Pergamon Press), 1983.

Parloff, M. B., & Datta, L. (1965). Personality characteristics of the potentially creative scientist. In J. H. Masserman (Ed.), *Communications and community.* (*Science and Psychoanalysis, 8*), pp. 91–106.

Parloff, M. B., Datta, L., Kleman, M., & Handlon, J. H. (1968). Personality characteristics which differentiate creative male adolescents and adults. *Journal of Personality, 36,* 528–552.

Perkins, D. N. (1981). *The mind's best work.* Cambridge, Mass.: Harvard University Press.

Piaget, J. (1951). *Play, dreams and imitation in childhood.* New York: Norton.

Piaget, J. (1952). *The origins of intelligence in children.* New York: International Universities Press.

Poland, N. (1978, July-August). The most fascinating family in Britain. *Harvard Magazine, 81,* 29–32, 56–59.

Roe, A. (1952). *The making of a scientist.* New York: Dodd, Mead.

Runco, M. A., & Albert, R. S. (1984a). *Ideational originality in the divergent thinking of academically gifted and nongifted children.* Manuscript submitted for publication.

Runco, M. A., & Albert, R. S. (1984b, April). The threshold of intelligence and creativity. Paper presented at the Annual Convention of the Western Psychological Association, Los Angeles.

Sattler, H. N. (1982). *Assessment of children's intelligence.* Philadelphia: Saunders.

Scarr, S., & McCartney, K. (1983). How people make their environments: A theory of genotype environment effects. *Child Development, 54,* 424–435.

Scarr–Salapatek, S. (1975). Genetics and the development of intelligence. In F. D. Horowitz (Ed.), *Review of Child Development* (Vol. 4), 1–57.

Schaefer, C. E. (1970). *Manual for the Biographical Inventory – Creativity.* San Diego: Educational and Industrial Testing Service.

Simonton, D. K. (1978). History and the eminent person. *Gifted Child Quarterly, 22,* 187–195.

Southern, M. L., & Plant, W. T. (1968). Personality characteristics of very bright adults. *Journal of Social Psychology, 75,* 119–126.

Stanley, J., Keating, D. P., & Fox, L. H. (Eds.) (1974). *Mathematical talents: Discovery, description, and development.* Baltimore: Johns Hopkins University Press.

Strout, C. (1968). William James and the twice-born sick soul. In R. S. Albert (Ed.), *Genius and eminence: The social psychology of creativity and exceptional achievement* (pp. 374–385). New York: Oxford University Press (Pergamon), 1983.

Subcommittee on Education (1972). *Education of the gifted and the talented: Report to the Congress of the United States.* Washington, D.C.: U.S. Government Printing Office.

Terman, L. M. (1954). The discovery and encouragement of exceptional talent. *American Psychologist, 9,* 221–230.

Thorndike, E. L. (1926). *The measurement of intelligence.* New York: Teachers College Press.

Walberg, H. S., Rasher, S. P., & Hase, K. (1978). IQ correlates with high eminence. In R. S. Albert (Ed.), *Genius and eminence: The social psychology of creativity and exceptional achievement* (pp. 52–56). New York: Oxford University Press (Pergamon), 1983.

Wallach, M. A. (1970). Creativity. In P. H. Mussen (Ed.), *Carmichael's manual of child psychology* (Vol. 1, pp. 1211–1272). New York: Wiley.

Wallach, M. A., & Kogan, N. (1965). *Modes of thinking in young children.* New York: Holt, Rinehart & Winston.

Wiener, N. (1958). *Ex-prodigy.* Cambridge, Mass.: MIT Press.

Wild, C. (1965). Creativity and adaptive regression. *Journal of Personality and Social Psychology, 2,* 161–169.

Winner, E. (1982). *Invented worlds: The psychology of arts.* Cambridge, Mass.: Harvard University Press.

Winnicott, D. W. (1976). *The maturational processes and the facilitating environment.* London: Hogarth Press and the Institute of Psychoanalysis.

Yarrow, L. J., & Peterson, F. A. (1976). The interplay between cognition and motivation in infancy. In M. Lewis (Ed.), *Origins of intelligence* (pp. 379–399). New York: Plenum Press.

Zuckerman, H. (1977). The scientific elite: Nobel Laureates' mutual influences. In R. S. Albert (Ed.), *Genius and eminence: The social psychology of creativity and exceptional achievement* (pp. 241–252). New York: Oxford University Press (Pergamon), 1983.

Part V

Explicit-theoretical approaches: domain-specific theory

16   Youths who reason exceptionally well mathematically

Julian C. Stanley and Camilla Persson Benbow

The topic of this volume is conceptions of giftedness. It is somewhat anomalous that the present chapter is included in such a volume. The Study of Mathematically Precocious Youth (SMPY) is not concerned much with conceptualizing giftedness. Obviously, many children are clearly talented intellectually and need educational assistance. SMPY concentrates its efforts on helping such youths and devising novel educational alternatives for them. Thus, its staff has not spent much time contemplating the psychological underpinnings of giftedness. This necessitates our taking a different emphasis than in other chapters of this volume. We shall first describe our operational definition of mathematical giftedness and its meaning. Then we shall outline the rationale of our program.

The following quotation illustrates SMPY's position well:

What is particularly striking here is how little that is distinctly psychological seems involved in SMPY, and yet how very fruitful SMPY appears to be. It is as if trying to be psychological throws us off the course and into a mire of abstract dispositions that help little in facilitating students' demonstrable talents. What seems most successful for helping students is what stays closest to the competencies one directly cares about: in the case of SMPY, for example, finding students who are very good at math and arranging the environment to help them learn it as well as possible. One would expect analogous prescriptions to be of benefit for fostering talent at writing, music, art, and any other competencies that can be specified in product or performance terms. But all this in fact is not unpsychological; it simply is different psychology. (Wallach, 1978, p. 617)

What is mathematical precocity?

SMPY's indicator of mathematical talent is simply a high score at an early age on the mathematics section of the College Board's Scholastic Aptitude Test (SAT-M). This may appear narrow. We feel, however, that its elegance lies in its simplicity and objectivity. Moreover, few would argue that such

This is a revision and extension of Stanley (1977). We thank Barbara S. K. Stanley for considerable editorial assistance and Lois S. Sandhofer for her excellent word-processing work in preparing the manuscript.

ability does not indicate a high level of cognitive functioning. Although some students may be missed by this criterion, we identify more youths who *reason* exceptionally well mathematically than we can handle.

SAT-M is the major instrument of the Johns Hopkins Talent Searches (Stanley, Keating, & Fox, 1974; George, 1979). It was designed for above-average high school juniors and seniors to measure their mathematical reasoning ability (Donlon & Angoff, 1971). We, however, use it mainly to test seventh-graders, who are approximately 5 years younger. We call them talent search participants. Few of these students have received formal opportunities to develop their abilities in algebra and beyond (Benbow & Stanley, 1982a, 1982b, 1983d). For example, we have found that among the top 10% of our talent search participants (i.e., those eligible for our fast-paced summer programs in mathematics), a majority do not know even first-year algebra well. Thus, they must begin their mathematics studies with Algebra I.

Therefore, these students are demonstrably unfamiliar with mathematics from algebra onward. Yet many of them are able to score highly on a difficult test of mathematical reasoning ability. Presumably, this could occur only by the use of extraordinary ability at the "analysis" level of Bloom's (1956) taxonomy. Thus, we previously concluded that the SAT-M must function far more at an analytic reasoning level for the talent search participants than it does for high school juniors and seniors (Benbow & Stanley, 1981, 1983d).

Although it is not yet well known how precocious mathematical reasoning ability relates to "mathematical reasoning ability" in adults, SMPY has a procedure any researcher can reproduce (many have) and enables selection of populations with high tested ability. Criticisms of whether we are measuring "true" mathematical reasoning ability are at present beside the point. If a test can predict achievement in specific aspects of later life fairly well, it is of value regardless of the precise nature of the ability measured. If the test does predict high achievement, then we may want to establish exactly what it measures or what mathematical reasoning ability may be. SMPY's purpose is in part to determine the predictive validity of the SAT-M. Our work to date indicates that it does predict relevant criteria (e.g., Benbow & Stanley, 1983a).

Finally, SMPY has sought already evident ability, rather than some presumed underlying potential that has not yet become manifest. Thus, we have not worried about late bloomers. As a matter of fact, we are not convinced that many late bloomers in terms of ability exist. It is possible but unlikely to find a student whose SAT scores jump greatly in 1 year, for example over 200 points more than other students his or her age. We at SMPY feel that late bloomers are usually the result of early lack of motivation or test sophistication rather than of ability. In order to prevent late blooming or no blooming at all among the mathematically gifted, one of the authors (Stanley) founded SMPY.

Why mathematical reasoning ability

Persons often ask why we chose mathematical reasoning ability rather than something else, or even why we decided to concentrate on one type of talent rather than studying all sorts. The answer is that we wanted to steer a careful course between excessive specialism and overly broad coverage.

Sharply limited resources made this decision inevitable. Even for the first 2 years, after the study was funded by the Spencer Foundation in 1971, it did not have a single full-time worker. After that there was just one. Small wonder that we did not also select initially for other talents such as verbal reasoning ability, athletic prowess, musical talent, and leadership potential! No matter how hard we might work, relatively little could be done by us for that varied a group.

Given the need to specialize, it seemed sensible to choose an ability closely related to major subjects in the academic curricula of schools in the United States. Because we planned to help intellectually talented youths improve their education, it also appeared wise to start at as early a grade and age level as the maturation of the chosen ability permitted. Moreover, in order to capitalize on the precocious development of this ability by greatly accelerating school progress in the subject matter area concerned, it was necessary to choose school subjects much more highly dependent for their mastery on manifest intellectual talent than on chronological age and the associated life experiences. These considerations led to our choosing mathematical reasoning as the ability and the best of the standard courses in mathematics, the mathematical sciences, and the sciences as the subjects on which to focus directly. We did not want to develop curricula in mathematics, but instead wanted to help mathematically talented boys and girls use their abilities more effectively in the various academic areas. We encouraged curricular flexibility by schools (e.g., Benbow & Stanley, 1983b, 1983c; Stanley & Benbow, 1982, 1983).

We were aided in this choice by more than just armchair considerations. Great precocity in mathematics and the physical sciences has been documented by such writers as Cox (1926) in the second volume of Terman's *Genetic Studies of Genius* series,[1] Bell (1937), Roe (1951), Lehman (1953), Kramer (1974), and Zuckerman (1977). The only clear competitor was musical composition, where the almost unbelievably early accomplishments of Saint-Saens, Mozart, and Mendelssohn are well known (e.g., see Schonberg, 1970). This ability does not articulate well with school curricula, however, nor do we have the knowledge or facilities to nurture young composers. We eliminated chess because it is not an academic discipline.

Why IQ scores are not used

This may be the place to decry what we at SMPY perceive to be vast over-emphasis on the Stanford–Binet or Wechsler-type overall IQ in planning academic experiences for brilliant children. If one takes a group of students who all have exactly the same Stanford–Binet IQ (say, 140), one does not have a group homogeneous with respect to such special abilities as mathematical reasoning. The IQ is a global composite, perhaps the best *single* index of general learning rate. One can, however, earn a certain IQ in a variety of ways, for example, by scoring high on memory but much lower on reasoning, or vice versa. *It is illogical and inefficient to group students for instruction in mathematics mainly on the basis of overall mental age or IQ.* Often this is done and students who lag behind in the class are accused of not being well motivated, when in fact they simply do not have as high aptitude for learning mathematics as some in the class who have the same IQ. These considerations also apply to other academic subjects, such as history or English literature.

It is difficult to form a group of students really homogeneous for instruction in a given subject even when one uses all the psychometric and other knowledge about them that can be gathered. To rely primarily on the IQ for this purpose, as do quite a few city and state programs for intellectually talented youths, seems curious. An obvious corollary is that students should be grouped for instruction separately for each subject and that these groupings should be free to change from year to year. Administrative or political convenience is the probable cause of undue reliance on a single grouping measure such as IQ. Now that computer scheduling is available, however, this justification for an ineffective process is weakened.

Why SAT-M score is the initial criterion

We wanted to find youths who at an early age (mostly 12 or 13) were already able to *reason* extremely well with simple mathematical facts, students who even before taking or completing the first year of algebra would reason mathematically better than the average college-bound male 12th-grader does. (Performance is compared against college-bound male 12th-graders because that is the College Board's most stringent norm group.) It seemed to us likely that a reasoning test would predict success in later mathematics, at least through differential equations, far better than would items measuring learned concepts, learned algorithms, and computational speed and accuracy.

We also needed a mathematical reasoning test difficult enough that our average examinee would at age 12 score on it halfway between a chance score and a perfect score. Also, the test should have enough "ceiling" so that virtually no perfect scores would occur.

In addition to the considerations of reasoning content and appropriate difficulty, we wanted a professionally prepared, carefully standardized, reliable test for which several well-guarded ("secure") forms existed and for which well-known, meaningful interpretations of scores were available. High scores on the test should command immediate attention and respect at both the high school and college levels.

These considerations led to pilot studies of the SAT-M, which required only a little knowledge of algebra and geometry.[2] To ensure that testees were given equal opportunity to score well on it, however, we gave them plenty of practice materials. Because reasoning mathematically involves knowledge of some elementary mathematics, this was essential in order to smooth out partially differences in mathematical training. We did not want scores to depend much on rote knowledge of mathematical concepts or on computational ability, as the usual test of mathematical skills does.

In 1969 our first examinee, an obviously brilliant 13-year-old 8th-grader, scored 669 on SAT-M, the 91st percentile of college-bound male 12th-graders. On the verbal part of SAT (SAT-V), he scored 590, the same percentile of the same norm group. Another 13-year-old 8th-grader, on whom we tried the test the next year, scored 716 on M and 608 on V. Others scored similarly, some even higher. Extremely few scored near the perfect score on M or even close to the maximum on V. It seemed likely, then, that SAT-M would be excellent for identifying the level of mathematical reasoning ability we sought among seventh and eighth graders. SAT-V could provide additional assessment of overall mental age as well as level of verbal reasoning ability.

As has been shown in several publications, especially Stanley et al. (1974) and Keating (1976), for the students we tested in our talent searches (i.e., generally the top 3% on the mathematics part of standardized achievement tests administered by the students' schools), SAT-M and SAT-V did indeed prove suitable in both content and difficulty. The mean score on each test was appropriately between the chance- and perfect-score levels. The highest scores were almost never perfect.

It would be rare, indeed, for a person to have excellent mathematical *reasoning* ability and yet be inferior to average thinkers in verbal *reasoning* ability. SMPY did not want to identify mere calculating freaks (Barlow, 1952; Smith, 1984). Though its participants are not chosen explicitly for high IQ, virtually none of them seems to have average or below-average IQs.

Students who made high scores on the SAT-M (e.g., 500 or more) in one of our six talent searches, conducted between 1972 and 1979, were considered mathematically precocious. A score of 500 is the 51st percentile of male college-bound 12th-graders. Our programs were directed at these boys and girls who are estimated to reason better mathematically than 99 percent of their age-mates.

Whenever one uses a test and has a fixed point above which the examinee is considered "successful," however, the issue of false positives and false negatives arises. Some examinees whose true ability is right at the criterion will have a good day and equal or exceed it, whereas others will have a bad day and score somewhat below it. On another occasion the situation would have been reversed. (About two-thirds whose true ability is exactly the criterial score, 500, would be expected to score not more than approximately 30 points above or below it, i.e., 470–530.) Thus, we developed a safeguard against false negatives: Whereas the talent-search SAT is taken in January of the seventh grade, examinees who miss the criterion may retake the test on their own in later months to qualify for programs.

False positives are less of a concern than false negatives. The fallacious addition of even as much as 30 points to their score (e.g., 500 when the true score is 470) may give examinees a slightly exaggerated view of their precocity and therefore a higher, but not unattainable, standard for achieving.

Why identification began at the junior high school level

Elementary mathematics is, from the standpoint of the learner, heavily an algorithmic and deductive system, though for those who create it there are usually strong intuitive and aesthetic elements (e.g., Hardy, 1969; Polya, 1973). Unlike understanding philosophy or great novels such as Tolstoy's *War and Peace*, personal experience outside the classroom and maturation closely tied to chronological age seem not essential for learning mathematics well. Certain types of reasoning ability and Piagetian formal-operations status, however, are necessary for mastering subjects such as high school algebra. These develop in various individuals at vastly different ages.

A startling example will illustrate that young students can develop advanced thought processes at an early age. At age 10, one of SMPY's participants made the highest grade in a state college introductory computer science course. He was competing with 7 other exceptionally able, older students and 12 adults. Before his 11th birthday, he had completed at Johns Hopkins most of a second-level computer course, on which he earned a final grade of A. At age 11 he earned, by a score of 4 on the BC level of the Advanced Placement Program examination, credit for two semesters of calculus at Johns Hopkins. This is no ordinary boy, of course. His Stanford–Binet IQ at age 8 was 190, and he had been in our special fast-mathematics classes for 2 years. He graduated from Johns Hopkins at age 18 in 1982, Phi Beta Kappa. Currently, he is the top student in a major law school. He is not, however, nearly the most precocious youth we have discovered.[3]

Thus, SMPY's extensive experience and the studies by Keating (1975) and Keating and Schaefer (1975) indicated that the intellectually top 2% of students in the fifth grade have the necessary abilities sufficiently developed to learn Algebra II and other precalculus courses well. Extremely few could suitably begin studying these before the fifth grade. Because algebra is not usually offered until junior high school, however, the seventh grade seemed a practicable point to start.

Another reason to begin identification in the seventh grade is that many able students can learn precalculus mathematics *far* more quickly than schools ordinarily permit. The first year of algebra usually causes serious motivational problems for such youths. Regardless of how advanced their ability is, seldom are they permitted to take this subject before the eighth or ninth grades. Then, no matter how much Algebra I the student can already do or how quickly he or she could learn the material, the student is usually lock-stepped into at least 180 class periods throughout the school year. Mathematically highly precocious youths need vastly less exposure than that to what is for them an extremely easy subject. This is especially true when the student has already had one or more years of "modern" mathematics that may have included much algebra covertly. Several dramatic examples from our experience will illustrate the mathematically talented youth's dilemma.

A 12-year-old seventh grader who scored 760 on SAT-M in SMPY's 1974 talent search asked permission to join his junior high school's eighth-grade Algebra I class in February. This was refused on the grounds that he already had missed more than half the course. He insisted on being given a standardized test covering the first year of the subject. On this he made a perfect score, 40 right in forty minutes, which is 2 points above the 99.5th percentile of national norms for ninth-grade students who have been in that type of class all year. On seeing this achievement, the teacher agreed with the boy that he was indeed ready to join the class! Instead, he took a college mathematics course that summer and easily earned a grade of A. As a high school senior, he represented the United States well in the International Mathematical Olympiad contest.

At the end of the sixth grade a student took second-year algebra in summer school without having had first-year algebra; his final grade was A. By the end of the eighth grade he had earned credit by examination for two semesters of college calculus. A year later he had completed third-semester calculus by correspondence from a major university, earning A as his final grade. At age 21 he graduated from a top university with majors in mathematics, physics, and humanities.

A student learned 2 1/2 years of algebra well by being tutored while in the fifth and sixth grades. He continued, by means of tutoring, with a high-level course in geometry. His tutor in geometry was a 16-year-old freshman at Johns Hopkins who enrolled for honors advanced calculus (final grade, A) and other subjects that most 19-year-olds would find extremely difficult. He, too, condensed his mathematics radically.

A 6-year-old boy in California mastered 2 years of high school algebra. At age 7 he enrolled in a standard high school geometry course but found it too slow-paced and therefore finished the book on his own before Christmas. He also taught himself trigonometry. Before age 7 1/2 he had scored at the 99th percentile on standardized tests of Algebra I–III, geometry, and trigonometry. His SAT-M score at age 7 was 670, the 91st percentile of college-bound male high school seniors.

An 8-year-old boy in Australia scored 760 (the 99th percentile) on SAT-M, even though he was unaccustomed to taking multiple-choice tests.

Several girls have accelerated their progress in mathematics considerably, though not as much as the boys just discussed. One of them graduated from high school a year early while being the best student in SMPY's second high-level college calculus class. She went on to earn a bachelor's degree in computer engineering from an outstanding university and then a master's degree in computer science and a Master of Business Administration degree.

Many other such examples could be given (e.g., see Stanley, 1974, 1976a-f) to show that the usual high school pace in Algebra I–III, geometry, trigonometry, analytic geometry, and the calculus is far from optimum for boys and girls who reason extremely well mathematically. Algebra I is particularly virulent, because being incarcerated in it for a whole year gives the apt student no really appropriate way to behave. He or she can daydream, be excessively meticulous in order to get perfect grades, harass the teacher, show off knowledge arrogantly in the class, or be truant. There is, however, no *suitable* way to while away the class hours when one already knows much of the material and can learn the rest almost instantaneously as it is first presented. Boredom, frustration, and habits of gross inattention are almost sure to result. Therefore, SMPY identifies youths before they begin their precalculus training, and attempts to intervene educationally.

We are amazed that even more youths do not sustain obvious academic injury, and suspect that the actual damage is far greater than it seems. At least, it appears uncomfortably likely that motivation for mathematics may suffer appreciably in all but those few students devoted to the subject. After such snail-pacing in high school precalculus and calculus – often, 5 1/2 years or more – the number of top minds still excited by mathematics or its applications may be few.

For these reasons SMPY conducted its first three annual mathematics talent searches (1972–1974) among seventh- and eighth-graders, but also did special work among sixth-graders and a few students even younger than that. Beginning in December of 1976 the SMPY staff specialized even further to identify only seventh-graders. In SMPY's talent searches, students who were already known to be in the top 3% in mathematical ability on standardized achievement tests administered by their schools applied and participated by taking the SAT test. The talent searches initially surveyed only the Greater Baltimore area. They then grew. Since 1979 the Johns Hopkins Center for the Advancement of Academically Talented Youth (CTY)[4] annually surveys the entire Northeast and the Middle Atlantic states, from Virginia through Maine. CTY's western talent search encompasses Alaska, California, Hawaii, Oregon, Washington, and western Canada.

Students whose mathematical reasoning abilities proved to be superb were encouraged to move fast through the high school mathematics sequence, beginning with Algebra I or skipping it and *soon* having calculus so well learned that college credit for it could be obtained. They were also offered a smorgasbord of accelerative opportunities, such as skipping grades and graduating from college early. Somewhat less able entrants were given less drastic suggestions but were nevertheless encouraged to speed up their progress in mathematics and science. A dozen years of experience have shown that youths able and eager to move ahead can do so readily if they and their parents are resolute and persistent in their search for suitable ways.

Probably the best opportunities currently available are the academic, fast-paced summer programs offered by CTY and its counterparts at Duke and Northwestern universities. During these 3- or 6-week programs students can learn precalculus, calculus, high school biology, chemistry, and physics, writing skills at four levels, German, American history, computer science at three levels, Latin, and so on.

These classes are based on or adapted from the many fast-paced mathematics classes pioneered by SMPY between 1972 and 1979. In such classes, apt students were grouped homogeneously according to knowledge of mathematics. Details about these are contained in Fox (1974, 1976) and Stanley (1976b). Calculus can also be learned quickly by mathematically apt youths, as George and Denham (1976), George (1976), Stanley (1976b), Bartkovich and George (1980), Mezynski and Stanley (1980), Bartkovich and Mezynski (1981), and Mezynski, Stanley, and McCoart (1983) document rather fully.

Why not conduct a controlled experiment?

Because experimentation is a strong force in psychology and in my own background (e.g., Campbell and Stanley, 1966; Stanley, 1973), we were tempted to set up SMPY as a rigorously controlled experiment. On reflection, however, the initial SMPY staff came to believe that there were cogent reasons for not doing so. Some of those considerations were the following:

1. We were rather sure that the smorgasbord of accelerative educational opportunities we planned to offer the "experimental" subjects in the study were much more likely to help than to harm them. Therefore, it would be inadvisable to withhold such opportunities from a portion of the subjects (probably half of them) who in a controlled experiment would be assigned randomly to a "control" group.
2. There were not likely to be enough extremely high scorers to make the numbers in both the experimental and the control group sufficiently large to yield statistically powerful or precise comparisons between groups and

subgroups. It seemed more sensible to take the ablest subjects and mass the experimental efforts on them.

3. The procedures, principles, and techniques that SMPY planned to develop would be disseminated widely by the press and in speeches, letters, articles, books, and newsletters, so withholding knowledge of opportunities from a control group of subjects would be impossible. The control group would be exposed substantially to influences designed only for the experimental group, and that type of contamination would greatly weaken or even nullify the experiment.

4. By not having a control group from which certain presumably beneficial opportunities and information were withheld, it is possible to keep the study completely on an aboveboard basis, with no need to deceive anyone about anything. This openness is important in gaining the confidence of the students, their parents and teachers, and the general public.

5. Certain comparisons could be made by matching and other quasi-experimental procedures. Fox (1976) did this in her study of sex differences in mathematical aptitude and achievement, as have other SMPY researchers in trying to determine how well a certain special procedure worked (e.g., Benbow, Perkins, and Stanley, 1983; Pollins, 1983).

6. A great deal of SMPY's analysis of the results of its programs depends heavily on case-study clinical methods, using all known information about each individual with as much insight as can be mustered on the basis of considerable experience with many mathematically precocious youths (see Hudson, 1975). Burt (1975, p. 138) stated this point especially clearly:

> With human beings, when the problem is primarily psychological, statistical studies of populations should always be supplemented by case studies of individuals: early histories will often shed further light on the origin and development of this or that peculiarity. Tests should be supplemented by what Binet called the *methode clinique*, and interpreted by introspective observations, designed to verify the tacit assumption that they really do test what they are intended to assess. After all, each child is a complex and conscious organism, not a mere unit in a statistical sample.

Fortunately, many of SMPY's procedures yield results so different from the usual ones that the effects are obvious. For instance, it is almost preposterous to suggest that if SMPY had not found a local youth when he was an overage sixth-grader and helped him in many ways to move ahead educationally fast and well, he would, nevertheless, have been graduated from a major university at barely 17 years of age and become an assistant professor at 21. The youngest recipient of a bachelor in 1971 at Johns Hopkins was 19 years, 10 months old (Eisenberg, 1977). Two years later, under SMPY's influence, the youngest was 17 years, 7 months old, and 3 months later he had completed a master's degree also. Now 17-year-old graduates are frequent (see Stanley & Benbow, 1983). Similar strong observations could be made about most of SMPY's programs, such as the effects of the fast-paced classes.

Four sequential aspects of SMPY

The first book-length report about SMPY's initial work (Stanley, Keating, & Fox, 1974) was entitled *Mathematical Talent: Discovery, Description, and*

Development. To emphasize those three *D*'s and a fourth *D*, *dissemination* of our findings, we sometimes abbreviate that title as MT:D⁴. *Discovery* is the identification phase during which the talent is found. *Description* is the phase during which the most talented students are tested further, affectively and cognitively, and otherwise studied a great deal. This leads to the prime reason for SMPY, the *development* phase. During it the youths who were found and studied are continually helped, facilitated, and encouraged. Each is offered a smorgasbord of special educational possibilities (see Stanley & Benbow, 1982) from which to choose whatever combination, including nothing, best suits the individual. Some splendid mathematical reasoners try almost everything at breakneck speed, whereas others do little special. SMPY offers as much educational and vocational counseling and guidance as its resources permit, both via memoranda and individually as requested.

Most studies of intellectually gifted children are heavy on description but light on educational facilitation. From the start the SMPY staff was determined to intervene strongly on behalf of the able youths it found. Thus, discovery and description were seen as necessary steps leading to emphasis on accelerating educational development, particularly in mathematics and related subjects. SMPY promotes curricular flexibility or acceleration.

Why acceleration rather than enrichment is stressed

There were both logical and empirical reasons why we chose to emphasize educational acceleration rather than enrichment. Our rationale was that the pacing of educational programs must be responsive to the capacities and knowledge of individual children. As Robinson (1983) eloquently stated, this conclusion is based on three principles derived from developmental psychology. The first such principle is that learning is a sequential and developmental process (e.g., Hilgard & Bower, 1974). The second is that there are large differences in learning status among individuals at any given age. Although the acquisition of knowledge and the development of patterns follow stable sequences, children progress through them at varying rates (Bayley, 1955, 1970; George, Cohn, & Stanley, 1979; Keating, 1976; Keating & Stanley, 1972; Robinson & Robinson, 1976).

The final such principle is that effective teaching involves assessing the student's status in the learning process and posing problems slightly exceeding the level already mastered. Work that is too easy produces boredom; work that is too difficult cannot be understood. Hunt (1961) referred to this as "the problem of match, which is based on the premise that learning occurs only when there is an appropriate match between circumstances that a child encounters and the schemata that he/she has already assimilated into his/her repertoire" (p. 268).

The implication of the three principles delineated by Robinson (1983) is that the pace of educational programs must be adapted to the capacities and knowledge of individual children. SMPY found adapting existing curricula and making them available to younger students rather than writing new curricula to be most productive in meeting this need.

We did consider enrichment, however. There seemed to be four main kinds of educational enrichment: busywork, irrelevant academic, cultural, and relevant academic. In our opinion, for reasons to be stated, only the third (cultural) is well suited to mathematically highly precocious youths. It does not, however, meet their needs in mathematics or in the other academic subjects.

Busywork is a well-known but usually unfortunate way for some teachers to keep their brightest students occupied while the class goes on with its regular work. If often consists of having gifted children do a great deal more of the subject they have already mastered, but at the same level as the class they have surpassed.

One of our eighth-graders, with a Stanford–Binet IQ of at least 187, was asked by his algebra teacher to work every problem in the book, rather than just the alternate problems the rest of the class was assigned. Because he already knew Algebra I rather well and needed to work few problems, he resented this burdensome chore. The busywork proved to be a powerful motivator, however. After that year, he took all of his mathematics at the college level. First, though, while he was still 12 years old this precocious youth took the regular introductory course in computer science at Johns Hopkins and earned a final grade of A. During the following summer he took a course in college algebra and trigonometry at Johns Hopkins, earning a B. From then on, at a local college for two academic years and two more summers, he took college mathematics through the calculus and linear algebra and 2 years of college chemistry, with all A's. At age 15 he entered Johns Hopkins as a full-time student with 30% of the sophomore year completed. Three years later he graduated with a major in electrical engineering and began graduate work in computer science at MIT on a National Science Foundation Graduate Fellowship. Thus, in a rather perverse sense, his teacher had done him a great favor. Without SMPY's discovering him, however, he would probably have been forced to sit a whole year in each of numerous high school mathematics courses far below his capabilities. Instead, by age 24 he had a PhD degree in computer science from MIT.

Irrelevant academic enrichment consists of not providing the type of advanced stimulation the brilliant student needs, such as faster-paced mathematics for the mathematically precocious. Instead, all high-IQ youths are offered a special academic course, nonacademic work such as games (e.g., chess), or creativity training largely divorced from subject matter. Although this may be splendid for those whose major interest is tapped, it does not assuage the mental hunger of the mathematically oriented (see Stanley, 1954, 1958, 1959).

Cultural enrichment consists of providing certain cultural experiences that go beyond the usual school curriculum and therefore do not promote later boredom. Examples are music appreciation, performing arts, and foreign languages such as Russian, Chinese, and Classical Greek (see Mill, 1924; Packe, 1954; and Wiener, 1953). Early experiences with speaking modern foreign languages and learning about foreign cultures also fit this pattern. The latter may be a type of stimulation that parents and teachers of high-IQ youths could provide from the early years. These do not, however, meet the specialized academic needs of the intellectually talented.

The fourth and last type of enrichment is what we term *relevant academic*. It is likely to be both the best short-term method and one of the worst long-term ones. Suppose, for instance, that an excellent, forward-looking school system provides a splendid modern mathematics curriculum for the upper 10% of its students from kindergarten through the seventh grade, and then in the eighth grade these students begin a regular Algebra I course. How bored and frustrated they are almost sure to be! It is not educationally or psychologically sound to dump these highly enriched students into the mainstream. Yet that kind of situation often occurs. Only if the kindergarten through 12th-grade curriculum is considered can this failure of articulation be prevented. Even then, a superb 13-year mathematics program without strong provisions for college credit would merely defer the boredom and frustration until the college years.

Therefore, none of these types of enrichment was felt to be suitable for the mathematically talented student. None would provide such students an appropriate mathematics education at an appropriate pace and also prevent boredom in later years. The problem of "match" that Hunt had discussed would not be solved. For the preceding logical reasons we felt strongly that any kind of enrichment except perhaps the cultural sort will, without acceleration, tend to harm the brilliant student. Therefore, high-level, accelerative instruction was deemed the most suitable alternative.

Furthermore, there is excellent support for acceleration in the professional literature. Wiener (1953, 1956), Bardeen (Young, 1972), Watson (1968), Fefferman (Montour, 1976b), Wolf (Keating, 1976, see index; Montour, 1976a), and others have benefited greatly from it professionally. Norbert Wiener had his baccalaureate at 14 and his PhD degree at 18. Charles Louis Fefferman had his baccalaureate at 17 and his doctorate at barely 20; by age 22 he was a full professor of mathematics at the University of Chicago. Five years later he was the first winner of the National Science Foundation's $150,000 Waterman Award. Before age 30 he had won the prestigious Field Medal in mathematics and become a member of the National Academy of Sciences.

John Bardeen, twice a Nobel laureate in physics, completed high school at age 15. Merrill Kenneth Wolf, now a prominent neuroanatomist and talented pianist, was graduated from Yale University in 1945 shortly after becoming 14 years old. James Watson had his PhD degree at age 23 and before he became 25 had done with Francis Crick the work that later earned them a Nobel Prize. These examples could go on and on. Counterexamples, such as the ill-fated William James Sidis (Montour, 1975, 1977), who was graduated from Harvard College at age 16 but failed badly thereafter, are rare.

Terman and Oden (1947, pp. 264–66) found that the typical member of Terman's gifted group was graduated from high school about a year early. They advocated a moderate amount of acceleration for gifted youths. Hollingworth (1942), who worked with even abler children than the average of Terman's group, recommended considerable acceleration for them.

The University of Chicago's extensive experience with early entrance and fast progress in college during the 1930s showed it was indeed a feasible approach for certain students. After this program was largely abandoned because of financial and other reasons, the Fund for the Advancement of Education (1953, 1957) set up studies at a number of colleges and universities to admit well-qualified students at the end of the 10th or 11th grade. These were judged to be markedly successful.

Hobson (1963) and Worcester (1956) showed that, when properly arranged, early entrance to public school was beneficial. It seems to us especially unfortunate that their work is not well known to most educational administrators, because its scope, practicality, and clarity make the findings hard to ignore.

Perhaps the most comprehensive study of educational acceleration was the splendid monograph by Pressey (1949). Anyone who can read it carefully and still oppose such acceleration certainly has the courage of his or her preconvictions. Pressey, Hobson, Worcester, and others reveal that opposition to acceleration is founded largely on emotionalized prejudices rather than facts. (Also, see Friedenberg, 1966.) We do not know of a single careful study of actual accelerants that has shown acceleration not to be beneficial, though armchair articles against it abound (see Daurio, 1979; Pollins, 1983; Robinson, 1983).

Furthermore, Lehman (1953), a psychologist, teamed up with a specialist in each of various fields to study the ages at which the greatest creative contributions were made by eminent scientists, scholars, and prodigies of other kinds. The typical age at which eminent mathematicians and physical scientists made their most highly rated achievements was lower than the average age at which the PhD degree in those fields is awarded in the United States. Many brilliant young men and women are still students when according to logic and history they should be independent researchers.

As a cautionary note, however, the eagerness of the brilliant individual to move ahead rapidly is crucial. If the youth is reluctant to take a particular accelerative path, such as going into Algebra I early, taking a college course, or skipping a grade, probably he or she should not be urged to do so. Unfortunately, many boys and girls are not allowed by their teachers, guidance counselors, principals, or even sometimes their parents to make calm, rational decisions about such matters. They may get so much bad advice that they give up in confusion. Many are simply forbidden to use a particular method of acceleration.

In summary, the SMPY staff believes that offering each splendid mathematical reasoner a varied assortment of accelerative possibilities and letting him or her choose an optimum combination of these to suit the individual's current situation is far superior to so-called special academic enrichment.

Why educational planning is done with the child directly

From its inception SMPY has tried to communicate chiefly with youths themselves, rather than through their parents. Reports of results of the testing competition have gone to them, even including discussion of percentile ranks on national norms and the like. We have also written them letters in response to their queries or their parents'. It is our belief that contacts of the facilitating agency, such as SMPY, should be mainly through the youth, even though he or she may be only 9 or 10 years old. After all, a child that age whose Stanford–Binet IQ is 170 or more (and SMPY seldom deals with any that young unless they are that bright) has a mental age of at least 15 years.

Moreover, we want youths to take charge of their own academic planning early and to use their parents and us as means for implementing their own decisions. Some parents object to this approach, of course. If communication from the beginning is with the student, such friction is usually minimized.

Self-pacing as inappropriate neo-enrichment versus individualized group pacing

When we propose accelerative opportunities for mathematically highly talented youths, the school is likely to counter by offering to let them proceed "at their own pace." In practice, this usually means still sitting in the too-slow class, such as first-year algebra, while working ahead in the book and perhaps into Algebra II. Common sense and observation tell us that this is not likely to work well for most students, no matter how able. Any student that autonomous and well motivated would probably have little use for school. Our model is definitely not self-pacing, whether in the crude way described above or by means of programmed instructional materials.

Programmed instructional materials are almost sure to contain too many steps, and too small ones, for mathematically extremely able students. Also, such materials do not usually lend themselves to group-paced stimulation.

Most of our precocious youths do not perform well against an abstract standard, such as number of chapters or frames completed. Similarly, a track man
or woman does not usually run well alone or a tennis player perform his or
her best against a weak opponent. Most of our students who have tried self-
pacing or correspondence-study courses move far less swiftly and well than
they do in special fast-paced mathematics classes. Therefore, we consider the
group-pacing feature essential for most persons (cf. Macken et al., 1976), but
with full allowance for some students to forge ahead far faster than others.
It is a group-mentor, rather than a group-instructional, approach.

The group-mentor approach produces astoundingly good results. Skeptics
should read about some of SMPY's fast-mathematics classes: Wolfson I (Fox,
1974; Stanley, 1976b; Benbow et al., 1983); Wolfson II (George & Denham,
1976); the summers of 1978 and 1979 (Bartkovich & Mezynski, 1981); and
calculus (Stanley, 1976b; Mezynski & Stanley, 1980; Mezynski et al., 1983).

Effects of SMPY program participation

In this chapter we have delineated only our success stories to illustrate the
use of our educational options. This is because they are the most useful.
Obviously, students in SMPY's programs have met varying success. Some
students can race through a three-week precalculus class and finish the entire
precalculus sequence, whereas a few have great difficulty completing even
Algebra I. Ability and motivation are two factors influencing this (Fox, 1974;
Favazza, 1983). Interest is another. A student interested in many different
things or preoccupied with another activity is not going to have much time
or mental energy to spend learning precalculus. Yet that person may still feel
that he or she benefited from the class.

Therefore, it is difficult to determine what criteria describe failure and also
when to decide if a student has failed. The following example illustrates the
point well. One of the highest achieving students in SMPY's second fast-paced
mathematics class entered Johns Hopkins at age 16. He got terribly involved
with computers, however, and began neglecting his classwork. After earning
poor grades and committing several fairly serious computer pranks, he dropped
out. At that point he might have been considered an academic failure. Nevertheless, he became a successful computer consultant. Several years later he
returned to Hopkins, finished his baccalaureate with honors, and soon won
a truly major national award.

Actually, the numbers who do not succeed at a high level in our programs
are small. This is partly because participation has been voluntary. No person
was forced to enter college early or skip a grade. Thus, most students unlikely
to succeed in our programs select themselves out.

Anecdotes are not scientific evidence, however. This necessitated that SMPY
systematically follow up students to study their development and to evaluate

SMPY's programs. Those in SMPY's first three talent searches have been studied approximately 5 years after initial contact. Their development was traced through high school (Benbow, 1981, 1983; Benbow & Stanley, 1982b). Students who had scored at least 370 on SAT-V or 390 on SAT-M (the mean scores of a national random sample of high school females) were sent an 8-page printed questionnaire. Over 91% of 2,188 SMPY students participated by completing the survey. The general conclusion of the study was that SMPY students had fulfilled their potential in high school.

Relative to appropriate comparison groups, SMPY students were superior in both ability and achievement, expressed stronger interests in mathematics and the sciences, were accelerated more frequently in their education, and were more motivated educationally, as indicated by their desire for advanced degrees from difficult schools. Over 90% were attending college, and approximately 60% of those were planning to major in the sciences. The results suggested strong relationships between mathematical talent of students in grade seven or eight and subsequent course-taking, achievements, interest, and attitudes in high school. SMPY's identification procedure was effective in selecting students in the seventh grade who achieve at a superior level in high school, especially in science and mathematics (Benbow, 1981, 1983).

In addition to studying the development of mathematically talented students, the longitudinal study provides useful data for evaluating lasting effects of SMPY's various methods in facilitating the education of its students. It was found, for example, that the successful participants in SMPY's first fast-paced precalculus classes achieved much more in high school and college than the equally able invitees who had not participated. They were also much more accelerated in their education than the nonparticipants. The former were satisfied with their acceleration, which they felt did not detract from their social and emotional development. Furthermore, there appeared to be no evidence to justify the fear that accelerating the rate of learning produces gaps in knowledge or poor retention (Benbow et al., 1983). Similar results were found for those students who graduated from *college* before age 19 (Stanley & Benbow, 1983; Benbow & Stanley, 1983a) and the less accelerated students in the follow-ups (Benbow, 1981, 1983). Most of the SMPY students felt that SMPY had helped them at least some, while not detracting from their social-emotional development (Benbow, 1981, 1983). This was true even for the students with whom the staff of SMPY had not had much contact.

Predictive validity of SAT-M

The above findings attest to the predictive validity of the SAT-M. In addition, SAT-M and SAT-V proved to have great value for predicting which students would be able to accelerate their mathematical education radically. Of course, motivational factors proved crucial within the high-scoring group. Without considerable ability of the SAT-M and SAT-V types, however, even highly motivated students could not race ahead successfully in mathematics and related areas. For example, in the fast-paced summer precalculus programs the amount of mathematics learned was best predicted by the SAT-M score (Fox, 1974; Favazza, 1983).

We have found that the SAT-M score scale is valid right up the the top-reported score, 800, *if* the criteria themselves have enough "ceiling" for the group. For instance, in the usual eighth- or ninth-grade Algebra I class, variation in this ability would probably make little difference in apparent success of students at SAT-M levels 500, 600, 700, or 800, because all of these exceed the mathematical reasoning demands of the course. Paying attention and doing homework and tests carefully are probably better determiners of grades among these high scorers than are differences of the order of even 100 to 300 points. Put a 500 SAT-M scoring individual into a fast-paced, homogeneously grouped Algebra III class designed for students scoring at least 700 on SAT-M, however, and he or she is unlikely to be able to keep up. There are reports that a test of appropriate difficulty loses its validity at some point short of the top of its score scale. Most such reports are actually commentaries on the lack of ceiling of the criterion, rather than intrinsic dropping-off of validity of the predictor. This is especially true when both the predictor and the criterion variables are ability-test scores.

Benefits to students

The benefits to SMPY's participants are numerous. Among them are the following:

1. Increased zest for learning and life, reduced boredom in school, and therefore a better attitude toward education and other activities.
2. Enhanced feelings of self-worth and accomplishment.
3. Reduction of egotism and arrogance. At first this may seem counterintuitive, but repeatedly we have observed that SMPY students who learn with their intellectual peers in rigorous settings, such as special fast-mathematics classes, tend to develop more realistic understanding of their ability. These youths learn that, compared with national norms on standardized tests, they are superb, but less spectacular relative to each other. In regular mathematics classes, the typical SMPY participant earns such good grades with so little effort that the temptation to feel superior is strong. For example, the 190-IQ boy who by age 11 had done extremely well in two college computer-science courses and on the Advanced Placement Program examination in college calculus seemed far less egotistical than he was before entering one of our special precalculus classes at age 10. In the SMPY courses, he had to work hard to maintain an average rank, whereas as an accelerated sixth-grader he was vastly overqualified for all his regular subjects.
4. Far better educational preparation than they otherwise would get, especially in mathematics, which is basic to many disciplines.

5. Better qualifications for the most selective colleges and improved chance of being admitted to them.
6. Getting into college, graduate school, and a profession earlier, thus having more time and energy for creative pursuits.
7. Increased opportunities to explore more specialties and hobbies.
8. More time to explore various careers before marriage.
9. Less cost. Most accelerative procedures save the student and/or the parents money. Even skipping the last year of junior high school and going into senior high school a year early eliminates a year that the student must be supported at home. Eight credits earned by means of an Advanced Placement Program examination in calculus were worth nearly $2,300 of tuition at Johns Hopkins in the fall of 1984, and such costs tend to rise almost every year. Graduating from college in 3 years rather than 4 saves about one-fourth of all costs and can lead to paid full-time employment a year earlier than otherwise.
10. Being an unusually well-prepared, advanced, entrant to college often brings the student to the attention of professors, who help him or her get started on important research early. This, in turn, usually leads to better graduate school opportunities, including improved financial support there. For example, five of SMPY's six radically accelerated youths who were graduated from college in 1977 at ages 15 to 18 won National Science Foundation 3-year graduate fellowships (Nevin, 1977; *Time*, 1977).
11. It seems likely that accelerants will have considerably greater success in life, both professionally and personally, than if held age-in-grade (Stanley & Benbow, 1983). That likelihood may, however, depend rather strongly on the accelerant's ability to acquire the necessary tacit knowledge (Wagner & Sternberg, 1985).

Benefits to society

Presumably, whatever helps a sizable group of talented individuals use their abilities better should also benefit the larger society. It is easy to see that a number of the points made above about benefits to SMPY participants themselves fall into this category. Below are listed a few other, somewhat related, gains that society itself can expect from the four *D*'s of SMPY and similar programs.

1. Students superbly prepared to major in the mathematical sciences, physical sciences, quantitative social sciences, and other areas where mathematical talent and keen analytical ability are essential or helpful.
2. More years of professional contribution and effective adulthood.
3. More income and sales taxes paid over a longer period of time.
4. Happier, more effective citizens who should understand better how to educate their own children.
5. Reduced cost of education. The policies and activities that SMPY espouses save school systems and colleges money rather than increase educational expenditures. When a student who already knows first-year algebra is moved into Algebra II, room for another pupil is created in the Algebra I class. Also, the teacher is free to work more effectively with the class, because a potential distracter or irritant has been removed. When a student skips an entire school grade, the cost of educating him or her that year is saved. If several years of precalculus mathematics can be learned in one year, a great saving of time and resources ensues. Passing introductory college calculus

by examination increases room in the class and enriches the next mathematics course by moving an able, well-motivated student directly into it. Students who go through selective colleges in 3 years rather than the usual 4 enable those schools to handle more students.

It would be naïve to assume that special policies and provisions for mathematically highly talented youths do not require any extra efforts. Much of the identification, study, and implementation, however, can be done by regular personnel in the mathematics supervisor's office. Even if in a strict cost-accounting sense the mathematically precocious were to cost a little extra, it would be an almost negligible amount relative to the expenditures for other types of special education within most school systems.

An often overlooked factor reducing the cost of working with intellectually gifted youths is the tremendous output one often gets for small inputs. A few instructional minutes spent with a brilliant youth can produce amazing results. This contrasts sharply with the much greater amount of time that must be devoted to a slow learner in order to get even moderate gains. Similarly, counseling SMPY participants and their parents by memorandum, telephone, letter, or case conference does not usually require a great deal of time but often produces striking changes in their education.

The two sentences with which I ended the first chapter of the first volume of *Studies of Intellectual Precocity* seem appropriate here: "Expensive curricular adjustments are made, quite justifiably, for slow learners. It is past time that fast learners get the much less costly 'special education' they deserve" (Stanley, 1974, p. 19).[5]

Scarce resources and elitism

But even after the above points, some readers may still feel that any special attention to highly precocious youths is an unwarranted and unnecessary diversion of scarce resources. Won't the talented boy or girl get along well with the regular resources of the school? Don't elective courses and the considerable array of honors-type subjects in senior high school (calculus being an example) take care of the needs of the gifted satisfactorily? Why provide more for those who already have so much? Isn't that elitism and, therefore, contrary to the American way of life? One could argue endlessly about the philosophical content of these questions. Empirically, however, the answer is clear: Many of the youths in the top few percent of their age-mates with respect to mathematical reasoning ability can learn mathematics and related subjects faster and better than the curricula of most schools permit. If held to the age–grade lock-step, a large percentage of them will develop poor work habits and lose interest in the area. Even those who do not would usually benefit from better opportunities. Thus, a laissez-faire policy for education of the mathematically talented is misguided. Perhaps "genius will out," but much of the superior talent with which SMPY deals is unlikely to do so if unaided.

Talent versus genius

Many persons seem hostile toward intellectually talented youths, perhaps a little less so toward those splendid in mathematics than toward the verbally precocious. This contrasts sharply with the American public's generally favorable attitudes toward prodigies in music and athletics. Friedenberg (1966) and Stanley (1974), among others, have discussed how deep-seated this prejudice is. Expressions such as the following abound in literature back to Shakespeare's time: "Early ripe, early rot"; "So wise so young, they say, do never live long"; "For precocity some great price is always demanded sooner or later in life"; and "Their productions . . . bear the marks of precocity and premature decay" (Stanley, 1974, pp. 1–2).

We noted earlier that one disguise for dislike of the intellectually talented is to argue that they need no special help; it is assumed that they will succeed well educationally without it. Another tactic we have noticed is the comparison of a highly able youth with Gauss, Euler, Fermat, Galois, Pascal, Newton, or (especially) Einstein, a sort of reductio ad absurdum denigration of the former's intellectual talent by asserting that it is not the rarest genius. Terman encountered a great deal of this. Some reviewers criticized him because in his one-state sample, identified in a short while, he did not discover anyone who later became a worthy successor to the greatest musicians, artists, and writers of all time. Some insight into problems of defining and predicting genius may be obtained from Albert (1975) and Bell (1937).

Obviously, in SMPY's and CTY's 11 annual talent searches thus far in the Northeast we do not expect to have located or helped produce Nobel laureates, much less successors to Gauss or Einstein. To find someone even of the caliber of Norbert Wiener (1953, 1956) is perhaps more than we can reasonably expect.

On the other hand, we believe that SMPY is helping a number of exceptionally able young men and women go far beyond what they would probably have done without our intervention. That is sufficient for us: effective enhancement of talent, rather than the creation of genius. We might have been able to help a lonely, awkward person such as Wiener use his great talents better at an earlier age, and probably Einstein would have scored quite high in a contest like ours had he deigned to enter it, but those two men are examples of persons who somehow achieved magnificently anyway. If one has already thrown a coin and it has landed with the "head" side up, what is the probability of *that* occurrence? This is a foolish question, of course, but no more simplistic than reasoning from the success of Einstein and Wiener that great intellectual talent will lead inevitably to success. Those country churchyards chronicled by the poet Thomas Gray long ago hold their share of "mute, inglorious" Wieners and Einsteins as well as of Miltons. We suspect that many classrooms also serve as tombs for mathematical talent.

A strong bond

SMPY's top participants differ considerably in most personal characteristics except age. Some are tall and others are short. Some are introverted, others are extroverted. Some are much better verbal reasoners than others (range, 280–760V before age 13). Some are males and others are females. In fact, they probably differ at least as much from each other as do youths their age who are only average mathematically. These students have one important thing in common, however: They entered a challenging mathematical aptitude search and scored extremely well on a difficult mathematical reasoning test designed to be used with above-average students three to five years older than they. This powerful commonality reminds us of the famous lines from Rudyard Kipling's "The Ballad of East and West":

> Oh, East is East, and West is West, and never the
>   twain shall meet,
> Till Earth and Sky stand presently at God's great
>   Judgment Seat;
> But there is neither East nor West, Border, nor
>   Breed, nor Birth,
> When two strong men stand face to face, though
>   they come from the ends of the earth!

Read Kipling's male-chauvinistic "two strong men" as "mathematically highly precocious youths" and you have a summing-up of the rationale for SMPY. We believe that mathematical talent transcends sex, circumstance, and nationality and mandates special educational treatment of mathematical prodigies with respect to their area(s) of great talent. We consider accelerative procedures crucial because – to paraphrase Robert Browning – "a mathematically precocious youth's reach should exceed his or her grasp, or what's an educational system for?" We at SMPY will continue helping to extend both the reach and the grasp of youths who reason extremely well mathematically.[6]

Notes

1 It is well for the reader to keep in mind the nature of these five volumes, the years in which they appeared, and the fact that their publisher (the Stanford University Press) has kept the whole series in print for more than half a century. References are as follows: Terman (1925), Cox (1926), Burks, Jensen, and Terman (1930), and Terman and Oden (1947, 1959). Work reported in those volumes has been extended by Oden (1968), Sears and Barbee (1977), R. Sears (1977), and Ohanian (1977).
2 For SAT's history and rationale, see Downey (1961).

3 Even more psychometrically precocious was the boy of Chinese background who at age 10 years, 1 month scored 600 on SAT-V and 680 on SAT-M, and a year later scored 710V and 750M. (For his further achievements, see Stanley and Benbow 1983.) SMPY's youngest college graduate thus far is Jay Luo, born April 4, 1970, who received his BS degree in mathematics with honors from Boise (Idaho) State University in May of 1982. In the fall of 1982 he enrolled as a graduate student in mathematics at Stanford University. In 1985, at age 15, Mr. Luo began his fourth year there.

4 In 1979, SMPY helped create at Johns Hopkins the Office of Talent Identification and Development (OTID), now called the Center for the Advancement of Academically Talented Youth (CTY), to run the talent searches and conduct special educational activities. CTY, directed by Dr. William G. Durden, has done so since 1980.

5 The other eight volumes of that SIP series are by Keating (1976), Stanley, George, and Solano (1977, 1978), George, Cohn, and Stanley (1979), Fox, Brody, and Tobin (1980), Bartkovich and George (1980), Fox and Durden (1982), and Benbow and Stanley (1983a).

6 For some complementary or contrasting points of view, see Feldhusen (1983), Feldman (1979), Gallagher (1979), Laycock (1979), Michael (1983), Renzulli (1977), Tannenbaum (1983), Torrance (1977), and Wallach (1978).

References

Albert, R. S. (1975). Toward a behavioral definition of genius. *American Psychologist, 30* (2), 140–51.

Barlow, F. (1952). *Mental prodigies: An enquiry into the faculties of arithmetical, chess and musical prodigies, famous memorizers, precocious children and the like, with numerous examples of "lightning" calculations and mental magic.* New York: Philosophical Library.

Bartkovich, K. G., & George, W. C. (1980). *Teaching the gifted and talented in the mathematics classroom.* Washington, D. C.: National Education Association. [Obtainable from NEA Distribution Center, the Academic Building, Saw Mill Road, West Haven, Connecticut 06515]

Bartkovich, K. G., & Mezynski, K. (1981, Spring). Fast-paced precalculus mathematics for talented junior high students: Two recent SMPY programs. *Gifted Child Quarterly, 25*(2), 73–80.

Bayley, N. (1955). On the growth of intelligence. *American Psychologist, 10*, 805–818.

Bayley, N. (1970). Development of mental abilities. In P. H. Mussen (Ed.), *Carmichael's manual of child psychology* (3rd ed., Vol. 1). New York: Wiley.

Bell, E. T. (1937). *Men of mathematics.* New York: Simon & Schuster.

Benbow, C. P. (1981). *Development of superior mathematical ability during adolescence.* Unpublished doctoral dissertation, Johns Hopkins University.

Benbow, C. P. (1983). Adolescence of the mathematically precocious: A five-year longitudinal study. In C. P. Benbow and J. C. Stanley (Eds.), *Academic precocity: Aspects of its development* (pp. 9–29). Baltimore: Johns Hopkins University Press.

Benbow, C. P., Perkins, S., & Stanley, J. C. (1983). Mathematics taught at a fast pace: A longitudinal evaluation of the first class. In C. P. Benbow & J. C. Stanley (Eds.), *Academic precocity: Aspects of its development* (pp. 51–70). Baltimore: Johns Hopkins University Press.

Benbow, C. P., & Stanley, J. C. (1981). Mathematical ability: Is sex a factor? *Science, 212,* 118–119.

Benbow, C. P., & Stanley, J. C. (1982a, Spring). Intellectually talented boys and girls: Educational profiles. *Gifted Child Quarterly, 26*(2), 82–88.

Benbow, C. P., & Stanley, J. C. (1982b, Winter). Consequences in high school and college of sex differences in mathematical reasoning ability: A longitudinal perspective. *American Educational Research Journal, 19*(4), 598–622.

Benbow, C. P., & Stanley, J. C. (Eds.) (1983a). *Academic precocity: Aspects of its development.* Baltimore: Johns Hopkins University Press.

Benbow, C. P., & Stanley, J. C. (1983b). Constructing bridges between high school and college. *Gifted Child Quarterly, 27,* 111–113.

Benbow, C. P., & Stanley, J. C. (1983c). Opening doors for the gifted. *American Education, 19*(3), 44–46.

Benbow, C. P., & Stanley, J. C. (1983d). Sex differences in mathematical reasoning ability: More facts. *Science, 212,* 1029–1031.

Bloom, B. S. (Ed.). (1956). *Taxonomy of educational objectives: Handbook 1. The cognitive domain.* New York: McKay.

Burks, B. S., Jensen, D. W., & Terman, L. M. (1930). *Genetic studies of genius: Vol. 3. The promise of youth: Follow-up studies of a thousand gifted children.* Stanford, Calif.: Stanford University Press.

Burt, C. L. (1975). *The gifted child.* New York: Wiley.

Campbell, D. T., & Stanley, J. C. (1966). *Experimental and quasi-experimental designs for research.* Chicago: Rand McNally.

Cox, C. M. (1926). *Genetic studies of genius: Vol. 2. The early mental traits of three hundred geniuses.* Stanford, Calif.: Stanford University Press.

Daurio, S. P. (1979). Educational enrichment versus acceleration: A review of the literature. In W. C. George, S. J. Cohn, & J. C. Stanley (Eds.), *Educating the gifted: Acceleration and enrichment* (pp. 13–63). Baltimore: Johns Hopkins University Press.

Donlon, T. F., & Angoff, W. H. (1971). The Scholastic Aptitude Test. In W. Angoff (Ed.), *The College Board admissions testing program.* Princeton, N.J.: College Entrance Examination Board.

Downey, M. T. (1961). *Carl Campbell Brigham: Scientist and educator.* Princeton, N. J.: Educational Testing Service.

Eisenberg, A. R. (1977). Academic acceleration and the relationships between age and grade-point average. Baltimore: Study of Mathematically Precocious Youth, Department of Psychology, The Johns Hopkins University.

Favazza, A. (1983). *The relationship of verbal ability to mathematics achievement in a fast-paced precalculus program.* Unpublished doctoral dissertation, The Johns Hopkins University.

Feldhusen, J. F. (1983). Eclecticism: A comprehensive approach to the education of the gifted. In C. P. Benbow & J. C. Stanley (Eds.), *Academic precocity: Aspects of its development* (pp. 192–204). Baltimore: Johns Hopkins University Press.

Feldman, D. H. (1979). The mysterious case of extreme giftedness. In A. H. Passow (Ed.), *The gifted and the talented: Their education and development* (pp. 335–351). The Seventy-eighth Yearbook of the National Society for the Study of Education, Part I. Chicago: University of Chicago Press.

Fox, L. H. (1974). A mathematics program for fostering precocious achievement. In J. C. Stanley, D. P. Keating, & L. H. Fox (Eds.), *Mathematical talent: Discovery, description, and development* (pp. 101–125). Baltimore: Johns Hopkins University Press.

Fox, L. H. (1976). Sex differences in mathematical precocity: Bridging the gap. In D. P. Keating (Ed.), *Intellectual talent: Research and development* (pp. 32–54). Baltimore: Johns Hopkins University Press.

Fox, L. H., Brody, L., & Tobin, D. (Eds.). (1980). *Women and the mathematical mystique.* Baltimore: Johns Hopkins University Press.

Fox, L. H., & Durden, W. G. (1982). *Educating verbally gifted youth.* Bloomington, Ind.: Phi Delta Kappa Educational Foundation.

Friedenberg, E. Z. (1966). The gifted student and his enemies. In E. Z. Friedenberg, *The dignity of youth and other atavisms* (pp. 119–135). Boston: Beacon Press.

Fund for the Advancement of Education of the Ford Foundation. (1953). *Bridging the gap between school and college.* New York: Research Division of the Fund.

Fund for the Advancement of Education of the Ford Foundation. (1957). *They went to college early.* New York: Research Division of the Fund.

Gallagher, J. J. (1979). Issues in education for the gifted. In A. H. Passow (Ed.), *The gifted and the talented: Their education and development* (pp. 335–351). The Seventy-eighth Yearbook of the National Society for the Study of Education, Part I. Chicago: University of Chicago Press.

George, W. C. (1976). Accelerating mathematics instruction for the mathematically talented. *Gifted Child Quarterly, 20*(3), 246–261.

George, W. C. (1979). The talent-search concept: An identification strategy for the intellectually gifted. *Journal of Special Education, 13*(3), 222–237.

George, W. C., Cohn, S. J., & Stanley, J. C. (Eds.). (1979). *Educating the gifted: Acceleration and enrichment.* Baltimore: Johns Hopkins University Press.

George, W. C., & Denham, S. A. (1976). Curriculum experimentation for the mathematically talented. In D. P. Keating (Ed.), *Intellectual talent: Research and development* (pp. 103–31). Baltimore: Johns Hopkins University Press.

Hardy, G. H. (1967). *A mathematician's apology.* Cambridge University Press.

Hilgard, E. R., & Bower, G. H. (1974). *Theories of learning* (4th ed.). Englewood Cliffs, N.J.: Prentice-Hall.

Hobson, J. R. (1963, Spring). High school performance of underage pupils initially admitted to kindergarten on the basis of physical and psychological examinations. *Educational and Psychological Measurement, 33*(1), 159–170.

Hollingworth, L. S. (1942). *Children above 180 IQ Stanford–Binet: Origin and development.* New York: World Book.

Hudson, L. (1975). *Human beings: The psychology of human experience.* New York: Doubleday (Anchor Books).

Hunt, J. M. (1961). *Intelligence and experience.* New York: Ronald Press.

Keating, D. P. (1975). Precocious cognitive development at the level of formal operations. *Child Development, 46*, 276–280.

Keating, D. P. (Ed.). (1976). *Intellectual talent: Research and development.* Baltimore: Johns Hopkins University Press.

Keating, D. P., & Schaefer, R. A. (1975). Ability and sex differences in the acquisition of formal operations. *Developmental Psychology, 11*(4), 531–532.

Keating, D. P., & Stanley, J. C. (1972). Extreme measures for the exceptionally gifted in mathematics and science. *Educational Researcher, 1*(9), 3–7.

Kramer, E. A. (1974). *Nature and growth of modern mathematics* (2 vols.). New York: Fawcett World Library.

Laycock, F. (1979). *Gifted children.* Glenview, Ill: Scott, Foresman.

Lehman, H. C. (1953). *Age and achievement.* Princeton, N.J.: Princeton University Press.

Macken, E., van den Heuvel, R., Suppes, P., & Suppes, T. (1976). Home-based computer-assisted instruction for gifted students. *Home-based education: Needs and technological opportunities* (pp. 49–71). Washington, D.C.: National Institute of Education, U.S. Department of Health, Education, and Welfare.

Mezynski, K., & Stanley, J. C. (1980, November). Advanced placement oriented calculus for high school students. *Journal for Research in Mathematics Education, 11*(5), 347–355.

Mezynski, K., Stanley, J. C., & McCoart, R. F. (1983). Helping youths score well on AP examinations in calculus, chemistry, and physics. In C. P. Benbow & J. C. Stanley (Eds.), *Academic precocity: Aspects of its development* (pp. 86–112). Baltimore: Johns Hopkins University Press.

Michael, W. B. (1983). Manifestation of creative behaviors by maturing participants in the Study of Mathematically Precocious Youth. In C. P. Benbow & J. C. Stanley (Eds.), *Academic precocity: Aspects of its development* (pp. 38–50). Baltimore: Johns Hopkins University Press.

Mill, J. S. (1924). *Autobiography of John Stuart Mill.* New York: Columbia University Press.

Montour, K. M. (1975, May 15). Success vs. tragedy. *ITYB* [Intellectually Talented Youth Bulletin, published by SMPY], *1*(9), 3.

Montour, K. M. (1976a, March 15). Merrill Kenneth Wolf: A bachelor's degree at 14. *ITYB* 2(7), 1–2.

Montour, K. M. (1976b, April). Charles Louis Fefferman: Youngest American full professor? *ITYB*, 2(8), 2.

Montour, K. M. (1977). William James Sidis, the broken twig. *American Psychologist, 32*(4), 265–279.

Nevin, D. (1977, October). Young prodigies take off under special program. *Smithsonian*, 8(7), 76–82, 160.

Oden, M. H. (1968, February). The fulfillment of promise: 40-year follow-up of the Terman gifted group. *Genetic Psychology Monographs*, 77(1st half), 3–93.

Ohanian, P. B. (1977). A musically and artistically talented family nearly half a century later. In J. C. Stanley, W. C. George, & C. H. Solano (Eds.), *The gifted and the creative: A fifty-year perspective* (pp. 66–72). Baltimore: Johns Hopkins University Press.

Packe, M. S. J. (1954). *The life of John Stuart Mill*. New York: Macmillan.

Pollins, L. M. (1983). The effects of acceleration on the social and emotional development of gifted students. In C. P. Benbow & J. C. Stanley (Eds.), *Academic precocity: Aspects of its development* (pp. 160–178). Baltimore: Johns Hopkins University Press.

Polya, G. (1973). *How to solve it* (2nd ed.). Princeton, N.J.: Princeton University Press.

Pressey, S. L. (1949). Educational acceleration: Appraisals and basic problems. *Bureau of Educational Research Monographs* (No. 31). Ohio State University, Columbus.

Renzulli, J. S. (1977). *The enrichment triad model: A guide for developing defensible programs for the gifted and talented*. Mansfield Center, Conn: Creative Learning Press.

Robinson, H. B. (1983). A case for radical acceleration: Programs of The Johns Hopkins University and the University of Washington. In C. P. Benbow & J. C. Stanley (Eds.), *Academic promise: Aspects of its development* (pp. 139–159). Baltimore: Johns Hopkins University Press.

Robinson, N. M., & Robinson, H. B. (1976). *The mentally retarded child* (2nd ed.). New York: McGraw-Hill.

Roe, A. (1951). A psychological study of eminent physical scientists. *Genetic Psychology Monographs, 43*, 121–239.

Schonberg, H. C. (1970). *The lives of the great composers*. New York: Norton.

Sears, P. S., & Barbee, A. H. (1977). Career and life satisfactions among Terman's gifted women. In J. C. Stanley, W. C. George, & C. H. Solano (Eds.), *The gifted and the creative: A fifty-year perspective* (pp. 28–65). Baltimore: Johns Hopkins University Press.

Sears, R. R. (1977). Sources of life satisfactions of the Terman gifted men. *American Psychologist, 32*(2), 119–128.

Smith, S. B. (1984). *The great mental calculators: The psychology, methods, and lives of calculating prodigies, past and present*. New York: Columbia University Press.

Stanley, J. C. (1954). Is the fast learner getting a fair deal in your school? *Wisconsin Journal of Education, 86*(10), 5–6.

Stanley, J. C. (1958, Spring). Providing for the gifted by means of enrichment of the curriculum. *Bulletin of the Wisconsin Association of Secondary School Principals*, pp. 5–7.

Stanley, J. C. (1959). Enriching high-school subjects for intellectually gifted students. *School and Society*, 87(2151), 170–171.

Stanley, J. C. (1973). Designing psychological experiments. In B. B. Wolman (Ed.), *Handbook of general psychology* (pp. 90–106). Englewood Cliffs, N.J.: Prentice-Hall.

Stanley, J. C. (1974). Intellectual precocity. In J. C. Stanley, D. P. Keating, & L. H. Fox (Eds.), *Mathematical talent: Discovery, description, and development* (pp. 1–22). Baltimore: Johns Hopkins University Press.

Stanley, J. C. (1976a). Use of tests to discover talent. In D. P. Keating (Ed.), *Intellectual talent: Research and development* (pp. 3–22). Baltimore: Johns Hopkins University Press.

Stanley, J. C. (1976b). Special fast-math classes taught by college professors to fourth- through twelfth-graders. In D. P. Keating (Ed.), *Intellectual talent: Research and development* (pp. 132–159). Baltimore: Johns Hopkins University Press.

Stanley, J. C. (1976c, March). The student gifted in mathematics and science. *NAASP* [National Association of Secondary School Principals] *Bulletin, 60*(398), 28–37.

Stanley, J. C. (1976d, April). Tests better finder of great math talent than teachers are. *American Psychologist, 31*(4), 313–314.

Stanley, J. C. (1976e, Spring). The case for extreme educational acceleration of intellectually brilliant youths. *Gifted Child Quarterly, 20*(1), 66–75, 41.

Stanley, J. C. (1976f). Concern for intellectually talented youths: How it originated and fluctuated. *Journal of Clinical Child Psychology, 5*(3), 38–42.

Stanley, J. C. (1977). Rationale of the Study of Mathematically Precocious Youth (SMPY) during its first five years of promoting educational acceleration. In J. C. Stanley, W. C. George, & C. H. Solano (Eds.), *The gifted and the creative: A fifty-year perspective* (pp. 75–112). Baltimore: Johns Hopkins University Press.

Stanley, J. C., & Benbow, C. P. (1982). Educating mathematically precocious youths: Twelve policy recommendations. *Educational Researcher, 11*(5), 4–9.

Stanley, J. C., & Benbow, C. P. (1983, Summer). Extremely young college graduates: Evidence of their success. *College and University, 58*(4), 361–371.

Stanley, J. C., George, W. C., & Solano, C. H. (Eds.). (1977). *The gifted and the creative: A fifty-year perspective*. Baltimore: Johns Hopkins University Press.

Stanley, J. C., George, W. C., & Solano, C. H. (Eds.). (1978). *Educational programs and intellectual prodigies*. Baltimore: Study of Mathematically Precocious Youth, Department of Psychology, The Johns Hopkins University.

Stanley, J. C., Keating, D. P., & Fox, L. H. (Eds.). (1974). *Mathematical talent: Discovery, description, and development*. Baltimore: Johns Hopkins University Press.

Tannenbaum, A. J. (1983). *Gifted children: Psychological and educational perspectives*. New York: Macmillan.

Terman, L. M. (1925). *Genetic studies of genius: Vol. 1. Mental and physical traits of a thousand gifted children*. Stanford, Calif.: Stanford University Press.

Terman, L. M. (1954). Scientists and nonscientists in a group of 800 gifted men. *Psychological Monographs, 68*(7) (Whole No. 378, 44 pages).

Terman, L. M., & Oden, M. H. (1947). *Genetic studies of genius: Vol. 4. The gifted child grows up*. Stanford, Calif.: Stanford University Press.

Terman, L. M., & Oden, M. H. (1959). *Genetic studies of genius: Vol. 5. The gifted group at mid-life: Thirty-five years' follow-up of the superior child*. Stanford, Calif.: Stanford University Press.

Time. (1977). Smorgasbord for an IQ of 150. *109*(23), 64.

Torrance, E. P. (1977). Creatively gifted and disadvantaged gifted students. In J. C. Stanley, W. C. George, & C. H. Solano (Eds.), *The gifted and the creative: A fifty-year perspective* (pp. 173–196). Baltimore: Johns Hopkins University Press.

Wagner, R. K., & Sternberg, R. J. (1985). Practical intelligence in real-world pursuits: The role of tacit knowledge. *Journal of Personality and Social Psychology, 49*, 436–458.

Wallach, M. A. (1978). Care and feeding of the gifted. *Contemporary Psychology, 23*, 616–617.

Watson, J. D. (1968). *The double helix: A personal account of the discovery of the structure of DNA*. New York: Atheneum.

Wiener, N. (1953). *Ex-prodigy*. Cambridge, Mass.: MIT Press.

Wiener, N. (1956). *I am a mathematician*. Cambridge, Mass.: MIT Press.

Worcester, D. A. (1956). *The education of children of* above-average *mentality*. Lincoln: University of Nebraska Press.

Young, P. (1972). The transistor's coinventor makes history with a super-cold superprize. *National Observer, 11*(50), 1, 22.

Zuckerman, H. (1977). *Scientific elite: Nobel Laureates in the United States*. New York: Free Press.

17   Cognitive issues in the development of musically gifted children

Jeanne Bamberger

Little is known about the development of children who demonstrate extraordinary musical ability at an early age. However, there is growing anecdotal evidence to suggest that as they approach adulthood they face a critical turning point in their careers. I have termed this period of critical reappraisal the "midlife crisis" – midlife for those whose public careers may have begun at 5 or 6 (Bamberger, 1982).

For some of these prodigious individuals this is the end of development and the end of their promising careers; for some it is a painful period of reassessment and reflection that they pass through successfully – a passage from early prodigiousness to adult artistry.

Although undoubtedly a multitude of factors contribute to this midlife crisis – social, maturational, and career issues – I have proposed that specifically cognitive changes are a significant contributing factor as well (Bamberger, 1982). In particular I have argued that during this period young performers undergo significant changes in their internal representation of musical structure itself.

To pursue these proposals it seemed essential, first, to gain some insight into the nature of mental representations that serve young performers so well. That is, if we could gain a better understanding of these earlier cognitive structures, we might then be more likely to understand the changes that occur during the later critical periods. In considering the transition from early prodigiousness to adult artistry, then, we need to be able to answer the question Transitions *from* and conflicts *with* what?

In an effort to do so, I have made close observations of five musically gifted children between the ages of 7 and 10 in their natural working environments and also in experimental task situations. In brief, these studies have led to the following conclusions and implications:

1. Gifted young performers have an unusual capacity for representing musical relations to themselves in multiple ways. This is seen in observations of their

The work reported here was supported by a grant from the Spencer Foundation.

388

everyday work, and also in experimental situations, as an ability to move their attention freely among the complexity of intersecting musical dimensions that together give unique coherence to even a single moment in a composition.

2. At the same time, in the work of practicing, in lessons, and in the children's extraordinary abilities for all-at-once imitation, they neither represent nor name these multiple dimensions as separate, individual realms. Rather they are represented as a single network – the reciprocal result of intertwined, intersecting relations.

3. Although specific experimental evidence remains still to be generated, it is possible, with these initial findings, to speculate on the nature of changes that earlier representations may undergo during the transitions associated with adolescence. Consider the following: In experimental situations, the younger children's multiple representations of musical structure could be *artificially* teased apart, even made to come into conflict with one another. But in adolescence, multiple dimensions and their internal representations similarly come apart, but now quite *spontaneously*. During this period of transition with its natural need to reflect, to question and analyze, complexly interactive dimensions are not only named separately but are perhaps even reified. In practicing, focus shifts among these now differentiated dimensions, priorities among them are weighed, and decisions become self-conscious as possibilities are considered that may project particular meanings for a given passage.

4. As a result, the functional reciprocity within the network of representations that so characterizes younger performers – and the easy, all-at-once imitation it made possible – no longer works.

5. This leaves gifted adolescents with a new problem, namely, one of developing means for coordinating these now separate musical dimensions and their underlying representations – representations that before seemed to function as a single, reciprocally interactive web in guiding their performance actions and decisions. And if they succeed in carrying out this cognitive reorganization, then the critical period can become an effective transition from the remarkable but nonreflective performance of the prodigious child to the thoughtful but still spontaneous artistic performance of the adult.

Having made these speculative comments, I shall concentrate the rest of my discussion on the observations in natural settings and on the children's work in the experimental task situations. In my conclusions I shall return briefly to their implication for an understanding of the midlife crisis.

Observations in natural settings

Observations were carried out in the context of the Young Performers Program at the Longy School of Music in Cambridge, Massachusetts. Over a period of 6 months I observed 5 gifted young violinists between the ages of 7 and 11. These children were part of a group of 16 gifted performers between the ages of 7 and 12 who made up the junior group in the program.[1] Activities in the program occupy the full day (9:00 to 5:30) on Saturdays. The children attend regular schools during the week.

Observations included all the usual activities the children participated in:

private violin lessons, chamber music rehearsals and coaching sessions, theory classes, orchestra rehearsals, master classes and public performances. In addition, I had follow-up interviews with teachers and coaches and also continuing informal discussions with parents.

Definition of terms

The term *musical dimensions* ordinarily refers to features and relations *given* in a piece – pitch, pitch-relations as generated by a sequence of pitches, durations, phrase structure, accent structure, melodic and harmonic functions, texture, instrumentation, and the like. *Internal representation* ordinarily refers to a mind and to the features and relations of some process or some phenomena that are taken to be "representable" in or by a particular mind. But put this way, we have a patently untenable formulation because it does not allow us to account for demonstrably different "hearings" or "interpretations" of a piece that occur across analyses or performances by different individuals or by the same individual at different times.

We cannot assume that elements and relations of a unique composition are simply *given* by the score, but we must assume rather that there are crucial interactions between the presented phenomenon and the active mental processes of a particular mind as it shapes that phenomenon. In turn, what we take to be "representable" by various minds can only be inferred from observations of an individual's actions, judgments, decisions, or descriptions in response to some phenomenon presented to him. From these external responses we can, for example, say something about an individual's implicit assigning of priorities among musical dimensions, even what he has access to, or takes to exist as possible entities and possible relations as these lead to a particular performance or even a particular "hearing." Thus, in analyzing the children's work I make the assumption that musical dimensions and internal representations are in a dynamically reciprocal relation to one another.

Results and discussion: fields of attention

It was in observations of teachers and students in natural settings that evidence initially emerged for the claim concerning multiple representations of musical elements and relations. The use of such multiple representations was seen in the continuing shifts in focus of attention during lessons and chamber music coaching sessions. Later, as a result of close analysis, I identified particular contexts within which these shifts occurred. I have given the name *fields of attention* to these contexts.

Fields of attention can be characterized as conceptual mini-worlds within which ordinary work and learning take place – conversation, instruction, practicing. The robustness of the fields is evidenced in that units of description and kinds of language are unique to each field separately. In turn, we can infer that each field entrains differing units of internal representation, differing ontologies. The fields of attention are important because they spawn the use of different sensory modalities, different media, and different symbol systems. As such they provide possibilities for different ways of conceptualizing, even seeing or hearing the same moment in a piece, as well as different ways of solving the same problem. The fields of attention are, then, the contexts in which the repertoire of multiple internal representations develops.

I shall first characterize each of the four fields studied thus far and then give two brief examples of moves through them taken from an actual violin lesson.

The instrument and actions on it. Given the violin as instrument, pitch and melodic configurations are represented as *places and distances between places* on the four violin strings. These are, in turn, represented as *configurations of actions*. The internal feel for the physical interaction of hand and arm with the geography of the instrument takes the form of a kinesthetic internal representation of a musical passage – what we might call the "image" of a passage in the hand. In this field, violinists refer most particularly to "bowing and fingering." For example, a particular pitch might be referred to as "third finger on the E string." Common problems in this field involve decisions concerning whether to play a passage in "first or second position" when position refers to the various possible relations between the place of a pitch on one or another string and its fingerings.[2] Bowing, in turn, involves decisions as to whether to play a passage in "one bow" or to change, for instance, from "up-bow" to "down-bow." Bowing relates to and influences decisions concerning rhythm, phrasing, accent, dynamics, and more. In this field, then, a passage or a whole piece is represented as what I have called a "felt path" – a learned sequence of actions on a familiar instrument that on the largest scale results in the performance of an entire composition.

Notation – the score. The score provides *symbolically* encoded information for these same pitches and rhythms. But clearly the information encoded as notes on the staff is fundamentally different in *kind* from that internally represented as a felt path on an instrument. Interestingly, marks indicating fingering and bowing are constantly written on or added to the score by student or teacher or chamber player. These markings become, then, another layer of the score that contains a different kind of information from the notes as encoded in standard music notation. The process, in turn, becomes an important means for coordinating the kinesthetic instrument field with the symbolic notation field.

Sound. Here, pitch and rhythm as well as tone, dynamics, and the like are what are actually produced on the spot by the performer and the instrument. In turn, the field includes inner, imagined sound toward which the performer is striving. The latter is often acquired by listening to recordings or through imitation of the teacher's example. In particular it involves, on the local level, listening back to one's own playing so as, for instance, to adjust for playing in tune. Or, on a more global level, matching one's immediate, live actions to models such as those mentioned earlier. Here, representation is in terms of sound itself, as this is actively held in memory and as it is produced.

Musical structure. This field has a somewhat different, perhaps more abstract, status. It includes attention, on one hand, to smaller structural relations of a piece such as groupings of events into figures, and on the other, to larger relations such as where figures return and how they are developed, as well as the long line of a piece as it moves toward a climax and then to its resolution. This field was exemplified in one session when the teacher, after working on intonation, bowing, and fingering, said, "Now let's look at what holds the piece together." Here, pitch–rhythm configurations are represented as functional entities embedded in the unique context of *this* piece. Unlike in the other fields of attention, the focus is not on a medium (instrument, sound, score) but rather on the more abstract relations that give a piece its coherence.

   Two small examples from an actual violin lesson should make the robustness of these fields vividly clear. The teacher, helping his student with a difficult passage, moved her attention rapidly through three different views of the same passage, each view belonging to a different field:

Teacher's comments:	*Field of attention:*
"You have three times the same figure, here."	(Structure)
"It's written so you can't notice it."	(Score)
"Use the same bowing, then you'll feel that they are the same."	(Instrument)

And later in the same lesson the teacher said:

"And now we come once more to the beginning."	(Structural function)
"It's like a memory – vague."	
"Don't play it so loud."	(Sound/instrument)

   In the first example the teacher focuses on repetition of a figure ("three times the same figure") that is important to the *structural* design of the piece. However, the way it's written, in the *score*, obscures this repetition ("It's written so you can't notice it"). But by shifting focus from the score to the medium of the instrument and to the kinesthetic modality ("Use the same bowing"), the sameness of the figures emerges because they "feel . . . the same."

In the second example, the use of an explicit image ("like a memory") serves as another instance of the same process. Pointing first to the *structural* function of the passage, a return (" . . . once more . . . the beginning"), the teacher brings the student to another view of "return" by suggesting a qualitatively similar experience in other media ("memory – vague"). The teacher then moves quickly on to how to project this function in the media of the *instrument* and *sound* – quite simply, "Don't play so loud." But this last simple directive becomes more than that through its association with the other views of the passage, all of which *coalesce into \ a single performance* that expresses both feeling and form.

In both examples we see student and teacher experimenting with same and different as they move through the modes and media associated with the various fields of attention: A repeated figure can *look* different in notation but must be made to *sound* the same on the instrument; a passage can be the same in pitch – a return – but still played so as to sound different.

Through the easy moves among these fields of attention, learning becomes an evolving process of building a repertoire of *possible* representations. As a configuration is seen now with one focus of attention, now with another, media, sensory modalities, and the multiple dimensions of musical structure evolve together through a process of dynamic interaction. And most important, although the fields of attention can, on careful analysis, be identified and named as separate foci, the easy movement among them keeps them functionally interconnected, mappable onto one another – an actively intertwined web.[3]

This functional, nonanalytic interactiveness is perhaps best seen in the children's capacities for all-at-once imitation. That is, while the children are encouraged in lessons to work on a passage in many different ways, they also learn by the wholistic *feel* of "doing as I do." For example, the child listens to and attentively watches his teacher play a particular passage and plays it back replete with the same bodily gestures and with the same subtlety of detail. Children imitate the playing of their fellow students; public performances are watched with intense concentration; and recordings by great artists are listened to repeatedly. The results are often quite remarkable. For instance, I watched children playing a game of "guess the performer": One child would imitate the performance of a well-known artist with such accuracy that the others could, indeed, recognize the mimicked artist, differentiating this performer's performance from the next.

Although there may be a kind of internal, tacit analysis involved in this ability to imitate, it is not interrupted by description; it is explicitly nonreflective. Indeed, exposing it to scrutiny is almost to be feared: " . . . it won't work if you think about it."

Experimental tasks

Subjects for the experiments were the five children from the Young Performers Program – three girls aged 8 and 9 and two boys aged 7 and 9, respectively. Four older children (aged 11 and 12) were also asked to do the tasks in an earlier pilot study. The children worked individually in sessions of about 45 minutes. All sessions were videotaped.

Materials for the task were Montessori bells. Each of these mushroom-shaped metal bells stands on its own wooden base and is thus free to be moved about. *All the bells look alike*, but when struck with a small mallet each plays a particular pitch. For this task the children were given 11 bells that together included all the pitches of the C-major scale plus three matched pairs – two C's, two G's, two E's. The bells were set out on the table in an arbitrarily mixed array.

The task had three parts: The first was a construction task where the children were asked to "make the tune 'Twinkle, Twinkle Little Star' with the bells." The children were encouraged to move the bells about in any way they liked. Second, when the children had finished with the construction of the tune, they were given pencil and paper and asked to "put down some instructions so a friend who walked into the room right now could play the tune on your bells as they are arranged on the table." Third, when the children had completed their instructions, they were shown "instructions" different from theirs and asked to make another arrangement of the bells so these alternate instructions would work to play the same tune.

Rationale. The sequence of tasks was chosen initially because I had considerable data on the same tasks from three quite different groups of subjects – musically untrained children of about the same age (7–10 years old); musically untrained adults (mostly MIT students and faculty); and musically trained adults (MIT students with at least 5 years of music instruction). The tasks, then, served as an initial probe for possible differences between the gifted children on one hand, and subjects in the comparison groups on the other.

Second, the tasks were designed to bring to the surface and to tease apart multiple representations by explicitly *disturbing the structures of the familiar fields of attention*. It was expected that if these familiar structures were significantly disturbed, multiple representations that are reciprocally interactive, and thus hidden in normal working situations, would come apart. That is, they would be seen operating in isolation from one another, functioning in new kinds of interactions, and possibly even coming into conflict.

The construction task disturbs the familiar structure of the instrument field in a major way: For example, pitch configurations associated with a particular piece (like "Twinkle," which all the children had played on both the violin and the piano) or commonly played figures such as scales or chord passages in a given key are represented, held in mind or in the hand, as configurations of spatial moves – what I have called "felt paths." When confronted, then, with a collection of objects (bells) that include familiar pitch-making relations but now scattered about in an arbitrary, nonlinear way, the bases for representing pitch relations are profoundly disturbed. In fact, expert instrumentalists faced with this experimental situation report a strong sense of disorientation reflected not only in their general confusion at the outset, but even in their confusion about what they are hearing when they *play* the bells – is a sequence of pitches "going up" or "going down"? And because the bells all look alike, leaving the player without even relative size to distinguish one from another, the player has neither spatial nor visual cues to go on but only his immediate apprehension of isolated pitch relations. The *sound* field is thus disengaged from its intersections with the *instrument* field. As a result, the fields of attention, along with their common interactions, are seriously disturbed, and perhaps most poignantly because of the confounding of familiarity with unfamiliarity.

The effect of these disturbances was seen specifically in the construction task as shifts in focus among the features associated with the various dimensions of the tune. These shifts were made concrete as the children worked within the dimensional constraints of the task itself.

Multiple dimensions of the tune and the task. Some of the multiple dimensions of the tune "Twinkle, Twinkle" that came into play in work on the tasks are shown in Figure 17.1.

Along the *structural* dimension, the diagram shows the two-level hierarchical structure of the tune: A B + A ′ represents the larger sections of the melody while A.1, A.2, and B.1 represent smaller subsections or phrases within these larger sections. The two identical A-sections function as both beginning and ending, while B functions as a middle.

Along another dimension, *pitch relations*, the arrows in the diagram indicate the direction of *pitch motion*. Notice that pitch direction is generally up in A.1 and down in A.2. However, within A.1 there is a leap from C up to G, and a local reversal of direction from A down to G, again. The inner figure, G-A-G, serves to extend the single pitch, G. The boxed pitches show the downward progression that begins in A.1 and continues across the phrase boundary into A.2 so as to fill in the initial pitch-gap between C and G.

Along with these aspects of pitch relations, all of which play an important role in the children's work, there is the dimension of *pitch function*. Notice that all the pitches in the tune are already present by the completion of Section A, and, indeed, the two primary pitches, C and G, have already been used twice within this section. Although the same pitch is thus used several times, its meaning or function within the melody changes significantly with each situation in which it occurs. The pitch, G, for instance, occurs first in the middle of Phrase A.1 on the word *twinkle*, where it is approached by a leap

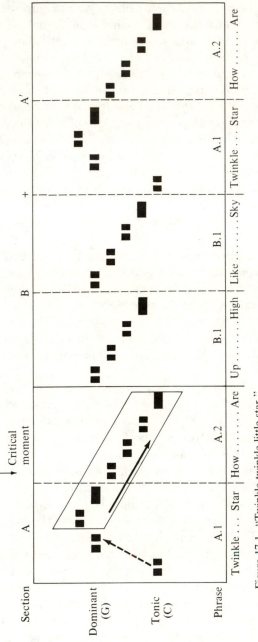

Figure 17.1. "Twinkle twinkle little star."

from below; it is followed by itself and then left by going up, stepwise, to A. This same G occurs again at the end of A.1 on the word *star*, but here it is approached from above, has a longer duration as compared with its previous appearance, and, most importantly, is a *phrase boundary* and thus has a different *structural function*. Thus the two events are the same only with respect to pitch property; in every other way multiple dimensions intersect so as to give different meanings to the two events. Similar differences in dimensions and function can be found between the two C's that begin and end Section A.

It is not surprising, then, that some subjects hear two events of the same pitch as different. These subjects are responsive to the unique situational context in which each occurs. In contrast, other subjects are able to focus on the single dimension, pitch, that both events share, and these subjects hear the two events as the same. These contrasting responses are important in understanding the differences among trained and untrained subjects, as well as the shifts in strategies observed in the work of the gifted children.

In addition to the multiple dimensions of the tune, the construction task itself has a number of important dimensions. The following terms refer to these various dimensions and their relevant entities:

1. Bell-pitch: An object (bell) with the property, pitch-P (e.g., G-bell, F-bell, etc.)
2. Bell-path: The spatial arrangement of bells-pitches on the table as made in constructing the tune.
3. Action-path: The sequence of actions made on the bell-path in playing the tune.
4. Tune-path: The sequence of pitch-events as they occur in the tune.
5. Felt-path: An internalized sequence of actions for playing common configurations or a whole piece on a familiar instrument.
6. Relevant spaces:
   a. Table-space
      Work-space – the area occupied by the cumulating bell-path; the space where the work and the results of construction take place. Search-space – the area occupied by the unused bells in the mixed array.
   b. Pitch-space: Higher or up, associated with moving right; lower or down associated with moving left. Also – steps or leaps.

Results and discussion: construction task

Given, then, the multiple intersecting dimensions of the tune and task, and given that the fields of attention were disturbed in a major way, it is not surprising that internal representations associated with them did emerge separately, in new kinds of interactions and also in conflict with one another. Evidence was found, explicitly, in the gifted children's shifts in strategies during the construction task. *And shifts in strategy occurred during the course of each child's work*. Further, with each strategy shift, priorities changed with

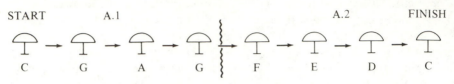

Figure 17.2. Figural bell-path.

respect to features associated with fields of attention and/or dimensions of musical structure as these intersected with dimensions of the task itself.

But the most striking finding was that in this regard the gifted children differed dramatically from subjects in the comparison groups. These subjects differed in quite explicit ways across groups, but within any one group, *subjects maintained a single, consistent strategy throughout the entire course of their work on the task.*

To make this important difference quite clear, I shall describe the *singular* construction strategies of trained and untrained subjects (both children and adults) and then give some brief examples of *shifts* in strategies among the gifted children.

Construction strategies of subjects in the comparison group. The construction strategy used by musically untrained subjects can be characterized as follows:

1. Always add new bells to the cumulating bell-path in their order of occurrence in the tune.
2. Always add a new bell for next-in-tune to the right of the just previous bell in the cumulating bell-path.
3. There must be a new bell for each pitch-event in the tune.

The result is a row of bells (bell-path) matched one-for-one with the sequence of pitch-events in the tune. Further, there is a one-to-one correspondence between bell-path and action-path – that is, subjects play the tune by simply moving always to the right or "straight ahead" without ever turning back or playing any one bell more than once except where there is immediate repetition of a pitch in the tune. Thus, for example, untrained subjects need to use two different bells for the two occurrences of the same pitch, G, in Phrase A.1. For these subjects, each is a new event in the onward flow of the piece. They neither hear nor recognize the two events as sharing a common property but rather attend to the differences in function generated by the particular intersections of all the other dimensions.

The bell-path and action-path for phrases A.1 and A.2 are shown in Figure 17.2. I have called this a *figural* strategy because subjects focus primarily on the unique shape of the tune-as-figure as it emerges over time. (See Bamberger, 1980, 1981, and Bamberger and Schön, 1979.)

In contrast, musically trained subjects begin the task of building the tune by putting to themselves a previous task, namely, to "put the bells in order."

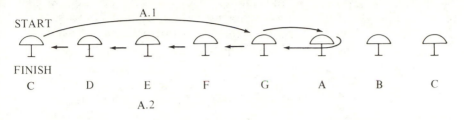

Figure 17.3. Formal bell-path.

Uncomfortable and disoriented at the outset, these subjects "put themselves in order" by first ordering the mixed array of bells from lowest to highest with the order proceeding from left (low) to right (high). In short, they build a C-major scale. Once the bells have been thus ordered in their work-space, these subjects simply play the tune *on* the previously ordered set. The ordered set, then, serves as a familiar fixed reference structure within which they can easily find the sequence of pitch-events that make up this particular tune. But unlike untrained subjects, trained subjects must move backward and forward on their bell-path and they must sometimes use the same bell more than once – that is, for events of the same pitch when these occur in different positions in the tune-path (Figure 17.3). I have called this strategy *formal* because subjects focus on the tune as it relates to, or maps onto, the formal structure of the fixed reference scale.

As a result of their consistent and singular construction strategies, untrained and trained subjects differ both in the bell-paths they make and in their action-paths on them. For untrained subjects, given a particular tune, it is the bell-path that is unique to the tune, the action-path remaining constant across tunes. For trained subjects, given a particular tune, it is the action-path that is unique to that tune while the bell-path remains constant across tunes. These strategies appear to be robustly consistent *within* the two groups. The gifted children, in striking contrast, switch their strategies significantly as their work evolves.

The gifted children: multiple representations. At the outset of their work, all five gifted children seemed to be proceeding like their untrained peers. And interestingly, older children in the program (11- to 12-year-olds) began the task like musically trained subjects by formally ordering the bells from low to high. In contrast, these younger children began by searching for each bell-pitch as it was needed in the tune, figurally adding them to their cumulating bell-path in order of occurrence from left to right:

But with the next event all the children made a switch in strategy as compared with the untrained groups. Acting now more like gifted older subjects, the children *reversed the direction* of their action-paths, turning back on the word *star* to play the previous G-bell again:

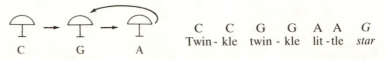

C   C   G   G   A A   G
Twin- kle twin - kle lit -tle *star*

What we see here is another dimensional focus: Although tune-events were first represented and added to the bell-path as simply *next-in-tune* (like figural subjects), on this move the children recognize this new event (like formal subjects) as not only next-in-tune but *lower-than* the previous event (A) as well as the *same in pitch* as the earlier G.

But as a result of their multiple foci, the children are left with a mixed representation of the tune in their work-space and, given what happens next in the tune, a problematic situation. The issue is, What to do with the F on the word *How* . . . that begins Phrase A.2?

C   C   G   G   A   A   G   ⫶   F   F   E   E   D   D   C
                                How   I   won–der what you are

The critical moment. The problems the children face at this critical moment typify the conflicts among multiple dimensions that emerged. They can be formulated as follows:

P.1 If the children follow their initial figural strategy – more like untrained subjects, the next bell-pitch (F) would be represented as *next-in-tune* and added "after" or to the right of the A-bell at the end of the current bell-path. However, this move would not take into account the *downward pitch-motion*, F<G<A, that continues on from A.1 into A.2. At the same time it would be inconsistent with a figural straight-ahead action-path because the previous A-bell would be interposed:[4]

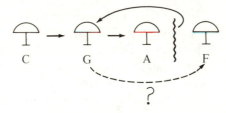

C   G   A   F

?

P.2 If they follow their new strategy – more like formal subjects, the next pitch (F) would be represented as *lower-than* the previous G-bell and would be added to its left. However, the C-bell already occupies that position in their work-space as a result of their initial figural strategy – C and G were originally placed next to each other because of *order of occurrence* in the tune.

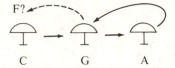

In confronting the problematic situation, the children made different choices implicitly assigning differing priorities with respect to these multiple possible dimensions. As illustration, we shall look at the moves of two of the children, Keith and Rebecca, at this critical moment (Tables 17.1 and 17.2).

Keith clearly sets himself the problem described as P.2. At Move 1, thinking of the F as lower-than the previously struck G-bell, he appropriately moves left *on his bell-path* – appropriately, that is, if the bells were ordered low-to-high. Striking the C-bell, which is in fact occupying that position as a result of his initial figural strategy, he confronts the conflict! "Backing up" (moving right) at Move 2, he identifies F, now as a *place* in the low–high ordering: "Yeah, it goes there." Finding the F-bell in his search-space at Move 3, he resolves the conflict by giving the problematic F-bell double meaning. That is, he recognizes F as *next-in-tune* but also *lower-than* G and *higher-than* C. As evidence, we see him push the C-bell left (at Move 4) and insert the F-bell in the space he has provided for it (at Move 5). Continuing with this procedure, he inserts the remaining bells in *order of occurrence* in the phrase (F E D). But simultaneously taking into account *downward pitch-motion*, he positions them according to their order in the *low–high series* (D E F). He has, then, invented a kind of double classification strategy – each added bell is both next-in-tune and also lower-than.

And, as a result of his new double classification strategy, the pitch-gap between C and G also visibly emerges. That is, at the outset, when Keith's focus was primarily on next-in-tune, he had appropriately juxtaposed the C- and G-bells (as one would, in fact, in notating the tune). But as he adds to his focus the dimension, direction of pitch-motion (as one does in following a familiar felt-path), he realizes in *table-space* the previously nonrepresented *pitch-space* between C and G. In doing so, Keith also transforms the unique sequence of pitch-events in *this* tune (C G A) into the generalizable, property-ordered sequence, the low–high ordered series (C D E F G A).

But notice the difference between Keith's process and that of older, trained subjects: Keith's low-high ordered series evolves *as a result of the particular structure of the tune and in the course of the construction process itself*. This is in marked contrast to older subjects, who feel the need first to orient themselves by building the complete, fixed-reference scale. Only with the scale almost literally "in hand" are they then able to find the tune *on* it.

Rebecca, in contrast, sets herself the problem described as P.1 (Table 17.2). At Move 4, she thinks of F as simply *next-in-tune* as she places it at the end of her cumulating bell-path. But at Move 8 her attention shifts to thinking of F as the *first in Phrase A.2* and also as *higher-than* E. Unlike Keith, she

Table 17.1. *Keith*

Moves		Description
1	C G A	Continues his action-path to left, gently striking the C-bell currently, immediately left of the G-bell; K. pauses.
2	C G A	Swings his mallet between C- and G-bells and says, "Yeah, it has to go here."
3		Moves into search-space, finds F-bell.
4	C C G A	Leaving F-bell where it is, goes back to workspace. Moves C-bell to the left leaving a space between C- and G-bells.
5	C F G A	Picks up bell from search-space and inserts it in space between C- and G-bells.
6	C F G A	New bell-path.
7–12		Continues with same procedure inserting E- and D-bells.
	C D E F G A	Completed bell-path.

START

FINISH

C   D   E   F   G   A

Action-path for Section A′

(C C G G A A G $\frac{3}{2}$ F F E E D D C)

Table 17.2. *Rebecca*

Moves		Description

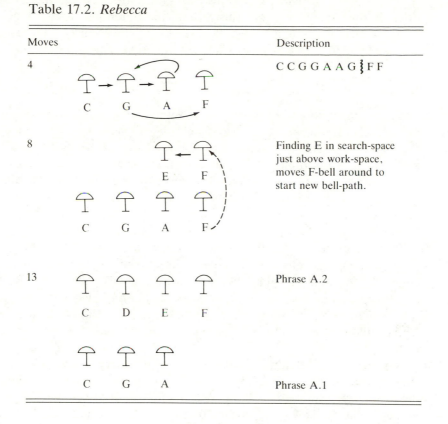

4	C C G G A A G ⅜ F F
8	Finding E in search-space just above work-space, moves F-bell around to start new bell-path.
13	Phrase A.2
	Phrase A.1

solves her problem by giving priority to *phrase structure*. This is seen in her two separate bell-paths, one representing and playing A.1, the other A.2. And notice that each is a self-contained entity – one C-bell functions as the *beginning* of A.1 and this is different from the second C-bell that functions as the *ending* of A.2.

In the process of constructing the tune, we have seen the children represent what may too easily seem to us the *same event* variously as:

1. Recognizable "sound" (in searching)
2. Next in a unique sequence of events
3. Lower-than or higher-than another event
4. A place on a felt-path on an instrument
5. A place in a stable, internal reference structure
6. A place and a function within a structural entity (phrase)

As expected, then, multiple dimensions did emerge separately, were co-ordinated in new ways, and also came into conflict. And in the solutions to conflict, we saw the children variously assign priorities among these dimensions. In turn, we gained some insight into the children's internal representations of these dimensions – representations that, in their functional reciprocity, are usually hidden as long as the fields of attention remain intact.

Notation task 1: making a notation

As in any invention of an instrumental notation, the fundamental question in this task was how to use the two dimensions of paper-space, together with some kinds of marks in it – graphics, symbols, words – so as adequately to represent to a performer an already organized instrument-space and a sequence of actions in it, that will result in a performance of the intended tune. In looking at the children's notations, then, I asked: How are particular graphics, symbols, words, as well as paper-space itself, used and what are they meant to represent?

The instructions for the first notation task were as follows: "Put down on paper some instructions so that a friend who walked into the room right now could play 'Twinkle' on your bells as they are arranged on the table." Because all of the children read conventional music notation, they could have used *it* to complete the task. But interestingly, none of them did so. Instead, each of the children took the task to be one *inventing* a notation specific to this task.

As a result, the children's notations are particularly interesting because they show the children inventing a way of representing the tune in a different medium (paper and pencil) along with the invention of symbols, as well as graphics that would work as "instructions" for playing the tune. Because all the children did so, the notations quite literally provide further evidence for their abilities to make multiple representations as well as further evidence from which to infer multiple internal representations.

Results and discussion

Each of the children made a unique set of instructions that, however, can be grouped into two types of notational strategies, which I have called *coordination* and *correspondence*, respectively. Figure 17.4, copies of instructions made by Keith and Rebecca for Sections A and B, illustrates each type.

The notations make a striking contrast. Keith uses his lineups of numbers to coordinate two dimensions of the tune, each with its own internal organization – the unique internal structure of this tune, and the general structure of ordered pitch-properties. His procedure is as follows: Using his low–high ordering of bells on the table as a fixed reference, he tacitly assigns the numbers 1–6 to the ordered series. Each number is a name that stands for the fixed position of a bell in instrument-space as well as the position of its

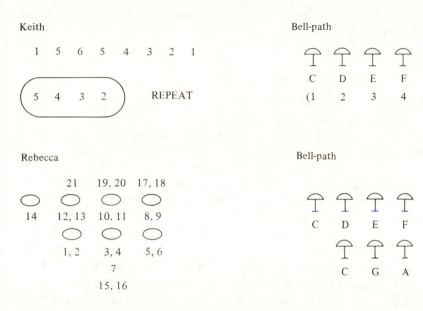

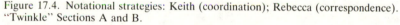

Figure 17.4. Notational strategies: Keith (coordination); Rebecca (correspondence). "Twinkle" Sections A and B.

pitch-property in the ordered series. Having done so, Keith uses the *symbols alone* as objects to be manipulated. The numbers going left to right in paper-space show the unique *temporal* sequence of events in the tune; the numbers themselves show the fixed *position* of each event along the bell-path in instrument-space.

Notice that Keith's strategy allows him to coordinate three distinct kinds of paths, each with its own meaning and its own trajectory – his bell-path, action-path, and notation-path. Thus, left–right on the bell-path is *low–high*; left–right along the notation-path shows the *temporal sequence* of unique tune-events, and each of these is, in turn, different in trajectory from the forward and backward movements of the action-path on the bells in *playing* the tune.

Rebecca's strategy is described as one of correspondence because she makes a direct correspondence between her bell-path in instrument-space and pictures in paper-space. That is, instead of coordinating dimensions by manipulating symbols, like Keith, Rebecca draws pictures of the bells taking them, so to speak, one-for-one from instrument-space and putting them into paper-space. Her pictured bells, then, mark fixed places in both *spaces*, leaving numbers to mark unique "places" in *time*. Focusing her attention on moving numbers about on the pictures, she directly mirrors on paper the distance, direction, and sequence of her actions in actually playing the bells in "real" space. Rebecca's instructions resemble a trail map imposed on a pictured terrain: Following the sequence of numbers through the terrain gives you the path to your destination.

Notation task 2: alternative notations

In this final task I showed each of the children a notation for playing "Twinkle" on the bells that was significantly different from their own and asked them to see if they could "make it work." As in their constructions, once again, the children in the gifted group differed dramatically from subjects in the comparison groups. Both musically trained and untrained subjects in these groups found it difficult, often impossible, to make sense of notations other than their own. In marked contrast, all but one of the children in the gifted group were able almost instantly to grasp the sense of an alternative notation and, where necessary, to rearrange their bell-paths so that the new notation would "play the same tune." In each case I gave subjects in the gifted group and in the comparison groups notations that were strategically different from their own. For example, I gave to Keith, as well as to adult trained subjects, a notation that was typical of untrained, figural subjects to be played on their "straight-ahead" bell-path:[5]

(1	2	3	4	5	6	7	8)
C	G	A	G	F	E	D	C

1 1 2 2 3 3 4 5 5 6 6 7 7 8

Figural bell-path   Figural notation-path

The task required these subjects first to understand the alternate meaning of numbers – actions on the bells in correspondence with the bell-path – and second, actually to rearrange their own low–high, fixed reference bell-path to make an order-of-occurrence bell-path.

In turn I gave Rebecca, as well as figural, untrained subjects, a notation that was typical of formal trained subjects:

(1	2	3	4	5	6	7	8)
C	D	E	F	G	A	B	C

1 1 5 5 6 6 5 4 4 3 3 2 2 1

Formal bell-path   Formal notation-path

These subjects were required to understand the use of numbers, *without any pictures* corresponding to the bells, to grasp that the numbers were names for spatial position in the property-ordered, low–high fixed reference structure, and also to rearrange their own bell-paths from order of occurrence to lowest-to-highest.

Although it is not surprising that untrained subjects were unable to make sense of the alternative notation I gave them, it is of critical significance that adult, trained subjects also had serious difficulties with the task. When confronted with an order-of-occurrence notation – 1 1 2 2 3 3 4 5 5 6 6 7 7 8 – they found themselves initially at a loss. After some thought, they typically did try to reorder their own prebuilt scale to put bells in order of occurrence. But in doing so they frequently became confused. At one moment they would appropriately take a number to refer to the position of a bell in the *sequence of tune-events*, but at the next moment the meaning of even that number would, so to speak, slip away and they would return to their familiar notation taking the number to mean *position in the scale*.[6]

Some were, of course, able to complete the restructuring called for by the notation, but many found it too painful to extricate themselves from their confusions, and simply gave up. For these experienced musicians, then, the conventional notation scheme, in which numbers stand for what are called "degrees" of the scale, is apparently so thoroughly internalized that these names have become almost built-in, *undetachable properties* of the pitches themselves. Indeed, for adult musicians the numbers carry with them a whole cluster of meanings, particularly in relation to a key: The number 5, for instance, is almost unalterably associated with the "5th degree" of the scale and also, of course, a place along the felt-path associated with a given key on their instruments. In short, the numbers have acquired deeply internalized meanings; for users to give these up not only disturbs their understanding of notation but, if given other meanings, their whole internalized network of tonal relations is put into disarray, including their all-important felt-path relationships.

Not so for the younger gifted children. Of the three who had made a fixed reference, property-ordered bell-path, using numbers as names for positions in this reference, all were able, with just a quick glance at the alternative notation, to make sense of it! That is, they were able to understand the numbers as referring to order of occurrence in the tune and to rearrange their bell-rows appropriately so as to make a straight-ahead, order-of-occurrence bell-path. And this included finding and adding, with no hesitation, new G- and C-bells in the appropriate places (C G A *G* F E D *C*).

All but one of the children (including one who made a correspondence notation) were able to restructure their representations of the tune. But this should not be surprising. Recall that adult trained subjects in the construction task began by prebuilding the C-major scale, using it then as a necessary fixed reference within which to *find* the tune. But all of the gifted children during the construction task had already made multiple representations of the tune in the process of constructing it – implicitly analyzing and redescribing it in-action along the way. Indeed, in doing so, they all had made, at some point, similar reconstructions and coordinations between the two kinds of "lineups" for pitch structures – property-order and tune-order – as required in the alternative notation task. And yet their ability to do so in the context of the new notation task seems further evidence for their effective use of multiple *internal* representations, for mapping them onto *external* descriptions, and their unusual capacity for moving freely from one representation to another, for seeing one *as* the other.

The gifted children's behavior is in most striking contrast to adult musicians who may be more consistent, more predictable, but perhaps are so because for them the connections between notation and internal representation are locked into one another – fixed, like dead metaphors. This difference has, I believe, crucial implications for the transitions that occur during the critical period between childhood extraordinary performance and adult artistry. I shall return to these implications in the conclusions.

Conclusions

In the introduction I argued that gifted young performers have an unusual capacity for representing musical elements and relations to themselves in multiple ways. Initial evidence for this claim came from observations of the children in their everyday work, where I identified at least four fields of attention each with its own languages of description and its own internal entities.

But I also tried to emphasize that while an observer can, on analysis, identify these separate foci, the children neither name nor think of them as separate, individual realms; they are, in practice, a single, interactive network.

But in the artificial situations of the experimental tasks, multiple representations were, as expected, teased apart. With the familiar structures of the fields of attention disturbed, we saw evidence of these multiple representations as the children arranged and rearranged their bells, shifting their focus of attention among various possible dimensions of musical structure. We saw representations functioning independently of one another in new kinds of interactions and also coming into conflict. And in this process we were able to gain some insight into the multiple *internal* representations that otherwise tend to remain buried in the simultaneity that characterizes performance in situ.

In this regard the younger gifted children differed strikingly from their musically untrained peers and also from adult, trained subjects. In both of these comparison groups, subjects used a single strategy throughout the construction task and in all of their work focused consistently on a limited set of particular dimensions.

In both the construction and notation tasks there was another rather striking kind of evidence for the children's capacities for multiple representations, namely, their changing use of what I have called paths or "lineups." Such paths were used in various media and with various trajectories in space to represent differing structured dimensions of the tune. But because neither pitch-relations nor their unfolding in time literally occupy space, the children's various uses of the conventions associated with the meanings of such lineups served as important clues to possible internal representations. Further, because these conventions cross over media and fields of attention (words, numbers, notations, instrumental geography, pitch-properties, structure), the meanings a child had given to a lineup easily changed. The confluence of *where* a pitch-object is in space with *what* is its meaning or function continued to influence and confound each other, sometimes creating conflict and confusion, sometimes leading to insight. Although representations did, then, come apart, the children seemed to have an unusual capacity for putting them back together again in new ways.

But perhaps the most significant finding came in the alternative notation task. Although musically trained adult subjects found it difficult, sometimes impossible, to make sense of a notation other than their own formal ones, all but one of the younger gifted children were able to do so.

This finding, perhaps more than any other, seems to distinguish the young gifted children from adult trained subjects. For these younger children, internal representations of musical structure are not yet fixed in their attachments to the conventional meanings associated with external notation systems; internal representations are, rather, still mobile, still evolving, easily mappable onto one another – a kind of movable feast of possible interconnections.

Implications for the midlife crisis

I want to argue now that what we may be seeing in the artificial task situations is a small-scale anticipation of the kinds of cognitive disequilibrium that occur on a much larger scale during the later transition into adulthood.

To understand this conjecture, it is important to consider a fundamental difference between the activities of the tasks and the children's ordinary musical activities: What we are seeing in the task situations are the children's capacities to *analyze and describe* – neither of which can be said to characterize their everyday work. Analysis and description were obviously involved in the notation tasks, but the construction task also involved the children in analysis (albeit in-action) and in description – at times out loud in words, like Keith, at times tacitly as they resolved conflict by making new lineups. Even the results of construction were sometimes partial descriptions of tune structure, such as Rebecca's phrase rows.

In turn, analysis and description ask the children consciously, even self-consciously, to *reflect on* understandings, actions, and perceptions along with the reciprocal relations among them – things they usually could take for granted. Thus it seems likely that this necessity for reflection both contributed to and resulted in the moments of cognitive disequilibrium. And these were the moments, in turn, that triggered the "liberation" of separate dimensions from their usually interwoven web. But it was also reflection that led to insight and to the invention of new ways of coordinating these now separate representations.

Now, my argument, as intimated above, is that the constellation of behaviors that emerged in the artificial and imposed task situations is similar in some important respects to that which occurs naturally, spontaneously during the critical transition into adulthood. And the crucial connection lies, I believe, in the causal relations between reflection, disequilibrium, and the subsequent invention of new "coordinating schemes" – i.e., the developmental dialectic described variously by Piaget (1960), Strauss (1981), Feldman (1980), and others.

Given a very short time span, this dialectic seems aptly to describe behavior in the experimental situations. But here the situation was artificially contrived to *create* conflict and then reflection: An overly familiar, musically obvious tune was placed in a spatially and kinesthetically unfamiliar environment, resulting in such confusion and conflict that previously well-functioning, thoroughly interactive representations came apart.

Although there is yet only anecdotal evidence to go on, I want to propose that a similar dialectic may characterize the midlife crisis, but with some important differences: The instability associated with this critical period is a function of *natural* developmental growth occurring over a long time span and resulting from the *inner* need for reflection. But as in experimental situations, such self-conscious reflection "liberates" problems and conflicts that seemed not to exist before. Choices must be made between *possible* meanings that now emerge and that, in their multiplicity, are often elusive; and conflicts must be resolved, in turn, between *possible* performance decisions that might project these various meanings. This flux of possibilities leads to analysis and description – to looking *at* what before we looked *through*. In this process, details become detached from the larger design, dimensions are disassembled, and their previously effective interactions break down. It is like a driver looking at the streaks on the windshield instead of looking through the windshield so as to guide his actions in the traffic beyond. Just so, reflection here leads, for example, to looking *at* the score – a possible source of answers but also a source of puzzlement – instead, as previously, looking *through* it as a transparent guide to actions on the instrument beyond.

As a result of reflection on actions and on underlying assumptions, dimensions become articulated in all their particularity, and with this, previously confident and well-functioning performance also seems to break down. As one 16-year-old performer told me, "It's easy to feel like your playing has gotten worse because now we're listening and hearing so much more." As in the experimental tasks, reflection has spawned disequilibrium but now "for real"; these teenage gifted performers are faced with the problem of building new means for coordinating multiple dimensions, that is, for constructing coherence. They can focus on separate fields of attention, developing each along its own independent trajectory. However, as it did for the younger children, this may later mean weighing priorities, for example, between the instrument and structure domains: "Sometimes a bowing works technically but not phrasewise, so you have to decide on priorities." Or, at times, technique (the instrument field) may be torn off from attention to structure: "I've been practicing the Saint-Saens cello concerto just for technique; I haven't even thought about 'the music' yet."

In other cases the fear of flux can lead to ritualizing, rigidly fixing connections. For example, well-practiced, common configurations on the instrument (what I have called felt-paths) can become undetachably linked to notation, sound, and even meaning. Then – unlike with the younger children, for whom these attachments are still mobile – units of action, of perception, of notation become locked into one another for instant security and retrieval. This solution to disequilibrium accounts, I believe, for the confusions experienced by adult nongifted subjects in the alternative notation tasks.

However, as I have made clear elsewhere (Bamberger, 1981), truly artistic performance depends on multiple representations functioning in reciprocal interaction with one another in such a way that events can be related in all their dimensional complexity. This new integration would mark the success of the work of cognitive reorganization. As Artur Schnabel put it:

The mature performer works for those rare inspirations when his conception of the score becomes one with its physical realization in performance. At such moments, technique is more than just the disciplined functioning of the body at the command of the ear: It grows into a physical activity which in turn may stimulate the imagination. If all goes well, the conception materializes and the materialization redissolves into conception.

On this view, then, the midlife crisis must be seen as a period of serious cognitive reorganization. There can be neither return to imitation and the unreflective, spontaneous "intuitions" of childhood, nor a simple "fix-up." As in the microcosm of the experimental situations, reflection that leads to disequilibrium can also be the means toward the inventions of new and more powerful understandings. Just as in other creative acts, the macro-process is one of evolution and transformation, of almost literally coming to see in a new way.

It remains now to test this view in the musical workplace. This might mean longitudinal case studies that would follow up some of the younger children studied thus far, and perhaps might also include case studies of those who are in the midst of this transition from youthful promise to adult artistry. One could hope that such studies will lead to insights that will find their way back into the real-world musical workplace of lessons, chamber music rehearsals,

theory classes, and public performance, to help gifted young performers tra-
verse the often rocky road into successful adult careers.

Notes

1 The children are admitted to the program on recommendation of their teachers and by audition.
   Although none of them is being "exhibited" as a "professional child prodigy," they are playing
   at a very high level. For example, I heard good public performances of Bach, Vivaldi, and
   Mozart violin concerti as well as performances of Mozart, Haydn, and Borodin string quartets.
   At this early point in their development, it is reasonable to assume that each *could* go on to
   become a professional musician.
2 "Fingering" in itself involves an interesting use of multiple representations. The same pitch
   can be found or made in a number of different places on the violin. Thus, in a quite concrete
   sense violinists can represent the same pitch to themselves in multiple ways. In fact, each
   instantiation of a single pitch has associations, even unique qualities: The pitch, A, played on
   the open A string sounds and feels quite different from that same pitch played on the D string
   with the second finger in second position. In a very real sense, then, an object to which we
   give the same name (A), and that is in the same place on the musical staff, can be represented
   in meaning and in "feel" as quite different objects.
3 When the teachers were shown examples such as those just described and others, they greeted
   them with a mixture of surprise and recognition. They were surprised, on one hand, to see
   how explicitly they shifted their language and their students' focus of attention. On the other
   hand, once seen, the fields of attention and the moves among them seemed so familiar as to
   be obvious. I take this response not as disconfirmation of the importance I have given to the
   fields of attention but, on the contrary, as reinforcing their functional reality. Further, although
   shifts in focus of attention may seem obvious to musicians, the ability to shift attention along
   with the multiple representations the shifts entrain are, I believe, a significant aspect characterizing the development of musical intelligence. The teacher's reactions reminded me of a
   comment of Wittgenstein's: "The aspects of things that are most important to us are hidden
   because of their simplicity and familiarity. (One is unable to notice something – because it is
   always before one's eyes.) The real foundations of enquiry do not strike a man at all. Unless
   that fact has at some time struck him. And this means: we fail to be struck by what, once
   seen, is most striking and powerful" (Wittgenstein, 1953, p. 50). It would be interesting to
   know if there are analogous fields of attention and shifts in focus among them in the development of intelligence in other domains.
4 "Straight-ahead" is meant to include here immediately repeated strikes on the same bell, as
   in:

   C   G   A

5 The musically untrained children usually also drew pictures of the bells, as Rebecca did.
6 Their feelings of confusion and disorientation here were similar and directly related to their
   initial response to the bells when they were scattered about on the table at the outset of the
   construction task. And incidentally, readers may find *themselves* confused by this time. Although careful reading may lead to extrication, the sense of confusion may itself give the
   reader a feel for what I have called "multiple intersecting dimensions of musical structure,"
   especially as these are represented in various spaces, with various trajectories (left–right and
   right–left), in different notation systems, and in different media.

References

Bamberger, J. (1980). Cognitive structuring in the apprehension and description of simple rhythms. *Archives de Psychologie*, *48*, 171–199.

Bamberger, J. (1981). Revisiting children's descriptions of simple rhythms. In S. Strauss (Ed.), *U-shaped behavioral growth*. New York: Academic Press.

Bamberger, J. (1982). Growing-up prodigies: The midlife crisis. In D. H. Feldman (Ed.), *Developmental approaches to giftedness*. San Francisco: Jossey-Bass.

Bamberger, J., and Schön, D. A. (1979). The figural-formal transaction. Division for Study and Research in Education, MIT (Working Paper No. 1).

Feldman, D. (1980). *Beyond universals in cognitive development*. Norwood, N.J.: Ablex.

Piaget, J. (1960). *The psychology of intelligence*. Totowa, N.J.: Littlefield, Adams.

Strauss, S. (Ed.). *U-shaped behavioral growth*. New York: Academic Press.

Wittgenstein, L. (1953). *Philosophical investigations*. New York: Oxford University Press.

Wolff, K. (1972). *The teaching of Artur Schnabel*. New York: Praeger.

Part VI

Conclusions and integration

18   Two levels of giftedness: shall ever the twain meet?

Robert S. Siegler and Kenneth Kotovsky

The chapters in this volume discuss pathbreaking research with two populations of gifted people: children who are doing well in school and on IQ tests, and adults who have made eminent contributions in their fields. Although the same label, "gifted," is applied to members of both groups, many obvious differences distinguish them. The purpose of this chapter is to discuss the findings that are emerging about the two groups, the gap that exists between research on one and research on the other, and whether and how this gap might be bridged.

The discussion is divided into three sections. The first section focuses on definitional issues: How can giftedness be defined, and can a single definition be applied to both groups of gifted people? The second section examines the descriptive characteristics of gifted people that emerge from the present research: What are gifted people like at the time when they are being studied, and how do gifted people become gifted? The third section outlines implications of the research reported in this volume: How might educational practice and future research be improved? In all three sections, the relation between research on intelligent children and research on eminent adults will be a recurring theme.

Definitional issues

When the term *giftedness* is used, a certain stereotype comes to mind. Within this stereotype, giftedness is a single quality that is manifested throughout a person's intellectual performances. It is measurable by a single quantitative index, an IQ score. It is present as a potential from early in life, or it is never present; you either are gifted or you are not. It applies to a person, not a product.

The definitions of giftedness advanced in this volume are remarkable both for the degree to which they disagree with this popular stereotype and for the degree to which they agree with each other. Csikszentmihalyi and Robinson, Feldhusen, Feldman, Gallagher and Courtright, Haensley, Reynolds, and Nash, Renzulli, Tannenbaum, and Sternberg all define giftedness as

417

involving multiple qualities. These qualities are not just intellectual. All of the investigators argue that giftedness involves social and motivational properties as well. All view IQ scores as inadequate measures of giftedness. Task commitment, high self-concept, and creativity are explicitly mentioned by many or all of these researchers as being among the defining qualities of giftedness.

This consensus definition seems much more realistic than the popular stereotype. It also points the way to promising research on such topics as the way in which the *profile* of gifted people's abilities differs from the norm. However, there is one large unresolved definitional issue that we feel merits detailed consideration. This involves the advisability of including the two groups of gifted people alluded to above – intelligent children and eminent adults – under a single definition.

Renzulli distinguishes quite clearly between the two populations. He labels one group creative–productive gifted, and the other, schoolhouse gifted. Schoolhouse giftedness involves learning and test taking, is ordinarily measured by IQ tests, and is, to a degree, an enduring property of people. Creative–productive giftedness, in contrast, involves development of creative products, is measured by the quality of those products, and may reflect a once-in-a-lifetime effort.

Research reported in this volume suggests that the two types of giftedness involve many additional differences as well. Creative–productive giftedness is ordinarily manifested in achievements that take months or years. Schoolhouse giftedness typically is manifested in achievements that take hours, days, or, occasionally, in the case of projects, weeks. In part because of these different time frames, creative–productive giftedness seems to require high levels of task commitment. In contrast, people can do well on IQ tests and in many school courses with relatively little commitment to the educational task. Creative–productive contributions are defined by the standard of all contributions that have ever been made in that field. The products of schoolhouse giftedness are judged against more local competition. These and other inherent differences between the two types of giftedness are noted in Table 18.1.

Other differences between schoolhouse and creative–productive giftedness are not inherent but are highly correlated with the distinction. When we talk about schoolhouse giftedness, we select our population on the basis of childhood achievements. When we talk about creative–productive giftedness, we select our population on the basis of adult achievements. Creative–productive giftedness can involve contributions in extremely narrow domains. Schoolhouse giftedness usually demands reasonable levels of achievement over considerably broader domains. In research on creative–productive giftedness, past achievements are emphasized. In research on schoolhouse giftedness, the emphasis is on what future accomplishments may be possible.

Table 18.1. *Dimensions of differences between schoolhouse-gifted and crea-tive–productive gifted people*

Dimension	Schoolhouse gifted	Creative–productive giftedness
Typical age at which studied	Children	Adults
Nature of contributions	Learning what is known	Discovery
Level of achievement	Very good	Profound
Time frame to achieve goal	Minutes to months	Months to years
Role of creativity	Often unnecessary	Necessary
Level of task commitment required	Variable	High
Level of self-concept required	Variable	High

Many of these factors emerge in Albert and Runco's, Csikszentmihalyi and Robinson's, Feldman's, Gruber's, and Tannenbaum's compelling arguments for the importance of the *fit* between eminent contributors and the field of their contribution. As these contributors indicate, creative innovations require a meshing of an individual's talents, personality, and institutional resources with the issues of the time and the larger cultural context. The requirements for eminent contributions may differ at different times, even within a single field. In the second half of the 19th century, scientists without superior mathematical ability could make fundamental contributions to understanding of genetics and evolution. Scientists with similar abilities might not be able to make comparable contributions today.

The fit between the individual and the field is important for both intellectual and motivational reasons. A superior fit allows the individual to learn quickly and deeply the material in the field. It also can motivate the dedication of huge amounts of time and effort that is so critical for even a person of superior intellectual gifts to acquire the knowledge base from which to make eminent contributions. Such meshing is required only to a minor extent in performance in the classroom, and not at all in performance on IQ tests. It is no accident that a fair number of children perform excellently in all subjects, but that eminent contributions are almost always limited to one or two areas.

These differences make ties between research on the two types of giftedness quite tenuous. The difficulty is evident in considering the role of creativity in each type. As the name implies, creativity is inherently part of creative–productive giftedness. Eminent contributions are by almost any reasonable definition creative. However, the relation between schoolhouse giftedness and creativity is less certain. Children can have high IQs and perform extremely well in school without great creativity. Further, no one knows whether creative–productive adults were especially creative as children.

Some researchers have attempted to transcend this difficulty by fiat: Simply include creativity in the definition of giftedness, with the definition presumably applying to children as well as adults. For example, creativity is one of the three rings within Renzulli's model. Haensly, Reynolds, and Nash cite the ability "to see possibilities where others do not" as a crucial quality in giftedness. Another example is Feldman's emphasis on children's novel accomplishments as being an important "part of the creative process."

What if, however, creativity in childhood is unrelated to creativity in adulthood? As Feldhusen notes, "creativity or divergent thinking tests offer no compelling evidence of validity links to creative production in adulthood." This lack of linkage may be due to adequate tests of creativity not yet having been developed. Another possibility, however, is that the linkages simply do not exist. All of the dimensions of difference between schoolhouse and creative–productive giftedness cited in Table 18.1 apply equally to differences between the levels of creativity shown among the top 5% or 20% of children and those shown by the far less than 1% of adults whose achievements would be labeled creative–productive. Especially important is the fact that creative–productive contributions often require innovation in only the most limited of domains. Within the domain of writing, creative writers of historical novels would not necessarily be creative writers of short stories. Within the domain of short-story writing, creative writers of short stories about suburban Connecticut towns would not necessarily be creative writers of short stories about sports. Within the domain of sports short-story writing, creative writers of short stories about the colorful characters surrounding boxing in the 1920s would not necessarily be creative writers of short stories about the reactions of the late 1940s Brooklyn Dodgers to the racial integration of their baseball team. Whether a child is generally creative may be at best weakly linked to whether he or she as an adult will be extremely creative at any one activity.

The predictive problem becomes even more daunting when we realize that there is no guarantee that an adult who could be exceptionally creative at an activity will ever find that activity. Even if the individual does find an activity in which he or she shows exceptional talent, there is no guarantee that he or she will find it sufficiently rewarding to make it a life's work.

The divide between schoolhouse and creative–productive giftedness explains many of the differences among the definitions discussed in the first part of the book. Simply put, most of the definitions seem intended for a reference group either of schoolchildren or of creative producers, but not of both. For example, Haensley et al. include conflict and commitment as two of their four defining qualities. These make sense when discussing creative–productive adults, but are not easily applicable when discussing schoolhouse-gifted children. Similarly, the Marland definition discussed by Gallagher and Courtright, among others, is clearly directed at schoolchildren. The emphasis is being "capable of high performance," not on having made any outstanding contribution. These differing definitions reflect different conceptions of giftedness, but not ones that can be ordered along an evaluative dimension. Each seems a reasonable characteristic of one of the two populations of gifted people.

In our view, Jackson and Butterfield are to be commended for clear thinking on this issue. They have unambiguously defined the type of giftedness they were addressing as involving superior early performance, whether on IQ tests or in specific domains such as reading. This cutting of the Gordian knot certainly does not preclude other researchers from studying eminent contributors or from documenting parallels in the mechanisms underlying schoolhouse and creative–productive giftedness. Its biggest effect, however, may be in facilitating research on high-performing children, a worthy enterprise in its own right.

The characteristics of gifted performance

One of the most heartening qualities of the research described in this book is the number and variety of mechanisms that have been proposed to account for gifted performance. These mechanisms can be categorized according to the level of detail at which they characterize processing. They fall into four groups: elementary information processes, processes that operate on the products of these elementary processes, rules and strategies that combine several operations on products of elementary information processes, and global analyses of the system's traits. The four levels of analysis can be distinguished by their time frame and by their specificity. Elementary information processes are the most rapidly executed and the most fully specified. Trait-level processes refer to mechanisms of the longest duration, and are the least precisely specified. The other two categories fall in between. We will discuss examples of each level of analysis in turn. Then we will examine the advantages and disadvantages of characterizations at the different levels.

Elementary information processes

Superiority in elementary information processes provides an appealing account of the origins of giftedness. A major source of the appeal is generality. Differences in how efficiently information is stored in memory or in how efficiently stored information is retrieved would influence performance in many domains. Another source of appeal is the relative precision of current understanding of these processes. Compared with our understanding of more global constructs such as creativity and metacognition, we understand much better what goes on in memory scanning and other elementary processes.

Jackson and Butterfield nicely reviewed work on the role of elementary information processes in giftedness. They noted several differences between high-IQ and average-IQ children. Much of the evidence derives from performance on the Sternberg memory-scanning task. High-IQ children are less affected by increases in memory set size, and their absolute rate of scanning is faster. Other information derives from performance on the Posner name identity–physical identity task. High-IQ children are faster at retrieving information from memory than are their lower-IQ peers. Interestingly, as Borkowski and Peck noted, the correlations between performance on these tasks and IQ are much stronger for children than for adults. One possibility is that asymptotic levels of mastery of these processes exist, and that the main difference between children of different IQs is in the rate at which they reach these asymptotic levels.

Davidson and Sternberg provide evidence that gifted children are superior to average-IQ peers in how efficiently they execute another elementary information process, encoding. The gifted children's advantage in solving problems was especially great on problems that demanded encoding some information and ignoring other information. Sternberg also hypothesizes that gifted children are superior in another elementary process, automatization.

An interesting regularity of these studies of elementary information processes is that they all deal with schoolhouse giftedness. The tasks are not profound; they would seem to demand intelligence rather than creativity or task commitment; and the gifted subjects are intelligent children or college students. It would be interesting to know the status of creative–productive people on these tasks; this would be a valuable focus for future research on giftedness.

Operations on the products of elementary information processes

Davidson and Sternberg studied two mechanisms that are likely to be of broad importance in gifted performance: combination and comparison. Combination, the putting together of separate units of information to solve problems where no one piece of information would suffice, has high face validity as a contributor to giftedness. Comparison, the relating of new information to existing knowledge and the extraction of dimensions of similarities and differences between the two, has similarly high face validity. Davidson and Sternberg provide the same type of high-quality converging evidence for the importance of these two mechanisms in gifted performance that they provide for the role of encoding. They show that gifted children combined and compared information more successfully, and benefited less from aids that made execution of the processes easier, than did nongifted children.

Additional evidence for the potential role of processes that operate on the products of elementary information processes comes from a computer simulation developed by Siegler and Shrager (1984). The simulation learns addition and subtraction problems by associating answers it generates with the problems. Starting with no knowledge of specific problems, but with general problem-solving procedures such as putting up fingers and counting them, the simulation's performance eventually resembles closely 5-year-olds' performance. It comes to be like the children in which strategies it uses, which particular errors it makes, the relative frequency of errors on different problems, the relative solution times on different problems, and the close relations among frequency of errors, solution times, and overt strategies on each problem.

Analyses of children's errors on addition problems revealed a striking regularity. In the set of problems that was presented, 10 problems involved either an ascending series of numbers (e.g., $2+3$ or $2+4$) or a tie (e.g., $2+2$ or $3+3$). On all 10 of these problems, the most frequent error was the answer one greater than the second number. Thus, the most frequent error to $2+3$ was 4 and the most frequent error to $4+4$ was 5. The result seemed to be due to a kind of semantic priming in which the children's associations from the counting string interfered with their addition and led to their stating as the answer the number that was next in the counting string. Formal modeling within the computer simulation revealed that suppressing this irrelevant association led to considerably faster learning. By analogy, ability to suppress irrelevant associations might distinguish faster human learners from slower ones.

In these operations on elementary information processes, as in the elementary processes themselves, all of the empirical research to date has been with intelligent children. Again, presenting similar tasks to eminent contributors seems of inherent interest, and might help reveal parallel mechanisms distinguishing renowned contributors from their less renowned peers.

Analyses of rules and strategies

In investigations of adult cognitive psychology, cognitive development, and retardation, differences in rules and strategies have accounted for many differences in performance. The same might be expected to hold true in studying giftedness. It is not surprising, then, that some of the most convincing findings in this volume involve analyses at this level.

As shown in Table 18.2, the relation between gifted and nongifted people's rules and strategies logically might involve progress either through the same developmental sequence or through a different developmental sequence. In fact, all of the research reported in this volume seems to indicate similar developmental sequences for gifted and normal children. The Ferretti and Butterfield (1983) research was illustrative. Gifted children, average children, and retarded children all used the same rules on the balance scale. The higher the IQs of the children, the more advanced the rule they used at a given age.

Table 18.2. *Levels of analysis of giftedness* (*selected works, this volume and elsewhere*)

I. Elementary information processes (EIPs)
   A. Encoding (Davidson & Sternberg)
   B. Rate of retrieval from memory (Hunt)
   C. Memory scanning (Keating & Bobbitt)
II. Processes that operate on products of EIPs
   A. Selective combination (Davidson & Sternberg)
   B. Selective comparison (Davidson & Sternberg)
   C. Suppression of related but irrelevant operations (Siegler)
III. Rules and strategies
   A. Same developmental sequence
      1. Faster progression without specific experience (Ferretti & Butterfield)
      2. More types of experiences help (Davidson; Borkowski & Peck)
      3. Faster learning from experience (Davidson; Sternberg; Jackson & Butterfield; Borkowski & Peck)
   B. Different developmental sequences
      1. Skip strategies within usual sequences
      2. Invent different strategies
IV. Trait-level descriptions
   A. Intelligence (just about everybody)
   B. Creativity (just about everybody)
   C. Metacognition (just about everybody)
   D. Critical life experiences
      1. Midlife crises (Bamberger)
      2. Familial strife (Albert & Runco)
      3. Crystallizing experiences (Walters & Gardner)

However, the identities of the rules themselves were the same. Thus, given no special experience, gifted children used the same rules as nongifted children, just acquiring them at younger ages.

Ferretti and Butterfield, Sternberg and Davidson, and Borkowski and Peck all found more rapid learning of new facts and strategies, and learning from a wider range of experiences, among gifted children than among nongifted ones. The range of tasks on which this pattern was evident – balance scales, insight problems, vocabulary learning, and memory strategies – was ample demonstration of the view that intelligence is related to the ability to learn. An especially nice methodological feature of all of these studies was their control for degree of initial knowledge. Ferretti and Butterfield assessed children's rules and compared the learning of children with different IQs but with the same initial rule. Sternberg and Davidson presented esoteric vocabulary items, which almost no one would have encountered previously, in the context of very simple passages that everyone could easily understand. These procedures avoided the commonly found problem that, in many experiments, children who learn more already possess greater amounts of directly relevant knowledge.

In contrast to these plentiful demonstrations of accelerated sequences of the same strategies and of faster and more flexible learning, no evidence was reported of different developmental sequences in which children skipped strategies or invented totally different strategies. This may reflect the validity of Jackson and Butterfield's and Borkowski and Peck's operating assumption that gifted children's thinking is much like that of their MA equivalents, as has often proved the case with retardates. Another possibility, however, is that studying other tasks and other populations will reveal that gifted people sometimes invent unusual strategies. Consider the approach used by one unusually intelligent 4-year-old who participated in the Siegler and Shrager (1984) study. When presented problems that she did not know, she often put up her fingers and counted them. Some of the problems had sums greater than 10, however, which made it difficult to execute the counting-fingers strategy. This one girl, alone among the more than 100 children we have observed, devised a novel strategy for dealing with this problem. She whistled. Given the problem $7 + 5$, she might count from 1 to 10 and then whistle twice and say 12. Such atypical strategies, by their very nature, require careful observation of exactly what people are doing. They also may be more frequent when people are just learning a skill than when they have mastered it to a higher degree. Thus, such novel strategies are not easy to document, but they can be revealing of the types of unusual insights that may distinguish gifted from nongifted people.

Once again, all or almost all analyses at the level of strategies involved studies of schoolhouse-gifted children. A possible welcome exception was Bamberger's study of musically gifted children. Reading about these children, it was difficult to know just how gifted they were relative to other young music students. If the children turn out to be exceptionally gifted, the study would constitute a welcome bridging of the gap between studies of the two populations.

Trait-level characterizations

Many characterizations of both schoolhouse giftedness and creative–productive giftedness are at the level of trait descriptions. Generally high intelligence is referred to by almost all investigators as an important part of giftedness. Specific intelligences are emphasized by Feldman, Feldhusen, Tannenbaum, Walters and Gardner, and a number of others. Insight, creativity, and metacognitive skills are among the other qualities frequently said to define giftedness.

Analyses at this level have several advantages. They are useful for communicating with nonspecialists. They often are as precise as is possible, for example, when the aim is to study great geniuses of the past. They also may summarize a variety of more particular ideas.

Perhaps the strongest recommendation for trait-level descriptions of giftedness is the interesting accounts of transition processes that they have yielded. One of the most stimulating is Walters and Gardner's discussion of the role of crystallizing experiences in the development of mathematicians, musicians, and visual artists. The notion of crystallizing experiences presumes that some people's biological makeups predispose them to be interested in, and exceptionally skillful at, certain domains if they receive the right type of experience. At young ages, the effect of the crystallizing experience is to strengthen interest and increase understanding of the domain as a whole; at older ages, it functions to stimulate interest in some particular approach or area within the domain. The number of geniuses who have reported such experiences suggests that such experiences are real and that they can have a lasting impact. The contrast between music and mathematics, in which such experiences are commonly reported, and visual arts, in which they are not, is especially tantalizing. It may mean, as Walters and Gardner suggest, that the importance of such experiences in stimulating cognitive growth is greatest in domains that are relatively remote from everyday experience.

Bamberger's notion of the midlife crisis is another intriguing trait-level idea about transition processes. The hypothesis that young musicians usually represent music in a wholistic way, and that older musicians more often represent it in a dimensionalized way, parallels the representational development hypothesis that has been proposed to explain a wide variety of perceptual and cognitive changes (Kosslyn, 1978). To the best of our knowledge, other investigators have not related acquisition of formal operations to developmental changes in artistic domains. Bamberger's hypothesis thus extends Piagetian ideas about developmental changes in an interesting direction.

Csikszentmihalyi and Robinson extend these developmental notions to include four types of developmental discontinuities: those pertaining to the field, to the domain, to cognitive development, and to life-span transitions. In doing so, they make contact with Eriksonian as well as Piagetian theory. An interesting issue raised by their notions about these transitions concerns the relations among the different sources of development. One way of viewing these relations would be to posit that each source of development constitutes a veto factor. To become an eminent contributor, an individual must be good enough along each dimension to surmount its hurdles. Tannenbaum explicitly adopts this approach in his chapter. We wonder, though, whether excellence in one dimension may not be sufficient to overcome deficiencies in others. For example, if a dancer is brilliant in his movements, but not very advanced in his general cognitive and socio-emotional development, would this impose a serious barrier to his success? Did Norbert Wiener's lack of social skills limit his mathematical and scientific success? The dynamics of gifted performance thus may be considerably more complex than a simple multiple-threshold model would suggest.

Another issue raised by Csikszentmihalyi and Robinson's account concerns the arbitrariness of fields. They comment that "There being no 'natural' talents, their number and kind depend entirely on the distinctions we are willing to make." They then raise the intriguing example of the game *mo*, which requires skillful discrimination between colors and sizes, agility, and high alcoholic tolerance. The *mo* example is useful in illustrating the simultaneous roles of culture and biology in all human activities. We think it important, however, to note a possible limitation of the example as an analogy to naturally occurring fields within which people display talent. There is no reason to think that there is any correlation in ability along the three dimensions of *mo*. People who are good at discriminating colors seem, a priori, to be as likely to have high alcoholic capacity as low. This would not seem likely to be true for the dimensions critical to being a great physicist, a fine musician, or a top baseball player. In physics, for example, mathematical aptitude, ability to design and understand experiments, and ability to write concisely and coherently would seem to be at least moderately correlated. Csikszentmihalyi and Robinson might reply that these correlations are the result of common cultural factors pressing people to perform well or poorly on all dimensions relevant to physics expertise. This is one possibility, but another possibility is that disciplines are "natural kind" concepts, and that the correlations that seem to exist result from inherent relations among different aspects of the human intellect.

Albert and Runco's ideas about how people become creative represent the most explicit ideas expressed in the volume about how personality contributes to the development of giftedness. One appealing idea is that many eminent people are motivated by "others" not having performed adequately. The role of self-criticism is also noted, as is the importance of becoming absorbed in problems without immediate personal ramifications. Especially interesting is the evidence Albert and Runco present that disagreements in attitudes between mothers and fathers of high-IQ boys are associated with creativity in these children.

The hypothesis that children's experiencing parental disagreement contributes to the children's later creativity at first runs counter to the intuition that pleasant, concordant homes would provide the most secure bases from which to explore the world. More careful thought, however, reveals that the two ideas are not inconsistent. Supportive homes are not necessarily ones where parents are similar, or even ones where the parents get along with each other. It is at least imaginable that one or both parents may become *more* invested in a child's success as other aspects of family relationships founder. Another possibility is that parental differences engender in some children a degree of self-sufficiency, or even withdrawal from social activities, and a substitution of intellectual pursuits. Yet another possibility is that the intuition is simply incorrect. Tolstoy once ventured the opinion that all happy families are similar, but each unhappy family is different. Some of these differences may provide powerful incentives for dedication to a task and eventual creative contributions.

Borkowski and Peck propose a different type of role for parents in their children becoming gifted. They suggest that parents perceive the efficiency of their children's information-processing system early in life. If parents think the child is exceptionally intelligent, they react by providing greater intellectual stimulation. This greater intellectual stimulation leads to the children developing greater metacognitive awareness. From Borkowski and Peck's description, there is no reason not to think that all children would develop superior metacognitive skills if their parents thought they were intellectually gifted. A type of Pygmalion experiment thus seems suggested.

These hypotheses about how transitions to giftedness occur illustrate the strength of trait-level descriptions – they stimulate people to think interesting thoughts and postulate interesting relations. Such characterizations also have several disadvantages, however. These can be illustrated in the context of the metacognition construct.

Many contributors to this volume emphasize metacognition as a key feature distinguishing gifted people from others: Gallagher and Courtright, Haensly, Reynolds, and Nash, Jackson and Butterfield, Sternberg, and Borkowski and Peck, among them. The construct is posited not only as a dimension of description but also as a causal factor. But what exactly is metacognition? Sometimes it is used to mean conscious knowledge of which strategies to use in which situations. Other times it is used to describe any transfer of training. Yet other times it is used to mean filling in the gaps of instructional procedures. Even investigators who emphasize the term do not agree with each other as to where its domain begins and ends. Jackson and Butterfield claim that Sternberg's and Davidson's constructs of selective encoding, selective combining, and selective comparing are instances of metacognition. Sternberg and Davidson disagree.

This multiplicity of uses raises a question: Is metacognition the 1980's equivalent of *g*? Ability to learn, to generalize, to go beyond the information given, and to use strategies flexibly and appropriately are all attributes of that venerable construct. How exactly does metacognition differ? Metacognition also has encountered a number of difficulties in the area in which it has received the greatest study, cognitive development. Empirical relations between measures of metacognitive knowledge and performance have frequently not been found where expected. Borkowski, Peck, Reid, and Kurtz's (1983) finding is quite representative in this regard, as indicated in a review by Cavanaugh and Perlmutter (1982). Even when such relations do appear, it often is unclear exactly how metacognition influenced performance. Beyond this, no one knows how well the various mental operations that are said to constitute metacognition correlate with each other. In other words, we have no measure of construct validity, despite the construct having been used quite widely for a full decade.

Another type of problem with metacognition, a problem common to many trait descriptions, is that phenomena that superficially should be explained by the construct often have their explanations in quite different sources. The Siegler and Shrager research on learning of arithmetic can be used to illustrate. A basic finding in that investigation was that children used overt strategies, such as counting their fingers, most often on the most difficult problems. This was an adaptive course of action in that it struck a balance between speed and accuracy demands. Children were more accurate when they used the overt strategies than when they retrieved an answer and stated it. On the other hand, the overt strategies took longer to execute than did retrieval. Thus, the children used retrieval when they could do so accurately, and used the more time-consuming overt strategies when they alone would yield accurate performance.

This phenomenon would seem exactly the type that prompted formulation of the metacognition construct: children seeming to choose among alternate strategies in an intelligent way. Further experimentation, however, revealed that children's metacognitive knowledge was not responsible for the relation. The knowledge simply was insufficient to account for the very strong relations that were present in the children's arithmetic performance. Rather, the source of the relations lay in the nature of the memory system. The workings of that system enabled children to arrive at intelligent strategies, despite the fact that at no point did they ever evaluate the advisability of different strategies and choose one of them. This discussion is not the best place to describe in detail the way in which the memory system produces this effect. However, the work has convinced us that phenomena that might on the surface seem to be inherently metacognitive in nature may have fundamentally different explanations. More generally, it points to the danger of using trait-level terms as explanations. They may seem to explain more than they actually do.

Evaluation of description at different levels

The levels of description of giftedness can be compared on at least four criteria: specificity, predictive accuracy, success of related theories in explaining other developmental and individual differences, and instructional implications. The ordering of the levels on the criterion of specificity was indicated earlier. Descriptions of elementary information processes are the best specified. Saul Sternberg's account of memory scanning, for example, specifies all or virtually all of the processing that goes on in the second or so required to perform the task. The completeness of the accounts drops off as the time frames increase. Thus, we can specify almost none of the processes that occur in creativity. Indeed, any one example of these trait-level constructs may include such different processes from any other example of the same construct, that it is impossible to specify in any detail the processes characteristic of the construct.

A second criterion is predictive accuracy. The trait-level construct of intelligence was frequently criticized, both for its lack of specificity of processes and for its "only" accounting for a moderate percentage of variance in later occupational success. Yet none of the research reported in the volume, nor any other that we know about, can be said to do better. It has not been demonstrated that other constructs predict later contributions more successfully than does IQ, or even that the other constructs in combination with IQ allow more accurate prediction. For those who believe that childhood giftedness and adult eminent contributions are related, and who believe that giftedness involves more than intelligence, establishing such predictive validity seems crucial. What is needed, in a sense, is a new psychometrics that has the advantage of psychological revealingness and specificity without sacrificing the old virtue of accurate prediction. Of course, if giftedness in childhood and giftedness in adulthood are viewed as fundamentally discontinuous phenomena, no predictor would be expected to do especially well, and the problem of prediction becomes less urgent.

A third dimension for evaluating the levels of analysis is how much variance in performance each seems to account for. It is here that the second and third levels excel. Research on individual differences has indicated that variation in strategies and in processes that operate on the output of elementary information processes accounts for many large differences between people of differing intelligence and differing cognitive styles (Cooper & Regan, 1982). Research on developmental differences has revealed a similar picture (Siegler & Richards, 1982). The studies reported in this book suggest that the same picture is emerging in the study of gifted children. Among the most striking empirical relations reported are those from Davidson's analysis of insight problems, Jackson and Butterfield's analysis of the balance scale, and Sternberg's analysis of vocabulary acquisition. All of these analyses were directed at processes at a middling level of specificity and temporal duration.

The fourth evaluative dimension involves whether plausible instructional implications can be drawn from the research. On this criterion, the second, third, and fourth levels of analysis seem to hold the most potential. Elementary information processes would be difficult if not impossible to train. Even if children differed on these processes and the differences were educationally important, teachers probably could do little to help. In contrast, educational potential was demonstrated at the three more general levels. Davidson demonstrates that children can be taught to combine elementary information processes through selective encoding, combination, and comparison in ways that help them to solve insight problems. Jackson and Butterfield demonstrate how instruction on the balance scale can build from the children's existing strategies. Renzulli's revolving door program and Stanley and Benbow's SMPY program demonstrate how educational programs emphasizing global qualities, such as creativity and mathematical talent, can be effective.

What general evaluations can be drawn? Viewed across the four criteria, it seems that the second and third levels have been the most productive. They combine fairly specific analyses, ability to account for sizable portions of variance in performance, and good educational potential. The analyses of elementary information processes fall short on the last two of these; the trait-level analyses fall short on the first two. We suspect that considerable progress will be made in the next few years in studies of giftedness examining gifted people's strategies and their procedures for combining elementary information processes.

Implications for educational practice

Educating gifted children involves three basic decisions: Should such children be given special education? If they should, then how should participants in such programs be selected? And once they are selected, what instruction should they be given? Research reported in this volume has important implications for each of these issues.

The authors in this volume seem to agree that special education for gifted children is appropriate. Stanley and Benbow discuss the issue in greatest detail. As they note, improving the education of gifted children might allow these children later to contribute more to society. The children also might enjoy their education more, and be less bored, if they were challenged by other intelligent children. Finally, all children deserve an appropriate education; intelligent children may not be able to receive one in traditional classrooms.

How children can be selected for special education seems more controversial. Identifying gifted children necessitates deciding what dimensions to consider as relevant to giftedness and deciding how stringently to set cutoff criteria. Traditionally, IQ has been the primary dimension, often the only dimension, that has been considered in identifying academically gifted children. As mentioned earlier, a number of investigators in the present volume argue for broadening these criteria. For example, Renzulli argues for including creativity and motivation, as well as reasonably high intelligence. If we accept the argument that all of these characteristics are important in giftedness, we might at first be surprised and disappointed at Renzulli's statement that, in practice, the selection criteria for admission to his revolving door program resemble those of traditional programs in their heavy reliance on IQ.

Practical demands often force recognition of hard truths, however. Suppose that children were admitted to Renzulli's program on the basis of unstandardized assessments of creativity and motivation. Would the results be preferable to those obtained by relying entirely on IQ? It is possible that such a system would work well, but there are reasons for doubt. One such reason is to be found in the clinical psychological literature on statistical versus clinical prediction. Despite clinicians' often expressed confidence in their prognoses of their patients' outcomes, it has been found again and again that simple unweighted regression equations predict more accurately.

The point can perhaps be made more poignantly with regard to the Ochoa case cited by Renzulli. Ochoa came from a Spanish-speaking home. He apparently was given an IQ test at a young age and scored poorly on it, due to his lack of knowledge of English. Ochoa then was placed in a school for retarded children, where he stayed until he finished high school. He then registered for the Navy, and took another intelligence test. By this time, he knew English well and scored above 130 on the test. He was allowed to enroll in officers' candidate school, and eventually become a professor at a college in California.

The Ochoa case is often cited as evidence of the evils that result from relying on IQ tests. Because of the initial test results, he was misclassified for the rest of his elementary and high school education. A completely opposite moral might be more reasonable, though. Ochoa's performance on the Navy's IQ test was what rescued him from injustice. All of the teachers, psychologists, and other school personnel whom he encountered failed to do this. They either did not recognize his ability or did not care sufficiently to secure a more appropriate education for him.

One conclusion that follows from this story is that there is a need to develop reliable and well-standardized measurement instruments that assess creativity, task commitment, need for achievement, metacognitive knowledge, and other factors potentially relevant to giftedness. Designing such measurement instruments would also have the desirable side effect of enabling researchers to determine the predictive validity of these constructs. Lacking such instruments, multistage selection procedures such as those used in Renzulli's revolving door program seem like an excellent idea. Indeed, creativity, task commitment, and the other qualities may prove to be sufficiently domain-specific that useful general tests cannot be developed. If this is the case, careful observation of the products children produce may prove to be the most practical way to improve on intelligence tests as assessment devices. This is already done in the areas of music, drawing, and sports, without obvious undesirable consequences. Such an approach, within a multistage selection process, would allow evidence of task commitment to be a part of the selection process as well as a goal of educational design.

The next issue concerns how stringently to set admission criteria. Renzulli argues persuasively for widening the net, that is, to admit 15% or 20% of children, rather than the traditional 2% or 5%, to special classes. Perhaps by providing this larger percentage of children with smaller classes, more individualized instruction, and opportunities to explore topics in depth, we could increase the number of people destined to make eminent contributions as adults.

This may well be sound educational practice for all children. However, given the limited predictive validity from current educational placement measures to adult contributions, limiting the program to any size subset of children seems arbitrary. Why not give all children the education most likely to promote eminent contributions? Renzulli reports that children in the 80th to 95th percentile benefited from his revolving door program as much as children above the 95th percentile. Why stop at the 80th percentile? Why not put all children in small classes with their intellectual peers and expose all of them to revolving door opportunities? Why not emphasize task commitment and creativity at all levels of educational selection?

The third instructional issue involves how best to educate gifted children. Renzulli and Stanley and Benbow report large-scale successful efforts in this direction. Interestingly, these two admirable programs take strikingly different approaches to gifted education. Stanley and Benbow set a high test-score criterion for admission, Renzulli, a relatively low one. Stanley and Benbow emphasize acceleration, Renzulli emphasizes projects that are most easily thought of as a form of enrichment. Stanley and Benbow's program results in children eventually attending classes with much older children, Renzulli's does not. Perhaps the most appealing aspect of Stanley and Benbow's program is that it gives truly precocious children the chance to realize their potential. Perhaps the most appealing aspect of Renzulli's program is that it gives children who might not initially appear exceptional the chance to realize their potential.

Despite these differences, both programs seem successful in motivating children to achieve and in providing conditions under which they can achieve. The success may in large part be due to two common qualities of the programs. One is that both programs give children the opportunity to spend more than the usual amount of time at one pursuit. The experience may create greater than usual excitement during the learning process. It also may help inculcate a taste for the type of detailed understanding that underlies later eminent contributions. Another similarity is the close interaction between an adult teacher and each child that both programs appear to facilitate. The special circumstances of these programs, where children are working intensely in a single area over a prolonged period and the pupil–teacher ratio is very low, seem likely to promote mentor–protégé relations.

How can such motivating relationships be developed when circumstances are less ideal? One strategy would be for academic instructors to emulate some of the techniques of athletic coaches. Perhaps because the athletic performance of high school students constitutes a serious product for many people, coaches have a long tradition of emphasizing dedication, self-confidence, the overcoming of obstacles, and other motivational qualities. These qualities may be just as essential for intellectual achievements as for athletic ones. Thus, we might do well to look to the athletic field for more than entertainment.

Implications for research

What will be the most fruitful approaches for research on giftedness in the next 5 or 10 years? Which issues will prove to be both interesting and tractable to currently available methods? Below we hazard a few predictions.

One useful approach would be to focus on people in the process of becoming productive–creative contributors to a field, for example, high school students who win Westinghouse Science Competition prizes, who publish articles in nationally circulated magazines, or who have their drawings shown in major exhibits. Members of these groups are of special interest for two reasons. They already have made creative contributions – they have not just learned to perform well on tests – but they are still in the process of becoming eminent. In all likelihood, some will become truly eminent, others will become typical producers in the field of their early contribution, others will move on to another field entirely. Studying them can help bridge the gap between the study of schoolhouse-gifted children and creative–productive adults.

A second valuable type of research would be to study in greater detail what benefits children obtain from gifted education programs. Recall the problem of arbitrariness of criteria for selecting children to participate in gifted education classes. One way to solve the problem would be to demonstrate that children who met the placement criteria derived greater benefit from the programs than children who did not.

A third valuable research initiative would be to demonstrate predictive and construct validity for the constructs being used to describe and explain giftedness. At present, we do not know whether alternative measures of metacognition correlate any more highly with each other than they do with measures of other constructs. Our ignorance about the convergent and discriminant validity of creativity is nearly as great. Evidence of the long-term stability of these constructs and their generality across domains is similarly lacking. Before we can feel confident of the role of these abilities in intelligence, generally, and in giftedness, in particular, we must obtain these types of evidence. The new psychometrics of Davidson and Sternberg represents a praiseworthy start in this direction.

The final research recommendation is that researchers start building computer simulations, or other formal models, of gifted performance and of the development of giftedness. Modeling gifted performance would require detailed specification of the processes involved and of the knowledge base on which such processes operate. Modeling the development of gifted perform-ance would require specification of an initial state of a potentially gifted person, a set of transition processes, a set of experiences on which the tran-sition processes would operate, and the end state that would be embodied in the model of gifted performance. Artificial-intelligence simulations of expert knowledge, especially ones that learn from their experience, represent one move in this direction. However, they are not as concerned with psychological plausibility as would be models constructed by people interested in giftedness per se.

What would be the advantages of constructing such models? One advantage would be that building them would force their authors to be explicit about how the hypothesized mechanisms work. Another would be that the models would demonstrate that the hypothesized mechanisms were sufficient to ac-count for gifted performance or for the development of gifted performance in some domain. Finally, building developmental models might go a long way toward bridging the gap between schoolhouse and creative–productive gift-edness. The models could specify the processing characteristics that led to schoolhouse-gifted performance, the transition mechanisms that constituted gifted potential, the types of experiences that could lead to realization of that potential, and the end state of creative–productive giftedness. Building such developmental models of giftedness would pose large challenges, but their successful completion would go a long way toward resolving many of the issues raised in this volume.

References

Borkowski, J. G., Peck, V., Reid, M. K., & Kurtz, B. (1983). Impulsivity and strategy transfer: Metamemory as mediator. *Child Development, 54*, 459–473.

Cavanaugh, J. C., & Perlmutter, M. (1982). Metamemory: A critical examination. *Child Development, 53*, 11–28.

Cooper, L. A., & Regan, D. (1982). Attention, perception, and intelligence. In R. J. Sternberg (Ed.), *Handbook of human intelligence*. Cambridge University Press.

Ferretti, R. P., & Butterfield, E. C. (1983). Testing the logic of instructional studies. Paper presented at the Gatlinburg Conference on Mental Retardation/Developmental Disabilities, Gatlinburg, Tennessee.

Kosslyn, S. M. (1978). Imagery and cognitive development: A teleological approach. In R. S. Siegler (Ed.), *Children's thinking: What develops?* Hillsdale, N.J.: Erlbaum.

Siegler, R. S., & Richards, D. D. (1982). The development of intelligence. In R. J. Sternberg (Ed.), *Handbook of human intelligence*. Cambridge University Press.

Siegler, R. S., & Shrager, J. (1984). A model of strategy choice. In C. Sophian (Ed.), *Origins of cognitive skills*. Hillsdale, N.J.: Erlbaum.

Author index

Alba, J. W., 204, 221
Albert, R. S., 13–14, 69, 128, 140, 332, 333, 334, 339, 342, 345, 350, 351, 353, 354, 381, 419, 427
Algozzine, B., 104
Allen, L., 29
Alvino, J., 62
Amabile, T. M., 115, 280
Anastasi, A., 38
Anastaziow, N. S., 120
Angoff, W. H., 362
Arend, R., 141
Aschmer, M., 98, 99
Ashby, W. R., 30
Astin, A. W., 67
Atkinson, J. W., 47–8
Atkinson, R. C., 185

Bahlke, S., 251
Baker, C. T., 29
Baldwin, A., 104
Bamberger, J., 17–18, 274, 289, 388, 398, 411, 425, 426
Barbee, A. H., 27, 382n1
Barclay, C. R., 169
Barlow, F., 298, 365
Baron, J., 137
Barron, F., 69, 343, 351
Bartkovich, K. G., 369, 376
Baumgarten, F., 298, 299
Baumrind, D., 339, 340
Bayley, N., 371
Becker, G., 337
Beery, R., 42
Bell, E. T., 363, 381
Belmont, J. M., 168, 171
Benbow, C. P., 16–17, 113, 362, 363, 370, 371, 376, 377, 379, 431, 433
Benton, A. L., 153
Bereiter, C., 286
Bernal, E., 104, 105
Bernstein, M., 239
Berrington, H., 332, 339

Biemiller, A. J., 156, 172
Binet, A., 10, 95–6, 102, 129, 266, 370
Birch, J. W., 128
Bloom, B. S., 46, 67, 69–70, 76–7, 100, 114–15, 118, 124–5, 276, 310, 334, 362
Blum-Zorman, R., 32, 38
Bobbitt, B. L., 162, 163, 164, 185, 187, 188
Bolus, R., 120
Boring, E. G., 26
Borkowski, J. G., 8, 9, 163, 169, 170, 173, 182, 186, 188, 189, 190, 197, 422, 424, 425, 428
Borland, J. H., III, 38
Bower, G. H., 371
Bradley, M., 129
Brannigan, A., 266
Bransford, J. C., 187, 197
Bringuier, J. C., 303
Brody, E. B., 348
Brody, N., 348
Bronowski, J., 95
Brookover, W. G., 41
Brown, A. L., 96, 99, 158, 159, 164, 169, 171, 173, 177, 183–4, 185, 186, 188, 189, 286
Brown, R. T., 142
Bruch, C., 105
Bryant, N. E., 185
Burke, R. J., 203
Burks, B. S., 382n1
Burks, G. S., 41
Burt, C. L., 370
Butterfield, E. C., 7–8, 9, 156, 163, 165, 166, 168, 169, 170, 171, 172, 173–4, 175, 177, 178, 421–2, 423, 424, 425, 428, 430–1

Campbell, D. T., 69, 369
Campbell, E., 249–50
Campione, J. C., 96, 99, 164, 169, 173, 174, 177, 178, 183, 184, 185, 186, 189
Carroll, J. B., 39, 156, 201
Carter, K. R., 37, 273
Cattell, R. B., 122, 224, 342, 350
Cavanaugh, J. C., 169, 173, 190, 428

437

Cellerino, M. B., 80
Chambers, J. A., 69
Chandler, M., 100
Chase, W. G., 288, 289, 293
Chaunsey, H., 349
Chennells, P., 347
Chi, M. T. H., 156, 164, 167–8, 171, 176,
    177, 187
Chissom, B., 141
Cleland, L. N., 156, 167, 172
Cohen, R. L., 185, 188, 191
Cohn, S. J., 371
Colangelo, N., 46
Coleman, J. S., 47
Coleman, W., Jr., 93
Collins, E., 101
Collins, J., 289
Converse, H. D., 36
Conway, B. E., 239
Cooper, C., 83
Cooper, L. A., 161, 163, 164, 430
Corriher, S. E., 170, 184, 188
Corsale, K., 187, 197
Courtright, R. D., 5, 417–18, 420–1, 428
Covington, M. V., 42
Cowell, Henry, 37
Cox, C. M., 27, 41, 69, 349, 363, 382n1
Craik, F., 188
Crick, F. H. C., 137, 140
Cronbach, L. J., 37, 236, 288
Crutchfield, R. S., 67, 69, 350
Csikszentmihalyi, M., 11–12, 13, 38, 275, 279,
    280, 289, 337, 417–18, 419, 426–7
Cullinan, D., 129
Curtis, M. E., 172

Dabrowski, K., 94
Datta, L., 350
Daurio, S. P., 47, 374
Davidson, J. E., 8–9, 137, 151, 154, 156–7,
    174–6, 177, 178, 202, 204, 207, 209, 219,
    231, 232, 422, 424, 430, 434
Davis, F. B., 39–40
Davis, J. C., 68
Dearborn, W. F., 29
DeFries, J. C., 99, 130
DeGroot, A. D., 250–1
DeHaan, R. F., 101, 122, 123
Delisle, J. R., 82, 270, 277
Dellas, M., 72
Dempster, F. N., 185, 188, 191
Denham, S. A., 369, 376
Detterman, D. K., 182
Dettman, D. F., 46
DeVillis, R. F., 187
Dick, W., 118, 122
Donlon, T. F., 362
Downey, M. T., 382n1
DuBois, P. H., 53

Dugas, J., 187
Dyson, F., 255

Edlind, E. P., 136
Eiduson, B. I., 350
Eisenberg, A. R., 370
Ekstrom, R. B., 209
Ellis, N., 96, 99
Ellison, R. L., 29
Erikson, E. H., 12, 271, 272, 275–6, 280, 426
Esquirol, 128–9
Estes, W. K., 37, 96, 286
Eysenck, H. J., 129, 135
Eysenck, M., 135

Favazza, A., 378
Fekman, D. H., 160
Feldhusen, J. F., 5–6, 113, 115, 120, 121, 124,
    417–18, 425
Feldman, D. H., 12–13, 36–7, 38, 117, 118–
    19, 157, 237, 268, 270, 285, 286, 287,
    288, 289, 290, 291, 292, 293, 295, 296,
    297, 298, 299, 302, 307, 334, 410, 417–
    18, 419, 420, 425
Ferguson, T. J., 271, 282
Ferrara, R. A., 164
Ferretti, R. P., 156, 170, 171, 173–4, 175, 177,
    178, 423, 424
Fischer, K. W., 291
Flack, J. D., 125
Flavell, J. H., 171, 182, 188
Ford, M. E., 186
Fox, L. H., 104, 343, 362, 369, 370–1, 376,
    378
Franco, L., 275
Franks, J. J., 187
Freedman, D. G., 269
Freeman, F. S., 87
French, E., 39–40
French, J. W., 209
Freud, S., 300, 347
Friedenberg, E. Z., 374, 381
Frost, N., 185
Frost, R., 256
Fulbright, M., 142

Gagne, R. M., 118, 122
Gaier, E. L., 72
Gallagher, J. J., 5, 30, 98, 99, 100, 101, 417–
    18, 420–1, 428
Galton, F., 10, 26–7, 70–1, 95, 96, 101, 341
Garber, H., 121
Gardner, H., 13, 269, 270, 277, 289, 291, 293,
    296, 302, 308, 346, 425, 426
Gardner, M. K., 226
Gear, G., 104
Geis, M. F., 170, 184, 188
George, W. C., 362, 369, 371, 376
Gesell, A., 89

Getzels, J. W., 34, 38, 48, 103, 137, 151, 265, 274, 275, 279, 280, 337, 343
Ghiselin, B., 293, 297
Gibson, J., 347
Gilchrist, M. B., 43
Gill, M. M., 258
Glaser, R., 156, 168, 178
Globerson, T., 163, 164
Goertzel, M. G., 27, 46, 115
Goertzel, T. G., 27, 46, 115
Goertzel, V., 27
Goldberg, R. A., 186
Goldsmith, L. T., 291, 297
Goodman, N., 231, 322
Gove, F. L., 141
Gowan, J. C., 60, 138
Gruber, H. E., 11, 12, 13, 14, 17, 112, 117, 248, 250, 252, 253, 254, 261, 265, 289, 293, 296, 297, 419
Gubbins, J., 82
Guilford, J. P., 29, 38–9, 69, 72, 77, 96, 98, 103, 109, 121, 122, 224

Haensly, P. A., 6, 7, 133, 134, 136, 138, 141, 142, 143, 417–18, 420, 428
Hall, W. B., 343, 350
Halstead, W. C., 135
Hardy, G. H., 319, 366
Harmon, L. R., 67, 69
Harper, T., 138
Hase, K., 349
Havighurst, R. J., 101, 122, 123, 271, 272, 276
Hayes, J., 289, 310
Head, H., 135
Healy, J., 156, 167
Heber, R., 121
Hebert, T., 80
Heims, S., 316
Helmreich, R. L., 119
Helson, R., 67, 69, 350
Hildreth, G., 129
Hilgard, E. R., 371
Hill, A. L., 155, 166
Hilton, T. L., 349
Hobson, J. R., 374
Holland, J. L., 67
Hollingworth, L. S., 35, 151, 299, 302, 344, 374
Holmes, B., 22
Holzman, T. G., 156, 163, 164, 165–6, 172
Honzik, M. P., 29
Horn, J. L., 39, 113, 121, 122, 184, 187
Hoyt, D. P., 68
Hubner, J. J., 120
Hudson, L., 67, 370
Hughes, H. H., 36
Hunt, E., 185–6, 201, 202
Hunt, J. M., Jr., 93, 100, 371, 373
Huttenlocher, J., 167

Huttenlocher, P. R., 167

Inhelder, B., 294–5
Itard, J., 129

Jackson, N. E., 7–8, 9, 156, 160, 163, 167, 172, 421–2, 425, 428, 430–1
Jackson, P. W., 103, 151, 265, 343
Jenne, W., 98, 99
Jensen, A. R., 100, 129, 184, 226, 228, 234, 294
Jensen, D. W., 27, 382n1
Jones, E., 336
Jones, J., 58

Kagan, J., 130
Kaltsounis, W., 136
Kaplan, E., 228
Karlsson, J. L., 129
Karnes, F., 101
Keating, D. P., 37, 159, 160, 162, 163, 164, 177, 185, 186, 187, 188, 343, 349, 350, 362, 365, 366, 370–1, 373
Kellas, G., 187
Keller, E. F., 250
Keniston, K., 338
Ketcham, R., 119–20
Ketron, J. L., 121, 239
Kingsley, M. E., 170, 187, 188
Knapp, J. R., 39
Koeske, R. D., 168
Kogan, N., 352
Köhler, W., 203
Kolloff, M. B., 120
Kosslyn, S. M., 426
Kotovsky, K., 18
Kough, J., 122, 123
Kramer, E. A., 363
Kranz, B., 105
Kreutzer, M. A., 188
Krinsky, S. G., 159, 160
Kubie, L. S., 342
Kübler-Ross, E., 133
Kuhn, T. S., 142, 338, 341
Kurtz, B. E., 182, 189, 190

LaBerge, D., 233
Langer, S. K., 276
Lansman, M., 202
Larkin, J., 288, 293
LaRossa, C., 295
Laski, H. J., 45
Lauwerys, J. A., 22
Laycock, F., 36, 348, 349
Legendre, A. M., 316
Lehman, H. C., 43, 255–6, 363, 374
Leonard, C., 188
Leresche, K., 251
Lesgold, A. M., 161, 172

Lesser, G. S., 39–40
Lewin, K., 259
Lewis, J., 104–5, 185
Lindauer, B. K., 188
Lockhart, R., 188
Lockspeiser, E., 307
Lorge, I., 35
Lucito, L., 99, 104
Ludwig, G., 129
Luecking, E., 100
Lunneborg, C., 185, 186
Lutz, S. W., 67

McCartney, K., 335
McCauley, C., 162, 187–8
McClearn, G., 99
McClelland, D. C., 337
McCoart, R. F., 369
McCurdy, H. G., 27, 46, 71
MacFarlane, J., 29
Macken, E., 376
MacKinnon, D. W., 69, 71, 84, 103, 112, 117,
    118, 120, 124, 146, 337, 338, 342, 343,
    347, 350, 351
McNemar, Q., 39, 69
Maier, N. R. F., 203, 221
Manuel, F. E., 260
Marjoribanks, K., 352
Marland, S. P., Jr., 30, 64–5, 101, 104, 123,
    420–1
Martinson, R., 47
Maruyama, M., 256
Maslow, A. H., 342
Masson, D., 256–7
Medawar, P., 32
Mednick, M. T., 67
Mednick, S. A., 342
Mensch, I., 129
Mercer, J., 104–5
Merton, R. K., 140, 338
Messick, S. B., 137
Mezynski, K., 369, 376
Michael, W. B., 117
Miles, C. C., 26
Mill, J. S., 373
Miller, A. I., 253, 261
Mitchell, J. O., 47
Mitchell, R. F., 190
Mönks, F. J., 271, 282
Montour, K. M., 373, 374
Morris, C. D., 187
Morrison, P., 254
Munday, L. A., 68
Myers, M. G., 163

Nash, W. R., 6, 141, 417–18, 420, 428
Neisser, U., 56, 239
Nelson, V. L., 29
Nevin, D., 379

Newell, A., 96, 225
Newland, T. E., 105, 157–8, 177
Nicholls, J. C., 71, 72
Nicholls, J. G., 116, 118, 119
Nichols, R. C., 42

Oden, M. H., 27, 43, 69, 104, 118, 120, 271,
    332, 374, 382n1
Oglesby, K., 101
Ohanian, P. B., 382n1
Omelich, C. L., 42
Ormrod, J. E., 37, 273
Ornstein, P. A., 187, 197
O'Sullivan, J. T., 197

Packe, M. S. J., 373
Pais, A., 253, 261
Paris, S. G., 188
Parloff, M. B., 67, 350
Peck, V. A., 8, 9, 163, 170, 173, 422, 424,
    425, 428
Pellegrino, J. W., 156
Perfetti, C. A., 161, 172
Perkins, D. N., 203, 204, 221, 338
Perkins, S., 370
Perlmutter, M., 173, 428
Perry, R. B., 255
Peterson, A., 41
Peterson, F. A., 334
Phenix, P. H., 22
Piaget, J., 11, 12, 13, 14, 37, 96, 141, 161,
    229, 273, 274, 276, 281, 286, 287, 288,
    289, 294–5, 296, 303, 345, 347, 410, 426
Piechowski, M. M., 31, 32
Plant, W. T., 351
Plomin, R., 99, 130
Poland, N., 334–5
Pollins, L. M., 370, 374
Polya, G., 366
Posner, M. I., 186, 190
Powell, J. S., 121, 228
Prentky, R. A., 129
Pressey, S. L., 46, 374
Pressley, M., 197
Pribram, K. H., 258
Price, I. A., 209
Purpura, D., 100

Raaheim, K., 229
Rasher, S. P., 349
Rees, E., 168
Regan, D. T., 162, 163, 164, 430
Reid, M. K., 182, 428
Reis, S. M., 53, 57, 76, 80, 81, 82, 85, 132
Renzulli, J. S., 4–6, 30, 31, 41, 53, 54, 57, 59,
    66, 76, 79, 80, 81, 82, 83, 85, 103–4,
    105, 108, 113, 116, 123, 132, 134, 151,
    224, 242, 264, 270, 277, 417–18, 420,
    431–3

note

Revesz, G., 298
Reynolds, C. R., 6, 129, 135, 136, 139, 142, 417–18, 420, 428
Reynolds, M. C., 128
Richards, D. D., 158, 163, 164, 430
Richards, J. M., Jr., 67
Ringness, T. A., 119–20
Roberts, N. M., 133, 134, 138, 142, 143
Robinson, H. B., 29, 40, 371–2, 374
Robinson, J. A., 170, 187, 188
Robinson, N. M., 371
Robinson, R. E., 11–12, 13, 417–18, 419, 426–7
Roe, A., 27, 34, 69, 71, 333, 342, 349, 350, 363
Roeder, C., 136, 137
Roth, S. F., 172
Rothney, J., 29
Runco, M. A., 13–14, 342, 345, 419, 427
Russell, C., 22

Sameroff, A., 100
Samuels, J., 233
Sandberg, T., 185, 188, 191
Sattler, H. N., 348
Saussure, F. de, 278
Scarr, S., 335
Scarr-Salapatek, S., 130, 334, 336
Schaefer, C. E., 352
Schaefer, R. A., 366
Schnabel, A., 411
Schon, D. A., 398
Schonberg, H. C., 363
Schopenhauer, A., 129
Schwartz, S., 186
Sears, P. S., 27, 382n1
Sears, R., 37, 382n1
Selby, C., 93
Shapiro, R. J., 72
Shavelson, R. J., 120
Shiffrin, R. M., 185
Shiver, D., 142
Shrager, J., 422, 424, 429
Siegler, R. S., 18, 158, 163, 164, 170–1, 288, 293, 422, 425, 429, 430
Siladi, D., 168
Simon, H., 96, 225, 288, 289, 293
Simon, Th., 95, 129
Simonton, D. K., 341
Smith, L. H., 53, 57, 76, 80, 132
Snow, R. E., 176, 177, 236
Snyder, R. T., 119–20
Snyder, S. S., 290, 291, 295, 297
Sokol, L., 113
Solano, C. H., 47
Sontag, L. W., 29
Sosniak, L. A., 46, 69–70, 124–5
Southern, M. L., 351
Spearman, C. E., 38, 202

Spence, J. T., 119
Sperry, R. W., 275
Spiegel, M. R., 185
Sroufe, L. A., 141
Stanley, J. C., 16–17, 116, 134, 334, 343, 349, 362, 363, 365, 368, 369, 370–1, 373, 376, 377, 379, 381, 431, 433
Stanton, J. C., 120
Stein, B. S., 187
Stein, M. I., 69
Sternberg, R. J., 9, 10, 15, 31, 55–6, 62, 96, 108, 113, 118, 121, 122, 131, 137, 151, 154, 156–7, 168, 172, 174–6, 177, 178, 184, 197, 201, 202, 204, 207, 209, 219, 224, 225, 226, 227, 228, 229, 230, 231, 232, 233, 239, 288, 293, 379, 417–18, 422, 424, 428, 429, 430, 434
Stewart, M., 186
Strauss, S., 410
Sulloway, F. J., 253, 258
Sumption, M., 100

Tannenbaum, A. J., 4, 5, 6, 11, 47, 116, 117, 123, 151–2, 155, 178, 182, 242, 303, 417–18, 419, 425, 426
Taylor, C. W., 29
Terman, L. M., 27–8, 30, 43, 56, 63, 69, 70–1, 95, 96, 102, 104, 118, 120, 151, 271, 303, 349, 363, 374, 382n1
Thomas, S., 411
Thomas, T., 101
Thorndike, E. L., 57, 345
Thorndike, R. L., 294
Thrower, N., 298
Thurstone, L. L., 29, 96, 202
Tjossem, T., 100
Torrance, E. P., 72, 103, 116–17, 134, 136, 209, 268–9
Trotman, F. K., 46

Vaillant, G. E., 43
Vernon, P. E., 38, 69
Voss, J. F., 37
Vygotsky, L. S., 178

Wachs, T. D., 184
Wagner, R. K., 233, 379
Walberg, H. J., 69
Walberg, H. S., 349
Walker, C. C., 30
Wallach, M. A., 67, 72, 285, 294, 352, 361
Walters, J., 13, 425, 426
Ward, V., 83–4
Watson, J. D., 137, 140
Webb, R., 159
Weber, M., 45
Wechsler, D., 96, 187
Weil, E. M., 227

Weinberg, R. A., 130
Weisberg, R. W., 204, 221
Weiss, P., 101
Wellman, H. M., 182
Wells, H. G., 247
Werner, H., 228
Wertheimer, M., 203, 258
Werts, C. E., 84
Westfall, R. S., 252
Whitmore, J., 108
Wiener, N., 373
Wild, C., 342
Wing, C. W., Jr., 67
Winner, E., 337, 342

Winnicott, D. W., 342
Wittgenstein, L., 412n3
Witty, P. A., 43, 64, 100, 155
Witty, S., 289
Wolf, R., 45–6
Worcester, D. A., 374

Yalow, E., 176, 177
Yarrow, L. J., 334
Young, P., 373
Ysseldyke, J., 104

Zeaman, D., 96, 99
Zuckerman, 69, 333, 341, 363

Subject index

ability(ies), 70, 116, 124, 131, 152, 376; *see also* specific abilities; talents
  belief in one's, 69, 75, 100
  in gifted responses, 130, 131, 132, 133–4, 136, 139, 140
  kinds of, 224
above-average abilities, 4–5, 31, 41, 244
  in three-ring conception of giftedness, 65, 66–9, 72, 73, 75, 76, 80, 82, 85, 87, 88, 103, 123–4
abstract thinking, 66, 75, 97, 274
academic ability, 71, 72–3; *see also* schoolhouse giftedness
academic advancement, 94–9
academic aptitude, specific, 30, 65, 101–2, 123, 348
academic performance, 176
academic success, 67–8
acceleration, 47, 57, 77, 80, 86, 134, 433
  and costs of education, 379–80
  enrichment versus, 277, 371–5
  SMPY, 369, 371
  studies of, 373–4, 377
accommodation, 130–1, 229, 294, 345, 346, 347
achievement, 62, 69, 116, 119, 281, 283, 291, 293, 418
  age of, 256–8, 320, 374
  assessment of need for, 432
  crystallizing experience and, 309
  defined, 119
  drive for, 70, 75, 118
  early, 253, 255, 258
  family in, 332
  motivation, 5, 6, 45–6, 112
  prediction of lifetime, 348–9
  self-concept and, 41–2
  specific, 117–18
  tests, 67, 87, 107
achievement, extraordinary, 252
  giftedness and, 261–2
action information, 78–80, 86–7
adaptation, 9, 130–1, 141, 344

to environment, 55, 56, 108, 223, 225, 230, 235–7, 240, 344, 345
to novelty, 28, 56, 75, 108
adolescence, 18, 112, 271, 272, 274, 281, 311
  cognitive change in, 389
  origins of creative work in, 247
adult creativity
  early giftedness and, 247, 248, 249, 250, 253
  problem finding in, 274–5
adult development, 11
adult giftedness, 18, 33, 112
adult productivity, childhood giftedness as potential for, 151, 153, 154, 430
adults, study of, 41–2
adults, eminent, differences from intelligent children, 417, 418–21
age
  of achievement, 256–8, 320, 374
  and appearance of talent, 81, 330
  in crystallizing experience, 310, 312–16, 329
  and measurability of aptitudes, 39–40
  and reasoning ability, 366
analogies, 205, 226
analysis, 136, 138, 276–7, 409–10
anomalous talents, 4, 5, 25–6, 123
anxiety in families of creative children, 339, 340; *see also* tension
apathy, 142
application, 121, 226
aptitude(s), 29, 34, 124, 283, 327, 345–6
  special, 34, 35, 38–40, 49
  tests, 57, 66, 67
aptitude–treatment interactions, 176, 177
art, 12, 23–4, 123, 124, 278, 279, 281
artistic talent, 122, 136, 268
artists, 25, 34, 272, 275
  creative behavior of, 337–8
  social pressures on, 279
  values of, 343
arts (the), 45, 113
assessment; *see also* measurement
  of creativity, 116–17
  in giftedness, 125, 136, 292–3

assessment (*cont.*)
  instruments 104, 132, 136, 432
  of intelligence (*see also* intelligence tests), 96,
    122
  of newly emerging skills, 277
  of school programs, 81–3
  of self-concept, 114
  of talent, 113–14, 116
assimilation, 229, 294, 345, 346
association, 94, 97
  irrelevant, 423
athletics, 255, 278, 281
attention, 96, 97, 98, 133, 142–3, 291, 293
attitude, in gifted responses, 130
attributional assumption, 266, 269, 270
automatization, 223, 224, 225, 232–3, 234,
    240, 241, 422
  of information processing, 9, 56, 75, 108,
    185, 229
autonomy, 117, 272, 274, 281
average/gifted child comparisons, 156, 158,
    159, 162–3, 164–6, 169–71, 174, 175–6,
    183–4, 186–9, 190, 193, 277, 422, 423–4
  insight problems, 208, 210–13, 215, 217,
    219–20
  thinking strategies, 273
awareness, 137

balance-scale problems, 170, 173–4, 424, 430,
    431
behavior; *see also* performance
  creative, 333, 336–40
  intelligent, 56, 223–4, 345–7
  self-concept and, 120
  strategic, purposeful, 183, 186, 187–8, 189,
    190
behavioral perspective, 37, 287
Berkeley Studies, 29
Biographical Inventory of Creativity (BIC), 105,
    352, 353
biographical observation (method), 15
biographies, 28, 322; *see also* creative lives
  crystallizing experience in, 311, 312–22, 323,
    329, 330
  of eminent people, 27, 115–16, 141–2, 342
biological intelligence, 135, 308, 345–6
bodily–kinesthetic intelligence, 13, 308
boredom (student), 368, 371, 373, 378, 431
boys, gifted, 332–57
brain, 21, 93, 96, 136, 266, 300, 346
brainstorming, 141
breakthrough(s), 22, 24, 142, 296, 297
burnout, 86
business executives, 25, 238–9
busywork, 372

California Psychological Inventory (CPI), 334,
    342, 350, 351, 352, 353
canalization, 332, 334, 336, 345

candidate selection, 341–2; *see also* identifica-
    tion of gifted and talented; Talent Pool(s)
capitalization, 236, 237
career(s), 14, 131, 333, 343
  goodness of fit with, 335–6
  luck, chance in, 48
career choice, 42
  in achievement of eminence, 336, 350
  environmental selection in, 27, 237–8
  as existential act, 341
  experiential demands of, 333–4
case studies, 88, 160, 255–6, 411
  method of, 15, 248, 370
catalytic forces, 291, 292, 302–3
  in development of prodigy, 300, 301
  novelty as, 297–8
categorical clustering, 168, 169, 170
celebrity status, 23–4
chance (luck), 47–8, 49, 85, 112, 152, 273,
    297, 309
  in emergence of giftedness, 34, 35, 47–8
chess, 156, 168, 250–1, 267, 288–9, 299, 302
child development, 11; *see also* development;
    stage development
child rearing, 46–7, 340
childhood (phase), 17, 49, 352
  origins of creative work in, 247, 248, 249,
    250, 253
  relation of creativity in, to adult creativity,
    312–20, 419–20
childhood giftedness, 151–2, 155
  and adult creativity, 247, 248, 249, 250, 253
  difference from eminence in adults, 417, 418–
    21
  as potential for adult productivity, 151, 153,
    312–20, 430
  in school, 18 (*see also* schoolhouse
    giftedness)
  studies of, 157–77
children, 32–4, 112
  cognitive development of, 37–8 (*see also* cog-
    nitive development; stage development)
  prejudice against gifted, 381
choice of instrument in domain, 324–5, 330
classification, 94, 97, 99
closed domains, 278
clustering of concepts, 96, 123
clustering-rehearsal strategy, 192
coalescence, 6, 7, 132, 133, 134, 136–9, 140, 143
cognition, 7, 9, 10, 15, 44, 87, 124, 278, 337
  and creative behavior, 336
  deficiency as delay, 160
  in development of musically gifted children,
    388–413
  differences in, 152, 154, 156, 158, 161–79,
    191 (*see also* individual differences)
  sources of drives in, 345
cognitive components, *see* cognitive process(es)
cognitive development, 15, 37–8, 96, 98–9,

352; *see also* developmental differences, in cognition
and change in talent, 12, 271, 273–6, 277, 280–4, 388, 389, 408
discontinuity in, 426
evenness/unevenness in, 160–1
metacognition in, 428–9
rules and strategies in, 423–5
cognitive disequilibrium, 409–11
cognitive dissonance, 141
cognitive efficiency (theory), 161–4, 169, 177
cognitive functions, 288, 289, 293
universal, 290
cognitive process(es), 9, 38, 151, 177
in chess, 250–1
in insight, 204–8
cognitive psychology, 156, 249, 274, 423
cognitive reorganization, 389, 411
cognitive stages, transition points in, 273–5, 276
cognitive style, 116, 135, 250, 346–7, 430
cognitive theory, 7–11, 15–16, 184, 198
indifference to time, 254
intellectual functioning in, 288, 289–90, 292, 299
coherence, 411
"co-incidence," 300, 301–2, 303
combination, 137, 422
combination rule, 56, 240–1
commitment, 6, 118–19, 132, 133, 134, 142–3; *see also* task commitment
in definition of giftedness, 420
early, 255
communication, 123, 132
necessity of, 138–9
comparison, 121, 137, 226, 422
compensation, 236, 237
competitiveness, 118, 119
complexity, 339, 343, 351
component(s), 184, 225, 240
comparison of, 197–8
defined, 225
componential model, 121, 122
componential subtheory (intelligence), 31, 55, 56, 223, 224–9, 240
computer simulation(s), 96, 422–3, 434–5
concentration, 255
Concept Assessment Kit, 159
concept projection task, 230–1
conception(s) of giftedness, 3–18, 112–27, 239–40, 264
designed to promote research, 151–81
issues in study of, 54–63
limits of current, 152–4
conceptualization, 17
concrete operations, 273, 274, 275, 277
conflict, 6, 132, 133, 134, 140–2, 143
in cognitive change in musical representations, 388, 394, 397, 403–4, 408, 410

in creative behavior, 338
in definition of giftedness, 420
in family, 340, 351
conformity, 340, 343, 344
conservation, 159, 296
of energy, 345, 346–7
construct validity, 429, 434
construction task (musical structure), 394–404, 407, 408–9
consumers of knowledge, 33, 34, 59
content, 39, 133, 224
content domains, 202
context, 6, 132, 133, 134, 139–40, 143, 228
characteristics of, 291, 292
interaction with, 12
contextual subtheory (intelligence), 15, 55, 56, 131, 224, 235–40, 241
control processes, 185, 188, 198, 225
convergent thinking, 40, 98, 103
coordinating schemes, invention of new, 410, 411
coordination (strategy), 404
correspondence (strategy), 404
CPI, *see* California Psychological Inventory (CPI)
creative behavior, *see* creativity
creative lives, 255–8, 342
study of, 103, 117, 248, 249–50, 252, 254, 255, 262, 293
traits of, 68–9, 71, 337
creative or productive thinking, *see* definition(s) of giftedness, USOE
creative personality profile, 340–4, 350–1
creative-productive giftedness, 58–9, 60, 76, 87–8, 134
components of, 115–16
developmental model for, 53–92
differs from schoolhouse giftedness, 418–21, 434, 435
creative thinking, 141, 258–9
creative work, 247, 252, 254, 259, 261–2, 293
creativity, 4–5, 9, 31, 41, 108, 112, 116, 122, 123–4, 265; *see also* childhood (phase)
academic ability and, 72–3
achievement of eminence and, 333, 336–40
assessment of, 116–17, 432
associated with schizophrenia, 129
convergent/discriminant validity of, 434
in creative-productive giftedness, 419–20
as criterion of giftedness, 431, 432
defined as blend of processes and values, 340–1
in developmental view, 287, 296
as domain-specific talent, 6
in educational practice, 103, 433
fluency and, 135
in giftedness, 49, 116–17, 151, 224, 242,

creativity (*cont.*)
    248–9, 418, 425
    and intelligence, 13, 336, 345, 347
    knowledge of, 128
    knowledge in, 118
    nonintellectual factors in, 82
    personality sources of, 351–3
    in psychometric approach, 294
    in schoolhouse giftedness, 419–20
    social significance of, 296
    specification of processes in, 430
    tests of, 71–2, 103, 112, 116–17, 203, 292,
        420
    in three-ring conception of giftedness, 65, 71–
        2, 73, 75, 76, 80, 85, 86–7, 88, 103
    training of, 372
    transformed into eminence, 14 (*see also* child-
        hood giftedness)
    ways of being, 347
criticism, 75
    in creative behavior, 336–7, 427
cross-racial adoption studies, 130
crystallized intelligence, 122, 184, 187
crystallizing experience (the), 13, 306–31, 426
    commonness of, 309–10, 311
    defined, 309
    initial, 309, 310, 312–14, 315, 319, 325,
        329
    occurs in isolation, 322, 323
    refining, 309, 310, 314–15, 319, 325, 329
cues, cuing, 134, 175, 206, 211–13, 214–15,
        216–18
    in decontextualization, 228
    in insight problems, 208, 219
cultural differences and educational concept of
        giftedness, 104–5
cultural enrichment, 372, 373
cultural expectations and expression of talents,
        11–12, 264, 267–8, 270, 273, 275, 279–
        80, 283, 284, 296
cultural factors in giftedness, 53, 56, 250–1,
        300, 303, 340–1
    and contributions of eminent adults, 419
    and development of talent, 24, 264–84
    and domain development, 269, 322, 330
    and intelligence, 345
curiosity, 75, 134, 346
curriculum, 39, 47, 373
    compacting, 57, 77
    domains of, talent areas in, 124
    modification of, for gifted and talented, 85–6,
        277, 372

decisions, 121, 225
decoding skills, 167, 172, 185–6, 193
decontextualization, 228
dedication, 69, 75, 152
deductive problems, 208, 209, 210–11
definition(s) of giftedness, 4, 100–1, 128, 348,

    417–21; *see also* educational definition of
        giftedness
conservative–liberal continuum, 63–4
contextual, 235
differs across societies, 347
Feldhusen, 5–6
implicit and explicit theories, 10
imposed by researchers, 130
as model, 73
multifaceted, 130–4
operational, 17, 96
and performance on Piagetian tasks, 160
psychosocial (proposed), 32–4
purposes and criteria for, 54–5
Renzulli, 4–5, 31, 88–9
static, 133
Tannenbaum, 4, 48–9
Terman, 29
USOE, 30, 64–5, 101–2, 123, 348, 420–1
deprivation, 84
development, 7, 12, 14, 60–1, 426; *see also*
        cognitive development; psychosocial
        development
    crossing paths of, 280–4
    in SMPY, 371
    uneven, 322
    unusual, abnormal, 94
developmental dialectic in musical "midlife cri-
        sis," 410–12
developmental differences, 187, 429, 430
    in cognition, 152, 154, 156, 158, 161, 164,
        177
developmental discontinuities, 426
developmental level and crystallizing experience,
        319–20; *see also* age, in crystallizing
        experience
developmental potential (DP), 31
developmental psychology(ists), 14, 15, 141,
        288, 371
developmental theory, 11–16, 17, 130, 285–305
diagnosis, 37, 227
digital processes, 322
discipline(s), 118, 123
discontent, disapproval, in creative behavior,
        336–7, 338, 342, 344
distinctions (among people), 3; *see also* individ-
        ual differences
divergence, 138, 347
divergent thinking, 40–1, 98, 112
    in creative behavior, 342, 343
    tests of, 72, 116, 151, 352, 353, 420
domain(s), 5, 12, 118, 303; *see also* field(s)
    changing requirements of, and change in tal-
        ent, 271, 275–8, 281–3
    in crystallizing experience, 309, 315, 319,
        320, 329–30, 426
    defined by society, 265, 267, 270–1
    of developmental discontinuity, 426
    necessity of, in prodigiousness, 300

nonuniversal development, 288–90
reorganization of structure of, 287
selection of, 291, 292, 293
social organization of, 279 (*see also* field[s])
stability of, 278
universal or culture dependent, 269
variations within, 267–71
domain-relevant skills, 115–16
domain-specific knowledge, 168, 178, 187, 197
domain-specificity, 14, 16–18, 287, 293, 302, 432
of adult giftedness, 419
of creativity, 420
of developmental stages, 13
dramatic talent, 122, 123

early admittance (school), 374
early intervention studies, 130
ecological factors, 5, 6, 108
economic talents, 22
education; *see also* school(s)
in achievement of eminence, 333, 341, 350
in development of creativity, 14, 341
differentiated, 178–9
education for gifted and talented, 25, 72–3, 76, 88–9, 93, 101, 103, 116, 142, 431–4; *see also* programming for gifted and talented
admission criteria for, 113, 114, 125, 432–3, 434 (*see also* identification of gifted and talented)
concepts of giftedness and, 61–2
evaluation of, 47
purposes of, 59–60
research issues for, 177–9
use of IQ scores in, 363–4 (*see also* SMPY)
educational definition of giftedness, 5
academically advanced, 100–7
policy implications of, 93–111
educational experience(s), 85, 160
educational placement measurements, 3
predictive validity of, 432–3, 434
educational practice, 93, 98–9, 132–4
harm to student in, 368
implications of research for, 417, 431–4
educational programs, 130; *see also* programming for gifted and talented
pacing of, 371, 372, 375–6
educational talents, 22; *see also* schoolhouse giftedness
educators, *see* teachers
efficiency, 8, 9, 184–5, 188, 189, 190, 191, 198; *see also* cognitive efficiency (theory); perceptual efficiency
of mental processing, 135, 136, 137
in reading, 172
effort, 255, 419; *see also* hard work
in extraordinary achievement, 252, 289, 333
ego-involvement, 119
ego strength (system), 75, 259–61, 262

elaboration, 103, 255, 191, 193
elementary information processes, 18, 421–2
specificity of, 429–30
elitism, 83, 380–1
eminence, 13–14, 26–7, 101, 128
achievement of, 332–57
attained, likely, 350
frequency of, 349
qualification in, 34
eminent individuals, 71, 134, 136, 374
study of, 46, 129
encoding, 137, 186, 187, 193, 226, 227, 422; *see also* selective encoding
endurance, 69, 75
energy, 88, 114
enrichment, 47, 433
versus acceleration, 277, 371–5
kinds of, 372–3
Type I, II, III (three-ring concept), 77–8, 79, 80, 87, 134
environment, 48, 49, 134, 152, 287, 292
adaptation, selection, shaping of, 9, 223, 225, 235–8, 240
and crystallizing experiences, 319–20
and emergence of talent, 34, 35, 44–7
factors influencing giftedness, 27, 83–5, 100, 153, 343
family, home, 198, 352–3
interaction of individual with, 14–15, 344, 345
interaction with heredity, 100
manipulation of, 344, 345
in psychological intelligence, 135
role in intelligence, 129–30
in stage development, 298
environmental presses, 352–3
equilibration, 141, 294
error, tolerance for, 339
evaluation, 95, 98, 240, 265; *see also* assessment; measurement
evaluation (operation), 276–7
evolution (theory), 205, 232, 260, 289, 293
excellence, 22, 25, 34, 75, 93, 125, 273
criteria for, 265, 268, 278
domain-specific, 426
precursors of, 265
requirements for, 49
striving for, 112
exceptional intelligence, contextual definition of, 235
exceptionality, giftedness and, 335–6; *see also* extraordinariness
executive level, 97, 98, 136, 137–8, 140, 184, 185, 186–9, 190, 196, 198, 225
expectations, 120, 133, 294, 428
brought to crystallizing experience, 307
parental, 334, 335, 340
experience(s), 9, 66, 105, 332, 426, 435; *see*

experience(s) (*cont.*)
    also crystallizing experience (the); educational
       experience(s)
    complex, 283
    early, and achievement of eminence, 332, 333
    foreshadowing, 297
    forms of, 31–2
    points using intelligence in, 223–4
    provided by environment, 320
    and self-concept, 120
experience-producing agents, 334
experience-selecting agents, 333–4
expert systems, 293, 435
expertise, focused, 311
explicit theories
    cognitive theory, 3, 7–11, 15–16
    developmental theory, 3, 11–16
    domain-specific theory, 16–18
exposure to field(s), 308
expression, 96, 332, 336
extraordinariness, 248, 267

facilitators of giftedness, 34, 49
    nonintellective, 34, 35, 40–4
factor analysis, 29, 39, 201
factor theories of intelligence, 184, 220
failure, 34, 42, 120, 376–7
false positives and negatives, 365–6
falsifiability, 3
family, 44, 45, 46–7, 300, 312, 332–6, 427–8
    and achievement of eminence, 332, 333, 350,
       352–3, 354
    of creative/effective children compared, 339–
       40
    and development of independence, 339
    histories, 14, 334–5, 350
    and intelligence, 344
    as nurturing agency, 112
    as organizer, 14
    position, 85
    presses of, 334–5, 336
fear of flux, 411
feedback (mechanism), 96
feelings, 40, 42, 343
Fels Institute, 29
felt paths, 391, 395, 397, 411
field(s), 113, 289, 291, 292; *see also* domains
    arbitrariness of, 427
    contact with materials of, 308, 309, 330–1
    developmental discontinuity, 426
    fit of individual with, 325, 419, 420
    necessity of, in prodigiousness, 300
    selection of, 292, 293
    shifting requirements of, and change in talent,
       271, 278–80, 281
fields of attention (musically gifted children),
    390–3, 398, 408, 409, 411
    disturbed, 394–5, 408
flexibility, 75, 103, 117

fluency, 75, 103, 135
fluid intelligence, 122, 184
foresight, 136–7, 140
formal operations, 37, 38, 112, 273, 274, 277,
    366, 426
    rules in, 173–4
formal training, 308, 316
free recall problems, 170, 184
freedom from inferiority feelings, 70, 75
frustration, 84, 368, 373
fulfillment, factors linking promise with, 34–48

g factor, 29, 38, 428
    defined, 35
general intellectual ability, 5, 6, 32, 40, 125,
    155, 156, 201–2, 224
    in concept of giftedness, 34, 35–8, 112–13,
       121–2
    defined, 66, 75
    stability of, 151
    in USOE definition of giftedness, 30, 65,
       101–2, 123, 348
general interest assessment techniques, 86
generalizability
    of extraordinary responses, 139–40
    of research findings, 18
generalization, 99
    tests of, 192, 193, 196
generativity, crisis of, 272, 273
Genetic Studies of Genius series, 27, 363
genius, 21, 28, 30–1, 41–2, 71, 133, 273
    crystallizing experience, 426
    defined, 95, 128, 353–4
    in developmental view, 287
    emphasis on, 26–7
    frequency of, 341, 353–4
    incipient, 353
    as madness, 128–9
    mental health of, 43
    and talent, 276, 381–2
Gestalt psychologists, 203, 258–9
gestalten, giftedness as special case of,
    143–6
gift(s), 265
    concept of, 247, 248, 261
    discovery of, 306–31
    innate, 256
    kinds of, 247–52
gifted (the), 53, 54
    definition of, 5, 61–3, 71, 93, 108, 109
    distinct from potentially gifted, 60–1
    numbers of, 310
    profile of abilities, 418
    traits of, 129
Gifted and Talented Children's Education Act of
    1978, 101
gifted behavior(s) (performance), 61–3, 155
    characteristics of, 421–31
    definition of, 73–83

development of, 83
opportunities for display of, 80–1
gifted children; *see also* childhood giftedness
characteristics of, 157–8
number of, 266–7
studies of, 157–77, 264
gifted pool, *see* Talent Pool(s)
gifted responses, 130, 134, 140, 142
shaped by individual, 134
variable nature of, 133
giftedness, 9, 62, 116, 128–48; *see also* conceptions of giftedness, definition(s) of giftedness, talent(s)
and achievement of eminence, 332–57
assumptions about, 151–2, 154–5
causes of, 35, 182, 421
consensus on, 23
as continuum of abilities, 28
development of, 12, 14, 60–1, 62, 273–4, 283, 334
in developmental view, 287
differences in, 80, 136
experience-producing/experience-selecting agent, 334, 335
factors in, 31, 72
fostering, 178–9
generality of, 116, 121
as heredity phenomenon, 29
intuitive descriptions of, 177
levels of analysis of, 18
models of, 183–5, 191, 308–10
must be manifest, 135
as organizer, 335
plurality of, 8, 9, 241, 242, 302, 418
predictive and construct validity in, 434
reification of, 266–7, 283
as stable trait, 264, 282
temporal constitution of, 271–84
two levels of, 55–9, 417–35
unitary and multiple, 268–70
goals, 142, 345
career, 343
change across life-span, 271–3, 274
high and difficult, 112, 125, 259–60, 261
integration toward, 70, 118
single-minded pursuit of, 255
goodness of fit, 235, 236, 237
family/giftedness, 335–6
giftedness/career demands, 333–4
individual/domain, 309
individual/field, 419
person/environment, 345
task/solution, 347
grandparents, 334
greatness, *see* eminence
group factors, 38, 101, 108
Guinness Book of World Records, 4, 25, 267

Handbook of Human Intelligence, 96

hard work, 31, 69, 70, 74, 125; *see also* effort
Harvard Growth Study, 29
hat rack problem, 203, 221
heredity, 29, 48, 70, 85, 95, 99–100, 116
in biological intelligence, 135
in intelligence, 129–30, 308
hero(es), as role model, 340, 351
higher-order processes, 10–11, 16, 172, 225
variation across domains, 276–7
highly creative persons (term), 71
historical forces, circumstances, 11, 45, 248, 292, 340, 344
home(s), 46–7, 427; *see also* family; environment
homuncular view of giftedness, 270
"homunculus" (the), 225
human extraordinary, self-construction of, 247–63
Hunter Aptitude Scales for the Gifted, 39–40
Hunter College Elementary School, New York City, 39
hyperlexia, 167
hypothesis testing, 135, 154

idea(s), 40, 88, 137, 138, 142
necessity of communication of, 138–9
new, 48, 96, 112, 116, 295
ideally intelligent individual (the), 239–40
identification(s), 343, 351
identification and recall, 161
identification of gifted and talented, 7, 17, 30, 53, 54, 55, 57–8, 61, 62–3, 80, 88, 89, 93, 132, 178, 201, 277, 380, 431–2; *see also* assessment; measurement
absolute approach in, 63
children missed in, 153
composite index in, 116
early, 100
in educational practice, 94, 101, 102–3, 104–7, 109
plan for, 76–81
prognostic value of, 273
restrictive, 63–4
scales used in, 123
shifts in social expectations and, 280, 296
for SMPY, 366–9, 371, 377
in sociocultural model, 270–1
in three-ring model, 81, 83–4, 86–7
identity, 272, 273, 274, 281
idiot savant, 135, 155–6, 166–7
illumination in creative experience, 342; *see also* crystallizing experience (the); insight
imagery, 342, 343
imaginational mode (overexcitability), 32
imitation, 389, 393, 411
implicit theories, 3, 4–7, 10, 11
impulsiveness, 137

independence, 134
  as trait in creative behavior, 338–9, 343, 344
individual (the), 11, 12, 14–15, 134
  development, 94
  focus on, 4, 5, 152, 154–5, 418
  internal/external worlds of, 55, 56
  qualities of (in giftedness), 289–92, 302, 303
  in social context, 21–2
  varied responses in, 131
individual differences, 5, 184, 186, 287, 429,
    430
  as concept of giftedness, 100, 107t, 108, 109,
    293
  in crystallizing experiences, 329
  in developmental view, 287–8
  measurement of, 95–9
  in memory performance, 170, 171, 188
  in multiple intelligences, 308
  in perceptual efficiency, 185–6
  study of, 94
individual differences in cognition, 152, 154,
    156, 158, 177, 184, 191, 198
  in cognitive efficiency, 161–4
  in knowledge, 164–9
  in metacognition, 171–6
  in strategy use, 169–71
individual differences in intelligence, 201, 221,
    240, 345
  basis of, 99–100
  insight in, 202, 206–7, 214, 219–20, 222
  variables in, 346
individuality, 117
  of creative persons, 342, 343–4
inductive reasoning, 226–7
  insight problems and, 208, 209, 210, 211
  problems of, 164–6, 172
inference, 121, 184, 226
influence, 132
information, *see also* selective encoding, combi-
    nation, and comparison
  available to creative person, 342, 343
  defined, 38
  durability of, 185
  role in giftedness, 117–18
  stored, 100 (*see also* information storage and
    retrieval)
information processing, 30, 66, 95, 101, 102,
    108; *see also* automatization, of information
    processing; elementary information
    processes
  ability, 135, 308
  components (triarchic theory), 223, 240
  creativity and, 337
  differences between gifted and regular chil-
    dren, 189–90
  efficiency, 187, 188
  insightful, 219–22
  intellect as, 38
  levels of, 135

in model of intelligence, 184–5
operations in, 96–7, 98
parental observation of early, 198
speed of, 161–2, 197
style of, 136
tasks of, 187
information-processing theory(ies), 121, 130,
    201, 202, 219, 220–1
  intellectual functioning in, 288, 290, 292, 293
information processor, brain as, 30
information storage and retrieval, 96, 97, 184
  effect on performance, 421–2
  efficiency of, 185, 186, 189, 190
  speed of, 162–3, 202
informational organization, principles of, 344,
    345
innovation, 420; *see also* novelty
  in creativity, 49, 419
insanity, 128–9
insight, 8–9, 10, 136, 137, 140, 143, 157, 320
  cognitive disequilibrium and, 409, 410–11
  logical–mathematical problems of, 174–5, 176
  "moments" of, 254
  "nothing-special" views of, 203, 204, 221
  role of, in giftedness, 201–22, 425
  special-process views of, 203–4, 221
insight problems, 151, 154, 203, 204, 207, 208,
    219–20, 221, 424, 430
  ability to deal with novelty, 231–2
  convergent–discriminant validation, 208–11,
    219
inspiration, 203, 411; *see also* insight
  sources of, 342, 343
instruction, 160, 165, 178; *see also* training
  implications of descriptions of giftedness for,
    429, 430–1
  individualized, 433
  in strategy use, 169, 173–4, 175
instructional gaps, filling in, 174, 176, 196,
    319, 428
instrument (music), as field of attention, 391,
    392, 393, 395, 411
intellect
  defined, 38
  superior general, 49
intellective attributes, 31–2
intellectual ability/aptitude, 100, 108, 122, 202
  memory correlates, 185–6
intellectual achievement
  extreme instances of, 300
  significant and exceptional, 202, 219, 220
intellectual giftedness, triarchic theory of, 223–
    43
intellectual mode (overexcitability), 31–2
intellectual talent, 122
intelligence, 37, 95–6, 108, 128–9, 201–2, 223,
    336; *see also* IQ
  and ability to learn, 424

and achievement of eminence, 332, 333, 336, 341, 342, 344–7, 349–53
  concept(s) of, 55–9, 113
  and creativity, 13, 67, 69, 116–17, 336, 345
  defined, 26, 38, 345
  extremes in, 129–30
  forms of, 13, 308
  as function of insight abilities, 206, 207–8, 220, 221
  giftedness and, 129, 135–6, 425
  increase/decrease in, 121, 267–8
  index of, 241
  models of, 183, 184–5, 186, 189
  modifiability of, 121
  multifactor theory of, 38–9, 121–2, 189–90
  multiple, 269, 270, 277
  predictive and construct validity in, 430, 434
  "raw," unmediated, 310, 311, 315, 329, 330
  in schoolhouse giftedness, 422
  social context of, 266–7
  theory of, 184, 198, 224
  universal/relativistic, 236, 237
  variations in, 129–30 (*see also* individual differences in intelligence)
  as what test measures, 96
intelligence tests, 17, 87, 98, 156, 159, 203
  assumptions of, 104
  predictive validity of, 66, 67–9
  what they measure, 29, 96, 113
intelligent behavior, 223–4
  components of, 345–7
  learning, planning, execution, evaluation of, 56
interaction(s) (interactionism), 12, 14–15, 78; *see also* goodness of fit
  early talent and domain distinctions, 319
  giftedness as product of, 135–6, 285
  of heredity and environment, 100
  of individual and environment, 34, 287
  of individual skills and cultural values, 269, 270
  in three-ring conception of giftedness, 66, 73, 75–6, 83, 87–8, 103–4, 123–4
interest(s), 343, 376
  intrinsic, 116, 118
internal representations, definition, 390
internal representations of musical structure, 391, 392
  change in, 388
  in construction task, 395–404, 407
  disintegrated, reintegrated, 409, 410, 411
  multiple, 388–9, 390, 394, 397–8, 408–9, 411, 426
  network of, 389, 393, 408
  in notation tasks, 404–8
  unified in children, 409, 411
interpersonal intelligence, 13, 308
interpersonal relationships, 350

intervention(s), 17, 334
  SMPY, 368, 371
interviews
  with master teachers, 311, 314, 320–9, 330
  as research strategy, 173, 290, 238
  in study of family in achievement of eminence, 335
intimacy, 272, 273
intrapersonal intelligence, 13, 308
intuition(s), 117, 411
inventions, 48
IQ, 34, 41, 266, 285, 292, 293, 294; *see also* intelligence
  childhood potential and, 27–9
  and divergent thinking, 117
  of eminent persons, 349
  and family environment, 353
  and giftedness, 29, 35–8, 40, 62, 417, 418
  in identification of gifted and talented, 113, 431, 432
  and insight, 207
  intelligence and, 26
  process variables and, 46
  relations with special aptitudes, 39–40
IQ cutoff score, 29, 58, 62, 63, 65, 266, 267, 348
  Terman's, 335
IQ scores, 187
  consistency of, 29
  inefficient for instructional grouping, 363–4
  stability of, 153
  and success in school, 57–8
IQ tests, 57, 94, 201, 220, 417, 418, 421
  insight problems and, 232
  as predictors of adult creativity, 274, 275
isolation-of-variables strategy, 10, 16

job opportunities, 29; *see also* career(s)
  in quota talents, 24–5
Johns Hopkins Center for the Advancement of Academically Talented Youth (CTY), 368–9, 381
Johns Hopkins Talent Searches, 362, 368–9, 377, 381
judgmental skills, 238–9
justification, 121, 226

knowledge, 8, 115–16, 122, 139, 259
  acquisition, 112, 371
  bases, 118, 184, 185, 228, 434–5
  in chess, 250
  as component of intelligence, 186, 187
  components of acquisition of, 9, 31, 174, 225, 227–9, 231, 241
  domain-specific, 168, 178, 187, 197
  individual differences in, 164, 168–9

knowledge (*cont.*)
  measurement of, 190, 197
  perspective of, 160, 164–9, 177
  role in giftedness, 117–18

laboratory experiments, 15, 94
  time scale in, 254–5
language, 46, 129, 135, 136, 278
large-sample methods, 11, 15
late bloomers, 17, 257–8, 274, 362
lawyers, 4, 25
leadership, 116, 122, 123
  ability, in USOE definition of giftedness, 30, 65, 101–2, 123, 348
learning, 28, 123, 176, 204, 223, 418
  ability, 154, 345–7, 428
  action information in, 79–80
  assessment of, 344
  contextually determined, 228
  versus development debate, 286
  excitement in, 433
  formal, 348
  gifted/average comparison, 424
  IQ and, 336
  operations in, 347
  opportunities for, 46
  role in giftedness, 117–18
  sequential and developmental process, 371
  situations, 58
  skills, metamemory in, 189–96
  status, differences among individuals, 371
  style, 133, 136; *see also* cognitive style
lesson-learning giftedness, 57, 60, 72, 87; *see also* schoolhouse giftedness
level of aspiration, 259–60
levels of analysis, 421–31
life-span
  criteria for excellence at points in, 265
  development of giftedness across, 14, 15, 17, 154
  individual capacity for action changes across, 264, 270, 271–3, 283
  transitions in, 12, 426
life-style, 103
linguistic intelligence, 13, 308
locus of control, 82–3
logical–mathematical intelligence, 13, 308
logical–mathematical reasoning ability, 158, 159–60
long-term memory (LTM), 97, 162–3, 164, 185–6, 202
longitudinal studies, 271, 283, 411; *see also* Terman longitudinal study
  of achievement of eminence, 349–53
  of gifted boys and their families, 332–57
lower-order processes, 10–11, 172

macro-developmentalists, 286–90
madness, genius and, 128–9
maintenance tests, 192, 193, 196

map drawing, 290–1, 294–8
mapping (component), 121, 184, 226
Marjoribanks Family Press Inventory, 334, 335
masculine/feminine in personality, 342–3
mastery
  process of, 290, 291, 292, 296, 299, 300, 301, 302
  rate of, 422
match, problem of, 371, 373, 420
math–science ability, 136
  and achievement of eminence, 336, 344, 349–53
mathematical reasoning ability, 156, 362
  choice of, in SMPY, 363, 364, 365
mathematical talent, 113–14, 265, 280, 330
mathematically precocious youth, 361–87
mathematicians, 32, 280, 426
  crystallizing experiences, 315–20
  development and, 281–2
mathematics, 16–17, 66, 69, 113, 255–6, 278; *see also* Study of Mathematically Precocious Youth
  assessment of talent in, 113–14
  cognitive development and demands in, 275
  crystallizing experiences in, 306, 311, 320
  early appearance of talent in, 330
  mental processes in, 322
measurement, 40–1, 49, 94, 95; *see also* assessment; testing; tests
  of ability to deal with novelty, 230–2
  of contextually directed intelligence, 238–40
  of creativity, 72
  criteria for, in domains, 278
  of giftedness, 73, 132, 264, 274, 417, 418
  of individual differences, 95–9
  of insight, 202, 203, 208–11, 221
  instruments of, 5, 107, 432
  of intellectual giftedness, 223, 224, 225, 228–9, 232, 233–4, 240–1
  of intelligence, 27–8, 35, 37, 56–7, 66, 201–2, 221, 345, 348 (*see also* intelligence tests)
  of IQ, 266 (*see also* IQ; IQ tests)
  of perceptual efficiency, 185
  precision in, 267
  of special abilities, 67
mechanical talent, 122
mechanisms
  in gifted performance, 421–31, 435
  underlying intelligent behavior, 223, 224–9, 240
memory, 66, 75, 94, 97, 98, 103, 122, 291, 293; *see also* long-term memory (LTM); short-term memory (STM); working memory
  capacity of slots in, 185
  correlation with giftedness, 163–4
  feats of, 156
  individual differences in, 170, 171, 188
  influenced by domain-specific knowledge, 168

modes of, 99
scanning, 185, 421, 422, 429
span, 185
and strategy selection, use, 424, 429
tasks, 190
Mensa, 351
mental abilities, 202
latent, 201
mental health (status), 43
mental operations, 93, 94, 95–9, 103, 224
defined, 39
for metacognition, 428–9
mental process, 16, 40, 130, 136, 347
measured in intelligence tests, 96
multifaceted, 29
uneven development of, 322
mental processing; *see also* information processing; processing
in differences in giftedness, 136
divergence in abilities in, 131
purposeful and unique, 139, 140
mental reorganization(s), 291
mental retardation, *see* retarded (the),
retardation
mental testing movement, 30; *see also* tests
mentors, 115, 300, 433
meta-awareness, 136, 137, 428
metacognition, 7–8, 10, 15, 99, 102, 136, 169,
171–6, 178, 185, 186, 421, 434
as component of intelligence, 184, 188–9,
198
defined, 171, 188
in giftedness, 425, 428–9
metacognitive knowledge, 432
metacomponents, 9, 31, 121, 184, 225–6, 240,
241
metalearning, 43–4
metamemory, 8, 190
and emergence of strategic behavior, 191–6
in gifted children, 182–200
metaphors, 205
micro-developmentalists, 286–90
midlife crisis (in development of musically
gifted children), 388, 389, 409–12, 426
minority students, 104–5, 106
mnemonic strategies, 163, 168
models, modeling, 73, 165, 423
of giftedness, 183–5, 191, 308–10, 434–5
of inductive reasoning, 165
of intelligence, 55, 96, 183, 184–5, 186, 189
in problem solving, 205
monitoring, 184, 196, 225
moral talents, 22, 265, 267, 270
motivating relationships, 433–4
motivation, 6, 10, 15, 16, 100, 108, 116, 123;
see also task commitment
to achieve, 5, 6, 41, 45–6, 112, 114–15
in chess, 250
and creativity, 103, 112
in identification of gifted, 431, 432

defined, 69
in giftedness, 7, 118–19, 125, 242, 418
in goodness of fit, 419
intrinsic/extrinsic, 119, 259, 280
in music, 251
obstacles and, 141
of parents, 334
and success in SMPY, 376, 377–8
and talent, 326–7, 328–9, 330
as variable in intelligence, 346
motivators, 119
multiple intelligences theory (MI theory), 13,
308, 309, 310–12, 322, 328, 329, 330
multiple talent(s), 29–30, 64
music, 16, 17–18, 23–4, 67, 123, 251–2, 278,
289, 302, 308, 381
crystallizing experiences, 306–7, 311, 312–
15, 320
early appearance of talent in, 330
mental processes in, 322
precocity in, 363
self-training in, 316
musical dimensions, definition, 390
musical intelligence, 13, 308
musical structure, 388, 392–3, 395, 398, 402,
412
musical talent, 122, 136, 265, 330
musically gifted children, 425, 426
cognitive issues in development of, 388–413
musicians, 274, 426
crystallizing experiences, 312–15
and social pressures, 279–80

National Commission on Excellence in Education, 93
National Merit Scholarship Finalists and Scholars, 42–3
naturalistic assumption(s), 266, 269, 283, 284
naturalistic observation (method), 15
nature/nurture controversy, 37, 129–30, 266
negative feelings, sublimation of, in creativity,
337
"networks of enterprise," 293
neurological organization, 269, 270
neurology, 99–100
neurotransmitters, 99–100
Nobel Prize, 341
nonintellective facilitators, 34, 35, 40–4
nonintellective factors (traits), 30, 31–2, 49, 65,
70
in childhood giftedness, 152
in creative–productive accomplishment, 71,
83
nonverbal reasoning tests, 105, 234
notation tasks (music), 404–9
notational processes, 322
novelty, 9, 223, 224, 225, 229–32, 233, 234,
240, 241, 295, 296–8, 420
adaptation to, 28, 56, 75, 108

numerical reasoning, 66, 75; *see also* mathematical reasoning ability
nurturance, 27, 33, 105, 109, 112, 129, 134, 153, 265
  in family, 46–7
  of talent, 122, 124

"objective" tests, 3, 87
observation, 128
obstacles, 140–2, 143
occupations; *see also* career(s)
  as talents, 124
oddity learning tasks, 183–4
open domains, 278
open-mindedness, 117
openness
  to experience, 75, 146, 342
  to personality and creative potential, 352
opportunities, 12, 46, 100
  and development/expression of creativity, 341
  informing, 14, 333
  nurturing, 112, 114
organization of mental powers, indivisibility of, 29
originality, 58, 75, 103; *see also* novelty
overachievers, 293–4
overexcitability, 31–2
oversensitivity, 94

paired-associate learning, 184
paired-associate task, 191–2, 193
paradigms, 142
parent–child dissimilarity, 351–2
parent–child relationship, 334, 339–40
parental loss, 332, 339
parents, 120, 291, 292, 312, 373, 427–8
  development and early experience of, 334, 335
  permissive, 340
  personality profile, 84–5, 350–3
  recognition of giftedness by, 183, 198
  role in achievement of eminence, 332, 334, 350–3, 354
  role in motivation, 115
passion, 118, 250
passivity, 337, 338
patterns, 293, 371
peers, 44, 47, 291, 300
penicillin, 24, 205, 232
perception, 69, 96, 204
  of self, 120
perceptual efficiency, 185–6, 189, 190, 193
  as fundamental characteristic of giftedness, 189, 190, 191, 194, 196, 198
perceptual–logical reasoning, 160, 161
perfectability of human beings, 45
performance, 25, 34, 45, 114, 125, 161, 171, 266–7; *see also* behavior; product(s)
  actualization of, 30
  in assessment of talent, 113
  difference of extraordinary from ordinary, 289–90, 291, 292
  as domain specific, 302
  giftedness defined as, 12, 95, 101, 104, 105, 152, 154–7, 161, 166
  motivation in, 280
  process variables and, 45–6
  school, 107
  self-concept and, 41–2
  three-ring conception of giftedness in, 73
performance components, 31, 121, 225, 226–7, 241
performing skills, 48
perseverance, 69, 75, 273
persistence, 41, 70, 118, 134, 138, 140, 142; *see also* commitment
person–environment interaction, 14–15, 344, 345
personality, 33, 118, 291, 332, 352
  and achievement of eminence, 332, 333, 334
  conflicts in creativity, 337
  and creative behavior, 338–44, 350–1
  and creativity in children, 117
  factors influencing giftedness in, 70, 83–5, 427
  in family, 14, 334
  of geniuses, 27, 41–2
  masculine/feminine in, 342–3
  of parents, 84–5, 334, 336, 340, 350–3
  in psychological intelligence, 135
  stability of, 153
  traits, 34, 49, 71
personological traits, 40–4
photography, 67
physical talent, 122
physics, 69, 113, 261
Piagetian perspective, 286
  and childhood giftedness in, 158–61, 177
Piagetian stages, 160–1; *see also* stage development
planfulness, 136, 137, 140
planning, 123, 223, 225, 240
plastic arts, 278
poetry, 278
Posner letter matching task, 190, 422
potential, 40, 49, 134, 265, 329, 341
  antecedents of, 351–2
  childhood giftedness as, 28, 151, 153
  for crystallizing experience, 331
  giftedness as, 49, 284, 417
  and IQ, 27–9
  personality in fulfillment of, 42–3
  predictive of future accomplishment, 128
  realization of, 265, 283, 433
  shaped by cultural expectations, 270
  unrecognized, 270, 420

utilization of, 292
potentially gifted (the)
    distinct from gifted, 60–1
    initial state of, 435
Power (P) factor, 135
practice, 308, 389
    chess, 250
    and talent, 326
precocity, 17, 32–4, 99, 116, 255, 258, 270, 276
    defined, 361–2
    desire for self-advancement and, 41
    developmental, 37–8, 160
    in math, 361–87
    prejudice against, 381
    variability in, 160
prediction(s), 27, 35, 48, 264, 270, 274–5, 420
    of adult productivity, from childhood giftedness, 130, 151, 152, 249
    clinical versus statistical, 432
    of evaluation(s) of intelligence, 239–40
    of genius, 381
    of individual differences, 186
    of intelligence, 348
    of lifetime achievement, 348–9
    in mathematical reasoning, 362
    from school success, 280
    of strategic behaviors, 183
    through tests, 67–9, 72, 274, 294, 349, 362
predictive validity, 432
    description of giftedness, 429, 430
    educational placement measurements, 432–3, 434
    IQ, 36–7
    SAT-M, 377–8
    of tests, 66, 67–9, 72, 274, 294, 349, 362
predispositions, 112, 426
    brought to crystallizing experience, 307, 314, 324, 326–7
prior knowledge, 204, 217, 220, 221, 424
problem finding, 38, 44, 337, 341
    versus problem solving, 274–5, 280, 281
problem-finding ability, 345, 346
problem identification, 69, 75, 137, 141
problem orientation
    in creativity, 341, 343–4
    of intelligence, 336, 345–7
problem-oriented operations, 347
problem solving, 28, 44, 69, 96, 103, 121, 277, 337
    ability, 239–40, 314–15, 345–7
    creative, 134, 341, 347
    creative thinking as, 258–9
    deliberate, 185
    and intelligence, 203
    metacognition in, 171–6
    musically gifted children, 391, 403–4
    versus problem finding, 274–5, 280, 282
    processing components in, 178

reasoning in, 98
    skills prerequisite to, 351
    strategies in, 169–71, 188
    styles of, 38
    time in, 254
problems
    real, 134
    slightly exceeding level mastered, 371
    ways gifted deal with, 43–4
process analyses, 156
process variables, 45–6
processes of intellectual functioning, 12–13, 286
    specification of, 434
processing, 177; *see also* information processing; mental processing
    automatic, 197 (*see also* automatization)
    components of, 177–9, 184, 435
    holistic, 136
    level of detail of, 421–31
    of products of information processes, 18, 421–3, 430–1
    of response, 132
prodigies, 13, 156, 265, 267, 274, 283, 290, 292, 381
    age of achievement, 374
    defined, 299, 301
    lacking in visual arts, 320
    math, 316
    study of, 298–302
prodigiousness, 25
    transition to adult artistry, 388, 389, 408, 409–12
producers of knowledge, 33–4, 59
product(s), 26, 30, 39, 224; *see also* creativity; performance
    as assessment instruments, 113, 432
    eminence as, 332
    emphasis on, 417, 418
    factors in great, 34
    new, 112
    socially valued, 151, 152, 153
production skills, 48–9
productivity, 45, 339
    eminence as, 128
professional achievement, 67–9
programming for gifted and talented, 53, 54, 55, 57, 58, 61, 63, 73, 80, 81, 87, 88, 89, 157, 270, 277; *see also* curriculum; education for gifted and talented
    differentiated, 153
    using three-ring conception, 81–3
promise; *see also* potential
    and fulfillment, 34–48
prompting, 173–4, 175
propensities, 131, 291
Protestant ethic, 45
provincials (intelligence), 224
psychiatry, creative behavior in, 337–8

psychic reorganization, 272, 273, 286
psychoanalysis, 336, 337–8
 family in, 334
psychological defenses, lack of, in creative process, 342
psychological development, 256
psychological intelligence, 135–6, 137
psychological model (perspective), 5, 26–32, 101
psychological research, 96
psychological vigilance (concept), 135
psychological well-being and achievement of eminence, 350
psychology, creative behavior in, 337–8
psychometrics, 10, 27, 200–1, 220–1, 285, 287, 293, 294, 430, 434
 giftedness in, 302
 prodigies in, 299, 300
 theory without, 30–1
psychomotor ability, 124, 136
 in USOE definition of giftedness, 30, 65, 101–2, 123, 348
psychomotor mode (overexcitability), 31–2
psychosocial approach, 4, 6, 11, 21–52
 proposed definition of giftedness in, 32–4
psychosocial development, 43
 and change in talent, 271–3, 275–6, 280–4
psychosocial excellence, 265
public good (the), 60
pupil–teacher ratio, 433
purpose, 262
purposiveness, 235

qualitative differential (average/gifted), 277
quantification, 267
quantitative analysis, in age of achievement, 256–8
quantitative differential (average/gifted), 277
Quiz Kids, 237–8
quota talents, 4, 24–5, 26, 123

Raven Progressive Matrices, 37, 105, 159, 234
reaction time, 187–8, 190, 221
reaction time tests, 161
reading, 156, 229, 232–3
reading ability
 precocious, 153, 163, 167, 172
 and self-concept, 120
reasoning, 94, 97–8, 231
 ability, 160, 169, 345–6, 365–6
 insight in, 203
 scientific, 156
 syllogistic, 227
 tests, 220
recall, 187, 193, 195, 196, 197
recognition, 140, 142–3, 162, 204
reflection, 136, 137, 409–11
rehearsal strategy, 187–8

reinforcement, 134, 265
relativity (theory), 253
relevance, environmental, 235, 240
relevance information, 218, 219
relevant academic enrichment, 372, 373
remediation, 227
renown, 41
representation, 161
representational development hypothesis, 426
repression, lack of, in creative persons, 342, 343
research, 8, 11
 concept(s) of giftedness in, 61, 62–3, 88–9, 151–81
 empirical, 3, 11, 16, 248
 individual differences in cognition, 177–9
 two levels of giftedness and, 417, 418, 419, 422, 434–5
research skills, strategies, 11, 15, 16, 134
resource development, allocation, 226, 300
resource scarcity and education of gifted, 380–1
response(s), 121, 134, 137, 226, 240
 alternative, 135
 choice of, 97
 to conflict, 140–2
 to context, 140
 divergent, 347
 dynamic, 130–1, 133
 extraordinary, 136–7, 138, 139–40, 141, 142
 flash-in-the-pan, 140
 processing of, 132
 selective, 338
retarded (the), retardation, 99, 128–9, 423, 425
 deficits of, 182
 studies of, 153, 157
retarded/average children comparisons, 154, 156, 158, 160, 163, 164, 169, 170, 171, 173, 176, 177, 186
retention components, 31
Revolving Door Identification Model (RDIM), 76–83, 270, 431–2, 433
reward(s), 7, 119, 280
role(s), 279–80, 308
role models, 339, 340, 343, 351
rules and strategies, 18, 97–8, 184
 combining operations on products, 421, 423–5, 431
 in problem solving, 170–1, 173–4

satisfaction, and creative/intelligent behavior, 347
scarcity talents, 4, 23, 24, 25, 26, 123
schizophrenia, 129

Scholastic Aptitude Test (SAT), 17, 113, 116, 203, 274, 344, 349, 350
  predictive validity of, 377–8
  use in SMPY, 361, 362, 364–6, 377
school(s), 32, 33, 44, 84, 93, 94, 266, 348
  and development of giftedness, 350
  motivation in, 280
  as nurturing agency, 28, 112
  prediction of success in, 48
  and talents, 24, 25, 26
schoolhouse giftedness, 18, 57–8, 60
  versus creative–productive giftedness, 418–21, 434, 435
science
  assessment of talent in, 113–14
  commitment in, 143
  conflict in, 142
  creative, 338
  precocity in, 363
  and society, 45
scientific revolutions, 142
scientific talent, 122
scientific theories, 338
scientists, 32, 34, 117, 419
  creative behavior of, 338
  insight in, 205–7
  values of, 343
score (music), 391, 392
sculptors, sculpture, 67, 69
seeing possibilities where others do not, 132, 134, 140, 420
selection, 30, 121
  of environment, 55, 56, 223, 225, 230, 237–8, 240
selection (for gifted programs), 3, 17, 57, 59, 67, 268, 431–3, 434; *see also* education for gifted and talented, admission criteria for; identification of gifted and talented
  bases of, 418
  multistage process of, 432
  use of tests in, 68–9, 73
selective encoding, combination, and comparison, 137, 174–6, 228, 428, 430
  in insight, 8, 204–6, 207–8, 211–21, 231–2
self-advancement, desire for, 41
self-concept, 5, 6, 41–2, 112, 119–21, 125, 272, 418
  academic, 82–3
  aspects of, 120
  assessment of, 114
  of creative person, 103, 341
  in creativity, 112, 259
  crystallizing experience and, 308, 309
self-confidence, 41, 69, 70, 75
self-constructive activity, 248–63
self-criticism in creative behavior, 337, 427
self-definition, 341
self-fulfillment, 59–60, 342

self-knowledge, 259
self-management, 174–5, 176, 251
self-mobilization, 11, 258–61, 262
self-pacing, 375–6
self-report, 72, 105
self-teaching, 316–19, 323, 330
self-worth, 42, 378
semantic organization, 184, 186
sensitivity, 75, 341, 344, 346
  to significant problems, 338
sensorimotor learning, 273–4, 278
sensual mode (overexcitability), 31–2
setting(s)
  modification of, 130–1
  real, 134
  response to, 139
  sociocultural, 224
  specific and varied, 130–1, 132, 133
sexual identity, 343
shaping environment, 55, 56, 223, 225, 230, 236–7, 240
short-term memory (STM), 97, 163, 164, 165
sibling studies, 99, 129
single-mindedness, 255, 258, 273
situations, 5, 56, 339
  novel, 230, 241 (*see also* novelty)
skills, 19, 24–5, 48–9, 262; *see also* ability; talent
  brought to crystallizing experience, 307, 315
  latent, 309
slow learners, 380
SMPY, *see* Study of Mathematically Precocious Youth (SMPY)
social class, 45
social competence, 239, 240
social factors, 11, 44, 248, 279–80, 302–3
  in definition of giftedness, 100, 103–4, 418
  in identification of gifted, 104–5
social intelligence, 109
social skills, 350
social structure(s), 45
  progression in, 12
social talents, 22
socialization, 340
  professional, 341
society
  and education for gifted, 59–60, 267, 379–80, 431
  and giftedness, 4, 7, 21–52, 94, 132, 265–7, 347–8, 296
sociocultural context(s), 152, 224, 235
sociocultural factors; *see also* cultural factors; social factors
  in constitution of domains, 267–8, 269
  in constitution of giftedness, 265–7
sociocultural groups, comparison of intelligence across, 224, 234

sociocultural model, implications of, 270–1
socioeconomic status, 14, 83–5, 334
socio-emotional aspects of development, 15, 16
spatial intelligence, 13, 136, 308
spatial relations, 66, 75
special education, 28, 380; *see also* education
    for gifted and talented
specialization, 22, 29, 38
specialness, feeling of, 11, 258–61
specific abilities, defined, 66–7, 75
specificity
    description of giftedness, 429–30, 431
    gifted performance, 421
speed, 220–1, 226
Spencer Foundation, 363
stabilty
    assumption of, 154–5
    of childhood markers of giftedness, 153
    of creativity, 86
    of domains, 278
    of giftedness, 57, 116, 151, 270, 281, 285
    of intelligence, 95
    of talent, 11–12, 264
    three-ring conception of giftedness, 85–7
stage development, 12, 14, 159, 286, 287
    and change in giftedness, 271, 281–4
    movement in, 294, 295
    in prodigies, 299, 300–1
    as sequences of stages, 13, 423–5
    transition mechanisms in, 285, 291, 295–8,
        299, 302
Stanford Achievement Test, 189
Stanford-Binet Intelligence Scale, 63, 96, 151,
    344, 348, 363–4
"stars," 236–7
status, 279
status information, 78–9, 85, 87
status variables, 45
stereotype(s), 47, 104, 417, 418
    early-start, 255, 256
Sternberg memory-scanning tasks, 187–8, 422
"stick-to-itiveness," 136, 138, 142; *see also*
    persistence
stimulation, 86–7, 115, 373
    interpersonal, 115
    provided by parents, 198, 428
stimuli
    combination or comparison of, 226
    environmental, 134, 152
strategic behavior, metamemory and, 191–6
strategic skills, 189
strategies, 184; *see also* rules and strategies
    assessment of, 190
    execution of, 226, 227
    of gifted children, 190, 429
    instruction in use of, 173–4, 177–8
    invention of, 425
    monitoring of, 196
    selection of, 232

shifts, during musical construction task, 397–
    9, 400, 408, 409
    use of, 168, 169–71, 186, 187–8, 428
"street-smartness," 9
strength of character, 41
stress, intrafamily, 340
structure-of-intellect model, 38–9, 77, 96, 103,
    121, 122
student(s)
    benefit of SMPY to, 378–9
    crystallizing experiences, 323–5, 330
    role of, 58–9, 78
    with special needs, 122
Study of Mathematically Precocious Youth
    (SMPY), 17, 116, 349–50, 361–87, 431
    effects of participation in, 376–7
    reports, 370–1
    sequential aspects of, 370–1
subcomponents, 225
subject matter, fascination with, 69, 71
subjectivity (measurement), 64, 72
success, 34, 120, 376–7, 379
    in school, as predictor of success in life, 280
    tacit understandings in, 238–9
    traits in, 327–8
suppression, lack of, in creative persons, 342
symbol systems, 94, 278, 308, 309, 311, 315
    continuous, analog, 322
    music, 391, 404, 405
synergistic reaction, 132
synthesis, 33, 138, 276–7
System of Multicultural Pluralistic Assessment
    (SOMPA), 104–5

tacit knowledge, 379
tacit understandings, 238–9
talent(s), 112, 113–14, 131, 136, 291
    achievement of, 309
    classification of, 4
    and creativity, 338
    and cultural expectations, 11–12, 296
    defined, 124
    development of, 7, 14, 264–8, 271, 287, 329
    differentiated, 29–30
    diversity within domains of, 32–3
    domain-specificity of, 5, 6
    early, and adult accomplishment, 312–20, 330
    enhancement of, 381–2
    extreme, 138
    versus genius, 381–2
    matching to task, 140
    and motivation, 326–7, 328–9, 330
    nature of, 22–26, 268–71, 284
    perception of, by teachers, 325–9
    "raw," 312
    reification of, 270
    socially defined, 21, 268, 296, 427
    special, 5, 6, 115–16, 122–5, 156–7
    stability of, 11–12, 264

time lines in development of, 282f
versus training, 310
unitary and multiple, 268–70
unrecognized, 382
Talent Pool(s), 29, 33, 81, 85, 87, 277
identification of, 76–7
target population, and definition of giftedness,
55
task(s), 5, 12, 229, 233
analysis of, 176
demands of, 133
focus on, 140
on intelligence tests, 156
involvement with, 118–9, 259
matching abilities to, 140
for measuring giftedness, 223
motivation, 115–6
novel, 229–30
in research on giftedness, 153–4
theory of performance of, 228
task commitment, 4–5, 31, 41, 123–4, 151,
224, 418, 422; *see also* commitment
assessment of, 432
emphasis on, in educational practice, 433
prerequisite of giftedness, 7
in three-ring conception, 65, 69–71, 72, 73,
75, 76, 80, 82, 85, 86–8, 103
task selection, 220
two-facet subtheory and, 233–4
task solution
in novelty, 230, 231–2
stages of, 226
taxonomy of educational objectives, 276–7
teacher rating scales, 105, 107
teachers, 4, 25, 47, 59, 79, 80, 115, 120, 133,
291, 292, 300, 373, 375
awareness of crystallizing experiences of students, 323–5, 330
crystallizing experiences of, 323–4, 330
and definition of giftedness, 33
inspiring, 29
perception of talent in students, 323, 325–9
relation with children, 433
teaching, effective, 371
technical knowledge, 276, 277
technical skills, 115–16
tension, 146, 346
creativity as response to, 342
Terman longitudinal study, 27–9, 35–7, 41, 43,
96, 104, 118, 332, 348, 374, 381
terminology, 109
test-taking giftedness, 9, 57
testing, offgrade, 17, 116, 362
tests, 14–15, 56–7, 73, 85, 378, 432; *see also*
intelligence tests; IQ tests
in assessment of eminence, 349
of creativity, 71–2, 103, 112, 116–17, 203,
292, 420
culture-free, 234

of divergent thinking, 72, 112, 116, 151,
352, 353, 420
generalization, 192, 193, 196
and identification of gifted, 58, 59, 62, 63,
64, 116 (*see also* IQ cutoff score)
of innate intelligence, 113
"objective," 87
predictive validity of, 66, 67–9, 72, 274, 294,
349, 362
situational, 87
theory, 220; *see also* explicit theories; implicit
theories
without psychometrics, 30–1
in research, 16
thinking, 107, 134; *see also* convergent thinking; divergent thinking
creative, 141, 258–9
process models of, 76–7
thought
development of, 273–4
as interaction, 269
three-ring conception of giftedness, 4–5, 53–92,
116, 123–4, 420
discussion of, 83–9
research underlying, 63–5
threshold effect, 69, 76
threshold level(s), 34, 35, 117, 122
vary across domains, 49
Thurstone Primary Mental Abilities Test (PMA),
39, 40
time
in achievement, 289, 291
attentive, 133, 142–3
commitment of, 82
and contribution of eminent adults, 419
in creativity, 258, 261
and development of talent, 264–84
frame(s) of, 418, 421, 429
and giftedness, 140, 271–84
spent on talent field, 70, 433
spent in thinking, 252–5
Torrance Tests of Creative Thinking, 117, 209
trained/untrained subjects and musical construction task, 397, 398–9, 406–7, 408, 409,
410
training, 86–7, 134, 430–1; *see also* instruction;
self-teaching
and achievement, 308, 310–11, 334
creativity, 372
of intelligence, 113, 121, 241
and presence/absence of crystallizing experience, 323, 325, 329
requirement of early, 330
strategy use, 183, 191–6, 197
studies of, 189, 191–6
trait-level processes, 18, 421, 425–9, 430, 431
traits, 294
transfer, 99, 173–4, 175, 191, 193–6, 197, 428
components of, 31

transfer (*cont.*)
  tests of, 183
transformation, early gifts to creativity (T[G to
  C]), 248–9, 250, 252, 258
transformation of early giftedness into achievement of eminence, 312–20, 333, 351
transition mechanisms, 426, 435
  in stage development, 285, 290–4, 295–8,
  299
traumatic experience, 84
triarchic theory of intellectual giftedness, 223–43
triarchic theory of intelligence, 9, 55–6, 108,
  131, 224
tripartite theories of intelligence, 224
tryouts, 113; *see also* performance
twin studies, 99, 129
two-facet subtheory (intelligence), 55–6, 223–4,
  229–34, 240
Type II errors, 128, 132

underachievers, 31, 61, 108, 293–4
understanding
  detailed, 433
  new, 118
universalism and relativism of intelligence, 224
universals, 15, 38, 290
usefulness (as test), 3–4

values, 14, 64, 350
  and creativity, 338, 343
  family, 14, 332, 333, 334, 340
  as variable in intelligence, 346
variance (performance), explanation of, 429,
  430–1
verbal ability, 122, 159, 186, 228, 239, 240
verbal reasoning, 66, 75, 122, 136, 156, 159

verbal tests, 234
veto factor(s), 426
visual artists, 426
  crystallizing experiences, 307, 311, 320–2,
  330
visual or performing arts
  training in, 330
  in USOE definition of giftedness, 30, 65,
  101–2, 123, 348
visualization, 122, 169
vocabulary acquisition, 430
vocabulary learning, 228–9, 424

Wechsler (test), 363–4
Wechsler Intelligence Scale for Children, 348
Wechsler Intelligence Scale for Children – Revised (WISC-R), 189, 190, 344
Western civilization, 265
  talents valued in, 22, 24
What Ever Happened to the Quiz Kids?, 237–8
word fluency, 66, 75
word-span tests, 190
work; *see also* creative work; hard work
  done by creative adults, 248, 252–3
  habits, 380
  involvement in, 70, 71
  prediction of success in, 48
  style, 116
working memory, 162, 163, 165–6
world-class performers, 100

younger children/older children comparisons,
  156, 160, 163, 164, 169

zone of proximal development, 178